tive Mansion,

Washington; .... , 186 .

ago our fathers brought

a new nation, conceived

to the proposition that

al "

a great civil war, testing

any nation so conceived,

ng endure. We are met

of that war. We have

of it, as a final rest-

GRAND INAUGURATION BALL,

TO BE GIVEN BY THE

12th Ward Democratic Association of Philadelphia,

AT THE ASSEMBLY ROOMS, LOUISIANA AVENUE,

WASHINGTON CITY,

ON TUESDAY EVENING, MARCH 3rd, 1857.

COMMITTEE ON INVITATIONS.

Charles W. Carrigan,   Charles S. Lincoln,   Charles M. Howell,   Col. Wm. Selden,
Hon. Joshua Vansant,   William Flinn.

LADIES' TICKET.

Henry Dunlap,
TREASURER.

The
AMERICAN
HERITAGE
HISTORY
of the
PRESIDENCY

by

MARCUS CUNLIFFE

and

the Editors of
AMERICAN HERITAGE
The Magazine of History

Editor in Charge
KENNETH W. LEISH

Published by
American Heritage Publishing Co., Inc.

Book Trade Distribution by
Simon and Schuster

On a bronze door at the U.S. Capitol, the first presidential inauguration is depicted. Chancellor Livingston administers the oath to Washington; at right is the Vice President, John Adams.

AMERICAN HERITAGE
BOOK DIVISION

MANAGING DIRECTOR
Richard M. Ketchum

GENERAL EDITOR
Alvin M. Josephy, Jr.

Staff for this Book

EDITOR
Kenneth W. Leish

ASSOCIATE EDITORS
David Jacobs
Michael Harwood

ART DIRECTOR
Chester Prosinski
Assistant: Margaret Chou

PICTURE EDITORS
Wesley Day
Carla Davidson

COPY EDITOR
Ellen C. Ehrlich
Assistant: Helen C. Dunn

ASSISTANT EDITOR
Susan D. Eikov

EDITORIAL ASSISTANT
Hilary E. Abramson

AMERICAN HERITAGE
PUBLISHING CO., INC.

PRESIDENT
James Parton

CHAIRMAN, EDITORIAL COMMITTEE
Joseph J. Thorndike

EDITOR, AMERICAN HERITAGE MAGAZINE
Oliver Jensen

SENIOR ART DIRECTOR
Irwin Glusker

PUBLISHER, AMERICAN HERITAGE MAGAZINE
Darby Perry

Embroidered in 1861, the cloth on
this page honored Abraham Lincoln,
who had pledged to save the Union.

CONTENTS

Introduction

The inauguration of Ulysses S. Grant (left) in 1873

A torchlight parade in Denver, Colorado, celebrating the

On Inauguration Day, 1897, the new President, William McKinley, turned to his predecessor Grover Cleveland and remarked, "What an impressive thing it is to assume tremendous responsibilities!" McKinley's first term was highlighted by a brief, victorious war with Spain; there were few moments of domestic crisis and relatively little criticism of the popular Chief Executive. Yet in September, 1899, McKinley said of the Presidency, "I have had enough of it, Heaven knows! I have had all the honor there is in this place, and have had responsibilities enough to kill any man." Nevertheless, he sought a second term in 1900; "the call of duty," he explained, outweighed personal desires.

Today the Presidency of the United States is more than ever a killing job. The office that was created by the founders of a new nation in 1787 and shaped by men of greatness and vision has evolved into a position of unprecedented power—but

election of Benjamin Harrison as President in 1888.   *Presidents Wilson and Taft, on Inauguration Day, 1913*

that power is accompanied by danger and frustration. Why then do men continue to seek it? Why do they plead, bargain, and bludgeon their way to a presidential nomination? A partial answer is that the Presidency exists and that someone must occupy it; it is natural that men of ability and ambition should strive to attain the highest office that the nation can bestow. An American seeking the Presidency must also be confident that he is the best man for the job, that he is most capable of coping wisely with the plethora of problems facing the United States. The opportunity to guide a great nation, to secure or retain peace and prosperity, to fulfill the American Dream—and by so doing earn an indelible place in history beside Washington, Lincoln, Franklin Delano Roosevelt, and other presidential giants—is clearly irresistible to ambitious Americans convinced of their own capability. In the nuclear age, when a misstep in foreign policy can result in the obliteration

Franklin and Eleanor Roosevelt on one of his four Inauguration Days

Chief Justice Earl Warren administers the

of humanity, when social injustices cry out for amelioration, no Chief Executive is likely to share the sentiments of Theodore Roosevelt, who wrote that although the Presidency "has been very wearing . . . I have thoroughly enjoyed it, for it is fine to feel one's hand guiding great machinery." To a beleaguered President, a remark of Harry Truman's may seem more apt: "There is no exaltation in the office of the President of the United States—sorrow is the proper word."

On Inauguration Day, however, there is exaltation. It is a majestic, solemn, and hopeful moment when a President-elect—chosen by his fellow citizens—raises his right hand and repeats after the Chief Justice the portentous oath first sworn by George Washington in 1789: "I do solemnly swear that I will faithfully execute the Office of President of the United States, and will to the best of my Ability, preserve, protect and defend the Constitution of the United States."—THE EDITORS

presidential oath to Dwight D. Eisenhower at the Capitol in 1957.   *The Kennedys on Inauguration Day, 1961*

MINERVA DICTATING THE CONSTITUTION TO

PART

I

THE INVENTION OF THE PRESIDENCY

"The executive Power shall be vested in a President of the United States of America."

THE CONSTITUTION OF THE UNITED STATES

Minerva, the Roman goddess of wisdom, dictates the Constitution to Young America in this allegorical frieze at the U.S. Capitol.

CHAPTER ONE

The Office Created

Fifty-five delegates arrived in Philadelphia during the spring and summer of 1787, empowered to propose revisions to the Articles of Confederation, under which the newly independent United States was governed. When the Convention adjourned in September they had drafted an entirely new Constitution instead. There had been a good deal of disagreement and moments of near-deadlock. Several delegates had serious doubts as to the wisdom of the final document; a few refused to sign it.

The discussions in Independence Hall had been conducted in secret (knowledge of the proceedings is derived largely from James Madison's daily notes, which were not published until 1840, four years after his death). As word of the Convention's decisions spread to the outside world reactions were mixed. The new Constitution was debated all over again, in newspapers and in pamphlets, in conversation and in correspondence, in state legislatures and in state ratifying conventions. To take effect the document had to be ratified by at least nine of the thirteen states. Not until June, 1788, was the necessary total secured. Rhode Island, which had sent no delegates to Philadelphia, voted heavily against the Constitution in a popular referendum. Antifederalists—men opposed to the Constitution in whole or in part—put up a stout fight in other states. The Federalists carried the day by only 57 votes to 47 in New Hampshire. And even though George Washington had lent his great prestige to the Philadelphia Convention by attending, with some reluctance, and by consenting to preside over its sessions, his own state, Virginia, approved the document by only 89 votes to 79. New

York, the eleventh state to ratify the Constitution, followed the example of Virginia and Massachusetts in insisting that various amendments be given prompt consideration. North Carolina was so concerned about these additions that ratification was withheld pending proof that the first Congress convened under the Constitution would respect its obligation.

One of the novel features of the Constitution that aroused alarm was the provision for a single Executive, the President. Under the Articles of Confederation there was a President of Congress; but the office was merely a chairmanship and was not to be held for more than one year in any three. The immediately acceptable notion was that of a plural Executive, in which power was shared by a committee or council. When the idea of a single Executive was first broached at Philadelphia by James Wilson of Pennsylvania, Madison noted that it was greeted with an embarrassed pause. Edmund Randolph of Virginia then voiced the objection that was evidently in the minds of a number of delegates. The temper of Americans, he said, was "adverse to the very semblance of monarchy"; a single executive figure would be "the foetus of monarchy."

Although the Convention swallowed its misgivings and approved the proposal, the cry was taken up again in the ratification controversies. In Virginia Washington's old friend George Mason, who had been at Philadelphia but had declined to sign the Constitution, argued against the Executive. The President would have far too much scope, he said, in being (under Article II, Section 2) "Commander in

Chief of the Army and Navy of the United States and of the Militia" when it was called into federal service, and in being empowered to make treaties and appoint public officials with the advice and consent of the Senate. Mason disliked the overlapping of executive and legislative functions that such provisions entailed. There should, he thought, have been a small council of state that would give "proper information and advice"; the chairman could serve as Vice President. Without such a council, Mason warned, the President would "be directed by minions and favorites; or he will become a tool to the Senate —or a Council of State will grow out of the principal officers of the great departments." From this defect had also sprung "that unnecessary (and dangerous) officer the Vice-President, who for want of other employment is made president of the Senate, thereby dangerously blending the executive and legislative powers, besides always giving to some one of the States an unnecessary and unjust pre-eminence over the others." In short, George Mason saw the proposed Constitution as a scheme for an elective monarchy. So did his fellow Virginian, the eloquent patriot and ex-governor Patrick Henry. A "squint toward monarchy" was Henry's expressive phrase during the Virginia ratifying convention. James Monroe, speaking against the Constitution in the same convention, was worried by the method of electing the President. He assumed that candidates would seldom gain the clear majority of votes that would enable the proposed Electoral College to decide the matter. The election would then, according to the Constitution, be thrown to the House of Representatives, where each state would have one vote. How easily, Monroe speculated, could the "chair of the United States . . . be approached and achieved, even contrary to the wishes of the people. . . ." Given the prevailing "ardent spirit of liberty," treason and subversion were improbable; but anyone capable of digesting the lessons of history could not help but be uneasy for the future of the United States.

Others echoed these objections. Rawlins Lowndes, a South Carolina legislator, said that the Constitution was "the best preparatory plan for a monarchical government he had read." A colleague, James Lincoln, who like George Mason was worried by the President's re-eligibility for office at the end of his four-year term, declared that "this mighty, this omnipotent governor-general" could well remain in office for "fourteen times four years," and "may hold it so long that it will be impossible without a revolution, to displace him."

Thomas Jefferson, having received news of the Constitution while serving as American minister in Paris, liked some provisions but was extremely uneasy at the possibility of presidential re-election. "Reason and experience," he wrote to John Adams in November, 1787, "prove to us that a chief magistrate, so continuable, is an officer for life. When one or two generations shall have proved that this is an office for life, it becomes on every succession worthy of intrigue, of bribery, of force, and even of foreign interference. It will be of great consequence to France and England to have America governed by a Galloman or Angloman. Once in office, and possessing the military force of the union, without either the aid or check of a council, he would not easily be dethroned, even if the people could be induced to withdraw their votes from him. I wish that at the end of the 4. years they had made him for ever ineligible a second time." A month later in a letter to James Madison, Jefferson reiterated that "I . . . greatly dislike . . . the abandonment . . . of the necessity of rotation in office, and most particularly in the case of the President. Experience concurs with reason in concluding that the first magistrate will always be re-elected if the constitution permits it. He is then an officer for life."

There was strenuous opposition to the proposals for a President in some of the Northern states. One of the most influential Antifederalists was Governor George Clinton of New York. Writing a series of letters to the *New-York Journal* over the pen name CATO, Clinton predicted in accents of horror and woe that the President would "be surrounded with expectants and courtiers." His patronage power, his control of the armed forces, his "unrestrained power of granting pardons for treason, which may be used to screen from punishment those whom he had secretly instigated to commit the crime, and thereby prevent a discovery of his own guilt," his entrenchment in office for four long years: these factors proved to Clinton that "if the president is possessed of ambition, he has power and time sufficient to ruin his country." Taking another tack, Clinton asked whether there was any essential difference between the "powers and prerogatives" of the American President and those of the English monarch. Although the Constitution merely stipulates that the Executive "shall . . . receive . . . a compensation," Clinton said that the President was bound to be paid enough "to appear with the splendor of a prince." He was also "a constituent part of the legislative power," since his approval was required for all federal legislation. He had great latitude of action in foreign affairs. "Therefore these powers, in both president and king, are substantially the same."

The Founding Fathers were more violently assailed for their work at Philadelphia in a series of articles published between February and April, 1788, in *The Freeman's Journal; Or, The North-American Intelligencer*. The author of the articles, PHILADEL-PHIENSIS, is believed to have been Benjamin Workman, a tutor at the University of Pennsylvania. He detected a "conspiracy," devised "by an infernal junto of demagogues," to consolidate "our thirteen free commonwealths" into a "*despotic monarchy*." Lacking precise evidence for the charge, he argued that its truth was self-evident: "Who can deny but the *president general* will be a *king* to all intents and purposes, and one of the most dangerous kind too—a king elected to command a standing army. Thus our laws are to be administered by this *tyrant*; for the whole, or at least the most important part of the executive department is put in his hands." This "*President-general . . .* is vested with powers exceeding those of the most *despotic monarch . . .* in modern times." Why had the conspirators destroyed the chances of American happiness by framing "a system of oppression that must involve in its consequences the misery of their own offspring"? Like other subsequent imaginers of conspiracies, the writer found corroboration, and further proof of depravity, in apparently unpromising material. The mean and dastardly Founding Fathers had betrayed their country and their own children merely in "hopes of obtaining some lucrative employment, or of receiving a little more homage from the rest of their fellow creatures. . . ." It was a strange diagnosis of a gathering that embraced old Benjamin Franklin, the austere and dignified Washington, and the scholarly James Madison, even if the later careers of a few of the delegates—the financier Robert Morris, or the imperiously ambitious Alexander Hamilton—lent a little color to such suspicions.

In fact, practically all the forebodings of the Antifederalists are more likely to amuse than to impress modern readers. With the hindsight of nearly two centuries, one knows that the system worked out very much better. The Presidency did not turn out to be an elective monarchy. Its incumbents have not proved to be in "office for life." The interfusion of executive and legislative functions, while sometimes a cause of friction and confusion, has justified itself as a wise improvement upon the theoretically ideal but practically unworkable plan of a perfect separation of powers. Not surprisingly, more attention has been devoted to those who analyzed the new Constitution sympathetically—Hamilton, Madison, and John Jay, for example, who contributed the eighty-five impressive letters of *The Federalist* in 1787 and 1788—than to those who assailed it. Thus Hamilton appears an easy winner over Monroe and Clinton. Monroe wrung his hands at the opportunities for corruption (and worse) created by the method of electing the President. In *The Federalist* No. 68, Hamilton at his most sweetly reasonable pointed out that the mechanism of the Electoral College would give the people a say in the process, and exclude from it senators and representatives: "The process of election affords a moral certainty, that the office of President will never fall to . . . any man who is not in an eminent degree endowed with the requisite qualifications. Talents for low intrigue, and the little arts of popularity, may . . . suffice to elevate a man to [the governorship of a state]; but it will require other talents, and a different kind of merit, to establish him in the esteem and confidence of the whole Union. . . . It will not be too strong to say, that there will be a constant probability of seeing the station filled by characters preëminent for ability and virtue." Too rosy a picture? Perhaps. But it was in the main accurate, which is more than can be said for Monroe's prophecy.

Clinton insisted that the Presidency would hardly differ from the British monarchy. Hamilton's devastating answer appeared in *The Federalist* No. 69. "The President of the United States would be an officer elected by the people for *four* years; the king of Great Britain is a perpetual and *hereditary* prince. The one would be amenable to personal punishment and disgrace [through impeachment]; the person of the other is . . . inviolable. The one would have a *qualified* negative upon the acts of the legislative body; the other has an *absolute* negative. The one would have a right to command the military and

While George Mason (above, left) and Patrick Henry (center) were eloquently opposing ratification of the controversial new Constitution in Virginia, Alexander Hamilton (right) was vigorously advocating its immediate adoption by New York State.

naval forces of the nation; the other, in addition to this right, possesses that of *declaring* war [a right reserved to Congress in the Constitution], and of *raising* and *regulating* fleets and armies [likewise, a responsibility of Congress] by his own authority. The one would have a concurrent power [with the Senate] in the formation of treaties; the other is the *sole possessor* of the power of making treaties. The one would have a like concurrent authority in appointing offices; the other is the sole author of all appointments. . . . The one has no particle of spiritual jurisdiction; the other is the supreme head and governor of the national church! What answer shall we give to those who would persuade us that things so unlike resemble each other? The same that ought to be given to those who tell us that a government, the whole power of which would be in the hands of the elective and periodical servants of the people, is an aristocracy, a monarchy, and a despotism."

It is obvious that if some of the Federalist arguments smacked of special pleading, so did those of the Antifederalists. Clinton, for example, was the powerful governor of a powerful state. His disapproval was not directed toward executive authority as such, but toward federal, centralized executive authority. The Antifederalists were on the whole less opposed to a single Executive than to some other aspects of the Constitution—notably the absence of a bill of rights, which was a common feature of the post-Revolutionary state constitutions. Most of them overcame their scruples fairly quickly once the new Constitution took effect. Some years before his death in 1799 Patrick Henry, reversing his position, had become a vehement Federalist. Jefferson wrote to his friend Francis Hopkinson in March, 1789, that he would not wish to make further criticisms of the re-eligibility rule while George Washington was at the helm, as he had full confidence in "our great leader." Henry hoped the potentially dangerous provision would be amended as soon as Washington had stepped down from the Presidency. But Jefferson himself was President a few years later, and he then saw no harm in imitating Washington's example of what he called "voluntary retirement after 8 years." In the same way James Monroe ceased to be apprehensive of the dreadful problem of election to the Presidency; he too would have eight years in office.

By the same token, one is puzzled by the anxiety over the President's powers as Commander in Chief expressed by the Antifederalists in what Hamilton called their "parade of imaginary horribles." The New York ratifying convention suggested that the President be prevented from taking the field at the head of his troops "without the previous desire of Congress." But the standing Army of the United States numbered less than one thousand men in the late 1780's. A generation later, despite America's increase in population and territory, the Army would consist of about ten thousand men. Nor would Presidents show much enthusiasm for assuming personal command. During the Whisky Rebellion, Washington accompanied the federal forces as far as Bedford, Pennsylvania; but the only other such instances in America's long history would be "little Jemmy" Madison's somewhat farcical appearance at the inglorious defeat at Bladensburg, Maryland, in 1814, and one or two brief prodding exercises attempted by Abraham Lincoln.

As for the President's "unrestrained power of granting pardons," it is true that Article II, Section 2, of the Constitution gave him the right to "grant Reprieves and Pardons for Offences against the United States, except in Cases of Impeachment." But this privilege of clemency would if anything be invoked too sparingly by Presidents. When Eugene V. Debs was sentenced in 1918 to ten years' imprisonment for seditious opposition to the war, President Wilson did not intervene; the war had been over for three years when President Harding pardoned Debs with the genial observation that "personally he is of a very clean and lovable character."

Today's Americans know, then, that the Presidency evolved into a wholesome and stable institution. It has been a great success, as success is commonly measured. Accepting this evaluation as a commonplace of history, one is apt to underestimate or misunderstand the problems facing the Constitution makers during that hot summer in Independence Hall.

Their task—one that many of them had probably not intended to undertake—disclosed itself as the invention of a new form of government. It would be novel in several ways. Like the Articles of Confederation, it would prescribe a dual or federal system conceding some powers to the central executive-legislative government and reserving others to the thirteen semisovereign states. It would be looser and more democratic than the monarchico-aristocratical governments of Europe, yet it would furnish the "energy"—a favorite word among the Federalists—that men such as Washington, Jay, and Hamilton thought was alarmingly absent in the Articles. A majority of the Philadelphia delegates were "Federalists" in the broad sense of wishing to impart more energy to the central government. Beyond that goal, certainty and unanimity ceased. They were venturing into dangerous country, the maps of which were conjectural and daunting: "Here be wild beasts" was, so to speak, inscribed in the blank spaces.

The Founding Fathers could seek inspiration from two types of material. There were the actual examples of other nations, historical and contemporary, and of the former colonies that composed the United States; and there were the theoretical commentaries on government, above all those of John Locke, William Blackstone, and Charles de Secondat et de Montesquieu. None of these provided reassurance. History seemed to show that loose federations such as those of the Greek city-states were too parochial and too jealous of one another to survive. On the other hand, well-knit societies like that of ancient Rome slid into corruption: the Republic became the Empire of the twelve Caesars. The picture at the time of the Convention was equally dismal. Almost every country in the known world was ruled by a hereditary monarch. Some of them—Victor Amadeus II of Sardinia, Ferdinand IV of Naples, Gustavus III of Sweden, Frederick II of Prussia (who died the year before the Philadelphia Convention, having occupied the throne for forty-six years)—were absolute or would-be absolute rulers. Others—Louis XVI of France, Charles III of Spain, Leopold I of Tuscany, Catherine the Great of Russia—were known as enlightened or benevolent despots. Whatever the type of monarchy, there tended to be a tussle between the ruler and the aristocracy, each seeking power at the expense of the other.

The few exceptions yielded no comfort to the Founding Fathers. In Switzerland, where there was no king, there was instead a jostling collection of cantons, which were split over religious issues and controlled by a small group of rich families. In Holland there was a qualified monarchy in the shape of the Stadholder; but William V, who was then the ruler, was mournfully ineffectual. For one hundred and fifty years Poland had had an elective monarchy. The results were lamentable, as Jefferson knew when he complained in 1787 that the proposed American President "seems a bad edition of a Polish King." In Poland every election was an open invitation to conspiracy, both within the country and on the part of neighboring nations. The nobility in the Polish Diet, or parliament, held the power, but they managed it so irresponsibly that it was useless; they refused even to be bound by majority rule.

The example of Britain might have seemed more relevant. In different ways Locke, Blackstone, and

Montesquieu all praised the real or supposed features of British government: a monarch capable of ruling, yet restrained by Parliament from behaving despotically; a sensibly balanced and mixed constitution embodying a separation of functions; a vigorous tradition of libertarianism reinforced by a body of common law. At the outset of the Revolution, some Americans had allowed themselves to believe that the British king, George III, would use his prerogative to uphold their liberties. Swiftly disillusioned, they convinced themselves that neither the British nor any other monarchy would be desirable for the United States. The hereditary principle was objectionable; so were the inevitable accompaniments of monarchy—titles, sinecures, ecclesiastical hierarchies, "expectants and courtiers." Many Americans became convinced of the dangers of monarchy by reading Thomas Paine's rousing pamphlet *Common Sense*, which is said to have sold one hundred and twenty thousand copies within three months of its publication in 1776. Paine was one of the first and certainly one of the most effective debunkers of the hallowed institution of kingship. "There is something exceedingly ridiculous," he announced, "in the composition of monarchy; it first excludes a man from the means of information, yet empowers him to act in cases where the highest judgment is required." A few pages later he asked: "Why is the constitution of England sickly, but because monarchy hath poisoned the republic, the crown hath engrossed the commons? In England a king hath little more to do than to make war and give away places; which in plain terms, is to impoverish the nation and set it together by the ears. A pretty business indeed for a man to be allowed eight hundred thousand sterling a year for, and worshipped into the bargain!"

The lessons of history and the examples of other contemporary nations demonstrated that America had to avoid both a monarchy and the rule of a clique—whether such a group was known as an aristocracy or an oligarchy. But could the word "rule" logically be applied to the rule of the many— to a government without energy and without the vesting of authority in a small group of men, to a government presided over by one supreme figure? Some believed that the experiment was worth making, if only because the alternatives were so ominous. Some felt that the United States under the Articles of Confederation was healthy and reason-

ably strong. Why be alarmed by one small uprising— led by Daniel Shays, a dissatisfied Massachusetts farmer—in 1786? "A little rebellion now and then is a good thing, & as necessary in the political world as storms in the physical," Jefferson assured Madison in a letter written in January, 1787. The Philadelphia Convention, he insisted in November of the same year, had been "too much impressed by the insurrection of Massachusetts: and in the spur of the moment they are setting up a kite to keep the hen yard in order."

Others read the signs very differently. Madison received another letter, from George Washington, who was becoming convinced that his dreams of peaceful retirement at Mount Vernon were about to be shattered. Washington saw in Shays' Rebellion proof of "the want of energy in our governments. . . . Thirteen Sovereignties pulling against each other, and all tugging at the foederal head," he warned, "will soon bring ruin on the whole. . . . We are fast verging to anarchy and confusion!"

Washington and other men of his outlook were sure that the Articles were to blame. The "foederal head" was toothless. Executive power was in the hands of Congress, and its hands were feeble. Originally, under the Continental Congress, the executive departments had been run by committees, such as the board of five members that superintended the treasury. When the Articles were ratified, separate departments, with officials at their head, came into being. But government by committee continued, without any formal separation of executive and legislative functions. In consequence individual states did much as they pleased.

Nor were the states as a whole in strong executive hands. They had begun to draft new constitutions for themselves in 1776. To some extent they repeated the structures of colonial days, replacing the royal or proprietary governors with chief executives—who were known as presidents in Delaware, New Hampshire, and Pennsylvania, and were elsewhere styled governors. There had been acute friction between the colonial governors and their legislatures, with the latter grimly hanging on to their control of appropriations. These memories, and the augmented distaste for British institutions resulting from the Revolution, made the drafters of state constitutions doubly determined to emphasize the primacy of the legislative over the executive branch. In eight states

Governor George Clinton of New York opposed the Constitution but approved of strong state executives, as the broadside below, concerning Daniel Shays' rebellion, suggests.

BY HIS EXCELLENCY

George Clinton, Efq.

Governor of the STATE of NEW-YORK, General and Commander in Chief of all the Militia, and Admiral of the Navy of the fame.

A Proclamation.

HEREAS His Excellency JAMES BOWDOIN, Efq; Governor of the Commonwealth of Maffachufetts, did iffue his proclamation, bearing date the ninth day of this inftant month of February, fetting forth, that the General Court of the faid Commonwealth had, on the fourth day of the faid month declared, that a horrid and unnatural rebellion had been openly and traiteroufly, raifed and levied againft the faid Commonwealth, with defign to fubvert and overthrow the conftitution and form of government thereof, and further fetting forth, that it appeared that Daniel Shays, of Pelham, and Luke Day, of Weft Spring-

the governor was actually chosen by the legislature. Pennsylvania's president was elected by the legislature from an upper chamber or council of twelve, which collectively formed the executive. Such councils were provided in other states. In New York the governor had to share his veto power and other powers with a council of revision. In North and South Carolina he was allowed no right of veto. Ten of the thirteen states limited the governor's term of office to one year. In only two states, New York and Delaware, was he allowed a three-year term. The governor of Virginia, Edmund Randolph, regarded himself as simply "a member of the executive." Jefferson remarked of the Virginia constitution: "All the powers of government, legislative, executive and judiciary, result to the legislative body." As in the national Congress of the 1780's, the outcome of legislative supremacy was—according to the Federalists, at any rate—muddle, inefficiency, and bad feeling. In reacting against executive encroachments, the states had gone to the other extreme, legislative overlordship. If the new Constitution could be criticized for seeking to establish a "Polish King," America in the 1780's could be portrayed as a country at the mercy of one principal Polish Diet and thirteen subsidiary ones.

This was the heart of the problem for the delegates at Philadelphia. Murphy's Law of Politics—"If anything bad can happen, it will"—had not then been formulated. But those attending the Convention would have known exactly what he meant. History, the state of affairs in Europe, and their own experience of government in America combined to admonish them that the correct mixture of elements might be as hard to achieve as the alchemists' elixir of eternal life. To change the metaphor, one might say that government in relation to the competing needs of a nation was like a single sheet for a double bed. It could not cover the whole surface; the art was to dispose it as equitably and effectively as possible. Or, to return to the actual words at Philadelphia, the problem of a rightly balanced Executive was, according to the shrewd Gouverneur Morris, the most difficult of all: "Make him too weak: the Legislature will usurp his power. Make him too strong: he will usurp on the Legislature."

Almost every conceivable answer was put forward in Philadelphia before the weary delegates settled upon the Constitution in its final form. The most audacious proposal came from Alexander Hamilton in the course of a five-hour speech. He wanted a stronger central government and Executive than had previously been suggested. Indeed he advocated a replica of the British system, "the best in the world." There should be a single Executive, or "Governour," who would be virtually a monarch, an upper house to hold office for life (or during good behavior), and a popularly elected lower house. No one made an immediate favorable response to his plan. He had come near to saying the unsayable. Yet the notion of monarchy had survived after the beginning of the Revolution in curiously clandestine ways. In May, 1782, one of General Washington's officers, Colonel Lewis Nicola, had hinted to his commander that bearing in mind "the weakness of republics" and the "benefits of a mixed government," something on the lines of the British monarchy could be "readily adopted" in the United States; and who was better fitted to wear that crown than Washington himself? Washington quickly condemned the suggestion for being "big with the greatest mischiefs that can befall my Country." It is certain that he had no yearning for a throne. Nevertheless the idea of an American monarchy reappeared, as a fear if not as a hope. The young lexicographer Noah Webster feared a military *coup d'état* in 1785.

"Shall we have a king?" John Jay asked Washington the following year, after analyzing the weaknesses of the existing government. In 1787 Mrs. Mercy Warren, sister of the Massachusetts patriot James Otis, maintained that "many of the younger Class, particularly the students of Law and the youth of fortune and pleasure, are crying out for a monarchy and a standing army to support it." It is conceivable that Nathaniel Gorham, one of the Massachusetts delegates to the Philadelphia Convention, might have been prepared at one stage to support a plan for a monarchy, at least for New England. While the Convention was in progress, wild rumors circulated that the delegates were about to recommend a Hanoverian bishop, Frederick Augustus, the second son of George III, as king of the United States. The rumor was totally unfounded; it was thought to have emanated from a band of Connecticut royalists. In later ratification controversies Luther Martin of Maryland, who had refused to sign the Constitution, claimed that no less than twenty of the fifty-five delegates at Philadelphia had been in favor of a con-

solidated national government of a monarchic nature.

At the opposite pole from Hamilton's scheme were sundry proposals that envisaged the executive as a separate branch of government but differed as to its shape. The most cautious proposals, typified by the early remarks of Roger Sherman of Connecticut and by the plan that William Paterson of New Jersey had introduced, leaned toward a plural Executive. Others advocated a single Executive held in check by an advisory council. Congress would select the Executive, who would be debarred from immediate reappointment and would be subject to removal by the legislature. The Executive would have no veto power. Congress would control foreign policy by retaining the power to declare war and to make treaties. Such formulas drew upon the Articles of Confederation and more especially upon those state constitutions that applied drastic curbs to executive authority—Georgia's for instance, which restricted the governor to a single one-year term in any three-year period.

Later proposals that won acceptance specified a single Executive, not chosen by Congress, who would be re-eligible for appointment. If removable, he would be so only by impeachment on specific charges. He should have the right to veto legislation, a prime voice in the choice of judicial, diplomatic, and other important figures, a comparable though not absolute power in the management of foreign affairs, and various additional prerogatives, including the power to pardon offenders for all except the gravest crimes against the state. The delegates who advocated an energetic executive branch had taken a close look not only at the British government but at the situation of those states, notably New York and Massachusetts, in which the governor had considerable authority. Indeed, by drawing selectively from the state constitutions, it was possible to find sanction for every feature of a strong national Executive in one or another of these charters of Americanism.

New York was the best case of an active, efficient, popular administration. The governor, re-eligible for election indefinitely, held office for a term of reasonable length. The constitution vested in him "the supreme executive power and authority of the State." He was declared commander in chief of the militia, and even admiral of New York's navy; he could pardon offenders; he could call the legislature into special session, or dismiss it; he was required to pre-

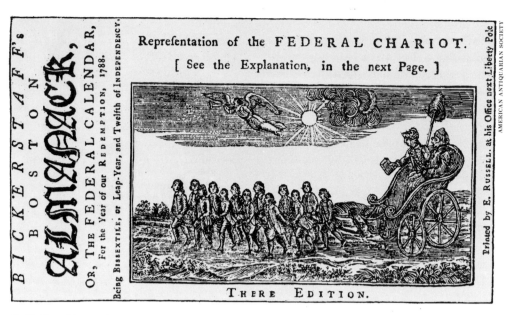

Pulled by thirteen freemen, Washington and Franklin are depicted above escorting the Constitution and "Cap . . . of American Freedom" to ratification and the country's "political Salvation."

sent a miniature State of the Union (or rather State of the State) report to each session, and to "take care that the laws are executed." He had fairly generous appointive and veto powers. He was popularly elected. By the test of experience, New York was a well-governed state. Its executive head, George Clinton, who had been first elected in 1777, was re-elected in 1780, 1783, and 1786—and would continue in the governorship for a total of eighteen consecutive years. Nor did it seem to matter greatly what term of office was prescribed. A competent and well-liked governor would remain firmly in office. This was borne out in Connecticut, where Jonathan Trumbull was chief executive from 1769 to 1786 under a system of annual elections, and in New Jersey, where Governor William Livingston had been returned to office every year since 1776—and would be re-elected annually until 1790.

Emboldened by such considerations, the group of delegates who believed in a strong Executive found that week by week the Convention was more inclined to listen sympathetically. Once they could agree on the idea of a single Executive, and once they perceived the advantages of a system that mingled executive and legislative operations ("Ambition must be made to counteract ambition," as James Madison nicely put the point in *The Federalist* No. 51), the initial premises shaped the evolution of the debate.

The presiding presence of George Washington did

much to encourage the process, although Washington himself did not play an active part in discussion. His standing was unique. He had served as commander in chief of the Continental Army for eight and a half years, accepting merely his expenses as financial return. Entrusted with extraordinary powers, he had quietly tendered his commission to Congress and returned to private life as a planter at Mount Vernon. Everyone knew him to be above suspicion and without overweening ambition. Everyone knew too that with the ratification of the new Constitution it would be unthinkable to name any man but him America's first true President. Gazing at this large, imposing, reticent personage as he took the chair each day, the Philadelphia delegates saw in him the living embodiment of their groping efforts to define the presidential essence. When the Constitution had been completed, signed, and sealed and the delegates had gone home, one of them—Pierce Butler of South Carolina—candidly admitted that he did not think the powers vested in the President "would have been so great had not many of the members cast their eyes towards General Washington as President, and shaped their ideas . . . by their opinions of his Virtue."

There were other reasons why the delegates moved toward the conception of a single and potentially strong Executive. One was that in the later stages of the Convention an identity of interests developed between the Federalist bloc and the representatives of small states. From different motives both were willing to uphold the position of the Executive against the large states reluctant to surrender the privileges of wealth and population. A second reason was that the advocates of a strong Executive, once they had refuted the accusation that they were cryptomonarchists, had a more positive and compelling brief than their opponents. They also exhibited most of the talent at Philadelphia, although they were by no means unanimous on every issue. Men of the caliber of Madison and Oliver Ellsworth of Connecticut might have had misgivings; they were nevertheless capable of a dispassionate insight that led them to prefer the risks of autocracy to those of anarchy. Assailed by fewer doubts, James Wilson and Gouverneur Morris of Pennsylvania, Rufus King and Elbridge Gerry of Massachusetts, Charles Pinckney and John Rutledge of South Carolina, and of course New York's glitteringly talented Alexander Hamilton, all urged their colleagues toward the ultimate goal of a rejuvenated national government.

Gradually the business of the Convention was divided among committees, in each of which the Federalist contingent played a crucial role. Ellsworth, Wilson, and Rutledge were members of the five-man Committee on Detail, whose task was to frame a tentative draft constitution. (It was this body, and more particularly James Wilson, that probably made the decision to call the Executive "President" instead of "Governor" or "Governour," the designations favored by Hamilton and followed in the first rough outline prepared for the Committee on Detail by Edmund Randolph. Wilson was no doubt influenced by the use of the term "President" in a previous plan submitted by Charles Pinckney, and by the constitution of his own state of Pennsylvania, which then described its executive as "president.")

At a subsequent stage several important loose ends were referred to the charmingly named Committee on Postponed Matters and Unfinished Business. This body put forward sympathetic recommendations on such intricate problems as the method of electing and removing the President, his appointive powers, and the extent of his authority in negotiating treaties. In the last ten days of the Convention, its provisional decisions were polished by the Committee on Style and Arrangement, which assigned Gouverneur Morris to write a final draft. Indeed he imparted more than polish to certain sections. By choosing the precise phraseology that he wanted (in company with Hamilton, Madison, and Rufus King), Morris was able to express his "own notions" without "alarm [to] others": to steer the document in as Federalist a direction as he dared. Thirty-nine delegates were both present and willing to sign the finished Constitution on September 17, "in the Year of our Lord"—who was not otherwise mentioned in the text—"one thousand seven hundred and Eighty seven and of the Independence of the United States of America the Twelfth. . . ."

So, in the course of inventing a new government, the Founding Fathers had invented a new head of government, the President.

As many historians have noted, and as the men of Philadelphia were abundantly conscious, the Constitution was a medley of compromises. The single sheet had been pulled to and fro across the double bed. Its final position was determined by sheer exhaustion as well as by wisdom. At least the delegates could feel that they were exhausted because they had debated the problems of government thoroughly. For example, Article II simply states that the President "shall hold his Office during the Term of four Years." A letter from Madison to Jefferson, written a month after the delegates adjourned, reveals how much discussion had preceded the bare wording of such clauses:

"As to the duration in office, a few would have preferred a tenure during good behaviour—a considerable number would have done so in case an easy & effectual removal by impeachment could be settled. It was much agitated whether a long term, seven years for example, with a subsequent & perpetual ineligibility, or a short term with a capacity to be re-elected should be fixed. In favor of the first opinion were urged the danger of a gradual degeneracy of re-elections . . . into first a life and then a hereditary tenure, and the favorable effect of an incapacity to be reappointed on the independent exercise of the Executive authority. On the other side it was contended that the prospect of necessary degradation would discourage the most dignified characters from aspiring to the office, would take away the principal motive to ye faithful discharge of its duties—the hope of being rewarded with a reappointment . . . and instead of producing an independent administration . . . would render the [President] more indifferent to the importance of a place which he would soon be obliged to quit forever, and more ready to yield to the encroachments of the Legislature of which he might again be a member."

It was involved prose, for one of several involved and "much agitated" issues. Madison could have added that only at a late stage was the four-year term with re-eligibility substituted for a single seven-year term.

The Chief Executive was not given as much power as some of the delegates would have wished. Not all were satisfied with the provisions that enabled Congress to override the President's veto, or with the extent to which the Senate might assert its views on foreign policy. On the other hand, the Executive was stronger than some thought desirable. More than a century of Constitution worship elapsed before the historian Charles A. Beard felt the need to remind Americans that their Founding Fathers had been mostly men of property, prominent in their communities, and conservatively inclined. This statement would not have been news to the Antifederalists. To stress that the Constitution was a product of its time—of a particular moment in American history when a significant number of influential and articulate citizens thought their country had reached a crisis—is not to impute wicked designs to the

Founding Fathers. Diagnosing an emergency, they managed to incorporate in the Constitution what might almost be called emergency powers for the Executive.

In much the same way, New York happened to have a strong executive because conditions in the state during the years of the Revolutionary War had been extraordinary, and because the leading patriots were substantial, conservative persons. If the Philadelphia meeting had taken place twenty or even ten years later, and if the country had continued to struggle along under the Articles of Confederation, it is quite likely that the changes recommended would have been much less sweeping and would have still retained the principle of legislative supremacy. True, the presidential powers outlined in the 1787 Constitution were potential rather than actual. The Founding Fathers, as befitted serious-minded innovators, had an exceptional sense of posterity. They wanted their work to last. The Constitution, like Washington's Farewell Address and the Monroe Doctrine, has achieved a timeless fame, as if it and they were conceived out of timeless wisdom. No doubt the Constitution makers were right—given the later development of American history—to create an executive branch and to allow it the opportunity to display energy, just as Washington's and Monroe's pieces of

POGHKEEPSIE,
July 2d, 1788.

JUST ARRIVED
BY EXPRESS,

The Ratification of the New Conſtitution by the Convention of the State of Virginia, on Wedneſday the 25th June, by a majority of 10 ; 88 agreeing, and 78 diſſenting to its adoption.

When the ninth state, New Hampshire, ratified it on June 21, 1788, the Constitution became operative. As this broadside proclaims, Virginia ratified on June 25. New York approved in July.

advice have proved highly relevant to later generations. Yet in common with these other examples of statecraft, the Constitution was produced in response to the urgent demands of its day. It was the happy, somewhat fortuitous outcome of prescience and jitters. If Washington, Hamilton, and the rest had not believed the "American empire" to be in imminent danger of "disunion, anarchy and misery" (Hamilton's words at the end of June, 1787), the Constitution would probably not have worn anywhere near as well. A related paradox is that those who, like Jefferson, remained calm and saw no reason for jitters have seemed to posterity not dispassionate or imaginative enough. They would, in declining to be stampeded into emergency measures, have bequeathed to posterity an instrument of government altogether too time-bound.

This is not to assert that the 1787 Constitution was entirely new. Although they were innovators, the men of Philadelphia did not regard themselves as revolutionaries. They had no interest in novelty for its own sake; their concern was to fashion a system of government that would operate efficiently and that would be supported by Americans. One way of enlisting support was to draw upon the immediate precedent of state constitutions such as that of New York. Yet even if they had desired to fabricate an utterly new system, they would not have been able to move beyond the dominant conceptions of the age. The writers they consulted—Locke, Blackstone, Montesquieu, John Adams' *A Defence of the Constitutions of the Governments of the United States of America* —all affirmed the same eighteenth-century doctrine: checks and balances, mixed governments, separation of powers, the entrusting of an indefinable amount of prerogative to the Executive. The Philadelphia Constitution may be seen as a classic sample of the thinking of the Enlightenment. It is useful to consider the role of the President defined by the Constitution as a figment of the imagination of the Enlightenment: an equivocal, dream-personage who could claim immortality only by assuming mortal form and undergoing the ordeal by experience that began in 1789 and has not yet ended.

The Constitution was not brand-new. Nor was it a complete guide to American federalism. Napoleon once said that constitutions should be "short and obscure." A certain guile worthy of Napoleon was apparent in some of the Founding Fathers' tanta-

lizingly brief statements. Gouverneur Morris was content to let future generations puzzle out everything that might be implied in the Delphic utterance, "The executive Power shall be vested in a President . . ." and to let them weigh this against the equally oracular declaration that "all legislative Powers herein granted shall be vested in a Congress. . . ." The overlapping of executive and legislative functions was a deliberate application of eighteenth-century theorizing. So was the distinction drawn between them. (As Montesquieu observed in his *L'Esprit des Lois*, "When the legislative and executive powers are united . . . there can be no liberty; because apprehensions may arise, lest the same monarch or senate should enact tyrannical laws. . . .") But much of the Constitution was vague, either because the delegates concealed disagreement by using a form of words open to multiple interpretation, or else because they were not able to anticipate the vast range of difficulties that would arise when the Constitution was tested. They built friction into the document intentionally, as a safeguard against corruption and dictatorship. Some of the friction generated later they did not foresee and would not have deemed healthy. Some difficulties would be resolved by constitutional amendments. Four of the twenty-five changes sanctioned by amendment would deal with election to or tenure of the Presidency—although many commentators feel that the Twenty-second Amendment, which restricts the President to two terms, creates more difficulties than it solves.

The Constitution, praised all over the world for its wisdom and longevity, was not a perfect document. Its Antifederalist opponents, though sometimes foolish, inconsistent, and shortsighted, raised questions that have lingered on disquietingly. Could or should one man have the possibility of so much power? Was he entitled to it? Was he superhuman enough to carry such a burden? As the final chapter of this book notes, many experts on American government wish to reopen the old debate as to the viability of a single Executive. Nor were critics of the Constitution entirely unjustified when they grumbled that the Federalists recommended their handiwork in diverse ways to diverse audiences. Abraham Lincoln once said that the incompatible arguments of a rival politician reminded him of a Yankee peddler's claim that the clothes he was selling were "large enough for any man, small enough for any boy." In the same way, the Antifederalists could point out that whereas *The Federalist* papers ridiculed Clinton's comparison of the President with the British king, Alexander Hamilton had, according to well-founded rumor, recommended a strong American Executive on exactly the same grounds. Could Edmund Randolph (who did not sign the document), remembering Madison's vital role at Philadelphia and in the ratification controversy, believe his colleague wholly sincere when Madison told him in May, 1789, that "I see and *politically feel* that [the Presidency] will be the weak branch of the Government"? If Madison was sincere, how could he remain closely associated with the new Federalist administration? How could Jefferson become one of the executive heads, as Secretary of State, in the administration? Were there two or more conceptions of the power of the Presidency, ranging from strong to weak, beneath the apparent consensus of Philadelphia?

The critics of the Constitution were apt to harp tiresomely on the theme of monarchy. The word was often merely a catchall, a convenient term of abuse. Yet they were right to draw the parallel, as Edward S. Corwin stressed. In his words, the Presidency was "designed in great measure to reproduce the monarchy of George III with the corruption left out, and also of course the hereditary feature." In part because the eighteenth century could not imagine a totally nonmonarchic Executive, in part because of their reading, in part because they wished to emulate the best features of the British system, and in a few cases because they secretly admired the pomp and circumstance of a mixed monarchic government, the Founding Fathers actually devised a type of elective monarchy, just as the critics said. It was as if they had placed the Polish king in the British context, which was modified in turn by the American context.

The President, though the Constitution nowhere said so, was meant by some of the delegates to symbolize the United States, much as the British crown symbolized the British realm. A President is supposed to preside, with dignity and detachment, over affairs from which he is somewhat removed. This quasi-monarchic dream was ideally personified in George Washington, the "Father of his Country." Better still, he was not an actual father. Having no sons of his own, he could never be the founder of a dynasty. Instead Americans could and did name their own sons after him. One such beneficiary, the writer Washington Irving, caught the truth of the transfer of regality in his tale of Rip Van Winkle. Rip, having fallen asleep for twenty years on the eve of the Revolution, returns to his village in bewilderment. He discovers among other alterations that the old Dutch inn has become the Union Hotel. On the inn sign "he recognized . . . the ruby face of King George, under which he had smoked so many a peaceful pipe; but even this was singularly metamorphosed. The red coat was changed for one of blue and buff, a sword was held in the hand instead of a sceptre, the head was decorated with a cocked hat, and underneath was painted in large characters, GENERAL WASHINGTON."

There is a story that at the close of the Philadelphia Convention Benjamin Franklin returned to his lodgings to be greeted by this query from his landlady: "Well, Mr. Franklin, what have you given us, a republic or a monarchy?" His enigmatic answer was: "A republic—if you can keep it." Almost every book on the Constitutional Convention or on the history of the Presidency cites Pierce Butler's confession that delegates were stimulated to grant "full great" powers by shaping their ideas around the virtuous and awesome figure of General Washington. The conclusion of Butler's letter is less often quoted: "So that the Man, who by his Patriotism and Virtue, Contributed largely to the Emancipation of his Country, may be the Innocent means of its being, when He is lay'd low, oppress'd."

It was an alarming observation, indicative of quite profound uneasiness. Had the Constitution makers invented a workable mechanism of government or a monster—or possibly a mere figurehead behind whom the real struggle for control would be carried on by heads of executive departments, members of the Senate, or others? Only time would reveal the answer. No matter how ingenious and theoretically perfect the Constitution might be, the office of the President could develop beneficially for the nation only if George Washington accomplished a miracle of discretionary firmness, if his fellow countrymen displayed more than average good sense and harmony, and if luck or Providence smiled upon the risky scheme. Nearly every precedent of history taught that the plan would fail, or at any rate be transformed into a creature unpredictably strange in its lineaments.

1787 - 1789

The Presidency in Documents

Alexander Hamilton's brilliant defense of the Constitution before a predominantly hostile New York convention led to that state's ratification of the new form of government. On June 27, 1788, the day he gave the speech outlined by delegate John McKesson (above), Hamilton sent a letter to Madison, inquiring into the status of the Virginia convention. That day Madison was writing him, also—to report that Virginia had ratified.

Advice
from History

The men who invented the Presidency in Philadelphia in 1787 were not bound by a long national tradition. Even so, they were deeply affected by the past. Early in the year, John Adams had written in London that the creators of the American state governments had "adopted the method of a wise architect, in erecting a new palace for . . . his sovereign." Such an architect, said Adams, would read the best writers, examine the most famous buildings to see how well they had survived the passing years, and then choose the ideas that seemed most useful to his own structure. Similarly, in devising the national Executive, the writers of the Constitution called not only on their own sentiments and experience, but also on those of lawmakers and philosophers throughout history.

Plato

In his fourth-century-B.C. dialogue Laws, *the Greek philosopher, speaking as the Athenian Stranger, addressed these thoughts to two companions—one a citizen of Sparta—as they journeyed to the temple of Zeus.*

. . . if any one gives too great a power to anything, too large a sail to a vessel, too much food to the body, too much authority to the mind, and does not observe the mean, everything is overthrown, and, in the wantonness of excess runs in the one case to disorders, and in the other to injustice, which is the child of excess. I mean to say, my dear friends, that there is no soul of man, young and irresponsible, who will be able to sustain the temptation of arbitrary power—no one who will not, under such circumstances, become filled with folly . . . when this happens, his kingdom is undermined, and all his power vanishes from him. And great legislators who know the mean should take heed of the danger. . . .

. . . A God, who watched over Sparta, seeing into the future, gave you two families of kings instead of one; and thus brought you more within the limits of moderation. In the next place, some human wis-

dom mingled with divine power, observing that the constitution of your government was still feverish and excited, tempered your inborn strength and pride of birth with the moderation which comes of age, making the power of your twenty-eight elders equal with that of the kings in the most important matters. But your third saviour, perceiving that your government was still swelling and foaming, and desirous to impose a curb upon it, instituted the Ephors, whose power he made to resemble that of magistrates elected by lot; and by this arrangement the kingly office . . . duly moderated, was preserved, and was the means of preserving all the rest. . . .

. . . there are two mother forms of states from which the rest may be truly said to be derived; and one of them may be called monarchy and the other democracy. . . . Now, if you are to have liberty and the combination of friendship with wisdom, you must have both these forms of government in a measure . . . no city can be well governed which is not made up of both. . . .

Aristotle

Pupil of Plato and tutor to Alexander the Great, Aristotle was frequently cited in early American commentaries on government. The following remarks concerning the enrichment of public magistrates appear in Politics.

. . . But above all every state should be so administered and so regulated by law that its magistrates cannot possibly make money. In oligarchies special precautions should be used against this evil. For the people do not take any great offence at being kept out of the government—indeed they are rather pleased than otherwise at having leisure for their private business—but what irritates them is to think that their rulers are stealing the public money; then they are doubly annoyed; for they lose both honour and profit. If office brought no profit, then and then only could democracy and aristocracy be combined; for both notables and people might have their wishes gratified. All would be able to hold office, which is the aim of democracy, and the notables would be magistrates, which is the aim of aristocracy. And this result may be accomplished when there is no possibility of making money out of the offices; for the poor will not want to have them when

Plato   *Aristotle*   *Machiavelli*

there is nothing to be gained from them—they would rather be attending to their own concerns; and the rich, who do not want money from the public treasury, will be able to take them; and so the poor will keep to their work and grow rich, and the notables will not be governed by the lower class. . . .

Niccolò Machiavelli

In his sixteenth-century Discourses, *the pragmatic Florentine statesman and political philosopher advocated a strong executive. Machiavelli emphasized, however, that effective checks on executive power must be provided.*

. . . truly, of all the institutions of Rome, this one [dictatorship] deserves to be counted amongst those to which she was most indebted for her greatness and dominion. For without some such an institution Rome would with difficulty have escaped the many extraordinary dangers that befell her; for the customary proceedings of republics are slow, no magistrate or council being permitted to act independently, but being in almost all instances obliged to act in concert one with the other, so that often much time is required to harmonize their several opinions; and tardy measures are most dangerous when the occasion requires prompt action. And therefore all republics should have some institution similar to the dictatorship. . . .

. . . there are two things to be considered; namely,

the manner in which the authority is bestowed, and the length of time for which it is given. For when full power is conferred for any length of time (and I call a year or more a long time) it is always dangerous. . . . at the creation of a Dictator, the Tribunes, the Consuls, and the Senate all remained with their respective powers, of which they could not be deprived by the Dictator. And even if he could have removed any one from the consulate or from the Senate, yet he could not abrogate the senatorial order and make new laws himself. So that the Senate, the Consuls, and the Tribunes, remaining in full authority, served as it were as a guard to watch that the Dictator did not transcend his powers. . . .

John Locke

A leading exponent of the theory that government properly rests on the continuous consent of the governed, Locke was of prime importance to American political thought. The selections below are from Concerning Civil Government, Second Essay, *published in 1690.*

. . . The legislative power is that which has a right to direct how the force of the commonwealth shall be employed for preserving the community and the members of it. Because those laws which are constantly to be executed, and whose force is always to continue, may be made in a little time, therefore there is no need that the legislative should be always in being, not having always business to do. . . . it may be too great temptation to human frailty, apt to grasp at power, for the same persons who have the power of making laws to have also in their hands the power to execute them, whereby they may exempt themselves from obedience to the laws they make, and suit the law . . . to their own private advantage, and thereby come to have a distinct interest from the rest of the community, contrary to the end of society and government. . . .

. . . it is necessary there should be a power always in being which should see to the execution of the laws that are made, and remain in force. And thus the legislative and executive power come often to be separated.

. . . There is another power in every commonwealth which one may call natural, because it is that which answers to the power every man naturally had before he entered into society. For though in a commonwealth the members of it are distinct persons, still, in reference to one another, and, as such, are governed by the laws of the society, yet, in reference to the rest of mankind, they make one body, which is, as every member of it before was, still in the state of Nature with the rest of mankind, so that the controversies that happen between any man of the society with those that are out of it are managed by the public, and an injury done to a member of their body engages the whole in the reparation of it. So that under this consideration the whole community is one body in the state of Nature in respect of all other states or persons out of its community.

. . . This, therefore, contains the power of war and peace, leagues and alliances, and all the transactions with all persons and communities without the commonwealth, and may be called federative. . . .

. . . These two powers, executive and federative, though they be really distinct in themselves . . . one comprehending the execution of the municipal laws of the society within itself upon all that are parts of it, the other the management of the security and interest of the public without with all those that it may receive benefit or damage from, yet they are always almost united. . . .

. . . they are hardly to be separated and placed at the same time in the hands of distinct persons. For both of them requiring the force of the society for their exercise, it is almost impracticable to place the

The delegates to the Convention were profoundly influenced by the writings of Montesquieu (above), who had advocated the separation of powers and checks and balances.

force of the commonwealth in distinct and not subordinate hands, or that the executive and federative power should be placed in persons that might act separately, whereby the force of the public would be under different commands, which would be apt some time or other to cause disorder and ruin. . . .

. . . When the legislative hath put the execution of the laws they make into other hands, they have a power still to resume it out of those hands when they find cause, and to punish for any mal-administration against the laws. The same holds also in regard of the federative power, that and the executive being both ministerial and subordinate to the legislative. . . .

. . . Where the legislative and executive power are in distinct hands, as they are in all moderated monarchies and well-framed governments, there the good of the society requires that several things should be left to the discretion of him that has the executive power. For the legislators not being able to foresee and provide by laws for all that may be useful to the community, the executor of the laws, having the power in his hands, has by the common law of Nature a right to make use of it for the good of the society, in many cases where the municipal law has given no direction, till the legislative can conveniently be assembled to provide for it; nay, many things there are which the law can by no means provide for, and those must necessarily be left to the discretion of him that has the executive power in his hands, to be ordered by him as the public good and advantage shall require; nay, it is fit that the laws themselves should in some cases give way to the executive power, or rather to this fundamental law of Nature and government—viz., that as much as may be all the members of the society are to be preserved. . . .

. . . This power to act according to discretion for the public good, without the prescription of the law and sometimes even against it, is that which is called prerogative; for since in some governments the law-making power is not always in being and is usually too numerous, and so too slow for the dispatch requisite to execution, and because, also, it is impossible to foresee and so by laws to provide for all accidents and necessities that may concern the public, or make such laws as will do no harm, if they are executed with an inflexible rigour on all occasions and upon all persons that may come in their way, therefore there is a latitude left to the executive power to do many things of choice which the laws do not prescribe. . . .

Montesquieu

Eighteenth-century historians noted that the stability of governments seemed to be related to how carefully the powers of making and administering laws were distributed. Charles Louis de Secondat, Baron de La Brède et de Montesquieu, gave an explanation for this relationship in his The Spirit of the Laws, *published in 1748. Montesquieu, whose name was mentioned often during American constitutional debates, particularly admired the English system of government, which is under discussion in the following selection from his book.*

. . . When the legislative and executive powers are united in the same person, or in the same body of magistrates, there can be no liberty; because apprehensions may arise, lest the same monarch or senate should enact tyrannical laws, to execute them in a tyrannical manner. . . .

Were the executive power not to have a right of restraining the encroachments of the legislative body, the latter would become despotic; for as it might arrogate to itself what authority it pleased, it would soon destroy all the other powers.

But it is not proper, on the other hand, that the legislative power should have a right to stay the executive. For as the execution has its natural limits, it is useless to confine it; besides, the executive power is generally employed in momentary operations. . . .

But if the legislative power in a free state has no right to stay the executive, it has a right and ought to have the means of examining in what manner its laws have been executed; an advantage which this government has over that of Crete and Sparta, where the Cosmi and the Ephori gave no account of their administration.

But whatever may be the issue of that examination, the legislative body ought not to have a power of arraigning the person, nor, of course, the conduct, of him who is entrusted with the executive power. His person should be sacred, because as it is necessary for the good of the state to prevent the legislative body from rendering themselves arbitrary, the moment he is accused or tried there is an end of liberty.

In this case the state would be no longer a monarchy, but a kind of republic, though not a free government. But as the person entrusted with the executive power cannot abuse it without bad counsellors, and such as have the laws as ministers, though the laws protect them as subjects, these men may be examined and punished—an advantage which this government has over that of Gnidus, where the law allowed of no such thing as calling the Amymones to an account, even after their administration; and therefore the people could never obtain any satisfaction for the injuries done them. . . .

Here then is the fundamental constitution of the government we are treating of. The legislative body being composed of two parts, they check one another by the mutual privilege of rejecting. They are both restrained by the executive power, as the executive is by the legislative.

These three powers should naturally form a state of repose or inaction. But as there is a necessity for movement in the course of human affairs, they are forced to move, but still in concert.

As the executive power has no other part in the legislative than the privilege of rejecting, it can have no share in the public debates. It is not even necessary that it should propose, because as it may always disapprove of the resolutions that shall be taken, it may likewise reject the decisions on those proposals which were made against its will. . . .

John Adams

A Defence of the Constitution of the Governments of the United States of America *was written while Adams was in London as envoy to England. It was his answer to A. R. J. Turgot and other French philosophers who criticized the state constitutions in America for dividing the powers of government after the British model. Volume I of the* Defence *was published before the Constitutional Convention met and was read by many delegates. Parts of the last chapter are excerpted here.*

According to M. Turgot's idea of a perfect commonwealth, a single assembly is to be possessed of all authority, legislative, executive, and judicial. It will be a proper conclusion of all our speculations upon this, the most interesting subject which can employ the thoughts of men, to consider in what manner such an assembly will conduct its deliberations, and exert its power. The executive power is properly the government; the laws are a dead letter until an administration begins to carry them into execution. Let us begin then with this. If there is an army to raise, this single assembly is to appoint all its officers. . . . Here is an endless source of debate and delay. When there are two or more candidates for a commission, and there will generally be several, how shall an assembly of five hundred or one hundred men, collected from all the most distant parts of a large state, become informed of the merits and pretensions of each candidate? . . . All the officers of revenue, police, justice, must be appointed in the same way. Ambassadors, consuls, agents to foreign countries, must be appointed too by vote of assembly.—This branch of business alone would fill up the whole year, and be more than could be done. An assembly must be informed before it can act. The understanding and conscience of every member should be clearly satisfied before he can vote. Information is to be had only by debate, and examination of evidence. Any man may see that this must be attended with difficulty; but no man, who has not seen the inside of such an assembly, can conceive the confusion, uncertainty, and procrastination of such proceedings. The American provincial congresses had experience enough of this. . . . In the second place, there never was yet a people who must not have somebody or something to represent the dignity of the state, the majesty of the people, call it what you will—a doge, an avoyer, an archon, a president, a consul, a syndic; this becomes at once an object of ambition and dispute, and, in time, of division, faction, sedition, and rebellion. . . . Will it be said that the assembly shall appoint committees to try causes? But who are to make these appointments? Will not a few haughty palatines in the assembly have influence enough to determine the election in favour of their friends? and will not this make the judges the tools of a party? If the leaders are divided into parties, will not one prevail at one year, and another the next? and will not this intro-

Franklin's prerevolutionary cartoon prophesied that England would lose her colonies.

duce the most wretched of servitudes, an uncertain jurisprudence? Will it be said that the assembly shall appoint committees for the nomination of officers? The same intrigues, and greater struggles, would be introduced for the place of a committee-man; and there would be frequent appeals from those committees to the body that appointed them. Shall the assembly appoint a governor or president, and give him all the executive power? Why should not the people at large appoint him? Giving this power to the assembly will open a wider door to intrigue for the place; and the aristocratical families will be sure, nine times in ten, to carry their choice in this way; and, what is worse, the first magistrate will be considered as dependent on every obscure member of the house, but in reality he will be dependent only on a dozen or a score, perhaps on two or three, of the whole. He will be liable to daily motions, debates, and votes of censure. Instead of thinking of his duty to the people at large, he will confine his attention chiefly to the assembly, and believe, that if he can satisfy them, or a majority of them, he has done his duty.... As the executive power, the essence of government, is ever odious to popular envy and jealousy, it will ever be in the power of a few illustrious and wealthy citizens to excite clamours and uneasiness, if not commotions and seditions, against it. Although it is the natural friend of the people, and the only defence which they or their representatives can have against the avarice and ambition of the rich and distinguished citizens, yet such is their thoughtless simplicity, they are ever ready to believe that the evils they feel are brought upon them by the executive power. How easy is it then for a few artful men, among the aristocratical body, to make a president, thus appointed and supported, unpopular, though he conducts himself with all the integrity and ability which his office requires? ...

Separate the legislative and executive powers, Adams said, and place executive responsibility in one man.

... the unity, the secrecy, the dispatch of one man, has no equal; and the executive power should be watched by all men; the attention of the whole nation should be fixed upon one point, and the blame and censure, as well as the impeachments and vengeance for abuses of this power, should be directed solely to the ministers of one man....

The Articles of Confederation

The government of the Union was entrusted to a single deliberative body—"the united states in congress assembled." Moreover, the Articles of Confederation, ratified in 1781, placed great dependence on the good faith and cooperation of the states. The Congress was given no effective means to enforce its decisions, and those executive powers it was allowed were almost meaningless.

Article IX. The united states in congress assembled, shall have the sole and exclusive right and power of determining on peace and war, except [those cases in which a state "be actually invaded by enemies, or shall have received certain advice of a resolution being formed by some nation of Indians to invade such state, and the danger is so imminent as not to admit of a delay till the united states in congress assembled can be consulted . . ."]—of sending and receiving ambassadors—entering into treaties and alliances, provided that no treaty of commerce shall be made whereby the legislative power of the respective states shall be restrained from imposing such imposts and duties on foreigners as their own people are subjected to, or from prohibiting the exportation or importation of any species of goods or commodities, whatsoever—of establishing rules for deciding in all cases what captures on land or water shall be legal, and in what manner prizes taken by land or naval forces in the service of the united states shall be divided or appropriated—of granting letters of marque and reprisal in times of peace—appointing courts for the trial of piracies and felonies committed on the high seas and establishing courts for receiving and determining finally appeals in all cases of captures....

The united states in congress assembled shall also be the last resort on appeal in all disputes and differences now subsisting or that hereafter may arise between two or more states. [A legal process for settling these disputes by a congressional court was outlined.] ... and the judgment and sentence of the court ...

shall be final and conclusive; and if any of the parties shall refuse to submit to the authority of such court, or to appear to defend their claim or cause, the court shall nevertheless proceed to pronounce sentence, or judgment, which shall in like manner be final and decisive, the judgment or sentence and other proceedings being in either case transmitted to congress, and lodged among the acts of congress. . . .

The united states in congress assembled shall also have the sole and exclusive right and power of regulating the alloy and value of coin struck by their own authority, or by that of the respective states—fixing the standard of weights and measures throughout the united states—regulating the trade and managing all affairs with the Indians, not members of any of the states, provided that the legislative right of any state within its own limits be not infringed or violated—establishing or regulating post-offices from one state to another . . . and exacting such postage on the papers passing thro' the same as may be requisite to defray the expences of the said office—appointing all officers of the land forces, in the service of the united states, excepting regimental officers—appointing all the officers of the naval forces, and commissioning all officers whatever in the service of the united states—making rules for the government and regulation of the said land and naval forces, and directing their operations.

The united states in congress assembled shall have authority to appoint a committee, to sit in the recess of congress, to be denominated "A Committee of the States," and to consist of one delegate from each state; and to appoint such other committees and civil officers as may be necessary for managing the general affairs of the united states under their direction—to appoint one of their number to preside, provided that no person be allowed to serve in the office of president more than one year in any term of three years; to ascertain the necessary sums of money to be raised for the service of the united states, and to appropriate and apply the same for defraying the public expences—to borrow money, or emit bills on the credit of the united states, transmitting every half year to the respective states an account of the sums of money so borrowed or emitted,—to build and equip a navy—to agree upon the number of land forces, and to make requisitions from each state for its quota . . . which requisition shall be binding. . . .

Article X. The committee of the states, or any nine of them, shall be authorized to execute, in the recess of congress, such of the powers of congress as the united states in congress assembled by the consent of nine states, shall from time to time think expedient to vest them with; provided that no power be delegated to the said committee, for the exercise of which, by the articles of confederation, the voice of nine states in the congress . . . is requisite.

In Convention

The Constitutional Convention was scheduled to begin on May 14, 1787, but a quorum of states was not represented in Philadelphia until May 25. On that day the delegates chose George Washington as their presiding officer and began to work. Nearly four months later, on September 17, they adjourned for the last time, their new Constitution completed. There were no newspaper reports of their sessions; they had agreed to keep the proceedings secret in order that public reaction might not influence the frankness of their discussions. The extant records of these meetings, the most momentous in American history, are contained largely in the sketchy official journal and in the notes of the men who attended—particularly in the journal of James Madison of Virginia. Except when otherwise noted, Madison's journal (as edited by Max Farrand and published in 1966 by Yale University Press) is the source of the following material.

The Virginia Plan

On May 29 the young governor of Virginia, Edmund Randolph, presented a working draft of the Constitution to the Convention. Probably composed chiefly by Madison, the draft included a provision for an executive branch.

7. Resd. that a National Executive be instituted; to be chosen by the National Legislature for the term

Philadelphia's State House, now known as Independence Hall, was the site of the Constitutional Convention in 1787.

of   years, to receive punctually at stated times, a fixed compensation for the services rendered, in which no increase or diminution shall be made so as to affect the Magistracy, existing at the time of increase or diminution, and to be ineligible a second time; and that besides a general authority to execute the National laws, it ought to enjoy the Executive rights vested in Congress by the Confederation.

8. Resd. that the Executive and a convenient number of the National Judiciary, ought to compose a council of revision with authority to examine every act of the National Legislature before it shall operate . . . and that the dissent of the said Council shall amount to a rejection, unless the Act of the National Legislature be again passed . . . by   of the members of each branch.

One Executive, or Several?

On June 1 James Wilson of Pennsylvania, seconded by Charles Pinckney of South Carolina, moved that the national executive powers be lodged in a single person.

. . . A considerable pause ensuing and the Chairman asking if he should put the question, Docr. Franklin [Benjamin Franklin of Pennsylvania] observed that it was a point of great importance and wished that the gentlemen would deliver their sentiments on it before the question was put.

Mr. Rutledge [John Rutledge, delegate from South Carolina]. . . . said he was for vesting the Executive power in a single person, tho' he was not for giving him the power of war and peace. A single man would . . . administer the public affairs best.

Mr. Sherman [Roger Sherman of Connecticut] said he considered the Executive magistracy as nothing more than an institution for carrying the will of the Legislature into effect, that the person or persons ought to be appointed by and accountable to the Legislature only, which was the depositary of the supreme will of the Society. As they were the best judges of the business which ought to be done by the Executive department, and consequently of the number necessary from time to time for doing it, he wished the number might not be fixed, but that the legislature should be at liberty to appoint one or more as experience might dictate. . . .

Election and Term

Wilson's motion was postponed, and the Convention went on to other questions, including how to choose the Executive and how long he (or they) should serve.

. . . Mr. Wilson said he was almost unwilling to declare the mode [of election] which he wished to take place, being apprehensive that it might appear chimerical. He would say however at least that in theory he was for an election by the people; Experience, particularly in N. York & Massts, shewed that an election of the first magistrate by the people at large, was both a convenient & successful mode. The objects of choice in such cases must be persons whose merits have general notoriety.

Mr. Sherman was for the appointment by the Legislature, and for making him absolutely dependent on that body, as it was the will of that which was to be executed. An independence of the Executive on the supreme Legislative, was in his opinion the very essence of tyranny if there was any such thing.

Mr. Wilson moves that the blank for the term of duration should be filled with three years, observing at the same time that he preferred this short period, on the supposition that a re-eligibility would be provided for. Mr. Pin[c]kney was for seven years.

Mr. Sherman was for three years, and agst. the doctrine of rotation [ineligibility for a second term] as throwing out of office the men best qualified to execute its duties.

Mr. Mason [George Mason of Virginia] was for seven years at least, and for prohibiting a re-eligibility as the best expedient both for preventing the effect of a false complaisance on the side of the Legislature towards unfit characters; and a temptation on the side of the Executive to intrigue with the Legislature for a re-appointment.

Mr. Bedford [Gunning Bedford of Delaware] was strongly opposed to so long a term. . . . [Suppose] the first magistrate should be saddled on it for such period and it should be found on trial that he did not possess the qualifications ascribed to him, or should lose them after his appointment. An impeachment he said would be no cure for this evil, as an impeachment would reach misfeasance only, not incapacity. He was for a triennial election, and for an ineligibility after a period of nine years.

The Electoral College

The Convention settled tentatively on seven-year terms. The next day James Wilson put forward a plan for elections that joined popular choice with conservative checks.

. . . "That the States be divided into   districts: & that the persons qualified to vote in each district for members of the first branch of the national Legislature elect   members for their respective districts to be electors of the Executive magistracy. that the said Electors of the Executive magistracy meet at   and they or any   of them so met shall proceed to elect by ballot, but not out of their own body   person   in whom the Executive authority of the national Government shall be vested." . . .

King Making?

Wilson's resolution was defeated. It was agreed that no one should hold the executive office for more than a single term. Two days later the question of how many persons

should comprise the executive branch was taken up again. Some of the delegates believed that a single Executive would be too much like a royal monarch, or that the people of the United States would think so.

. . . Mr. Wilson. . . . [said] All know that a single magistrate is not a King. . . . All the 13 States tho' agreeing in scarce any other instance, agree in placing a single magistrate at the head of the Governmt. The idea of three heads has taken place in none. . . . Among three equal members, he foresaw nothing but uncontrouled, continued, & violent animosities; which would not only interrupt the public administration; but diffuse their poison thro' the other branches of Govt., thro' the States, and at length thro' the people at large. . . .

The one-man Executive was then accepted by the Convention, but George Mason, who had not been present for the vote, continued to oppose it. This speech, found among his papers, was probably delivered on June 4.

. . . The chief Advantages which have been urged in favour of Unity in the Executive, are the Secrecy, the Dispatch, the Vigour and Energy which the Government will derive from it; especially in time of war. —That these are great Advantages, I shall most readily allow—They have been strongly insisted on by all monarchical Writers—they have been acknowledged by the ablest and most candid Defenders of Republican Government; and it can not be denied that a Monarchy possesses them in a much greater Degree than a Republic—Yet perhaps a little Reflection may . . . lead us to enquire whether there is not some pervading Principle in Republican Governments which sets at Naught . . . this boasted Superiority. . . . [and which] is to be found in the Love the Affection the Attachment of the Citizens to their Laws, to their Freedom, and to their Country. . . .

We have not yet been able to define the Powers of the Executive; and however moderately some Gentlemen may talk or think upon the Subject, I believe there is a genera[l] Tendency to a strong Executive and I am inclined to think a strong Executive necessary—If strong and extensive Powers are vested in the Executive, and that Executive consists only of one Person; the Government will of course degenerate . . . into a Monarchy. . . . If the Executive is vested in three Persons, one chosen from the northern, one from the middle, and one from the Southern States, will it not contribute to quiet the Minds of the People, and convince them that there will be proper attention paid to their respective Concerns? Will not three Men so chosen bring with them, into Office, a more perfect and extensive Knowledge of the real Interests of this great Union? Will not such a mode of Appointment be the most effectual means of preventing Cabals and Intrigues between the Legislature and the Candidates for this Office? . . . Will it not be the most effectual means of checking and counteracting the aspiring Views of dangerous and ambitious Men, and consequently the best Security for the Stability and Duration of our Government upon the invaluable Principles of Liberty? . . .

Veto Power

On June 4 the delegates also debated the eighth proposition in the Virginia Plan, "that the executive and a convenient number of the National Judiciary" should be able to reject any act approved by the legislature unless the act was repassed by Congress by a specific margin.

. . . Mr. Gerry [Elbridge Gerry of Massachusetts] doubts whether the Judiciary ought to form a part of it, as they will have a sufficient check agst. encroachments on their own department by their exposition of the laws, which involved a power of deciding on their Constitutionality. . . . It was quite foreign from the nature of ye. office to make them judges of the policy of public measures. He moves to postpone the clause in order to propose "that the National Executive shall have a right to negative any Legislative act which shall not be afterwards passed by   parts of each branch of the national Legislature. . . .

Mr. Wilson thinks. . . . If the Legislative Exẽtiv & Judiciary ought to be distinct & independent, The Executive ought to have an absolute negative. Without such a Self-defence the Legislature can at any moment sink it into non-existence. He was for varying the proposition in such a manner as to give the Executive & Judiciary jointly an absolute negative. . . .

Docr. Franklin. . . . had had some experience of this check in the Executive on the Legislature, under the proprietary Government of Pena. The negative of the Governor was constantly made use of to extort money. No good law whatever could be passed without a private bargain with him. . . . He was afraid, if a negative should be given as proposed, that more power and money would be demanded, till at last eno' would be gotten to influence & bribe the Legislature into a compleat subjection to the will of the Executive.

A move to vest the Executive with an absolute negative on legislation was beaten down, but it was also tentatively agreed at the same time that he should share the veto power with no one. On June 6 the argument began again.

. . . Mr. Madison. . . . observed that the great difficulty in rendering the Executive competent to its own defence arose from the nature of Republican Govt. which could not give to an individual citizen that settled pre-eminence in the eyes of the rest, that weight of property, that personal interest agst. betraying the National interest, which appertain to an hereditary magistrate. In a Republic personal merit alone could be the ground of political exaltation, but it would rarely happen that this merit would be so pre-eminent as to produce universal acquiescence. The Executive Magistrate would be envied & assailed by disappointed competitors: His firmness therefore wd. need support. He would not possess those great emoluments from his station, nor that permanent stake in the public interest which wd. place him out of the reach of foreign corruption: He would stand in need therefore of being controuled as well as supported. An association of the Judges in his revisionary function wd both double the advantage and diminish the danger. . . .

Mr. Gerry thought the Executive, whilst standing alone wd. be more impartial than when he cd. be covered by the sanction & seduced by the sophistry of the Judges.

Mr. King [Rufus King, a delegate from Massachusetts]. If the Unity of the Executive was preferred for the sake of responsibility, the policy of it is as applicable to the revisionary as to the Executive power. . . .

Col Mason was for giving all possible weight to the revisionary institution. The Executive power ought to be well secured agst. Legislative usurpations on it. The purse & the sword ought never to get into the same hands. . . .

Roger Sherman

Elbridge Gerry

Rufus King

Choosing the Executive

It had become obvious that it would be difficult to frame an acceptable system for picking the Executive. On June 9 Elbridge Gerry tried his hand at finding a solution.

. . . Mr. Gerry . . . moved "that the National Executive should be elected by the Executives of the States whose proportion of votes should be the same with that allowed to the States in the election of the Senate." [At that point state membership in the Senate was to be allotted by population.] . . . He proposed . . . appointing by the State Executives as most analogous to the principle observed in electing the other branches of the Natl. Govt.; the first branch being chosen by the *people* of the States, & the 2d. by the Legislatures of the States. . . .

Mr. Randolph urged strongly the inexpediency of Mr. Gerry's mode. . . . The confidence of the people would not be secured by it to the Natl. Magistrate. The small States would lose all chance of an appointmt. from within themselves. Bad appointments would be made; the Executives of the States being little conversant with characters not within their own small spheres. [Also they] . . . being in fact dependent on the State Legislatures will generally be guided by the views of the latter. . . . A Natl. Executive thus chosen will not be likely to defend with becoming vigilance & firmness the national rights agst. State encroachments. Vacancies also must happen. How can these be filled? He could not suppose

either that the Executives would feel the interest in supporting the Natl. Executive which had been imagined. They will not cherish the great Oak which is to reduce them to paltry shrubs. . . .

Strength and Balance

For more than five weeks, the Convention paid little attention to the Executive, as it tried to decide whether to create a national government or continue the Confederation, and how the legislature would be composed. On July 17 it returned at last to the question of the Executive. The goal was to give the office the power and independence that would allow those who held it to act energetically and compete effectively with the legislature, but to provide checks so that an Executive could not overwhelm the legislature, or be invulnerable to public disapproval. Should the legislature choose him?

. . . Mr. Governr. Morris [Gouverneur Morris of Pennsylvania] was pointedly agst. his being so chosen. He will be the mere creature of the Legisl: if appointed & impeachable by that body. He ought to be elected by the people at large, by the freeholders of the Country. . . . If the Legislature elect . . . it will be like the election of a pope by a conclave of cardinals. . . .

Mr. Sherman thought that . . . the people at large . . . will never be sufficiently informed of characters, and besides will never give a majority of votes to any one man. They will generally vote for some man in their own State, and the largest State will have the best chance for the appointment. If the choice be made by the Legislre. A majority . . . may be made necessary to constitute an election. . . .

Col. Mason. . . . [thought] it would be as unnatural to refer the choice of a proper character for chief Magistrate to the people, as it would, to refer a trial of colours to a blind man. The extent of the Country renders it impossible that the people can have the requisite capacity to judge of the respective pretensions of the Candidates. . . .

How long should he serve? Should he be eligible for re-election? Should he be impeachable? Why should not the people elect him? Morris gave his opinions during debate on July 19, after Maryland's Luther Martin had moved that the Executive "be ineligible a 2d. time."

. . . Our Country is an extensive one. We must either then renounce the blessings of the Union, or provide an Executive with sufficient vigor to pervade every part of it. . . . One great object of the Executive is to controul the Legislature. The Legislature will continually seek to aggrandize & perpetuate themselves. . . . It is necessary then that the Executive Magistrate should be the guardian of the people, even of the lower classes, agst. Legislative tyranny. . . . What effect will [Martin's motion] have? 1. it will destroy the great incitement to merit public esteem by taking away the hope of being rewarded with a reappointment. It may give a dangerous turn to one of the strongest passions in the human breast. . . . Shut the Civil road to Glory & he may be compelled to seek it by the sword. 2. It will tempt him to make the most of the Short space of time allotted him, to accumulate wealth and provide for his friends. 3. It will produce violations of the very constitution it is meant to secure. In moments of pressing danger the tried abilities and established character of a favorite Magistrate will prevail over respect for the forms of the Constitution. . . . Can no better establishmt. be devised? If he is to be the Guardian of the people let him be appointed by the people? . . . let him not be impeachable. Let him be of short duration, that he may with propriety be re-eligible. . . . He suggested a biennial election of the Executive. . . . Again, it might be objected that two years would be too short

a duration. But he believes that as long as [the Executive] should behave himself well, he would be continued in his place. . . .

Mr. King did not like the ineligibility. He thought there was great force in the remark of Mr. Sherman, that he who has proved himself to be most fit for an Office, ought not to be excluded by the constitution from holding it. . . . the people at large would chuse wisely. There was indeed some difficulty arising from the improbability of a general concurrence of the people in favor of any one man. On the whole he was of opinion that an appointment by electors chosen by the people . . . would be liable to fewest objections. . . .

Mr. Butler [Pierce Butler, from South Carolina] was agst. a frequency of the elections. Geo & S.C. were too distant to send electors often.

Mr. Elseworth [Oliver Ellsworth of Connecticut] was for 6 years. If the elections be too frequent, the Executive will not be firm eno'. There must be duties which will make him unpopular for the moment. There will be *outs* as well as *ins*. His administration therefore will be attacked and misrepresented.

Mr. Williamson [Hugh Williamson, North Carolina delegate] was for 6 years. The expence will be considerable & ought not to be unnecessarily repeated. If the Elections are too frequent, the best men will not undertake the service and those of an inferior character will be liable to be corrupted. . . .

For the first time the Convention voted for an electoral system: the electors would be chosen by the state legislatures, and the Executive would serve six-year terms and would be eligible for re-election. The next day, July 20, the topic of impeachment of the Executive was debated.

. . . Mr. Pinkney & Mr Govr. Morris moved to strike out this part of the Resolution. Mr P. observd. he ought not to be impeachable whilst in office . . .

Mr. Govr. Morris. He can do no criminal act without Coadjutors who may be punished. In case he should be re-elected, that will be sufficient proof of his innocence. Besides who is to impeach? Is the impeachment to suspend his functions. If it is not the mischief will go on. If it is the impeachment will be nearly equivalent to a displacement, and will render the Executive dependent on those who are to impeach. . . .

Mr. Madison—thought it indispensable that some provision should be made for defending the Community agst the incapacity, negligence or perfidy of the chief Magistrate. The limitation of the period of his service, was not a sufficient security. He might lose his capacity after his appointment. He might pervert his administration into a scheme of peculation or oppression. He might betray his trust to foreign powers. The case of the Executive Magistracy was very distinguishable, from that of the Legislative or of any other public body, holding offices of limited duration. It could not be presumed that all or even a majority of the members of an Assembly would either lose their capacity for discharging, or be bribed to betray, their trust. Besides the restraints of their personal integrity & honor, the difficulty of acting in concert for purposes of corruption was a security to the public. And if one or a few members only should be seduced, the soundness of the remaining members, would maintain the integrity and fidelity of the body. In the case of the Executive Magistracy which was to be administered by a single man, loss of capacity or corruption was more within the compass of probable events, and either of them might be fatal to the Republic. . . .

Mr. Govr. Morris,'s opinion had been changed by the arguments used in the discussion. He was now sensible of the necessity of impeachments, if the Executive was to continue for any time in office. . . . When we make him amenable to Justice however we should take care to provide some mode that will not make him dependent on the Legislature.

2 that in case of any flagrant partiality or error, in the nomination, it might be fairly presumed that ⅔ of the 2d. branch would join in putting a negative on it. 3. that as the 2d. b. was . . . now to be composed of equal votes from all the States, the principle of compromise which had prevailed in other instances required in this that their shd. be a concurrence of two authorities, in one of which the people, in the other the states, should be represented. The Executive Magistrate wd be considered as a national officer, acting for and equally sympathising with every part of the U. States. If the 2d. branch alone should have this power, the Judges might be appointed by a minority of the people, tho' by a majority of the States, which could not be justified on any principle as their proceedings were to relate to the people, rather than to the States. . . .

Mr. Elseworth. . . . [said] The Executive will be regarded by the people with a jealous eye. Every power for augmenting unnecessarily his influence will be disliked. As he will be stationary it was not to be supposed he could have a better knowledge of characters. He will be more open to caresses & intrigues than the Senate. The right to supersede his nomination [of Judges] will be ideal only. A nomination under such circumstances will be equivalent to an appointment.

Mr. Govr. Morris. . . . [noted] It had been said that a jealousy would be entertained of the Executive. If the Executive can be safely trusted with the command of the army, there can not surely be any reasonable ground of Jealousy in the present case. . . .

Power to Appoint

It was agreed that the Executive should be subject to impeachment. On July 21 the Convention discussed Madison's motion that the Executive be empowered to pick federal judges and that the Senate be able to veto his appointments, but only if a two-thirds majority agreed.

. . . Mr. Madison stated as his reasons for the motion. 1 that it secured the responsibility of the Executive who would in general be more capable & likely to select fit characters than the Legislature, or even the 2d. b. of it, who might hide their selfish motives under the number concerned in the appointment-

Election by the Legislature

For the time being, however, the power of appointing judges was retained by the Senate. In the next few days the delegates demonstrated clearly how fluid their concept of the Executive still was. Not really liking the electoral system as it was then framed, they returned to appointment by the legislature, although that did not fully please them either. On July 25 Williamson made a suggestion that eventually helped solve the problem.

. . . Mr. Williamson was sensible that strong objections lay agst an election of the Executive by the Legislature. . . . The principal objection agst. an election by the people seemed to be, the disadvantage under which it would place the smaller States. He suggested as a cure for this difficulty, that each man should vote for 3 candidates. One of these he observed would be probably of his own State, the other 2. of some other States; and as probably of a small as a large one.

Mr. Govr. Morris liked the idea, suggesting as an amendment that each man should vote for two persons one of whom at least should not be of his own State.

Mr Madison also thought something valuable might be made of the suggestion with the proposed amendment of it. The second best man in this case would probably be the first, in fact. The only objection which occurred was that each Citizen after havg. given his vote for his favorite fellow Citizen wd. throw away his second [vote] on some obscure Citizen of another State, in order to ensure the object of his first choice. But it could hardly be supposed that the Citizens of many States would be so sanguine of having their favorite elected, as not to give their second vote with sincerity. . . .

Mr. Gerry—A popular election in this case is radically vicious. The ignorance of the people would put it in the power of some one set of men dispersed through the Union & acting in Concert to delude them into any appointment. . . .

Thorny Questions

On July 26 the Convention turned over its business to a committee of detail, with instructions to write a draft of the Constitution as it then stood. The committee reported back on August 6; the sections on the Executive included appointment by the legislature for a single seven-year term, the veto power, command of the armed forces, and provision for impeachment and removal. The officer was at last given a name: the President. The fierce feelings engendered by the long debate were evident in a memo jotted down that day by James McHenry of Maryland.

. . . N.B. Saw Mr. Mercer [John Francis Mercer of Maryland] make out a list of the members names who had attended or were attending in convention with for and against marked opposite most of them —asked carelessly what question occasioned his being so particular upon which he told me laughing that it was no question but that those marked with a for [about twenty] were for a king. I then asked him how he knew that to which he said no matter the thing is so. . . .

Debate on the Executive began again four days later. Some delegates felt he should have to meet certain standards besides those of appropriate age and citizenship.

. . . Mr. Pinkney. . . . thought it essential that the members of the Legislature, the Executive, and the Judges—should be possessed of competent property to make them independent & respectable. . . . he should not think of less than one hundred thousand dollars for the President. . . .

Doctr Franklin expressed his dislike of every thing that tended to debase the spirit of the common people. . . . Some of the greatest rogues he was ever acquainted with, were the richest rogues. . . . This Constitution will be much read and attended to in Europe, and if it should betray a great partiality to the rich—will not only hurt us in the esteem of the most liberal and enlightened men there, but discourage the common people from removing to this Country. . . .

How much, if any, of the war-making power should be given the President? The matter came up on August 17.

. . . Mr Pinkney opposed the vesting this [war-making] power in the Legislature. Its proceedings were too slow. It wd. meet but once a year. The Hs. of Reps. would be too numerous for such deliberations. The Senate would be the best depositary, being more acquainted with foreign affairs, and most capable of proper resolutions. . . .

Mr Butler. The Objections agst the Legislature lie in a great degree agst the Senate. He was for vesting the power in the President, who will have all the requisite qualities, and will not make war but when the Nation will support it.

Mr. Madison and Mr Gerry moved to insert "*declare*," striking out "*make*" war; leaving to the Executive the power to repel sudden attacks.

Mr Sharman [Sherman] thought it stood very well. The Executive shd. be able to repel and not to commence war. . . .

Mr Gerry never expected to hear in a republic a

motion to empower the Executive alone to declare war. . . .

The next day the Convention debated whether or not some sort of Cabinet ought to be specified in the Constitution.

. . . Mr. Elseworth observed that a Council had not yet been provided for the President. He conceived there ought to be one. . . . composed of the President of the Senate—the Chief-Justice, and the Ministers as they might be estabd. for the departments of foreign & domestic affairs, war finance, and marine who should advise but not conclude the President.

Mr. Pinkney. . . . [said] the President shd. be authorized to call for advice or not as he might chuse. Give him an able Council and it will thwart him; a weak one and he will shelter himself under their sanction.

Mr Gerry was agst. letting the heads of the departments, particularly of finance have anything to do in business connected with legislation. He mentioned the Chief Justice also as particularly exceptionable. These men will be so taken up with other matters as to neglect their own proper duties. . . .

If the President died, resigned, was removed from office, left the country, or became disabled, who should take his place as Chief Executive? As matters stood on August 27, the Senate's presiding officer was the next in line.

. . . Mr. Govr. Morris objected . . . to the President of the Senate being provisional successor to the President and suggested a designation of the Chief Justice.

Mr. Madison added as a ground of objection that the Senate might retard the appointment of a President in order to carry points whilst the revisionary power [the veto] was in the President of their own body, but suggested that the Executive powers during a vacancy, be administered by the persons composing the Council to the President.

Mr Williamson suggested that the Legislature ought to have power to provide for occasional successors. & moved that the last clause . . . relating to a provisional successor to the President be postponed.

Mr Dickinson [John Dickinson of Delaware] 2ded. the postponement. remarking that it was too vague. What is the extent of the term "disability" & who is to be the judge of it? . . .

Eighty-one-year-old Ben Franklin addresses James Madison and George Washington at the Constitutional Convention.

The Final Debates

Dickinson's query was never answered, despite the plethora of talk about the Executive. The delegates were repeating all the old arguments without being able to agree, and on August 31 they finally threw up their hands and turned the question, along with others that had not been decided, over to a committee of eleven—one member from each of the states then in attendance. The committee's proposals were offered on September 4.

. . . [The President] shall hold his office during the term of four years, and together with the Vice President, chosen for the same term, be elected in the following manner.

Each State shall appoint in such manner as it's Legislature may direct, a number of Electors equal to the whole number of Senators, and Members of the House of representatives to which the State may be entitled in the legislature.

The Electors shall meet in their respective States, and vote by ballot for two Persons, of whom one at least shall not be an inhabitant of the same State with themselves.—and they shall make a list of all the Persons voted for, and of the number of votes for each, which list they shall sign and certify, and transmit sealed to the seat of the general Government, directed to the President of the Senate.

The President of the Senate shall in that House open all the certificates, and the votes shall be then and there counted—The Person having the greatest number of votes shall be the President, if such number be a majority of the whole number of the Electors and if there be more than One, who have such Majority, and have an equal number of votes, then the Senate shall choose by ballot one of them for the President: but if no Person have a majority, then from the five highest on the list, the Senate shall choose by ballot the President—and in every case after the choice of the President, the Person having the greatest number of votes shall be Vice President: but if there should remain two or more, who have equal votes, the Senate shall choose from them the Vice President. . . .

. . . The Vice President shall be ex officio [in virtue of his office], President of the Senate, except when they sit to try the impeachment of the President, in which case the Chief Justice shall preside, and excepting also when he shall exercise the powers and duties of President, in which case, and in case of his absence, the Senate shall chuse a President pro tempore—The Vice President when acting as President of the Senate shall not have a vote unless the House be equally divided. . . .

[The President] shall be removed from his office on impeachment by the House of representatives, and conviction by the Senate, for treason or bribery, and in case of his removal as aforesaid, death, absence, resignation or inability to discharge the powers or duties of his office the Vice President shall exercise those powers and duties until another President be chosen, or until the inability of the President be removed. . . .

These proposals set off new, sometimes angry debates.

Mr. Gorham [Nathaniel Gorham of Massachusetts] disapproved of making the next highest after the President, the vice-President, without referring the decision to the Senate in case the next highest should have less than a majority of votes. as the regulation stands a very obscure man with very few votes may arrive at that appointment. . . .

Mr. Madison was apprehensive that by requiring both the President & vice President to be chosen out of the five highest candidates, the attention of the electors would be turned too much to making candidates instead of giving their votes in order to a definitive choice, Should this turn be given to the business, the election would in fact be consigned to the Senate altogether. It would have the effect at the same time, he observed, of giving the nomination of the candidates to the largest States. . . .

Col: Mason confessed that the plan of the Committee had removed some capital objections. . . . It was liable however to this strong objection, that nineteen times in twenty the President would be chosen by the Senate, an improper body for the purpose. . . .

Mr. Baldwin [Abraham Baldwin, Georgia delegate] thought the plan not so objectionable when well considered, as at first view. The increasing intercourse among the people of the States, would render important characters less & less unknown; and the Senate would consequently be less & less likely to have the eventual appointment thrown into their hands.

Mr. Wilson. . . . thought the plan on the whole a valuable improvement. . . . He thought it might be better however to refer the eventual appointment to the Legislature than to the Senate, and to confine it to a smaller number than five of the Candidates. . . . [One] reason for preferring the Legislature to the Senate in this business, was that the House of Reps. will be so often changed as to be free from the influence & faction to which the permanence of the Senate may subject that branch. . . .

The electoral debate resumed once more on September 6.

. . . Mr. Williamson suggested as better than an eventual choice [of the President] by the Senate, that this choice should be made by the Legislature, voting *by States* and not *per capita*.

Mr. Sherman suggested the House of Reps. as preferable to "the Legislature", and moved, accordingly,

To strike out the words "The Senate shall immediately choose &c." and insert "The House of Representatives shall immediately choose by ballot one of them for President, the [delegation] from each State having one vote."

. . . Mr· Randolph moved . . . "The legislature may declare by law what officer of the U. S—shall act as President in case of the death, resignation, or disability of the President and Vice-President; and such officer shall act accordingly until the time of electing a President shall arrive."

Mr. Madison observed that this, as worded, would prevent a supply of the vacancy by an intermediate election of the President, and moved to substitute— "until such disability be removed, or a President shall be elected—" . . . which was agreed to [as part of the Randolph motion]. . . .

. . . "The vice President shall be ex officio President of the Senate" [being debated]

Mr. Gerry opposed this regulation. We might as well put the President himself at the head of the Legislature. The close intimacy that must subsist between the President & vice-president makes it absolutely improper. He was agst. having any vice President.

Mr Govr Morris. The vice president then will be the first heir apparent that ever loved his father—If there should be no vice president, the President of the Senate would be temporary successor, which would amount to the same thing.

Mr Sherman saw no danger in the case. If the vice-President were not to be President of the Senate, he would be without employment, and some member by being made President [of the Senate] must be deprived of his vote, unless when an equal division of votes might happen in the Senate, which would be but seldom. . . .

Mr. Williamson [a member of the Committee of Eleven], observed that such an officer as vice-President was not wanted. He was introduced [by the committee] only for the sake of a valuable mode of election which required two to be chosen at the same time. . . .

Presidential powers were also discussed that day, beginning with a resolution that the President "shall nominate & by & with the advice and consent of the Senate, shall appoint ambassadors . . . ministers . . . Judges of the supreme Court," and other officers whose appointments the Constitution did not allocate.

. . . Mr. Wilson objected to the mode of appointing, as blending a branch of the Legislature with the Executive. Good laws are of no effect without a good Executive; and there can be no good Executive without a responsible appointment of officers to execute. Responsibility is in a manner destroyed by such an agency of the Senate—He would prefer the Council proposed by Col: Mason [containing two senators each from the Northern, Middle, and Southern sections], provided its advice should not be made obligatory on the President. . . .

Mr. Govr. Morris said that as the President was to nominate, there would be responsibility, and as the Senate was to concur, there would be security. As Congress [of the Confederation] now make appointments there is no responsibility. . . .

. . . "The President by and with the advice and consent of the Senate shall have power to make Treaties"—"*But no treaty shall be made without the consent of two thirds of the members present*"—this last being before the House.

Mr Wilson thought it objectionable to require the concurrence of ⅔ of the Senate which puts it in the power of a minority to control the will of a majority. . . .

Mr King concurred in the objection. . . .

Mr. Madison moved to insert after the word "treaty" the words "except treaties of peace" allowing these to be made with less difficulty than other treaties—It was agreed to. . . .

Mr. Madison then moved to authorize a concurrence of two thirds of the Senate to make treaties of peace, without the concurrence of the President. . . . The President he said would necessarily derive so much power and importance from a state of war that he might be tempted, if authorized, to impede a treaty of peace. . . .

Mr. Govr Morris thought the power of the President in this case harmless; and that no peace ought to be made without the concurrence of the President, who was the general Guardian of the National interests. . . .

"and may require the opinion in writing of the principal officer in each of the Executive Departments, upon any subject relating to the duties of their respective offices." being before the House

Col: Mason said that in rejecting a Council to the President we were about to try an experiment on which the most despotic Governments had never ventured—The Grand Signor himself had his Divan. [He advocated a six-man sectional council.] . . .

Doctor Franklin 2ded. the motion. We seemed he said too much to fear cabals in appointments by a number, and to have too much confidence in those of single persons. . . . He thought a Council would not only be a check on a bad President but be a relief to a good one.

Mr. Govr. Morris. The question of a Council was considered in the Committee [of Eleven], where it was judged that the Presidt. by persuading his Council—to concur in his wrong measures, would acquire their protection for them . . .

Mr. Dickinson was for a Council. It wd. be a singular thing if the measures of the Executive were not to undergo some previous discussion before the President . . .

The Convention nevertheless elected not to provide for a council in the Constitution. The work of the delegates was nearly finished. On September 8 the Constitution went to the Committee of Style for polishing, and on September 17 most of the delegates signed the printed document. Sections pertinent to the Executive follow.

In Article I

. . . The House of Representatives shall chuse their Speaker and other Officers; and shall have the sole Power of Impeachment. . . .

The Vice President of the United States shall be President of the Senate, but shall have no Vote, unless they be equally divided.

The Senate shall chuse their other Officers, and also a President pro tempore, in the Absence of the Vice President, or when he shall exercise the Office of President of the United States.

The Senate shall have the sole Power to try all Impeachments. When sitting for that Purpose, they shall be on Oath or Affirmation. When the President of the United States is tried, the Chief Justice shall preside: And no Person shall be convicted without the Concurrence of two thirds of the Members present.

Judgment in Cases of Impeachment shall not extend further than to removal from Office, and disqualification to hold and enjoy any Office of honor, Trust, or Profit under the United States; but the Party convicted shall nevertheless be liable and subject to Indictment, Trial, Judgment and Punishment, according to Law. . . .

Every Bill which shall have passed the House of Representatives and the Senate, shall, before it become a Law, be presented to the President of the United States; If he approve he shall sign it, but if not he shall return it, with his Objections to that House in which it shall have originated, who shall enter the Objections at large on their Journal, and proceed to reconsider it. If after such Reconsideration two thirds of that House shall agree to pass the Bill, it shall be sent, together with the Objections, to the other House, by which it shall likewise be reconsidered, and if approved by two thirds of that House, it shall become a Law. But in all such Cases the Votes of both Houses shall be determined by Yeas and Nays, and the Names of the Persons voting for and against the Bill shall be entered on the Journal of each House respectively. If any Bill shall not be returned by the President within ten Days (Sundays excepted) after it shall have been presented to him, the Same shall be a Law, in like Manner as if he had signed it, unless the Congress by their Adjournment prevent its Return, in which Case it shall not be a Law.

Every Order, Resolution, or Vote to which the Concurrence of the Senate and House of Representatives may be necessary (except on a question of Adjournment) shall be presented to the President of the United States; and before the Same shall take Effect, shall be approved by him, or being disapproved by him, shall be repassed by two thirds of the Senate and House of Representatives, according to the Rules and Limitations prescribed in the Case of a Bill. . . .

[Congress shall have power] To make all Laws which shall be necessary and proper for carrying into Execution the foregoing Powers, and all other Powers vested by this Constitution in the Government of the United States, or in any Department or Officer thereof. . . .

No Title of Nobility shall be granted by the United States: And no Person holding any Office of Profit or Trust under them, shall, without the Consent of the Congress, accept of any present, Emolument, Office, or Title, of any kind whatever, from any King, Prince, or foreign State. . . .

Article II

Section. I. The executive Power shall be vested in a President of the United States of America. He shall hold his Office during the Term of four Years, and, together with the Vice President, chosen for the same Term, be elected, as follows:

Each State shall appoint, in such Manner as the Legislature thereof may direct, a Number of Electors, equal to the whole Number of Senators and Representatives to which the State may be entitled in the Congress: but no Senator or Representative, or Person holding an Office of Trust or Profit under the United States, shall be appointed an Elector.

The Electors shall meet in their respective States, and vote by Ballot for two Persons, of whom one at least shall not be an Inhabitant of the same State with themselves. And they shall make a List of all the Persons voted for, and of the Number of Votes for each; which List they shall sign and certify, and transmit sealed to the Seat of the Government of the United States, directed to the President of the Senate. The President of the Senate shall, in the Presence of the Senate and House of Representatives, open all the Certificates, and the Votes shall then be counted. The Person having the greatest Number of Votes shall be the President, if such Number be a Majority of the whole Number of Electors appointed; and if there be more than one who have such Majority, and have an equal Number of Votes, then the House of Representatives shall immediately chuse by Ballot one of them for President; and if no Person have a Majority, then from the five highest on the List the said House shall in like Manner chuse the President. But in chusing the President, the Votes shall be taken by States, the Representation from each State having one Vote; A quorum for this Purpose shall consist of a Member or Members from two thirds of the States, and a Majority of all the States shall be necessary to a Choice. In every Case, after the Choice of the President, the Person having the greatest Number of Votes of the Electors shall be the Vice President. But if there should remain two or more who have equal Votes, the Senate shall chuse from them by Ballot the Vice President.

The Congress may determine the Time of chusing the Electors, and the Day on which they shall give their Votes; which Day shall be the same throughout the United States.

No Person except a natural born Citizen, or a Citizen of the United States, at the time of the Adoption of this Constitution, shall be eligible to the Office of President; neither shall any Person be eligible to that Office who shall not have attained to the Age of thirty five Years, and been fourteen Years a Resident within the United States.

In Case of the Removal of the President from Office, or of his Death, Resignation, or Inability to discharge the Powers and Duties of the said Office, the Same shall devolve on the Vice President, and the Congress may by Law provide for the Case of Removal, Death, Resignation or Inability, both of the President and Vice President, declaring what Officer shall then act as President, and such Officer shall act accordingly, until the Disability be removed, or a President shall be elected.

The President shall, at stated Times, receive for his Services, a Compensation, which shall neither be encreased nor diminished during the Period for which he shall have been elected, and he shall not receive within that Period any other Emolument from the United States, or any of them.

Before he enter on the Execution of his Office, he shall take the following Oath or Affirmation:—"I do solemnly swear (or affirm) that I will faithfully execute the Office of President of the United States, and will to the best of my Ability, preserve, protect and defend the Constitution of the United States."

Section. 2. The President shall be Commander in Chief of the Army and Navy of the United States, and of the Militia of the several States, when called into the actual Service of the United States; he may require the Opinion, in writing, of the principal Officer in each of the executive Departments, upon any Subject relating to the Duties of their respective Offices, and he shall have Power to grant Reprieves and Pardons for Offences against the United States, except in Cases of Impeachment.

He shall have power, by and with the Advice and Consent of the Senate, to make Treaties, provided two thirds of the Senators present concur; and he shall nominate, and by and with the Advice and Consent of the Senate, shall appoint Ambassadors, other public Ministers and Consuls, Judges of the supreme Court, and all other Officers of the United States, whose Appointments are not herein otherwise provided for, and which shall be established by Law: but the Congress may by Law vest the Appointment

The Picture Exhibition.

UNION:
Or, the Twelve
Federal Pillars.

When this children's primer was printed, the Union consisted of twelve states; Rhode Island did not join until May, 1790.

of such inferior Officers, as they think proper, in the President alone, in the Courts of Law, or in the Heads of Departments.

The President shall have Power to fill up all Vacancies that may happen during the Recess of the Senate, by granting Commissions which shall expire at the End of their next Session.

Section. 3. He shall from time to time give to the Congress Information of the State of the Union, and recommend to their consideration such Measures as he shall judge necessary and expedient; he may, on extraordinary Occasions, convene both Houses, or either of them, and in Case of Disagreement between them, with Respect to the Time of Adjournment, he may adjourn them to such Time as he shall think proper; he shall receive Ambassadors and other public Ministers; he shall take Care that the Laws be faithfully executed, and shall Commission all the Officers of the United States.

Section 4. The President, Vice President and all civil Officers of the United States, shall be removed from Office on Impeachment for, and conviction of, Treason, Bribery, or other high Crimes and Misdemeanors.

In Article VI

. . . The Senators and Representatives before mentioned, and the Members of the several State Legislatures, and all executive and judicial Officers, both of the United States and of the several States, shall be bound by Oath or Affirmation, to support this Constitution; but no religious Test shall ever be required as a Qualification to any Office or public Trust under the United States.

Ratification

Publication of the proposed Constitution touched off a war of speeches and letters to newspapers. Since nine of the thirteen states had to ratify the compact before it became operative, there was still a chance that its opponents could defeat it and thereby retain the old, toothless government of the Confederation. The battle was fierce.

Cato v. Caesar

CATO *was the nom de plume used by Governor George Clinton of New York for his letters against the Constitution. The identity of* CAESAR, *author of the following letter, is in doubt, although some contemporaries believed that Alexander Hamilton was the writer. It appeared in the New York* Daily Advertiser *in October, 1787.*

. . . Cato tells us . . . that the new constitution comes sanctioned with the approbation of General Washington; and, though he appears to have some reverence for that great patriot chief, yet he very sagaciously observes, that the *best and wisest man may err*; and thence asserts, that every man in *politics*, as well as in religion, ought to judge for himself. This paragraph needs no comment . . . but with all deference to Cato's penetration, I would recommend to him, instead of entering into fruitless discussion of what has come from so many *clear heads* and *good hearts*, to join his fellow-citizens, and endeavor to reconcile this *excellent constitution* to the *weak*, the *suspicious*, and the *interested*, who will be chiefly opposed to it, as soon as possible. I would also advise him to give his vote (as he will probably be one of the Electors) to the American Fabius [Washington]; it will be more healthy for this country, and *this state*, that he should be induced to accept of the presidency of the new government, than that he should be solicited again to accept of the command of *an army*. . . .

Clinton was not frightened off. The fourth CATO *letter was printed in the* New-York Journal *on November 8.*

. . . It is remarked by Montesquieu, in treating of republics, that *in all magistracies, the greatness of the power must be compensated by the brevity of the duration, and that a longer time than a year would be dangerous.* It is, therefore, obvious to the least intelligent mind to account why great power in the hands of a magistrate, and that power connected with considerable duration, may be dangerous to the liberties of a republic, the deposit of vast trusts in the hands of a single magistrate, enables him in their exercise to create a numerous train of dependents . . . and the duration of his office for any considerable time favors his views, gives him the means and time to perfect and execute his designs, *he therefore fancies that he may be great and glorious by oppressing his fellow-citizens, and raising himself to permanent grandeur on the ruins of his country.* . . .

The ten miles square [provided for, but not located geographically, by the Constitution], which is to become the seat of government, will of course be the place of residence for the president and the great officers of state . . . [there will be found] *ambition with idleness—baseness with pride—the thirst of riches without labor—aversion to truth—flattery—treason—perfidy—violation of engagements—contempt of civil duties—hope from the magistrate's weakness; but above all, the perpetual ridicule of virtue*—these, he remarks, are the characteristics by which the courts in all ages have been distinguished. . . .

It is a maxim in republics that the representative of the people should be of their immediate choice; but by the manner in which the president is chosen, he arrives to this office at the fourth or fifth hand, nor does the highest vote, in the way he is elected, determine the choice, for it is only necessary that he should be taken from the highest of five, who may have a plurality of votes. . . .

. . . wherein does this president, invested with his powers and prerogatives, essentially differ from the king of Great Britain (save as to name, the creation of nobility, and some immaterial incidents, the offspring of absurdity and locality). . . .

The Federalist

Hamilton may not have been CAESAR, *but he was* PUBLIUS *of* The Federalist, *in which he answered the criticisms of Clinton and others. The following selections are from the sixty-seventh and sixty-ninth essays.*

The constitution of the executive department of the proposed government, claims next our attention.

There is hardly any part of the system which could have been attended with greater difficulty in the arrangement of it than this; and there is, perhaps, none which has been inveighed against with less candor or criticised with less judgement.

Here the writers against the Constitution seem to have taken pains to signalize their talent of misrepresentation. Calculating upon the aversion of the people to monarchy, they have endeavored to enlist all their jealousies and apprehensions in opposition to the intended President of the United States; not merely as the embryo, but as the full-grown progeny, of that detested parent. . . . they have not scrupled to draw resources even from the regions of fiction. The authorities of a magistrate, in few instances greater, in some instances less, than those of a governor of New York, have been magnified into more than royal prerogatives. He has been decorated with attributes superior in dignity and splendor to those of a king of Great Britain. He has been shown to us with the diadem sparkling on his brow and the imperial purple flowing in his train. He has been seated on a throne surrounded with minions and mistresses. . . . We have been taught to tremble at the terrific visages of murdering janizaries, and to blush at the unveiled mysteries of a future seraglio. . . .

The President of the United States would be an officer elected by the people for *four* years; the king of Great Britain is a perpetual and *hereditary* prince. The one would be amenable to personal punishment and disgrace; the person of the other is sacred and inviolable. The one would have a *qualified* negative upon the acts of the legislative body; the other has an *absolute* negative. The one would have a right to command the military and naval forces of the nation; the other, in addition to this right, possesses that of *declaring* war, and of *raising* and *regulating* fleets and armies by his own authority. The one would have a concurrent power with a branch of the legislature in the formation of treaties; the other is the *sole possessor* of the power of making treaties. The one would have a like concurrent authority in appointing offices; the other is the sole author of all appointments. The one can confer no privileges whatever: the other can make denizens of aliens, noblemen of commoners: can erect corporations with all the rights incident to corporate bodies. The one can prescribe no rules concerning the commerce or currency of the nation; the other is in several respects the arbiter of commerce, and in this capacity can establish markets and fairs, can regulate weights and measures, can lay embargoes for a limited time, can coin money, can authorize or prohibit the circulation of foreign coin. The one has no particle of spiritual jurisdiction; the other is the supreme head and governor of the national church! What answer shall we give to those who would persuade us that things so unlike resemble each other? . . .

Virginia Convention

By the end of May, 1788, eight states had ratified the Constitution. The Virginia convention met on June 2, and during the debate James Monroe, a future Chief Executive, attacked the Presidency as it was conceived by the Founding Fathers. In referring to the President's "own council," he reflected the widely held belief that the senators would be the President's chief advisers.

. . . Let us now consider the responsibility of the president. He is elected for four years, and not excluded from re-election. Suppose he violates the laws and constitution, or commit[s] high crimes, by whom is he to be tried? By his own council—by those who advise him to commit such violations and crimes? . . . He commands the army of the United states till he is condemned. Will not this be an inducement to foreign nations to use their arts and intrigues to corrupt his counsellors? . . . How is he elected? By electors appointed according to the directions of the state legislatures. . . . A combination between the electors might easily happen. . . . Contemplate this in all its consequences. Is it not the

New Yorkers held a parade to celebrate the impending ratification of the Constitution in 1788. One of the floats was a twenty-seven-foot replica of a frigate. It was christened in honor of Alexander Hamilton, who led the fight for ratification.

object of foreign courts to have such a man possessed of this power, as would be inclined to promote their interests? . . . Foreign nations may, by their intrigues, have great influence in each state, in the election of the president, and I have no doubt but their efforts will be tried to the utmost. Will not the influence of the president himself have great weight in his re-election? The variety of the offices at his disposal, will acquire him the favor and attachment of those who aspire after them, and of the officers, and their friends. He will have some connexion with the members of the different branches of government. They will esteem him, because they will be acquainted with him, live in the same town with him, and often dine with him. This familiar and frequent intercourse will secure him great influence. I presume that when once he is elected, he may be elected forever. . . .

. . . It appears to me that it would have been dangerous, if congress could intermeddle with the subject of religion. . . . It is apprehended that Jews, Mahometans, Pagans, &c., may be elected to high offices under the government of the United States. Those who are Mahometans, or any others, who are not professors of the christian religion, can never be elected to the office of president or other high office but in one of two cases. First, if the people of America lay aside the christian religion altogether. . . . Another case is, if any persons of such descriptions, should, notwithstanding their religion, acquire the confidence and esteem of the people of America by their good conduct and practice of virtue, they may be chosen. I leave it to gentlemen's candor to judge what probability there is of the people's choosing men of different sentiments from themselves. . . .

North Carolina Convention

New Hampshire ratified the Constitution on June 21; four days later Virginia became the tenth state to do so. Antifederalist New York fell in line at the end of July. Only two states did not ratify before the new government was organized. Intractable Rhode Island, which had not even sent delegates to the Convention, withheld its approval until May 29, 1790. North Carolina decided to withhold its approval until Congress submitted a bill of rights to the states, despite the eloquent speeches of James Iredell at a convention held in July, 1788:

. . . I met by accident with a pamphlet this morning, in which the author states, as a very serious danger, that the pope of Rome might be elected president. I confess this never struck me before, and if the author had read all the qualifications of a president, perhaps his fears might have been quieted. No man but a native, and who has resided fourteen years in America, can be chosen president. . . . A native of America must have very singular good fortune, who after residing fourteen years in his own country, should go to Europe, enter into romish orders, obtain the promotion of cardinal, afterwards that of pope and at length be so much in the confidence of his own country, as to be elected president. . . . Sir, it is impossible to treat such idle fears with any degree of gravity. . . .

First in Peace

Meanwhile, the man whom Americans thought of as the very personification of their best selves contemplated the possibility of being chosen President. In April, 1788, George Washington wrote about it, wryly and wistfully, to a former comrade in arms, the Marquis de Lafayette.

. . . In answer to the observations you make on the probability of my election to the Presidency (knowing me as you do) I need only say, that it has no enticing charms, and no fascinating allurements for me. However, it might not be decent for me to say I would refuse to accept or even to speak much about an appointment, which may never take place: for in so doing, one might possibly incur the application of the moral resulting from that Fable, in which the Fox is represented as inveighing against the sourness of the grapes, because he could not reach them. All that it will be necessary to add, my dear Marquis, in order to show my decided predilection, is, that, (at my time of life and under my circumstances) the encreasing infirmities of nature and the growing love of retirement do not permit me to entertain a wish beyond that of living and dying an honest man on my own farm. Let those follow the pursuits of ambition and fame, who have a keener relish for them, or who may have more years, in store, for the enjoyment. . . .

COLONIAL WILLIAMSBURG

THE WHITE HOUSE COLLECTION

Break with the Past

Despite their successful rebellion against England, the American states in 1787 still seemed likely to "hang separately," as Ben Franklin had warned they might in 1776. Liberty was triumphant over King George III (above, left) and *all* collective authority; the states were badly divided. Was there no way for them to combine effectively for common purposes? Drawing on history, philosophy, and contemporary politics for guidelines, the delegates to the Constitutional Convention invented a new government and an office that their presiding officer, Washington (above, right), would be the first to fill.

Executive power in the Roman Republic was shared largely by two institutions dominated by the wealthy classes: the Senate and two annually elected consuls. However, the tribunes, chosen by and from the plebeians, could veto any Senate measure, and all citizens could participate in the election of government officials. At right, the face of a coin minted in 137 B.C. depicts a Roman casting his ballot. Below, promoting two candidates—Julius Polybius and Holconius Priscus—is an election campaign notice that was discovered on the wall of a clothing shop in the ruined city of Pompeii.

At right, in the Roman Senate in 63 B.C., the patrician consul Cicero assails a demagogic candidate for the consulship. However, popular support brought Julius Caesar to power soon thereafter.

Ancient Precedents

Debating reform of their own government, the delegates looked back to the ancient republics. Virginia's George Mason spoke for democracy: "The Love the Affection the Attachment of the Citizens" to the state had "enabled the little Cluster of Grecian Republics to resist, and almost constantly to defeat the Persian Monarch. . . ." Some had doubts that a national government could be both strong and fair to all states and urged continuation of the Confederation. Mason wanted a plural Executive, representing all sections. Warned Pennsylvania's James Wilson, "The Kings of Sparta & the Consuls of Rome prove . . . the factious consequences of dividing the Executive. . . ." More important, not even the Greek confederacies had lasted long: the states had been too contentious. And republics such as Rome had ended in tyranny.

"Kingly Government"

"There is a natural inclination in mankind," noted old Benjamin Franklin, "to Kingly Government. It sometimes relieves them from Aristocratic domination. They had rather have one tyrant than five hundred." It appeared to many eighteenth-century Americans that democratic institutions were hobbled and ultimately perverted by tugs of war between classes for rights, power, and wealth. Monarchic systems, they felt, were steadier, and many thought that limited monarchies, such as England's, were among the best governments in the world. "It [is] certain," said John Dickinson, a Delaware delegate to the Constitutional Convention, "that equal blessings [have] never yet been derived from any of the republican form." But the delegates assembled at Philadelphia also believed, as Luther Martin of Maryland expressed it, that "the first principle of government is founded on the natural rights of individuals"—rights with which kings seemed certain to interfere.

The English had a long history of placing limitations on the power of their kings. In 1215, English barons forced King John to sign the Magna Charta (left), granting them personal and political liberties. In 1649, Charles I was executed (above) and the monarchy temporarily ceased to exist; it was restored in 1660 when King Charles II came to power.

The English System

England's King George III seemed tyrannical enough to Americans, but he was actually restricted to a degree that horrified the other European monarchs. The British upper class exercised considerable control through the great families that supplied government administrators; that was to be expected. But the strong Parliament, under aristocratic command, was unique, and in the eighteenth century the wealthy and educated led efforts to limit the king further; in 1782 they forced the king to name their choice, rather than his, for Prime Minister. Yet the king retained the power of executive appointment. He could dissolve the legislature at will. He could veto legislation, although sovereigns had not done so in years, since they were able to buy votes when necessary. The king alone had power to declare war and make treaties. He headed a state church. And all this came to him through inheritance—even when, like George III, he was unstable to the point of madness.

To English conservatives, pomp and ceremony were time-honored traditions. But to liberals, they were symbols of corruption and inherited pre-eminence. Above is Thomas Rowlandson's satirical depiction of the "best families" on their way to a royal levee. At right, in a painting by Henry Briggs, King George III presents a sword to Admiral Lord Howe.

Since the thirteenth century, the English Parliament had developed from a body empowered to ratify taxes to a bicameral legislature that represented public opinion and possessed broad lawmaking powers and the right to unseat a king. During the Commonwealth of

the seventeenth century Parliament's powers were confirmed, although even after the Restoration the monarch had considerable control over the composition of Commons and Lords. Above, William Pitt the Younger, Prime Minister in 1787, addresses Commons.

"Dangerous Commotions"

If the English system seemed to Americans too likely to result in infringements on liberty, the other European governments offered even less to emulate, and more to avoid. Russia's Catherine the Great and Spain's Charles III tried to behave like enlightened rulers. But despotism, corruption, and privilege were still the most common characteristics of monarchy. Even in Poland, where the king was elected, there was little of value to draw on; the "Election of the supreme Magistrate is attended with the most dangerous commotions," warned James Wilson. "The Polish nobles have resources & dependents which enable them to appear in force, and to threaten the Republic as well as each other." James Madison pointed to the "eager interference" of the other European sovereigns in those elections. What about systems that were closer in form to the American Confederation in 1787? Unfortunately, all the European confederacies were of negligible value as examples, since they had so long been bound up with, and thus dependent on, the Continental community. They were also weak and unsound. In the Dutch and German confederations, the smaller states were under the control of the larger, or they sustained themselves by outside alliances. And, as Alexander Hamilton of New York noted, "the Swiss cantons have scarce any Union at all, and have been more than once at war with one another. . . ."

Reports of the corruption and cruelty of monarchies horrified Americans. Catherine the Great of Russia (left, below) usurped the power of her husband, Peter III; he died mysteriously soon after. Selim III (at a court ceremony, left) was the first ruler of the Ottoman Empire in many years who had not spent time in a cage; the custom was to imprison heirs to the throne so they could not meddle in politics. (The weak-mindedness of Selim's predecessor was attributed to his forty-three-year-long incarceration.) In Spain, Charles IV (below) dishonored the memory of his reforming father by his dissoluteness.

Feudalism, which assigned every man his place and kept him there, was shaken by the Reformation and the Enlightenment. But the old order—personified by rulers such as Maria Theresa of Austria and Frederick the Great of Prussia (in a diplomatic chess game, right, under the eye of Mars)—was still holding out. Even when monarchs attempted reform, the ruling classes resisted, clinging to an uncertain status quo. "Après nous le déluge," said Madame de Pompadour, mistress of Louis XV of France. She was not far wrong: Louis XVI, who was crowned in 1775 (below), was guillotined in 1793.

CÉRÉMONIE DU SACRE
DE LOUIS XVI
le 11 Juin 1775.

Natural Rights

The *sine qua non* of the Constitution writers was to embody in their system the philosophy of the Enlightenment. The Protestant Reformation that began in the sixteenth century proclaimed that each man was responsible for his own faith and behavior; all men were equal before God; institutions were answerable to individuals, not the other way around. These beliefs sired the concept of the "natural rights of man" in relation to the state, a theory of individual equality promoted brilliantly by eighteenth-century writers, particularly in France (where the king nonetheless remained absolute until the American rebellion provided inspiration for violent change). Although in Europe tradition and privilege—represented by nobles, clergy, and royal families—made orderly democratic reform appear impossible, the United States had no such entrenched institutions, and had already produced a new, freer society. But the radicals wanted more; they railed at the limitations on suffrage and the checks and balances of state constitutions that aimed at providing stability as well as liberty. Some of them demanded that Americans create completely representative—that is to say, legislative—government. But most of the delegates to the Constitutional Convention were unconvinced of the wisdom of the masses; and it was the failure of legislative government on a national scale that had brought them together in Philadelphia.

Article 10.th

The solemn Ratifications of the present Treaty expedited in good & due Form shall be exchanged between the contracting Parties in the Space of Six Months or sooner if possible to be computed from the Day of the Signature of the present Treaty. In Witness whereof we the undersigned their Minister Plenipotentiary have in their Name and in Virtue of our Full Powers signed with our Hands the present Definitive Treaty, and caused the Seals of our Arms to be affixd thereto.

Done at Paris, this third Day of September, In the Year of our Lord one thousand seven hundred & eighty three.—

D Hartley   John Adams.   B Franklin   John Jay

The Treaty of Paris (above), signed on September 3, 1783, ended the war for independence with the recognition of American sovereignty. Many in England welcomed this result; the kerchief, right, glorifying Washington and other Revolutionary heroes was printed in England. The treaty also ceded the Old Northwest to the new nation, opening the way to the Pacific but reinforcing a central question: How, in an area the size of America, could the government be both effective and responsive to local needs? Hamilton argued that however important home rule might be, the Confederation could not contend with the problems facing it when individual states were more powerful than the central council. "With me," responded Pennsylvania's James Wilson, "it is not a desireable object to annihilate the state governments. . . . In all extensive empires a subdivision of power is necessary." Agreed, said Hamilton in his reply, but if the new national government did not have unlimited powers, "the rivalship of the States would gradually subvert it."

AMERICA PRESENTING AT THE ALTAR OF LIBERTY MEDALLIONS OF HER ILLUSTRIOUS SONS

The Confederation

American government in 1787 consisted of thirteen state structures, in most of which the legislatures were supreme. Under the Articles of Confederation, they sent—when they saw fit to do so—representatives to "the united states in congress assembled" at New York, where the nation's business was conducted. Congress' powers were limited, and the Confederation was hampered by lack of cooperation, fierce competition between states, and fiscal instability. An economic crisis resulting in part from the weakness of Congress had led to a commercial convention at Annapolis in 1786; representatives of five states had attended, and had taken the opportunity to call for a convention to amend the Articles and, implicitly, to strengthen the government. That fall an uprising of debt-ridden farmers in Massachusetts had lent a sense of urgency to the request, and early in 1787 Congress had called the Convention.

Commonwealth  of Massachusetts.

By His EXCELLENCY

JAMES BOWDOIN, Esquire,

Governour of the Commonwealth of Massachusetts.

A Proclamation.

WHEREAS information has been given to the Supreme Executive of this Commonwealth, that on Tuesday last, the 29th of August, being the day appointed by law for the sitting of the Court of Common Pleas and Court of General Sessions of the Peace, at *Northampton*, in the county of *Hampshire*, within this Commonwealth, a large concourse of people, from several parts of that county, assembled at the Court-House in *Northampton*, many of whom were armed with guns, swords and other deadly weapons, and with drums beating and fifes playing, in contempt and open defiance of the authority of this Government, did, by their threats of violence and keeping possession of the Court-House until twelve o'clock on the night of the same day, prevent the sitting of the Court, and the orderly administration of justice in that county:

AND WHEREAS this high-handed offence is fraught with the most fatal and pernicious consequences, must tend to subvert all law and government; to dissolve our excellent Constitution, and introduce universal riot, anarchy and confusion, which would probably terminate in absolute despotism, and consequently destroy the fairest prospects of political happiness, that any people was ever favoured with:

I HAVE therefore thought fit, by and with the advice of the Council, to issue this Proclamation, calling upon all Judges, Justices, Sheriffs, Constables, and other officers, civil and military, within this Commonwealth, to prevent and suppress all such violent and riotous proceedings, if they should be attempted in their several counties.

AND I DO hereby, pursuant to the indispensible duty I owe to the good people of this Commonwealth, most solemnly call upon them, as they value the blessings of freedom and independence, which at the expence of so much blood and treasure they have purchased—as they regard their faith, which in the sight of GOD and the world, they pledged to one another, and to the people of the United States, when they adopted the present Constitution of Government—as they would not disappoint the hopes, and thereby become contemptible in the eyes of other nations, in the view of whom they have risen to glory and empire—as they would not deprive themselves of the security derived from well-regulated Society, to their lives, liberties and property; and as they would not devolve upon their children, instead of peace, freedom and safety, a state of anarchy, confusion and slavery,—I do most earnestly and most solemnly call upon them to aid and assist with their utmost efforts the aforesaid officers, and to unite in preventing and suppressing all such treasonable proceedings, and every measure that has a tendency to encourage them.

GIVEN at the COUNCIL-CHAMBER, in BOSTON, this second day of September, in the year of our LORD, one thousand seven hundred and eighty-six, and in the eleventh year of the Independence of the United States of AMERICA.

JAMES BOWDOIN.

By his Excellency's command.

JOHN AVERY, jan. Secretary.

BOSTON: Printed by ADAMS and NOURSE, Printers to the GENERAL COURT.

The proclamation above asked the support of all state officials against the rebellion in the Bay State. It took six months to bring the insurgents, commanded by Daniel Shays, to heel.

America's Solution

The states might not be really united under the Articles of Confederation, but would the attempts to make the Union stronger lead to the creation of a worse condition—aristocracy, monarchy, despotism? Many feared so. Although only Hamilton openly espoused the idea of an elective American king, rumors were flying that as many as twenty of the fifty-five delegates wished to establish an American throne; that, in fact, some of them had even secretly designated a prince of the British blood royal as first of the line. Meanwhile, the Convention slowly worked out a plan for an executive department. It was, as Madison later wrote Thomas Jefferson, a "peculiarly embarrassing" task; the composition of the Executive would be a crucial indicator of the framers' intent in the Constitution. "On the question whether it should consist of a single person, or a plurality of co-ordinate members," wrote Madison, "on the mode of appointment, on the duration in office, on the degree of power, on the re-eligibility, tedious and reiterated discussions took place." From the debates emerged an Executive personified in one man, who could be elected—in a process that began with the states—to as many four-year terms as his performance justified and politics allowed. He would be responsible for the administration of the laws and for the command of the armed forces, but he would be sharply restricted by the powers of the legislature; Congress would be able to remove him from office for "Treason, Bribery, or other high Crimes and Misdemeanors." The President would be able to veto legislation, but all lawmaking would begin in the Congress, which could override his veto with a two-thirds majority. The raising of troops and declaration of war would be legislative responsibilities. The Chief Executive could conclude treaties and could nominate advisers, but in both cases the Senate's approval was mandatory. In short, the President of the United States would be strong enough to provide effective leadership, but accountable to the Congress and the people for his actions.

Three prominent framers of the Constitution were James Madison, far left, major architect of the Virginia plan, and Pennsylvania's Gouverneur Morris, top, and James Wilson. Wilson fought for the electoral system of choosing the Executive; Morris wrote most of the document's final draft.

It was rumored that proponents of the monarchic system intended to place on an American throne the second son of George III—Frederick Augustus, Duke of York and Albany, Prince-Bishop of Osnabrück. He became British commander in chief in 1798. The portrait above was painted in 1823.

"We the People"

The Presidency was only one symbol of the Constitution's greatest import: America was a nation—partly unwillingly and out of necessity, but a nation nonetheless. The Constitution made the whole Union—"We the people of the United States," and their representatives who gathered in the national Capital—capable of executing national purpose even when that purpose might disadvantage a minority or a region. National law, passed by the Congress and signed by the President, was to be superior to local law. There would be a national judiciary. Yet democratic principles were to be sustained on the national level—by frequent elections and by competition between institutions answerable to the public: the state and national governments, the two houses of Congress, and the national judiciary, legislature, and executive.

Of the signing of the Constitution (depicted below by Thomas Rossiter), James Madison wrote: "Whilst the last members were signing it Doctr. Franklin [second from left] looking towards the Presidents Chair [right], at the back of which a rising sun happened to be painted, observed to a few members near him, that Painters had found it difficult to distinguish in their art a rising from a setting sun. I have, said he, often and often in the course of the Session, and the vicissitudes of my hopes and fears as to its issue, looked at that behind the President [George Washington] without being able to tell whether it was rising or setting: But now at length I have the happiness to know that it is a rising and not a setting Sun."

INDEPENDENCE HALL

Order of Procession,

In honor of the establishment of the CONSTITUTION of the United States.

To parade precisely at Eight o'Clock in the Morning, of FRIDAY, the 4th of JULY, 1788, proceeding along *Third-street* to *Callowhill-street*; thence to *Fourth-street*; down *Fourth-street* to *Market-street*; thence to the Grounds in Front of *Bush-hill.*

I.
AN Officer, with twelve Axe-men, in frocks and caps.

II.
The City Troop of Light-Horse, commanded by Colonel *Miles.*

III.
INDEPENDENCE.
John Nixon, Esq; on horseback, bearing the staff and cap of Liberty—The words "*4th July, 1776*," in gold letters, pendant from the staff.

IV.
Four Pieces of Artillery, with a detachment from the Train, commanded by Captains *Morrell* and *Fisher.*

V.
ALLIANCE WITH FRANCE.
Thomas Fitzsimons, Esq; on horseback, carrying a flag, white ground, having three fleurs-de lys and thirteen stars in union, over the words "*6th February, 1778*," in gold letters.

VI.
Corps of Light-Infantry, commanded by Capt. *Claypoole*, from the 1st regiment.

VII.
DEFINITIVE TREATY OF PEACE.
George Clymer, Esq; on horseback, carrying a staff, adorned with olive and laurel, the words "*3d September, 1783*," in gold letters, pendant from the staff.

VIII.
Col. *John Shee*, on horseback, carrying a flag, blue field, with a laurel and an olive wreath over the words—"WASHINGTON, THE FRIEND OF HIS COUNTRY"—in silver letters—the staff adorned with olive and laurel.

IX.
The City Troop of Light Dragoons, commanded by Major *W. Jackson.*

X.
Richard Bache, Esq; on horseback, as a Herald, attended by a trumpet, proclaiming a New Æra—the words "NEW ÆRA," in gold letters, pendant from the Herald's staff, and the following lines,
Peace o'er our land her olive wand extends,
And white rob'd Innocence from Heaven descends;
The crimes and frauds of Anarchy shall fail,
Returning Justice lifts again her scale.

XI.
The Hon. *Peter Muhlenberg*, Esq; Vice-President of Pennsylvania, on horseback, carrying a flag, blue field, emblazoned—the words "*17th September, 1787*," in silver letters, on the flag.

XII.
Band of Music.

XIII.
The Honorable Chief-Justice M'Kean,
The Hon. Judge Atlee, The Hon. Judge Rush, (in their Robes of Office)
In an ornamented Car, drawn by six horses, bearing the CONSTITUTION, framed, fixed on a staff, crowned with the Cap of Liberty—the words—"THE PEOPLE," in gold letters, on the staff, immediately under the Constitution.

XIV.
Corps of Light-Infantry, commanded by Capt. *Heysham*, from the 3d regiment.

XV.
Ten Gentlemen, representing the States that have adopted the Fœderal Constitution, *viz.*
1. *Duncan Ingraham*, Esq; — New-Hampshire,
2. *Jonathan Williams*, jun. Esq; — Massachusetts.
3. *Jared Ingersoll*, Esq; — Connecticut.
4. Hon. Chief Justice *Brearley*, — New-Jersey.
5. *James Wilson*, Esq; — Pennsylvania.
6. Col. *Thomas Robinson*, — Delaware.
7. Hon. *J. E. Howard*, Esq; — Maryland.
8. Col. *Febiger*, — Virginia.
9. *W. Ward Burrows*, Esq; — South-Carolina.
10. *George Meade*, Esq; — Georgia.
Bearing distinguishing flags and walking arm in arm, emblematic of Union.

XVI.
Colonel *William Williams*, in armour, on horseback, bearing a Shield, emblazoned with the arms of the United States.

XVII.
The Montgomery county Troop of Light-Horse, commanded by *James Morris*, Esquire.

XVIII.
An ornamented Car, drawn by four horses, bearing Captain *Thomas Bell*, carrying the Flag of *The United States*,—Monsieur *Barbé de Marbois*, Flag of *France*,—Mr. *Hennekin*, Flag of *The United Netherlands*,—Mr. *Helstead*, Flag of *Sweden*,—Mr. *Locke*, Flag of *Prussia*,—*Thomas Barclay*, Esquire, Flag of *Morocco*,—States in alliance with *America.*

XIX.
The Judge, Register, Marshal, and other Officers of the Court of Admiralty, with their insignia.

XX.
Wardens of the Port, and Tonnage Officers.

XXI.
Collector of the Customs, and Naval Officer.

XXII.
The Surveyor-General, Receiver-General, Secretary, and other Officers of the Land Office.

XXIII.
Register, Recorder of Deeds, and Comptroller-General.

XXIV.
Peter Baynton, Esq; and Colonel *Isaac Melcher*, as an American and an Indian, smoaking the Calumet of Peace, in a carriage drawn by two horses.

XXV.
GRAND FŒDERAL EDIFICE, on a carriage drawn by ten horses, containing Messrs. *Hilary Baker*, (*George Latimore*,) *John Wharton*, *John Nesbitt*, *Samuel Morris*, *John Brown*, *Tench Francis*, *Joseph Anthony*, *John Chaloner* and *Peter Ozias*, citizens of the Union—
Attended by the House-carpenters.

XXVI.
Corps of Light Infantry, commanded by Captain *Rose*, 5th regiment.

XXVII.
The Agricultural Society, headed by their President, *S. Powel*, Esq;

XXVIII.
The Farmers, headed by *Richard Peters*, *Richard Willing*, *Samuel Meredith*, *Isaac Warner*, *George Gray*, *William Peltz*, —— *Burkhart* and *Charles Willing*, with ploughs, &c.

XXIX.
The Manufacturing Society, with the spinning and carding machines, looms, &c. headed by *Robert Hare*, Esq;

Corps of Light Infantry, commanded by Capt. *Robinson*, from the 6th regiment.

The Marine Society, with their insignia.

The Fœderal Ship, The UNION, commanded by *John Green*, Esq; Captain *S. Smith*, *W. Belcher* and Mr. *Mercer*, Lieutenants, with a proper crew of Officers and Seamen.

The Pilots of the Port, with a Pilot Boat.

Boat Builders, with a Barge.

The Ship-carpenters, Sail-makers, Rope-makers, Block-makers and Riggers.

The Merchants and Traders of the city and liberties of Philadelphia, headed by *Thomas Willing*, Esq; with their insignia—followed by the Merchants Clerks.

Corps of Light Infantry, commanded by Capt. *Spreat*, from the 4th regiment.

TRADES and PROFESSIONS.

XXX.
1. Cordwainers,

XXXI.
2. Coach-painters,

XXXII.
3. Cabinet and Chair-makers,

XXXIII.
4. Brick-makers,

XXXIV.
5. Painters,

XXXV.
6. Porters,

XXXVI.
7. Watch-makers,

XXXVII.
8. Fringe and Ribband Weavers,

XXXVIII.
9. Bricklayers,

XXXIX.
10. Taylors,

XL.
11. Instrument-makers, Turners and Windsor Chair-makers,

XLI.
12. Carvers and Gilders,

XLII.
13. Coopers,

XLIII.
14. Plane-makers,

XLIV.
15. Whip Manufacturers,

XLV.
16. Black-smiths, White-smiths, Nail-smiths and Bell-hangers,

XLVI.
17. Coach-makers,

XLVII.
18. Potters,

XLVIII.
19. Hatters,

XLIX.
20. Wheel-wrights,

L.
21. Tin-plate Workers,

LI.
22. Skinners, Breeches-makers and Glovers,

LII.
23. Tallow-chandlers,

LIII.
24. Butchers,

LIV.
25. Printers, Stationers and Book-binders,

LV.
26. Saddlers,

LVI.
27. Stone-cutters,

LVII.
28. Bakers,

LVIII.
29. Gun-smiths,

LIX.
30. Copper-smiths,

LX.
31. Gold-smiths, Silver-smiths and Jewellers,

LXI.
32. Distillers,

LXII.
33. Tobacconists,

LXIII.
34. Brass-founders,

LXIV.
35. Stocking Manufacturers,

LXV.
36. Curriers,

LXVI.
37. Druggists,

LXVII.
38. Upholsterers,

LXVIII.
39. Sugar-refiners,

LXIX.
40. Brewers,

LXX.
41. Peruke-makers and Barbers,

LXXI.
42. Ship-chandlers,

LXXII.
43. Engravers,

LXXIII.
44. Plaisterers,

Corps of Light Infantry, commanded by Capt. *Rees*, from the 2d regiment.

The Civil and Military Officers of Congress in the City.

His Excellency the PRESIDENT, and the SUPREME EXECUTIVE COUNCIL.

The Justices of the Common Pleas and the Magistrates.

Sheriff and Coroner, on horseback.

City Wardens.

Constables and Watchmen.

The gentlemen of the Bar, headed by the Honorable *Edward Shippen*, Esquire, President of the Common Pleas, and *William Bradford*, Esquire, Attorney-General, followed by the Students of Law.

The Clergy of the different denominations.

The College of Physicians, headed by their President, Dr. *Redman.*

Students of the University, headed by the Vice-Provost, and of other Schools, headed by their respective Principals, Professors, Masters and Tutors.

The County Tooop of Light Horse, commanded by Major *W. Macpherson*, bringing up the rear of the the whole.

Major *Fullerton* to attend the right wing——Colonel *Mentges* the left wing.

On the UNION GREEN, at Bush-hill, Mr. WILSON will deliver an Oration, suited to the day; after which a Collation will be prepared for the company.

The following gentlemen, distinguished by a white feather in the hat, are Superintendants of the procession. General *Mifflin*, General *Stewart*, Colonel *Proctor*, Colonel *Gurney*, Major *Moore*, Major *Lenox*, Mr. *Peter Brown*, Colonel *Will*, Colonel *Marsh.*

To add to the entertainment of the day, ten vessels will be prepared and paraded as follows, one representing *New-Hampshire*, opposite the Northern-Liberties,—the next for *Massachusetts*, opposite Vine-street,—*Connecticut*, opposite Race-street,—*New-Jersey*, Arch—*Pennsylvania*, Market—*Delaware*, Chestnut—*Maryland*, Walnut—*Virginia*, Spruce—*South-Carolina*, Pine—and *Georgia*, South-street. The RISING SUN, under the command of Captain *Philip Brown*, will be anchored off Market-street, and superbly dressed. At night she will be handsomely illuminated.

By Order of the Committee of Arrangement,
Francis Hopkinson, Chairman.

Philadelphia: Printed by HALL and SELLERS.

"The New Roof"

On June 21, 1788, New Hampshire ratified the Constitution; it was the ninth state to do so, enough to start the machinery of the new government. Virginia—a key state—ratified four days later. On Independence Day Philadelphia, proud home of the Constitutional Convention, saw an enormous celebration: ships on the Delaware flying colorful pennants, bells ringing, guns booming, speeches, and a "Federal Procession" (left) a mile and a half long. "And let the people's motto ever be/ 'United thus, and thus united, free!'" exulted a poem by Francis Hopkinson, chairman of the procession. Not everyone was happy, of course. In Albany, New York, Antifederalists burned a copy of the Constitution, which led to a riot. But the general mood was one of confidence in the document that Hopkinson called the New Roof.

En route to his inauguration in 1789, the first President elected under the Constitution is greeted in Trenton, where, on December 26, 1776, his army had routed the Hessians.

PART

THE FORMATIVE YEARS

*"As the first of every thing,
in our situation, will serve
to establish a Precedent, it is
devoutly wished on my part,
that these precedents may
be fixed on true principles."*

GEORGE WASHINGTON

*The Washingtons' receptions were formal
and regal. Martha is on the dais in this
painting; the President is in the center.*

CHAPTER TWO

The Office Defined and Tested

Professor Rexford Guy Tugwell, a onetime adviser to Franklin D. Roosevelt, writes that when the Philadelphia framers approved Article II of the Constitution, the one that describes the President, "none . . . could have had any very definite picture of the official they had created—except that he would be very much like Washington."

Washington himself, to judge from his correspondence, was much impressed by the level of debate at Philadelphia. It was, he told his French friend the Marquis de Lafayette in February, 1788, "little short of a miracle" that delegates from so many different states should have been able to agree on a system "so little liable to well founded objections." He thought the distribution of responsibility ingenious and prudent. Unlike Lafayette and Jefferson, he was not worried by the possibility that a President might continue in office for more than one term. "I can see no propriety," he informed Lafayette, "in precluding ourselves from the services of any man, who on some great emergency shall be deemed universally, most capable of serving the Public."

General Washington fully realized that he was regarded as the indispensable person for the post. "It is to little purpose," Alexander Hamilton wrote, "to have *introduced* a system, if the weightiest influence is not given to its firm *establishment*, in the outset." Lafayette among others begged the general "not to deny your acceptance of the office of President for the first years. You only can settle that political machine." Every finger pointed at Washington.

His own reactions were understandable. He was flattered to be held in such universal esteem. With more good sense and perhaps greater freedom of maneuver than some of his successors would have, he determined—and announced to acquaintances—that he would assume the Presidency "unfettered by promises"; he would not feed "the expectations of *any man living* for my assistance to Office." He well knew, as he wrote to a correspondent, that "the first transactions of a nation, like those of an individual upon his first entrance into life, make the deepest impression, and . . . form the leading traits in its character. . . ." In short, neither he nor any other patriot could decline to lend his services to the new government. When the electors made their choice known officially, the result was an extraordinary demonstration of confidence, of an order that would never be vouchsafed to any other American Chief Executive. Each elector had two votes; each gave one of his votes to Washington, making him the unanimous choice for President. (Second in the list of preferences was John Adams of Massachusetts, who thus became Vice President.) When Washington considered that among the electors were such Antifederalist war horses as Patrick Henry, he could indeed feel gratified.

Otherwise he was one of the most reluctant men ever to become President. Some of his reasons were personal. Too much of his life had already been spent in public service, away from his beloved Mount Vernon. Although he was only fifty-seven—three years older than what would become the average age of Presidents at inauguration—Washington was weary and in poor health. Above all he was nervous. At Philadelphia he had heard more learned men than he expound the drawbacks of constitutional government. He did not feel that he was equipped to deal with the "ocean of difficulties" that lay ahead. It was one thing to practice elementary plantation bookkeeping, quite another to contemplate the tangled mass of America's national and state debts. The strength of local and factional feeling displayed in some of the ratification controversies gave promise of a stormy passage. There were dozens of opportunities for wrangling over the new Constitution.

Being human, George Washington had snatched at the faint chance that the government might "be just as happily and effectually carried into execution without my aid." When he received the formal notice of his election and saw that all escape routes were barred, he "bade adieu to Mount Vernon, to private life, and to domestic felicity, with a mind oppressed with more anxious and painful sensations than I have words to express."

Within a few weeks he was feeling his way forward cautiously amidst general acclaim. He was installed in reasonable comfort in a rented house in New York, the temporary Capital of the reconstituted Union. He had taken the oath of office prescribed in the Constitution: "I do solemnly swear that I will faithfully execute the Office of President of the United States, and will to the best of my Ability, preserve, protect and defend the Constitution of the United States." He had delivered an appropriately modest yet dignified ten-minute Inaugural Address. Since Congress was assembling with a dilatoriness characteristic of the old days under the Articles of Confederation, there was no sudden press of business. Washington and Congress therefore had time to deal with sundry matters of protocol.

Such questions were not of tremendous consequence, but in the early stages it seemed important to get things right. Washington consulted Vice President Adams and two newly appointed figures, Chief Justice John Jay and Secretary of the Treasury Alexander Hamilton, by inviting their answers to a set of written queries:

"1st. Whether a line of conduct, equally distant from an association with all kinds of company on the one hand and from a total seclusion from Society on the other, ought to be adopted by [the President]? and, in that case, how is it to be done?

"2d. What will be the least exceptionable method of bringing any system, which may be adopted on this subject, before the public and into use? . . .

"4th. Whether it would tend to prompt impertinent applications and involve disagreeable consequences to have it known, that the President will, every Morning at eight Oclock, be at leisure to give Audience to persons who may have business with him?

"5th. Whether, when it shall have been understood that the President is not to give general entertainments in the manner the Presidents of Congress have formerly done, it will be practicable to draw such a line of discrimination in regard to persons, as that six, eight or ten official characters (including in the rotation the members of both Houses of Congress) may be invited . . . to dine with him on the days fixed for receiving Company, without exciting clamours in the rest of the Community?

"6th. Whether it would be satisfactory to the public for the President to make about four great entertainments, in a year on such great occasions as . . . the Anniversary of the Declaration of Independence. . . .

"8th. Whether, during the recess of Congress, it would not be advantageous to the interests of the Union for the President to make the tour of the United States, in order to become better acquainted with their principal Characters and internal Circumstances, as well as to be more accessible to numbers of well-informed persons, who might give him useful information and advices on political subjects? . . ."

Hamilton's answer, which was more or less in accord with Adams' and Jay's, was that "men's minds are prepared for a pretty high tone in the demeanor of the executive, but I doubt whether for so high a one as in the abstract might be desirable. The notions of equality are . . . too general and too strong. . . ." This view probably concurred with Washington's own sentiments. He had always liked to live in style, dressing handsomely and entertaining on a generous scale. As President he felt that a still higher and more formal style was necessary. He decided that because of his office he could no longer accept private invitations. Instead, he and Lady Washington (as she was sometimes called) invited others to levees, dinners, theater parties, and ceremonial receptions. Some recipients of these invitations, such as the scornful Senator William Maclay of Pennsylvania, complained that the affairs were too reminiscent of a royal court. The President bowed to his guests— there were no handshakes—and at the dinner table,

Maclay reported, conversation was stiff and desultory, since initiative was left to the President, who was not a sparkling conversationalist.

No doubt some of these functions were too solemn and punctilious. Maclay and other critics were, however, unfair in not realizing that the Presidency was more than the man who occupied it. It was a symbolic office, which most Americans then and later expected to see maintained with a degree of panache. The striking feature of Washington's questions is the awareness of public sensitivity they revealed. He was asking how he might best reconcile the elevation of the office with American ideas of equality and with the necessity of being accessible to "persons who may have business" with the President.

He was certainly less agitated by problems of protocol than John Adams, who was more of an American democrat than he was given credit for. Adams' writings were often misinterpreted. Because of his diplomatic experience in London and elsewhere, Adams had no doubt that a monarchy would be wrong for America. As a connoisseur of political systems, however, he appreciated the British solution; he considered European countries not yet ready to dispense with royal government; and he was honest enough to admit that the kings he had met were not more stupid than other men. Nevertheless Adams, the "Duke of Braintree," amused and irked certain members of the Senate, over which he presided. He was satisfied when the Senate suggested that the President be officially known as "His Highness, the President of the United States of America, and Protector of their Liberties." He was dismayed when the House of Representatives chose the simple title —"President of the United States"—given in Article II of the Constitution. "What," he asked "will the common people of foreign countries, what will the sailors and soldiers say, 'George Washington, President of the United States'? They will despise him to all eternity." Adams was not as foolish as this remark makes him sound. It should be noted that he was talking of the foreign, not the American, reaction. People who insist on giving their stay-at-home companions bits of wisdom culled from travel overseas are never popular. But Adams was correct in his own terms. European society, especially that of courts, teemed with titles and ranks. American prestige, he thought, would be jeopardized without such protective coloration—as American diplomats

Washington (left) meets with his Cabinet: Henry Knox, Alexander Hamilton, Thomas Jefferson, and Edmund Randolph.

would discover when they attended functions in plain clothes instead of court dress and were occasionally mistaken for servants. Nor were titles unimportant within the United States. Foreign travelers would claim that Americans, while lacking in some forms of deference or courtesy, were pretentious in other ways: they addressed one another as "Major," "Colonel," "General"—and, of course, as "Judge." In this context, "Mr. President" acquired the glamour of understatement.

In his Inaugural Address Washington announced that he would prefer to receive no salary, although the Constitution spoke of a "compensation"; he wished only to be reimbursed for expenses (as when he had been commander in chief). Perhaps he had been impressed by Benjamin Franklin's argument at Philadelphia against a presidential salary. Franklin had cited British precedent and had maintained that if a "Post of Honour" became a "Place of Profit" it would make America's Chief Executive a greedy schemer. The framers rightly believed that this would be more likely to happen if he was not paid a reasonable salary. In 1789 Congress fixed the President's annual salary at $25,000. The Secretaries of State and of the Treasury were to receive $3,500, and the Vice President, $5,000. These figures were to remain fixed until 1873, when the President's and

Vice President's emoluments were doubled to $50,000 and $10,000 respectively. John Adams, always touchy and considerably less wealthy than George Washington, no doubt meditated on the apparent conclusion that Congress estimated the value of a President at five times that of his deputy.

Washington's advisers concurred in his view that it would be useful for the President to make extensive trips while Congress was recessed. He traveled around the Northeastern states in the summer of 1789 (skipping Rhode Island, which he did not visit until it had ratified the Constitution in 1790), and made a long tour of the Southern states in 1791. The performance never became standard for Presidents. John Adams, for example, headed home to Braintree (Quincy), Massachusetts, each summer—and stayed so long that he was accused of neglecting his job. But Monroe imitated Washington by touring the North in 1817, the year of his inauguration, and Andrew Jackson traveled among the Yankees in 1833—receiving an honorary degree from Harvard in the process. To their delight both men were welcomed by immense, applauding crowds. For them as for Washington and for nearly all the later Presidents, there was a peculiar thrill in these contacts with ordinary Americans. In some almost magical way—as if the President were like the giant Antaeus, whose strength depended upon contact with the earth—Chief Executives who traveled about the Union usually found that they were more refreshed than fatigued by the journeying, the hubbub, and the succession of banquets and testimonial speeches.

Before he set out on his visit to the Northeast, Washington began to establish more workaday precedents. Congressional enactments provided for the first executive departments and for the apparatus of a Supreme Court and a number of federal district and circuit courts. The Department of State absorbed and extended the functions of the former Department of Foreign Affairs. Washington appointed Jefferson Secretary of State, although he was still in France and was not able to take office until March, 1790. Henry Knox of Massachusetts, a congenial associate of Revolutionary War days, was named Secretary of War. The Departments of State, of War, and of the Treasury (with Hamilton at its head): these made up the modest total of executive departments in 1789. Congress also created the office of Postmaster General—which would not be-

come an executive department until 1872—to control the postal service that Benjamin Franklin had once supervised. It was not an overwhelming task in that formative time. The Postmaster General, Samuel Osgood, was urged to occupy a desk in the same room with his few clerks, so that he could keep an eye on their handling of the mails. A more important office in the executive circle was the Attorney Generalship, a post that had been established along with the Supreme Court by the Federal Judiciary Act of 1789. Washington's choice for Attorney General was a fellow Virginian, Edmund Randolph, who had reconciled his objections to the new Constitution. He had been helped to do so by the President's allusion in his Inaugural Address to the government's obligation to encourage additional guarantees in the shape of amendments. Twelve amendments were in fact proposed in the House of Representatives; ten were eventually ratified by the states and incorporated in the Constitution as the Bill of Rights in December, 1791.

The executive branch began modestly. Even in 1800, when Adams' administration was nearing its end, the accumulation of paper was so frugal that the entire archives of the executive departments could be stowed in seven packing cases for the move to the new Capital. But this did not mean that there was no work to be done. Washington was able to employ experienced secretaries, such as William Jackson, who had acted as secretary to the Philadelphia convention. Even so, the press of business was considerable, ranging from routine matters such as signing commissions to more intricate questions.

Washington often invited Jefferson, Hamilton, and others to breakfast to discuss papers he had sent to them the previous day. Sometimes he would ask officials to report to him individually. The administrative historian Leonard D. White, who has made a close study of the first years of the Presidency, concludes that Washington was a capable, hard-working administrator. His wartime years, when he was largely concerned with matters of supply, equipment, promotion, and recruitment as well as with strategy and tactics, had obliged him to maintain a copious correspondence. As President he seemed the master of administrative detail—signifying formal approval of schemes submitted by executive heads, sending outlines of plans to be expanded, seeking opinions on the constitutionality of legislation or on policy matters, and requesting drafts of his various public papers.

When Jefferson became President in 1801 he outlined Washington's system as a model for his own heads of departments (whose number had been increased by the formation in 1798 of a Navy Department). Every item of business, recalled Jefferson, had been seen at some stage by President Washington, even if it had been addressed to a particular executive head. "If a doubt of any importance arose, he reserved it for conference. By this means, he was always in accurate possession of all facts and proceedings in every part of the Union, and to whatsoever department they related; he formed a central point for the different branches; preserved an unity of object and action among them; exercised that participation in the suggestion of affairs which his office made incumbent on him; and met himself the due responsibility for whatever was done."

In part Washington was instituting a mechanism for dealing with the miscellaneous matters of executive government; in part he was seeking guidance on problems that might be of greater import. During his first administration he used James Madison, who was then a member of the House of Representatives. It was Madison who drafted the first version of Washington's intended Farewell Address when the President anticipated retirement in 1793. Their contacts became less frequent as Madison developed views in opposition to those of the administration.

Washington also sought the advice of the Supreme Court—only to be told in effect that the Court meant to preserve its separation from the executive branch. When, for instance, he asked the Court to assist him in untangling the legal questions involved in the Neutrality Proclamation of 1793, he was told that the justices did not consider it their function to advise the Chief Magistrate. It had seemed possible that Washington would form a close liaison with the Senate. As the Upper House of Congress, the Senate was somewhat analogous to the governors' councils of colonial days; it numbered only twenty-six men initially—a reasonably intimate circle—and its constitutional duty to "advise and consent," especially on foreign policy questions, required it to have regular dealings with the President. But the separation of powers specified in the Constitution proved stronger than the potential affinity between President and Senate. When the first test came there was a fiasco. Wishing to make a treaty with some Indian tribes, Washington duly notified the Senate and appeared before it on August 2, 1789. The treaty was read out. There followed an uneasy silence broken by muttering; the President waited for senatorial approval and his audience fidgeted until its less bashful spokesmen intimated that they would like time (and privacy) in which to make up their minds. According to Senator Maclay, Washington behaved irritably and impatiently. If so, he quickly learned his lesson. When he returned to the Senate after an adjournment, he was elaborately polite—but he never repeated the experiment. Thereafter Presidents would deal with the Senate indirectly.

The conferences that Jefferson recalled were attended by Washington, the Secretaries of State, of War, and of the Treasury, and the Attorney General (the Postmaster General was not brought into the circle until 1829, under Jackson). Washington asked Adams to be present at one meeting during his absence, but after that Adams was never again included in these high-ranking deliberations—not out of rudeness, but simply because the Vice President had no useful role. The Attorney General was invited because of the appearance of crucial legal problems (such as the constitutionality of the Bank of the United States, which had been chartered in 1791) and also because Edmund Randolph was a gifted man whom the President had known for many years.

In 1792 and 1793 the group met with increasing frequency, but they never became friends. Jefferson recollected that Washington's executive heads had been "equally divided by as marked an opposition of principle as monarchism and republicanism could bring into conflict." He and Hamilton, he remembered, had been "daily pitted . . . like two cocks." Knox had usually sided with Hamilton, and Randolph had been somewhat more independent.

The vital point is that a new governmental body, not mentioned in the Constitution, was evolving: the Cabinet. In a way, it had been foreseen and was an inevitable outcome; for as Washington himself wrote at the end of the Philadelphia discussions: "The impossibility that one man should . . . perform all the great business of the state I take to have been the reason for instituting the great departments, and appointing officers therein to assist the supreme magistrate in discharging the duties of his trust." Charles Pinckney had talked of a "Cabinet Council" during the debates on a plural Executive. In a sense, Washington's Cabinet—the word seems to have been first applied to the group by Madison in 1793—was such a body. Washington probably compared its meetings to the councils of war that he had summoned during the Revolution. It was military custom not to undertake a major operation without the advice and consent of the senior officers in an army. More than once Washington, though commander in chief, had rejected his own plan in the face of adverse comment from his generals.

His later habit was to consult his executive heads, require them to express their opinion, and arrive at a sort of collective decision. However, President Washington during Cabinet meetings, as in his military career, was much more than *primus inter pares*. Indeed there was an important difference. His generals had been appointed by Congress; his Cabinet was appointed by him and could be removed by his sole decision—a power of which he dramatically if sadly availed himself in 1795 when he dismissed Edmund Randolph, the Secretary of State, on suspicion of improper dealings with a French diplomat. Jefferson, for all his democratic airs, believed that the American Cabinet system had proved a success because unlike the Directory in revolutionary France it had a genuine head. In 1811, when his own Presidency was over, Jefferson claimed that his eight-year administration had "presented an example of harmony in a cabinet of six persons, to which perhaps history has furnished no parallel." Yet he doubted whether this rapport would have been possible but for "the power of decision in the President. . . ."

So the federal government acquired a Cabinet. By 1800 the institution and its name were accepted without question. The Cabinet underwent some changes while Washington was still President. He had not enjoyed the cleavage between Hamilton and Jefferson. He had enjoyed still less the emergence of a party, or "faction," which, coalescing around Madison and Jefferson, was opposed to the general policy of his administration. After Hamilton and Jefferson had resigned their offices, and after the President had perhaps wrongly condemned Randolph, Washington announced that if possible, he would no longer "bring a man into an office of consequence . . . whose political tenets are adverse to the measures which the general government are pursuing. . . ." To do so would be "political suicide." This development was

to be permanent: since 1795, Presidents have occasionally appointed Cabinet members who were affiliated with a rival party, but never at the risk of creating dissension within the ranks of the government.

Other aspects of the Cabinet were less permanent. Occasionally a Cabinet officer has exerted great influence over a President. But on the whole the Cabinet, an extraconstitutional body, has had a fluctuating existence and has tended to be replaced by other advisers chosen at presidential will either from within a select group of Cabinet favorites or from among men who, like those in Andrew Jackson's "Kitchen Cabinet," held no executive office at all.

In federal appointments as a whole Washington had to reckon with a necessity that would govern the calculations of all his successors. The requisite art was that of spreading appointments geographically in an effort to placate different sections of the country. For Washington and his immediate successor, John Adams, a more pressing problem was to persuade good men to accept federal posts. According to the historian Stephen Kurtz, none of the major figures who served the first two Presidents could avoid financial hardship. At the outset there were floods of applicants for federal employment. But within a few years the cost of living doubled. Alexander Hamilton resigned from the Treasury Department in 1795 mainly because he could no longer support his family. John Marshall, having no independent source of income, was forced to decline the invitation to become Attorney General in 1795. Patrick Henry and Charles Cotesworth Pinckney were other prominent Southerners who had to refuse invitations from the President. One result was that the chief posts tended to be filled by relatively well-to-do men. But they were as anxious as Washington to escape the ordeal of office, some because they felt they had already served their time in the Revolution or in the Continental Congress, and some because they found government at the state level more rewarding. There might have been a disastrous deterioration in the quality of federal administrators had salaries not been increased by the Jeffersonian Republicans. This increase helped to sustain the prestige of federal service. So did various intangible factors, including the social pleasures and the chances for forming connections provided by life in the Capital. At any rate, all but the most menial places in the executive bureaus came to be filled by Americans who prided themselves on their good families and superior educations. Even Andrew Jackson, with his zeal for rotation in office, made only a small dent in the genteel hierarchy of the District of Columbia. (Central bureaucracies, and bureaucrats' wives, do not differ much from generation to generation or from country to country.)

The issue of the President's prime responsibility for appointing to office might have been thorny. Instead Congress, initially deferential to Washington, readily conceded to him the right to choose his own officials, judges, and diplomats—and the still more crucial right to dismiss appointees without explaining his reasons. In later decades the Senate hardly ever rejected Cabinet nominations, although it sometimes contested the President's will on other appointments. As for the removal power, it had been firmly specified in the statutes establishing the first executive departments and was underlined by the precedents of the first six Presidencies. Although the Senate censured Andrew Jackson for having dismissed Treasury Secretary William J. Duane, Jackson undoubtedly won the purely constitutional argument. The summary of the historical background of Jackson's April, 1834, protest to the Senate is worth quoting. The original debate in Congress, in 1789, said Jackson, had "covered the whole ground, embracing the Treasury as well as all the other Executive Departments, [but] arose on a motion to strike out of the bill to establish a . . . Department of State, a clause declaring the Secretary 'to be removable from office by the President of the United States'. . . . It was perceived that these words did not convey the sense of the House of Representatives in relation to the true source of the power of removal. With the avowed object of preventing any future inference that this power was exercised by the President in virtue of a grant from Congress, when in fact that body considered it as derived from the Constitution, the words . . . were struck out, and . . . a clause was inserted in a provision concerning the chief clerk of the Department, which declared that 'whenever the said principal officer shall be removed from office by the President . . . or in any other case of vacancy,' the chief clerk should . . . have charge of the papers of the office." In other words, the change had been made "for the express purpose of declaring the sense of Congress that the President derived the power of removal from the Constitution. . . ."

This engraving of "Giorgio Washington" appeared in a book published in Milan in 1815. He looks decidedly Italian.

The removal power was an apparently straightforward matter; but not even this point was settled forever. As John Quincy Adams later remarked, the American system of federal government with checks and balances was the most complicated in the world. Adams conceded in his *Jubilee of the Constitution*, printed in 1839, that the right of removal, "like all other discretionary powers, is susceptible of great abuse. . . ." At that point he could not resist the temptation to take a sidelong swipe at his old enemy Jackson. But having once been President himself, Adams was quick to defend the office by adding that any procedure curtailing the presidential prerogative would be still more liable to abuse. (No matter how negative their conception of the Presidency, every one of Andrew Johnson's predecessors must have turned in his grave in 1868 when Congress impeached that luckless Chief Executive mainly on the ground that he had dismissed his Secretary of War in violation of a congressional law.)

Andrew Jackson's critics in the Senate challenged his removal power partly because some felt that the Secretary of the Treasury occupied a special position among the executive heads. This conception, like so

A Japanese history of the United States, printed in the 1850's, featured this depiction of the first President.

many others, began in President Washington's time. Historians still debate the underlying truth, which concerns Alexander Hamilton's role as envisaged by himself, Jefferson, Congress, and his President. In all likelihood Hamilton did think of or try to encourage a pattern of American executive government based on that of Britain, in which Washington would represent the king and Hamilton, the prime minister. He was supported in such a view by the knowledge that England's vigorous young prime minister, William Pitt, also directed financial policy as chancellor of the exchequer and first lord of the treasury. The act of Congress that created Hamilton's department seemed to specify that he maintain a special relationship with the House, which he interpreted as requiring him to attend debates like a minister in Parliament. Problems over debts, banks, currency, and the like were both urgent and fundamental. The President was not an expert on economics. Hamilton, while financially honest, was an unscrupulous as well as an extremely industrious and quick-witted person who could not resist meddling in Thomas Jefferson's domain of foreign affairs or attempting to run the War Department. His beliefs notwithstanding, he was elaborately courteous to President Washington.

According to Jefferson, who made his views clear to the President, Hamilton was sheltering behind Washington's prestige and treating the President as a ceremonial figure of no real substance. This theory would seem to be borne out by Hamilton's remark, after the President's death, that Washington was *"an Aegis very essential to me."* Among recent historians, Joseph Charles, Jr., considered Hamilton the dominant figure among Washington's advisers. Certainly Washington accepted Hamilton's main proposals, despite the opposition of Jefferson and of numerous thoughtful Americans. Another historian, Alexander DeConde, portrayed Washington as "slow of mind," and said "he took his ideas and theories, without much question, from Hamilton."

It is intriguing to consider how the Presidency might have evolved if Hamilton had had his way. An exceptionally ambitious and brilliant sequence of Treasury Secretaries might have assumed executive initiative, relegating the President to a mainly honorific role like that of the president in other republican systems. Or, of course, the Secretaryship of State might have become the focus of real power; it was the senior executive post, and especially in the first years was thought to embrace not only foreign responsibilities but also certain domestic ones (such as the new federal mint). Two factors appear to have regulated matters differently. One was the chilly response of Congress to Hamilton's overtures—a response reinforced by the unequivocal statement in the Constitution (Article I, Section 6) that "no Person holding any Office under the United States, shall be a Member of either House during his Continuance in Office." Hamilton's efforts to present his recommendations on the floor of the House were rebuffed. In January, 1790, Congress decided that all future reports from the Secretary of the Treasury were to be submitted in written form.

The second factor, already mentioned, was Washington's hold over his executive heads. Those who ridiculed him as ignorant and ponderous took care not to do so within reach of his formidable wrath; indeed most of them waited until he was dead. He had too commanding a presence to allow familiarity, let alone condescension. He was too experienced to be taken in by flattery or specious arguments. When he failed to grasp the subtleties of a problem he was careful to listen to contrary opinions. And if he depended upon Hamilton, Hamilton undoubtedly depended upon him. As Jefferson testified, the first President held the balance between bitterly incompatible viewpoints. The position was uncomfortable for him, yet oddly enough it gave him additional stature. Neither group could afford to do without him at the head of affairs. Both begged him, wholeheartedly if for complex reasons, to remain for a second term. In consenting he settled the future pattern of the Presidency in several ways. One of these was to ensure that the President was master in his own executive domain. In Washington's second term the splenetic divisions of party politics perhaps made him more susceptible to the opinions that Hamilton —who was by then a private citizen—voiced in his letters to the President. But that situation may be left until a later chapter, which deals with politics and the Presidency.

Relations between Washington and his legislature developed politely in various ways. He vetoed only two congressional bills during his eight years of power, confining himself to a few minor issues and explaining that they conflicted with the Constitution or were undesirable. There seemed little cause for alarm over entrusting the President with this semiregal attribute (though incidentally, if those who sought to draw a parallel between the President and the British monarch had wished to make the comparison favorable to the king, they could have disclosed that the royal veto had lain unused since the early eighteenth century). The next five Presidents were equally sparing in their vetoes.

Nor was there much difficulty with the annual State of the Union messages that Presidents Washington and Adams delivered in person before Congress. The only initial awkwardness came from exaggerated formality: Congress at first answered messages from the President by tendering messages of appreciation. Later, as partisan feeling became intense, there were grumblings that Washington's annual addresses too closely resembled the British "Speech from the Throne" that opened each session of Parliament. With this criticism in mind, Jefferson abandoned the precedent set by Washington and Adams and simply transmitted his messages to Congress, where they were read aloud by a clerk. His method would be followed until 1913, when Woodrow Wilson, the twenty-eighth Chief Executive, reverted to the old style—not to revive a ritual but to demonstrate his conception of a re-energized Presidency.

Congressional prickliness sometimes took mean and foolish shapes. On some early issues, however, their jealousy of presidential style was to prove wiser than they realized. For instance, Alexander Hamilton's 1792 draft of an "Act for Establishing a Mint" stipulated that Washington's head should be stamped on all coins of the United States. It was a gracious gesture for which there was precedent; but it was the wrong type of precedent, the type applied to reigning monarchs. The act was amended. Thereafter, with an aversion to overmighty symbols that other new nations would have been well advised to imitate, the United States commemorated rather than celebrated its Chief Magistrates. Not until they were dead might their likenesses be reproduced on currency or (a later, consequential decision) on postage stamps. It could be added that the nation carried caution to an excess of parsimony in not making financial provision for ex-Presidents. Washington was not a pauper and lived less than three years after he relinquished the Presidency, but John Adams had to scrape along for a quarter of a century after his term in the White House. Jefferson, Madison, and Monroe, who survived after office for seventeen, nineteen, and six years respectively, were far from prosperous. Not until 1958 would pensions be authorized for former Presidents. And even if money was no problem, a suitable occupation was. For many years the majority of ex-Presidents either buried themselves in retirement (some to write justificatory memoirs) or frequented the corridors of power in hopes of re-election. John Quincy Adams was one of the few to plunge into a second active career—in his case, as a redoubtable member of the House.

The precedents set by Washington and John Adams in the field of foreign policy are hard to interpret, because both men were challenged within their own circle of advisers and because party feeling was as violent as it has ever been in American history. Both Presidents, it may be said, acted promptly, intelligently, and courageously—Adams in such a spirit of defiant rectitude that he alienated most of his Federalist supporters as well as his Republican opponents, and so denied himself the chance of re-election in 1800. There was by no means universal acceptance of the powers that the first two Presidents appeared to be claiming for the executive branch. The situation was dangerous and intractable. The

United States owed an actual and a figurative debt to France for assistance in the Revolutionary War and was allied to France by the treaties of 1778. When the French Revolution erupted, all men of liberal views rejoiced. When the Revolution became more extreme and the French not only established a republic but also guillotined their king, Louis XVI, and his queen, Marie Antoinette, Washington had to mediate between furiously divergent lines of policy. To recognize the French republic in its new phase was to sanction extremism and to jeopardize American neutrality in the Franco-British war that had broken out and was to continue with only two short interruptions until the final overthrow of Napoleon at Waterloo in 1815. To withhold recognition, entirely or in part, was to incur the enmity of the only other republican creation of the modern world and to favor monarchic England.

Washington did not manage to solve the insoluble problem of presidential control of foreign policy. His Neutrality Proclamation of 1793, however, was the first of many such presidential directives to the nation. His decision in this instance, like his decision not to receive the French republican-revolutionary minister Citizen Edmond Genêt, seemed to Jefferson and Madison to constitute an infringement on the privileges of the legislature. Congress was the branch that decided whether to declare war. A presidential neutrality proclamation prejudged the issue. A presidential claim that the duty of formally receiving representatives included the power to refuse to receive them would mean that the Executive could present Congress with a *fait accompli* by having prejudged whether or not to enter into friendly relations with another country.

Washington did not entirely carry the day; Congress asserted itself by passing the Neutrality Act of 1794—the first of several such demonstrations of congressional control over war and peace. Nor was Hamilton's far-reaching analysis of presidential authority well received at the time. He claimed that there was a vital and intentional difference between legislative and executive powers in the wording of the Constitution. Legislative power was limited by the words "herein granted." Since there was no similar qualification in the grant of executive power, Hamilton said, the President was therefore empowered to do anything not specifically prohibited in the Constitution. Gouverneur Morris' joker had come to

the surface; it remained a joker in the pack, though some players of the federal government game would insist that it was not a true card at all.

Nevertheless, with Hamilton's emphatic support, President Washington held his general position. In his second administration he emerged successfully from an angry challenge by the House of Representatives. He had sent John Jay to make a treaty with Britain. The resultant document, signed in 1794, was highly unpopular. The House demanded that Washington furnish copies of Jay's instructions and all other papers relevant to the negotiation. Of the arguments advanced, the most plausible was that of Albert Gallatin of Pennsylvania—a man almost as resourceful as Hamilton—who was to serve as Jefferson's Secretary of the Treasury. Gallatin said that according to the Constitution, treaties had the force of law and were therefore a form of law. The House was a lawmaking body; hence it must have a say in the ratification of treaties or it would be surrendering its legislative authority. A little perplexed and annoyed by the truculence of Congress, Washington consulted Hamilton, who gave him the answer he no doubt wished to hear. Hamilton also offered an additional theory that must have stiffened Washington's resolve—that the opposition might be collecting material in order to impeach the President. At any rate Washington used Hamilton's words to reply impenitently that he could not furnish the papers. The concurrence of the House was not required to validate a treaty; he was obliged to maintain "the boundaries fixed by the Constitution."

In these early, inconclusive struggles between Executive and legislature over foreign policy, Washington and Adams were aided not merely by the pseudonymous writings of Hamilton but also by such Federalist stalwarts as John Marshall. At the height of Adams' troubles over his policy toward France, Marshall declared forthrightly in the House that "the President is the sole organ of the nation in its external relations, and its sole representative with foreign nations." Fighting words at the time, they would gradually become a commonplace of American constitutionalism. One consideration that weakened congressional intransigence was that ordinary citizens were showing a disturbing aptitude for conducting private diplomacy. Congress passed a law against such enterprises—and in so doing weakened its own case, for the law (known as the Logan Act and still in the statute book) was entitled an "Act to Prevent Usurpation of Executive Functions."

In domestic as in foreign affairs, Washington upheld the dignity of his office. His critics alleged that, egged on by Hamilton, he took altogether too strong a stand in suppressing the "whisky rebels"—Western Pennsylvanians who revolted against a tax on their chief product. Washington called out the militia, threatened to march at their head, and inspected the force before it went off (though not, after all, under his personal command). But he had not done anything unconstitutional. What he had done was to demonstrate the power of the federal government—and thereby, the power of the Presidency. Similarly, in the period between 1797 and 1799, when relations with France were strained and war seemed imminent, John Adams displayed the inclinations of a strong President despite derision and abuse. He called Congress into special session and requested an increase in the size of the regular Army. He then stubbornly resisted Federalist pressure to go to war with France. Although he was an unpopular and little-respected figure when his term ended, he could feel that he had sustained the honor of the Adams family and that of the presidential office. Being an Adams, he rated the one as highly as the other.

Pierce Butler, one of the Founding Fathers, had feared that Washington might be the innocent means by which his country would be "oppress'd." Too much trust was being placed in the office of President because he would occupy it: no one would be able to succeed him. Looking back on the evolution of the Presidency, one is impressed by the smoothness of succession. Washington was followed by his Vice President, John Adams, in 1797, Adams by his Vice President, Jefferson, in 1801. Then came a period of inheritance—Madison from Jefferson, Monroe from Madison, John Quincy Adams from Monroe—in which each President was followed by his Secretary of State. All but the Adamses had two terms in office; all but the Massachusetts Adamses were Virginians.

The succession *was* smooth, considering what opportunities for discord there were and how abrupt and fearful—at least for the Federalists—was the so-called Revolution of 1800 when their party had to yield office to the Jeffersonian Republicans. The tact and the indication of a basic consensus in President Jefferson's Inaugural Address of 1801 ("We are all Republicans, we are all Federalists") have been properly emphasized in surveys of American history.

It is important, though, to remember how intricate the problem of succession was, and in particular how indeterminate the role of the Vice President was. As Lucius Wilmerding, Jr., explained in *The Electoral College*, the framers of the Constitution gave much thought to what should happen if the President should fall ill or die. Their solution was to fasten upon the Vice President; the Constitution states plainly: "In Case of the Removal of the President from Office, or of his Death, Resignation, or Inability to discharge the Powers and Duties of the said Office, the Same shall devolve on the Vice President. . . ."

The difficulty was that a Vice President might suddenly find himself burdened with the full responsibility of the Chief Magistracy. The United States could not afford to let such a burden devolve upon a person of mediocre ability. It was therefore imperative to ensure that the Vice President would be a man worthy of the Presidency. The method adopted was in theory brilliantly effective. Article II of the Constitution defines the mode of choosing the Chief Executive: "Each State shall appoint . . . a Number of Electors, equal to the whole Number of Senators and Representatives to which the State may be entitled. . . . The Electors shall meet in their respective States, and vote by Ballot for two Persons, of whom one at least shall not be an Inhabitant of the same State with themselves." The Article also specifies that if no candidate should have the necessary majority or if there should be a tie, the ultimate choice would rest with the House of Representatives (or with the Senate if the possible Vice Presidents were tied after the President had been chosen). Despite these intricacies, the intention is clear: "In every Case, after the Choice of the President, the Person having the greatest Number of Votes of the Electors shall be the Vice President."

In short, the framers deliberately refrained from distinguishing between the President and Vice President, at least so far as election was concerned. The electors would each vote for two men, either of whom they would be happy to see as President. As Senator Uriah Tracy of Connecticut defined the system in 1803, the runner-up "can have no existence until the first character is designated, and then seems to be discovered, not elected." By this beautifully simple mechanism they would obtain, New Jersey Federalist Elias Boudinot said, "the second best character in the union to fill the place of the first, in case it should be vacated by any unforeseen accident." The succession would be immediate and smooth. Not only would the Vice President be a man of parts; through his activity as President of the Senate he would be familiar with the working of the government.

The mechanism failed. John Adams was the first of a long line of "second best characters" who felt they had been consigned to limbo. After less than a year in office he confided to his wife: "My country has in its wisdom contrived for me the most insignificant office that ever the invention of man contrived or his imagination conceived." He was a nobody, and an embarrassing nobody, mistrusted by the Senate and superfluous in the executive branch.

Worse still for Adams' self-esteem, the electors soon came to view the Vice Presidency in the same way. They did not plump for the two best men; instead they began to discriminate sharply between the man they wanted for President and the other figure for whom they were obliged to vote. The elections of 1789 and 1792 worked satisfactorily because all were agreed on their candidate for the Presidency. In 1796 and 1800 there was no such unanimity: when the nation was split into Federalist and Republican camps, the system disclosed its weaknesses. If the electors of one party gave all their votes equally to two men, and if they were the stronger party, things could still go badly. A few additional votes from other electors might give the Presidency to the victors' second choice. Or, as happened in 1796, the Presidency might go to a leading figure of one party (Adams) and the Vice Presidency to one of his chief rivals (Jefferson). The first of these two unwelcome alternatives threatened the country in 1800, when the Republican electors gave an equal number of votes to Jefferson and to Aaron Burr, and the decision passed to the House of Representatives. Burr was clearly meant for the Vice Presidency. The Republicans as a whole were dismayed at the prospect of having him as President.

When Jefferson was at last installed in office—the Federalists in Congress had decided to support him rather than Burr—the Republicans began to press for a constitutional amendment. They feared that in the 1804 national election the Federalists would, by juggling electoral votes, elect a Federalist Vice President and so repeat the Republican maneuver of 1796. The Federalists argued for abiding by the intentions of the framers. Senator James Hillhouse of

Connecticut said, "Your amendment proposes to persuade the people that there is only one man of correct politics in the United States. Your Constitution provides a remedy against this, and says you must bring forward two." Nevertheless, the Twelfth Amendment—specifying that the electors were to cast two distinct ballots, one for President and one for Vice President—was fashioned in Congress, and was duly ratified by the states in time to ensure that Thomas Jefferson would be re-elected to the Presidency in 1804 and that his Vice President would be of the same political persuasion. The election of 1804 set a new precedent: the Vice President (George Clinton of New York) was, while a man of reasonable standing, selected not because he was considered of presidential timber but because he could lend geographical or other support to the ticket.

Although Jefferson never relished the public exposure of high office, in 1797 he wrote to an acquaintance that he had enjoyed being Vice President. "The second office of the government is honorable and easy," he said, "the first is but a splendid misery." He and John Adams were undoubtedly distinguished holders of the second office. But after 1804 its stature dwindled. With a few exceptions, Vice Presidents would be picked because they came from a particular state, or because the party wished to put some old war horse out to graze. After Jefferson only one ex-Vice President, Martin Van Buren, would gain the Presidency by election instead of by inheritance through death. The names of some of the Vice Presidents illustrate the decline. Only a scholar would be likely to have much to say about Daniel D. Tompkins, who entered office in 1817, or Richard M. Johnson (1837), or George M. Dallas (1845), or William R. King (1853). The contrast between the renown of Lincoln and the obscurity of his first Vice President, Hannibal Hamlin, speaks for itself.

Among other significant developments during the first fifteen to twenty years of the new government was a change in its location. After some debate and bargaining, a site along the Potomac, between Maryland and Virginia, was chosen for the federal district. The first two sessions of Congress were held in New York. From 1791 until 1800, while the new city was being planned, Philadelphia was the Capital. The move to the permanent Capital, named Washington in honor of the "Father of his People," took place in the autumn of 1800. To some of its early inhabi-

A NATIONAL HYMN

TUNE CHINA. BY L. GRIFFING

Composed to be sung on the 14th. of May 1841; the day recommended by the PRESIDENT, to be set apart as a day of fasting and prayer, by the people of the United States, on account of the death of Gen. Wm. H. Harrison.

1.

ALMIGHTY GOD! Oh, hear our moan!
  We lift our voice in prayer;
Oh! make our country's cause thy own,
  Take us beneath thy care.

2.

We mourn our Chieftain laid in dust;
  We feel thy chastening rod:
We know thy judgments all are just:
  But oh! have mercy GOD!

3.

Be thou our council, thou our guide,
  Keep us from every ill;
And may the man call'd to Preside,
  Learn, and obey thy will.

An 1841 broadside depicted Harrison's death and announced a day of mourning proclaimed by his successor. Tyler, the former Vice President, is unequivocally called President.

tants it seemed a good deal less permanent than New York or Philadelphia. John Adams arrived there at the beginning of November, in the melancholy closing months of his Presidency. His wife joined him a few weeks later. She reported to their daughter that although the Executive Mansion was habitable, it was barely so. "There is not a single apartment fin-ished. . . . We have not the least fence, yard, or other convenience, without, and the great unfinished audi-ence room I make a drying-room of, to hang up the clothes in. The principal stairs are not up, and will not be this winter. . . ."

It was a cheerless winter for the Adamses. Perhaps it is no wonder that the second President vacated the White House (as it would later be known) with such unseemly haste that he did not attend the inaugural ceremony for his successor Thomas Jefferson. (Twenty-eight years later his son John Quincy Adams also left the Capital without attending Andrew Jackson's inauguration. They have been the only two Presidents thus far to reveal the exasperation that several have nourished inwardly.) For many years the Capital, especially to foreign observers, seemed peculiarly rural and makeshift. Washington was the Brasilia of its day.

Still, by degrees it took on life and form. Less than one year after Abigail Adams hung the washing in "the great unfinished audience room," Jefferson entertained one hundred guests there at a July Fourth celebration. Instead of bowing, like his Federalist predecessors, he shook hands to indicate the informality of the Republican regime. The change was inevitable in a society that was growing demonstratively more egalitarian; but the precedent would leave his successors with an occupational ailment whose symptoms were aching arms and swollen fingers.

Jefferson's informality on this occasion symbolized an attempt to put the ship of state "on the Republican tack." He did not, for example, end his Presidency by issuing a Farewell Address; that was too regal for the Jeffersonians. In dress, in general behavior, and in his close contacts with his associates in Congress, Jefferson showed that he did not believe the presidential mold had hardened.

In some respects he was correct, although it remained to be seen whether his experiments would conduce to an efficient government. Some problems awaited future crises. There was, for example, the question of succession after a President died in office. In 1841, only one month after his inauguration, William Henry Harrison died. Perhaps the Whigs had made a mistake in picking a candidate who was then sixty-eight years old—the oldest on record. Perhaps Harrison had made a mistake in exposing himself to the elements for an hour and three quarters while he read the longest Inaugural Address on record—and caught a cold that developed into pneumonia. At any rate the Whigs found themselves with a Vice President, John Tyler, who subscribed to none of their policies. The country found itself confronted with a constitutional riddle: What was Tyler's status?

Some students of American constitutional history have maintained that the Founding Fathers did not intend that the Presidency should actually devolve upon the Vice President, but simply that the "powers and duties" of the office should be entrusted to him as an emergency measure. Ex-President John Quincy Adams was among Tyler's contemporaries who asserted that he had no right to call himself the President when he was only "Acting President." Tyler, however, did not hesitate to assume the office. He was sustained in his view by Secretary of State Daniel Webster; eight weeks later Congress recognized him as full President and the issue died down.

The Presidency would, however, remain the center of seemingly endless controversy. Nevertheless the first few Chief Executives, sometimes consciously and sometimes unwittingly, defined its basic nature. Their successors, whether or not they fully understood or liked the process, were to be fixed within certain intangible yet real modes. There was a genetic element in the office. The business of protocol is a case in point. The Federalist initiators approved of a degree of ceremony: Jefferson and Madison did not. Yet with James Monroe, the White House saw a level of formality and magnificence that no Federalist President could have surpassed.

President after President would also discover that the post was beset with cares. After the measured succession of the Virginia dynasty, the Presidency was in theory open to all contenders. The desire to be President afflicted American men by scores and hundreds. The handful who gained the prize found it, as Jefferson had foretold, a "splendid misery." There were the major battles with Congress and the constant lesser guerrilla clashes. There were the annoying attacks by waspish journalists and pamphleteers. There was the sickening importunacy of office seekers, the lack of privacy, the strain of social functions. (Sometimes, as Rexford Tugwell remarked, the social aspects are an almost intolerable strain on presidential couples unused to entertainment on the grand scale; several Presidents' wives have suffered breakdowns.) There was the grind of routine and the swamping of small office staffs whenever an emergency increased the press of business. There was the dense, clammy heat of the Washington summer climate. Almost no President who was re-elected had a second term as popular as his first. This was true of Washington, of Jefferson, of Madison, and of Jackson. Euphoria yielded to acrimony. The knowledge that no President would care to challenge Washington's precedent after eight years had much to do with this recurrent phenomenon of second-term gloom. Once the end was in sight for a President and his power was waning, criticism became sharper and more open, applause briefer and more perfunctory. Then there was the final anticlimax of being out of office—a relief so sudden that some Presidents seemed to languish afterward and die prematurely.

Jefferson was present at a meeting in 1793 at which George Washington exploded with anger on hearing a piece of scurrility aimed at him. The President declared that he had "never repented but once the having slipped the moment of resigning his office, & that was every moment since, that by god he had rather be on his farm than be made *emperor of the world*, and yet they were charging him with wanting to be a king." Near the end of his life John Adams reflected that "no man who ever held the office of President would congratulate a friend on obtaining it." Adams added, repeating an aphorism of Louis XIV's: "He will make one man ungrateful, and a hundred men his enemies, for every office he can bestow." In 1807 Jefferson said: "I am tired of an office where I can do no more good than many others, who would be glad to be employed in it. To myself, personally, it brings nothing but unceasing drudgery and daily loss of friends."

Those who followed Jefferson have left similar testimony. One consolation did cheer the Adamses and Jefferson and bring them together again, although they were not able to savor it until the calm of old age. They were the forerunners, the Founding Fathers. They had experienced bitter rivalry; they had not always been discreet or sensible. But they could finally believe that they had fought together in more than one sense. Through their strife they had fashioned a nation and a government, a government of laws whose precise meaning was open to debate but whose import was beyond question. Believing this, the veterans of Philadelphia and primordial Washington could believe that posterity would thank them even if their contemporaries failed to do so.

CHAPTER THREE

The Presidency Consolidated

In the early days of the American republic Alexander Hamilton predicted that a time would come "when every vital question of state will be merged in the question, 'Who will be the next President?'" His prediction was borne out, in large part because the Presidency became the apex of the political contest between excited and organized national parties. But there were other factors.

Among these factors the first in time and perhaps also in significance was the Presidency of George Washington. In his second administration he had been the target of considerable criticism, and for some years after his death Jeffersonian Republicans hesitated to sing his praises, since his name and reputation were being appropriated by the Federalists for partisan purposes. For example, the Washington Benevolent Societies, which were promoted by the Federalists, were political clubs despite their pretense of charitable patriotism. This factionalism soon disappeared: thenceforward the first President's name would be associated with the national Capital, with towns, counties, lakes, and mountains, or with the blameless "Washingtonian" temperance movement. Washington was once more the Father of his Country. In retrospect, all Americans were ready to pay tribute to him. His birthday was a national holiday; his Farewell Address was read aloud each year in Congress.

With the decades these rituals would become automatic and would lose some of their impact. But they were not empty gestures, even if those who participated gradually forgot exactly whom, or rather what, they were honoring. They were actually

honoring the establishment of a stable society—a society created through the necessarily disrupting process of a revolution. In *The First New Nation*, published in 1963, Seymour M. Lipset illuminated the situation by comparing the early history of the United States to that of the many subsequent countries —particularly those African nations that achieved independence in the twentieth century—that have had to face the complex task of existing and thriving under a new instrument of government. There is, as Lipset said, an acute difficulty in legitimizing the new authority immediately after repudiating the old. Authority cannot be created overnight, nor can it be imposed. It must be willingly recognized by those subject to it, through their active participation. Success is possible only if the population is broadly united and sympathetic to parliamentary mechanisms. Otherwise, the result will be an authoritarian government with no organic base of support.

A further complication is that new countries need symbols around which to affiliate, decisive leadership, and a sense of an actual transfer of authority from the former ruling power—a set of conditions rarely fulfilled. The requirements were met, however, for the United States; and George Washington was, next to the generally high level of American political sophistication, the prime agent. (Having seen him, Abigail Adams enthused that he looked more like a king than George III, whom she had also seen.)

His actions as President were commendable. Yet as a symbol of the new government he was almost more important to the United States for what he was than for what he did. The hiatus was over, the ma-

86

chine was running again, the movement was forward. One can guess what a jolt the new government would have suffered if President Washington had died from either of the two serious illnesses that afflicted him during his first term. Or, if he had felt too much like a king, or had become a vengeful party chieftain determined to run for re-election in 1800—as a few desperate Federalists urged him to do—what chaos might have befallen America?

Instead, there came the healing, bandaging influences of mere usage, the lulling of repetitious ritual, the absorption in the daily detail of government, the increment of folklore and precedent and tradition. (The long continuance of John Marshall as Chief Justice of the Supreme Court also helped form what Walter Bagehot called the cake of custom. The Court's decisions were not welcomed by everyone, but they were accepted, and in emphasizing the centrality of the federal government, they indirectly asserted the centrality of the executive branch. Although Jefferson detested Marshall, he never made a frontal attack upon him; he knew that John Marshall, like Washington, was a person who by virtue of his office was enveloped in an impersonal dignity.)

According to Jefferson, an interesting conversation took place between Adams and himself in 1800, at a moment when it was becoming clear that Jefferson would win the presidential election. Adams said to him: "Well, I understand that you are to beat me in this contest, and I will only say that I will be as faithful a subject as any you will have." Jefferson replied: "Mr. Adams . . . this is no personal contest between you and me. Two systems of principles . . . divide our fellow citizens into two parties. . . . Were we both to die today, tomorrow two other names would be in the place of ours, without any change in the motion of the machinery. Its motion is from its principle, not from you or myself." Neither man was perhaps entirely sincere or candid. Adams' comment sounds double-edged; he may have used the word "subject" sarcastically and may have intended to imply that Jefferson would have no real following. Yet both men found it convenient to believe in the continuity of systems.

In his *Democracy in America*, written on the basis of a visit to the United States during Andrew Jackson's administration, Alexis de Tocqueville said that the Presidency was not of great importance, since all legislation was controlled by Congress. This conclusion may be regarded as an error—or at least a failure of vision—caused by relying too much on the views of such anti-Jackson men as Daniel Webster. But Tocqueville was correct when he pointed out the nationwide interest in political issues and the remarkable propensity for establishing voluntary organizations to effect changes through constitutional means. Americans were, so to speak, addicted to such involvements—a healthy addiction that was greatly encouraged by the profound constitutionalism of Washington and his immediate successors.

The early Presidents continually emphasized that their nation needed time in which to take shape. Every year counted; every administration added to the fabric. When the newly inaugurated Abraham Lincoln faced the gravest crisis since 1776, he must have derived comfort, if only a limited comfort, from the awareness that fifteen Presidents had held office before him. Several had confronted and survived possible disaster. Several had ennobled the office, or perhaps the office had ennobled them. Perhaps no other Presidents have suffered the full dread of unexplored hazards that Washington and Lincoln had to overcome. But at least Lincoln knew that there *was* a Union to revere and defend.

The continuity of the office had been maintained thanks to a certain amount of good luck. Washington did not die in 1789 or 1790. Luck attended President Jackson in 1835: when a madman armed with two pistols tried to shoot him, both weapons misfired. There was no sudden transfer of presidential power until William Henry Harrison died in 1841 and Vice President John Tyler, "His Accidency," became Chief Magistrate. Three years later, luck preserved Tyler and the stability of the Presidency; he narrowly missed death when an explosion occurred aboard the frigate *Princeton* killing the Secretary of State. It is possible that luck as well as prudence saved the life of President-elect Lincoln. He circumvented a rumored plot to kill him before he reached Washington by slipping quietly into the Capital. Although he was jeered at for having taken undignified or cowardly evasive action, Lincoln was quite right to be cautious. His death at that time might have brought about the collapse of the Union.

The example of George Washington and the stature of some of his successors, the organic rooting of the government over the decades, a measure of sheer luck—all these contributed to the consolidation of the Presidency. But did this consolidation go on continually or was it promoted by the strong Presidents and set back by weak ones? One difficulty in answering is that a great man such as Jefferson was not necessarily a great President; he may be deemed a great President by future generations because his posthumous prestige increased the renown of the Presidency. Another constant problem in historical causation is to decide how much any one individual can be said to define the character of his era. In his book *Andrew Jackson: Symbol for an Age*, published in 1955, John William Ward presented a persuasive interpretation of a man who embodied rather than set the tone of his times. Some historians believe that America's history, at least that of the nineteenth century, has been distorted by being portrayed largely as a history of the federal government and of presidential administrations. They concede that Americans were often engaged in political controversy and that they were excited by the quadrennial drama of presidential elections. But these historians argue that such concern was intermittent and usually directed toward local issues and the degree of attention to be paid to them in the otherwise remote purlieus of the Capital. It has also been claimed that except for occasional interludes, the Presidency was not dominant and not even particularly visible for most of the century after its establishment.

There is a valuable degree of truth in these views. The case of Thomas Jefferson illustrates the need to define terms. His reputation has had some startling ups and downs—which were charted in 1960 in Merrill Peterson's *The Jefferson Image in the American Mind*. The imposing monument to Jefferson in Washington, D.C., was not built until the early 1940's—under a Democratic administration. Although he now figures in all selective listings of outstanding Presidents, most scholars distinguish between his intellectual and executive accomplishments. They frequently quote John Marshall's comment to Alexander Hamilton in a letter written during the presidential campaign of 1800: "Mr. Jefferson appears to me to be a man, who will embody himself with the House of Representatives. By weakening the office of President he will increase his personal power. He will diminish his responsibility, sap the fundamental principles of the government, and become the leader of that party which is about to constitute the majority of the legislature."

Marshall's forecast was shrewd. Jefferson's sway depended upon intimate contact with Republican adherents in Congress. Gone were the lonely, trenchant assertions of John Adams; Jefferson dealt with the present, not with some abstract vision of the Executive, which might be vindicated decades or centuries thence. His public pronouncements invariably stressed the modesty of the executive function. In his first annual message he meekly promised: "Nothing shall be wanting on my part to inform, as far as in my power, the legislative judgment, nor to carry that judgment into faithful execution."

In this respect the Presidency under the Republicans did go into partial eclipse. The astronomical metaphor is helpful because it suggests the alternation of light and shadow that has characterized the stages of the Presidency. It suggests, too, that there was something ordained, or at least normal, in the alternation. Jefferson and his Virginian successors, Madison and Monroe, did not press for recognition of executive supremacy because they did not believe in it. They were reacting to the theories advanced by Hamilton—the most comprehensive claims made for the Presidency in the whole of America's first century under the Constitution. But they were not simply resisting Hamilton. They had an equally clear though by its nature seemingly negative view of the limits of federal power in relation to the states, and of executive power in relation to Congress.

In yet another respect the metaphor of eclipse is apposite. Eclipses are temporary. Jefferson was by no means the last President to pay assiduous court to Congress as the best method of getting his own way. He himself was no negligible figure. Hamilton disagreed with his friend John Marshall's estimate of their opponent. It was wrong, he wrote in January, 1801, to suppose that Jefferson "is an enemy to the power of the Executive," or that he favored the concentration of power in the House of Representatives. "It is a fact . . . that, while we were in the administration together, he was generally for a large construction of the executive authority and not backward to act upon it in cases which coincided with his views." In this instance Hamilton's memory was defective, or else he had special motives for wishing to portray Jefferson as a forceful person. But he was not altogether wrong. As Secretary of State and as President, Jefferson was "not backward . . . in cases

A mug honoring President Madison

If, as Hamilton believed, conspicuous assertion of prerogative was germane to the Presidency, the Virginia triumvirate was inadequate. The War of 1812 was frequently called Mr. Madison's War. But that appellation was a doubtful compliment: according to his critics, Madison's name was attached to the conflict not in honor but in blame for having let the nation slide into an unnecessary and inglorious struggle. The Monroe Doctrine, for which James Monroe is primarily remembered, actually owed more to Secretary of State John Quincy Adams than to its nominal author.

It is not feasible, then, to pretend that the Virginia dynasty notably strengthened the Presidency, either by intention or in effect. The national luck carried them through a number of painful crises. Of course luck is not a historical explanation: it is an excuse for not offering proper explanations. It may be said that the United States was lucky in the first third of the nineteenth century because it was remote from European conflicts. Once the Union had survived the first parlous decade of the new Constitution—a decade that was probably more a "Critical Period" than the 1780's, for which the term was coined—an interval without great shocks and controversies was needed. There have been few tranquil interludes in the nation's history. President Warren G. Harding has been ridiculed for his message of 1920, in which he said that "America's present need is not heroics but healing; not nostrums but normalcy; not revolution but restoration; not surgery but serenity." Yet this craving for uneventfulness, for being left in peace, was understandable in 1920, and still more so in 1810 or 1820. Americans have revealed a considerable appetite for social change, in the shape of new homes, new jobs, new ways of living. Their appetite for intellectual or institutional change has been far smaller. The strain of the one form of change has produced a longing for stability in the other realm.

In these respects it can be said that Jefferson, Madison, and Monroe, whether or not they deserve the credit, provided a period of normalcy for the government over which they presided. The administrations of the first two were not very serene, but at least they seemed not to add unnecessarily to the problems of their age by raising fundamental difficulties. When Jefferson retired from the Presidency in 1809, the lawyer-author William Wirt prepared a

which coincided with his views." His initiative in arranging the Louisiana Purchase was a less resounding executive gesture than is sometimes stated. He had not anticipated the outcome and was embarrassed at having committed the nation without congressional approval. Still, his embarrassment was on a reasonable scale. Other instances of his executive inclination were his astonishing feat in rushing the unpalatable Embargo Act through Congress in a single day and his occasional brushes with the federal courts. He was particularly incensed when a judge remarked that "the President's duties as chief magistrate do not demand his whole time, and are not unremitting." Jefferson retorted: "If he alludes to our annual retirement from the seat of government, during the sickly season, he should be told that such arrangements are made for carrying on the public business . . . that it goes on as unremittingly there, as if it were at the seat of government. I pass more hours in public business at Monticello than I do here [in Washington], every day; and it is much more laborious, because all must be done in writing."

Certainly he was not idle. He probably worked harder and gave more active guidance in promoting legislation than many later Presidents. True, his techniques were devious; and many of the forthright Jeffersonian dicta were, as his biographer Dumas Malone observed, not even noticed at the time because they were confined to private correspondence.

handsome and possibly fulsome tribute on behalf of the Virginia state legislature. The nation has learned to mistrust the slogan that the Democratic party of Jackson's day took as a legacy from Jefferson and put at the masthead of the Washington *Globe*: "The world is too much governed." But Wirt's theme of tolerance, tranquillity, and prosperity caught the essence of the Jeffersonian dream. He was in earnest, if not completely accurate, when he thanked the ex-President "for the model of an administration conducted on the purest principles of republicanism; For pomp and state laid aside; Patronage discarded . . . The monarchic maxim that a national debt is a national blessing, renounced. . . . Without the guilt or calamities of conquest, a vast and fertile region added to our country. . . . Peace with the civilized world, preserved through a season of uncommon difficulty and trial. . . ."

In relation to the Constitution, it might be said that in general the Virginia dynasty considered themselves more bound by the Tenth Amendment than given carte blanche by the preamble to the document, which states: "We the People of the United States, in Order to form a more perfect Union, establish Justice, inspire domestic Tranquility, provide for the common defence, promote the general Welfare, and secure the Blessings of Liberty to ourselves and our Posterity, do ordain and establish this Constitution for the United States of America." Wirt congratulated Jefferson for preserving the blessings of liberty; his other accomplishments could be interpreted as promoting the general welfare. But he had not achieved these results by declaring that as the official entrusted with the national well-being he was authorized, indeed obliged, to interpret his responsibilities broadly. Rather he had respected the spirit and the letter of the final amendment in the Bill of Rights. "The powers not delegated to the United States by the Constitution, nor prohibited by it to the States, are reserved to the States respectively, or to the people." In the same spirit Madison and Monroe declined to sponsor schemes for internal improvement, which they believed to be constitutionally up to the states.

Under John Quincy Adams, Monroe's successor, there was an attempt to build upon an older conception, which may be called Federalist although the maverick Adamses prided themselves on not having been orthodox Federalists. Perhaps Henry Clay's phrase, the "American System," is more appropriate. In his first annual message to Congress, in 1825, Adams insisted that "the great object of the institution of civil government is the improvement of the condition of those who are parties to the social compact. . . ." He therefore recommended a national university, an astronomical observatory, and a network of roads and canals. There was no extraordinary novelty in his proposals. Less than ten years earlier John C. Calhoun had been an enthusiastic advocate of internal improvements. Speaking in the House of Representatives in 1817, Calhoun had said, "The more enlarged the sphere of commercial circulation— the more extended that of social intercourse—the more strongly are we bound together—the more inseparable are our destinies. . . . Let us, then, bind the republic together with a perfect system of roads and canals. Let us conquer space." In similar language Adams said that "roads and canals, by multiplying and facilitating the communications and intercourse between distant regions and multitudes of men, are among the most important means of improvement." Nor was Adams the first to mention a national university. Washington and Jefferson had been as keen as Adams on providing higher education for American youths, instead of obliging them to go to Europe, where their sense of nationality was jeopardized. Washington left a bequest to help launch a federal university in the District of Columbia.

Yet Adams' schemes were either derided or ignored. He had no party organization to back him. He lacked the personal magnetism to fire the national imagination and impose his will. There is a revealing story that, turning the first sod of a new enterprise on a hot day, he removed his jacket to ease his work with the spade and was surprised when this homely gesture was applauded. It would not have occurred to him to court popularity by taking off his jacket. He made a double tactical error in his first annual message: "While foreign nations less blessed with that freedom which is power than ourselves are advancing with gigantic strides in the career of public improvement, were we to slumber in indolence . . . and proclaim to the world that we are palsied by the will of our constituents, would it not be to cast away the bounties of Providence and doom ourselves to perpetual inferiority?" In trying to stimulate national pride, he offended it by appearing to suggest that the United States was backward. (He also incidentally reminded the public that he, like his father, had spent many years abroad in foreign service—a patriotic duty in his eyes, but to the more chauvinist of his countrymen an absence casting doubt on his Americanism.) The appeal to American leaders not to be "palsied" by the parochialism and sluggishness of their constituents also alienated an electorate that was beginning to expect of its leaders not rebuke but the assurance that the people were the fount of wisdom.

But there are deeper reasons for Adams' failure. He was not merely the last representative in the Presidency of an outmoded style of social behavior: he was anachronistic in advocating a plan that was both ahead of and behind its time. His farsightedness, together with a forgivable tinge of exaggeration and self-pity, is apparent in a summary of his life that he prepared in 1837 for a Massachusetts biographer: "The great effort of my administration was to mature into a permanent and regular system the application of all the superfluous revenue of the Union to internal improvements. . . . In ten years from this day the whole Union would have been checkered over with railroads and canals. It may still be done half a century later and with the limping gait of state legislature and private adventure. I would have done it in the administration of the affairs of the nation. . . . The great object of my life, therefore, as applied to the administration of the government of the United States, has failed. The American Union, as a moral person in the family of nations, is to live from hand to mouth, and to cast away instead of using for the improvement of its own condition, the bounties of Providence." Only a few days before his death Adams reproached himself in his private diary for his inability to convey his vision to others: "I should have been one of the greatest benefactors of my country. . . . But the conceptive power of mind was not conferred upon me by my Maker, and I have not improved the scanty portions of His gifts as I might and ought to have done."

In common with other shy, gifted people John Quincy Adams was a compound of self-doubt and vanity. In his heart he may well have felt that the fault lay less with his Maker and himself than with his obtuse fellow citizens. If so, he was not far wrong. The neglect of what John Kenneth Galbraith calls the public sector in favor of the private sector has become a matter of urgent relevance to the twen-

tieth-century United States. Adams' aim was to bring about a situation recognizable to our generation under other names—of which the Great Society is one. He was not, it should be added, interested in his vision for the sake of aggrandizing the Presidency. He did not closely consider how his scheme was to be carried out. In this respect he revealed that he was not a practical politician. Later Presidents who would have sympathized with his general objectives would also regard him as a man with no real grasp of how his office operated. No President can afford to march out of step with his time or with his potential following. The Adams plan had no chance of success. But it deserved a better fate than that of an isolated signpost to a road not then taken—a road to power and dignity for the federal government, and so indirectly for the man in the White House.

Then came Andrew Jackson, one of the half-dozen major figures in the history of the Presidency. Some accounts have made him even more important than he was. Jackson was not swept into power by a wave of newly enfranchised democratic voters; the historian Richard P. McCormick has shown that the first decisive increase in voter participation came with the 1840 contest between Van Buren and Harrison. Nor did Jackson invent, or enter the Presidency by means of, the new device of the national nominating convention. Nor did his backers or the general public think of him in 1824 and 1828—the first two elections in which he was a presidential candidate—as a passionate democrat, an energetic leader, or as a man of firm political convictions. His initial reputation was that of a military hero, a courageous patriot, a successful Tennessee planter-judge, and a person with a fairly long and wide experience of public life who had been a member of both houses of Congress as well as a onetime military governor of Florida. The alarm expressed by men such as Daniel Webster at the prospect of having him in the White House was based on uncertainty rather than on any definite knowledge of what he might do. Nicholas Biddle, the debonair head of the Bank of the United States, was confident that Jackson would do nothing very drastic and so voted for him in 1828. Those who watched the inaugural ceremony in 1829 saw an old, thin, white-haired man, an apparently extinct volcano, so feeble that he had to be supported by two servants. Some wondered whether he had enough stamina to endure the fatigues of office.

Even when the frail old gentleman had begun to reveal that there was plenty of fire left in him, his actual policies were in the main either circumscribed or negative. He did not claim to be ushering in a new order; he felt rather that he was restoring America to the purity of the old Jeffersonian ideal. With this aim he recommended in his first two annual messages that Presidents should be restricted to a single term by a constitutional amendment and that they should be elected directly by the people. His vetoing of internal improvements bills was avowedly Jeffersonian. His opposition to Biddle's Bank was that of an old-line Republican; he knew how strenuously Jefferson had fought against Hamilton's First Bank of the United States, whose charter had been allowed to expire in 1811. The second creation was too much like the original and was—its critics alleged—established in 1816 only because the expenses of the War of 1812 necessitated a central banking system. Even in Jackson's most defiant executive messages there were often passages that taken in isolation sounded like pure Jeffersonianism: agrarian, libertarian, and hostile to consolidated government. Thus in his Bank veto of July, 1832, Jackson said: "Our Government [is not] to be maintained or our Union preserved by invasions of the rights and powers of the several States. . . . Its true strength consists in leaving individuals and States as much as possible to themselves. . . ." And in his Protest to the Senate of April, 1834, he spoke of his "anxious desire" to persuade his countrymen that "it is not in a splendid government supported by powerful monopolies and aristocratical establishments that they will find happiness or their liberties protection, but in a plain system, void of pomp, protecting all and granting favors to none, dispensing its blessings, like the dews of Heaven, unseen and unfelt save in the freshness and beauty they contribute to produce." In this traditional, Jeffersonian idea of a "plain" administration intended for a yeomanly society, the operations of government would be so minimal that they would be virtually "unseen and unfelt." It was a world away from John Quincy Adams' vision of a government of talents, which would enlighten the people and embellish the land. It was also a long way, apparently, from the later image of Jackson as "Old Hickory," the vigorous and democratic ruler whose example has been cited by every subsequent strong President.

There was no contradiction. Andrew Jackson pre-sented the case (as John Tyler was to do in a minor degree) of a forceful Executive who did not approve of a forceful federal government. In the present century it has seemed impossible to divorce one from the other. In the Jacksonian Era, when the main aim of the President was not to reform but to restore, his admirers saw no contradiction.

For them Andrew Jackson was a phenomenon to delight in. Scholars agree, despite various qualifications, that with Jackson a new element was added to the role of the Chief Executive. He was, as his contemporaries claimed, the People's President. The United States witnessed a modulation, in the phraseology of the sociologist Max Weber, from government by a "party of notables" to government by "a party of politicians." Jackson was—again in Weber's terminology—an outstanding example of charisma. He was a leader whose links with his supporters were intimate, unselfconscious, and reciprocal. Jacksonians identified themselves with him and he with them. J. G. Baldwin caught the essence of Jacksonianism in a sketch written in 1855. In the direct, impatient world of Tennessee, said Baldwin, "as face answereth to face in water, so must the popular favorite answer to the genius and character of the people. Only a bold, frank, decisive man could rise to power in such a community. He must shrink from no danger; he must fear no responsibility; he must wear no mask; he must wait for no cue; he must be able to appeal to the strong feelings and the manly common-sense of the people."

Baldwin noted that Jackson had almost no formal education (all his predecessors except George Washington had been to college). He lacked the ability to write lucidly and elegantly, and so entrusted the composition of his principal statements to subordinates such as Roger B. Taney, who drafted part of the Bank veto, and Edward Livingston, who wrote the Nullification Proclamation. Jackson was no orator, unlike his great Senate adversaries Clay, Webster, and Calhoun, or his wordy lieutenant, Senator Thomas Hart Benton. Although skill on the speaker's platform helped Lincoln and James Garfield win the Presidency and secured William Jennings Bryan the Democratic nomination in 1896, in an earlier day it was less essential. Indeed, none of the Presidents before Jackson was celebrated for oratory. Jackson had a more compelling asset. As Baldwin put it: "Swords, not words, were *his* arguments. . . . He could speak tersely, vigorously, movingly, but his words were the brief words of command. Action followed speech, as thunder the lightning. . . . With him, to think and to do were not so much two things as one."

Another perceptive observer, Jackson's biographer James Parton, said that the way to understand him was to remember his Scotch-Irish ancestry. His was the world of the clan. He was the clan chieftain, bound to his following by mutual ties of kinship and interest. In this intense camaraderie, loyalty was almost the highest virtue; betrayal, actual or fancied, was the worst crime and was answered with implacable hatred. Jackson's enthusiasms and antipathies were simple, direct, and wholehearted. He could be influenced by astute advisers; it was probably Martin Van Buren who persuaded him to go against expectation by vetoing the well-lobbied Maysville Road bill in 1830. On this and other occasions, he responded to lofty arguments as well as to personal ones. He believed in the Democratic-Republican cause but he also relished the notion of frustrating his enemies. The Maysville Road veto satisfied both his sense of doctrine and his desire to punish Henry Clay, whose state of Kentucky would have particularly benefited from the bill. Once Jackson's mind was made up, however, no amount of political counsel could convince him that he should change it.

Van Buren was fascinated by the power that a man of Jackson's temperament could wield. The clan was an admirable paradigm for the American political party. It did not preclude planning and organization of a highly professional order; the technique was to find a popular issue that would generate zeal and provide a rallying cry, and then to channel this surging, combative spirit into the party apparatus. Van Buren was also intrigued by the latitude allowed their leader by the clan members. Perhaps in his later writings he was a little wistful; for Van Buren was too dispassionately intelligent not to acknowledge that he had been a colorless successor to Jackson in the Presidency. It was splendid to be known as the People's President, or as the Hero of New Orleans. It was less gratifying to be dubbed, as Van Buren was, the Red Fox of Kinderhook or the Wizard of the Albany Regency. Old Hickory was a gloriously sturdy appellation; but what of the sting of being called the Mistletoe Politician—a parasite entwined about the Jackson tree? It was more flatter-

ing to be assailed as a tyrant than lampooned as an artful dodger; a Whig journalist once said of Van Buren, "he could take a piece of meat on one side of his mouth, a piece of bread on the other, and cabbage in the middle, and chew and swallow each severally while never mixing them together."

The discovery that interested the equable Van Buren was that the people demanded that a popular leader be like themselves, on a larger scale. They did not blame him unduly for inconsistency or for making mistakes: these were human foibles, of the kind the ancient Greeks imputed to their gods. What the people loved and warmed to was vitality, color, even idiosyncrasy, combined with courage and certitude. They did not examine too carefully how or where they were being led so long as they had confidence in their leader. Andrew Jackson's errors were forgiven and forgotten, or chuckled over, because his supporters felt that he was at one with them. An identification so complete made him irresistibly appealing —at least to those who identified with him. The anger of the opposition, the rival clan, only heightened the invigorating sense of Jacksonian solidarity. "The people believed in General Jackson," testified one contemporary, "as the Turks in their prophet." Thomas Hart Benton did not greatly exaggerate when he described Jackson's departure from the Capital at the end of his Presidency. According to Benton a great shout went up from the assembled crowd, a shout "such as power never commanded, nor man in power received. . . . It was the acclaim of posterity, breaking from the bosoms of contemporaries." In Baldwin's view, Andrew Jackson "impressed his name and character upon the country more deeply than any man, the father of his country only excepted, ever did. . . . He gave a fresh and awakening influence to the popular mind . . . and started the government and the people onward in a new and more impulsive career. He opened a new era in American politics. . . . He found a confederacy— he left an empire."

Whether Jackson's activities as party leader and pugnacious President had quite the wholesome grandeur that Baldwin attributed to them will be considered in future chapters. It should be apparent from Jackson's Jeffersonian feeling for states' rights that the "empire" he sustained was, so far as he was concerned, still a "confederacy." But there is no doubt of the essential if partial truth of the assessments quoted above, or of the essential novelty—within limits—of what he represented as a charismatic leader.

No President before him, not even "Long Tom" Jefferson, had come so near to basing his conception of the Presidency upon the proposition that the Chief Executive ruled for and by the people. Wherever the people were mentioned in the Constitution—in the preamble or in the Tenth Amendment—Jackson claimed to be their voice. He was, he said, "the representative and trustee of the American people." As such he claimed the right, in fact the duty, to defend his office against Congress and the Court, to strike down the Bank, to defeat the nullifiers, to establish the principle of rotation in office, and to advance his views through an administration newspaper, the Washington *Globe*, which (in Baldwin's phrase) was "a whole troop of cavalry and a pack of flying artillery besides." He was the popular will incarnate; but who were the people? How did Jackson know he represented them? Could a party leader speak for more than half of the people? Was such a leader apt to confuse the national welfare with his own prejudices? Was he in danger of mistaking coercion for persuasion? Did the rhetoric of popular democracy lend itself to cynical abuse? The answer to these questions would long be debated. What was beyond question, as Jackson rode off in his carriage toward The Hermitage in 1837, was that—for good or ill—the quality of the Presidency had changed. Thenceforward any assertive Chief Executive would be armed with additional precedents.

James K. Polk, President from 1845 to 1849, was a faithful Jacksonian in thought and in deed. He too was from Tennessee. The Democrats (as the former Jeffersonian-Republican party was by then known) called him Young Hickory. Like Jackson, Polk seized the opportunity of his final annual message to present a testament of faith. In keeping with the man and his time, Polk's speech was in large part a doctrinaire exposition of the excellencies of the Democratic ensemble. However, in the course of justifying his use of the veto, he also underlined the creed of his master: "If it be said that the Representatives in the popular branch of Congress are chosen directly by the people, it is answered, the people elect the President. If both Houses represent the States and the people, so does the President. The President represents in the executive department the whole people of the United States, as each member of the legislative department represents portions of them." There was a double implication in Polk's words. The Senate, not being the "popular" house of Congress, was perhaps less authentically representative than the President or the Lower House. And congressmen were less representative than the President, since they—he said—were only "responsible to the people of particular States or districts," while he was responsible to "an enlightened public opinion" and to "the people of the whole Union." As a representative of the people, Polk found the veto a dramatically effective device. It was, Tocqueville noted, "a sort of appeal to the people."

These Democratic contentions were not accepted by the Whigs. Answering Jackson in the Senate in 1834, Daniel Webster had scorned "the idea of this airy and unreal responsibility to the public. . . ." He had attacked the Jacksonian claim that "*the President is the direct representative of the American people.* . . . Now, Sir, this is not the language of the Constitution. The Constitution nowhere calls him the representative of the American people; still less, their direct representative. It could not do so with the least propriety." An apparent flaw in the reasoning of Jackson and Polk was that the President was not directly elected. How could a man picked by a few hundred members of the Electoral College, or—as in the special circumstances of 1801 and 1825—by a handful of congressmen, be considered the embodiment of anything so large and impalpable as "enlightened public opinion"? Jackson had had a ready and indignant answer. The Electoral College was an unreliable device. Through its malfunction, he had been cheated of the Presidency in 1825. He had secured more popular votes than John Quincy Adams; but he and the American public had both been thwarted. In consequence he had proposed a more democratic system of presidential election, but Congress had refused.

However, neither the Electoral College nor Congress was long able to withstand the general will of the American people. In 1828 they had undisputably placed Jackson in power. In 1832 he had tested the efficacy of the President's responsibility to the people by vetoing the Bank recharter, although it had passed the House by 107 votes to 86 and the Senate by 28 votes to 20. Jackson had been vindicated in the election: some 688,000 voters had rallied to him, as against some 530,000 for the coalition of enemies led by Henry Clay and William Wirt. He had his mandate. Clay and Biddle in private correspondence saw that Jackson's victory did amount to "a popular ratification" of his stand on the Bank issue.

By Polk's time there was the further sanction of the national nominating convention, which replaced the old congressional caucus. Grass-roots sentiment found expression through the convention delegates. The politicians said that the candidate could not help but be the man the people wanted. In Polk's case there was the inconvenient fact that he had hardly been mentioned for the Presidency in the Democratic newspapers. At the Baltimore convention in May, 1844, his name was not put in nomination until the eighth ballot and he was not nominated until the ninth. Still, he was declared the party's unanimous choice, and having won the election, he soon demonstrated that he, too, felt he had had a mandate. Even before he was inaugurated he told a crony that whether or not he managed to achieve harmony among the Democratic factions that had preferred other candidates, "in any event I intend to be *myself* President of the U.S."

The Polk mandate came partly from the knowledge that Andrew Jackson accepted him as a worthy Democratic standard-bearer, but mainly from the evident appeal of a party platform that called for a vigorous policy toward Oregon and Mexico. Polk's own stubborn, ungenial temperament reinforced the conviction that he had received a directive from the United States. As President he created difficulties for himself by behaving deviously, and by annoying his supporters in Congress to a degree surprising in one who had learned the ropes as Speaker of the House. He made the settlement of the Oregon boundary question more complicated than was necessary.

Nevertheless his record of accomplishment in one term was astonishing. His performance in the Mexican War is especially significant today. In the words of Leonard D. White, in *The Jacksonians*, "Polk gave the country its first demonstration of the *administrative* capacities of the presidency as a war agency. He proved that a President could run a war." He also made mistakes. Aside from the question of whether the war with Mexico was necessary, Polk managed to offend many of his subordinates, especially those in the Army and Navy. He was ungracious to and mistrustful of those who were Whigs.

He behaved abominably, though not without some provocation, to Nicholas Trist, the State Department chief clerk whom he dispatched to Mexico as his peacemaking agent. At times it seemed that he viewed his administration and the war as if they were on the same scale as his fairly recent tenure as governor of Tennessee. If he worked himself almost literally to death in the White House, the fault was in some degree his own. He would not devolve responsibility on his executive heads. He preoccupied himself with filling the hundreds of offices vacated as the result of a Democratic victory. He took the same trouble in scrutinizing the scores of applications for appointments to new Army regiments. When his Secretary of War, William L. Marcy, escaped the summer heat, the President more or less assumed the direction of the War Department. In his four-year term Polk spent only six weeks away from Washington. "He works from 10 to 12 hours in every 24," said a Washington editor. "He holds two Cabinets a week. He sees visitors two hours every day when the Cabinet is not employed. . . . He is also in frequent communion with his [department] secretaries." When the day's labors ended Polk recounted them in his diary, often at length, and brooded over his problems. Near the end of his term, Polk explained that "no President who performs his duty faithfully and conscientiously can have any leisure. If he intrusts the details . . . to subordinates constant errors will occur. I prefer to supervise the whole operations of the Government myself . . . and this makes my duties very great."

But even an administrative genius, no matter how brilliant and decisive, would have found the task overwhelming. Since Washington's era the population of the country had increased from four million to some twenty million. By the end of 1845 the original thirteen states had grown to twenty-eight. The press of public business had expanded accordingly. Administrative arrangements, however, remained primitive. Presidents in search of secretarial assistance usually paid sons or nephews out of the executive salary. Not until 1857 did Congress authorize additional expenditure to give the President his own private secretary. Whenever there was an unusual amount of activity in Washington the Executive was swamped. In this respect Polk's desperate labors to keep abreast of the material that poured in were a miniature prefiguration of Lincoln's nightmarish struggle during the Civil War. The executive branch was always on the edge of collapse, since it had no margin for sudden expansion. The lessons of Polk's administration were not pondered. Indeed, it was not only Lincoln who suffered the consequences. As late as 1898, confronted with the Spanish-American War, McKinley's Secretary of War Russell A. Alger was even more beset than Marcy had been; and McKinley himself was ready to exclaim with Polk, "I have had enough of it, Heaven knows! I have had all the honor there is in the place, and . . . responsibilities enough to kill any man."

A further lesson of Polk's administration was likewise ignored. Although by later standards the executive branch was still minuscule, it had grown enough to make strict supervision as difficult as it was necessary. In each department, the bureau heads followed their own inclinations and routines, despite what the White House or their immediate chiefs might ordain. Incurably suspicious and pertinacious, Polk was horrified to encounter the curious combination of laxity and inflexibility that continued to be noted in Washington long after his day. His Secretaries were sometimes unaware of decisions taken (or not taken) in their own departments. Orders were ignored or reinterpreted. Expenditure was occasionally slack to the point of corruption; each bureau exaggerated its needs as a matter of course. For a man of Polk's frugality, the administration was scandalously wasteful.

In comparison with some European governments, that of the United States was in fact reasonably honest, efficient, and economical. Yet Polk made a valuable contribution when in the midst of all his other burdens he formed himself into a one-man investigatory commission. His principal discovery was that there was no budgetary mechanism. In the Treasury Act of 1789 Congress had required the Secretary of the Treasury, not the President, to compile and submit estimates of income and expenditure. Alexander Hamilton, according to Leonard D. White, had set the precedent of not consulting the President. Monroe had complained in vain that he was being kept in the dark by his Secretary. John Quincy Adams had insisted on seeing the draft of the Treasury Department's annual report. It is doubtful, though, that Adams or any of his predecessors had scrutinized the estimates of the various departments.

In the general prosperity of the country such casualness had gone unnoticed. But with the Panic of 1837 a different mood began to appear. After his election in 1844, Polk, worried by the expenses of the Mexican War and devoted to the Republican principle of freedom from public debt, tried to institute a regular, thorough scrutiny of executive expenditure. In his view no one but the President could undertake such a chore. He was more prescient than he realized; but his opening salvos died away. After his departure the problem went back into limbo—one more task to be deferred until half a century later when the executive branch would begin to orchestrate the themes that rare, compulsive men like Polk had striven to play on a single instrument. The problem, of course, was that the symphony would still have to be conducted by one man—the President.

In fairness to Polk it must be noted that he got results. He used his Cabinet more effectively than anyone else had done. He kept the entire administration on the alert with his probings. If they had been as energetic and as competent as he, his task would have been appreciably lighter. He took the lead, within the Cabinet, in planning strategy, logistics, finance, and diplomacy. Although he was not always judicious, he was invariably vigorous; and that, as Van Buren said of Jackson, was at least half the battle. His predecessors had learned that the Presidency was, even in supposedly normal times, a demanding office. "Dignified slavery," Jackson called it; "toilsome and anxious probation" was Van Buren's phrase. Polk sighed that it was "no bed of roses." At least he could reflect that with Oregon, California, and New Mexico in American hands, Young Hickory had deserved his nickname. There was no doubt that the Mexican conflict was "Mr. Polk's War."

The inertia of the system, the institutionalized vendetta of party politics, and Polk's lack of personal charm, however, meant that his consolidation went largely unrecognized. The great crisis in the nation's history, and the great leap forward in the demonstration of executive authority, came in 1861 with the accession of Abraham Lincoln. Ironically enough he was, as David Donald emphasized in a brilliant essay, a "Whig in the White House." As an Illinois congressman, he had in January, 1848, voted for a resolution that maintained the Mexican War had been "unnecessarily and unconstitutionally begun by the President of the United States." As a faithful Whig, he believed that Jackson and Polk had exceeded the limits of executive authority. Yet this same man, as President, said, "I conceive that I may in an emergency do things on military grounds which cannot constitutionally be done by the Congress," and told a committee in 1862 that "as Commander in Chief of the Army and Navy, in time of war I suppose I have a right to take any measure which may best subdue the enemy." Although Polk had been an aggressive war leader and had shown how a President might display his talents as commander of the armed forces, he had not explicitly derived his claims to authority from the Commander-in-Chief clause of the Constitution. Edward S. Corwin said that until the Civil War it was "the forgotten clause." Then Lincoln, citing also his duty "to take care that the laws be faithfully executed," envisaged something known as the war power, which he thought entitled him to take amazing liberties in his first three months in office—a period when Congress was not in session and had not been summoned by him into special session. He created a ninety-day national Army from the state militias, after he had maneuvered over the provisioning of Fort Sumter and so in a way launched the Civil War. He called out forty thousand volunteers, doubled the regular Army and Navy, declared a blockade of the South, expended Treasury funds for unauthorized purposes, and in other respects behaved—his critics alleged—as if the Constitution did not exist.

Lincoln's justification, of course, was that in a dire emergency it was necessary to act in order to save the country. Without a country there would be no Constitution. In the light of the war powers exercised by twentieth-century Presidents, Lincoln's conduct seems entirely understandable and even circumspect—except possibly for the umbrella of martial law that permitted him to hold several thousand civilians in jail without due process. In the light of the Whig theory of the Presidency, his behavior was ominously reminiscent of Jacksonian "despotism." A legal brief contesting his assumptions of power argued that they made the President "the impersonation of the country" and empowered him to do whatever he pleased to " '*save the life of the nation*'. . . . This is to assert that the Constitution contemplated and tacitly provided that the President should be dictator, and all constitutional government be at an end whenever he should think that 'the life of the nation' is in danger."

Abraham Lincoln posed for the daguerreotype above in 1860, the year he was elected President of the United States.

In the abstract, such misgivings were eminently reasonable. There were disquieting denials of individual liberty during the Civil War years in the name of emergency. Constitutionalists were rightly concerned lest these emergency measures somehow acquire the sanction of usage—much as, for example, temporary buildings are apt to become permanently occupied. Nor could Congress lightly accept the President's apparent marauding in the no man's land between those two branches of government. Why, demanded Senator Charles Sumner, should "these vast War Powers" not pertain also to Congress? The President "is only the instrument of Congress, under the Constitution." Unless Congress upheld its rights, the American republic would be degraded "to one of those short-lived, vulgar despotisms appearing occasionally as a warning to mankind." Lincoln would have been delighted if he had known the opinion that Jefferson had expressed in a letter of 1810: "In time of peace the people look most to their representatives; but in war to the Executive solely."

But he would probably not have quoted the letter in any public answer to his critics. He was too clever to give offense where he could avoid it; and he agreed with the theoretical position of the Sumners and Wades and other vehement Republicans. He agreed because he had carried his old Whig views into the new Republican party. The paradox of Lincoln's Presidency was revealed by the kind of abuse that greeted him. He was assailed both as a dictator and as "timid and ignorant," "a political coward," a man "without any spinal column." In other words, he was accused both of having exceeded his authority and of having failed to exert it.

Some of the criticism came from Radical Republicans who thought the administration far too hesitant on the slavery issue. Some came from persons who felt that he lacked the magisterial presence they associated with his office. Ralph Waldo Emerson complained in 1863 that "you cannot refine Mr. Lincoln's taste, extend his horizon, or clear his judgment; he will not walk dignifiedly through the traditional part of the President of America. . . ." Some criticism was of the random variety that every President must learn to tolerate if he is to preserve his sanity. Lincoln's friend Ward Lamon reported an outburst from the President similar to one from George Washington: "In God's name! if any one can do better in my place than I have done, or am endeavoring to do, let him try his hand at it, and no one will be better contented than myself."

All such testimony indicates the dual character of Lincoln's Presidency. As Commander in Chief he acted the part of an almost ruthless Chief Executive. In attempting to preserve the Union and restore the peace, he behaved as if some spirit—the spirit of the office—were speaking through him. Otherwise he spoke very much in his own voice—that of a colloquial, wryly humorous, innately intelligent, half-deprecating Western politician, who had, like all successful politicians, dreamed of becoming President. Since he was a Whig, he had dreamed of being the kind of President that Henry Clay would have been. Part of him still visualized the office on Whig lines. It was this Lincoln who left to Congress most of the initiative in developing legislation: as President-elect he had said that he thought Congress "should originate, as well as perfect its measures, without external bias." For the same reason he made little use of the veto power; in this respect his only real challenge to Congress was a pocket veto of the Wade-Davis reconstruction bill, which he thought infringed upon the executive zone of responsibility. And possibly, although this point is less clear, his Whig political education accounted for his failure to dominate his Cabinet, or indeed to bring it into any regular system. Whatever the explanation, he gave his department heads far more scope for independent action than had Jackson or Polk.

Abraham Lincoln wielded more power than any of his predecessors because he had to. His Emancipation Proclamation was an example of his calm assertion of presidential prerogative in the face of whatever Congress or his Cabinet might deem the proper course. In any survey of the Presidency these assertions earn him a prominent place as an "aggrandizer." They were a high-water mark not reached again for almost half a century. In other respects Lincoln was a Jefferson rather than a Jackson. Unlike Jackson he did not stamp his name and his personality upon his era. Like that of Jefferson, his reputation was to a considerable extent posthumous. Only after he was dead, and the extraordinary quality of his thoughts and actions had become evident, did Lincoln join the ranks of the immortals among the Presidents. He enriched—and so consolidated—the office from the grave. Emerson and a multitude of others forgot their strictures and began to marvel.

The Place of Party Politics

Although the Constitution was silent on the matter, the framers and the nation's early leaders had decided views about political parties: they were against factions and parties and did not want them in the United States.

At best, as in eighteenth-century England, parties were seen as cynical, shifting alliances controlled by a circle of powerful families. The atmosphere was venal; lackeys and placemen jockeyed for recognition by the party of the "King's Friends" or that of his no less aristocratic opponents. (The contemptibility of this world was portrayed in *Gulliver's Travels*, in which Jonathan Swift mocked the pretensions of the rival factions in Lilliput—perhaps with an element of self-contempt, since his own career depended largely on his turning out political journalism on behalf of the Tory party.) At worst, the appearance of such groups spelled the doom of a society by splitting it into irreconcilably hostile segments.

Astute American theorists such as John Adams and James Madison were, of course, aware that their countrymen were not basically different from the rest of mankind, although American society was simpler and more wholesome than that of the Old World. In the famous tenth essay from *The Federalist*, which Madison wrote in 1787, he addressed himself to the problem of factions or parties as they might appear under the Constitution. He knew that "a landed interest, a manufacturing interest, a mercantile interest, a moneyed interest, with many lesser interests, grow up of necessity in civilized nations, and divide them into different classes, actuated by different sentiments and views." The United States,

Madison said, would be no exception—in fact it would be divided geographically or sectionally as well. He added, with impressive foresight: "The regulation of these various and interfering interests forms the principal task of modern legislation, and involves the spirit of party and faction in the necessary and ordinary operations of the government."

Yet taken as a whole Madison's essay is hardly a prediction of, still less a welcome for, the parties that were within a few years to burst upon the American scene. He regarded them as factions, which he defined as "a number of citizens, whether . . . a majority or minority of the whole, who are united and actuated by some common impulse of passion, or of interest, adverse to the rights of other citizens or to the permanent and aggregate interests of the community." To Madison parties were a necessary evil. They could not be avoided altogether, so they had to be brought under control by means of checks and balances. Madison's hope was twofold: first, that discord would be muted by the calmer, wiser counsels of elected legislatures, and second, that the abundance of rival interests within so large a republic would cause them to minimize one another. But in general his essay is pessimistic so far as actual parties are concerned. Even a minority interest, he conceded, might "clog the administration" and "convulse" society, though it could not accomplish total overthrow. Wise legislators ought to emerge; on the other hand, "men of factious tempers, of local prejudices, or of sinister designs, may by intrigue, by corruption, or by other means, first obtain the suffrages, and then betray the interests of the people." In short,

Madison's *Federalist* No. 10 does not look forward to the advent of the party system. And nowhere does he consider the possibility of two major parties, as distinct from an assortment, contending for the Presidency and for the legislative branch.

After a few years of government under the Constitution, prominent Americans seemed to share the apprehensions expressed by Madison. In March, 1789, Jefferson told Francis Hopkinson that he had never been willing to align his views on religion, philosophy, or politics with those of "any party of men.... Such an addiction is the last degradation of a free and moral agent. If I could not go to heaven but with a party, I would not go there at all."

When Vice President John Adams spoke of parties he specifically meant political units, and he was emphatic in his disapproval: "There is nothing I dread so much as the division of the Republic into two great parties, each under its leader.... This, in my humble opinion, is to be feared as the greatest political evil under our Constitution." The outcome, he thought, would be spleen and destructiveness. "As soon as one man hints at an improvement," he said, "his rival opposes it. No sooner has one party discovered ... any amelioration ... than the opposite party belies it ... misrepresents it, ridicules it ... and persecutes it." In his Farewell Address of 1796 George Washington warned his countrymen "in the most solemn manner against the baneful effects of the spirit of party.... It serves always to distract the public councils and enfeeble the public administration. It agitates the community with ill-founded jealousies and false alarms; kindles the animosity of one part against another; foments occasionally riot and insurrection."

To their surprise and dismay, Washington and Adams were faced by the very phenomenon that was so widely deplored. No wonder that they were slow to recognize it as unavoidable, and quite unable to consider it a potential benefit. While he was in office Washington never thought of his administration as that of a party but as national in outlook. True, in his second term he took care to appoint to executive offices only men whose sentiments were, like his own, "federal." But this did not mean he accepted the role of an opposition party. The Jeffersonian Republicans, later known as Democratic-Republicans, who challenged Washington's conduct of affairs, were not to him *the* opposition but simply opposition; faction,

and disloyal faction at that. He knew very well that the Republicans identified him with the Federalists; Jefferson informed him in 1792 that Alexander Hamilton's scheme was to "dismount" Washington from the Chief Magistracy and place him at the head of a party—the Federalist party. But Washington, reluctant to place the Federalist persuasion on a footing with the subversive "mobocracy," was still less prepared to agree that he might be in danger of losing his presidential impartiality. Only when he was out of office did he begin to show signs of acknowledging such an affiliation. He was still sure in 1798 that a "profest Democrat" was a man who "will leave nothing unattempted to overturn the Government of this Country." A year later—the last year of his life—Washington saw the situation more clearly. Explaining why he would not become a candidate for the 1800 presidential election, he observed that "principle, not men, is now, and will be, the object of contention." Even if he were to consent, he said, he "should not draw a *single* vote from the Anti-federal side; and of course, should stand upon no stronger ground than any other Federal well supported."

John Adams as President had an even more unsavory experience of the incipient spirit of party. Less elevated than Washington in the nation's regard, he caught the full blast of Republican opposition, an opposition tightly organized from within Congress. Feeling between the Republicans and the Federalists was intense: the stringent Alien and Sedition Acts were passed by the Federalist majority and approved by Adams in the hope that they would give him some protection from the barrage of Antifederalist abuse. He had—in Jefferson—a Republican Vice President. Worse still, Adams had to contend with the "Ultras," or "High Federalists," who looked to Hamilton for guidance and urged the President toward extreme policies. Adams had misguidedly continued his predecessor's Cabinet in office, and the principal Secretaries were markedly Hamiltonian. Vilified throughout his four years in office and defeated in the election of 1800 by a combination of Jeffersonians and Hamiltonians, Adams retired more firmly convinced than ever that parties might be the ruin of the United States.

The Jeffersonian opposition had understandably been quicker to visualize parties as a legitimate mechanism. By 1792 Madison had already been convinced. Jefferson himself, initially hesitant, had begun to grasp the point. At the end of 1795, still less partisan in mood than some of the admirers who were about to push him for the Presidency, Jefferson cautiously declared: "Were parties here divided merely by a greediness for office, as in England, to take a part . . . would be unworthy . . . but where the principle of difference is as substantial . . . as between the republicans and the Monocrats of our country, I hold it as honorable to take a firm and decided part. . . ."

Less than three years later Jefferson had arrived at a surprisingly modern assessment: "In every free and deliberating society there must . . . be opposite parties and violent dissensions and discords, and one of these, for the most part, must prevail over the other for a longer or shorter time. Perhaps this party division is necessary to induce each to watch and [relate] to the people the proceedings of the other."

Being the "outs," anxious to be "in," the Republicans showed more enterprise than the Federalists, both in Congress and in the country as a whole. Their more avowedly libertarian and egalitarian creed made it easier for them to broaden the base of their support. Both tactics and ideology led them to seek a grass-roots following and to employ sundry devices—canvassing, newspaper articles, slogans, tickets—that foreshadowed the present-day party structure. The passion of their beliefs and their genuine distrust of each other induced both parties to compete ferociously for office.

The origin of the American party system is a matter of great interest and complexity. Two points are of particular relevance: the role of the Presidency and the attitude of the various Presidents. Herbert Agar, Joseph Charles, William N. Chambers, and other students of American political history all agree that the Presidency was the vital prize in the system. Richard P. McCormick goes so far as to suggest that the contest for the Presidency was the prime function of American political parties. Perhaps this was not why parties originated; but once they existed, circumstances oriented political groups in this direction. The 1787 Constitution created a *national* political environment. In order to gain a hearing, local groups had to find representation within the federal government; and to do this they had to coalesce with other groups. Such loose coalitions were ineffective and wasteful of time and effort unless they could be unified by more permanent ties of organization and animated by larger enthusiasms and antipathies.

In European countries, political parties have been oriented toward the legislature, not the executive. Why did this not happen in the United States, especially since the first two Presidents revealed their distaste for parties? The answer obviously lies in the conception of the Presidency. In Europe the executive was usually a hereditary monarchy, not accessible to the competition of politics. In the United States, the fact that the Presidency was an elective office held for a relatively short term made it automatically subject to competition. If the Chief Executive had become a merely ceremonial figure, submissive to the dictates of Congress or of his Cabinet, the competition might have taken other forms. Instead Washington and Adams unwittingly thrust the office to the forefront of party politics by upholding its dignity. If the President was not to be a cipher, he had to be a person of incalculable potential. Even at a modest estimate, a political party active primarily in the legislature needed the concurrence of the executive branch. The emotions stirred by the elections of 1796 and 1800 ensured that these quadrennial contests would grip the national imagination. The fight for the Presidency became inextricably involved with other aspects of a nationwide battle—a battle for a whole administration, all the seats in the House of Representatives, one third of those in the Senate, and a large number (growing steadily as the principle of popular election replaced legislative selection) of governorships and other state and local offices. The "coattail" phenomenon was soon apparent. A minor candidate had more chance of recognition and victory if he could be associated with a national campaign. In 1796, for example, Massachusetts men were stimulated to re-elect Governor Samuel Adams by reminders that the issue was tremendous: "MONARCHY OR REPUBLICANISM." The ratification of the Twelfth Amendment before the 1804 election conferred a constitutional sanction upon an evolution not at all desired in 1787.

The Presidency of Thomas Jefferson set the seal on the Chief Executive's involvement in politics. Unlike Washington and Adams, he entered office and won re-election through the operation of a system that in the main he approved. In office he worked closely and smoothly with his congressional following. The man who in 1789 had proclaimed his intention to think for himself as a "free and moral agent" had become impatient with Republican legislators who would not stay in line. They were "wayward freaks," apt to "disturb the operations." The network of relationships that had been created in the 1790's by such pioneer politicos as John Beckley, clerk of the House in Washington's administration, was spread wider. Jefferson's devoted Secretary of the Treasury, Albert Gallatin, communicated to the Republican caucus in Congress the detail of what Jefferson wanted done. The executive branch also made use of key members of the standing congressional committees, which were beginning to multiply. Legislation was shepherded by unofficial but nonetheless active "floor leaders." Executive patronage was employed throughout the nation to reward the faithful.

Punishments were meted out to those who had lost favor with the President. A celebrated—some would say flagrant—case was that of John Randolph of Virginia. A master of sarcastic oratory, Randolph was singled out as House floor leader and chairman of the important Ways and Means Committee when he was only twenty-eight years old. During Jefferson's first administration Randolph's reputation stood high. He dined regularly with the President and was in almost daily touch with Gallatin or other Cabinet members. As floor leader he directed the repeal of the Judiciary Act and the impeachment of the vituperative Supreme Court Justice Samuel Chase—a chief villain in Republican eyes. As committee chairman, Randolph secured vital appropriations for the President.

However, he and Jefferson fell out, partly because he had failed to secure the conviction of Chase at the impeachment trial. The dinners ceased; the President found other channels of communication; Randolph was ousted from his floor leadership. He had, the President thought, become one of the wayward freaks—and indeed his subsequent career seemed to bear out the accusation. In 1813 another Republican contested Randolph's seat in the House and defeated him. By an odd coincidence Randolph's successful rival was a son-in-law of Thomas Jefferson's. (Randolph regained his seat in 1815, however.)

Jefferson maintained his hold over the Republican party because he was so clearly its most distinguished figure, because indirect leadership suited his talents, and because the Federalist party was in decline. Circumstances, however, worked against his successors Madison and Monroe. To the extent that they owed their nomination to the Republican caucus, they were regarded by Congress as its beneficiaries. And the gradual disappearance of the Federalists as a coherent, formidable opposition had the unexpected effect of weakening discipline within the Republican ranks. John Randolph, who for a quarter of a century after his own relegation to political impotence lost no opportunity to point to the same situation in other men's careers, said of Madison in 1811: "He is President *de jure* only. Who exercises the office *de facto* I do not know. . . ." By the end of Madison's first administration the executive office, or the power attached to it, was parceled out among the Speaker of the House (Henry Clay), the caucus in Congress, and the heads of congressional committees. Madison was not a complete nonentity, but there was an uncomfortable edge of truth in Randolph's gibe. Adams had been denied a second term because there had been too much opposition inside and outside his party. It could be said that Madison's second term proved either that even second-rate Presidents could be sure of re-election in wartime, or else that the office did not seem important enough to warrant putting someone else in his place.

Monroe suffered from the same afflictions as Madison. Outwardly all was well in the "Era of Good Feelings." The Republican caucus followed expectation in nominating Monroe: as Madison's Secretary of State he was the heir apparent. In the presidential election of 1816 he secured 183 electoral votes to the Federalist candidate's 34 votes. In 1820 Monroe was unopposed, a situation that had not occurred since 1789 and would never happen again. Every electoral vote except one went to him. With the collapse of the Federalists as a party capable of nominating a winning candidate, it appeared that perhaps the previous epoch of violent party spirit had been an aberration. The emergence of parties and their subsequent disintegration had coincided with the period when Europe was in the grip of the French Revolution and then the Napoleonic wars. The cleavage between the "Anglomen" of the Federalist group and the Republican "Gallomen" could have been interpreted as evidence that the United States should respect Washington's advice to have "as little *political* connection" with foreign nations as possible, and Jefferson's identical warning against "entangling alliances." The successful conclusion of the War of 1812 and the return of peace to Europe guaranteed America the immunity it sought. If an additional statement of intent was needed, it was provided in the Monroe Doctrine.

The period after the War of 1812 was a time to rejoice in America's harmony. It seemed possible that the Presidency might regain its full dignity as an honorable station raised far above petty faction. In this lofty frame of mind no less a figure than Andrew Jackson, the hero of New Orleans, recommended magnanimity to the newly elected Monroe in 1816: "Now is the time to exterminate the monster called party spirit. By selecting characters most conspicuous for their probity, virtue, capacity and firmness, without any regard to party, you will go far to, if not entirely eradicate those feelings, which, on former occasions, threw so many obstacles in the way of government; and perhaps have the pleasure of uniting a people heretofore divided. . . . Consult no party in your choice."

Jackson's views were in accord with those of Monroe. The new President wished to demonstrate the complete truth of Jefferson's conciliatory assertion, "We are all Republicans, we are all Federalists." He deliberately discounted party affiliation in distributing patronage. Although Monroe did not know it, he was following an opinion stated by ex-President John Adams in a letter of 1811. The President, Adams had said, "ought to select the men best qualified . . . for offices at his own responsibility," unimpeded by any other agency. Unless he could do so, "he must be the slave of the party that brought him in. He never can be independent or impartial."

There was, it appeared, a prevailing notion among high-minded Americans that parties were dead—and fortunately so. Monroe therefore reverted to Washington's initial practice of offering executive posts to the most eminent men in the land. The result, on paper, was a Cabinet of exceptional merit. Though Clay and Jackson refused office, Monroe succeeded in naming John Quincy Adams as his Secretary of State, John C. Calhoun as Secretary of War, William H. Crawford as Secretary of the Treasury, and William Wirt as Attorney General. When John Quincy Adams succeeded Monroe in 1825, he adhered to the same dignified assumption. In his Inaugural Address Adams announced:

"There still remains one effort of magnanimity, one sacrifice of prejudice and passion, to be made by the individuals throughout the nation who have heretofore followed the standards of political party. It is that of discarding every remnant of rancor against each other, of embracing as countrymen and friends, and of yielding to talents and virtue alone that confidence which in times of contention for principle was bestowed only upon those who bore the badge of party communion." In obedience to his own ideals Adams retained some of Monroe's Cabinet, brought in Henry Clay as Secretary of State, and offered posts to Jackson and Crawford although neither would accept.

It is worth repeating that of the first six Presidents, none, not even Jefferson, was wholly committed to the belief that political parties were essential to the United States. All except Jefferson and possibly Madison disliked most aspects of the party system, and strongly disliked the effect of politics upon the Presidency. Most of their successors have at one time or another regretted the partisan features of the office. Several have renewed the early efforts

In this Federalist cartoon, Jefferson and a devil try to destroy the government built by Washington and John Adams.

to rise above politics, in the sincere conviction that there is something anomalous in being both President of the United States and a party chieftain. A distaste so deeply rooted and so recurrent deserves to be studied sympathetically—though the consequences of attempted presidential impartiality have nearly always been unfortunate.

They were certainly unfortunate for Monroe and John Quincy Adams. Both failed to appreciate that when major parties disappeared they would be replaced by minor factions. Whatever the defects of the party system, it possessed a chain of command, a sense of purpose, a unifying quality. Factions, on the other hand, were fluid, personal, divisive, and conspiratorial. When issues were no longer at stake, and were no longer presented by contending national organizations, there was still contention among ambitious individuals. As before, the grand prize was the Presidency; but there was little semblance of grandeur in the struggle to attain it. In Monroe's Cabinet Adams, Calhoun, and Crawford were all keenly interested in becoming President. Outside the Cabinet, so were Clay, Jackson, and others. In the absence of party discipline the Republican caucus could no longer regulate the succession; support had to be intrigued for, and tended to form geographically, as each section responded to the appeal of a particular native son. Congress rather than the executive branch held the initiative. Clay remarked to Adams after Monroe's re-election that the President "had not the slightest influence on Congress. His career was considered as closed. There was nothing further to be expected by him or from him."

Poor Monroe knew that something was amiss. When the country was at war, or stirred by some internal controversy, he said plaintively, "the course is plain, and you have something to cheer and animate you to action, but we are now blessed with peace, and the success of the late war has overwhelmed the federal party, so that there is no division of that kind to rally any persons together in support of the administration." If he had been versed in the ancient techniques of unstable regimes he might have applied the principle of *divide et impera*—divide and rule—by setting his rivals at loggerheads. But he had no such guile. By declining to play the patronage game he lost all influence.

Looking back on the Era of Good Feelings, Martin Van Buren observed: "In the place of two great

By the Virtue, Firmness and Patriotism of

JEFFERSON & MADISON,

Our Difficulties with England are settled—our Ships have been preserved, and our Seamen will, hereafter, be respected while sailing under our National Flag.

An 1809 broadside praised Jefferson and Madison for avoiding war with England. They had really only postponed it.

parties arrayed against each other in a fair and open contest for the establishment of principles in the administration of Government which they respectively believed most conducive to the public interest, the country was overrun with personal factions." He blamed Monroe for aggravating the situation. The solution to the problem, as he saw it, was not to rejoice in the disappearance of parties but to work for their restoration. A rising young professional politician in the 1820's, Van Buren did not feel apologetic for his craft. On the contrary, he saw it as the way to rescue the United States from futile animosities. The lesson was clear to another of the new specialists in man-management, for whom politics was an endlessly absorbing and not entirely cynical occupation. This was Thurlow Weed, one of Van Buren's professional rivals in New York. Weed saw the need for a revision of the party system. He also saw the potential strength of John Quincy Adams, who could command a handsome block of votes (at least in New England). But, he noted sadly, "Mr. Adams during his administration failed to cherish, strengthen, or even recognize the party to which he owed his election [the National Republicans]; nor, as far as I am informed, with the great power he possessed did he make a single influential friend."

Personal and fortuitous factors have to be taken into account. Monroe could have shown an interest in the protracted debates over the Missouri Compromise (or compromises) between 1819 and 1821, rather than remaining aloof. He could have asserted himself more in the field of foreign policy. Adams, Monroe's successor, blundered after the disputed election of 1824. Appointed to the Presidency by the House of Representatives when he had, in fact, received fewer popular and electoral votes than Andrew Jackson, Adams appeared to indulge in a "corrupt bargain" by rewarding Henry Clay, who had turned the House in his favor, with the Secretaryship of State. Although there was almost certainly no "bargain" as such, the aggrieved Jackson was able to attract widespread sympathy as the victim of secret machinations, who had been deprived of his rightful office by a palace guard. After that, nothing went right for Adams. The Jackson men in his Cabinet were openly disloyal. Since both he and Monroe had retained several incumbent Cabinet members, the theory began to develop that the Cabinet's tenure might not end with each outgoing administration but would be continued in some semi-independent fashion. Halfway through his Presidency, Adams confessed in his diary that while he could not conceive what retirement would be like, it could not be "worse than this perpetual motion and crazing cares. The weight grows heavier from day to day."

Monroe and Adams had been at the mercy of circumstance. Jackson had guessed wrong along with them in 1816 when he had offered the conventional disparagement of party politics. His pronouncements as a presidential candidate in 1824 were equally conventional and demure, not out of cunning but rather because he and his managers had no clear idea of the new look in politics. The experts in what Van Buren called the "art and business of President-making" were feeling their way toward some fresh dispensation. Van Buren put his talents at the disposal of William H. Crawford of Georgia in the 1824 election. He may have been shrewd, but Crawford suffered a serious stroke and dropped behind in the competition. By the 1828 election, Van Buren was ready to back Andrew Jackson, who won. Within a fairly short period the clever men in politics perceived that the art of President making was inseparable from the art of party making.

They reached this conclusion without forming any particular conception of the Presidency as such. They were not concerned with nice constitutional arguments as to the Chief Executive's relationship to the legislature and the judiciary, or his authority in the realm of foreign affairs. They were interested in a strong Executive only to the extent that a forceful President might be a popular President, and

could be looked up to as a party leader instead of being cold-shouldered as Monroe and Adams had been. Their intention was not to innovate, but rather to return to the days when Thomas Jefferson had been in office and the Republican machinery had revolved with a contented hum. The lessons of Jeffersonian Republicanism were not mysterious. The desired formula comprised a President with a national reputation (which of course might also mean that he had a number of enemies); a well-knit party, able to reward the deserving and castigate the disloyal; an issue or two large and vital enough to arouse interest in all corners of the Union, and democratic enough to satisfy the Jeffersonian ideology; and an opposition that was, while not sufficiently powerful to win, sturdy enough to put up a reasonable fight.

The task was easier for the Republicans, or for what remained of the party by the latter half of the 1820's, than for the scattered and dispirited Federalists. The Republicans had retained whatever dominance and initiative were left. A revived party would be in tune with the impetus toward political democracy that was already manifesting itself in the abolition of suffrage restrictions, in the allotment of legislators to smaller electoral districts, and in the growing habit of subjecting governors and officials to popular election. Such a party could also claim direct inheritance from the Jeffersonian party. In fact Jackson frequently called himself a Republican although his party was officially styled Democratic. Opponents of "the Democracy," however, were distinctly unwilling to admit descent from the discredited Federalists. (It was an indication of James K. Polk's instinctive partisanship that he referred to the Whigs, as late as 1848, as the "Federal party.")

In other words, conditions were favorable for a fresh demonstration of the Jeffersonian approach to politics, although probably only a man of exceptional force could have contrived to take matters as far as Andrew Jackson did. The virtual collapse of the congressional caucus in 1820 had shown that some other device was needed. Jackson's defeat in the election of 1824, after he had won a sizable vote of confidence, dramatized the issue and filled him with an energizing desire for revenge. On this particular issue, majoritarian democracy and his own victory became synonymous for Jackson. In his first annual message of December, 1829, and again a year later in his second message to Congress, Jackson revealed that he still felt the sting of his earlier frustration. "To the people," he declared in 1829, "belongs the right of electing their Chief Magistrate; it was never designed that their choice should in any case be defeated, either by the intervention of electoral colleges or by . . . the House of Representatives." In both messages he recommended a constitutional amendment to permit free expression of the popular will. He was on familiar ground; amendments of this nature had been proposed several times in Congress in the previous decade, and had very nearly been carried. The suggested amendments and Jackson's recommendations were never passed for one cogent reason: the party in power preferred to stick to the known system, with all its manipulative possibilities, rather than take chances on a less controllable method. In 1829 and 1830 President Jackson still spoke as an outsider, a plain man unacquainted with political wiles.

In this guise he was more attractive to the populace than the Clays, Crawfords, and Calhouns. All three major groups contending for the Presidency in 1832—the Democratic party (by then formally labeled as such), the National Republicans (who soon became known as Whigs), and the short-lived Antimasonic movement—chose their candidates by means of national nominating conventions. King Caucus was dead. Much of the credit for the demise went to Jackson, though in actuality the Antimasonic convention preceded that of the Democrats by several months. Moreover, both of the other parties pioneered the introduction of party platforms in that election; the Democrats did not produce one of their own until 1840.

The Democrats had nevertheless done much to evolve a body of doctrine that cemented the party together, furnished ammunition against enemies, and was symbolized by Andrew Jackson. The first great manifesto appeared in Jackson's 1829 message to Congress, on the problem of rotation in office—whether men ought to hold governmental appointments indefinitely or be subject to removal. Once more he had Jeffersonian sanction, both in theory and in practice. He had the more recent support of the Tenure of Office Act of 1820, by which Congress had limited certain appointments to a maximum of four years as a check against corruption. And he was consistent in recommending that the Presidency itself be bound by the same principle of rotation, through restriction to a single four- or six-year term.

Among the arguments Jackson produced in favor of rotation was his celebrated assertion that the "duties of all public officers are, or at least admit of being made, so plain and simple that men of intelligence may readily qualify themselves for their performance; and I can not but believe that more is lost by the long continuance of men in office than is generally to be gained by their experience." No man, he said, had any "intrinsic right" to an official post. He wished to destroy the notion that an appointment was a form of property. He conceded that there might be cases of individual hardship; but rotation— "a leading principle in the republican creed"—would give "healthful action" to the whole system of government.

The personal factor that lent force to Jackson's words was obvious. He himself had succeeded in several careers—legal, military, political—without ever undergoing a laborious apprenticeship. This Tennessee outsider had been thwarted in 1824 by the coteries of the federal Capital. Even Cabinet members were beginning to assume that they held office almost indefinitely, like federal judges. One of Jackson's rivals for the Presidency, William H. Crawford, had occupied Cabinet posts continuously from 1815 to 1825. William Wirt, the Antimasonic candidate for President in 1832, had been Attorney General from 1817 to 1829.

What Jackson did not admit in his 1829 message was the influence of rotation upon political parties. He was neither a simpleton nor a hypocrite. It is reasonable to suppose that politics was a secondary concern for him. Not so for his lieutenants, whose operating rule was baldly stated by William L. Marcy: "To the victor belong the spoils of the enemy." Jackson himself warmed to the idea of politics as warfare, with no quarter given to unworthy foes. But he would have preferred the less crass discussion of the problem that appeared in a correspondence of 1828 between Postmaster General John McLean and young Edward Everett of Massachusetts. What, McLean asked, bound parties together? His answer was "the hope of office," with its "honors and emoluments." Administrations could not afford to neglect this political truth. John Quincy Adams had followed an opposite rule, "from pure motives," but "the People will not sustain it." The

No love was lost between President Jackson (left) and his two Whig antagonists, Daniel Webster (center) and Henry Clay (right). Both senators wanted desperately to win the Presidency, but never managed it.

earnest, respectable Everett, who was destined to become the most admired public orator of his time, agreed and added that in the United States, where there were no badges of honor such as titles, office was everything that men sought in the public sphere. "Truly incredible," he said, "are the efforts men are willing to make, the humiliations they will endure, to get it . . . while office is so passionately coveted, no party will sit still and see themselves postponed to their opponents in politics."

This candid and intelligent exchange revealed the variety of motives that impelled men to seek presidential office or to rally around those who did. Jackson did not abuse the spoils system during his administrations. Although the figures are disputed, it seems that he removed between 10 and 20 per cent of the approximately ten thousand holders of federal offices, and slightly more than a third of the six hundred officials whose appointment was the direct concern of the President. By later standards the total was modest and the application was, in general, honest. The wholesale massacre feared by anti-Jackson alarmists did not occur. The danger lay in the extension of the system to the indiscriminate degree practiced by Jackson's Postmaster General William T. Barry. Until Barry's incumbency the Postmaster General was not a member of the Cabinet and local postmasters were removed only for negligence or misconduct. Whig congressmen maintained that in six years of "Barry-mongering" there had been

nearly thirteen hundred removals of postal officials, usually without any explanation being given.

Barry was an exceptionally incompetent appointee whom Jackson eventually replaced. But rotation was a double-edged sword, apt to hurt all who wielded it. Old-style Republicans were worried by its implications. Ex-President Madison wrote in a private letter that the bribing and threatening entailed in the practice of wholesale rotation "could not fail to degrade any Administration." John Tyler, a future President, had similar misgivings. So did Thomas Ritchie, editor of the Richmond *Enquirer* and a sturdy Jeffersonian. "I go for reform," he assured Van Buren in March, 1829, when Jackson had been President less than a month, "but what is reform? . . . It surely is not to put out a good and experienced officer, because he was a decent friend of J. Q. Adams, *in order* to put in a heated partizan of the election of Gen. Jackson. . . . I trust that such a spirit of Reform will not come near to us in Virginia." Reform or abuse, no single development would give Presidents more problems or bind them more closely to the party apparatus than the application of the rotation principle.

Under Jackson, the Democratic-Republicans had as their President a figure of national repute who had not been associated with caucus politics. They had resourceful men such as Van Buren to plan strategy and distribute patronage. The next great step was to agree upon some issues that would arouse

FOUR • THE PLACE OF PARTY POLITICS

the martial enthusiasm of the whole party. Politicians well knew the value of such issues. One of William H. Crawford's congressional friends sighed in 1821 that if they could only "hit upon a few great principles and unite their support with that of Crawford," victory would be certain. The Jacksonians laid a general claim to being the democratic party, and intermittently professed a Jeffersonian attachment to states' rights. But the big issue they hit upon was the status of the Second Bank of the United States. It was a real issue, and an intricate one. Reduced to simple terms, the battle lay between Andrew Jackson, the People's President, and the "Monster Bank." Jackson was the ideal leader in the campaign, for he shared the fairly widespread American distrust of banks and made the fight vividly personal. Old Hickory was democracy's champion against the entrenched barons of the Bank; he was throwing down the gage at the feet of the Bank's chief henchman, Henry Clay of the "corrupt bargain." Senator Thomas Hart Benton was delighted by the controversy. "The Bank of the United States," he exulted, "is the turning point. That political engine of the federal monarchical party, will draw the lines between parties again."

And so it happened. Although the Democrats had no party platform in 1832, their campaign speeches hammered away at the Bank question. Jackson's Bank veto message was understandably denounced by his opponents as an incitement to class warfare. It was not quite that, but it was certainly excellent party propaganda. Jackson's victory in the 1832 election showed that the country was once more grouping into rival camps and that the Jacksonians were in a winning position. They were on the attack and they held the Presidency.

It is tempting to speculate that the national game of politics has influenced the development of the American version of football, which is elaborate, ritualized, episodic, somewhat arcane and therefore difficult for a novice to follow. Points are scored suddenly and in profusion. Possession of the ball is highly important: fumbling may give possession of the ball to the other team (party). The side that has possession must give proof of the ability to gain ground or it will lose possession to the other side. The most important person in these games is a nonparticipant, the coach, whose direction is, according to temperament, sometimes flamboyantly apparent and sometimes coolly concealed. The contract of an unsuccessful coach is not renewed. One might add a further analogy: other things being equal, the richest team is the likeliest to win.

During Jackson's Presidency one feature of old-style politics was missing. Van Buren's later writings refer to "two great parties" as the mark of a healthy system. This condition was not fulfilled in 1832 or in 1836. The Democrats were more or less unified; their opponents were not. Indeed in 1836 the coalition of anti-Jackson men, who called themselves Whigs, decided not to put forward one candidate but to let several run, partly in the hope that the election would have to be referred to the House of Representatives. As for Jackson, his 1829 and 1830 messages to Congress leave the impression that in those days he did not anticipate a straightforward division between two major national parties. The United States was apt, he said, to have a "multiplication of candidates for the Presidency."

By 1836 the Democrats were proud of their national standing as a major party, and quite naturally saw no reason to assist their enemies in consolidating. Theorists might recommend an almost exact parity of strength between two (and no more than two) parties; but the party in possession was not eager to oblige the theorists by building up its rivals. Nor, so long as the President might be picked in the House of Representatives, were the Whigs persuaded of the need to emulate the monolithic structure of the Democrats, especially since they were committed to the proposition that a powerful Executive was a national hazard.

The election of 1836 taught the Whigs a number of lessons. The negative lesson was that the multiple-candidate strategy had failed, even against the Democrats' relatively unimposing nominee, Martin Van Buren. A positive lesson was that the Whigs stood a good chance of winning in 1840 by emulating what the Democrats had done. They would have to capitalize upon the weaknesses of their foes. After eight years in office Jackson had alienated many powerful politicians; Van Buren had to be forced upon the reluctant Southern Democrats as the 1836 nominee. By 1840 a total of twelve years of Democratic rule would be bound to leave voters with a vague feeling that it was time for a change—since the millennium would, as usual, have failed to arrive under the incumbent administration.

The result of Whig cogitations was the choice of a Middle Western candidate of Southern birth, whose manner was dignified and who was portrayed as the hero of Tippecanoe—a battle against the Indians fought in 1811. William Henry Harrison was the nearest thing to Andrew Jackson, with Whig overtones. The successful campaign waged on his behalf against Van Buren marked the full emergence of what Richard P. McCormick calls the second party system. Most accounts of the "Log Cabin" saturnalia of 1840 stress the emptiness and imitativeness of the Whig campaign. There is the implication that in their lust for office the Whigs cynically outbid the Democrats. It is true that they lusted for office, and that having won they snatched at the spoils even more avidly than Jackson's or Van Buren's followers. It is also true that a few of the more austere Whigs expressed regret at the vote-catching vulgarities of the campaign. Much more significant, however, was the Whigs' readiness and skill in pitching their appeal at a popular level. This approach was not blind imitation of the Democrats but rather shrewd recognition of the political facts of life. The second party system, like that of the Republican-Federalist system, produced national organizations whose primary effort went into capturing the Presidency. What differentiated the second system was the elaboration and professionalism of these organizations, the small (though still not trivial) zone of disagreement as to party platforms, the dramatizing of the contest through the press, the state and national party conventions, and the campaign itself with its plethora of speeches, songs, and slogans. The voting figures reveal the effect of the system on the American public. In the election of 1840—an election supposedly rendered meaningless by farcical claims and accusations —78 per cent of those eligible to vote registered their preference. The figure was easily the highest recorded in a presidential contest up to that time. It would not be surpassed until the McKinley-Bryan battle of 1896. In other words, the lines had been drawn again. Presidents were—at least for the period between winning nomination and leaving office—the standard-bearers of their parties. As before, not all of them welcomed the role, which exposed them to indignity and additional controversy. The separation of powers implanted in the Constitution isolated them from their congressional cohorts, as if they were generals trying to command an army by remote control. As soon as the next election loomed, their authority began to dwindle unless they were clear favorites for renomination. As soon as they retired from the White House, unless like Jackson they had an exceptional hold over the party, they were apt to be put out to graze. In such cases they were symbols whose magic had evaporated. The scratched buttons, faded ribbons, and yellowed newspaper clippings that had borne their names ended up with other miscellaneous relics of the past in old desk drawers. This was the near-oblivion of democratic politics: ruthless, wasteful, and in the main desirable.

Thenceforward party politics pervaded American life. In 1841 a Whig administration followed Van Buren's Democratic term in office. In 1845 the Democrats returned to power with James K. Polk. In 1849 Zachary Taylor brought victory for the Whigs. In 1853 the Democrats once more celebrated a presidential inauguration—that of Franklin Pierce. The rapid alternations created an irresistibly congenial climate for the spoils system. It spread so far and so fast that every four years thousands of new faces were brought into the post offices, custom houses, and bureaus of the land, while the demand for places seemed always to outrun supply. In ceasing to be regarded as private property (if they had been so considered), the offices rotated in the whirligig of fortune had apparently become party property. The process affected an astonishing number of citizens, from the impecunious to the thrivingly ambitious.

The writer Nathaniel Hawthorne is an example of one of the impecunious, thrust in and out of office with dazing rapidity. Hawthorne was a Democrat and a fellow classmate at Bowdoin College of Franklin Pierce's. Pierce, a rising New Hampshire politician, helped him to secure a post in the Boston Custom House during Van Buren's administration. Harrison's victory left him unemployed. In came Polk; and presently Hawthorne was again a federal officeholder, this time as surveyor of the port of Salem, Massachusetts. His removal in 1849, after Taylor's election, aroused some local protest, but he was still removed: a humiliation he described feelingly in the preface to *The Scarlet Letter*. Hawthorne then wrote busily to replace his lost income. Among his literary products was a dutifully eulogistic campaign biography of Pierce, which was published during the election year 1852. Pierce's success brought a reward for Hawthorne—as for thousands of deserving Democrats—in the shape of a consulship at Liverpool.

The most exasperating consequence of the identification of politics with the Presidency was experienced by the Presidents themselves. Filling posts in their administration had always been a delicate and sometimes a burdensome responsibility. It became a nightmare. After Harrison's inauguration the White House was surrounded and invaded by a frantic crowd of office seekers. The President, trying to hold a Cabinet meeting, could not find a vacant room. He could not persuade the throng to leave him alone; they insisted that he receive their mass of papers on the spot and made him promise to attend to them. In desperation he agreed.

Polk, who augmented his difficulties through a fiercely partisan interpretation of his duties, came to loathe a process of which he theoretically approved. The pages of his diary are full of self-pity. In March, 1846, he wrote, "I am ready to exclaim, will the pressure . . . never cease! It is one year today since I entered . . . office, and still the pressure for office has not abated." Two and a half years later he was just as exasperated: "The office of President is generally esteemed a very high and dignified position . . . I think the public would not so regard it if they could . . . observe the kind of people by whom I

am often annoyed. I . . . must be accessible to my fellow-citizens, and this gives an opportunity to all . . . descriptions of people to obtrude themselves upon me. . . . There is no class of our population by whom I am annoyed so much, or for whom I entertain a more sovereign contempt, than for the professed office-seekers who have besieged me ever since I have been in the Presidential office."

In fact Polk more than once recorded the view that no President would ever again be re-elected. "The number of office seekers has become so large," he said in January, 1847, "that they probably hold the balance of power between the two great parties in the country, and if disappointed . . . under one administration they will readily unite themselves with the party and candidate of opposite politics . . . to increase their chances for place." In short, "the patronage of the Government will destroy the popularity of any President, however well he may administer the Government." The paradox was alarming: the absence of a vigorous party competition rendered the President powerless, but party competition, carried to its logical conclusion in the spoils system, had the same effect.

Polk was unduly despondent. Later Presidents learned to tolerate the system as an inevitable fea-

The Whig cartoon above, drawn during the 1852 campaign, shows General Winfield Scott pulling the President's chair away from Democrat Franklin Pierce, who says, "Look out. . . . Do you want to knock a feller's brains out?" But Pierce won the election.

ture of the office. Even Zachary Taylor, who had had forty years of continuous military service before reaching the Presidency, absorbed the notion from the American air he breathed. At the outset of his administration he assured Thurlow Weed that he did not intend to kick away the party ladder by which he had ascended—"colonels, majors, captains, lieutenants, sergeants, and corporals," he said, "are just as necessary to success in politics as they are to the discipline and efficiency of an army." Despite this robust attitude, Taylor no more learned to enjoy the pressure than did other Presidents. A caller at the White House early in Taylor's term found that sixty or seventy persons were ahead of him. The majority had come on harmless if tedious ceremonial errands; but there were "knots [of anxious supplicants] gathered in corners." In the argument over ratifying the 1787 Constitution, George Clinton had once predicted that the President would be "surrounded with expectants and courtiers." He had been right, except that the former far outnumbered the latter.

The only reasonable compromise open to Presidents was to tackle the unsavory task with dispatch and humor (with the consoling knowledge that some of the "career" federal bureaus were immune to recurrent evictions), and to avoid becoming unnecessarily embroiled. A delightful dead-pan note from President Lincoln illustrates the secret amusement to be extracted from a wretched business. It is an answer to one of thousands of people who pestered him for jobs: "My dear Madam, The most I can say is that when the time comes, if it be made to appear that the appointment of your friend to the Post-Office at Oskaloosa, will be as satisfactory to the people there, as would be that of any other person, he will probably receive it; otherwise not."

At the other extreme was the conduct of Lincoln's predecessor James Buchanan. Buchanan, who had been in politics as long as Taylor had been in the Army, tried to carry the rotation principle beyond the permissible limit. He offended party ethics by maintaining that although he was a Democrat who followed another Democrat, his administration was nevertheless new and ought to be given a free hand in removals and appointments. Even the spoilsmen objected to such a proposition. And Buchanan offended presidential ethics by urging federal appointees to secure his renomination in 1860. His attempt failed: again he had gone too far.

It is not surprising that civil service reform became an almost obsessive concern of righteous Americans in the generation after the Civil War. As Polk had suggested, the spoils system not only took too much of the President's time, it had a dangerous tendency to demean the executive office and to reintroduce an element of faction that often set the President at odds with members of his party in and out of Congress. When scholars discussed the history of the Jacksonian Era during the next three quarters of a century, few gave high marks to the People's President. Moisei Y. Ostrogorski, William Graham Sumner, and others blamed him for setting in motion the disastrous deterioration of American governmental service. They were too hard on him as a person, and not sympathetic enough to the conundrum of how to make government both popular and elevated. But they were justified in expressing disquiet. The ideology of democracy sounded perilously close to hypocrisy.

Other political aspects of the Presidency deserve discussion. One problem was the choice of an appropriate candidate. Most of the men who nursed presidential ambitions were politicians whose labors in the party cause entitled them to expect consideration. Yet the Presidency had an aura of remoteness, of symbolic majesty. Politicians were men who rolled up their sleeves and got their hands dirty. If they were suave, like Van Buren, they incurred suspicion as trimmers, artful dodgers, men without principle. In Calhoun's view, Van Buren was not "of the race of the lion or of the tiger; he belonged to a lower order—the fox." But politicians such as Calhoun were not foxy enough; their tigerish assertions of principle made them unacceptable. They were not "available." Out of expediency and out of some more elevated desire, the search was for candidates who were both "available" in the sense of not having made enemies and were also distinguished in some national sphere. The President was to be in and yet not of the political scene. He was to be introduced to it, not—if possible—spawned by it. Hence the attractiveness of military heroes: Washington, Jackson, Harrison, Taylor, Winfield Scott. Available soldiers had also to be civilian enough in outlook to refute the charge that they were fond of military despotism, standing armies, and social hierarchies. The professional politicians of the pre-Civil War decades might have felt frustrated if the stock of suitable military candidates had been abundant enough to fill the office in continuous succession. They could take heart from the defeat of General Scott at the hands of Brigadier General Pierce, who was more of a politico than a warrior. Like Pierce, however, they were quick to see the advantages of a military reputation. When a war came, ambition as well as patriotism set them scrambling for commissions.

In the Mexican War, James K. Polk probably played politics too hard. His dilemma was ironical. As President of the United States, he wished to defeat Mexico. As head of the Democratic party, he wished to secure the credit for victory to his own chosen people. He did his best by appointing Democrats to nearly all the new openings for brigadier and major generals. He was prepared to let a reasonable number of junior commissions go to the Whigs, but he found the congressional Democrats unwilling to yield the point and did not press it unduly. The great problem was that the Army's two most senior active generals, Taylor and Scott, were both Whigs. He did not think highly of them as soldiers; he detested them as Whigs. If they were permitted to win resounding victories, Polk would be presenting the rival party with a ready-made presidential candidate, perhaps two. If he withheld supplies and men he would be behaving despicably—and the disgrace might well rebound on the Democrats. The only solution, which he adopted with some eagerness, was to put a Democratic general in supreme command. The suggested person was Senator Thomas Hart Benton of Missouri, who had seen brief service in the War of 1812. But if Benton were made senior to Scott and Taylor he would have to be given the then nonexistent rank of lieutenant general. The preposterous plan was submitted to Congress and rejected only through strenuous Whig efforts. Polk, chagrined and tormented, had to watch the two Whig generals bring the war to a triumphant close. As he had feared, one of them—Taylor—received the Whig presidential nomination in 1848. (Four years later, Scott was the Whig nominee.) Polk vented his frustration in his diary, denouncing Taylor and Scott as unscrupulous politicians. When news of each victorious battle reached him, he merely complained that he ought to have been notified more promptly. He developed the peevish theory that generals did not win battles and ought not to be lauded; the real heroes, President Polk said, were the volunteer soldiers, most of whom happened to be Democrats.

Polk allowed political feelings to warp his judgment. What of Lincoln in the Civil War? He had the stigma of being a professional politician of unheroic antecedents; and, of course, he was a minority President, the nominee of a newly formed party. Most of the prominent Republicans distrusted or even despised him. Yet, according to David Donald, Lincoln showed superb political skill in controlling his party, in securing renomination when no one seemed enthusiastic for him, and in winning re-election—the first President since Jackson to accomplish the feat. Some historians would not lay so much stress on Lincoln's political sophistication. But David Donald is surely right to emphasize Lincoln's canniness, his ability to play hostile factions against one another, his adroitness in avoiding controversial statements of policy, and his Buchanan-like manipulation of patronage to turn votes his way. Unlike Buchanan, Lincoln succeeded in his maneuver.

Lincoln played the political game with shrewdness but without pettiness or rancor. He had the sagacity to convert his weakness into a kind of strength by establishing himself at the head of a coalition government. In 1864 he spoke of himself not as the Republican but as the National Union party nominee, and underlined the notion by welcoming the nomination of Andrew Johnson of Tennessee, a Union Democrat, as his running mate. He was not repudiating the idea of political parties, as Monroe and John Quincy Adams had misguidedly done. Rather, he was seeking to pull into his orbit everyone who would give him support—and perhaps eventually a vote. His relations with Congress were sometimes strained, however; he was not a President on the Jefferson model, hand and glove with the legislative branch.

The pros and cons of Lincoln's political strategy could be debated indefinitely. So could the advantages and disadvantages of an evolution that through the decades brought the Presidency into the arena of party politics. It might be argued that the process was one of deterioration. The best answer is that if the political hurly-burly could produce a Lincoln for President, and if he could so skillfully deploy his political experience without surrendering any of the essential grandeur of the executive office, then the history of the Presidency up to 1865 was on the whole a history not of decline but of successful adaptation.

bruary 13°
1793

165.

*Whereupon the Vice President de-
clared—*

*George Washington, unani-
mously elected President of the United
States for the period of four years, to com-
-mence with the 4th day of March next, ♦
and—*

*John Adams, elected by a plu-
rality of votes Vice President of the United States, for the same period, to commence with the 4th day of March next:*

*After which, the Vice President de-
livered the duplicate certificates of the
electors of the several States, received by
post, together with those which came
by express, to the Secretary of the Senate.*

The two Houses having separated—

On motion,

*The Senate adjourned to 11 o'clock to-
morrow morning.*

1789 - 1848
The Presidency in Documents

*The page above from the Senate Journal of 1793 records the formal an-
nouncement of George Washington's second unanimous election to the
Chief Magistracy. The one hundred and thirty-two electors had all
named him as one of their two choices. The Antifederalists had contested
second place by giving 50 votes to George Clinton. But John Adams
was named on seventy-seven ballots and was re-elected Vice President.*

Federalism

Commencing the operations of a new government was a complex and perilous task involving a host of questions. In what manner should a Chief Executive conduct his business with the Senate? How much initiative should he take in foreign affairs or in dealing with rebellion and antigovernment propaganda? Should changes be made in the rules for presidential elections? In many cases these answers came only through trial and error.

Seeking Consent

The Constitution directed that the President conclude treaties with the "Advice and Consent" of the Senate. Washington therefore appeared in the Senate chamber on August 22, 1789, to ask for advice on, and consent to, a treaty with the Cherokee Indians. Senator William Maclay, an outspoken, often caustic republican from Pennsylvania, recorded the event in his daily journal.

. . . The doorkeeper soon told us of the arrival of the President. The President was introduced, and took our Vice-President's chair. He rose and told us bluntly that he had called on us for our advice and consent to some propositions respecting the treaty to be held with the Southern Indians. Said he had brought General Knox [Henry Knox, Secretary of War] with him, who was well acquainted with the business. . . . General Knox handed him a paper, which he handed to the President of the Senate, who was seated on a chair on the floor to his right. Our Vice-President hurried over the paper. Carriages were driving past, and such a noise, I could tell it was something about "Indians," but was not master of one sentence of it. Signs were made to the doorkeeper to shut down the sashes. . . .

The President told us that a paper from an agent of the Cherokees was given to him just as he was coming to the Hall. He motioned to General Knox for it, and handed it to the President of the Senate. It was read. It complained hard of the unjust treatment of the people of North Carolina, etc., their violation of treaties, etc. Our Vice-President now read off the first article, to which our advice and con-

sent were requested. It referred back principally to some statements in the body of the writing which had been read.

Mr. Morris [Robert Morris of Pennsylvania] rose. Said the noise of carriages had been so great that he really could not say that he had heard the body of the paper which had been read, and prayed that it might be read again. . . . It was no sooner read than our Vice-President immediately read the first head over again, and put the question: Do you advise and consent, etc.? There was a dead pause. Mr. Morris whispered me, "We will see who will venture to break silence first." Our Vice-President was proceeding, "As many as—"

I rose reluctantly, indeed, and, from the length of the pause, the hint given by Mr. Morris, and the proceeding of our Vice-President, it appeared to me that if I did not no other one would, and we should have these advices and consents ravished, in a degree, from us.

Mr. President: The paper which you have now read to us appears to have for its basis sundry treaties and public transactions between the Southern Indians and the United States and the States of Georgia, North Carolina, and South Carolina. The business is new to the Senate. It is of importance. It is our duty to inform ourselves as well as possible on the subject. I therefore call for the reading of the . . . documents alluded to in the paper before us.

I cast an eye at the President of the United States. I saw he wore an aspect of stern displeasure. . . .

I had at an early stage of the business whispered Mr. Morris that I thought the best way to conduct the business was to have all the papers committed. My reasons were, that I saw no chance of a fair investigation of subjects while the President of the United States sat there, with his Secretary of War, to support his opinions and overawe the timid and neutral part of the Senate. Mr. Morris hastily rose and moved that the papers communicated to the Senate by the President of the United States should be referred to a committee of five, to report as soon as might be on them. He was seconded by Mr. Gunn [James Gunn of Georgia]. Several members grumbled some objections. Mr. Butler [South Carolina's Pierce Butler] rose; made a lengthy speech against commitment. . . .

I rose and supported the mode of doing business by committees; that committees were used in all public deliberative bodies, etc. I thought I did the subject justice, but concluded the commitment can not be attended with any possible inconvenience. Some articles are already postponed until Monday. Whoever the committee are, if committed, they must make their report on Monday morning. I spoke through the whole in a low tone of voice. Peevishness itself, I think, could not have taken offense at anything I said.

As I sat down, the President of the United States started up in a violent fret. *"This defeats every purpose of my coming here,"* were the first words that he said. He then went on that he had brought his Secretary of War with him to give every necessary information; that the Secretary knew all about the business, and yet he was delayed and could not go on with the matter. He cooled, however, by degrees. Said he had no objection to putting off this matter until Monday, but declared he did not understand the matter of commitment. He might be delayed; he could not tell how long. He rose a second time, and said he had no objection to postponement until Monday at ten o'clock. By the looks of the Senate this seemed agreed to. A pause for some time ensued. We waited for him to withdraw. He did so with a discontented air. Had it been any other man than the man whom I wish to regard as the first character in the world, I would have said, with sullen dignity.

I can not now be mistaken. The President wishes to tread on the necks of the Senate. Commitment will bring the matter to discussion, at least in the committee, where he is not present. He wishes us to see with the eyes and hear with the ears of his Secretary only. The Secretary to advance the premises, the President to draw the conclusions, and to bear down our deliberations with his personal authority and presence. Form only will be left to us. This will not do with Americans. But let the matter work; it will soon cure itself.

Neutrality by Proclamation

Maclay and Morris had helped to prevent the Senate from becoming, as some had feared, largely a council to the President rather than an independent branch of the legislature. Continuing to establish and test the boundaries of his office, President Washington on April 22, *1793, issued a proclamation of neutrality, an act that Antifederalists regarded as presidential usurpation of the congressional power to declare war and make peace.*

Whereas it appears that a state of war exists between Austria, Prussia, Sardinia, Great Britain and the United Netherlands on the one part, and France on the other, and the duty and interest of the United States require that they should with sincerity and good faith adopt and pursue a conduct friendly and impartial toward the belligerent Powers:

I have therefore thought fit by these presents to declare the disposition of the United States to observe the conduct aforesaid toward those Powers respectively; and to exhort and warn the citizens of the United States carefully to avoid all acts and proceedings whatsoever which may in any manner tend to contravene such disposition.

And I do hereby also make known, that whosoever of the citizens of the United States shall render himself liable to punishment or forfeiture under the law of nations by committing, aiding or abetting hostilities against any of the said Powers, or by carrying to any of them those articles which are deemed contraband by the *modern* usage of nations, will not receive the protection of the United States against such punishment or forfeiture; and further, that I have given instructions to those officers to whom it belongs to cause prosecutions to be instituted against all persons who shall, within the cognizance of the Courts of the United States, violate the law of nations with respect to the Powers at war or any of them.

Laws Faithfully Executed

During the antitax Whisky Rebellion of 1794, Washington asserted the new federal government's power to enforce its statutes—with troops, if necessary. The following excerpt is from his proclamation of September 25.

Whereas, from a hope that the combinations against the Constitution and laws of the United States, in certain of the Western counties of Pennsylvania, would yield to time and reflection, I thought it sufficient, in the first instance, rather to take measures for calling forth the militia than immedi-

Western Pennsylvanians rebelled against a tax on whisky in 1794. Above, the rebels jeer at a federal official whom they have tarred and feathered. Washington sent troops to quell the insurrection, thus demonstrating the strength of the new government.

ately to embody them; but the moment is now come, when the overtures of forgiveness, with no other condition than a submission to law, have been only partially accepted; when every form of conciliation not inconsistent with the being of Government has been adopted, without effect . . . when it is manifest, that violence would continue to be exercised upon every attempt to enforce the laws; when, therefore, Government is set at defiance, the contest being whether a small proportion of the United States shall dictate to the whole Union, and, at the expense of those who desire peace, indulge a desperate ambition;

Now, therefore, I, GEORGE WASHINGTON, President of the United States, in obedience to that high and irresistible duty, consigned to me by the Constitution, "to take care that the laws be faithfully executed;" . . . resolved, in perfect reliance on that gracious Providence which so signally displays its goodness towards this country, to reduce the refractory to a due subordination to the laws; do hereby declare and make known, that, with a satisfaction which can be equalled only by the merits of the militia summoned into service from the States of New Jersey, Pennsylvania, Maryland, and Virginia, I have received intelligence of their patriotic alacrity, in obeying the call of the present, though painful, yet commanding necessity; that a force, which, according to every reasonable expectation, is adequate to the exigency, is already in motion to the scene of disaffection; that those who have confided or shall confide in the protection of Government, shall meet full succor under the standard and from the arms of the United States; that those who having offended against the laws have since entitled themselves to indemnity, will be treated with the most liberal good faith, if they shall not have forfeited their claim by any subsequent conduct, and that instructions are given accordingly. . . .

Adams Elected

In 1796 Alexander Hamilton connived with Federalist electors from the South in an attempt to elect to the Presidency the party's nominal choice for Vice President, forty-six-year-old Thomas Pinckney of South Carolina, instead of its presidential nominee, John Adams. As a result, Adams defeated Thomas Jefferson by only three votes, and Jefferson, a Democratic-Republican, became Vice President. Because relations with France were strained at the time and because Jefferson was greatly respected in France, it was suggested that the new administration send him there as special ambassador. In a letter to Henry Knox on March 30, 1797, President Adams discussed the election and the proposal.

. . . It is a delicate thing for me to speak of the late election. To myself, personally, "my election" might be a matter of indifference or rather of aversion. Had Mr. Jay [John Jay of New York], or some others, been in question, it might have less mortified my vanity, and infinitely less alarmed my apprehensions for the public. But to see such a character as Jefferson, and much more such an unknown being as Pinckney, brought over my head, and trampling on the bellies of hundreds of other men infinitely his superiors in talents, services, and reputation, filled me with apprehensions for the safety of us all. It demonstrated to me that, if the project succeeded,

our Constitution could not have lasted four years. . . .
That must be a sordid people, indeed—a people destitute of a sense of honor, equity, and character, that could submit to be governed, and see hundreds of its most meritorious public men governed, by a Pinckney, under an elective government. Hereditary government, when it imposes young, new, inexperienced men upon the public, has its compensations and equivalent, but elective government has none. . . .

Your project has been long ago considered and determined on. Mr. Jefferson would not go. His reasons are obvious; he has a station assigned him by the nation, which he has no right to quit, nor have I any right, perhaps, to call him from it. . . . The circumstance of rank is too much. We shall never be respected in Europe while we confound ranks in this manner. In their eyes, the chief justice [Jay] was too much to send to England. . . .

If we wish not to be degraded in the eyes of foreigners, we must not degrade ourselves. What would have been thought in Europe, if the King of France had sent Monsieur, his eldest brother, as an envoy? What of the King of England, if he had sent the Prince of Wales? Mr. Jefferson is, in essence, in the same situation. He is the first prince of the country, and the heir apparent to the sovereign authority, *quoad hoc.* . . .

Void, and Not Law

Alarmed and offended by scurrilous attacks in opposition newspapers, and fearful that the demagogy of visiting European republicans would propel the stripling United States into war against England on the side of France, the Federalist majority in Congress passed several laws limiting the civil rights of those who criticized the Adams administration. Vice President Thomas Jefferson urged nullification of these hated alien and sedition laws in resolutions that the Kentucky state legislature subsequently passed and circulated to the other states, including Virginia. The following selection is from the Kentucky Resolutions of November 16, 1798.

VI. RESOLVED, That the imprisonment of a person under the protection of the laws of this Commonwealth on his failure to obey the simple order of the President, to depart out of the United States, as is

undertaken by the said act entitled, "An act concerning aliens," is contrary to the Constitution, one amendment in which has provided, that "no person shall be deprived of liberty without due process of law," and, that another having provided, "that in all criminal prosecutions, the accused shall enjoy the right to a public trial by an impartial jury, to be informed as to the nature and cause of the accusation, to be confronted with the witnesses against him, to have compulsory process for obtaining witnesses in his favor, and to have assistance of counsel for his defence," the same act undertaking to authorise the President to remove a person out of the United States who is under the protection of the law, on his own suspicion, without jury, without public trial; without confrontation of the witnesses against him, without having witnesses in his favor, without defence, without counsel, is contrary to these provisions also of the Constitution, is therefore NOT LAW, but utterly VOID and OF NO FORCE. . . .

The Electoral System

If the Electoral College voting proved inconclusive, the Constitution said, the House of Representatives was to choose a President from the leading candidates "immediately" after the ballots had been opened and tabulated. On March 28, 1800, Senator Charles Pinckney of South Carolina, who had been a delegate to the Constitutional Convention, explained the Founders' intent.

. . . The best and most generally admired expounders of the English language, give this explanation of the word *immediately;* they say it means "instantly" —at the present time—without delay. This is the meaning the framers of the Constitution intended to give it, and it admits of no other. The plain, express, literal direction of that instrument therefore is, that in case of no election, the House of Representatives, voting by States, are *immediately,* that is instantly, and on the spot, without leaving the House in which they are then assembled, and without adjournment, to choose, out of the five highest candidates that have been voted for by the Electors, the one who is to be the Executive. . . .

. . . The Constitution directs that the Electors shall vote *by ballot,* and seal up and transmit their votes to the President of the Senate. It is expected and required by the Constitution, that the votes shall be secret and unknown, until opened in the presence of both Houses. To suffer them to be known, as heretofore, has been the practice, is unconstitutional and dangerous, and goes to defeat in some measure, the wise provisions of that instrument, in declaring, that when the House of Representatives are to elect, that it shall be done immediately. The Electors, therefore, ought never to divulge their votes. . . .

It is to be remembered, that around the seat of Congress will be placed all the open and accredited Ministers, as well as secret emissaries, of foreign Powers. Here too will be assembled the concealed leaders of domestic faction; all the arts and intrigues that have been used in Elective Governments in the Old World, will soon find their way among us; and if the Electors do not conceal their votes until the day appointed by law for opening them, and in case of no election by them, an immediate one by the House of Representatives does not take place, we shall soon have the scenes of Polish Diets and elections re-acted here, and in not many years the fate of Poland may be that of United America.

Wisely foreseeing this, the Constitution expressly orders that the Electors shall vote by ballot; and we all know, that to vote by ballot is to vote secretly; that the votes shall be sealed up, and not opened until the day appointed by law, and that if no election has been made by the Electors, an immediate one shall take place by the House of Representatives; that so far from appointing committees to receive memorials or petitions respecting the election, or decide upon it, or so far from having any right to delegate an authority on this subject, that Congress shall not themselves, even when in convention, have the smallest power to decide on a single vote; that they shall not have authority to adjourn for one moment, but shall instantly and on the spot, in case of no election by the Electors, proceed to the choice of a President, and not separate until it is determined.

Pinckney's words had no effect when the 1800 election produced a tie between Republicans Thomas Jefferson and Aaron Burr. Desperate to preserve control of the government, the Federalists tried to bargain with Burr, who was reputed to be more ambitious than statesmanlike. Historians believe that Burr was willing to be

chosen over the intended President, but the hardheaded Federalist from Delaware, James Bayard, told a quite different story in a letter to Hamilton on March 8, 1801.

. . . In one case I was willing to take Burr, but I never considered it as a case likely to happen. If by his conduct he had completely forfeited the confidence and friendship of his party, and left himself no resort but the support of the Federalists, there are many considerations which would have induced me to prefer him to Jefferson. But I was enabled soon to discover that he was determined not to shackle himself with Federal principles. . . .

. . . When the experiment was fully made, and acknowledged upon all hands to have completely ascertained that Burr was resolved not to commit himself, and that nothing remained but to appoint a President by law, or leave the government without one, I came out with the most explicit and determined declaration of voting for Jefferson. You can not well imagine the clamor and vehement invective to which I was subjected for some days. We had several caucuses. All acknowledged that nothing but desperate measures remained, which several were disposed to adopt, and but few were willing openly to disapprove. We broke up each time in confusion and discord, and the manner of the last ballot was arranged but a few minutes before the ballot was given. . . .

The means existed of electing Burr, but this required his coöperation. By deceiving one man (a great blockhead), and tempting two (not incorruptible), he might have secured a majority of the States. He will never have another chance of being President of the United States; and the little use he has made of the one which has occurred, gives me but an humble opinion of the talents of an unprincipled man.

Several attempts had already been made to pass a constitutional amendment requiring electors to designate which candidate they wanted for President and which for Vice President. The nearly disastrous election of 1800 induced the Republicans to advocate the change. When an amendment was voted on by the Senate in 1802, it was defeated by a single nay. New York's Gouverneur Morris had cast one of the nays, and in a letter to the president of the New York senate he defended his vote by explaining what the framers had had in mind when they had chosen not to demand such a specification.

Thomas Jefferson

John Adams

Aaron Burr

When this article was under consideration in the National Convention it was observed, that every mode of electing the chief magistrate of a powerful nation hitherto adopted is liable to objection. . . .

The evils, which have been felt in the present mode of election, were pointed out to the Convention; but, after due advisement, the other mode appeared more exceptionable. Indeed, if the present be changed, it might be better to abolish the office of Vice President, and leave to legislative provision the case of a vacancy in the seat of the first magistrate.

The Convention was aware, that every species of trick and contrivance would be practised by the ambitious and unprincipled. It was, therefore, conceived, that if in elections the President and Vice President were distinctly designated, there would generally be a vote given for one of only two rival Presidents, while there would be numerous candidates for the other office; because he, who wished to become President, would naturally connect himself with some popular man of each particular district, for the sake of his local influence, so that the Vice Presidency would be but as a bait to catch state gudgeons. The person chosen would . . . be perhaps unknown to the greater part of the community, and probably unfit for those duties, which the death of a President might call on him to perform.

The Convention not only foresaw, that a scene might take place similar to that of the last presidential election, but even supposed it not impossible, that at some time or other a person admirably fitted for the office of President might have an equal vote with one totally unqualified, and that, by the pre-

dominance of faction in the House of Representatives, the latter might be preferred. This, which is the greatest supposable evil of the present mode, was calmly examined, and it appeared that, however prejudicial it might be at the present moment, a useful lesson would result from it for the future, to teach contending parties the importance of giving both votes to men fit for the first office.

Convention records neither support nor deny Morris' contentions. It may well be that he reported accurately. But he was also a Federalist, and, despite its waning strength, his party hoped to be a decisive factor in the election of 1804. If the system were not changed, the Republicans might try to avoid a repetition of the 1800–1801 election by giving their second choice a few less votes than their first, and the Federalists might therefore elect one of their own Vice President. Or they could vote for the Republican vice presidential candidate, to make him President. The Federalists therefore opposed changing the system. But in 1802 their contingent in Congress was reduced, permitting passage of the Twelfth Amendment, which was ratified on September 25, 1804.

The Electors shall meet in their respective states, and vote by ballot for President and Vice-President, one of whom, at least, shall not be an inhabitant of the same state with themselves; they shall name in their ballots the person voted for as President, and in distinct ballots the person voted for as Vice-President, and they shall make distinct lists of all persons voted for as President, and of all persons voted for as Vice-President, and of the number of votes for each,

119

which lists they shall sign and certify, and transmit sealed to the seat of the government of the United States, directed to the President of the Senate;—The President of the Senate shall, in the presence of the Senate and House of Representatives, open all the certificates and the votes shall then be counted;— The person having the greatest number of votes for President, shall be the President, if such number be a majority of the whole number of Electors appointed; and if no person have such majority, then from the persons having the highest numbers not exceeding three on the list of those voted for as President, the House of Representatives shall choose immediately, by ballot, the President. But in choosing the President, the votes shall be taken by states, the representation from each state having one vote; a quorum for this purpose shall consist of a member or members from two-thirds of the states, and a majority of all the states shall be necessary to a choice. And if the House of Representatives shall not choose a President whenever the right of choice shall devolve upon them, before the fourth day of March next following, then the Vice-President shall act as President, as in the case of the death or other constitutional disability of the President.—The person having the greatest number of votes as Vice-President, shall be the Vice-President, if such number be a majority of the whole number of Electors appointed, and if no person have a majority, then from the two highest numbers on the list, the Senate shall choose the Vice-President; a quorum for the purpose shall consist of two-thirds of the whole number of Senators, and a majority of the whole number shall be necessary to a choice. But no person constitutionally ineligible to the office of President shall be eligible to that of Vice-President of the United States.

Virginia Dynasty

With the defeat of John Adams in 1800, Virginia, the home of republicanism, became politically dominant for twenty-four years. Three consecutive Virginian Presidents—Jefferson, Madison, and Monroe—served two terms each. In general they considered Congress the supreme branch of government, and represented the strict-constructionist school of constitutional interpretation. There were, however, several notable exceptions.

Securing a Continent

In 1803 Jefferson convinced Congress that it should appropriate two million dollars to buy the French territory at the mouth of the Mississippi. That year he also commissioned Meriwether Lewis and William Clark to make an exploratory trip up the Missouri River. Napoleon proved willing to sell not only New Orleans, but a huge area that included much of the American West; it would cost the United States a sum much larger than that originally appropriated, but Jefferson considered it a bargain. When he heard the good news from France he called Congress into session to receive, on October 17, 1803, a message urging prompt acceptance.

. . . Congress witnessed at their late session the extraordinary agitation produced in the public mind by the suspension of our right of deposit at the port of New Orleans, no assignment of another place having been made according to treaty. . . .

Previous, however, to this period we had not been unaware of the danger to which our peace would be perpetually exposed whilst so important a key to the commerce of the Western country remained under foreign power. Difficulties, too, were presenting themselves as to the navigation of other streams which, arising within our territories, pass through those adjacent. Propositions had therefore been authorized for obtaining on fair conditions the sovereignty of New Orleans and of other possessions in that quarter interesting to our quiet to such extent as was deemed practicable, and the provisional appropriation of $2,000,000 to be applied and accounted for by the President of the United States, intended as part of the price, was considered as conveying the sanction of Congress to the acquisition proposed. The enlightened Government of France saw with just discernment the importance to both nations of such liberal arrangements as might best and permanently promote the peace, friendship, and interests of both, and the property and sovereignty of all Louisiana which had been restored to them have on certain conditions been transferred to the United States by instruments bearing date the 30th of April last. When these shall have received the constitutional sanction of the Senate, they will without delay be communicated to the Representatives also for the exercise of their functions as to those conditions which are within the powers vested by the Constitution in Congress.

Whilst the property and sovereignty of the Mississippi and its waters secure an independent outlet for the produce of the Western States and an uncontrolled navigation through their whole course, free from collision with other powers and the dangers to our peace from that source, the fertility of the country, its climate and extent, promise in due season important aids to our Treasury, an ample provision for our posterity, and a wide spread for the blessings of freedom and equal laws. . . .

Should the acquisition of Louisiana be constitutionally confirmed and carried into effect, a sum of nearly $13,000,000 will then be added to our public debt, most of which is payable after fifteen years, before which term the present existing debts will all be discharged by the established operation of the sinking fund. When we contemplate the ordinary annual augmentation of impost from increasing population and wealth, the augmentation of the same revenue by its extension to the new acquisition, and the economies which may still be introduced into our public expenditures, I can not but hope that Congress in reviewing their resources will find means to meet the intermediate interest of this additional debt without recurring to new taxes, and applying to this object only the ordinary progression of our revenue. Its extraordinary increase in times of foreign war will be the proper and sufficient fund for any measures of safety or precaution which that state of things may render necessary. . . .

The Executive as Judge

Thomas Jefferson had not corresponded with John Adams for years; partisan feelings still rankled. But at the death of Jefferson's daughter, whom the Adams family had loved, Abigail Adams' reserve broke and she wrote a letter to the President. This began a brief exchange in which she and Jefferson succeeded mainly

in opening old wounds. In September, 1804, in answer to her remonstrance against his freeing persons jailed under the sedition law, President Jefferson voiced a unique attitude toward checks and balances and toward the Chief Magistracy as defender of the Constitution.

. . . You seem to think it devolved on the judges to decide on the validity of the sedition law. But nothing in the constitution has given them a right to decide for the executive, more than to the Executive to decide for them. Both magistracies are equally independant in the sphere of action assigned to them. The judges, believing the law constitutional, had a right to pass a sentence of fine and imprisonment, because that power was placed in their hands by the constitution. But the Executive, believing the law to be unconstitutional, was bound to remit the execution of it; because that power has been confided to him by the constitution. That instrument meant that it's co-ordinate branches should be checks on each other. But the opinion which gives to the judges the right to decide what laws are constitutional, and what not, not only for themselves in their own sphere of action, but for the legislature and executive also in their spheres, would make the judiciary a despotic branch. . . .

Embargo

Jefferson's response to British and French harassment of American trade during the Napoleonic Wars was to prod his majority in Congress into passing a series of embargo acts, which forbade trade with any foreign country. The program was ruinous along the seacoast, but despite the cries of "Tyrant!" Jefferson went to extreme lengths to enforce cooperation. The regular Army and Navy were used against Americans. Coastal trade was restricted arbitrarily. One presidential proclamation declared a state of insurrection around Lake Champlain, where the greatest crime was actually only smuggling. In the Senate on November 29, 1808, James Hillhouse of Connecticut remarked on that proclamation and on the hated embargo in a widely reprinted speech.

. . . The senate will recollect that the last session of congress was closed on the 25th of April; and, although the proclamation was dated the 19th of that month, no intimation thereof, or of the state of the country to which it referred, was given to congress by the president of the United States. The proclamation was published in Vermont, April 30, and in the National Intelligencer, printed at the seat of government, on the 13th of May. Here was an official document, issuing from the same high authority that recommended the embargo, declaring to the nation, and to the world, that there existed so great uneasiness and discontent on account of the embargo, as to induce the forming of unlawful combinations to resist its execution, too powerful to be suppressed by the ordinary process of law, and which required the employment of a military force. Superadd to this, that our small standing army, and the whole naval force in actual service, were put in requisition. . . .

These circumstances present a melancholy view of our situation. An *embargo* recommended under the influence of the great popularity of the president, and *professed* to be laid for preserving in safety our vessels, our seamen and merchandise, and saving the honour, and vindicating the rights of our country, had become so unpopular, before the close of the session of the congress which imposed it, that in the president's opinion, it could not be executed by the ordinary process of law, and through the mild medium of courts of justice; so that it had already become necessary to call in the aid of an armed force.

I could have hoped it would not have been found necessary to employ the American navy to cruize against our own commerce; and little did I expect that the army I had so recently voted to raise, for the purpose, as I supposed, of opposing foreign aggression, would be required to point their bayonets at the breasts of their fellow citizens.

Making War

In times of national crisis the United States has tended to look to the President rather than to Congress for leadership and initiative. On June 1, 1812, as he moved the country toward what he considered an unavoidable war, James Madison addressed to Congress a special message about the deteriorating relations with Britain.

. . . Without going back beyond the renewal in 1803 of the war in which Great Britain is engaged,

and omitting unrepaired wrongs of inferior magnitude, the conduct of her Government presents a series of acts hostile to the United States as an independent and neutral nation.

British cruisers have been in the continued practice of violating the American flag on the great highway of nations, and of seizing and carrying off persons sailing under it, not in the exercise of a belligerent right founded on the law of nations against an enemy, but of a municipal prerogative over British subjects. . . .

The practice, hence, is so far from affecting British subjects alone that, under the pretext of searching for these, thousands of American citizens, under the safeguard of public law and of their national flag, have been torn from their country and from everything dear to them; have been dragged on board ships of war of a foreign nation and exposed, under the severities of their discipline, to be exiled to the most distant and deadly climes, to risk their lives in the battles of their oppressors, and to be the melancholy instruments of taking away those of their own brethren.

Against this crying enormity, which Great Britain would be so prompt to avenge if committed against herself, the United States have in vain exhausted remonstrances and expostulations, and that no proof might be wanting of their conciliatory dispositions, and no pretext left for a continuance of the practice, the British Government was formally assured of the readiness of the United States to enter into arrangements such as could not be rejected if the recovery of British subjects were the real and the sole object. The communication passed without effect.

British cruisers have been in the practice also of violating the rights and the peace of our coasts. They hover over and harass our entering and departing commerce. To the most insulting pretensions they have added the most lawless proceedings in our very harbors, and have wantonly spilt American blood within the sanctuary of our territorial jurisdiction. . . .

Under pretended blockades, without the presence of an adequate force and sometimes without the practicability of applying one, our commerce has been plundered in every sea, the great staples of our country have been cut off from their legitimate markets, and a destructive blow aimed at our agricultural and maritime interests. . . .

Not content with these occasional expedients for

laying waste our neutral trade, the cabinet of Britain resorted at length to the sweeping system of blockades, under the name of orders in council. . . .

In reviewing the conduct of Great Britain toward the United States our attention is necessarily drawn to the warfare just renewed by the savages on one of our extensive frontiers—a warfare which is known to spare neither age nor sex and to be distinguished by features peculiarly shocking to humanity. It is difficult to account for the activity and combinations which have for some time been developing themselves among tribes in constant intercourse with British traders and garrisons without connecting their hostility with that influence and without recollecting the authenticated examples of such interpositions heretofore furnished by the officers and agents of that Government.

Such is the spectacle of injuries and indignities which have been heaped on our country, and such the crisis which its unexampled forbearance and conciliatory efforts have not been able to avert. . . .

We behold, in fine, on the side of Great Britain a state of war against the United States, and on the side of the United States a state of peace toward Great Britain.

Whether the United States shall continue passive under these progressive usurpations and these accumulating wrongs, or, opposing force to force in defense of their national rights, shall commit a just cause into the hands of the Almighty Disposer of Events, avoiding all connections which might entangle it in the contest or views of other powers, and preserving a constant readiness to concur in an hon-

orable reestablishment of peace and friendship, is a solemn question which the Constitution wisely confides to the legislative department of the Government. In recommending it to their early deliberations I am happy in the assurance that the decision will be worthy the enlightened and patriotic councils of a virtuous, a free, and a powerful nation. . . .

As Madison indicated to Congress, a threat to national security was rising in the West, where the Shawnee chief, Tecumseh, was trying to organize the Indian nations to resist the white man's encroachment on Indian lands. The Madison administration was convinced that the Indian movement was due not to American casualness about observing treaties with the Indians, but to agitation by the British. Modern scholarship has disproved this assertion. Once war had been declared, however, Tecumseh—who was later killed by United States forces at the Battle of the Thames—did join the British. Madison's message to an Indian delegation, below, was an attempt to neutralize and pacify the tribes. The "eighteen fires" that he mentioned were the states of the Union; the "one little fire" was Canada; and Malden, near the city of Detroit, was Britain's border outpost.

MY RED CHILDREN,— You have come through a long path to see your father, but it is a straight and a clean path, kept open for my red children who hate crooked walks. I thank the Great Spirit that he has brought you in health through the long journey, and that he gives us a clear sky and a bright sun for our meeting. I had heard from General Clarke [William Clark, governor of Missouri Territory], of the

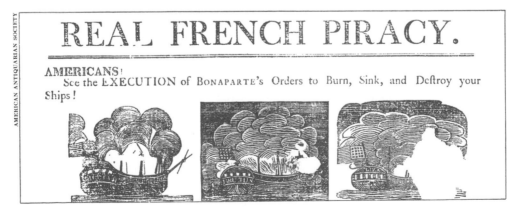

This broadside, distributed by Boston Federalists in 1808, was designed to convince Massachusetts voters that the French, not the British, were the real enemy of the United States.

good dispositions of several of the Nations on and West of the Mississippi, and that they shut their ears to the bad birds hovering about them for some time past. This made me wish to see the principal chiefs of those bands. I love to shake hands with hearts in them. . . .

A father ought to give good advice to his children, and it is the duty of his children to hearken to it. The people composing the 18 fires are a great people. You have travelled through their Country. You see they cover the land as the stars fill the sky, and are thick as the trees in your forests. Notwithstanding their great power, the British King has attacked them on the great water beyond which he lives. He robbed their ships, and carried away the people belonging to them. Some of them he murdered. He has an old grudge against the 18 fires, because, when he tried to make them dig and plant for his people beyond the great water, not for themselves, they sent out warriors who beat his warriors; they drove off the bad chiefs he had sent among them, and set up good chiefs of their own. The 18 fires did this when they had not the strength they now have. Their blows will now be much heavier, and will soon make him do them justice. It happened when the 13 fires, now increased to 18, forced the British King to treat them as an independent nation, one little fire did not join them. This he has held ever since. It is there that his agents and traders plot quarrels and wars between the 18 fires and their red brethren, and between one red tribe and another. Malden is the place where all the bad birds have their nests. There they are fed with false tales against the 18 fires, and sent out with bloody belts in their bills to drop among the red people, who would otherwise remain at peace. It is for the good of all the red people, as well as the people of the 18 fires, that a stop should be put to this mischief. Their warriors can do it. They are gone and going to Canada for this purpose. They want no help from their red brethren. They are strong enough without it. The British, who are weak, are doing all they can by their bad birds to decoy the red people into the war on their side. I warn all the red people to avoid the ruin this must bring upon them. And I say to you, my children, your father does not ask you to join his warriors. Sit still on your seats, and be witnesses that they are able to beat their enemies and protect their red friends. This is the fatherly advice I give you. . . .

President James Monroe

A Reluctant Veto

In the Jeffersonian view, any enlargement of federal responsibility through an implied powers interpretation of the Constitution would open the door to all sorts of federal interference in local matters. James Monroe's veto of the Cumberland Road bill on May 4, 1822, was based on that idea. The road then extended from Cumberland, in Maryland, to Wheeling, on the Ohio River.

Having duly considered the bill entitled "An act for the preservation and repair of the Cumberland road," it is with deep regret, approving as I do the policy, that I am compelled to object to its passage and to return the bill to the House of Representatives, in which it originated, under a conviction that Congress do not possess the power under the Constitution to pass such a law.

A power to establish turnpikes with gates and tolls, and to enforce the collection of tolls by penalties, implies a power to adopt and execute a complete system of internal improvement. A right to impose duties to be paid by all persons passing a certain road, and on horses and carriages, as is done by this bill, involves the right to take the land from the proprietor on a valuation and to pass laws for the protection of the road from injuries, and if it exist as to one road it exists as to any other, and to as many roads as Congress may think proper to establish. A right to legislate for one of these purposes is a right to legislate for the others. It is a complete right of jurisdiction and sovereignty for all the purposes of internal improvement, and not merely the right of applying money under the power vested in Congress to make appropriations, under which power, with the consent of the States through which this road passes, the work was originally commenced, and has been so far executed. I am of opinion that Congress do not possess this power; that the States individually can not grant it, for although they may assent to the appropriation of money within their limits for such purposes, they can grant no power of jurisdiction or sovereignty by special compacts with the United States. This power can be granted only by an amendment to the Constitution and in the mode prescribed by it.

If the power exist, it must be either because it has been specifically granted to the United States or that it is incidental to some power which has been specifically granted. If we examine the specific grants of power we do not find it among them, nor is it incidental to any power which has been specifically granted.

It has never been contended that the power was specifically granted. It is claimed only as being incidental to some one or more of the powers which are specifically granted. The following are the powers from which it is said to be derived:

First, from the right to establish post-offices and post-roads; second, from the right to declare war; third, to regulate commerce; fourth, to pay the debts and provide for the common defense and general welfare; fifth, from the power to make all laws necessary and proper for carrying into execution all the powers vested by the Constitution in the Government of the United States or in any department or officer thereof; sixth and lastly, from the power to dispose of and make all needful rules and regulations respecting the territory and other property of the United States.

According to my judgment it can not be derived from either of those powers, nor from all of them united, and in consequence it does not exist. . . .

Monroe Doctrine

The Monroe Doctrine, stated in Monroe's seventh annual address to Congress, on December 2, 1823, expressed the national desire to be let alone by quarrelsome Europe and also an intent to dominate the hemisphere.

. . . At the proposal of the Russian Imperial Government, made through the minister of the Emperor residing here, a full power and instructions have been transmitted to the minister of the United States at St. Petersburg to arrange by amicable negotiation the respective rights and interests of the two nations on the northwest coast of this continent. A similar proposal had been made by His Imperial Majesty to the Government of Great Britain, which has likewise been acceded to. . . . the occasion has been judged proper for asserting, as a principle in which the rights and interests of the United States are involved, that the American continents, by the free and independent condition which they have assumed and maintain, are henceforth not to be considered as subjects for future colonization by any European powers. . . .

It was stated at the commencement of the last session that a great effort was then making in Spain and Portugal to improve the condition of the people of those countries, and that it appeared to be conducted with extraordinary moderation. It need scarcely be remarked that the result has been so far very different from what was then anticipated. Of events in that quarter of the globe, with which we have so much intercourse and from which we derive our origin, we have always been anxious and interested spectators. The citizens of the United States cherish sentiments the most friendly in favor of the liberty and happiness of their fellow-men on that side of the Atlantic. In the wars of the European powers in matters relating to themselves we have never taken any part, nor does it comport with our policy so to do. It is only when our rights are invaded or seriously menaced that we resent injuries or make preparation for our defense. With the movements in this hemisphere we are . . . more immediately connected, and by causes which must be obvious to all enlightened and impartial observers. . . . We owe it, therefore, to candor and to the amicable relations existing between the United States and those powers to declare that we should consider any attempt on their part to extend their system to any portion of this hemisphere as dangerous to our peace and safety. With the existing colonies or dependencies of any European power we have not interfered and shall not interfere. But with the Governments who have declared their independence and maintained it, and whose independence we have, on great consideration and on just principles, acknowledged, we could not view any interposition for the purpose of oppressing them, or controlling in any other manner their destiny, by any European power in any other light than as the manifestation of an unfriendly disposition toward the United States. In the war between those new Governments and Spain we declared our neutrality at the time of their recognition, and to this we have adhered, and shall continue to adhere, provided no change shall occur which . . . shall make a corresponding change on the part of the United States indispensable to their security. . . .

The New Politics

The Virginia dynasty ended with Monroe, and a new era in presidential elections began in 1824. As there was no heir apparent, the White House was within the reach of five Republicans. The ensuing scramble was marked by the deals and trades and tasteless contentiousness that were to become an essential part of national campaigns. The race ended in the House of Representatives, where John Quincy Adams, second to Andrew Jackson in electoral voting, was made President by the votes of Henry Clay, who had been fourth. Adams showed poor judgment by promptly naming Clay Secretary of State, a move that reinforced the character of the new politics and helped make his Presidency difficult and frustrating.

Internal Improvements

John Quincy Adams' vision of American greatness was linked to national projects that Jeffersonians thought unconstitutional. In his annual address on December

6, 1825, Adams suggested various federal aid programs, and advocated federal sponsorship of a national university, an observatory, canals, roads, and explorations.

. . . The great object of the institution of civil government is the improvement of the condition of those who are parties to the social compact, and no government, in whatever form constituted, can accomplish the lawful ends of its institution but in proportion as it improves the condition of those over whom it is established. . . .

The Constitution under which you are assembled is a charter of limited powers. After full and solemn deliberation upon all or any of the objects which, urged by an irresistible sense of my own duty, I have recommended to your attention should you come to the conclusion that, however desirable in themselves, the enactment of laws for effecting them would transcend the powers committed to you by that venerable instrument which we are all bound to support, let no consideration induce you to assume the exercise of powers not granted to you by the people. But . . . if [the] powers . . . enumerated in the Constitution may be effectually brought into action by laws promoting the improvement of agriculture, commerce, and manufactures, the cultivation and encouragement of the mechanic and of the elegant arts, the advancement of literature, and the progress of the sciences, ornamental and profound, to refrain from exercising them for the benefit of the people themselves would be to hide in the earth the talent committed to our charge—would be treachery to the most sacred of trusts.

The spirit of improvement is abroad upon the earth. It stimulates the hearts and sharpens the faculties not of our fellow-citizens alone, but of the nations of Europe and of their rulers. While dwelling with pleasing satisfaction upon the superior excellence of our political institutions, let us not be unmindful that liberty is power; that the nation blessed with the largest portion of liberty must in proportion to its numbers be the most powerful nation upon earth, and that the tenure of power by man is, in the moral purposes of his Creator, upon condition that it shall be exercised to ends of beneficence, to improve the condition of himself and his fellow-men. While foreign nations less blessed with that freedom which is power than ourselves are advancing with gigantic strides in the career of public improvement, were we to slumber in indolence or fold up our arms and proclaim to the world that we are palsied by the will of our constituents, would it not be to cast away the bounties of Providence and doom ourselves to perpetual inferiority? . . .

Resignation

Elected at last in 1828, Jackson brought new strength and determination to the Presidency. But he was elderly and ill, and reluctant to serve more than four years. During a horseback ride with Secretary of State Martin Van Buren in 1830, Jackson suggested that he might resign the Presidency after winning re-election. Below is Van Buren's account of the incident, written in 1854.

. . . It was during one of our rides over the Georgetown Hills, in the autumn of 1830. . . . He spoke of the resolution he had formed at the period of his election to serve only one term and, referring to the seemingly insurmountable obstacles which had since arisen to the fulfillment of this intention and to the probability of the early developments of the opposition against his administration which had for some time been in course of preparation, said that his thoughts had been turned to the selection of some middle course by which his wish for an early retirement might be gratified without hazarding the accomplishment of the measures he had entered upon and the success of which he deemed essential to the national welfare. He had not, he added, been able to hit upon any plan so promising as that I should stand for the Vice Presidency on the ticket with him at the next election and, if successful, that he should resign in one year, or, if it should be necessary, at the expiration of the second year of his new term. The feelings with which this proposition was received are as fresh in my recollection as they were at the moment it was made. I could neither be ignorant of, nor insensible to the large share of personal kindness towards myself which had given birth to this suggestion beside his constant desire to promote the public interest; and that consideration, in addition to the earnestness with which he habitually embraced propositions which occupied his mind for some time before he brought them forward, demanded great circumspection in giving the requisite answer to it. But

I could see nothing but danger to myself in the proposition and, as I thought, to his own great popularity, and was deeply sensible of the necessity of giving to it a prompt negative. . . .

Jackson and the Bank

In vetoing recharter of the Second Bank of the United States on constitutional grounds (July 10, 1832), despite earlier Supreme Court rulings that the Bank was constitutional, Jackson claimed a presidential right to independent interpretation of the Constitution—the same position Jefferson had taken. The Bank became the major issue of the 1832 election. Perhaps most important, Jackson used the question to restate the President's role as the single representative of all the people.

. . . The bank is professedly established as an agent of the executive branch of the Government, and its constitutionality is maintained on that ground. Neither upon the propriety of present action nor upon the provisions of this act was the Executive consulted. It has had no opportunity to say that it neither needs nor wants an agent clothed with such powers and favored by such exemptions. There is nothing in its legitimate functions which makes it necessary or proper. . . .

It is to be regretted that the rich and powerful too often bend the acts of government to their selfish purposes. Distinctions in society will always exist under every just government. Equality of talents, of education, or of wealth can not be produced by human institutions. In the full enjoyment of the gifts of Heaven and the fruits of superior industry, economy, and virtue, every man is equally entitled to protection by law; but when the laws undertake to add to these natural and just advantages artificial distinctions, to grant titles, gratuities, and exclusive privileges, to make the rich richer and the potent more powerful, the humble members of society—the farmers, mechanics, and laborers—who have neither the time nor the means of securing like favors to themselves, have a right to complain of the injustice of their Government. There are no necessary evils in government. Its evils exist only in its abuses. If it would confine itself to equal protection, and, as Heaven does its rains, shower its favors alike on the high and the low, the rich and the poor, it would be an unqualified blessing. In the act before me there seems to be a wide and unnecessary departure from these just principles.

Nor is our Government to be maintained or our Union preserved by invasions of the rights and powers of the several States. . . .

Experience should teach us wisdom. Most of the difficulties our Government now encounters and most of the dangers which impend over our Union have sprung from an abandonment of the legitimate objects of Government by our national legislation, and the adoption of such principles as are embodied in this act. Many of our rich men have not been content with equal protection and equal benefits, but have besought us to make them richer by act of Congress. By attempting to gratify their desires we have in the results of our legislation arrayed section against section, interest against interest, and man against man, in a fearful commotion which threatens to shake the foundations of our Union. It is time to pause in our career to review our principles, and if possible revive that devoted patriotism and spirit of compromise which distinguished the sages of the Revolution and the fathers of our Union. If we can not at once, in justice to interests vested under improvident legislation, make our Government what it ought to be, we can at least take a stand against all new grants of monopolies and exclusive privileges, against any prostitution of our Government to the advancement of the few at the expense of the many, and in favor of compromise and gradual reform in our code of laws and system of political economy. . . .

Rebellious State

South Carolina reacted to the passage of the Tariff of 1832 by calling a convention to declare the tariff null and void in that state. On November 6, thirteen days before the convention met, Jackson moved to deal with the crisis in a practical way by sending secret orders to the federal collector of duties at the port of Charleston.

. . . Upon the supposition that the measures of the convention, or the acts of the legislature may consist, in part, at least, in declaring the laws of the United States imposing duties unconstitutional, and null and void, and in forbidding their execution, and the collection of the duties within the State of South Carolina, you will, immediately after it shall be formally announced, resort to all the means provided by the laws . . . to counteract the measures which may be adopted to give effect to that declaration.

For this purpose you will consider yourself authorized to employ the revenue cutters which may be within your district, and provide as many boats, and employ as many inspectors, as may be necessary for the execution of the law, and for the purposes of the act already referred to. You will, moreover, cause a sufficient number of officers of cutters and inspectors to be placed on board, and in charge of every vessel arriving from a foreign port or place, with goods, wares, or merchandise, as soon as practicable after her first coming within your district, and direct them to anchor her in some safe place within the harbor, where she may be secure from any act of violence, and from any unauthorized attempt to discharge her cargo before a compliance with the laws; and they will remain on board of her at such place until the reports and entries required by law shall be made, both of vessel and cargo, and the duties paid, or secured to be paid to your satisfaction, and until the regular permit shall be granted for landing the cargo; and it will be your duty, against any forcible attempt, to retain and defend the custody of the said vessel, by the aid of the officers of the customs, inspectors, and officers of the cutters, until the requisitions of the law shall be fully complied with; and in case of any attempt to remove her or her cargo from the custody of the officers of the customs, by the form of legal process from State tribunals, you will not yield the custody to such attempt, but will consult the law officer of the district, and employ such means as, under the particular circumstances, you may legally do, to resist such process. . . .

Should the entry of such vessel and cargo not be completed, and the duties paid, or secured to be paid, by bond or bonds, with sureties to your satisfaction, within the time limited by law, you will, at the expiration of that time, take possession of the cargo, and land and store the same at Castle Pinckney, or some other safe place, and in due time, if the duties are not paid, sell the same, according to the direction of the 56th section of the act of the 2d of March, 1799; and you are authorized to provide such stores as may be necessary for that purpose. . . .

The anti-Jackson cartoon above shows the President and Van Buren, on an ass, losing a race with Henry Clay, who supported the Bank of the United States. Actually, Jackson won his fight against the Bank.

Censure

Re-elected in 1832, Jackson began the following fall to remove federal money from the Bank of the United States, which had three years left on its charter. The money was deposited instead in a number of state banks. Outraged, the Senate officially censured Jackson, who responded with a formal protest on April 15, 1834.

It appears by the published Journal of the Senate that on the 26th of December last a resolution was offered by a member of the Senate, which after a protracted debate was on the 28th day of March last modified by the mover and passed by the votes of twenty-six Senators out of forty-six . . . viz:

Resolved, That the President, in the late Executive proceedings in relation to the public revenue, has assumed upon himself authority and power not conferred by the Constitution and laws, but in derogation of both.

. . . Without notice, unheard and untried, I thus find myself charged on the records of the Senate, and in a form hitherto unknown in our history, with the high crime of violating the laws and Constitution of my country.

It can seldom be necessary for any department of the Government, when assailed in conversation or debate or by the strictures of the press or of popular assemblies, to step out of its ordinary path for the purpose of vindicating its conduct or of pointing out any irregularity or injustice in the manner of the attack; but when the Chief Executive Magistrate is, by one of the most important branches of the Government in its official capacity, in a public manner, and by its recorded sentence, but without precedent, competent authority, or just cause, declared guilty of a breach of the laws and Constitution, it is due to his station, to public opinion, and to a proper self-respect that the officer thus denounced should promptly expose the wrong which has been done.

In the present case, moreover, there is even a stronger necessity for such a vindication. By an express provision of the Constitution, before the President of the United States can enter on the execution of his office he is required to take an oath. . . .

I do solemnly swear (or affirm) that I will faithfully execute the office of President of the United States and will to the best of my ability preserve, protect, and defend the Constitution of the United States.

The duty of defending so far as in him lies the integrity of the Constitution would indeed have resulted from the very nature of his office, but by thus expressing it in the official oath or affirmation, which in this respect differs from that of any other functionary, the founders of our Republic have attested their sense of its importance and have given to it a peculiar solemnity and force. Bound to the performance of

129

this duty by the oath I have taken, by the strongest obligations of gratitude to the American people, and by the ties which unite my every earthly interest with the welfare and glory of my country, and perfectly convinced that the discussion and passage of the above-mentioned resolution were not only unauthorized by the Constitution, but in many respects repugnant to its provisions and subversive of the rights secured by it to other coordinate departments, I deem it an imperative duty to maintain the supremacy of that sacred instrument and the immunities of the department intrusted to my care by all means consistent with my own lawful powers, with the rights of others, and with the genius of our civil institutions. To this end I have caused this my *solemn protest* against the aforesaid proceedings to be placed on the files of the executive department and to be transmitted to the Senate. . . .

The resolution above quoted charges, in substance, that in certain proceedings relating to the public revenue the President has usurped authority and power not conferred upon him by the Constitution and laws, and that in doing so he violated both. Any such act constitutes a high crime—one of the highest, indeed, which the President can commit—a crime which justly exposes him to impeachment by the House of Representatives, and, upon due conviction, to removal from office and to the complete and immutable disfranchisement prescribed by the Constitution. The resolution, then, was in substance an impeachment of the President, and in its passage amounts to a declaration by a majority of the Senate that he is guilty of an impeachable offense. As such it is spread upon the journals of the Senate, published to the nation and to the world, made part of our enduring archives, and incorporated in the history of the age. The punishment of removal from office and future disqualification does not, it is true, follow this decision, nor would it have followed the like decision if the regular forms of proceeding had been pursued, because the requisite number did not concur in the result. But the moral influence of a solemn declaration by a majority of the Senate that the accused is guilty of the offense charged upon him has been as effectually secured as if the like declaration had been made upon an impeachment expressed in the same terms. Indeed, a greater practical effect has been gained, because the votes given for the resolution, though not sufficient to authorize a judg-

ment of guilty on an impeachment, were numerous enough to carry that resolution. . . .

The President of the United States, therefore, has been by a majority of his constitutional triers accused and found guilty of an impeachable offense, but in no part of this proceeding have the directions of the Constitution been observed. . . .

Campaign Ardor

Having helped Jackson gain the White House in 1828 by means of a lowbrow assault on John Quincy Adams' lack of workingman's calluses, Van Buren was the target of a similar attack when he stood for re-election. Charles Ogle of Pennsylvania vividly demonstrated the spirit of 1840 in a speech to the House on April 14.

The House being in Committee of the Whole on the bill making appropriations for the civil and diplomatic expenses of the Government for the year 1840, Mr. OGLE, of Pennsylvania, moved to amend the bill by striking out the following clause: "For alterations and repairs of the President's house and furniture, for purchasing trees, shrubs, and compost, and for superintendence of the grounds, three thousand six hundred and sixty-five dollars."

Mr. OGLE said: Mr. Chairman, I consider this a very important item in the bill—not as to the amount, but as to the principles involved in it. . . .

. . . I resist the principle on which it is demanded as anti-democratic—as running counter in its tendency to the plain, simple, and frugal notions of our republican People. And I put it to you, sir, and to the free citizens of this country, whose *servant* the President is, to say whether, in addition to the large sum of ONE HUNDRED THOUSAND DOLLARS which he is entitled to receive *for a single term of four years*, they are disposed to maintain, for his private accommodation, A ROYAL ESTABLISHMENT *at the cost of the nation?* Will they longer feel inclined to support their *chief servant* in a PALACE *as splendid as that of the Caesars, and as richly adorned as the proudest Asiatic mansion?* . . .

. . . seeing that gallant and victorious general [William Henry Harrison] maligned and libelled day by day in the "official organ" of Martin Van Buren as a "red petticoat hero" and "superannuated dotard," I feel impelled by a strong sense of duty to cast aside every sentiment of mere delicacy and to "cry aloud and spare not" the abettor, the encourager, and the responsible accessary of those base libels. . . .

. . . You will remember that, by the act of the 25th of February, 1825, the sum of $5,000 was appropriated for "*levelling*," grading, &c., the President's square, and that the Administration of that day took measures to carry into effect the intention of Congress, by digging down the knolls, and by filling up the hollows, and in this manner *levelling* or making plain and flat the surface of the ground. But. . . . mere meadows are too common to gratify the refined taste of an exquisite with "sweet sandy whiskers." He must have undulations, "beautiful mounds, and other contrivances," to ravish his exalted and etheral soul. Hence, the reformers have constructed a number of clever sized hills, every pair of which, it is said, was designed to resemble and assume the form of AN AMAZON's BOSOM, with a miniature knoll or hillock on its apex, to denote the n—ple. Thousands of the People's dollars have been thrown away on these silly fancies, which are better adapted to please the sickly and vicious taste of palace dandies, than to gratify . . . plain, republican freemen. . . .

I am disposed to believe, Mr. Chairman, that the present occupant of the palace is not a "*real genuine*" locofoco, hard-handed democrat. He can't have the "*right stripe.*" You may depend upon it something must be out of gear. Why, sir, he loves tassels, rosettes, and girlish finery almost as much as a real "Bank Whig" loves "hard cider." By the act of the 3d of March, 1837, Congress appropriated twenty thousand dollars "*for furniture of the President's House;*" I quote the language of the law, "*for* 'FURNITURE' *of the President's House.*" . . . I would, therefore, respectfully inquire whether "*silk tassels and rosettes*" [on which some of the appropriation was spent] are considered household *furniture*, in the legitimate democratic meaning of the word? I ask, sir, whether "*silk tassels and rosettes*" can be democratically inventoried as part and parcel of the household *furniture* of a hard-handed locofoco? Are "*silk tassels and rosettes*" hereafter to be written down, deemed, and taken in the same category with frying pans, oaken chests, chaff-bags, and crout tubs? As well might the honest citizen of Tulpehacken valley, who garnishes his 8 by 10 looking glass with a string of blue-jay, yellow-hammer, whittaker, and mockingbird eggs, call those speckled eggs household furniture. . . .

Mr. Chairman, in my opinion, it is time the people of the United States should know that their money goes to buy for their plain hard-handed democratic President, knives, forks, and spoons of gold, that he may dine in the style of the monarchs of Europe. The fact, however, is impudently denied, not only by *Mr. Van Buren's* "*organ,*" the Globe, but by all the locofoco papers throughout the country. When a certain lawyer, in Columbus, Ohio, told a farmer in his neighborhood that the President had a dinner service of gold, the locofoco paper published in that place, and called the "*Ohio Statesman,*" made so fierce an attack upon him that the poor man was frightened, and actually retracted the statement—though it was as true as preaching. . . .

Now, sir, I would advise this Whig lawyer not to be quite so timid hereafter as to retract statements based upon substantial facts. . . . Oh! sir, how delightful it must be to a real genuine locofoco to eat his *paté de foie gras, dinde desossé, and salade à la volaile* from a SILVER PLATE with a GOLDEN KNIFE AND FORK. And how exquisite to sip with a GOLDEN SPOON his *soupe à la Reine.* . . .

. . . I had thought that it was bad enough for the farmers, mechanics, and laborers of the country to provide hay and pasturage for Mr. Van Buren's race and carriage horses; to pay for the manure on his potato, celery, cauliflower, and asparagus beds; to pay the hire of a British gardener to topdress his strawberry vines, cultivate his vegetables, and construct bouquets for his palace saloons; but, sir, to HEM his DISH RAGS, pay for his LARDING NEEDLES and LIQUOR STANDS is still worse. Ay, sir, worse, if possible, than filling the apartments in the House of the American People with royal and imperial Wiltons [rugs], foreign cut wine coolers, French bedsteads, and one hundred dollar artificial flowers. It is worse, sir, because there is a degree of littleness in the thing which demonstrates as clearly as if it were written in characters of living light, that the soul of Martin Van Buren is so very, very, very diminutive, that it might find abundant space within the barrel of a miliner's thimble to perform all the evolutions of the whirling *pirouette* avec chasee a suivant, according to the liberal gesticulations practised by the most celebrated *danseurs.* . . .

The Whig campaign in 1840 stressed Harrison's patriotism and humble origins. Virginia's John Tyler was the ticket balancer.

Death and Succession

Was the Presidency actually re-created every four years by the suffrage of the American people, or was Martin Van Buren right when he commented, "The President under our system, like the king in a monarchy, never dies"? The question was not decisively answered until the ratification of the Twenty-fifth Amendment in 1967. But in April, 1841, despite some opposition, John Tyler of Virginia went a long way toward establishing the Presidency as an institution independent of death.

President Tyler?

Tyler's accession to the powers and duties of the Presidency dismayed many observers, including a former President, John Quincy Adams, who wrote in his diary:

. . . At thirty minutes past midnight, this morning of Palm Sunday, the 4th of April, 1841, died William Henry Harrison, precisely one calendar month President of the United States after his inauguration. . . .

The influence of this event upon the condition and history of the country can scarcely be seen. It makes the Vice-President of the United States, John Tyler of Virginia, Acting President of the Union for four years less one month. Tyler is a political sectarian, of the slave-driving, Virginian, Jeffersonian school, principled against all improvement, with all the interests and passions and vices of slavery rooted in his moral and political constitution—with talents not above mediocrity, and a spirit incapable of expansion to the dimensions of the station upon which he has been cast by the hand of Providence. . . . To that benign and healing hand of Providence I trust, in

humble hope of the good which it always brings forth out of evil. . . . this is the first instance of a Vice-President's being called to act as President of the United States, and brings to the test that provision of the Constitution which places in the Executive chair a man never thought of for it by anybody. This day was in every sense gloomy—rain the whole day.

Tyler did not agree that he was only Acting President. The Harrison Cabinet, composed of men who believed in the active federalism of Clay's American System—a philosophy that, as they well knew, Tyler did not share—nonetheless supported his assumption of the title of President. However, when Congress met at the end of May the matter was still being argued; and the legislators might have established the contrary precedent— that the Vice President never became President in name, but only in powers and duties. The succession question came up in the Senate on June 1. William Allen led the attack on John Tyler's assumption of the highest office.

Mr. ALLEN of Ohio . . . . said that, in the Constitution, he found the following words:

"In case of the removal of the President from office, or of his death, resignation, or inability to discharge the powers and duties of the said office, the same shall devolve on the Vice President, and the Congress may by law provide for the case of removal, death, resignation, or inability, both of the President and Vice President, declaring what officer shall then act as President, and such officer shall act accordingly, until the disability be removed, or a President shall be elected."

The first clause in this portion of the Constitution classified all the contingencies under which the Vice President shall discharge the duties and exercise the powers of President, and it made no distinction whatever between removal by death and removal by a temporary inability to discharge the functions of the Presidential office. If, therefore, the late President had been afflicted with a disease producing, for time, a state of mental alienation, he would on his recovery have been reinstated in all the powers of that high office to which the People had elected him. But a contingency of that kind was provided for in the Constitution in the very same words as the case of the President's death. It might, perhaps, be said that the question was an unimportant one, inasmuch as it had reference mainly to the title to be applied to a public officer. Now Mr. A. had not raised it with the remotest desire to withhold the dignity of the title of President from the present incumbent of the chair. His anxiety in the matter arose from this: if the Presidential office was indeed now held by the Vice President, that fact recognised the existence of a case where the highest office in the Republic may be held otherwise than by an election of the People. The consequences of establishing such a principle might hereafter become very serious; but if the powers and duties of the Presidential office attached, in consequence of the death of the President, to the Vice President, he still remaining Vice President, then he continued to hold only the office to which the people had elected him, and thus the beautiful symmetry of our system of free and popular Government was preserved. . . .

. . . Suppose a President of the United States should be of one political party, and at the same time [there was] a Vice President of another political party; suppose the country to be about equally divided between the two, and both parties mutually and highly incensed against each other; and under these circumstances, the President should be seized with a temporary illness, producing, for a time, such an alienation of mind as unfitted him for the discharge of his official duties, in consequence of which, those duties were discharged by the Vice President. After a time the President completely recovered. The question would then arise, which of the two officers should continue in the chair. And might we not justly fear, under such a state of things, a renewal of those fearful struggles for supreme power which had so often convulsed the Old World with civil war and deludged it in blood? The question of succession had oftener than any other destroyed the peace of nations. Here was a Vice President armed with the purse and the sword, in actual possession, standing against the claims of the President, now restored to health and reason; and not only so, but with half the citizens of the Republic at his back. What would become of the office? Was it to *vibrate* between the

two claimants? In what manner could a President of the United States—unimpeached, sane, and alive—cease to be President? There was none known to the Constitution. None. If John Tyler was now President of the United States, nothing but impeachment, removal, mental alienation, or death, would expel him from the office. [Thus] . . . though a President should be restored, a Vice President once discharging his duties might hold out, and the President chosen by the people must take his place as a private citizen. . . .

Allen failed to convince the Senate, and succession to the office was established as a precedent. From one standpoint it was a valuable precedent, since it assured that there would never be an automatic diminution in executive prestige, either at home or abroad, when a Vice President had to take over. On the other hand, Allen was right: because of the way the succession clause was written, Tyler's precedent would also have to be followed in case of presidential illness, and this was to cause the United States monumental problems, particularly during the administrations of Garfield and Wilson.

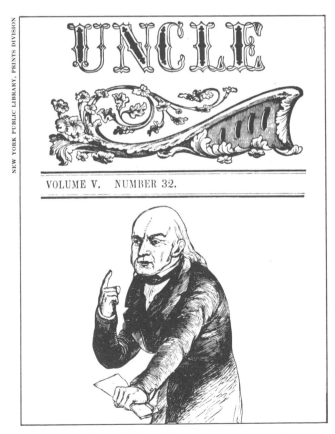

Congressman John Quincy Adams on an 1846 magazine cover

Harassments

Expansion and increasing sectional differences added to the complexity of governing the nation in the 1840's. Trying to cope with a multitude of problems, Presidents often found themselves thwarted by a willful Congress.

In Defense of the Veto

Nicknamed Old Veto because of his frequent use of the executive negative, John Tyler became anathema to the Whig leaders, whose nationalistic legislation he consistently opposed. On September 9, 1841, President Tyler defended the independence of the Chief Magistracy.

. . . I readily admit that whilst the qualified *veto* with which the Chief Magistrate is invested should be regarded and was intended by the wise men who made it a part of the Constitution as a great conservative principle of our system . . . yet it is a power which ought to be most cautiously exerted, and perhaps never except in a case eminently involving the public interest or one in which the oath of the President, acting under his conviction, both mental and moral, imperiously requires its exercise. In such a case he has no alternative. He must either exert the negative power intrusted to him by the Constitution chiefly for its own preservation, protection, and defence or commit an act of gross moral turpitude.

Mere regard to the will of a majority must not in a constitutional republic like ours control this sacred and solemn duty of a sworn officer. The Constitution itself I regard and cherish as the embodied and written will of the whole people of the United States. It is their fixed and fundamental law, which they unanimously prescribe to the public functionaries, their mere trustees and servants. This *their* will and the law which *they* have given us as the rule of our action have no guard, no guaranty of preservation, protection, and defense, but the oaths which it prescribes to the public officers, the sanctity with which they shall religiously observe those oaths, and the patriotism with which the people shall shield it by their own sovereign will, which has made the Constitution supreme. It must be exerted against the will of a mere representative majority or not at all. It is alone in pursuance of that will that any measure can reach the President, and to say that because a majority in Congress have passed a bill he should therefore sanction it is to abrogate the power altogether and to render its insertion in the Constitution a work of absolute supererogation. . . .

Polk versus Congress

An attempt to impeach Tyler because of his independence failed in 1843; no subsequent President until Andrew Johnson faced such a dire threat from Congress. Nevertheless, the legislature continued to block the Executive often—sometimes because that was its proper

This picture of a victorious moment in the Mexican War illustrated an 1848 book, Lives of General Taylor and General Scott.

function, but sometimes because of partisan antipathy to a Chief Executive and sometimes because Congress was too involved in its own intramural squabbles to pass needed legislation. James Knox Polk, trying to administer a war against Mexico, complained bitterly about congressional inaction on January 4, 1847:

. . . The truth is neither [Zachary] Taylor nor [Winfield] Scott are fit for the command of the army in the great operations in progress and which are contemplated. To add to my embarrassment, & it does greatly do so, Congress does not strengthen the Executive arm. Nearly half the session has passed and they are engaged in debates about slavery and party politics, and have passed none of the essential measures which I have recommended as indispensible to the vigorous & successful prosecution of the war. With a large nominal majority in both Houses, I am practically in a minority. The several cliques & sections of the Democratic party are manifestly more engaged in managing for their respective favourites in the next Presidential election, than they are in supporting the Government in prosecuting the war. . . . I will do my duty to the country and rejoice that with my own voluntary free will & consent I am not to be again a candidate. This determination is irrevocable. . . .

Appointments

The federal government, which had employed fewer than five thousand civilians in 1816, had more than twenty-six thousand employees in 1851. The President had to appoint many government officers himself, but he had no way of knowing the quality of most applicants. Polk discussed this problem in his diary on January 7, 1847.

. . . Many persons, members of Congress and others, called today; all of them or nearly all on what they may regard as the patriotic, but which I consider the contemptible business of seeking office for themselves or their friends. The passion for office and the number of unworthy persons who seek to live on the public is increasing beyond former example, and I now predict that no President of the United States of either party will ever again be reëlected. The reason is that the patronage of the government will destroy the popularity of any President, however well he may administer the government. The office-seekers have become so numerous that they hold the balance of power between the two great parties of the country. In every appointment which the President makes he disappoints half a dozen applicants and their friends, who, actuated by selfish and sordid motives, will prefer any other candidate in the next election, while the person appointed attributes the appointment to his own superior merit and does not even feel obliged by it. . . Another great difficulty in making appointments which the President encounters is that he cannot tell upon what recommendations to rely. Members of Congress and men of high station in the country sign papers of recommendation, either from interested personal motives or without meaning what they say, and thus the President is often imposed on, and induced to make bad appointments. When he does so the whole responsibility falls on himself, while those who have signed papers of recommendation and misled him, take special care never to avow the agency they have had in the matter, or to assume any part of the responsibility. I have had some remarkable instances of this during my administration. . . . shortly after the commencement of my administration I made an appointment upon the letter of recommendation of a Senator. I sent the nomination to the Senate at the last session and it was rejected, and, as I learned, at the instance of the same Senator who had made the recommendation. A few days afterwards the Senator called to recommend another person for the same office. I said to him, well, you rejected the man I nominated; O yes, he replied, he was without character and wholly unqualified. I then asked him if he knew upon whose recommendation I had appointed him, to which he replied that he did not. I then handed to him his own letter and told him that was the recommendation upon which I had appointed him. He appeared confused and replied, Well, we are obliged to recommend our constituents when they apply to us. . . .

The President and War

On February 19, 1848, the Treaty of Guadalupe Hidalgo, which ended the war with Mexico, arrived in Washington.

. . . Let me first state what I understand to be your position. It is, that if it shall become *necessary, to repel invasion*, the President may, without violation of the Constitution, cross the line, and *invade* the territory of another country; and that whether such *necessity* exists in any given case, the President is to be the *sole* judge.

Before going further, consider well whether this is, or is not your position. If it is, it is a position that neither the President himself, nor any friend of his, so far as I know, has ever taken. Their only positions are first, that the soil was *ours* where hostilities commenced, and second, that whether it was rightfully *ours* or not, *Congress had annexed it*, and the President, for that reason was bound to defend it, both of which are as clearly proved to be false in fact, as you can prove that your house is not mine. That soil was not ours; and Congress did not annex or attempt to annex it. But to return to your position: Allow the President to invade a neighboring nation, whenever *he* shall deem it necessary to repel an invasion, and you allow him to do so, *whenever he may choose to say* he deems it necessary for such purpose—and you allow him to make war at pleasure. Study to see if you can fix *any limit* to his power in this respect, after you have given him so much as you propose. If, to-day, he should choose to say he thinks it necessary to invade Canada, to prevent the British from invading us, how could you stop him? You may say to him, "I see no probability of the British invading us" but he will say to you "be silent; I see it, if you dont."

The provision of the Constitution giving the war-making power to Congress, was dictated, as I understand it, by the following reasons. Kings had always been involving and impoverishing their people in wars, pretending generally, if not always, that the good of the people was the object. This, our Convention understood to be the most oppressive of all Kingly oppressions; and they resolved to so frame the Constitution that *no one man* should hold the power of bringing this oppression upon us. But your view destroys the whole matter, and places our President where kings have always stood. . . .

Anxious Probation

. . . I must not be understood . . . as undervaluing the honor, dignity and usefulness of the Presidential office. No American citizen can fail to regard that position as, in every respect, the most exalted as it is the most responsible public trust that can be conferred. . . . But the extent to which personal happiness and enjoyment will be promoted by its possession is a question to be solved by the taste and temperament of the incumbent. There are men, and not a few, who derive so much pleasure from the mere possession of great power that any degree of dissatisfaction caused by its exercise is not too dear a price for the coveted indulgence, and the personal adulation which is sure to follow the footsteps of authority while it lasts fills the measure of their satisfaction. Those better regulated minds, however, whose gratification on reaching that high office is mainly derived from the consciousness that their countrymen have deemed them worthy of it and from the hope that they may be able to justify that confidence and to discharge its duties so as to promote the public good, will save themselves from great disappointments by postponing all thoughts of individual enjoyment to the completion of their labors. . . .

At the very head of their disappointments will stand those inseparable from the distribution of patronage, that power so dazzling to the expectant dispenser, apparently so easily performed and so fruitful of reciprocal gratification. Whatever hopes they may indulge that their cases will prove an exception to the general rule they will find, in the end, their own experience truly described by Mr. Jefferson when he said that the two happiest days of his life were those of his entrance upon his office and of his surrender of it. The truth of the matter may be stated in a word: whilst to have been deemed worthy by a majority of the People of the United States to fill the office of Chief Magistrate of the Republic is an honor which ought to satisfy the aspirations of the most ambitious citizen, the period of his actual possession of its powers and performance of its duties is and must, from the nature of things, always be, to a right minded man one of toilsome and anxious probation. . . .

BOTH: STANLEY KING COLLECTION

Choosing the President

The first President scarcely had to be picked. Having forged a provincial militia into a victorious national Army, having presided over men of sharp sectional and philosophical differences as they wrote a Constitution, George Washington was the very symbol of national unity, the logical and unanimous choice to head the new government. But Washington could not always be President, and the factions that developed had different ideas about who should replace him. Political parties formed, and with Washington's retirement began the great national sport, the contested presidential election. Rules, styles, and paraphernalia have changed over the years, but the drama remains because the judges—the people—may change their criteria from one contest to the next without notice. Thus, the Benjamin Harrison campaign item above notwithstanding, there can be no patent on winning systems. Harrison himself learned the lesson: in 1892, four years after defeating Grover Cleveland, he was defeated—by Grover Cleveland.

Bitter Contests

The constitutional method of choosing Presidents could not withstand the strain of contested elections. Since no provision had been made for political parties, the system whereby electors voted for two men without differentiating between their presidential and vice presidential choices produced an antagonistic team in 1796: Federalist John Adams and his Republican deputy, Jefferson, were not on speaking terms during much of the administration. They were rivals again in 1800, and because it seemed possible that they might reverse their roles, Jefferson's supporters made sure to cast their second vote for Aaron Burr, whom they intended to make Vice President. But Jefferson and Burr tied, and the result was a splenetic battle in the House, which ultimately chose Jefferson. The situation was rectified in 1804 by the Twelfth Amendment, and for twenty years thereafter the Democratic-Republicans—opposed only by the moribund Federalist party—held the White House.

Above is an oil painting on paper by Frederick Kemmelmeyer, a Baltimore artist, commemorating George Washington, the unanimous choice for first President of the United States.

REPUBLICANS

Turn out, turn out and save your Country from ruin !

From an *Emperor*—from a *King*—from the iron grasp of a *British Tory Faction*—an unprincipled banditti of British speculators. The hireling tools and emissaries of his majesty king George the 3d have thronged our city and diffused the poison of principles among us.

DOWN WITH THE TORIES, DOWN WITH THE BRITISH FACTION,

Before they have it in their power to enslave you, and reduce your families to distress by heavy taxation. Republicans want no Tribute-liars—they want no ship Ocean-liars—they want no Rufus King's for Lords —they want no Varick to lord it over them—they want no Jones for senator, who fought with the British against the Americans in time of the war.—But they want in their places such men as

Jefferson & Clinton,

The men who had set aside their differences to create a new nation in the eighteenth century were called upon to lead it in the nineteenth. The first six Presidents are shown on the French quilt at left. Clockwise around the eagle are George Washington, John Adams, John Quincy Adams, Thomas Jefferson, and James Monroe; James Madison is at far left. All but Washington had served as either Vice President or Secretary of State, and all were well qualified to be Chief Executive. Their political opponents did not, however, hesitate to warn the American people that the young United States would be ruined if they were elected, as the placard above, issued by the Democratic-Republicans in 1800, indicates.

LOOK ON THIS PICTURE, AND ON THIS.

In the Federalist poster above, Thomas Jefferson's opponents maintained that he was an unworthy successor to Washington.

PRESIDENCY!!!

This is the House that We* built.

TREASURY.

This is the malt that lay in the House that WE Built,

John Q. Adams,

This is the *MAIDEN* all forlorn, who worried herself from night till morn, to enter the House that WE built.

CLAY,

This is the *MAN* all tattered and torn, who courted the maiden all forlorn, who worried herself from night till morn to enter the House that WE built.

WEBSTER,

This is the *PRIEST*, all shaven and shorn, that married the man all tattered and torn, unto the maiden all forlorn, who worried herself from night till morn, to enter the House that WE Built.

CONGRESS,

This is the BEAST, that carried the Priest all shaven and shorn, who married the man all tattered and torn, unto the maiden all forlorn, who worried herself from night till morn, to enter the House that WE built.

CABINET,

These are the *Rats* that pulled off their hats, and joined the Beast that carried the Priest all shaven and shorn, who married the man all tattered and torn unto the maiden all forlorn who worried herself from night till morn to enter the House that WE built.

"OLD HICKORY,"

This is the *Wood*, well season'd and good, WE will use as a rod to whip out the RATS, that pulled off their hats and joined the Beast that carried the Priest all shaven and shorn, who married the man all tattered and torn, unto the maiden all forlorn, who worried herself from night till morn, to enter the House that WE Built.

NEW-YORK.

This is the *state*, both early and late, that will strengthen the Wood well seasoned and good, to be used as a rod to whip out Rats that pulled off their hats, and joined the beast that carried the Priest, all shaven and shorn, who married the man all tattered and torn unto the maiden all forlorn, who worried herself from night till morn to enter the House that WE Built.

FRE 'Y & ' R3?

On the American frontier, skins and corn were used as currency more frequently than dollars and cents. But as the 1828 election poster at left suggests, the National Republicans' connections with big-city financiers could be an effective campaign issue. Above is a ribbon commemorating Jackson's 1815 victory at New Orleans.

The People's Choice

The steady liberalization of suffrage laws and the final demise of the Federalist party did not immediately make the process of picking a President less cumbersome. Congressional caucuses, state party conventions, and state legislatures were still nominating candidates independently of one another in 1824; a four-man race that year produced healthy electoral and popular pluralities—but not the necessary majority—for Andrew Jackson. When supporters of candidate Henry Clay in the House of Representatives gave their votes and the victory to John Quincy Adams, the Jacksonians promptly complained of having been cheated by a "corrupt bargain." By 1828, however, all states but Delaware and South Carolina had instituted popular election of electors, and Jackson was not to be denied. The Antimasonic and National Republican parties held the first national nominating conventions in 1832. The Democrats held one also, but the renomination—and re-election—of Old Hickory was inevitable. In the new age of the common man, he was unbeatable.

In the 1824 print above, Jackson's ship blows up while Adams' heads toward the dock and victory. Like his father, victimized by rising Republicanism, John Quincy Adams would in 1828 fall to the rise of the common man. Below is an 1832 campaign coin. Jackson said that he would kill the National Bank and take the responsibility.

141

Dandy versus Hero

Jackson did not run for a third term in 1836, but the Democrats realized that a candidate endorsed by the popular President could not be beaten. The new Whig party contrived a roundabout route to defeat Jackson's choice, Martin Van Buren. Hoping to throw the election to the House of Representatives, where they were strong, the Whigs held a series of caucuses and state conventions, which named three different candidates. But Van Buren won a majority nevertheless, and the Whigs tried a different approach in 1840. Calling constant attention to Van Buren's fancy tastes and allegedly dandified ways, they nominated William Henry Harrison—the hero of Tippecanoe—and conducted a raucous, lowbrow campaign, thereby beating the Jacksonians at their own game. Old Hickory, self-made and roughhewn, had changed the image of the Presidency, and the victorious "Old Tip" was much closer to that image than was "Little Van." For years thereafter log cabin birth and frontier origin (real or invented) remained invaluable assets for presidential candidates.

In the cartoon above, symbolizing the 1836 election, Harrison (at left with Daniel Webster and Henry Clay) challenges Martin Van Buren, who is coached by Andrew Jackson and Thomas Hart Benton. Van Buren defeated Harrison and the two other Whig nominees that time, but four years later, a hard cider and log cabin campaign brought victory to Harrison. At right, he dispenses cider to voters while Jackson and Van Buren watch helplessly.

142

"HURRAH FOR OLD TIPPECANOE."

NEW YORK:

TURNER & FISHER, 52 CHATHAM STREET,

AND No. 11 NORTH SIXTH STREET, PHILADELPHIA.

Of whom may be had all the Principal Almanacs now Published.

The First Dark Horse

One month after his inauguration, Harrison became the first Chief Executive to die in office, and despite an ambiguous constitutional directive on the subject of succession, Vice President John Tyler assumed the office and title along with the responsibilities of the Presidency. Unlike Harrison, who had been nominated by the Whigs not because he was a statesman but because he looked like a winner, Tyler promptly proved impervious to Whig attempts to control him. Tyler's independence, exemplified by his periodic vetoes of Whig legislation, led to his repudiation by the party. As 1844 approached, the Whigs, assuming that Van Buren would be the Democrats' presidential nominee, decided not to look for another nonentity and gave Clay the opportunity to make his third bid for the White House. But it seemed likely that the dominant issue would be the annexation of Texas, and when Van Buren publicly agreed with Clay that the Texas question should not be debated during the campaign, Democratic leaders began to sour on him. The prospect of a party split sent worried Democrats off to The Hermitage to confer with Andrew Jackson; they returned not with the familiar name of one of the favorites, but with that of James K. Polk, former governor of Tennessee. Most Whigs smiled sheepishly and asked, "Who is Polk?" but Clay's alleged reaction was more prescient: "Beaten again!" Polk was the first dark horse in American election history. Texas did in fact become the main issue of the campaign, along with the Canadian boundary ("All of Oregon, all of Texas!" and "54° 40' or Fight!" were the Democratic slogans), and the unfamiliar Polk narrowly defeated Clay, who, after Jackson himself, was probably the best-known political figure in the country. The lesson was not lost on the politicians, and a dark horse candidate became a possibility at nominating conventions thereafter.

In a Whig cartoon of 1844, a balloon bearing Clay and his running mate, Theodore Frelinghuysen, floats off toward the Presidential Chair, while Polk and George Dallas lag behind. Former President Jackson tries to hold up Polk's deflated balloon, as Van Buren (the fox) remarks that he should have been the Democratic candidate. The cartoon notwithstanding, Polk won the election that November.

Like Harrison in 1840, Zachary Taylor (above) was nominated by the Whigs because they thought a military hero could win. Also like Harrison, Taylor died in office.

For the election of 1852 both parties returned to old successful formulas, the Whigs nominating a soldier, Winfield Scott (shown on the campaign souvenir above), and the Democrats a dark horse, Franklin Pierce (left). The dark horse won. In 1856 the new Republican party, a successor to disintegrated Whiggery, nominated John C. Frémont to oppose James Buchanan. The evasive Democratic platform did not, as predicted by the cartoon at right, cost Buchanan his victory; but the Presidency at that point was a prize of questionable worth.

Hollow Victories

The Mexican War was the last detour: the slavery issue would for years thereafter dominate presidential election campaigns. In 1848 the Whigs did the next best thing to ignoring the problem by nominating General Zachary Taylor, who seemed sympathetic to both North and South. Lewis Cass, the expansionist Democratic candidate, would probably have won had it not been for Martin Van Buren's antislavery candidacy on a third-party ticket, which cost Cass votes. Taylor died in office, and his successor Millard Fillmore did not look like a winner to the Whigs, so in 1852 they turned to another general, Winfield Scott; his rival, Franklin Pierce, pledged no further "agitation of the slavery question," and won the election. Thinking they could survive with such a noncommittal stand, the Democrats nominated James Buchanan in 1856. By then, a merger of Northern Whigs and Democratic freeholders had produced the new Republican party, which named John C. Frémont as its candidate. Buchanan was elected, and watched impotently as the nation divided.

"No Bargains"

"I authorize no bargains, and will be bound by none," wired Abraham Lincoln to his managers at the Republican convention of 1860. The intricacies and strategies of the President-choosing process had, he realized, produced a succession of compromised, weak Executives when circumstances had made strength of leadership essential. During the campaign he took the position that the Union must be preserved—period. After defeating two Democrats (the regular candidate and a Southern nominee) and a pro-Union conservative running as a Constitutional Unionist, he again refused to compromise; by the time of his inauguration the South had seceded. To Lincoln, the Civil War was a family tragedy, and he believed that the victors should bear no vindictiveness toward the losers. Stressing nonpartisanship, he ran for re-election in 1864 on the National Union ticket with a Democrat as his running mate.

The Currier and Ives cartoon above, "The National Game," celebrates Abraham Lincoln's "skunking" of his opponents in 1860. Constitutional Unionist John Bell (left) received 39 electoral votes. Runner-up in the popular balloting was regular Democrat Stephen Douglas, who nevertheless won only 12 electoral votes. Southern Democrat John Breckinridge (holding his nose), got 72. Lincoln's 180 gave him a majority and the Presidency.

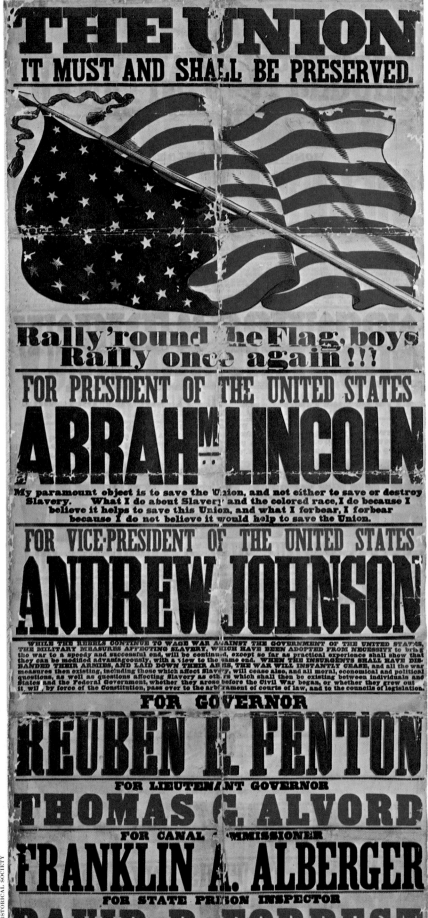

THE UNION
IT MUST AND SHALL BE PRESERVED.

Rally 'round the Flag, boys Rally once again!!!

FOR PRESIDENT OF THE UNITED STATES
ABRAH^M LINCOLN

My paramount object is to save the Union, and not either to save or destroy
Slavery. What I do about Slavery and the colored race, I do because I
believe it helps to save this Union, and what I forbear, I forbear
because I do not believe it would help to save the Union.

FOR VICE-PRESIDENT OF THE UNITED STATES
ANDREW JOHNSON

WHILE THE REBELS CONTINUE TO WAGE WAR AGAINST THE GOVERNMENT OF THE UNITED STATES, THE MILITARY MEASURES AFFECTING SLAVERY, WHICH HAVE BEEN ADOPTED FROM NECESSITY to bring the war to a speedy and successful end, will be continued, except so far as practical experience shall show that they can be modified advantageously, with a view to the same end. WHEN THE INSURGENTS SHALL HAVE DISBANDED THEIR ARMIES, AND LAID DOWN THEIR ARMS, THE WAR WILL INSTANTLY CEASE, and all the war measures then existing, including those which affect Slavery, will cease also, and all moral, economical and political questions, as well as questions affecting Slavery as others which shall then be existing between individuals and States and the Federal Government, whether they arose before the Civil War began, or whether they grew out of it, will, by force of the Constitution, pass over to the arbitrament of courts of law, and to the councils of legislation.

FOR GOVERNOR
REUBEN E. FENTON
FOR LIEUTENANT GOVERNOR
THOMAS G. ALVORD
FOR CANAL COMMISSIONER
FRANKLIN A. ALBERGER
FOR STATE PRISON INSPECTOR
DAVID P. FORREST

GEORGE F. NESBITT & CO., PRINTERS, CORNER PEARL AND PINE STREETS,

The Civil War produced a plethora of generals who became presidential candidates. General George B. McClellan, above, was the Democratic candidate in 1864, the year Lincoln ran as a National Unionist (left). Hannibal Hamlin had been replaced on the ticket by Johnson. Ulysses S. Grant, below, was the choice of Republicans in 1868.

A Stolen Election

Although the Radical Republicans narrowly failed to remove President Andrew Johnson from office in 1868, they rendered his administration virtually impotent and effected a harsh Reconstruction in the South. The election of General Ulysses S. Grant to the Presidency that year completed their seizure of power. Whatever their individual motives—which ranged from humanitarian concern for the emancipated slaves to simple vengefulness and greed for power—the Radicals managed to introduce one-party rule in a two-party nation. With the usually watchful opposition gagged, the administration became one of the most corrupt in the country's history. The only effective protest came from a reform movement within the Republican party. While the reformers did well in regional elections, the people did not associate the heroic Grant with the excesses of his cronies and political mentors, and in 1872 Grant swamped reformer Horace Greeley, 286 electoral votes to 66. Meanwhile, as carpetbag governments began to lose their grip, the Democratic party began to regain strength in the South, and as a result, in the nation. In 1876 the Democrats attempted to make their comeback with Governor Samuel J. Tilden, a New York reformer. His opponent was Rutherford B. Hayes of Ohio. Tilden won a majority of the popular votes, but there was a dispute about the vote in the carpetbag-ruled states of Louisiana, South Carolina, and Florida. An electoral commission was formed, with Republicans in the majority; voting strictly along party lines, it accepted the Republican electors of all three states and gave Hayes the victory by one electoral vote. Tilden could probably have insisted on a new ballot in the disputed states (it is assumed he would have won), but feelings were running high, and he accepted the decision of the commission to avoid bloodshed. Hayes became President, but Reconstruction was doomed, and two-party government returned to America.

When it accepted the Republican electors from three disputed states, the Electoral Commission of 1877 (shown in the House in a painting by Cornelia Adèle Fassett at right) confirmed the election of Rutherford Birchard Hayes to the Presidency. It is generally believed that the Democrats acceded to the decision with the understanding that the remaining federal troops would be removed from the South, ending carpetbag rule.

The Age of Bosses

The two-party system that had returned in strength to American politics by 1880 was a sham. There were great issues developing in the country—most of which revolved around the enormous growth of industry and finance—but the leaders of the rival parties scarcely noticed them. Political power, to a degree seldom equaled before or since in America, was meaningful for its own sake, rather than as a tool for governing by a certain philosophy. The base of power was the Presidency: to secure it was to secure the most jobs, control of custom houses and post offices, and positions of influence in business. Under these circumstances the political boss was not only inevitable, he was necessary; he was an accountant, a coach, a scorekeeper of favors dispensed and recovered. Whether he sought the Presidency for himself or for one of his men, he remained the principal producer and stockholder, and stood to profit or lose the most. The American voter was on to him: third and fourth parties appeared often and affected the outcome of every presidential election. Other citizens sold their votes rather cheaply—a sound estimate of their value.

When Senator James G. Blaine sought the Republican presidential nomination in 1880, he was blocked by rival boss Roscoe Conkling (touching Blaine in the cartoon above), who supported former President Grant. Opposite is a campaign advertisement for the compromise Republican ticket. Defeating Democrat General Winfield Hancock, President James A. Garfield seemed prepared to purge boss influence from government when he was assassinated.

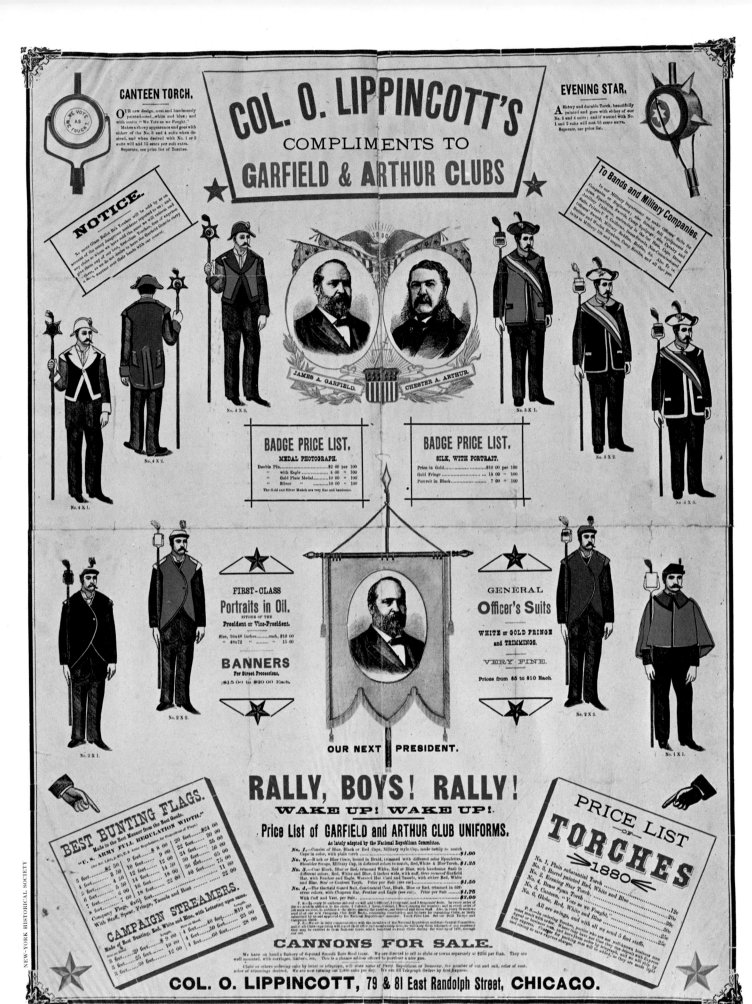

Slurs and Scandals

When Chester A. Arthur replaced the murdered James Garfield as President, he decided to stand up to his old mentor, Roscoe Conkling. Ironically, by decreasing Conkling's influence, he also weakened his support within the party, which spurned him in 1884 and gave James G. Blaine, Conkling's rival, the nomination. Blaine seemed unbeatable after the Republicans discovered that Grover Cleveland, the reform-minded Democratic candidate, was the probable father of an illegitimate child. But Cleveland won the voters' respect by candidly admitting that the child might be his. And Blaine's reputation as a wheeler-dealer, combined with his failure to repudiate promptly an anti-Catholic speech by a supporter, cost him votes, and as a result he lost the Presidency.

Above is an 1884 poster for the Grover Cleveland–Thomas A. Hendricks ticket, the first to win a presidential election for the Democratic party in almost thirty years.

In the 1884 Puck cartoon above, the unveiling of candidate Blaine reveals a body tattooed with symbols of all the deals with which he was associated. Puck also took a dim view of Greenback candidate Benjamin Butler and Equal Rights party nominee Belva Lockwood. Third parties affected the outcome of every election between 1880 and 1896. In 1888 the Prohibitionist vote was a factor in Cleveland's loss of New York and the election. At right is a Republican ribbon from 1888. Benjamin Harrison won a majority of the electoral votes that year while trailing Cleveland in popular votes.

Money and Vigor

Grover Cleveland was elected President again in 1892, but despite widespread disenchantment with the free-spending, probusiness Harrison administration, his margin was paper-thin. The reason was a third party, the Populists, who attracted more than a million votes. Four years later the two major parties paid special court to the growing grass roots vote. The Democrats nominated William Jennings Bryan, who, as expected, also won the Populist endorsement. The Republicans spent millions of dollars on an advertising campaign to make the name of their candidate, William McKinley, a household word. McKinley, protégé of Mark Hanna, a powerful Ohio politician, conducted a front-porch campaign, while Bryan traveled extensively on a meager budget. The voters loved listening to the eloquent Bryan condemn the gold standard, but they cast their votes for McKinley. The two rivals vied again in 1900 when McKinley, riding the crest of America's victory in the war against Spain, won by the first substantial margin in years. At their convention, Republican leaders had decided to "bury" Theodore Roosevelt, the noisy, reforming governor of New York, in the Vice Presidency, where he could do no harm. A year later McKinley was killed, and Roosevelt took charge. The rapport between the young, vigorous President and the people was unparalleled, and with their support he lifted presidential power and prestige from the doldrums in which they had been languishing since the death of Abraham Lincoln.

The Puck *cartoon opposite suggested accurately that Bryan's charge of imperialism would be no more effective against McKinley in 1900 than his "goldbug" charge had been in 1896. A keen judge of public opinion, the President had gone to war because he sensed the people wanted it; besides, the people were too exhilarated by the victory over Spain to take kindly to criticism of it. At the top of this page is an 1896 McKinley goldbug lapel pin. McKinley's campaign speeches favored the gold standard, which Bryan considered anathema. The button in the center was given away by the makers of ZigZag Chocolates, who combined support of Roosevelt with an advertising campaign in 1904—the year T. R. showed politicians used to squeakers what a landslide looked like. Below it is a William Howard Taft button worn by traveling salesmen. Taft defeated William Jennings Bryan in 1908.*

Clash of Giants

Because Theodore Roosevelt had been President of the United States, the American people had begun to take the office seriously, to respect it as they had not really respected it for decades. His Presidency had been personal and vital, and the people had taken him to their hearts. It was clear by 1912 that William Howard Taft, Roosevelt's hand-picked successor, was not the sort of President Americans wanted: T. R. had taught them to appreciate a dynamic Chief Executive who initiated action, rather than just reacted to events. But during his own administration Roosevelt had declared that he considered his first, three-year term a full one, and that since he opposed the idea of a third term, he would not run again. And so, while the electorate's affection for him was undimmed in 1912, the voters were not altogether receptive when he made it apparent that he would like to return to the White House. He was, after all, asking for a third term.

As the Republican convention of 1912 approached, Roosevelt took advantage of a new phenomenon in American politics, the presidential primary, which had been adopted in twelve states between 1910 and 1912. Roosevelt won 281 delegate votes in the primaries, to Taft's 71 and Robert La Follette's 36. But like most incumbents, Taft controlled the convention apparatus too firmly to lose the nomination. Roosevelt bolted, formed the Progressive, or Bull Moose, party, and ran against Taft and the Democratic nominee, Woodrow Wilson. The Bull Moose and Republican totals, when combined, exceeded Wilson's, but the Democrats captured the White House.

Reunified again in 1916, the Republicans nominated Charles Evans Hughes to oppose the re-election of Wilson. Although the President had had a distinguished first term in which tariff and banking reform had been enacted and legislation of significant social import had been passed, he was not, personally, the sort of man the people could feel particularly close to, and the election was tighter than it normally would have been at the end of a successful first administration. Nevertheless, Wilson won, largely because, as the slogan went, "He kept us out of war." In his second term, however, the war came to him; he entered it reluctantly and with great sorrow, and its aftermath destroyed him.

As if to compensate for the mediocrity of most of its late-nineteenth-century incumbents, the Presidency in the first two decades of the twentieth was dominated by the excellent men pictured on these pages. Theodore Roosevelt and Woodrow Wilson (left, top and bottom) gained votes by promising a better life for Americans; their programs were called the Square Deal and the New Freedom, respectively. Despite the lack of a similar catch phrase and of a real desire to be President, William H. Taft (above, campaigning in 1908) won one term in the White House, and enacted many of T. R.'s plans.

Normalcy

The frustrations following the Great War made the Republicans confident that they would win the election of 1920, and they looked only for a candidate who appeared statesmanly, and would do no harm in the campaign. From the famous smoke-filled room of the convention came the name of Senator Warren Harding, a name that was familiar only vaguely if at all to the majority of the electorate. Harding campaigned from his front porch, and as instructed, did no harm. His handsomeness probably did some good, for that year the ladies were voting for the first time. He was President for less than three years, and his death in office, as corruption of his cronies began to be exposed, was regarded by many as providential. His successor Calvin Coolidge got rid of the corruption but otherwise let well enough alone: Americans prospered, and probably would have elected him again in 1928. But he did not choose to run, and Herbert Hoover, who had served honorably as Secretary of Commerce, was rewarded with the Republican nomination. His defeat of Al Smith has been described with some distortion. While it is true that the religious issue hurt Smith, a Catholic, it seems unlikely that any Democrat could have unseated the Republicans as the economy continued its boom.

BOTH: STANLEY KING COLLECTION

The suggestion on Warren Harding's 1920 campaign badge (above, left) sounded good to Americans weary of Europe's troubles. The Coolidge thimble (above, right) was for the ladies, who made their second appearance at the polls in 1924. At right, Herbert Hoover's supporters in San Francisco turn out for a parade during the campaign of 1928. Hoover won some six million votes more than Democrat Al Smith of New York.

Hoover or Hearst?

A Rendezvous with Destiny

In 1932 Franklin Delano Roosevelt was a model presidential candidate. He was a proven vote getter, and as governor of New York—a traditional power base—he continued to add to his achievements while seeking the nomination. Both his name and face were assets; he had money, an energetic and popular wife, and a good relationship with the working press. His highly skilled managers were successful in securing delegate strength from all over the country, and their convention strategy was carefully planned. Nevertheless, there was something about the Roosevelt candidacy that seemed to make it an exception to the usual rules. For one thing, F. D. R. ignored the old taboo against appearing to want the nomination: he did want it and was not afraid to show it. For another—and this does not appear to have been a contrivance—the governor's candidacy gave the impression of having an irresistible force of its own. A series of preconvention polls, taken before the public politicking had begun, revealed that housewives and workingmen, intellectuals and the unemployed, people in and out of politics wanted Roosevelt to be President. Like any other candidate, Roosevelt needed an organization to win the nomination, but in his case the organization seemed necessary only to confirm a foregone conclusion. When he later told the nation that it had a rendezvous with destiny, the words sounded familiar and convincing coming from him, since he had seemed destined to become President. Together, destiny and the electorate were stronger than the traditional ban on third terms. F. D. R. was re-elected three times, and he remained President as long as he lived.

In 1932 newspaper publisher William Randolph Hearst supported John Nance Garner of Texas for the presidential nomination. When Garner accepted second place on the ticket, Roosevelt inherited Hearst's support. The cartoon on the opposite page suggests that Hearst was running the campaign ship; but Roosevelt's actions as President soon alienated the publisher. The photograph at left shows F. D. R. campaigning in a West Virginia mining community in 1932. The unionists' button (above, left) was probably used in the election of 1936, which Roosevelt won by a landslide. Alf Landon of Kansas captured only two states. F. D. R. was faced with more formidable opposition in 1940: the third-term issue (symbolized by the button above, right) and a more popular opponent, Wendell Willkie (on the matchbook, left). But Roosevelt won then and again in 1944, when he beat Thomas Dewey.

Truman's problems in 1948 were reflected in the cartoon above: Wallace would cost him votes, and Dewey's campaign was a well-financed, well-oiled mechanism. Below is an antiegghead cartoon regarding Stevenson's vocabulary in the 1952 race.

	EISENHOWER	STEVENS
ALA.	149,329	209,5
ARIZ.	90,338	51,87
ARK.	35123	4899
CALIF.	475,226	389,00
COLO.	102,871	61,97
CONN.	710,059	406,56
DEL	92,328	75,16
FLA.	512,308	361,09
GA.	136,077	227,
IDAHO	39,271	26,

Underdog and Shoo-in

The remarkable thing about the forty-first presidential election was the revelation that politicians, except for Harry Truman, had learned very little about the way Americans choose their Chief Executives. The Republicans and their candidate, Thomas Dewey, had the best organization and the most money, and all the polls predicted a Dewey landslide. The Democrats had tried almost frantically to find another candidate—preferably General Dwight Eisenhower, who refused them—and had settled on Truman only because he was the incumbent and there was no appealing alternative. Neither the left nor the right wing of the party liked him; so each broke away—the left to work for Progressive candidate Henry Wallace, the right to support Dixiecrat Strom Thurmond. True, radio had changed the nature of campaigning, but even in that area the Republicans had the advantage: Truman's twangy voice was no match for Dewey's rich baritone. The confident Dewey mouthed platitudes while Truman got on a train, made whistle-stop speeches, gave Congress, Republicans, and the people hell, and stunned the experts by winning. Never again would the Republicans take the electorate for granted—not even in 1952 when they had Eisenhower, probably the most popular man in America, as their candidate. Actually, that election was almost anticlimactic after the convention, to which Senator Robert A. Taft had come with what seemed to be sufficient delegate support to win. An Eisenhower candidacy—and almost certain victory in November—was an irresistible lure for the delegates, who switched to Ike. In a more adventurous mood, the Democrats nominated Governor Adlai E. Stevenson of Illinois, who was relatively unknown, an intellectual, and, as a divorced man, unelectable according to tradition. Stevenson did lose, but mainly because Ike was the closest thing in existence to an unbeatable candidate.

At left, the Eisenhowers and Richard M. Nixons celebrate their landslide re-election in 1956. When Ike was elected in 1952, he not only became the first Republican President in twenty years, but he brought many congressional Republicans with him. In later elections, however, the Democrats regained and held control of Congress despite Ike's own popularity.

The Primary Route

Senator John F. Kennedy was unusually young for a potential presidential candidate; he was, moreover, a Roman Catholic, and he lacked the support of his party's powerful congressional leadership. Nevertheless, he wanted the 1960 Democratic nomination, and with clever planning, a fine organization, and superb use of presidential primaries he got it. His most dramatic primary victory came in West Virginia, a poor, rural, and Protestant state where Kennedy's wealth, urbane manner, and religion had been expected to count heavily against him. Having won the nomination, he then disproved during the campaign the remaining charges against him—inexperience and immaturity—in a series of televised debates with his opponent, Vice President Richard M. Nixon. Kennedy won a narrow victory. Four years later, Republican Barry Goldwater won his party's nomination with equally good planning, organization, and use of primaries. But the election was not at all close. Goldwater, who had been insisting that Americans would elect a conservative if given the chance, carried his native Arizona and five southern states, losing all the rest to Lyndon B. Johnson.

Former President Harry S. Truman, who had denigrated John F. Kennedy and endorsed Senator Stuart Symington for the Presidency, loyally supported the Democratic candidate after he was nominated. The cartoon above comments on Truman's turnabout. At right is Kennedy campaigning.

At the Republican convention of 1964 (above), the conservatives, led by candidate Barry Goldwater, overwhelmed the party moderates. The Democrats (below) united behind incumbent Lyndon Johnson and were more harmonious, but the memory of Kennedy's assassination made for some somberness, too.

NATORIAL
ECTION
ROOM.
P STAIRS
ELEVATOR.

S DILLON
C. S. BRICE.
RUSSEL SAGE.
FIELD.
HUNTINGTON.

THE PRESIDENCY IN ECLIPSE

*"I shall on all subjects
have a policy to recommend,
but none to enforce against
the will of the people."*

ULYSSES S. GRANT

The cartoon at left, printed in Puck
*in 1890, implied that the Presidency
could be bought by rich politicians.*

CHAPTER FIVE

Suspicion of the Presidency

Most historians of America's Chief Magistracy chart its development as an intermittent yet irreversible increase in prestige and authority. In their view, power that has been successfully wielded by strong Presidents may be jeopardized by weak Presidents, but it is never quite lost.

Assessors of "strong" or "great" Presidents seem to agree that several of the first dozen Chief Executives fall into this honorific category. A collection of essays, *America's Ten Greatest Presidents*, edited by Morton Borden in 1961, paid that high compliment to no less than five among the first twelve: to Washington, John Adams, Jefferson, Jackson, and Polk. Moreover, such estimates invariably assume that what has been good for the Presidency has been good for the country. Edward S. Corwin was by no means condemning the tendency when he remarked in 1940 that "taken by and large, the history of the presidency has been a history of aggrandizement. . . ." He and other distinguished political scientists generally see the cumulative expansion of executive power as an index of national unity and power.

No doubt they are correct. But it is important to remember that the process has not been continuous, nor has it been uncontested. The growth of presidential power has perturbed many Americans who ought not to be dismissed as merely uninformed or hysterical. Corwin summed up the basis of their uneasiness and resentment when he said: "In short, the Constitution reflects the struggle between two conceptions of executive power: that it ought always to be subordinate to the supreme legislative power, and that it ought to be, within generous limits, autonomous

and self-directing; or, in other terms, the idea that the people are *re-presented* in the Legislature *versus* the idea that they are *embodied* in the Executive. . . ." The struggle, he added, has never entirely ceased.

For corroboration, one need look no further than the 1964 presidential campaign. In "My Case for the Republican Party, 1964," presidential candidate Senator Barry Goldwater expounded his ideas—extraordinary in view of the circumstances—on executive power. "We hear praise of a power-wielding, arm-twisting President who 'gets his program through Congress' by knowing the use of power. Throughout the course of history, there have been many other such wielders of power. There have even been dictators who regularly held plebiscites, in which their dictatorships were approved by an Ivory-soap-like percentage of the electorate. But their countries were not free, nor can any country remain free under such despotic power. Some of the current worship of powerful executives may come from those who admire strength and accomplishment of any sort. Others hail the display of Presidential strength . . . simply because they approve of the *result* reached by the use of power. This is nothing less than the totalitarian philosophy that the end justifies the means. . . . If ever there was a philosophy of government totally at war with that of the Founding Fathers, it is this one. To be a constitutionalist, it is at least as important that the use of power be legitimate as that it be beneficial."

This theme was a dominant one in Goldwater's campaign. Elsewhere he asserted that America's traditional and essential balance of power was being upset "by the trend toward increasing concentration of power in the Presidency.... *The more complete and concentrated executive power becomes, the greater will be the temptation to employ it to wipe out all opposing power....*"

It can be said that Goldwater was resoundingly defeated, and that he lost partly because he dealt in such hoary platitudes. He could not have hoped to scare the American people by warning them of dangers that had long ago disappeared, if indeed they had ever existed, in the United States. It could be noted, too, that he spoke as a senator: complaints of executive encroachments have been a standard feature of congressional oratory since 1789. He spoke, moreover, as an upholder of states' rights—another ancient source of hostility to centralized government. The significant point, however, is that after one hundred and seventy-five years of the Presidency, an honest if somewhat ingenuous candidate for the office could gain the confidence of a major party and the enthusiastic, if confused, agreement of millions of fellow citizens, by reiterating the old cry of executive encroachment, of presidential despotism. In fact the Republican party was no stranger to the cry. Throughout his successful campaign of 1952, General Dwight Eisenhower had stressed the need to end "executive usurpations of power" and "to restore the Congress to its rightful place in the Government."

The persistence of this fear deserves to be taken seriously. A central clue is provided by Professor Corwin's reminder that there have been two rival conceptions of executive power. The strong Presidents, their admiring biographers, and perhaps a majority of Americans have preferred the "autonomous and self-directing" conception. But a sizable number of weak Presidents and a numerous minority of Americans have preferred a limited executive acting negatively in response to congressional initiative, and taking no step to weaken the authority of individual states. The Founding Fathers appeared to tip the balance toward the first conception. Not all the Founding Fathers agreed, however, nor did many of their supporters. This minority was disposed to fight for its belief, and to regard all aspirants to the Presidency as guilty of nefarious designs until proved innocent. This meant that the men who actually achieved the Presidency were viewed with suspicion until the moment they left office. At the back of many minds was the dread of "monarchy," "tyranny," "usurpation"—a vocabulary of doubt and resentment employed again and again.

Of course the critics of Presidents often exaggerated, and knew they were exaggerating, for partisan purposes. Politicians avail themselves of whatever weapons are at hand. The fiercer the contest the less scruple they have in choice of weapons—including brickbats. "Waving the bloody shirt" against the Democrats (associating them with Southern secession) was a favorite tactic of Republicans after the Civil War. In the same way, the opposition party in the first half-century of American nationhood hoped to attract votes (partly through appealing to xenophobia) by accusing the administration of un-American inclinations toward monarchism.

Much of the criticism of George Washington was deliberately exaggerated along these lines. Could the more scurrilous journalists and pamphleteers who attacked him really have believed that he wanted to be king or that he was behaving like a hypocrite and an autocrat? They must have been conscious of the unfairness of describing him as one who "thundered contempt upon the people with as much confidence as if he sat upon the throne of Indostan," or of grumbling that "he receives visits. He returns none. Are these republican virtues? Do they command our esteem?" Another assailant pretended that the "improper influence" of Washington had deceived and "debauched" the American nation. "Let the history of the federal government," he went on, "instruct mankind, that the masque of patriotism may be worn to conceal the foulest designs against the liberties of a people."

The abuse heaped on Washington by Thomas Paine, a hero of early Revolutionary days, had a demented quality. Paine, living in France, had convinced himself that the United States was sliding back into British monarchico-aristocratical ways and that Washington was largely to blame. In a sixty-page open letter, written in 1796, Paine ranted that "you commenced your Presidential career by encouraging and swallowing the grossest adulation, and you travelled America . . . to put yourself in the way of receiving it. . . . John Adams has said (and John, it is known, was always a smeller after places and offices) . . . that as Mr. Washington had no child, the Presidency should be made hereditary in the family of Lund Washington [a cousin]. . . . He did not go so far as to say also, that the Vice Presidency should be hereditary in the family of John Adams. He prudently left that to stand upon the ground, that one good turn deserves another."

The interest of such scurrility lies not in its truthfulness, for it is invariably inaccurate as well as malignant, but in its underlying motivation. Two points should be noted. One is that these onslaughts represent a complex though largely irrational hostility to any person who achieves the combination of high office and celebrity that marks the Presidency. Merely to be President, no matter how deservingly or how modestly, is to attract venomous abuse. The second point is that this abuse reveals an irrational dislike of the power and social standing that makes the Presidency comparable—even if the comparison is somewhat farfetched—to an elective monarchy.

Three other factors help to account for the unpopularity that often surrounded the Presidency. The situation of Barry Goldwater, referred to previously, displays these factors, which are friction between Congress and the Executive, party politics, and states' rights. Power must rival power: that is the condition of a government of separated branches —a condition fully comprehended by Madison, Hamilton, and other Founding Fathers. Power acquired must necessarily be power acquired *from* some other branch. Each time a President successfully asserted an additional prerogative he laid up trouble for himself and his successors; Congress would be sure to strike back. Sometimes it would strike even when no offense had been given, just to keep in training. Of thirty-three items of possible legislation proposed by the undemanding Calvin Coolidge in his first annual message, for instance, Congress deigned to pass only one. A newspaper, looking at the record of Coolidge's relations with Capitol Hill, said, "Congress has devoted itself to bloodying the President's nose, boxing his ears, and otherwise maltreating him." The contest, which the modern political scientist James MacGregor Burns referred to as *The Deadlock of Democracy*, was even bloodier when vital and controversial issues were at stake. Burns argued that the United States long ago developed, and suffered from thereafter, not a two-party but a four-party system. Each of the two main parties, according to his analysis, has split into a presidential and a congressional bloc.

Whether or not Burns is correct, it is undeniable that members of the opposition party, sometimes assisted by disaffected congressmen from the administration party, often voiced intense suspicion of nineteenth-century Presidents. This suspicion was particularly virulent at times of crisis. A major source of complaint, exacerbated in wartime by the historic distrust of standing armies, was the President's patronage power. James Madison was a mild, scholarly man with a deep aversion to executive encroachments. When during the War of 1812 he asked for an increase in the size of the regular Army, John Randolph of Roanoke, Virginia (a member of his own party), protested that Madison was building up a "mighty apparatus of favoritism." The rival Federalist party accused Madison of scheming to place James Monroe at the head of the vastly expanded Army. Monroe, who was acting Secretary of War as well as Secretary of State, was Madison's most likely successor. "What a grasp at power is this!" exploded the Federalist politician Josiah Quincy of Massachusetts. His party was doubly indignant because the new officers' commissions were handed out almost exclusively to Republicans.

Similar fury was aroused during the Mexican War by James K. Polk's endeavors to gain political advantage for his own party. At the beginning of 1848, when the war was virtually over, President Polk asked for ten additional regular regiments and twenty volunteer regiments. A Whig congressman angrily maintained that the five hundred and forty or so new Army officers created by this increase were meant to help purchase the coming presidential election for the Democrats. Polk, said his critic, "already has much greater patronage than Washington, Madison, Jackson, or any other of his predecessors possessed, and I cannot . . . believe that the interests or honor of the country would be advanced by increasing it." The charge was comparable to the Whig complaint in eighteenth-century England that the King's power "has increased, is increasing, and ought to be diminished."

The states' rights controversy also fomented hostility toward any President who asserted the supremacy of the central government. In the days of the Virginia dynasty the issue was on the whole dormant. Jefferson, Madison, and Monroe genuinely believed in preserving the sovereign rights of the states. On several occasions they vetoed or discouraged bills providing federal funds for internal improvements, arguing that while such bills might be desirable they could not be sanctioned without the passing of a constitutional amendment. But Madison clashed with the governors of Massachusetts and Connecticut. Opposed to administration policy during the War of 1812, the New Englanders denied that Madison was empowered to call out the militias and use them outside the boundaries of their own states.

This dispute and others were fought out mainly in the Supreme Court, where Chief Justice John Marshall championed federal rather than state jurisdiction. But in 1832 there was a violent clash between Andrew Jackson and South Carolina caused by Southern objections to high tariffs. Jackson's prompt, unyielding response to the Palmetto State's defiance won him high praise from posterity and even from such unfriendly contemporaries as Daniel Webster. His Proclamation on Nullification is regarded as a key document in the history of federal control and as an example of his indomitable courage.

There is, however, another side to the story. South Carolina persisted in defying the Washington government partly because Jackson's previous conduct seemed to indicate that he too was a states' rights man. He had vetoed the Maysville Road bill of 1830 on strict-constructionist grounds. He had openly sympathized with the state of Georgia and had openly flouted John Marshall's Court in the controversy as to whether Georgia had the right to remove the Cherokee within its borders or whether—as the Supreme Court ruled—the Indians were wards of the federal government. The surprise and outrage of South Carolina were revealed in the resolutions that the state legislature approved as a reply to Jackson's Nullification decree:

"*Resolved*, That the proclamation of the President is the more extraordinary, that he had silently, and as it is supposed, with entire approbation, witnessed our sister state of Georgia avow, act upon, and carry into effect, even to the taking of life, principles identical with those now denounced by him in South Carolina."

How was his behavior to be explained? The obvious answer, according to John C. Calhoun and his fellow Carolinians, was that power had gone to the President's head. "King Andrew" was acting as capriciously and arrogantly as any European despot:

"*Resolved*, That the opinions of the President, in regard to the rights of the States, are erroneous and dangerous, leading not only to the establishment of a consolidated government in the stead of our free confederacy, but to the concentration of all powers in the chief executive.

"*Resolved*, That the declaration of the President . . . is rather an appeal to the loyalty of subjects, than to the patriotism of citizens, and is a blending of official and individual character, heretofore unknown in our state papers, and revolting to our conception of political propriety."

Historians have rightly stressed Jackson's importance in making the Presidency a far more vivid, personal, popular, and dynamic institution. Something new began with Andrew Jackson. Clinton Rossiter hinted at the reverse side of the coin when he remarked that "more than one such President a century would be hard to take." To see why Jackson's enemies regarded him as a baleful influence it is necessary to review the events of his administrations critically, as those events appeared to such opponents as Calhoun, Webster, and Clay.

Charles M. Wiltse, Calhoun's biographer, is one of the few modern scholars to have undertaken this task. The record of Jacksonian usurpation, he pointed out, contained several weighty charges. In the Peggy Eaton affair, for instance, Jackson had behaved (in the view of his enemies) with savage indiscretion. Mrs. Margaret Bayard Smith, a fairly sympathetic Washington hostess, reported that "the only excuse his best friends can make for his violence and imbecilities, is, that he is in his dotage." In the affair he treated his Cabinet and his Vice President with contempt. Indeed he replaced every member except one, his Postmaster General. Even earlier he had formed the habit of relying on a "Kitchen Cabinet" of editors and politicians. He established the Washington *Globe* as an administration newspaper, and used it and other Democratic publications to pervert the truth and to coerce his followers into unswerving obedience to the party line. He wrecked the ideal of an impartial, permanent civil service by sanctifying the cynical practice of rotation in office. He brought the code of a frontier bully into the White House. His crude, implacable clansman's outlook impelled him to believe that John Quincy Adams and Henry Clay had stooped to a corrupt bargain to keep him out of the Presidency. He broke off relations with his own Vice President when he discovered that Calhoun had disapproved of his highhanded activities as a military leader ten years earlier. Through his position on hard money, he earned the enmity of former supporters. In vetoing the recharter of the Second Bank of the United States, Jackson had defied well-informed public opinion and the wishes of both houses of Congress. In his eight years in office he used the veto twelve times —more than the eleven vetoes of all his predecessors. His Bank veto blatantly appealed to the common man and stirred up class war because it alleged that the friends of the Bank were friends of monopoly and aristocracy.

In the Cherokee cases, the President contended that he was not bound by the decisions of the Supreme Court. The executive, in his view (as docilely expounded in administration newspapers), was an independent, coordinate branch of the government, with the right to execute the Constitution according to executive interpretation. He made the challenge explicit in his Bank veto message of July 10, 1832. Although previous Supreme Court rulings (such as *McCulloch v. Maryland*, 1819, and *Osborn v. Bank of the United States*, 1824) had held that the Bank was constitutional, he refused to recognize such precedents. "If the opinion of the Supreme Court covered the whole ground of this act, it ought not to control and coördinate authorities of this Government," he said. "Each public officer who takes an oath to support the Constitution swears that he will support it as he understands it, and not as it is understood by others. . . . The opinion of the judges has no more authority over Congress than the opinion of Congress has over the judges, and on that point the President is independent of both."

When Jackson vetoed the Bank recharter in 1832, the original charter still had four years to run. He decided to kill the Bank at once by removing the government deposits and transferring them to state banks. He had to dismiss two Secretaries of the Treasury before he could find a third, Roger B. Taney, who was ready to do his bidding.

In this instance, as in the Peggy Eaton imbroglio, the President made clear his contempt for his Cabinet members. He had shown equal contempt for the judiciary. His opponents in Congress maintained that by vetoing so many of their bills, and by asserting in effect that he was the voice of the popular will, Jackson was guilty of similar contempt for the legislative branch. In the latter half of 1833 the Senate, in an unprecedented move, vented its displeasure by

In the anti-Jackson cartoon above, the President gaily dons Napoleon's clothes as Taney and Van Buren look on.

introducing two censure resolutions, one against Jackson and one against Taney. Both passed after protracted debate. What was at stake, said Calhoun, was not just a struggle over the Bank but "a struggle between the executive and legislative departments of the government."

Jackson's answer to the Senate was a lengthy message, by turns caustic and plaintive, which denounced the censure resolutions as unconstitutional, described them as an act akin to impeachment, and demanded that his reply be entered in the Senate's records. The request was refused. The Senate took further vengeance by refusing to confirm Taney's appointment as Secretary of the Treasury—the first time a Cabinet nomination had been rejected—and by postponing confirmation of his subsequent appointment to the Supreme Court.

If the Senate's display was vindictive, Jackson's opponents could contend that it was he who had loosed the vendettas of partisan politics upon the United States, and that they had been reluctantly obliged to follow suit. They saw proof of the vendetta instincts of Jacksonian democracy in the long campaign of Senator Thomas Hart Benton of Missouri (who had once fought a vicious duel-brawl with Jackson before becoming one of his supporters) to have the censure resolution expunged from the Senate journal and—a vulgarly melodramatic touch—to have "black lines . . . drawn around the entry." Benton at last got his way in January, 1837, by 24 votes to 19. "And now, sir," he declared in triumph, "I finish the task which, three years ago, I imposed on myself. Solitary and alone, and amidst the jeers and taunts of my opponents, I put this ball in motion. The people have taken it up and rolled it forward, and I am not anything in the vast mass which now propels it. In the name of the mass I speak. . . ."

Benton's demagogic cry rankled and lodged in the Whig memory. Apart from everything else, it was absurd to pretend that he had fought alone, sustained only by the people. In several states controlled by the Democrats, senators had been instructed by their respective state legislatures to vote with Benton. Some meekly obeyed; some, like John Tyler of Virginia, resigned their seats in protest.

Yet another grievance against "King Andrew" was that in his first and second annual messages, which advocated a mode of popular election for the President, he also recommended that the Chief Magistrate should be limited to "a single term of either four or six years." The reason he gave in the second message was that the President was the agent most subject to the temptation to exceed his powers. Was Andrew Jackson—who subsequently ignored his repeated dictum—not convicted out of his own mouth? He made sure that his followers nominated him for a second term; and as it neared its end, Calhoun was one of those who believed that Jackson was bent on a third term in office. Calhoun was wrong, of course, but he felt that he was essentially right: Jackson picked his own successor, Martin Van Buren, and forced him upon the party convention, together with a vice presidential nominee, Colonel Richard M. Johnson, who was so distasteful to some of the party faithful that he was actually hissed by the Virginia delegation. In the 1836 election Jackson's home state, Tennessee, indicated the extent of anti-Jackson feeling by handing its electoral votes to his antagonist Hugh Lawson White.

Benton's victory in the censure controversy was given an ironical twist in the election of 1840, when the Whigs settled part of the score against Jackson by engineering the defeat of his hand-picked favorite Van Buren. "I put this ball in motion," Benton had bragged. Whig demonstrators retaliated in 1840 by rolling a giant sphere from city to city, to the accompaniment of a jeering campaign song:

> What has caused this great commotion; motion, motion,
>   Our country through?
> It is the ball a rolling on.
> For Tippecanoe and Tyler too—Tippecanoe and
>   Tyler too.
> And with them we'll beat little Van, Van, Van;
> Van is a used up man.

The Whigs got their own back too by pretending that Van Buren, "King Matty," if not as fierce a tyrant as his predecessor, had at least developed a royal taste for gold dinner services, eau de cologne, and expensive wine:

> King Matty he sat in his "big white House,"
>   A curling his whiskers fine,
> And the *Globe* man, Blair, sat by his side,
>   A drinking his champagne wine, wine, wine,
>   A drinking his champagne wine.

The Whigs' speedy adoption of Democratic techniques, including the spoils system as well as the carnival type of election campaign, makes it appear that the charges of executive despotism against Jackson had no real substance. Van Buren's explanation was that the anti-Jackson men took up the cry because they had no other—once they discovered that the Bank contest was going against them. In his brilliant *Age of Jackson*, published in 1945, Arthur M. Schlesinger, Jr., agreed that "executive despotism" was a rallying cry for enemies of Jackson who otherwise had almost nothing in common. He conceded that "the fear of executive despotism . . . is no fancy, as the experience of the one-party states of the twentieth century clearly shows." But he thought it unlikely that "many raised this cry against Jackson who would not have fought him anyway." The charge of tyrant, Schlesinger added, "has been made against every strong democratic President by those whose interests he threatens." This statement is borne out by the administrations of Franklin D. Roosevelt and John F. Kennedy, which Schlesinger has also explored with admiring insight.

It may seem, then, that the violence of language hurled against Andrew Jackson is to be discounted. It would appear to be partisan rhetoric, and to testify more to envy and chagrin and congressional touchiness than to genuine alarm. Certainly most historians view the extreme instances of anti-Jacksonianism, during the period of the censure debates, in this way. A few well-known examples convey the tone of such indictments. In 1834 Chancellor James Kent of New York wrote to Justice Joseph Story, "I look upon Jackson as a detestable, ignorant, reckless, vain and malignant tyrant. . . . This American elective monarchy frightens me. The experiment, with its foundations laid on universal suffrage and our unfettered press, is of too violent a nature for our excitable people." Daniel Webster, fulminating in the Senate, declared that "the President carries on the government; all the rest are sub-contractors. . . . A Briareus sits in the centre of our system, and with his hundred hands touches everything, controls everything." Henry Clay, also in the Senate, said: "We are in the midst of a revolution, hitherto bloodless, but tending rapidly towards a total change of the pure republican character of the Government, and to the concentration of all power in the hands of one man." Governor Erastus Root of New York wrote to Clay to compliment him on his speech and to ask: "When will the mad career of the 'military chieftain' be checked? or is it never to meet with a check? Will a thoughtless multitude, led on by or encouraged by knavish politicians, always sing paeans of praise to the usurpations of a despot, if emblazoned with military renown?"

Calhoun echoed Clay's insinuations: "The Senator from Kentucky read a striking passage from Plutarch, descriptive of Caesar forcing himself, sword in hand, into the treasury of the Roman commonwealth. We are in the same stage of our political revolution, and the analogy between the two cases is complete, varied only by the character of the actors and the circumstances of the times. . . . The Senator said truly, and, let me add, philosophically, that 'we are in the midst of a revolution.'"

Those of the Whig persuasion, it could be said, derived their *raison d'être* from the theme of "King Andrew." The very name of their party (which originated in 1834) was an effort to draw a parallel between "Andrew I" and George III: in each case the cause of liberty was upheld by a Whig opposition. Or take Nathaniel Beverley Tucker's *The Partisan Leader*. This fantasy novel, published in 1836, is an expression of Southern states' rights sentiment. The work of a Virginian, it predicted a situation in which his state would be driven into a future rebellion against the federal government. But it is also a novel about usurpation. Written to prevent, if possible, the election of Van Buren, it treated him as though he would be certain to emulate "King Andrew" by becoming "King Matthew." In *The Partisan Leader* Van Buren has succeeded to the Presidency; moreover he has held office for twelve years with no intention of retiring from his "palace," the White House.

In December, 1838, the successful Whig candidate of 1840, William Henry Harrison, produced a set of promises that point by point were almost laughably non-Jacksonian: "If elected, I will: 1. Confine my service to a single term. 2. Disclaim all right of control over the public treasury. 3. Eschew any attempt to influence the elections. 4. Exercise due regard for laws passed by representatives of the people, and, within specified limitations, limit my exercise of the veto power. 5. Never suffer the influence of my office to be used for partisan purposes. 6. If requested, I will furnish to the Senate my reasons for removals from office. 7. Never suffer the executive 'to become the source of legislation' (expunging resolution)."

In the 1840 elections the Whigs were still harping on the same tune. Henry Clay, speechmaking on behalf of Harrison, repeated that Presidents should be restricted to one term. In a speech in Hanover County, Virginia, he reviewed recent history, emphasizing what was by then Whig doctrine. "Executive encroachment has quickly followed upon executive encroachment. . . ." Clay declared. "The nation has been in the condition of a man who, having gone to bed after his barn has been consumed by fire, is aroused in the morning to witness his dwelling-house wrapped in flames. So bold and presumptuous has the executive become, that, penetrating in its influence the hall of a co-ordinate branch of the government, by means of a submissive or instructed majority of the Senate, it has caused a record of the country to be effaced and expunged, the inviolability of which was guaranteed by a solemn injunction of the Constitution! . . ." The senator from Kentucky also made the ominous statement that "if the progress of executive usurpation were to continue unchecked, hopeless despair would seize the public mind, or the people would be goaded to acts of open and violent resistance."

Edwin C. Rozwenc, who in 1964 incorporated Clay's speech in a collection of source material on Jacksonian America, pointed out a weakness in the Whig position. Like Barry Goldwater in 1964, the Whigs in 1836, in 1840, and again in 1844 sought to narrow executive authority while at the same time recommending vigorous action by the federal government. There is perhaps a further interesting parallel. Goldwater struck an answering chord in his audiences when he expatiated on the spread of violence in America, and implied both that he would take firm action to end it and that the violence was in some way the fault of the Democratic administration. In Jackson's second administration and during the Presidency of Van Buren there appeared to be a frightening eruption of violence in the United States. In the fall of 1834 one New England periodical published an alarmist article entitled "The March of Anarchy"; another said that the previous year had produced "examples of outrage and violence altogether unprecedented in the annals of our country." *Niles' Register* claimed in September, 1835, to have recently clipped "more than 500 articles, relating to the various *excitements* now acting on the people of the United States, public and private! *Society seems everywhere unhinged.* . . ." In 1838 a young politician gave a talk on this subject to the Young Men's Lyceum of Springfield, Illinois. The speaker, Abraham Lincoln, who revered Henry Clay and yearned to follow in his footsteps, said that America faced serious danger from the "increasing disregard for law"— a disregard that could lead to the seizure of power by some exceptional man with the ambitions of "an Alexander, a Caesar, or a Napoleon." Edmund Wilson, pondering this utterance in 1962 in his book *Patriotic Gore*, suggested that Lincoln had unwittingly projected himself in the Napoleonic role. It seems more likely that in 1838 young Lincoln was thinking of Andrew Jackson.

To blame the Democrats for the alarming unrest of the 1830's was (as in the 1960's) as irresistible as it was unfair. Whatever the exact cause, many felt that something was wrong with America. Some believed that the trouble lay with Andrew Jackson and his usurpations. It is not quite enough to dismiss this uneasiness as party maneuvering, although there was certainly a tinge of blatant partisan exaggeration. Van Buren's explanation does not reveal why complaints at "King Andrew" began *before* the

Whigs had discovered their vulnerability on the Bank issue. In the 1832 election they were confident of defeating Jackson over the Bank. Even so, an anti-Jackson booklet of 1832, in the form of a nursery rhyme—"This Is the House that Jackson Built"— showed the monarchy accusation in full swing:

> And here is
> THE TYRANT
> Who, born to command,
> Is the curse of the country—the King of the land
> Against whom the people have taken their stand—
> The dotard of sixty—the plaything of knaves
> Who would make us obey him, or render us slaves.

Schlesinger's *Age of Jackson*, published the year Franklin D. Roosevelt died, was inevitably colored by the knowledge that F. D. R.'s powerful and prolonged stay in office had brought America through grave emergencies, domestic and foreign. It was natural that Schlesinger should be more interested in the positive than in the negative aspects of Jackson's reign. For this reason, no doubt, he did not mention the censure resolutions.

It is not necessary to believe that Jackson was a tyrant, or that either he or Van Buren had the faintest intention of becoming a king. But it is worth going into some detail about Andrew Jackson in order to see why many of his contemporaries were prepared to believe the assertion. His somewhat inconsistent, highly egocentric, and almost rabble-rousing Presidency followed a sequence of quiescent administrations in which no large demands were made on behalf of the executive branch. Nor, unlike Polk and Lincoln and Franklin D. Roosevelt, was Jackson confronted with a war situation (even if he indulged in some saber rattling against the French over a minor matter of unpaid debts), which would have obliged him to take vigorous action. Nor could it be said that the nation faced acute internal crises, with the possible exception of the Nullification controversy. The Bank war was of his own contriving. States' rights sensitivity, party spleen, and congressional jealousy of the Executive are not in themselves enough to explain why a Henry Clay, a Daniel Webster, and a John C. Calhoun may have honestly felt that Andrew Jackson was a menace to the nation. The alarm they expressed and the vocabulary they employed drew upon deep American suspicions, which were not allayed by the apparently harmless evolution of the Presidency after Jackson.

This brings us to subterranean and frankly speculative problems, which are barely touched on in the innumerable books that recount the history of the executive office or analyze its functions. Andrew Jackson was a figure of profound importance in the presidential succession, a man who demanded and received popular support on a scale never before experienced. In addition, he generated dislike and resistance of an intensity also previously unknown. He did things no earlier President had attempted. Something was also done to him, or almost done to him, that no previous President had experienced: someone tried to assassinate him with two pistols fired at point-blank range. Both weapons misfired, although when tested afterward they worked perfectly. Only luck saved the President.

A new hazard had been added to the office. Thirty years later, in April, 1865, the next effort at assassination succeeded: in the moment of Union victory John Wilkes Booth shot Abraham Lincoln in Washington. In 1881 the same fate claimed the life of President Garfield. In 1901 President McKinley was killed. The terrible tally was increased in November, 1963, with the slaying of John F. Kennedy in Dallas. Shortly before Kennedy's death, a man who had strapped some sticks of dynamite to himself had failed to carry through a scheme to blow the President to pieces while he was vacationing in Florida.

Between the assassinations of McKinley and Kennedy there were a number of abortive attacks. Ex-President Theodore Roosevelt was wounded in the chest by a bullet during his 1912 presidential campaign for re-election as a Progressive candidate. An attempt was made on the life of President-elect Franklin D. Roosevelt in February, 1933. The bullets missed him but killed Mayor Anton J. Cermak of Chicago and wounded several others. In 1950 a group of Puerto Ricans plotted to kill President Harry S. Truman. Although he escaped unhurt, one of the guards at Blair House (where he was then living) was killed and two were wounded.

These isolated acts of violence are generally regarded as meaningless events—wild gestures by wretched, unhinged creatures. Richard Lawrence, the man who had tried to kill Andrew Jackson, was an unemployed drifter, an English-born immigrant who believed that he was the rightful heir to the thrones of England and America, and that Jackson stood in his way. Lincoln's murderer, John Wilkes

Booth, was a flashy actor with delusions of grandeur. By the time he struck, allegedly on behalf of the Confederacy, it was too late for his assault to help the South, which lay in ruin. Charles J. Guiteau, who shot James Garfield in the back while the President waited for a train, was an unstable specimen of the breed known as disappointed office seekers and a member of the thwarted Stalwart wing of Garfield's Republican party. The good-natured McKinley was fired on by a self-styled anarchist, Leon Czolgosz, who had no connection with the American anarchist groups that he had halfheartedly sought to contact. Giuseppe Zangara, Franklin Roosevelt's would-be assailant, was another unemployed drifter, who had no idea what he might accomplish by taking the President's life. As for the shooting of Kennedy, we are in a nightmare realm. We do not know and perhaps shall never know whether Lee Harvey Oswald acted alone. The very pointlessness of his behavior has induced critics in the United States and elsewhere to invent an explanation if they could not discover one. So far, the event remains without plausible explanation. In the light of previous American assassinations the meaning might be that it was, in fact, meaningless.

In short, the series of attacks on the President, from Jackson to Kennedy, would appear to be nonpolitical in origin. If any comparison exists, perhaps it is with England. It is possible to cite the attempt to kill the prime minister, Sir Robert Peel, in 1843. The incident is remembered in the context of insanity; the case of the unsuccessful assassin, Daniel M'Naghten, who shot Peel's secretary by mistake, prompted the courts to formulate the M'Naghten rule for determining culpability for insane acts. Around the same time, there were three attempts on the life of young Queen Victoria. One of these, like certain of the American instances, seems to belong to the genre of black comedy. A pistol was pointed at the Queen by a deformed lunatic named Bean. In the melee he escaped arrest; before he was finally caught the police were rounding up every hunchback in London. In the past century England has revealed no tendency toward political or ideological killings.

General reasons are offered for the relative frequency of American assassination attempts. At least in comparison with Britain, the United States has accepted disorder and a high crime rate as almost an endemic condition in a mobile, heterogeneous,

UNITED PRESS INTERNATIONAL

John Wilkes Booth (left) assassinated Lincoln in 1865. In 1901 Leon Czolgosz (center) murdered McKinley. The bullet fired in 1881 by Charles J. Guiteau (right) need not have been fatal to James Garfield, but the medical care he received was inept.

and enormous country. England had its civil war more than two hundred years before the American Civil War, which, with all the deep unrest that occasioned, accompanied, and followed it, is in historical perspective a quite recent affair. Another obvious reason, given renewed prominence in the 1960's, is the availability of lethal weapons. It could be said that Yankee ingenuity and early techniques of mass production introduced the democracy of the pistol along with that of the ballot box: Colt and Deringer brought homicide within the reach of even the poorest citizen. (A Northern visitor to Dallas, Texas, shortly before the arrival there of President Kennedy, was told by a local acquaintance: "God made big people. And God made little people. But Colt made the .45 to even things out.") A third factor is the accessibility of the American President. Secret Service protection was not provided until after Czolgosz fatally wounded McKinley. Before (and after) that time the President was an easy target for assassination, not to mention personal insult, on the street, in travel, at the White House, or on the platform of some crowded hall.

A further though less obvious reason might be the effect of newspaper stories on the minds of potential American assassins. In the nineteenth and early twentieth century sensational attacks—sometimes by anarchists, sometimes by "patriots"—were made on heads of state all over the world. Felice Orsini

tried to kill Napoleon III in 1858, seven years before Booth burst into Lincoln's box at the theater. A quarter of a century before Theodore Roosevelt was wounded in the chest, the same thing happened to Bismarck in Germany. The list of actual killings, all of them front-page stories, is appallingly long. In 1868 the victim was Prince Michael of Serbia. In 1881, the year of Garfield's death, Czar Alexander II was brutally killed by a terrorist bomb. Anarchists dispatched President Carnot of France in 1894, Empress Elizabeth of Austria in 1898, and King Umberto of Italy in 1900. In 1903, in Serbia, Prince Michael's great-grandnephew Alexander was killed. The Russian minister of the interior, Plehve, was assassinated in 1904, the Portuguese king (Carlos) and crown prince in 1908. The prime ministers of Russia and Spain were murdered in 1911 and 1912. The killing of Archduke Ferdinand of Austria at Sarajevo in 1914 ignited World War I. And in recent years the tally has been increased by the assassinations of Mahatma Gandhi in India, Prime Minister Bandaranaike in Ceylon, and a host of other attacks —including those of French extremists on President De Gaulle.

Even so a puzzle remains. Including Lyndon B. Johnson, thirty-five men have occupied the Presidency. Four have been assassinated and attempts have been made to assassinate at least four others: eight murders or near-murders out of thirty-five. The actuarial chances are thus more than one in five that somebody will try to kill an American President, and about one in nine that he will succeed. It could be argued that the risks are actually greater. No one made an attempt on the life of the first six Presidents, from George Washington through John Quincy Adams. The danger began with Andrew Jackson, for reasons perhaps already plain. Omitting the first six Presidents, the odds that someone will attempt to kill the President stand at more than one in four.

Why such high odds when American Presidents are too hedged in by constitutional limitations to assume absolute power even if they wanted to? The vocabulary of the would-be assassins, lunatic though they may have been, reveals something. Lawrence brooded over the idea that Andrew Jackson was an actual king, though a usurper, who in the pursuit of his wicked aims had killed Lawrence's royal father. The man who shot Theodore Roosevelt shouted, "No third term!"

Although the application was insane, the vocabulary was drawn from everyday American discourse. As Louis Brownlow stated in *The President and the Presidency*, "Every President . . . with but one exception, when he has been in office has been denounced as a despot, as a tyrant, as a dictator, as one who was using the power of the government . . . to achieve his own personal ambitions. The only President who was not so denounced was William Henry Harrison: he lived only one month after he was inaugurated." The vocabulary had been suddenly and almost hysterically heightened in Jackson's time. Calhoun said in the Senate that Jackson's Bank depredations were "adding robbery to murder." Jackson claimed he had received five hundred letters from people threatening to kill him. So heated was the atmosphere that he himself believed the assassin had been hired by his enemies. Administration newspapers spread the theory. America witnessed an extraordinary moment when Calhoun, a former Vice President and a member of the United States Senate, rose from his seat to deny that he had plotted to kill the President.

Wild though Jackson's charges were, they contained a grain of truth. In a sense every enemy who called the President a tyrant or a Caesar was invoking the momentum of history. For the mentally unstable, or indeed for those literal-minded citizens who believed what they were told, America was succumbing to a despot. The lesson was plain, to Lawrence

and to Booth and no doubt to others who were not quite prepared to translate thought into deed: the tyrant must be struck down, the murderer murdered. *Sic semper tyrannis!* as Booth shouted: *ever thus to tyrants!* Was that not, after all, the sacred motto of Virginia, the Old Dominion? Had not Virginia's Thomas Jefferson declared that "the tree of liberty must be refreshed from time to time with the blood of patriots and tyrants"? Such blood was "its natural manure."

Every strong President was subject to this queerly sinister animus. Lincoln was stigmatized as a tyrant by Supreme Court justices and Northern editors as well as by the Confederacy. He was another Jackson, with his bypassing of Congress, his arrests of citizens who ventured to criticize him, his suppression of newspapers, his suspension of habeas corpus, his use of bayonets to enforce his decrees.

Senator Charles Sumner, indignant at Andrew Johnson's attempt to maintain Lincoln's initiative in determining Reconstruction policy, declared in 1865: "If something is not done the President will be crowned king before Congress meets." Johnson's retort to his critics, in February, 1866, was couched in the same extravagant idiom: "Men may talk about beheading and about usurpation, but when I am beheaded I want the American people to be witnesses. I do not want it, by innuendoes and indirect remarks in high places, to be suggested to men who have assassination brooding in their bosoms. . . ."

Theodore Roosevelt accused the newspapers of intensifying the emotions of his assailant. The problem of possible incitement through journalistic comment remained perplexing. A virulent example was provided in 1937. The confidential press reports of the McClure Newspaper Syndicate (whose service was distributed each week to some two hundred and seventy American newspapers) quoted an official of American Cyanamid as typical of right-wing reactions to Franklin Roosevelt's administration. This official, in remarks made at a private dinner in New York, apparently "asserted in so many words that 'the paranoiac in the White House' is destroying the nation, that a couple of well-placed bullets would be the best thing for the country, and that he for one would buy a bottle of champagne as quick as he could get it to celebrate such news." In the 1960's the columnist Westbrook Pegler—one of Roosevelt's most bitter critics—said of F. D. R. with unrepentant vehemence: "It is regrettable that Giuseppe Zangara hit the wrong man when he shot at Roosevelt in Miami. Roosevelt made many decisions in favor of Soviet Russia, beginning with his recognition of the Soviet Government [in 1933]. Thereafter he permitted the whole bureaucracy to be infested with spies. Anyone who opposed Roosevelt, or any of his henchmen, or designs, was labeled a 'hatemonger.' All right, if he acquired all this hate from people he set out to alienate, why deny it to him now?"

The idiom still had not changed by 1963. Five weeks before the Dallas catastrophe a Delaware newspaper informed its readers: "Yes, Virginia, there is a Santa Claus. His name right now happens to be Kennedy—let's shoot him, literally, before Christmas." The editor who wrote this advice scandalized some of his readers. But he did write it, and he did print it.

In the early years of the twentieth century, when the Presidency was suddenly being reactivated, there were a number of fantasy stories that were set in the future and that dealt with notions of violence, oligarchy, and usurpation in the United States. Sometimes, as in the 1912 novel *Philip Dru: Administrator; A Story of Tomorrow, 1920–1935*, written by Woodrow Wilson's friend and follower Colonel Edward M. House, the fantasy is enthusiastic. More often it is alarmist, as with a short story—written while Theodore Roosevelt was President—entitled "The Coup d'État of 1961." The author, Henry Dwight Sedgwick, was not a crank but a respected man of letters. In his story the American Presidency becomes the embodiment first of oligarchy and then of autocracy. A tycoon-superman named Campbell steps into the office and makes it both absolute and hereditary. The Constitution is so elastic, said Sedgwick, that he is able even to dispense with sessions of Congress. The United States acquires a royal dynasty—the Campbell dynasty.

To return from fantasy to fact, certain patterns begin to appear in the careers of those Presidents who have been special targets for suspicion. Strong executive heads would presumably be even more hated, and more subject to the charge of usurpation, if they sought re-election; and there is a correlation of sorts, although it is admittedly imperfect and conjectural. Four of the eight assassination attempts have been directed at Presidents—Jackson, Lincoln, McKinley, Truman—who had achieved re-election.

In a fifth case, that of Kennedy, it is reasonable to suppose that he would have won a second term. Although Theodore Roosevelt was not in office when he was shot, and had not, strictly speaking, been re-elected for a second term in 1904, he was nevertheless attempting to return to power, and, in effect, for a third term. A cartoon of the period showed him leaping blithely over a high "Anti-3rd-Term Wall," which was marked "Built by George Washington." In another hostile cartoon he brandished a scroll inscribed "THEODORE ROOSEVELT FOR EVER AND EVER"; in another he pinned up a proclamation signed "TR REX" that said: "*I* am the will of the people. . . . *I* chose myself to be leader. . . . *I* will have as many terms in office as *I* desire."

The other two intended victims, Garfield and F. D. R., do not fit the pattern, since Garfield had been in office for only four months and Roosevelt was merely President-elect. It is at least worth speculating that their offense, in the minds of the crazed men who fired at them, was that they had not yet become "legitimate" rulers. In the same way, perhaps, it is significant that attempted assassinations of Queen Victoria were confined to the early years of her long reign. She had followed the unpopular Hanoverian kings and was not even a male sovereign. Her "legitimacy" was therefore weak. Garfield, having secured the Republican nomination on the thirty-sixth ballot after an unedifying contest with General Grant (who would thereby himself have violated the third-term taboo), was immediately bedeviled by party feuds. In Guiteau's eyes, Garfield was thus not endowed with the prestige of the head of state, but was simply the victorious leader of a rival political machine. It was, lamented *Frank Leslie's Illustrated Newspaper*, "a thing of fearful omen that the assassin should have sought to justify the monstrous deed by considerations based on the spite and jealousy of a defeated faction, or the wrathful attitude of men whose sole grievance is their failure to share the spoils of office."

Both the strong Presidents and their haters are curiously involved in the language of monarchy—a language that has undergone little change from Washington's time to Lyndon Johnson's. A key word is "usurpation." Theodore Roosevelt, defending his conception of the Presidency in a letter to an English friend, boasted that "I have used every ounce of power there was in the office and I have not cared a rap for the criticisms of those who spoke of my 'usurpation of power'; for I knew that . . . there was no usurpation." John F. Kennedy developed a similar argument when he was campaigning for the office in 1960. He said that Woodrow Wilson "discovered that to be a big man in the White House inevitably brings cries of dictatorship. So did Lincoln and Jackson and the two Roosevelts. And so may the next occupant . . . if he is the man the times demand. But how much better it would be . . . to have a Roosevelt or a Wilson than to have another James Buchanan, cringing in the White House, afraid to move." Like Roosevelt, Kennedy drew a distinction between the good (or vigorous) Presidents and the bad (or inept) Chief Executives, between the Lincolns and the Buchanans.

It is possibly significant that no efforts have been made to assassinate Presidents in periods of war and other grave crises. At such times the nation draws together. The charge of usurpation seems relatively unimportant in face of the demand for leadership. Lincoln was assassinated when the crisis of the Civil War was over, McKinley when America had emerged triumphantly from the Spanish-American War. One point of this chapter, however, is that Buchanan survived, in common with every other unaggressive President; Lincoln, like several other aggrandizing Presidents, was shot at. And after each bold assertion of executive authority, for reasons to be explored later, there followed a marked reaction. After

Jackson no President until Lincoln had a second term. Lincoln's successor Andrew Johnson was vilified and even impeached. After Lincoln, with the exception of the unassertive Grant, no President until McKinley was re-elected for a second consecutive term. After the bold administrations of Theodore Roosevelt and Wilson came what Harold J. Laski called "the era of conscious abdication"—another monarchical word—"from power on the part of the president."

All strong Presidents, no matter how grateful posterity might be, have awakened the strange undercurrent of hatred, the persistent fear that the Founding Fathers had bequeathed a potential elective monarchy to the United States. The Kennedys were frequently referred to as a royal family, sometimes with affectionate mockery, more often with malice and suspicion. The latest example of the literature of antipresidential fantasy, Barbara Garson's pastiche *MacBird*, is bound by the same queer compulsion. Portraying Lyndon Johnson as the Macbeth-like assassin of Kennedy, it is a drama of monarchy and usurpation. The only novelty lies in the apparent assumption that all contenders for the throne would be illegitimate. In other respects it reveals obsessions akin to those of such bizarre bygone items as *The Adder's Den: or Secrets of the Great Conspiracy to Overthrow Liberty in America*, written in 1864. Its author, John Smith Dye, was a respectable if fanatical abolitionist, whose bête noire was not so much

One of the most vicious anti-Lincoln engravings appeared after the Preliminary Emancipation Proclamation was announced in 1862. With one foot stepping on the Constitution, a diabolic Lincoln uses ink from a devil's pot to write the Proclamation.

METROPOLITAN MUSEUM OF ART

the Presidency as the Confederacy. He was convinced that Southerners, who were led by Calhoun until his death in 1850, had, in fulfillment of their determination to overthrow the Union, fatally poisoned Presidents William Henry Harrison and Zachary Taylor. According to Dye, Southerners had also been behind the attack on Jackson in 1835, and had tried unsuccessfully to assassinate President-elect James Buchanan in 1857 and President-elect Lincoln in 1861.

To Lawrence in 1835 "King Andrew the First" was Andrew the usurper, the false king. All Presidents who are assertive are false kings in this peculiar yet intrinsic vocabulary. The assassins may be insane; yet they act out deep convictions and resentments, which are evidently shared by many of their countrymen.

There is a final reason why talk of usurpation and legitimacy seems appropriate in the profoundly republican American context. The President has a dual function. He is monarch and prime minister rolled into one. His task is both to rule and to govern. As head of state he symbolizes the American Union and speaks for every person in it. As head of government and party chief he must provide active direction, but he is the leader of a political machine. This development was inevitable. Yet it added to the inner doubts of Americans about the validity of presidential authority; and the first serious qualms came with Andrew Jackson. The President, this "elective monarch," upon inauguration becomes a part of the sacred fabric of national identity. Like a king, he never dies because the succession is automatic and instantaneous. But what is his legitimacy? There is a revealingly cynical definition in Ambrose Bierce's *The Devil's Dictionary:* "PRESIDENT, n. The leading figure in a small group of men of whom—and of whom only—it is positively known that immense numbers of their countrymen did not want any of them for President."

A man for whom many Americans did not vote, a partisan politician *against* whom many voted, suddenly becomes their almost-regal representative. In no less than fourteen elections the President has been elected without a popular majority. The margin in these and other elections has often been remarkably small. In 1864 Lincoln defeated Major General George B. McClellan by only about 400,000 out of more than 4 million votes, though his advantages

were considerable (and, unknown to him, probably included tampering with soldiers' ballot boxes). In 1880 Garfield squeaked by with a majority over his Democratic opponent Winfield Scott Hancock of fewer than 10,000 votes out of a total of more than 9 million. In 1960 Kennedy secured 49.94 per cent of the popular vote, a mere one-sixth of 1 per cent more than the Republican candidate Richard M. Nixon. It is, of course, a testimony to the soundness of American democracy that the results of such close contests are usually accepted with good-humored resignation by the defeated. It would be surprising, though, if an embittered minority did not brood over the outcome—especially with the knowledge that in certain districts the vote counting is not always overscrupulous, and that the tally of popular votes is distorted by the anachronistic workings of the Electoral College. In a country so wedded to a two-party system, frustration is heightened for those already discontented citizens who choose to cast their votes for presidential nominees of third (or even fourth or fifth) parties.

To sum up:
—The presidential office is disliked, feared, and suspected as well as admired and sought after and venerated.
—Strong Presidents, beginning with Andrew Jackson (though with premonitory rumblings even in the administration of George Washington), have by being strong stirred up deep resentments, which invariably express themselves as attacks on monarchical pretensions.
—The strong Presidents have been the ones most in danger of assassination.
—The danger is increased if they prolong their tenure through re-election.
—These resentments, which lie beneath the surface but bubble up periodically and are aggravated by political opponents and the press, may act upon the minds of the unstable, the failures, the men sick with anonymity. The assassins are to be understood as people behaving not inexplicably but within a national climate of opinion sometimes heavy with anger and accusation.

Two lines from Walt Whitman's "Starting from Paumanok" may serve as an epilogue:

And I will make a song for the ears of the President, full of weapons with menacing points,
And behind the weapons countless dissatisfied faces.

CHAPTER SIX

Authority in Abeyance

In 1848, a year of revolutions and fresh aspirations in Europe, the Swiss people framed a new republican constitution. They drew upon the American Constitution for several features; but they did not provide for a President because that office seemed to them an invitation to dictatorship. Their suspicion was based to some extent on what they had read of the American experience. They could, for example, have consulted the essay "Federal Government" published in 1840 by Abel Upshur, who was to become Secretary of State in Tyler's Cabinet. Upshur said the "most defective part" of the American Constitution was that relating to the executive branch; the prerogative of the President was described in dangerously "loose and unguarded terms," enabling him to claim far too much authority.

Forty-four years after Upshur's essay was published, another American, Henry C. Lockwood, wrote a book entitled *The Abolition of the Presidency*, in which he argued that the only way to rescue American liberty was to eliminate the Presidency— in other words, the single Executive—and replace it with an executive council on the Swiss model. There was, he maintained, a universal but perilous tendency to entrust rulership to one man: "Let a person be chosen to an office, with power conferred upon it equal to that of the Presidency of the United States, and it will make but little difference whether the law actually gives him the right to act in a particular direction or not. . . . He acts. No argument that the law has been violated will avail. . . . He is a separate power in himself. The lines with which we attempt to mark the limits of his power are shadowy and ill-

defined. A party . . . stands back of him demanding action. . . . The sentiment of hero worship . . . will endorse him."

The Swiss reaction of 1848 shows how seriously the rest of the world, as well as some Americans, took the criticisms of Jacksonian usurpation. Lockwood's volume reveals that in 1884 there was still uneasiness in the United States at the extension of executive authority achieved by Abraham Lincoln, even though Congress had hobbled and impeached Andrew Johnson, Lincoln's successor, had controlled Grant, and had kept Hayes and Arthur on the defensive. Lockwood was worried, too, by the way in which his countrymen had unthinkingly made General Grant President, knowing nothing about him except that he was presumably a strong man who would take command of the nation and issue orders for its salvation.

Lockwood's fears of the Presidency seem baseless in retrospect and—in the circumstances of his era— somewhat ludicrous. Surely he should have realized that if power had been usurped since the Civil War, it was Congress and not the Chief Executives who had done the usurping. Johnson had been impeached by the Senate on charges that amounted to an assertion that the President was subordinate to Congress. Thirty-five senators had voted to convict him, against nineteen for acquittal. Since a two-thirds vote was necessary to convict, the proceedings had failed—by one vote. Nevertheless, the executive branch had received the severest setback in its history.

Instead of striving to restore the prestige of the Presidency, General U. S. ("Unconditional Surrender") Grant, the hero of Vicksburg, the Wilderness, and Appomattox, virtually surrendered to Congress. His inadequacy was all too apparent to young Henry Adams, who had come to Washington after the Civil War hoping to make a public career, possibly as a political journalist. (As he said, all Adamses automatically gravitated to Washington.) He and his friends were convinced that the country needed "a reform President" to bring "the Senate back to decency," and that the task could be accomplished only by a man who was not a professional politician. At first he thought that Grant might be the man. If so, he resolved to help him. Writing of himself in the third person in his autobiography, Adams stated his intent to "support the executive in attacking the Senate and taking away its two-thirds vote and power of confirmation, nor did he much care how it should be done, for he thought it safer to effect the revolution in 1870 than to wait until 1920."

With this thought in mind, Adams went to hear the announcement of the Cabinet appointments of the newly inaugurated Grant. The list of names was so deplorable (it was composed chiefly of rich but woefully undistinguished personal friends of Grant's) that "within five minutes" it "changed [Adams'] intended future into an absurdity so laughable as to make him ashamed of it." Adams concluded unhappily that "a great soldier might be a baby politician."

Nevertheless, Lockwood's fear of presidential power was actually less eccentric than it sounds. His general argument was that powerful or impotent, a single Executive was unsatisfactory. Such opinions appeared with the creation of the office and have persisted as an undercurrent to the present day. It should be emphasized, also, that a majority of Presidents have themselves had misgivings about the power inherent in their position. Some have perhaps merely rationalized their own sluggishness or ineptitude. Others have believed in the necessary restriction of presidential authority not as an excuse for personal timidity but as a matter of genuine conviction. This Whig conception prevailed among Presidents in the years between Jackson and Lincoln, during almost the whole last third of the nineteenth century, again under President Taft (1909–1913), and again under the Republican administrations of the 1920's and the 1950's.

Certainly active Presidents make things difficult for their successors. In the seesaw contest between the executive and legislative branches, Congress strives to recover territory it has lost. A regular alternation may be discerned. After the initial executive period of Washington and John Adams there came the legislative interlude of the Virginia dynasty. After Andrew Jackson came almost twenty-five years of legislative dominance. After Lincoln Congress initiated a violent counterattack, of which Andrew Johnson bore the brunt. When one strong-willed President is succeeded by another, the double dose produces a correspondingly fierce reaction from Congress—as perhaps happened after Lincoln and the contumacious Andrew Johnson, or after the administrations of Franklin D. Roosevelt and Harry S. Truman. The reaction is heightened when, as usually happens, it coincides with a change of party: the "outs" tend to adopt the legislative, or Whig, conception of the Presidency as an additional weapon in their arsenal of criticism. But even when the succession remains in the hands of the same party, an incoming President may be at pains to disclaim the executive pretensions of his predecessor.

The most striking example of this phenomenon is the attitude of William Howard Taft. Having inherited office from Theodore Roosevelt in 1909, he discovered that such intractable problems as tariff revision had been neglected and bequeathed to him in aggravated form. Roosevelt's continued prominence on the national scene, even when he was trying to behave like a retired statesman, constituted a kind of interference with the new Executive. Moreover, in Taft's eyes, Roosevelt had weakened party unity by annoying the conservative wing of the Republicans. In claiming too much power, and in basing his claim on personal qualities, he had left a legacy of unrest. Taft explained his disapproval with considerable asperity after he left the White House, in a book entitled *Our Chief Magistrate and His Powers.* Annoyed that Roosevelt had compared himself to Lincoln, and Taft to Buchanan, Taft replied that the comparison was sheer egotism and that T. R.'s doctrine was unsound and unsafe. Like Lockwood he feared the possible consequences of those Presidents who "played their parts upon the political stage with histrionic genius and commanded the people almost as if they were an army and the President their Commander-in-Chief." Fortunately, said Taft, "there have always been men in this free and intelligent people of ours, who apparently courting political . . . disaster have registered protest against this undue Executive domination. . . ." He revealed his own discomfort and resentment by adding that although the cry of domination was often unjustified, "the fact that Executive domination is regarded as a useful ground for attack upon a successful administration, even when there is no ground for it, is itself proof of the dependence we may properly place upon the sanity and clear perceptions of the people in avoiding its baneful effects when there is real danger." It is a peculiar statement, and the more peculiar because it emanated from a former occupant of the White House. Taft seems to be saying that Presidents should preserve harmony by not rocking the political boat. He also apparently meant that the risk of executive domination is to be taken seriously and has great theoretical validity even when it is without actual foundation.

Although one must allow for a certain amount of pique, Taft's observations still merit attention. He had not become senile on retiring from the Presidency; he was a professor of law at Yale when he wrote his book, and would later be Chief Justice of the Supreme Court. He had had an unhappy four years in the White House, despite his administrative experience and his well-organized mind. He could not quite understand why his term had gone so badly. Although he could not bring the problem into focus, he was correct in believing that it involved the question of how much power the President ought to have, and where it was prudent to draw the line. Within his "proper sphere," Taft went on to say, the President had "great responsibilities and opportunities." But what were these?

The Chief Executives between Lincoln and McKinley faced the problem in acute form. Viewed in one way, they were men of no particular distinction under whose stewardship the office reached the nadir of its power. Seen in another way, all of them (except Grant and Benjamin Harrison) fought courageously and saved the Presidency from ignominious subjection to Congress. There is no doubt that these Presidents faced a weighty challenge. Andrew Johnson was denied the right to control his own Cabinet or to have more than a passive, minimal role in legislation. To earlier generations of Presidents the executive right of appointment and removal had seemed settled beyond dispute. Yet under Johnson it was repudiated by the Senate. During the impeachment proceedings a congressional spokesman, Benjamin F.

Butler, went so far as to say that the issue at stake was "whether the Presidential office (if it bears the prerogatives and power claimed for it) ought, in fact, to exist, as a part of the constitutional government of a free people." If the impeachment had succeeded, Benjamin F. Wade, president pro tempore of the Senate, would have become President in Johnson's place. According to rumor Wade would have then named Butler Secretary of State.

The threat went unfulfilled, but nothing in Grant's two administrations abated the challenge. In accepting the Republican nomination Grant defined his future role as that of a "purely administrative officer." He held the same opinion when he left office. As a soldier he had unquestioningly deferred to civil authority; during his Presidency he regarded Congress as the supreme civil authority. "The President very rarely appoints," he reportedly said, "he merely registers the appointments of members of Congress." Cocksure congressmen such as Roscoe Conkling treated Grant affably but with basic contempt. George F. Hoar, who was then just beginning a long and honorable congressional career, said later that during the Grant administration senators such as Conkling, John Sherman, Simon Cameron, Charles Sumner, and John "Black Jack" Logan "would have received as a personal affront a private message from the White House expressing a desire that they should adopt any course in the discharge of their legislative duties that they did not approve. If they visited the White House, it was to give, not to receive advice." John Sherman approvingly summed up the congressional position when he explained that "the executive department of a republic like ours should be subordinate to the legislative department. The President should obey and enforce the laws, leaving to the people the duty of correcting any errors committed by their representatives in Congress." Significantly, senators began to claim precedence over Cabinet members at social functions.

The first display of renewed presidential courage came when Rutherford B. Hayes deliberately ignored the hints and hopes of the Senate by preparing his own list of Cabinet nominations. In retaliation the Senate referred the entire list to committee scrutiny. After a great deal of delay and uproar Hayes got his way. He went on to contest the congressional phalanx by assailing one of its chief strongholds, the New York Custom House. When a com-

In 1882, President Arthur courageously vetoed a bill forbidding the immigration of Chinese for twenty years.

mission appointed by Hayes confirmed the corruption of the custom house Hayes removed two of the principals, including the collector, Chester A. Arthur. Another struggle ensued, with Conkling in the van, before Hayes once more imposed his will. He persisted with other nominations, cheered by the discovery that large sections of the public were as exasperated as he by the cynical misuse of the spoils system. By July, 1880, he could write, "I have had great success. No member of either house now attempts even to dictate appointments. . . . I began with selecting a Cabinet in opposition to their wishes, and I have gone on in that path steadily until now I am filling the important places of collector of the port and postmaster at Philadelphia almost without a suggestion even from Senators or Representatives!"

Emboldened by Hayes's defiance, James A. Garfield began his Presidency by appointing an enemy of Conkling's to the collectorship of the port of New York. "This," he wrote to a friend, "brings on the contest at once and will settle the question whether the President is registering clerk of the Senate or the Executive of the Nation." Garfield won a famous victory. Not only was his nominee finally confirmed by the Senate, but when the two New York senators, Conkling and Thomas C. Platt, ostentatiously re-

signed their seats to seek a vote of confidence from the New York assembly, the state legislators rebelled against them. Conkling's power was broken forever. Running (in retrospect) with the hare as well as the hounds, John Sherman made the statesmanlike comment that if Conkling and Platt had been vindicated by their assembly, "the President would have been powerless to appoint anyone in New York without consulting the Senators, practically transferring to them his constitutional power."

Murdered by a Republican Stalwart of the Conkling persuasion, Garfield was prevented from offering further proof of executive independence. The crime produced one benefit in the shape of the Pendleton Act of 1883, which heralded the gradual rescue of federal offices from the stranglehold of the spoils system. There was also the surprising discovery that Garfield's successor, Chester A. Arthur, had abandoned his spoilsman's outlook and was conducting his administration with dignity and some ability.

After Arthur, Grover Cleveland likewise displayed tenacity and shrewdness in resisting congressional inroads. The difficulty was that while the Presidency and the House of Representatives were in Democratic hands as a result of the elections of 1884, the Senate still retained a Republican majority. Cleveland, a product of New York local and state government, had visited Washington only once before his inauguration. The belief that he was a greenhorn in their world may have stimulated the senators to try to shatter him. Their technique was to delay several hundred of his appointments and to demand copies of the papers relating to these appointments. Cleveland refused in a ponderous but unmistakably decisive message, which ended: "Neither the discontent of party friends, nor the allurements constantly offered of confirmation of appointees conditioned upon the avowal that suspensions have been made on party grounds alone, nor the threat proposed in the resolutions now before the Senate that no confirmation will be complied with, are sufficient to . . . deter me from following in the way I am convinced leads to better government for the people."

Cleveland soon showed that he was nobody's fool. Even the vitriolic Senator John James Ingalls of Kansas, while pouring scorn upon political reformers, conceded that President Cleveland was "a very extraordinary man" and a puzzle—"the sphinx of American politics." Stories of his brusque treatment of office seekers and lobbyists became common. One such visitor related ruefully how, after an hour of affable conversation with the President, he thought the moment was opportune to introduce his particular interest. But as soon as he began, "I could see the process of congelation; and before I had half finished . . . the President was a monumental icicle. I became so thoroughly chilled that I broke off, took up my hat and said 'Good-night, Mr. President.'"

President Cleveland was particularly impatient of the many private bills designed to afford relief to the greedy as well as to the needy. Someone remarked that the American way in warfare was to take its soldiers straight from the plow and return them to the plow—with a pension. Most of the three hundred and one vetoes of Grover Cleveland's first term were of private pension acts. However, one or two of his vetoes, and several of Hayes's, were concerned with more important matters. Cleveland, Hayes, and Arthur all vetoed acts restricting Chinese immigration. Hayes resisted congressional blackmail by stoutly vetoing seven successive appropriation bills to which riders were attached. (By appending such riders to essential legislation, Congress tried to compel him to sanction repugnant provisions.) Hayes's veto messages stressed what was at stake. In one he said: "The new doctrine, if maintained, will result in a consolidation of unchecked and despotic power in the House of Representatives. A bare majority of the House will become the Government. The Executive will no longer be . . . an equal and independent branch of the Government. . . ."

With the exception of Grant the postwar Presidents thus did their best to counter the extreme assertions of legislative omnipotence. They won significant struggles with the Senate and the House. The Tenure of Office Act of 1867, used with such savage force to humiliate Andrew Johnson, was never afterwards used to browbeat the executive branch and was eventually repealed in 1887. The beloved argument of strong Presidents such as Jackson—that the Chief Magistrate was the embodiment of the popular will—was on occasion employed. Andrew Johnson referred specifically to Jackson in a speech in April, 1866. Johnson, too, regarded himself as "the Tribune of the people, and . . . I . . . intend to assert the power which the people have placed in me. . . . Tyranny and despotism can be exercised by many more rigorously . . . than by one." Hayes,

vetoing an army appropriation bill in 1879 because of its obnoxious rider, said: "The people of this country are unwilling to see the supremacy of the Constitution replaced by the omnipotence of any department of the Government." Cleveland assured the Senate of his determination to seek "better government for the people"; and in his book *Presidential Problems*, written in 1904, he reiterated that "the Presidency is pre-eminently the people's office." Occasionally there were episodes of Jacksonian or Lincolnian drama. In 1877 President Hayes dispatched regular troops to restore order in several states after labor strikes had erupted into violence. Cleveland, ignoring the protests of Governor Altgeld, sent soldiers into Illinois during the Pullman strike of 1894.

It may be argued, then, that the majority of post-Civil War Presidents did what they could despite severe handicaps. In the first place, it was a period of bitter and close competition between the two major parties. Other things being equal, the conditions might have favored the evolution of the President as a valued party generalissimo, directing the fight and using his personal and official magnetism to secure cohesion. Instead there tended to be a stalemate. Although the Republicans won three of the five presidential elections from 1876 to 1892, they secured a popular majority in none of them. Despite the apparent unevenness in party strength, and despite the apparent triumphs indicated in Electoral College votes, Republicans and Democrats ran almost neck and neck. In three of the five elections the gap between the winners and the losers in the two parties was under 1 per cent. The Republicans squeezed through with small margins in certain key states such as New York and Indiana. Under the circumstances, the temptation to bribery and fraud was irresistible. It may be impossible to buy all of the votes all of the time (and it is in any case unnecessary); the possibility of buying some of the votes some of the time lured politicians who were otherwise fairly upright men. The political history of the era is therefore full of "Burn-this-letter" skulduggery. There were many instances of secret directives such as the one sent in the 1888 election to loyal workers in Indiana by the National Republican Committee: "Divide the floaters into blocks of five and put a trusted man in charge of these five, with the necessary funds, and make him responsible that none get away, and that all vote our ticket." The impudence of some of the frauds and the elaborate ingenuity of others seem amusing today. But it would be a mistake to suppose that the men involved were not in earnest. The race was too close and the stakes too high to permit frivolity.

Worse still for effective government, the major parties rarely achieved simultaneous working majorities in both houses of Congress and control of the Presidency. The Democrats managed this for only two years, from 1893 to 1895. The Republicans were also usually hamstrung by the loss of at least one element in the system. Coherent legislative programs were unattainable. The Republican Hayes faced a Democratic House for the whole of his four years in office, and a Democratic Senate for his last two years. He suffered crippling disadvantages in having won the Presidency after an unsalubrious juggling with a few thousand crucial votes. In almost every sense a minority President, though personally honest, "His Fraudulency" the "*de facto* President" could not hope to give clear leadership. Other Presidents, while less marginally installed, were acutely aware that they held office without the sustenance of a comfortable majority.

Nor did it make much difference when the President and Congress were of the same political hue. Friction between the executive and legislative branches was inevitable unless the President tamely acquiesced in congressional supremacy. He could purchase peace only at the expense of his prerogative, as Grant and Benjamin Harrison did. Harrison, having defeated Cleveland in 1888, allowed himself to be instructed in his forthcoming duties by Senator Sherman, who wrote him: "The President should touch elbows with Congress. He should have no policy distinct from that of his party; and this is better represented in Congress than in the Executive." Less complaisant Chief Magistrates could have answered that it was not always feasible in a time of ferocious factionalism to know which of the rival wings constituted the true party. And patronage created monstrous difficulties. Even after the passage of the Pendleton Act and the extension of its merit system to cover more and more offices through the years, every administration was bedeviled with patronage squabbles. Over one hundred thousand posts were up for auction when Cleveland entered the White House. The dilemma of each President was that if he declined to play the patronage game he would win the approval of a handful of civil service reformers and satisfy his own conscience, but he would forfeit all chance of working with Congress. Jacob Dolson Cox, a perceptive congressman, said, "The experience of President Hayes proved that an administration which seeks to abolish the spoils system must expect to lose that appearance of leadership in legislation which has been sustained by the farming out of patronage. . . . In ordinary affairs a President who will not so purchase help will find his recommendations treated with slight respect, or even ostentatiously overruled." Indeed the "appearance of leadership," Cox said, was "in the main a sham." Congress often paid little or no attention to the legislative suggestions contained in Presidents' messages. Chester Arthur raised urgent matters involving law and order without any response whatsoever. His third annual message listed eight important recommendations including federal aid for education, a presidential succession law, and regulation of interstate commerce. Congress acted on only one of the eight, territorial government for Alaska, probably because such action would eventually provide votes, seats, and patronage. The much-quoted comment of the British observer James Bryce was not far from the mark. Bryce claimed that presidential messages might have no more effect on Congress than "an article in a prominent party newspaper."

In the 1840's James K. Polk had prophesied that the spoils system would prevent any future President from winning re-election; the struggle for loot would estrange him from Congress and commit power into the hands of the legislature. In the late nineteenth century it seemed that Polk's prophecy had come true. Except for the untypical wartime administrations of Lincoln, and those of the pusillanimous Grant, no President was re-elected for a second consecutive term until William McKinley in 1900. Chester Arthur, who became President when Garfield died, sought a nomination in 1884 but was denied it, and Grover Cleveland in 1888 and Benjamin Harrison in 1892 were beaten by the other party.

Lord Bryce had a close knowledge of and a considerable admiration for the United States. The main thesis of his influential book *The American Commonwealth*, published in 1888, was that the United States had to be seen as a whole, and that as a whole it worked extremely well. There were good reasons why the political and governmental systems had evolved as they had. But if the reasons were good, Bryce could not help but betray his conviction that the results were somewhat unfortunate. Men of education and social standing no longer entered politics, because more wealth and prestige were to be found in business and the law. The deterioration was cumulative. The higher the proportion of politicos such as New York's Roscoe Conkling and "Boss" Thomas Platt, and Ohio's Joseph B. "Fire-Alarm" Foraker, the smaller the number of persons of integrity who could be induced to live in such company. To Bryce, it followed that great men would not occupy the Presidency. Those nominated were usually party politicians of limited horizons. Indeed he thought that presidential horizons were limited. Great Presidents were created by great crises; and compared with the early years of the republic or with the agonies of the Civil War, the administrations of the Gilded Age seemed an anticlimax. Foreign affairs were limited to a contretemps with Chile, a scene in Samoa, a happening in Honolulu—events that seemed remote and theatrical to the average American.

Much of what Bryce wrote was true. As he correctly pointed out, "An American may, through a long life, never be reminded of the Federal Government, except when he votes at presidential and congressional elections, lodges a complaint against the post office, and opens his trunks for a custom-house officer.... His direct taxes are paid to officials acting under State laws. The State . . . registers his birth . . . pays for his schooling . . . marries him, divorces him . . . declares him a bankrupt.... The police that guard his house, the local boards which look after the poor, control highways, impose water rates, manage schools—all these derive their legal powers from his State alone."

The United States was still mainly oriented toward the local community and the state. There was no federal income tax. The Army and Navy were tiny, obscure bodies. The majority of congressmen came to Washington to intercede for their constituents, not to make national policy. The deficiency in Bryce's account—one that he shared with his American contemporaries—was that he underestimated the gravity of the nation's domestic problems, and the muted, puzzled, but nevertheless earnest and growing belief that something ought to be done.

Perhaps the most alarming factor of all, a weakness apparent in previous and in subsequent history,

was that by its very nature American federal government was not equipped to deal with complex, long-term issues. Weak executive leadership aggravated the problem. But even when the executive branch was strong and resourceful, the separation of powers and the peculiar rules of party government crippled policy making. A problem that could be solved in one swift stroke was sometimes resolved; but sustained scrutiny and protracted, systematic remedial action were almost invariably absent. Government direction was too divided and discontinuous. Because the two major parties were loose coalitions, they competed for public support mainly on matters calculated to please and attract the electorate. The spoils system was merely the most conspicuous example of an entire conception of federal party government: namely, a central agency for the distribution of rewards, bonuses, and concessions. Serious, unattractive, unrewarding matters of public policy were ignored or covered over by bland procrastinations that purported to be compromises. The rules of the political game stimulated legislators not to tackle such intractable areas but rather to make party capital out of them by pretending that the other party was to blame. It was the congressional equivalent of the children's party game of passing the hot potato, or of handing some other object around as rapidly as possible to avoid being caught with it when the music stopped. (The entire field of race relations, from the 1820's to the present, illustrates the evasive and impotent aspects of federal activity.) One result was the search for innocuous, "available" presidential candidates.

A pattern had emerged that still holds true. Those who would act positively are thwarted; the only room for maneuver lies with those who are skilled in the techniques of busy inactivity. Protest parties spring up to dramatize issues, but they have no hope of capturing the Presidency. Sometimes the knowledge that they are merely fringe movements makes them reckless, and their apparent irresponsibility alienates the general public. This weakness is not confined to the United States. It occurs in all democratic societies whose governments are mediated through political parties. Fortunately for the United States, a climate of reform eventually develops. When the need for change is finally recognized, the executive and legislative branches are capable of devising swift, decisive measures. But they do so because the President has finally taken the lead, or because the parties have concluded that they will lose seats if they do not satisfy public demand. In either case the initiative has come from ordinary citizens, not from Congress or the President. The party system had and still has many virtues. But it suffers from a desire to please where it should wish to instruct and correct. It has too often sought ephemeral popularity at the expense of permanent benefit.

In the Gilded Age federal government, executive and legislative, revealed these inadequacies as glaringly as at any time in the nation's history. Some of the reasons have been indicated, and there were others as well. The problems that arose in the United States were novel, intricate, and prodigious. The inevitable strains following the Civil War were heightened by the struggle over the control of Reconstruction waged between Andrew Johnson and Congress. The predicaments of the South were then distorted as Republicans and Democrats fought for Southern votes. Larger questions of economic welfare and civil rights were ignored in petty bargains over pork-barrel legislation and in cynical assessments of whether the Negro vote was an asset or a liability. Grant's plea, "Let us have peace," became not the noble ideal it might have been but a formula to justify private and partisan machinations.

There would have been some excuse for neglecting the South's ultimate welfare if the federal government had been preoccupied with other, even deeper issues of national welfare. Cleveland's annual message of December, 1888, near the end of his first term, revealed an awareness of what those issues were: "The fortunes realized by our manufacturers are no longer solely the reward of sturdy industry and enlightened foresight, but . . . they result from the discriminating favor of the Government and are largely built upon undue exactions from the masses of our people. The gulf between employers and the employed is constantly widening, and classes are

Mathew Brady photographed the House managers of Johnson's impeachment in 1868. Seated are Benjamin F. Butler, Thaddeus Stevens, Thomas Williams, and John A. Bingham. James F. Wilson, George S. Boutwell, and John A. Logan stand behind.

rapidly forming, one comprising the very rich and powerful, while in another are found the toiling poor. . . . Corporations, which should be the carefully restrained creatures of the law and the servants of the people, are fast becoming the people's masters."

There if ever was a summons to action. Nor was Cleveland springing a brand-new diagnosis upon the country. Ten years earlier Henry George's *Progress and Poverty* had eloquently analyzed the cleavage between the "house of Have" and the "house of Want." Books and magazine articles on the subject were beginning to appear with some frequency. Yet with few exceptions the entire United States—President, Congress, judiciary, populace—accepted the doctrines of laissez faire as an article of faith. An uncompromising scholar such as Professor William G. Sumner of Yale might challenge various sacred cows; but he did not deplore the consequences of an unregulated economic order because he genuinely believed in nonregulation. Like certain other intellectuals of his generation, indeed perhaps like the majority of college-educated Americans, Sumner exhibited an interesting mixture of complacence and pessimism known to its possessors as right thinking. ("Every right-thinking citizen will surely agree. . . .") He was complacent in that he could not conceive of a superior alternative to unbridled laissez faire. He was pessimistic in that he did not really consider democracy an admirable achievement. Not that he was stupid or malevolent. On the contrary, he was a man of intelligence and integrity. But he was enclosed—as, of course, most men are—by the beliefs of his time. The key belief, reinforced by such miscellaneous American dogmas as self-help, libertarianism, and states' rights, was still that in the United States that government was best that governed least.

The citizens most responsibly involved in improving the tone of government focused their energies on civil service reform. Note that it was the tone that preoccupied them, not the notion of vigorous action. Cleveland's 1888 message to Congress continued: "The existing situation is injurious to the health of our entire body-politic. It stifles . . . all patriotic love of country, and substitutes . . . selfish greed and grasping avarice. Devotion to American citizenship for its own sake . . . is displaced by the assumption that the Government, instead of being the embodiment of equality, is but an instrumentality through which especial . . . advantages are to be gained."

He went on to denounce the "communism of combined wealth and capital" as not less dangerous than the "communism of oppressed poverty and toil." "Communism of capital" was an arresting phrase. Cleveland employed the word "communism," however, merely to indicate his distaste for any organization that threatened property rights. The aims of the "goo-goos," or good government reformers, who commended his message, were limited to chasing the money-changers from the temple. The temple itself, the shrine of federalism, was to be purified but not energized. Their ideal was government as a kind of Hall of Fame stocked with frozen statues. Insofar as they confined themselves to condemning the spoils system, and to uttering general reproofs at rascally businessmen and corrupt legislators, the reformers made it still harder for a would-be powerful President to provide leadership. In a way, the ward heelers and party bosses had more insight than the gentleman-reformers. They were right, if for the wrong reasons, in insisting that despite Cleveland and his admirers, government is an instrumentality through which advantages are to be gained. The solution was not to stop the government from dispensing aid, but to make its assistance more efficient, more humanitarian, and far more complete. The politicians also knew that it was impossible for Presidents to behave with perfect neutrality. In attacking Conkling, the most Garfield could do was to give a patronage plum to the rival Blaine faction.

Being average, sensible Americans, the Presidents of the Gilded Age did not, except occasionally, recognize the opportunity that awaited them; or rather, that would await their successors in a more responsive climate of opinion. In their clashes with the congressional hegemony, Hayes, Garfield, and Cleveland were surprised and delighted to discover that public sympathy was with them and that the people would not tolerate blatant excesses on the part of their elected representatives. The proper presidential tactic was to strike a responsive chord in the electorate, especially through bold use of the veto, and claim a popular mandate for thoroughgoing reform. This strategy, however, was easier said than done in an era of congressional supremacy and of minority Chief Executives. The point to be emphasized is that the Presidents themselves had no wish to attempt an extension of the executive function.

Their defiance of Congress was courageous, and

provided an essential base for the operations of the Roosevelts and Wilsons of a later time. But they were fighting defensively to drive off their besiegers; they did not seize the initiative. In 1872, Rutherford B. Hayes was impressed by the argument of presidential candidate Horace Greeley and his supporters in the reform wing of the Republicans that corruption in government was greatly increased if the President held office for two terms, because unhealthily close links were forged between Executive and legislature. In accepting the Republican nomination in 1876, Hayes accordingly announced that he would never be a candidate for a second term, since he believed that "the restoration of the civil service to the system established by Washington and followed by the early Presidents can best be accomplished by an Executive who is under no temptation to use the patronage of his office to promote his own re-election. . . ." In his Inaugural Address of March, 1877, Hayes recommended a constitutional amendment similar to (although he did not actually say so) the Confederate constitution, which would have limited the President to a single term of six years. Cleveland also thought a single-term limitation would be wise. The idea was a solace to Chief Executives who hated the friction and uncertainty of the existing method. In 1915 former President William H. Taft remarked that it would have been better, "as it was at one time voted in the [Philadelphia] convention, to make the term of Presidency seven years and render him ineligible thereafter."

Another proposed reform, first suggested in the House of Representatives in 1864 and warmly endorsed by a Senate committee in 1881, was to allow department heads to sit in Congress. Two future Presidents strongly favored the idea. Congressman James A. Garfield wanted to readjust executive-legislative relations "so that there shall be greater responsibility to the legislative branch than there now is." In 1879 Woodrow Wilson, while still a senior at Princeton, published an article entitled "Cabinet Government in the United States," in which he warned that the nation's political maladies might prove incurable unless Cabinet members were made members of Congress and played a full part in the legislative process. There is no record of Garfield's attitude toward the idea when he was in the White House. Neither he nor President Wilson pressed the issue. The snag was that while the reform might have

made for greater legislative effectiveness, it almost certainly would have weakened the Presidency. The plan came to nothing. The executive branch limped along. Although Presidents, starting with Grant, were equipped with private secretaries at government expense, the job was at first deemed too menial to appeal to men of real ability. No new executive department was created between 1849, when Taylor appointed a Secretary of the Interior, and 1889, when the Department of Agriculture came into being. The Department of Commerce and Labor was not established until 1903.

Grover Cleveland was the toughest of the Gilded Age Presidents. In his *Twenty Years of the Republic*, Harry Thurston Peck quoted the story of an Englishman who was asked to explain the secret of Lord Palmerston's great political popularity: " 'Why,' said he, 'what the nation likes in Palmerston is his you-be-damnedness!' It was something of the same quality in Mr. Cleveland that caused the American people . . . to let their hearts go out to him. . . ." But Cleveland had little more than obstinacy to offer. His impatience with office seekers and pension hunters was close to mere irascibility; they disturbed his existence. His central idea was that the President must maintain his distance from Congress. It was a kind of Monroe Doctrine for the White House: he would not interfere with Capitol Hill if its agents refrained from interfering with him. The rule was too inert to vitalize the Presidency—which in any case Cleveland did not wish to do. In his second term he was closer to the Republicans than to the radicals of his own party. He had grown sententious: the Stuffed Prophet an unkind journalist called him.

As for Cleveland's sparring partner in the presidential ring, Benjamin Harrison was a person of good family and gentlemanly behavior but of no consequence. He was the perfect product of machine politics: presentable, decent, obliging, and too naïve to realize that his victory had been manufactured by thousands of industrious Republican politicians who took orders from the party directorate. For Cleveland and Harrison, in the new era of Populist discontent, "the people" were a slightly suspect entity apt to be troublemakers with an insufficient regard for the sanctity of property.

Striking evidence of the slump in presidential authority can be found in the era's polemic and imaginative literature. The authors and intellectuals who

CONTINENTAL HOTEL

But my dear they are for sale by all Hardware Stores in this country.

We cannot leave until we visit the Enterprise Mfg. Co. and order some of Mrs. Potts' **Cold Handle Sad Irons, like this.**

PRESIDENT AND MRS HAYES VISIT TO PHILADELPHIA

CULVER PICTURES

Nineteenth-century advertisers felt free to use pictures of Presidents to tout their products. Above, President Hayes and his wife discuss the desirability of an iron.

might have been expected to rally to the side of the Presidency rarely did so. More often their response was cynicism, disdain, despair. Men of good will such as Carl Schurz, Edwin L. Godkin (the brilliant editor of the *Nation*), Horace Greeley of the New York *Tribune*, Charles Francis Adams, and his son Henry Adams made their bid through the Liberal Republican movement in 1872. Their candidate, Greeley, who was also nominated by the Democrats, was resoundingly beaten. Although they occasionally made further efforts to defy the party organization, the reformers were almost always frustrated. They were quick to conclude that although the existing parties were beyond redemption, third parties and *ad hoc* coalitions were also doomed to failure, and the President would always be the prisoner of his party.

Having decided this, disillusioned figures such as Henry Adams tended to conduct themselves as if they were an invited audience at a bad play. Adams himself lived in Washington, hobnobbing with the few members of Congress or the executive branch who could match epigrams with him and his somewhat patronizingly witty Bostonian wife. They thought Hayes a provincial nobody, and Mrs. Hayes even worse. Their friend Henry James probably used Adams as his model in his short story "Pandora." The Adamsish character, discussing a dinner party, says: "Hang it, there's only a month left; let us be vulgar and have some fun—let us invite the President." Mrs. Adams, relating Washington gossip in

one of her weekly letters to her father, passed on with relish the absurd information that the Hayeses "suffer much from rats in the White House who run over their bed and nibble the President's toes."

The fictional President in Henry Adams' novel *Democracy*, published anonymously in 1880, epitomized the contempt American patricians felt for the succession of bores and boobies who had occupied the office for several decades—indeed, according to the Adams canon, ever since John Quincy Adams had been President. In the novel, the President began his career as a stonecutter in a quarry. Clumsy and inarticulate, he is unable to fashion his own Inaugural Address. In this instance Adams was probably aiming both at Grant and at Johnson, for he knew that his friend George Bancroft had composed Johnson's first message to Congress. Adams' account of a reception at the White House is a derisive parody of Rutherford and Mrs. Hayes; the fictional President's lady is a religious zealot who forbids wine, billiards, and cards, and will not receive women unless their bosoms and arms are amply clothed.

Such ridicule could be dismissed as individual malice, if it were not reinforced by so much other evidence that Presidents were regarded as nonentities by well-informed Americans. Adams' judgment was not faultless: he thought Benjamin Harrison was a good President, presumably because Harrison's prose and table manners were refined. But on more serious grounds the Presidents failed to make an impact, unless an unpleasant one. In radical circles, for example, the few episodes in which Presidents asserted their authority decisively seemed to prove that they were not true friends of the people. Johnson had appeared to most reformers not as a gallant Jacksonian but as an obstructionist bully. Hayes and Cleveland incurred dislike by using troops to intervene in labor disputes. No wonder the Populist platform of 1892 proposed to restrict the President to one term.

For the most part, however, reformers simply ignored the Presidency, not out of spleen but because it did not occur to them that Presidents could lead the nation to better things. Fertile though the reformers were in devising panaceas, they expected little or nothing of the federal government as a whole because they mistrusted it and because they too were bound by laissez-faire presuppositions. Henry George's *Progress and Poverty* offered a compelling view of the economic and social plight of the United States and a plausible remedy in his "Single Tax." Nothing but the tax, he seemed to believe, was required to cleanse the national stables. Other executive action would be irrelevant and probably harmful. In 1888, the year of Cleveland's moving yet negative message, Edward Bellamy published his enormously popular Utopian novel, *Looking Backward*. By portraying an ideal America of the year A.D. 2000, Bellamy delivered a powerful indirect indictment of the America of his own day, in which society is like a coach dragged along by the harnessed poor while the rich ride on top. His hero, returning to the Boston of 1887, is sickened by the spectacle of humanity "hanging on a cross," in a world of vicious and meaningless strife. Again, though, Bellamy's vision of the future left the federal government virtually out of the scheme. A cooperative economy is introduced. Everyone is obliged to serve as a state employee in an industrial army. Affairs are administered by a group of experienced businessmen. There is no mention of the President. He is apparently not even the chairman of the executive group.

A less familiar example is a novel by Francis Marion Crawford entitled *An American Politician*. Crawford, who thereafter specialized in romantic stories set in picturesque places, wrote his novel in 1884, no doubt under the stimulus of the presidential election of that year. It was the year when liberally inclined Republicans staged a limited revolt against the party candidate, James G. Blaine, the "continental liar from the State of Maine," by voting instead for the Democratic nominee, Grover Cleveland. The hero of Crawford's novel is a gentleman-reformer from Massachusetts, and a Democrat. His difficulty is that he does not approve of political parties, and cannot stomach the local breed of Boston Irish Democrats with whom he is obliged to deal. It seems that he will never win a campaign since he will not compromise his principles.

Crawford contrived an extraordinary piece of wish fulfillment to console his hero and his readers. He maintained that America's destinies were still in the hands of the patriciate, although for unexplained reasons their activities were clandestine. The hero, having passed muster, is brought under the wing of a mysterious inner council of three. The triumvirate is apparently rich, worldly, and powerful. They can maneuver as effectively as any clutch of senators or monopolists. They will ensure that the

hero plays a part in the federal government. The three secret leaders are members of "a small community of men which has existed from the earliest days of American independence. . . . It had frequently occurred that all the three members of the council simultaneously held seats in the senate. . . . More than one President since Washington had sat at one time or another in the triumvirate; secretaries of state, orators, lawyers, financiers, and philanthropists had given the best years of their lives to the duties of the council. . . ." In this latter-day Hamiltonian dream the nation was thus still governed by the wise and well-born. The interesting fact is that Crawford's dream was in 1884 pathetically at variance with the actual situation, and that although his was a dream of power, it was power wielded by a sort of Cabinet of which the President was merely one member—if he was a member at all.

While Crawford was writing his novel, Woodrow Wilson, by then a graduate student at Johns Hopkins, was busy with a doctoral thesis entitled *Congressional Government*, a lucid, confident exposition that was published in 1885. His views had not greatly altered since his essay of 1879. Wilson contended that since the Civil War the country had been "denied a new order of statesmanship to suit the altered conditions of government." But the very alteration inhibited statesmanship: the chief issues were too humdrum "to enlist feeling or arouse enthusiasm." And the American Constitution prevented leadership from being effective except in times of crisis. The Speaker of the House of Representatives had as much power as anyone through his right to appoint committee chairmen; but his prerogatives were "cramped and covert." The Presidency was "too silent and inactive, too little like a premiership and too much like a superintendency."

Wilson did not, however, deplore the lack of presidential authority; he took it for granted that "the business of the President, occasionally great, is usually not much above routine. Most of the time it is *mere* administration, mere obedience of directions from the masters of policy, the Standing Committees." What concerned Wilson was a closer relationship, on the British pattern, between the executive departments and Congress. Congress had inevitably become the dominant branch, in part because the standing committees had the time and the means to acquire specialized knowledge of multifarious issues.

By the same token Cabinets collectively knew far more about governmental matters than Presidents, who lived "by proxy; they are the executive in theory, but the Secretaries are the executive in fact." A modern President "must content himself with such general supervision as he may find time to exercise." Congress had become and had to remain the central force in federal government; Wilson apparently saw no function for the President beyond a rather vague role as the superintendent of the executive Secretaries, whom he should continue to appoint but whom Congress should "have the privilege of dismissing . . . whenever their service became unsatisfactory."

Later Wilson would change his ideas. But for the moment he was a faithful echo of the mood of the 1880's. One of the contemporary works that Wilson mentioned favorably was Alfred Stickney's *A True Republic*, which proposed to make the President a quasi-ceremonial figure responsible to the legislature, which could remove him by a two-thirds vote or continue him in office for life—like a federal judge—providing he behaved himself. A century earlier Antifederalists had feared that the President might become an elective monarch. By the Gilded Age, opinion had swung so far in the opposite direction that he was envisaged as precisely that—but a monarch without potency who would reign but not rule.

Some historians believe that in the 1890's the pendulum began to swing back again, thanks to the pugnacity of Cleveland and the more successfully genial administration of William McKinley, who seemed almost as skillful in working with Congress as Jefferson had been. If so, the liberal reaction was decidedly lukewarm. Serious magazines such as *The Arena* and *The Century* carried a number of articles on necessary political reforms. For instance, a justice of the supreme court of North Carolina, referring to a sign of activity on the part of Grover Cleveland, made the surprising claim in *The Arena* (in September, 1894) that "the weakness in our government is in the overwhelming weight of the executive and its constant tendency to grow. . . . But recently we have seen the *unprecedented* spectacle of the president, whose duty it is merely to execute the laws . . . publicly stating by a letter to a member of the legislative department, what legislation he desired. He appoints the judiciary. He can veto legislation. He can procure legislation by the use of patronage. Now, he goes further and simply tells Congress what he desires them

to do. From this to the Roman Empire, in which, under the emblems . . . of a republic, the executive was in fact the whole government, united in one person, is but a step." The author, Judge Walter Clark, recommended the elimination of the veto, the suppression of patronage, and the popular election of senators to oblige all branches of government to "understand their true positions as agents and servants of the sovereign people."

Such views were summarized and emphatically restated as late as 1897 in William D. P. Bliss's *The Encyclopedia of Social Reform*. "Very many believe," he wrote sourly, "that the Presidents of the United States have too much power." Others regarded them as too feeble, too unrepresentative. Among the authorities Bliss cited to support his implication that the Presidency was unsatisfactory were James Bryce and the distinguished civil service reformers Dorman B. Eaton and George W. Curtis. Eaton wished to confine the President to a single term of six years, Curtis to revive the Electoral College as a chamber that genuinely chose Presidents. The article asserted that Presidents were not properly chosen, and offered figures to demonstrate that in the 1896 election a shift of just over 20,000 votes in six marginal states would have brought victory for Bryan. Bliss also quoted approvingly from a radical petition to Congress asking for the abolition of the Presidency:

"It maintains the false, illogical, disorganizing theory—born in monarchy, and principally denying democracy—of the 'partition of powers.' In the democratic polity, all powers are derived from the people, and are no more capable of partition from and against each other than are the people. . . . It is a constantly menacing, constantly growing cause of danger to the republic—whose eventual ruin it must inevitably occasion."

The petitioners were almost back to the Articles of Confederation. They proposed, having got rid of Presidents, to transfer the executive functions to an "administrative commission, or Congressional ministry, to be chosen by Congress from their own body, or from among other competent citizens. . . ."

American history is full of surprises. One of the most intriguing is the process by which an office apparently despised or disliked by forward-looking citizens could within a few years leap into power and popularity. To judge from the literature of the Gilded Age, the change was neither desirable nor attainable.

The Folklore of the Presidency

From the close of Andrew Jackson's administration to the end of the nineteenth century the Presidency was—except under Abraham Lincoln—basically defensive and undramatic. In comparison with the extraordinary developments of the twentieth century the office lacked éclat. Those who wished to abolish it were, however, a small minority. If the Presidency was not accepted as the dominant element in the federal equation, it was nevertheless of great symbolic importance. Even a sluggish President was still the nation's first citizen, the ceremonial head of state, the welcomer of distinguished visitors, the receiver of deputations, the signer of bills and commissions, and the maker of speeches.

The Presidency continued to matter also to political machines. Third parties with no hope whatsoever of winning power built their organizations around a presidential candidate who became their figurehead and leader. To the Democrats and Whigs (or Republicans) the selection of a presidential nominee was a task of absorbing interest and prolonged scrutiny, reminiscent of the laborious search by which Tibetans used to choose their Dalai Lama.

A fundamental difference between the American and the Tibetan rituals was that in the United States the whole process was, at least theoretically, democratic. In other words, the explorations and incantations were ostensibly conducted in the open with maximum participation at all levels. When Jackson left the White House in 1837 the democratization of choice was well developed. The franchise was open to nearly all white males. National parties had elaborate structures linking every community in the land.

The congressional caucus was gone. In its place were the national party conventions, each preceded by numerous state and special-interest party conventions whose opinions were keenly observed by those politicians professionally involved in the art and business of President making.

The Presidency was also of boundless interest to the hundreds of Americans who, with varying degrees of justification, felt that the office might fall to them. Few of the outstanding congressmen of the century were able to renounce all thought of the Presidency. Ambitious wives nagged at them. Men from their own state sang their praises. Party followers hoping for preferment cast about for "coming men" around whom to rally. Hardheaded politicians encouraged a score of aspirants in order to test public response. Henry Clay, John C. Calhoun, Daniel Webster, Stephen Douglas, William H. Seward, and Salmon P. Chase were only a few among the well-known politicians of their day who thought they had the Presidency within their grasp. Lincoln typified innumerable Americans when he confessed that "from my boyhood up my ambition was to be President." Nor was the dream confined to congressmen.

With the advent of Jacksonianism it became clear that there were several routes that might lead to the White House. The most obvious starting point was a law career. All six of the disappointed candidates mentioned above received legal training. Of the first twenty-four men who actually served as President, all but five (Washington, William Henry Harrison, Taylor, Andrew Johnson, and Grant) had been admitted to the bar. The transition from law to politics was made easily. Some men, such as Daniel Webster, were able to shine simultaneously in both fields; in Webster's case, though, the combination may have weakened his presidential appeal by giving him a reputation as the advocate of rich men's causes.

Many candidates served an apprenticeship in state legislatures, as did Abraham Lincoln. It was also important for presidential aspirants to have gained some experience in the federal government, either as congressmen or as Cabinet members. Of the politicians nominated by the major parties for the Presidency or the Vice Presidency, Clay, Polk, Schuyler Colfax, and James G. Blaine had all served as Speaker of the House of Representatives. Madison, Fillmore, Lincoln, Hayes, Garfield, and McKinley had also been in the House. Monroe, John Quincy Adams, Van Buren, and Benjamin Harrison had been in the Senate. Andrew Jackson could claim membership in both houses of Congress, as could William Henry Harrison, Tyler, Pierce, Buchanan, and Andrew Johnson. Congressman Garfield was elected to the Senate in 1880, the year in which he was elected President. After the end of the Virginia dynasty, Cabinet membership was a less satisfactory entree, although Van Buren strengthened his position by serving as Jackson's Secretary of State. President Polk, who remembered the jostling for the Chief Magistracy that had characterized the executive departments in the previous twenty years, made his Cabinet members pledge not to seek the Presidency while they were in his administration; his Secretary of State, James Buchanan, bided his time and became President in 1857. Otherwise no Cabinet member rose to the White House until William Howard Taft, who when nominated in 1908 was Theodore Roosevelt's Secretary of War.

Although a firsthand knowledge of Washington, D.C., was valuable, it was not essential. Lincoln could never have been nominated on the strength of his one unspectacular term as a Whig congressman. His attraction depended considerably more on the reputation he had built up in his home state, Illinois. Similarly, Rutherford B. Hayes caught the eye of the Republican President makers not as a result of his two modest terms in the House of Representatives, in which his display of initiative was confined to recommending improvements for the Library of Congress, but through the record he had established as governor of Ohio. His opponent in the 1876 presi-

dential campaign, Samuel J. Tilden, had never served in Congress; his prowess at the bar and in state affairs had brought him to the governorship of New York. Horatio Seymour, the Democratic nominee in 1868, had also been New York's governor. Grover Cleveland was a third Democratic nominee from the Empire State who rose to the top of his party without benefit of a term in Congress. His fame was based on a succession of state offices—assistant district attorney and sheriff of Erie County, mayor of Buffalo—that culminated in the governorship. Polk had been governor of Tennessee as well as a member of Congress; so had Andrew Johnson. McKinley, a protégé of Hayes's, followed the same path as his mentor, via Congress and the governorship of Ohio. Indeed Woodrow Wilson speculated in his *Congressional Government* that since the Presidency was primarily an administrative office, those who held it could perhaps best prepare themselves by undertaking the essentially comparable task of governing a state.

There was also the backdoor entry, through the Vice Presidency. In an actuarial sense it was less of a gamble than any of the other possible ways. The accession of Tyler, Millard Fillmore, Andrew Johnson, and Chester A. Arthur within a period of forty years might have impelled presidential hopefuls to stake their hopes on accident. It certainly should have led Americans to give more thought to the succession problem. When Garfield died there was no one to follow Arthur in the succession. There was no Vice President, and the Republicans, who had lost their Senate majority when Conkling and Platt resigned in the spring of 1881, had prevented the election of a president pro tempore, who would have been next in line for the Presidency. If Arthur too had died before entering office an appalling hiatus would have been created. After he had been sworn in, President Arthur continually reminded Congress of the need to clarify the process in anticipation of future difficulties. But Congress merely toyed with the problem, which contained too many conundrums and provoked too much jockeying for legislative or party advantage. Above all, the Vice President was settled in national folklore as a sort of man without a country—"His Superfluous Excellency" in Benjamin Franklin's phrase.

In *Congressional Government*, Woodrow Wilson included a mere paragraph of dry wit on the Vice President: "His position is one of anomalous insignificance and curious uncertainty. . . . It is one of the remarkable things about him, that it is hard to find in sketching the government any proper place to discuss him. . . . He is simply a judicial officer set to moderate the proceedings of an assembly whose rules he has had no voice in framing and can have no voice in changing. . . . His chief dignity, next to presiding over the Senate, lies in the circumstance that he is awaiting the death or disability of the President. And the chief embarrassment in discussing his office is, that in explaining how little there is to be said about it one has evidently said all there is to say."

Daniel Webster, rejecting the offer of the Whig vice presidential nomination in 1848, had remarked: "I do not propose to be buried until I am really dead." The irony of his comment was that within two years it was the Whig President, Taylor, who was dead: Webster would have inherited the office he coveted. But such mortuary calculations did not figure in the plans of active politicians, partly, no doubt, because the "accidental Presidents" from Tyler to Arthur failed to add anything positive to the Chief Magistracy. The result was that vice presidential candidates were selected with only one thought in mind: to balance the ticket geographically. Such was the fate that lifted Congressman William A. Wheeler of New York to be Hayes's running mate. An adviser had told Hayes in 1876, "The ticket and platform should be of such character as to give the Republicans New York, Pennsylvania, and Indiana, or the first two certainly. This ticket would do it: Hayes and Wheeler." Hayes was too embarrassed to raise a question that he put instead to his wife: "I am ashamed to say, Who is *Wheeler?*"

There was a final way to the Presidency that was far removed from politics: the way of the military hero. George Washington's glory grew from his seven and a half years as commander in chief, and Andrew Jackson's from his miraculous victory in the Battle of New Orleans. Zachary Taylor and Ulysses S. Grant were professional soldiers. So were a quartet of unsuccessful candidates: Winfield Scott, the Whig nominee in 1852; John C. Frémont, the candidate of the new Republican party in 1856; George B. McClellan, chosen by the Democrats to run against Lincoln in 1864; and Winfield Scott Hancock, the Democratic contender in 1880. Some analysts have stressed the fact that a majority of American Presidents had undergone military service. William Henry Harrison,

Franklin Pierce, and James A. Garfield were presented to the electorate as General Harrison, General Pierce, and General Garfield on the strength of rank attained in three different wars. It has been maintained that far from being a disadvantage, a period of Army experience was a distinct asset for candidates. Certainly the Republican Presidents of the post-1865 era—Grant, Hayes, Benjamin Harrison, McKinley—had all made gallant records as officers in the Union army. Arthur had also been a general, if only a quartermaster general. The Republican charge against Cleveland in 1884, that he had ignominiously hired a substitute instead of fighting in the Civil War, might have cost him the election if his opponent, Blaine, had not also lacked a war record.

On the other hand, it has been argued that a professional soldier was an unlikely winner unless he could demonstrate that he was really a "citizen" soldier. In support of this view, it has been pointed out that George Washington was a special case and was without professional training; that Jackson too was unusual and was to some extent identified as a congressman; that Zachary Taylor was a most unmilitary figure who preferred not to dress in uniform and was not a West Pointer; and that Grant, the only graduate of the United States Military Academy to be elected President until General Dwight D. Eisenhower, was as unsoldierly as Taylor in appearance and outlook. Moreover, it is possible to generalize about the defeated military candidates. Scott, "Old Fuss and Feathers," was perhaps too fond of uniform to appeal to voters; and McClellan and Hancock were more typical West Pointers than Grant and were therefore less attractive to the electorate.

So many factors need to be taken into account that it is difficult to draw any reliable conclusions. Defeated or not, none of the nominees mentioned above would have been chosen by a major party if they had not seemed to be possible winners. Heroism on the battlefield stood any candidate in good stead, whether he was a professional soldier or merely a volunteer officer holding a temporary commission. (In 1948 President Truman was to reveal a traditional politician's response when he hinted to General Eisenhower—then still an active officer—that he might become the next Democratic President.) It was assumed that a man who had been a general was a proven leader. Professionals such as Taylor and Grant had the additional advantage of remoteness from the political scene. Their very innocence seemed a source of strength. They were uncontaminated by the political squabbles which titillated but also disgusted the American newspaper reader. Their hands would not be tied. Or, as the politicians could privately reflect, the Taylors and Grants might turn out to be malleable. The ideal military hero was a man with no previous political affiliation who, having suddenly burst into the limelight, discovered that his lifelong principles were, after all, in harmony with those of one of the major parties. Gideon Welles, the Secretary of the Navy during the Civil War, noted acidly in his diary that the Radical Republicans did not truly want Grant as their candidate when they began to pay him court, "but they are fearful he will be taken up by the Democrats."

It is doubtful whether Grant would have consented to be the Democratic candidate if their scouts had reached him first, given the favors Lincoln had shown him and the implication that the Democrats had been the disloyal party. But the latter reason induced the Democrats to seek soldier-candidates, so as to show that they had done as much as the Republicans to preserve the Union. In the fevered atmosphere of wartime, McClellan was an irresistible Democratic choice. Many Americans still believed he was the Union's greatest general, deprived of his destiny by the folly of the Lincoln administration. The usually sober *North American Review*, commenting on his candidacy in April, 1864, revealed that at least in emergencies a military hero was deeply appealing to the American public: "The imagination needs a single figure which it can invest with all those attributes of admiration that become vague and pointless when divided among a host. Accordingly, we impersonate in the general, not only the army he heads, but whatever qualities we are proud of in the nation itself. . . . There is nothing more touching than the sight of a nation in search of its great man, nothing more beautiful than its readiness to accept a hero on trust."

The nation very nearly did accept McClellan on trust and, of course, received Grant wholeheartedly. The counterview, expressed by *Harper's Weekly* in March, 1864—"the school of the soldier is not the school in which a President of the United States should be trained"—was not in itself enough to deny the election to McClellan. Virtually the same reservation had been expressed against Andrew Jackson,

the "military chieftain," and against Taylor. The invariable riposte was that despite his military garb the man in question was still a citizen. In 1880 Hancock's managers made a point of insisting that he and his party had always acknowledged the supremacy of the civil authority over the military. The weakness of his position was that he faced in Garfield a contender who had also fought bravely in the Civil War, and who had achieved fairly high rank with no previous grounding in the military profession. That he had returned to Congress halfway through the war, while Hancock soldiered on, was considered no discredit to Garfield. In the folklore of the Presidency it was possible to gain a reputation as a hero in a very short time. The most important quality to display, together with modesty and sterling worth, was versatility.

In most respects, then, the virtues looked for in military men did not differ fundamentally from those expected of candidates drawn from the more orthodox avenues of party politics. As W. Burlie Brown noted in his fascinating analysis, *The People's Choice: The Presidential Image in the Campaign Biography*, published in 1960, those qualities were amply indicated in the torrent of campaign literature that began to appear in Andrew Jackson's time. In the nineteenth century it was taken for granted that every candidate would be a Protestant of predominantly British (English, Scotch-Irish, Welsh) descent. The novelist William Dean Howells, who had written a campaign biography of Lincoln, later volunteered to perform the same task for his fellow Ohioan Hayes, perhaps in hopes of being rewarded with a congenial diplomatic assignment in Europe. Howells produced his potboiler in three weeks, and here and there allowed himself a touch of humor unusual in the genre, as when he alluded to another prerequisite for presidential nominees: "It is necessary that every American should have an indisputable grandfather, in order to be represented in the Revolutionary period by actual ancestral service, or connected with it by ancestral reminiscence." Nathaniel Hawthorne's campaign biography of Franklin Pierce supplied a splendid example of a candidate's patriotic ancestor: "On the 19th of April, 1775, being then less than eighteen years of age, the stripling was at the plough, when tidings reached him of the bloodshed at Lexington and Concord. He immediately loosened the ox chain, left the plough in the furrow, took his uncle's gun

. . . and set forth towards the scene of action."

Brown cited other unconsciously revealing passages. The candidate's father was almost always a plain, God-fearing, hard-working citizen like Van Buren's father, "a firm Whig in the Revolution," who instilled in his son "the maxims of piety, industry, economy and patriotism." The higher and gentler virtues of filial generosity, kindheartedness, domesticity, and the like were inculcated by a procession of candidates' mothers. The prototype of these was the glorified portrayal of George Washington's mother. True, George was supposed to have confessed to his father rather than his mother the mischief wrought by chopping down the celebrated cherry tree. But a story that had equal currency in the nineteenth century concerned young George's frank admission that he had broken in a favorite colt of the Widow Washington's so vigorously that it dropped dead. In the anecdote, his mother announced her pleasure in finding her son incapable of falsehood. The presidential candidate's mother, as he and his biographer wished to portray her and as the electorate was eager to picture her, was touchingly described in this classic delineation of Mrs. McKinley: "To see her, you must imagine a bright-eyed, motherly old lady, dressed in soft black, with a white lace collar around the throat and a cap of snow-white on her head. She is straight, well formed . . . and her hair is the color of frosted silver and combed so that the white strands curl just over the ears before they are tucked into the snowy cap."

With the shift in national tastes that took place in the last third of the century, stories of the candidate's boyhood changed from anecdotes of exemplary conduct to Tom Sawyerish tales of harmless pranks and physical activity. The shift is apparent in two different biographies of Rutherford Hayes. The first, written by the Reverend Russell H. Conwell, was almost as unblushing as the picture of young Washington presented seventy years earlier by the Reverend Mason Weems. Conwell said of Hayes: "During his attendance at the common school, he was always waiting at the steps of the old stone schoolhouse when the door was opened in the morning. . . . He did not splinter his desk with his penknife, nor throw paper balls or applecores at his neighbors . . . . He engaged in no quarrel with his schoolmaster, and he strictly obeyed every direction and command of his instructors." The second biographer followed

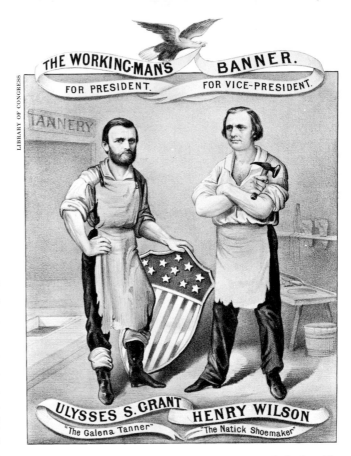

A Republican campaign poster of 1872 stressed the humble backgrounds of candidates Ulysses Grant and Henry Wilson.

the newer line by stressing in Hayes's boyhood "his overflowing jollity and drollery more distinctly than his ardor in study."

All the candidates, however, respected education. Several credited their success to devoted teachers. Several others—Pierce, Frémont, Blaine, Cleveland, McKinley—taught school before beginning their political careers. None, though, was unduly given to scholarship. As one of Grant's biographers observed, "A President"—he might have said a presidential candidate—"should not be a theorist or a bookworm." The aim of education was to rise in life, not to become a recluse. A man worthy of a nation's votes ought to have had a wholesome, rural upbringing, which indeed was not difficult for candidates to claim in the nineteenth century. If possible the candidate must have been born poor, better still in a log cabin like Pierce, Buchanan, Lincoln, and Garfield. *Log Cabin to White House* was the perfect title for a presidential biography. Many contain vignettes of the young hero, orphaned or otherwise alone, setting out to earn a living. Although Cleveland seemed excessively prosperous when the Democrats nominated him, his chronicler conjured up a pathetic memory of young Grover, employed as an office boy at three dollars a week and obliged to walk to work through the snow in flimsy shoes and no overcoat. Winfield Scott Hancock was probably as handicapped by not having had an impoverished childhood as by having graduated from West Point. The biographer of Horatio Seymour tackled a similar difficulty with his elegant subject by declaring that despite his worldly polish he was "only a plain farmer after all. . . . the proudest specimen of American yeomanry the world has ever looked upon." Playing his strong card, the biographer remarked that Seymour had, "while earnestly devoting himself to the tilling of the soil, been giving the best energies of his comprehensive mind to national affairs."

It is easy to make fun of this type of campaign literature, which was produced in haste (sometimes as a commercial venture) and was always intended to beatify a presidential hopeful. Yet well-known writers readily contributed their talents, and upright candidates did not hesitate to furnish details of their early lives. In these quadrennial displays of sentiment, the entire nation longed to be told that the candidates were not as other men. The nominee of the other party, they were determined to believe, was incompetent, misguided, perhaps villainous. Their own leader was by contrast a magnificent yet representative American, a person like themselves, who had been raised by force of character and by the presidential lottery to the height of fame. He was their champion. If he was a politician, his supporters were anxious to be reassured, and they inevitably were, that he was not a "mere politician" but a patriot, a loyal party man who bore the banner of the true political faith—whichever one it might be. If the voters were deceived, it was because they wanted to believe that it was possible to escape the trammels of everyday life. Rutherford B. Hayes was an honest man as well as a skillful politician. When Garfield emerged as the Republican candidate in 1880, President Hayes at once recorded in his diary, in all sincerity, the series of clichés by which the party should boost the new leader:

"We must neglect no element of success. There is a great deal of strength in Garfield's life and struggles as a self made man. Let it be thoroughly presented. In facts & incidents, in poetry and tales—in pictures —on banners, in representations, in processions, in watchwords and nicknames. How from poverty and

obscurity . . . he became a great scholar, a Statesman, a Major General, a Senator, a Presidential Candidate. Give the amplest details—a school teacher—a laborer on the canal—the name of his boat. . . . Once in about twenty years a campaign on personal characteristics is in order. Gen. Jackson in 1820–24—Gen Harrison in 1840—Lincoln in 1860— now Garfield. . . . Such struggles with adverse circumstances and such success! . . . He is the ideal candidate because he is the ideal self made man."

To Hayes the ballyhoo was beautiful because he was convinced that "we stand on the rock of truth." A campaign biography was like a secular sermon—a standing invitation to Americans to honor the nobility of their own transfigured existences. Walt Whitman felt a kindred stirring of exultation mixed with exaltation. "I know of nothing grander," he cried, "better exercise, better digestion, more positive proof of the past, the triumphant result of faith in human kind, than a well-contested national election."

Once a potential candidate had been identified he was propelled by a mounting tide of enthusiasm. In 1867, for example, Grant clubs sprang up all over the North. The National Union Club was formed in Philadelphia to secure him the Republican nomination. By the beginning of 1868 various magazines and newspapers had come out for him. A Central Grant Club was organized. In February, 1868, state conventions in New York, Indiana, and Wisconsin endorsed him. Before the opening of the national convention in Chicago, a Soldiers and Sailors Convention was staged in the same city; the convention wildly applauded an address by Grant's aged father and announced that everyone who had battled for the Union ought to be prepared to battle for Grant.

When the Republican convention assembled and duly nominated Grant on the first ballot, a curtain was raised to disclose a tableau especially created by the cartoonist Thomas Nast. In contest after contest Nast swayed voters with his boldly repulsive caricatures of politicians such as Greeley, Tilden, and Hancock, of whom he and his editor disapproved. On this occasion he was in a more solemn mood. He had painted on a back cloth a huge White House flanked by two pedestals labeled "Republican Nominee" and "Democratic Nominee" (the latter had not yet been chosen). General Grant was seated on the Republican pedestal. A figure of Columbia was pointing to the empty Democratic pedestal and saying, "Match him!'' Nast's design produced an ecstatic pandemonium on the convention floor. "Match him!" became a Republican campaign slogan. The party message, as Hayes would later say, was to be spread "in representations, in processions, in watchwords and nicknames." A more cynical party man might have added, "and in misrepresentations of the other side."

Some aspirants, including Salmon P. Chase, weakened their chances of nomination by appearing too eager. In keeping with the style set by Washington and John Adams and with the view that a candidate ought to stay above the fracas, the folklore of President making required possible nominees to behave almost as if they were oblivious to the campaign. Trying in vain to offset the feeling that Blaine was too nakedly interested in the Presidency, one of his supporters declared, "He is not a coy candidate. It is an honest aspiration and he indulged it like a man." In the nineteenth century a few candidates were genuinely reluctant to run. Horatio Seymour, the Democratic choice for 1868, was in earnest when he insisted that he had "not the slightest desire to occupy the White House; there is too much trouble and responsibility." He made three public announcements to this effect, and attempted to ensure his ineligibility by accepting the chairmanship of the convention. When his name was nevertheless put forward, Seymour told the delegates, "I must not be nominated by this Convention, as I could not accept the nomination if tendered." Twenty ballots later, with the convention in a state of near deadlock, the Ohio delegation reintroduced his name "against his inclination," as the Ohio spokesman said, "but no longer against his honor." Seymour was frantic. He protested that "when I said that I could not be a candidate, I *meant* it! . . ." However, while he was cooling himself in the foyer the convention nominated him. Resistance was futile after that, although in later days he described his failure to persist in his refusal as "the mistake of my life."

Such total reluctance was rare. The problem was that the ritual of indifference and hesitation made it impossible to distinguish between genuine modesty or unwillingness and counterfeit versions. Potential nominees such as Seymour or Grant, who were honestly of two minds whether to enter the race, were accused of excessive coyness. Men who actually desired nomination had to continue to disclaim and

dissemble. A visitor from another planet confronted with the performance might have decided that every public figure in the United States was either a nervous imbecile or a scheming hypocrite. An unfriendly acquaintance of General Winfield Scott's happened to travel with him aboard a Hudson River steamboat in June, 1839, when Scott had just begun to be mentioned as a possible Whig candidate for the 1840 contest. The passengers gave three cheers as Scott finally disembarked. He responded with a polite word of thanks. His caustic acquaintance said that the general "professed to deprecate being held up as a candidate for the presidency at this, or *any future time*—it is a hard part for him to play, but he does it with more discretion than some would have expected of him, and only overacts sometimes. . . ."

It was a hard part for anyone to play, though the skepticism of this particular report was justified by Scott's subsequent behavior. More sophisticated and levelheaded men than he learned to walk the narrow path of compromise by combining an air of personal detachment with the judicious promotional activity of their friends. At the present time, when more candid avowals are common, it is not easy to assess the inmost thoughts of potential presidential nominees of a bygone era. The diary of Rutherford B. Hayes is more baffling than revealing. His editor T. Harry Williams said that Hayes was "a curious mixture of idealism and practicality," at times "too high-minded for his own advancement, and at others . . . the most adept of politicians." Hayes noted in October, 1875, that if he won re-election as governor of Ohio, "I am likely to be pushed for the Republican nomination for President. This would make my life a disturbed and troubled one until the nomination six or eight months hence. If nominated, the stir would last until November a year hence." He appeared cool to the prospect—admittedly a distant one, since there were several other prominent candidates—and equally calm about the possibility of his losing the gubernatorial election, which would remove him from the presidential list.

By February, 1876, having been reinstated in the governorship, Hayes wrote that every day brought letters and callers on the subject of the Presidency: "I say very little. I have in no instance encouraged any one to work to that end. . . . I have said the whole talk about me is on the score of availability. Let availability do the work then." In other words he was available if he was "available." At the beginning of April he told himself, "I would be glad if now I could in some satisfactory way drop out of the candidacy." A few days later he observed: "In politics I am growing more indifferent. I would like it if I could now return to my planting and books at home." However, this entry in his diary is followed by a copy of a letter he had sent to one of the Ohio delegates to the forthcoming national convention—a letter politely affirming that he expected the courtesy of "the solid vote of Ohio" in the initial balloting. In later entries he transcribed various letters of support along with his answers, all of them models of discretion. His aim, as he told Garfield, was "not to lose my head, and to get through it without doing or saying anything unjust or even uncharitable towards competitors or their supporters. . . ." Luck was on his side. He had abided by the rules; the other Republican contenders stalemated one another and the nomination was his. How much did he want it? The truth was perhaps veiled from Hayes himself. Consciously or not, he was the servant of a complex code that had evolved through several decades.

Party conventions, too, were—much as in the twentieth century—highly stylized affairs, blending emotion and guile, exuberant horseplay and episodes of an almost mystical gravity. America's big and growing cities vied for the honor, publicity, and profit of acting as hosts. To attract the conventions they built immense auditoriums such as the Chicago Wigwam (a wooden structure, not a tent), where Lincoln was nominated, and the new Tammany Hall in New York. Ten thousand people crammed into the 1880 Republican convention hall in Chicago. The noise, the heat, and the confusion were both insufferable and intoxicating. Somewhere in the midst of the platitudes and the bargaining the delegates envisioned a united and regenerate party, which would be led into the promised land by Garfield, a spotless commander who had not sought the nomination but had been sought by it. "I nominate one whose name will suppress all faction and thrill the republic"; those words in support of Hancock at the Democrats' 1880 convention embodied the universal formula. A national convention was a combination religious revival meeting and stock exchange session. The vision, though it might prove a mirage, often possessed a strangely moving quality. As in revivalist meetings, it was compounded of penitence as well

as hope. Past follies were washed clean. Every good party man longed to believe that the candidate was as virtuous as his campaign biography said he was.

The convention mood could not have been sustained without minor rituals of reconciliation and unanimity. Hence the transfer of ballots to the winning candidate; hence the concern of defeated aspirants to congratulate the victor as rapidly and conspicuously as possible. If a man could not be a good winner, policy and party ethics enjoined on him the necessity of being a good loser. By the same token, party loyalty was esteemed a virtue almost beyond price. Young Theodore Roosevelt prided himself on having been a regular in 1884. When many of his fastidious friends bolted the party rather than vote for Blaine, he stood by his leader. He never doubted that he had done the right thing; once the army was on the march it was fatal to undermine the commander. Indeed, martial metaphors mingled with those of religion and commerce in the rich amalgam of President-making rhetoric.

Once nominated, a candidate was not expected to play an active part in the campaign. There were exceptions. William Henry Harrison set a precedent by making semipolitical speeches in 1836, and the fashion was repeated in 1840. Ex-President John Quincy Adams deplored this "revolution in the habits and manners of the people. . . . Electioneering for the Presidency has spread its contagion to the President himself, to his now only competitor, to his immediate predecessor. . . . The principal leaders of the political parties are travelling about the country from state to state and holding forth, like Methodist preachers, hour after hour, to assembled multitudes, under the broad canopy of heaven."

Party chiefs continued to stump the country in subsequent presidential election years. The candidates themselves, however, and the incumbent Presidents, reverted to an appearance of aloofness, and left the orating, parading, fund raising, and distribution of handbills and ribbons to the party machine. They were, of course, busy behind the scenes; but most stayed home. A misleading contemporary print showed Abraham Lincoln returning on horseback to his home in Springfield, Illinois, "after his successful campaign for the Presidency of the United States in October, 1860." He did not in fact stir from Springfield. The nearest he came to a campaign speech was a brief statement at a local Republican rally in

August. He declared that "it has been my purpose, since I have been placed in my present position, to make no speeches." After thanking the crowd and stressing that the cause that had brought them all together was far more important than any particular candidate, he excused himself and left the gathering to the orators. On the other hand, Stephen A. Douglas, who knew he had virtually no chance of victory, hurled himself into the fray with an admirable wholeheartedness. He even penetrated the South, which was by then enemy country for a Union Democrat. Some of his followers, though, felt that he had shown an indecent disregard for precedent. They circulated the unconvincing explanation that he was on a lyceum lecture tour, en route to visit his mother in New York. Cartoonists drew mocking maps of Douglas' zigzag itinerary "In Search of His Mother."

For twenty years thereafter the rule of reticence prevailed. In 1868 Grant hid in Galena, Illinois, his home town, to avoid the hurly-burly. Although he was persuaded to make a trip as far west as Denver, Colorado, in company with the popular Generals William T. Sherman and Philip Sheridan, no political speeches were delivered during the tour. Grant's opponent, Horatio Seymour, made some able but belated speeches in October, 1868. In 1876 Hayes did not leave Columbus, Ohio, except to attend the Centennial Exposition at Philadelphia on Ohio Day, which was less than two weeks before the election; he delivered a few short addresses, and was pleased that, as he put it, he had not "slopped over." In 1880 Garfield once more defied custom by undertaking an ambitious tour during which he spoke seventy times. Since he was a first-rate orator his boldness was forgiven. It was also understandable that underdogs such as William Jennings Bryan (another celebrated orator) might have to take the stump. In Bryan's case, there was another consideration: the predominantly Republican press of 1896 either maligned or ignored him. His exhausting travels in the North, West, and South were designed to take to the electorate a message that they might otherwise have never heard. But party funds and party organizations were not geared to such campaigning. One of his associates complained that Bryan had to make his own arrangements as he traveled. Since he had no special train, he sometimes had to get up in the middle of the night to reach his next engagement on time. A newspaper reporter traveling with him said that "Mr. Bryan has often been forced to carry his heavy grips from the train some distance up the street [and] that in one place he was forced to walk from the train up town, no arrangements having been made to have a carriage for him." But Bryan lost, and McKinley—waging a front-porch campaign from his home in Canton, Ohio —won. Not until 1928 did speaking tours by both major candidates become a regular feature of presidential elections. In any case, the politicos no doubt realized that other factors were more important than personal appearances—especially in an age when candidates were not required to be handsome and magnetic. By 1880, when campaign literature began to be produced in quantity, the torchlight era was over. The printed word seemed even more crucial than the spoken word. In 1896 the Republican National Committee alone sent out three hundred million leaflets—enough to supply four copies to every man, woman, and child in the country. Whatever was needed, from vote buying to processions, the Republicans had. That year a substantial campaign fund, raised by the energetic touting of wealthy backers, paid the expenses of a mobile task force of fourteen hundred Republican organizers. Without the intricate substructure of a major party a candidate could accomplish little, whether he barnstormed through every state or was content to receive an occasional delegation in his own parlor.

One element in presidential folklore persisted. It was not yet essential, though it was preferable, for a candidate to be a family man. Cleveland was a bachelor, whose campaign survived the scandal of an early liaison with a promiscuous lady of Buffalo. Nor need a candidate be a man of fine appearance and easy manners: a touch of the rough diamond was not amiss. But a nominee had to be at all costs a *serious* person. The ideal figure of the nineteenth century was James A. Garfield, self-made but eminently respectable. On his 1880 speaking tour, Garfield made a profound impression upon young Robert M. La Follette of Wisconsin, a future aspirant for the Presidency. "I heard him at Madison," La Follette recalled in his autobiography. "He was a very handsome man, of fine presence, dignity and power; splendid diction and a rather lofty eloquence. I do not remember a suggestion of humor.... I remember he impressed me more as a statesman and less as a politician than any of the men I had heard...."

William McKinley, the Republican presidential candidate in 1896, remained at his home in Canton, Ohio, throughout the campaign. Party leaders gave train fare to numerous delegations who came to Canton to hear McKinley speak from his front porch.

Candidates who indulged in humor, at least on public occasions, were suspect. None of the nineteenth-century Presidents was known as a humorist except Abraham Lincoln; although his drollery is admired today, many of his contemporaries were not amused. Even as late as 1894, Woodrow Wilson wrote primly in a magazine article that Lincoln's "mind never lost the vein of coarseness that had marked him grossly when a youth." Genial humor was all very well in local politics. A quick witticism on the floor of Congress was acceptable. One of the Whig leaders, Thomas Corwin of Ohio, acquired a national reputation for humor on the strength of a burlesque speech in the House of Representatives. But it should be added that he later believed his delight in humor had weakened his political reputation. If Lincoln had been known as Humorous Abe instead of Honest Abe he would not have reached the White House. His presidential prestige was threatened by his rumored fondness for little jokes. In 1863 Walt Whitman had to reassure friends that the President was really a wise person "underneath his outside smutched mannerism, and stories from third-class county barrooms (it is his humor)." Hostile commentators stressed a characteristic that was considered alien to the traditions of the Presidency. The New York *Herald* assailed him in 1864: "President Lincoln is a joke incarnated. . . . The idea that such a man as he should be the President . . . is a very ridiculous joke. . . . His debut in Washington society was a joke; for he introduced himself and Mrs. Lincoln as 'the long and short of the Presidency'. . . . His conversation is full of jokes. . . . His title of 'Honest' is a satirical joke."

Rutherford Hayes recorded in his diary the witticisms of his brilliant Secretary of State, William M. Evarts. He obviously appreciated them, as he did his children's riddles, which he also recorded. But there is no sign of one of his own jokes in Hayes's jottings. Presidents even more than candidates were expected to be above frivolity. In domestic life they could behave somewhat more relaxedly. Until the end of the century their daily life in the White House, despite the lack of privacy afforded by the building, was still on the whole concealed from the public. Writing in 1906, presumably in oblique disapproval of Teddy Roosevelt's much-publicized family, Harry Thurston Peck praised President Arthur as a gentleman who "kept the domestic side of his *ménage* a thing entirely apart from his official life. . . . Coarse-minded, peeping correspondents, male and female, found scant material here for vulgar paragraphs of kitchen gossip. There were published no foolish, nauseating chronicles of the 'daily doings' of the White House. The President's children were not photographed and paragraphed and made the subject of a thousand flat and fatuous stories. Beyond the veil of self-respecting privacy, which was drawn before the President's personal affairs, few ever penetrated."

206

McKinley's opponent, William Jennings Bryan (center), toured the nation in search of votes. But although the people greeted him enthusiastically, a majority cast their ballots for McKinley in the election. Four years later, McKinley beat Bryan again.

Peck was a snob. He did not consider Jefferson a worldly President on the level of Chester A. Arthur because "during his first term, he cultivated an ostentatious boorishness such as would have been impossible in a thoroughbred." Peck said too that probably not "even so great a man as Lincoln could have kept his powerful hold upon the masses had he not possessed some qualities which many of his truest friends deplored." Limited in such insights, Peck also overstated the view that "democracies prefer their idols to have feet of clay." The American people still expected their Presidents to behave as impeccably as did the heroes of genteel fiction and campaign biography. Toward the end of the century, however, they began to demand more evidence of the human side. When the middle-aged Grover Cleveland married a girl of twenty-one, public curiosity was perhaps bound to be stimulated. The appetite was fed by a swarm of newspaper correspondents—the *paparazzi* of 1886—who peered at Cleveland's honeymoon cottage through binoculars.

Cleveland was rightly indignant. But he had already alienated the newspaper fraternity. The power of the press to annoy Presidents was no novelty; it had been demonstrated again and again since the 1790's. Cleveland's mistake was in failing to see that American readers were developing more and more interest in the personal aspects of the Presidency. Perhaps this interest was a mark of the relative insignificance of the public side; perhaps it

foreshadowed the great awakening of interest in a rejuvenated office no longer so subject to the rules of political folklore. Cleveland became a prime target for journalistic censure and ridicule. When he seemed to neglect the obligatory rituals by going fishing on Memorial Day, he was accused of insulting the memory of the Union dead. The rumor that his culinary tastes were primitive led the press to picture him stuffing himself with "pig's feet, fried onions and a bottle of Extra Dry." Editors pretended that his sententious speeches were plagiarized from an encyclopedia or written by his overeducated sister. He retaliated by sending angry letters to editors and by denouncing "the silly, mean, and cowardly lies that every day are found in the columns of certain newspapers, which violate every instinct of American manliness, and in ghoulish glee desecrate every sacred relation of private life."

One must have some sympathy for Grover Cleveland. The yellow press *was* offensive and irresponsible. But the press as a whole, though capable of platitudes worse than those uttered by any President, had a satirical function that became increasingly evident in the Gilded Age, an era that was eminently satirizable. It is not altogether surprising that Ambrose Bierce, a man trained as a newspaper columnist, should have defined the Presidency in *The Devil's Dictionary* as "the greased pig in the field game of American politics." The method of selecting Cabinet members, for example, lent itself to mockery.

207

"Mr. Dooley" (Finley Peter Dunne) dealt with that subject after McKinley's election: "If 'twas one of the customs of this great republic of ours, for to appoint the most competent men for the places, he'd have a mighty small lot for to pick from. But, seein' as only them is eligible that are unfit he has the devils own time selectin'. . . . It may be hard for Mack, bein' new at the business, to select the right man for the wrong place. But I'm sure that he'll be advised by his friends, and . . . he'll have no trouble in findin' timber."

Some of the customs of the country were ripe for alteration. Some would remain unaltered. The folklore of the Presidency would not basically change for many years after McKinley, although there would be many changes in the way men acted once they were in office. Newspaper ridicule was often a recognition of the fundamental irreverence that paralleled the rather heavy ideology of Americanism. Americans were of two minds: they wished to respect and perhaps almost revere their leaders, but they were also disposed to laugh, to jeer, and to deflate the images they had themselves created.

Those fellow citizens who entered the presidential stakes were sometimes tormented and warped by ambition. The good-loser tradition, however, helped the unsuccessful to regain their equilibrium—as did the double consolation that they had not appeared to covet the office, and that in four years' time the dice might roll more fortunately. The presidential campaign of 1884, between Cleveland and Blaine, was vicious and heated, and hung upon the slenderest of majorities. Slightly over one thousand votes in New York State determined the outcome. Blaine, a prominent candidate since 1876, had the bitterest of pills to swallow. But custom had prevented the two candidates from abusing each other, though their henchmen did not shrink from the duty. And custom required that they should make gestures of reconciliation. Not long after Cleveland's inauguration, therefore, Blaine paid a courtesy call at the White House. He took the opportunity to ask a small political favor: Would the President be so kind as to continue in office the postmaster of Augusta, Maine, an old friend of Mr. Blaine's? The language of politics could be as delicate as the language of flowers. The defeated candidate was acknowledging the power of the victor—who was correspondingly gracious in return. The postmaster of Augusta kept his job.

If Cleveland had contrived to be always as genial the press, or the more reputable portion, might have treated him more kindly. For the style demanded of a President—and demanded with mounting insistence—was one of geniality that stopped somewhere short of levity and vulgarity and a long way short of arrogance. In his second term Cleveland struck unsympathetic witnesses as too self-centered, too much given to statements that sounded like edicts. The distinction was nicely put in a speech made by President Wilson in 1916. "Every man who takes office in Washington," he said, "either grows or swells." Cleveland was reproached, perhaps unfairly, for swelling instead of growing, whereas the unaffected geniality of his successor McKinley exactly caught the pitch of public expectation.

McKinley was not a giant, but the American electorate was not interested in gigantic figures. It wanted Presidents whose capacity was legendary only in the sense of conforming to the familiar legends of national folklore, which were only slightly larger than life-sized. As many historians have stated, the process of selection was erratic: a more discriminating electorate would probably have given a second term to John Quincy Adams, for instance, and would have preferred Seymour to Grant. In the main the voters got what they deserved. Or rather, the ennobling effect of the presidential office gave them something better than they deserved. A Hayes, an Arthur, or a McKinley, though commonplace enough in upbringing and outlook, rose sufficiently above his mediocre milieu to keep alive the democratic trust in man's ability to transcend himself. It is a trust that constitutes a magnificent naïveté.

The death of a Chief Executive in office was most indicative of the peculiar near-majesty of the Presidency. What is begrudged the living man is bestowed on him posthumously. This truth was excellently summarized in Wilfred E. Binkley's *The Man in the White House:* "The writer can never forget how he found his father, just after the news of McKinley's assassination had arrived, weeping as bitterly as if he had lost a child. So it was to others when Lincoln, Garfield, and Harding died in office. The son who protested to his foreign-born mother Harding's lack of merit when he found her weeping over news of the President's death got this significant response: '*Ach, aber er ist doch der Präsident*' ['Ah, but he is still the President']."

by whom the offence came, shall we discern there-in any departure from those divine attributes which the believers in a living God always ascribe to Him? Fondly do we hope— fervent-ly do we pray— that this mighty scourge of war may speedily pass away. Yet, if God wills that it continue, until all the wealth piled by the bond-man's two hundred and fifty years of unrequited toil shall be sunk, and until every drop of blood drawn with the lash, shall be paid by another drawn with the sword, as was said three thousand years ago, so still it must be said "the judgments of the Lord, are true and righteous altogether"

With malice toward none; with charity for all; with firmness in the right, as God gives us to see the right, let us strive on to finish the work we are in; to bind up the nation's wounds; to care for him who shall have borne the bat-tle, and for his widow, and his orphan— to do all which may achieve and cherish a just, and a lasting peace, among ourselves, and with all nations.

1849 - 1900

The Presidency in Documents

Lincoln's moving second Inaugural Address (the last section of the manuscript is reproduced above), was derided by the Chicago Times *in 1865: "We did not conceive it possible that even Mr. Lincoln could produce a paper so slip shod, so loose-jointed, so puerile, not alone in literary construction, but in its ideas. . . . He has outdone himself. He has literally come out of the little end of his own horn."*

Compromisers

The best of Presidents would have been hard put to provide effective leadership during the 1850's, a period in which the United States was splintered by the controversy over slavery and was hurtling toward civil war. But the men elevated to the Chief Magistracy were not the best. They were compromise choices, elected because it seemed unlikely that they would take and hold strong positions; they were expected to calm by temporizing, not to lead.

Surprising Strength

President Zachary Taylor—slaveholder, lifetime soldier, and political neophyte—stunned his more rabid Southern supporters by proposing that the expansion of slavery be halted, that its existence be guaranteed to the South, and that debates on the issue be removed from Congress. Then, in his first annual message, he suggested that New Mexico and California be admitted to the American Union as states, without a transitional period as territories. Taylor explained his motives in a special address to the Congress in late January, 1850.

. . . In advising an early application by the people of these [regions] for admission as States I was actuated principally by an earnest desire to afford to the wisdom and patriotism of Congress the opportunity of avoiding occasions of bitter and angry dissensions among the people of the United States.

Under the Constitution every State has the right of establishing and from time to time altering its municipal laws and domestic institutions independently of every other State and of the General Government, subject only to the prohibitions and guaranties expressly set forth in the Constitution of the United States. The subjects thus left exclusively to the respective States were not designed or expected to become topics of national agitation. Still, as under the Constitution Congress has power to make all needful rules and regulations respecting the Territories of the United States, every new acquisition of territory has led to discussions on the question whether the system of involuntary servitude which prevails in many of the States should or should

not be prohibited in that territory. The periods of excitement from this cause which have heretofore occurred have been safely passed, but during the interval, of whatever length, which may elapse before the admission of the Territories ceded by Mexico as States it appears probable that similar excitement will prevail to an undue extent.

Under these circumstances I thought, and still think, that it was my duty to endeavor to put it in the power of Congress, by the admission of California and New Mexico as States, to remove all occasion for the unnecessary agitation of the public mind. . . .

Trouble with Texas

During the debate over Taylor's controversial proposals, the status of California and New Mexico remained in doubt. A crisis arose when Texas, which claimed some of New Mexico's land, tried to establish jurisdiction in the disputed region, where federal forces were stationed to prevent a takeover. Texas began raising troops. In June, 1850, Army Lieutenant Alfred Pleasanton, who had been ordered to New Mexico, stopped off to see Taylor. He later recalled the President's words:

I have ordered the troops in New Mexico to be reinforced, and directed that no armed force from Texas be permitted to go into that territory. Tell Colonel Monroe (commanding in New Mexico) he has my entire confidence, and if he has not force enough out there to support him (and then his features assumed the firmest and most determined expression), I will be with you myself; but I will be there before those people shall go into that country or have a foot of that territory. The whole business is infamous, and must be put down.

New Mexico had no slaves, and it would apply for admission as a free state; that was one issue in the argument. Another was states' rights versus federal power. Representative Alexander Stephens of Georgia, who had supported Zachary Taylor for the Presidency, wrote angrily to the National Intelligencer *on July 3, 1850.*

. . . it seems that you hold it to be the "duty" of the "army" of the United States now stationed at Santa Fé to defend, without authority of law, the

THE KING OF TRUMPS.

An 1847 caricature of Taylor portrayed him as a cardboard hero. Names of the battles he had won adorn his garments.

military occupation of that portion of New Mexico lying this side of the Rio Grande against any attempt of Texas to maintain her claim by extending her jurisdiction over it.

Your right to entertain such an opinion it is not my object to question. But I wish to say to you, lest you may be mistaken in the opinions of others, that the first Federal gun that shall be fired against the people of Texas, without the authority of law, will be the signal for the freemen from the Delaware to the Rio Grande to rally to the rescue. Whatever differences of opinion may exist in the public mind touching the proper boundary of Texas, nothing can be clearer than that it is not a question to be decided by the *army*. Be not deceived, and deceive not others. "*Inter armes leges silent.*" When the "Rubicon" is passed, the days of this Republic will be numbered. You may consider the "gallant State of Texas" too weak for a contest with the army of the United States. But you should recollect that the cause of Texas, in such a conflict, will be the cause of the entire South. And whether you consider Santa Fé in danger or not, you may yet live to see that fifteen states of this Union, with seven millions of people, "who, knowing their rights, dare maintain them," cannot be *easily* conquered! "*Sapientibus verbum sat.*"

Executing the Law

Stephens' letter was printed on July 4; shortly thereafter the President fell ill, and on July 9 he died. Millard Fillmore of New York, who succeeded to the office, supported a compromise more favorable to the extension of slavery, and the threat of civil war temporarily subsided. One hotly debated feature of the Compromise of 1850 was the Fugitive Slave Law, which required Northerners to return escaped slaves to their owners. President Fillmore found the law distasteful, but signed it in the hope that peace might be maintained. On October 23, 1850, Fillmore wrote to Secretary of State Daniel Webster concerning enforcement of the controversial legislation.

. . . I have received a copy of Judge Woodbury's charge on the Fugitive Slave Law, and the Report of Judge Grier's opinion in a case before him, all manfully sustaining the constitutionality of the law, and manifesting a determined resolution to carry it out. I have also just received a joint letter from Judge Grier and Judge Keane, stating that a case has occurred before a commission in Pennsylvania where the execution of a warrant under that act was "forcibly and successfully resisted; the posse summoned to aid the officer having refused to act," and "inquiring whether upon the recurrence of an obstruction to his Process he will be entitled to call for the aid of such troops of the United States as may be accessible."

This you perceive presents a very grave and delicate question. I have not yet had time to look into it and regret much that so many of my Cabinet are absent, and especially yourself and the attorney general. These judges ask for a general order authorizing the employment of the troops in such an emergency; and I am disposed to exert whatever power I possess under the Constitution and laws, in enforcing this observance. I have sworn to support the Constitution. I know no higher law that conflicts with it; and that Constitution says, "the President shall take care that the laws be faithfully executed." I mean at every sacrifice and at every hazard to perform my duty. The Union must and shall be preserved, and this can only be done, by a faithful and impartial administration of the laws. I can not doubt that in these sentiments you are with me. And if you have occasion to speak I hope you will give no encouragement, even by implication, to any resistance to the law. Nullification can not and will not be tolerated. . . .

Diplomacy in Asia

President Fillmore turned briefly from domestic problems and cast his eyes toward Asia. He assigned Commodore Matthew Perry to take a letter, written in November, 1852, to the Mikado of Japan, whose people traditionally regarded all foreigners with deep distrust.

. . . We know that the ancient laws of your imperial majesty's government do not allow of foreign trade, except with the Chinese and the Dutch; but as the state of the world changes and new governments are formed, it seems to be wise, from time to time, to make new laws. There was a time when the ancient laws of your imperial majesty's government were first made.

About the same time America, which is sometimes called the New World, was first discovered and settled by the Europeans. For a long time there were but a few people, and they were poor. They have now become quite numerous; their commerce is very extensive; and they think that if your imperial majesty were so far to change the ancient laws as to allow a free trade between the two countries it would be extremely beneficial to both.

If your imperial majesty is not satisfied that it would be safe altogether to abrogate the ancient laws which forbid foreign trade, they might be suspended for five or ten years, so as to try the experiment. If it does not prove as beneficial as was hoped, the ancient laws can be restored. The United States often limit their treaties with foreign States to a few years, and then renew them or not, as they please.

I have directed Commodore Perry to mention another thing to your imperial majesty. Many of our ships pass every year from California to China; and great numbers of our people pursue the whale fishery near the shores of Japan. It sometimes happens, in stormy weather, that one of our ships is wrecked on your imperial majesty's shores. In all such cases we ask, and expect, that our unfortunate people should be treated with kindness, and that their property should be protected, till we can send a vessel. . . . We are very much in earnest in this.

Commodore Perry is also directed by me to represent to your imperial majesty that we understand there is a great abundance of coal and provisions in the Empire of Japan. Our steamships, in crossing the great ocean, burn a great deal of coal, and it is not convenient to bring it all the way from America. We wish that our steamships and other vessels should be allowed to stop in Japan and supply themselves with coal, provisions and water. They will pay for them in money, or anything else your imperial majesty's subjects may prefer; and we request your imperial majesty to appoint a convenient port, in the southern part of the Empire, where our vessels may stop for this purpose. We are very desirous of this.

These are the only objects for which I have sent Commodore Perry, with a powerful squadron, to pay a visit to your imperial majesty's renowned city of Yedo: Friendship, commerce, a supply of coal and provisions, and protection for our shipwrecked people. . . .

"No North, no South, no East, no West under the Constitution; but a sacred maintenance of the common bond, and a true devotion to the common brotherhood." FRANK PIERCE."

Franklin Pierce pledged to preserve the Union.

Self-restrictions

New Hampshire's Franklin Pierce, in his first annual address in December, 1853, expressed a Jeffersonian view of the role of the states in national government.

. . . I am deeply sensible of the immense responsibility which the present magnitude of the Republic and the diversity and multiplicity of its interests devolves upon me, the alleviation of which so far as relates to the immediate conduct of the public business, is, first, in my reliance on the wisdom and patriotism of the two Houses of Congress, and, secondly, in the directions afforded me by the principles of public polity affirmed by our fathers of the epoch of 1798, sanctioned by long experience, and consecrated anew by the overwhelming voice of the people of the United States.

Recurring to these principles, which constitute the organic basis of union, we perceive that vast as are the functions and the duties of the Federal Government, vested in or intrusted to its three great departments—the legislative, executive, and judicial—yet the substantive power, the popular force, and the large capacities for social and material development exist in the respective States, which, all being of themselves well-constituted republics, as they preceded so they alone are capable of maintaining and perpetuating the American Union. The Federal Government has its appropriate line of action in the specific and limited powers conferred on it by the Constitution, chiefly as to those things in which the States have a common interest in their relations to one another and to foreign governments, while the great mass of interests which belong to cultivated men—the ordinary business of life, the springs of industry, all the diversified personal and domestic affairs of society—rest securely upon the general reserved powers of the people of the several States. There is the effective democracy of the nation, and there the vital essence of its being and its greatness. . . .

Agitation

In 1854 the South demanded that the bill creating the territories of Kansas and Nebraska include repeal of the Missouri Compromise, which had excluded slavery from new territories in the northern part of the nation. Obviously, repeal would upset the balance so painfully wrought by the Compromise of 1850. President Pierce had promised to maintain that balance, but because he felt that Southern support was crucial to his administration, he agreed to back repeal. Congressman Benjamin Pringle of New York spoke for the outraged North in a speech to the House of Representatives on May 19, 1854.

. . . It seems, too, that the President is as fallible, as changeable as some other New Hampshire politi-

cians. In the last presidential contest he claimed to stand upon what was called the "Baltimore platform." He believed in the "*finality*" of the compromise measures of 1850. There was to be no more slavery agitation in any quarter. Every effort to disturb, by the repeal of these measures, the peace and quiet of the country, (which it was claimed these measures had secured,) was to be put down; and no longer ago than the commencement of the present session of Congress, we find the President, in his annual message, using the following language:

"It is no part of my purpose to give prominence to any subject which may properly be regarded as set at rest by the deliberate judgment of the people. . . . THAT THIS REPOSE IS TO SUFFER NO SHOCK DURING MY OFFICIAL TERM, IF I HAVE POWER TO AVERT IT, THOSE WHO PLACED ME HERE MAY BE ASSURED."

Now, instead of remaining true to his principles thus solemnly announced; instead of attempting to "avert," by his official power, the agitation of the troublesome question of slavery; instead of his performing his promise, *that the repose of the country should suffer no shock during his official term, if he had the power to prevent it*, we find him the very prince of agitators; we find the repeal of the "Missouri compromise" is made "*the measure*" of the Administration, and friends of the Administration are threatened with ostracism if they do not support it. Thank God, there are some noble spirits that do not quail before the threats and denunciations of the Executive, but stand up in all their pride of manhood "for freedom and the right!"

But the country was promised repose from agitation and excitement. Why, sir, compared with the agitation and excitement that will be awakened and started into life by the adoption of this wicked project, all former agitation and excitement will sink into utter insignificance and be forgotten. . . .

Furor Over Kansas

The Missouri Compromise was repealed, and Nebraska and Kansas became territories. In Kansas, proponents of slavery gained control of the government, although it was apparent to all that the majority of the territory's residents opposed slavery and would eventually have their way. Neither North nor South was happy. When the proslavery government wrote a constitution and asked to be admitted to the Union, President James Buchanan supported it and tried to justify his position in terms satisfactory to both sides. On March 30, 1858, Congressman W. L. Underwood of Kentucky pleaded for a more direct approach to the tense situation.

. . . Mr. Chairman, I would invite your attention to a most singular fact—singular, indeed, it would be if it did not recur in every phase of democratic policy and tactics. It is the rare and singular facility—I should rather call it *craft*—of the democratic party to give to all their measures a northern and a southern aspect. . . . They did apprentice work in the repeal of the Missouri Compromise, when they declared in the north it was a measure of freedom, and in the south that it was the unlocking of the Territories for the expansion of slavery; they did journeymen's work in their divers interpretations of squatter sovereignty, suited to all latitudes and localities; and they are doing master work now, when this very measure of the admission of Kansas under the Lecompton constitution is advocated by the President and his northern supporters as the *"promptest"* manner of prohibiting slavery in that State, whilst their southern brethren are advocating it, and are ready to split the Union about it, becauses it recognizes slavery north of 36° 30′—albeit, it shows its head there for a moment and disappears thenceforth forever. You are too familiar with the bold and ardent declarations of my southern friends to require me to cite instances to prove the burning zeal with which they contemplate and advocate admission under the Lecompton constitution. . . .

. . . Should not these bold contrasts, then, teach forbearance to our extreme southern friends? especially when they were told the other day on this floor, by one of their northern allies, that the north got the oyster whilst the south got the shell, in this division of the spoils. Are they not, at least, sufficient to silence the cry of "abolitionism," which, I doubt not, is preparing to be raised throughout the south against all those who shall dare to resist this measure, so really destructive of every principle the south should hold sacred and inviolate? But, Mr. Chairman, more than this, is it not time for us to have a straightforward and honest policy? Have we not been paltered with long enough in a double sense? How much longer will the south—or the north either —suffer itself to be deluded thus with fallacious hopes, having the word of promise kept to the ear but broken to the hope? For myself, I am weary of the Janus face and the forked tongue. . . .

Impotence

In 1860 Northern votes elected Abraham Lincoln President of the United States. South Carolina, having threatened for decades to secede from the Union, did so on December 20, and the other states of the Deep South pre-

Kansans opposed to slavery fire on a proslavery settlement in "Battle of Hickory Point," a drawing by S. J. Reader. Because of the bitter fighting that broke out there during Pierce's and Buchanan's terms, the territory became known as Bleeding Kansas.

pared to follow, convinced by their own rhetoric that Lincoln, despite his frequent avowals to the contrary, would immediately emancipate and enfranchise their slaves. In his last annual address to Congress, on December 3, a despairing James Buchanan had made an eloquent plea for national unity, while declaring the utter inability of the Chief Executive to help effect it.

. . . How easy would it be for the American people to settle the slavery question forever and to restore peace and harmony to this distracted country! They, and they alone, can do it. All that is necessary to accomplish the object, and all for which the slave States have ever contended, is to be let alone and permitted to manage their domestic institutions in their own way. As sovereign States, they, and they alone, are responsible before God and the world for the slavery existing among them. For this the people of the North are not more responsible and have no more right to interfere than with similar institutions in Russia or in Brazil.

Upon their good sense and patriotic forbearance I confess I still greatly rely. Without their aid it is beyond the power of any President . . . to restore peace and harmony among the States. Wisely limited and restrained as is his power under our Constitution and laws, he alone can accomplish but little for good or for evil on such a momentous question.

And this brings me to observe that the election of any one of our fellow-citizens to the office of President does not of itself afford just cause for dissolving the Union. This is more especially true if his election has been effected by a mere plurality, and not a majority of the people, and has resulted from transient and temporary causes, which may probably never again occur. In order to justify a resort to revolutionary resistance, the Federal Government must be guilty of "a deliberate, palpable, and dangerous exercise" of powers not granted by the Constitution. The late Presidential election, however, has been held in strict conformity with its express provisions. How, then, can the result justify a revolution to destroy this very Constitution? Reason, justice, a regard for the Constitution, all require that we shall wait for some overt and dangerous act on the part of the President elect before resorting to such a remedy. It is said, however, that the antecedents of the President elect have been sufficient to justify the fears of the South that he will attempt to invade their consti-

tutional rights. But are such apprehensions of contingent danger in the future sufficient to justify the immediate destruction of the noblest system of government ever devised by mortals? From the very nature of his office and its high responsibilities he must necessarily be conservative. The stern duty of administering the vast and complicated concerns of this Government affords in itself a guaranty that he will not attempt any violation of a clear constitutional right.

After all, he is no more than the chief executive officer of the Government. His province is not to make but to execute the laws. . . .

It may be asked, then, Are the people of the States without redress against the tyranny and oppression of the Federal Government? By no means. The right of resistance on the part of the governed against the oppression of their governments can not be denied. It exists independently of all constitutions, and has been exercised at all periods of the world's history. Under it old governments have been destroyed and new ones have taken their place. It is embodied in strong and express language in our own Declaration of Independence. But the distinction must ever be observed that this is revolution against an established government, and not a voluntary secession from it by virtue of an inherent constitutional right. In short, let us look the danger fairly in the face. Secession is neither more nor less than revolution. It may or it may not be a justifiable revolution, but still it is revolution.

What, in the meantime, is the responsibility and true position of the Executive? He is bound by solemn oath, before God and the country, "to take care that the laws be faithfully executed," and from this obligation he can not be absolved by any human power. But what if the performance of his duty, in whole or in part, has been rendered impracticable by events over which he could have exercised no control? Such at the present moment is the case throughout the State of South Carolina so far as the laws of the United States to secure the administration of justice by means of the Federal judiciary are concerned. All the Federal officers within its limits through whose agency alone these laws can be carried into execution have already resigned. We no longer have a district judge, a district attorney, or a marshal in South Carolina. In fact, the whole machinery of the Federal Government necessary for the distribution of remedial justice among the people has been demolished, and it would be difficult, if not impossible, to replace it.

The only acts of Congress on the statute book bearing upon this subject are those of February 28, 1795, and March 3, 1807. These authorize the President, after he shall have ascertained that the marshal, with his *posse comitatus*, is unable to execute civil or criminal process in any particular case, to call forth the militia and employ the Army and Navy to aid him in performing this service, having first by proclamation commanded the insurgents "to disperse and retire peaceably to their respective abodes within a limited time." This duty can not by possibility be performed in a State where no judicial authority exists to issue process, and where there is no marshal to execute it, and where, even if there were such an officer, the entire population would constitute one solid combination to resist him.

The bare enumeration of these provisions proves how inadequate they are without further legislation to overcome a united opposition in a single State, not to speak of other States who may place themselves in a similar attitude. Congress alone has power to decide whether the present laws can or can not be amended so as to carry out more effectually the objects of the Constitution. . . .

Lincoln

For years Presidents had tried to remain above the sectional argument and to avoid offending the moderate partisans of either North or South. The debate over slavery had thus taken place largely in Congress, and although the legislature had excoriated the problem instead of solving it, the Presidency had been eclipsed by Congress as the active force in government. But with a rebellion in progress, Lincoln regained the initiative for the Presidency—if only briefly. Humble, humane, politically astute, and far from doctrinaire in his attitudes toward the South, President Lincoln led the loyal states to victory, and set the United States on a path away from the morass into which the slavery issue had brought it.

The President Acts

By the time Lincoln was inaugurated all seven states of the Deep South had seceded and many federal installations had been seized by the Rebels. Fort Sumter, situated on an island off Charleston, South Carolina, was besieged. Convinced that some action had to be taken by the national government, President Lincoln prepared to send provisions to the federal fort. He wrote to the Secretary of the Navy, Gideon Welles, on March 29, 1861.

Sir: I desire that an expedition, to move by sea, be got ready to sail as early as the 6th. of April next, the whole according to memorandum attached; and that you co-operate with the Secretary of War for that object. Your Obedient Servant

A. Lincoln.

Navy Dept.
Stmrs Pocahontas at Norfolk, Pawnee at Washington, and Revenue Cutter Harriet Lane at N. York to be ready for sea with one months stores. Three hundred seamen to be ready for leaving the receiving ship at N. York.

War Dept.
Two hundred men at N. York ready to leave garrison—one years stores to be put in a portable form.

On April 4, Simon Cameron, the Secretary of War, sent a message to the commanding officer at Fort Sumter, Major Robert Anderson, in response to Anderson's warning that the fort's provisions were nearly gone.

Sir: Your letter of the 1st. inst. occasions some anxiety to the President.

. . . he had supposed you could hold out till the 15th. inst. without any great inconvenience; and had prepared an expedition to relieve you before that period.

Hoping still that you will be able to sustain yourself till the 11th. or 12th. inst. the expedition will go forward; and, finding your flag flying, will attempt to provision you, and, in case the effort is resisted, will endeavor also to reinforce you.

You will therefore hold out if possible till the arrival of the expedition.

It is not, however, the intention of the President to subject your command to any danger or hardship beyond what, in your judgment, would be usual in military life; and he has entire confidence that you will act as becomes a patriot and a soldier, under all circumstances.

Whenever, if at all, in your judgment, to save yourself and command, a capitulation becomes a necessity, you are authorized to make it.

Rebel artillery opened fire on Fort Sumter on April 12; thirty-four hours later Major Anderson surrendered, and on April 15 the President issued a proclamation.

Whereas the laws of the United States have been for some time past and now are opposed and the execution thereof obstructed in the States of South Carolina, Georgia, Alabama, Florida, Mississippi, Louisiana, and Texas by combinations too powerful to be suppressed by the ordinary course of judicial proceedings or by the powers vested in the marshals by law:

Now, therefore, I, Abraham Lincoln, President of the United States, in virtue of the power in me vested by the Constitution and the laws, have thought fit to call forth, and hereby do call forth, the militia of the several States of the Union to the aggregate number of 75,000, in order to suppress said combinations and to cause the laws to be duly executed.

The details for this object will be immediately communicated to the State authorities through the War Department.

I appeal to all loyal citizens to favor, facilitate, and aid this effort to maintain the honor, the integrity, and the existence of our National Union and the perpetuity of popular government and to redress wrongs already long enough endured.

I deem it proper to say that the first service assigned to the forces hereby called forth will probably be to repossess the forts, places, and property which have been seized from the Union; and in every event the utmost care will be observed, consistently with the objects aforesaid, to avoid any devastation, any destruction of or interference with property, or any disturbance of peaceful citizens in any part of the country.

And I hereby command the persons composing the combinations aforesaid to disperse and retire peaceably to their respective abodes within twenty days from this date.

Deeming that the present condition of public affairs presents an extraordinary occasion, I do hereby, in virtue of the power in me vested by the Constitution, convene both Houses of Congress. Senators and Representatives are therefore summoned to assemble at their respective chambers at 12 o'clock noon on Thursday, the 4th day of July next, then and there to consider and determine such measures as, in their wisdom, the public safety and interest may seem to demand. . . .

Habeas Corpus

Historians agree that the American President is most powerful in wartime. Certainly Lincoln did not hesitate to stretch to the utmost the executive prerogatives outlined in the Constitution. In a message to Congress on July 4, 1861, he defended one extraordinary move:

. . . Soon after the first call for militia, it was considered a duty to authorize the Commanding General, in proper cases, according to his discretion, to suspend the privilege of the writ of habeas corpus; or, in other words, to arrest, and detain, without resort to the ordinary processes and forms of law, such individuals as he might deem dangerous to the public safety. This authority has purposely been exercised but very sparingly. Nevertheless, the legality and propriety of what has been done under it, are questioned; and the attention of the country has been called to the proposition that one who is sworn to "take care that the laws be faithfully executed," should not himself violate them. Of course some consideration was given to the question of power, and propriety, before this matter was acted upon. The whole of the laws which were required to be faithfully executed, were being resisted, and failing of execution, in nearly one-third of the States. Must they be allowed to finally fail of execution, even had it been perfectly clear, that by the use of the means necessary to their execution, some single law, made in such extreme tenderness of the citizen's liberty, that practically, it relieves more of the guilty, than of the innocent, should, to a very limited extent, be violated? To state the question more directly, are all the laws, *but one*, to go unexecuted, and the government itself go to pieces, lest that one be

Lincoln and Jefferson Davis, the President of the Confederacy, are depicted as boxers in the cartoon above. Davis, a former senator and Secretary of War, was an ineffective Chief Executive and would have preferred to lead a Southern army.

Emancipation

Although the Preliminary Emancipation Proclamation of September 22, 1862 (below), and the subsequent decree of January 1, 1863, did not, in fact, free any slaves, they set the nation on a road that would lead to their actual emancipation. Lincoln had been forced to act by hardening antislavery opinion in the North.

. . . That on the 1st day of January, A.D. 1863, all persons held as slaves within any State or designated part of a State the people whereof shall then be in rebellion against the United States shall be then, thenceforward, and forever free; and the executive government of the United States, including the military and naval authority thereof, will recognize and maintain the freedom of such persons and will do no act or acts to repress such persons, or any of them, in any efforts they may make for their actual freedom.

That the Executive will on the 1st day of January aforesaid, by proclamation, designate the States and parts of States, if any, in which the people thereof, respectively, shall then be in rebellion against the United States; and the fact that any State or the people thereof shall on that day be in good faith represented in the Congress of the United States by members chosen thereto at elections wherein a majority of the qualified voters of such States shall have participated shall, in the absence of strong countervailing testimony, be deemed conclusive evidence that such State and the people thereof are not then in rebellion against the United States. . . .

Vice President Hannibal Hamlin of Maine, who favored emancipation of the slaves, congratulated President Lincoln after the first proclamation. The Chief Executive's pessimistic answer, written on September 28, follows.

My Dear Sir: Your kind letter of the 25th is just received. It is known to some that while I hope something from the proclamation, my expectations are not as sanguine as are those of some friends. The time for its effect southward has not come; but northward the effect should be instantaneous.

It is six days old, and while commendation in newspapers and by distinguished individuals is all that a vain man could wish, the stocks have declined, and troops come forward more slowly than ever.

violated? Even in such a case, would not the official oath be broken, if the government should be overthrown, when it was believed that disregarding the single law, would tend to preserve it? But it was not believed that this question was presented. It was not believed that any law was violated. The provision of the Constitution that "The privilege of the writ of habeas corpus, shall not be suspended unless when, in cases of rebellion or invasion, the public safety may require it," is equivalent to a provision—is a provision—that such privilege may be suspended when, in cases of rebellion, or invasion, the public safety *does* require it. It was decided that we have a case of rebellion, and that the public safety does require the qualified suspension of the privilege of the writ which was authorized to be made. Now it is insisted that Congress, and not the Executive, is vested with this power. But the Constitution itself, is silent as to which, or who, is to exercise the power; and as the provision was plainly made for a dangerous emergency, it cannot be believed the framers of the instrument intended, that in every case, the danger should run its course, until Congress could be called together; the very assembling of which might be prevented, as was intended in this case, by the rebellion. . . .

This, looked soberly in the face, is not very satisfactory. We have fewer troops in the field at the end of six days than we had at the beginning—the attrition among the old outnumbering the addition by the new. The North responds to the proclamation sufficiently in breath; but breath alone kills no rebels.

I wish I could write more cheerfully. . . .

Binding Wounds

The bitterness of war notwithstanding, Lincoln's main concern was for restoration of the Union. In a proclamation issued at the end of 1863 he offered full pardon to most of the Rebels and set up a simple method by which the Southern states could create governments that would make them full partners in the nation once more. In February, 1865, he made a new proposal to his Cabinet, but as this excerpt from Gideon Welles's diary reveals, the President was persuaded to abandon the idea.

Monday, 6. There was a Cabinet meeting last evening. The President had matured a scheme which he hoped would be successful in promoting peace. It was a proposition for paying the expenses of the war for two hundred days, or four hundred millions to the Rebel States to be for the extinguishment of slavery, or for such purpose as the States were disposed. This in few words was the scheme. It did not meet with favor, but was dropped. The earnest desire of the President to conciliate and effect peace was manifest, but there may be such a thing as so overdoing as to cause a distrust or adverse feeling. In the present temper of Congress the proposed measure, if a wise one, could not be carried through successfully.

I do not think the scheme could accomplish any good results. The Rebels would misconstrue it if the offer was made. If attempted and defeated it would do harm. . . .

The Confederacy was in its death throes. On March 4, Lincoln delivered his second Inaugural Address, in which he pleaded eloquently for forgiveness and justice.

. . . On the occasion corresponding to this four years ago, all thoughts were anxiously directed to an impending civil-war. All dreaded it—all sought to avert it. While the inaugeral address was being delivered from this place, devoted altogether to *saving* the Union without war, insurgent agents were in the city seeking to *destroy* it without war—seeking to dissol[v]e the Union, and divide effects, by negotiation. Both parties deprecated war; but one of them would *make* war rather than let the nation survive; and the other would *accept* war rather than let it perish. And the war came. . . .

. . . Fondly do we hope—fervently do we pray—that this mighty scourge of war may speedily pass away. Yet, if God wills that it continue, until all the wealth piled by the bond-man's two hundred and fifty years of unrequited toil shall be sunk, and until every drop of blood drawn with the lash, shall be paid by another drawn with the sword, as was said three thousand years ago, so still it must be said "the judgments of the Lord, are true and righteous altogether."

With malice toward none; with charity for all; with firmness in the right, as God gives us to see the right, let us strive on to finish the work we are in; to bind up the nation's wounds; to care for him who shall have borne the battle, and for his widow, and his orphan—to do all which may achieve and cherish a just, and a lasting peace, among ourselves, and with all nations.

The Executive In Jeopardy

The defeat of the Confederacy ensured the survival of the Union. But after Abraham Lincoln's death a new threat to constitutional government arose. Northern legislators sought to wrest executive power from the Presidency.

The Power of Dismissal

A Southerner—true to the Union, to be sure, but a native of a Confederate state—had inherited the Presidency. When Andrew Johnson made it clear that he in-

tended to follow Lincoln's program of compassionate Reconstruction, Congress used his Southern birth as an excuse to attack the program. One measure adopted by Congress to ensure that it and not the President would control Reconstruction was the Tenure of Office Act, which was passed over Johnson's veto in March, 1867. The law negated the Executive's traditional right to dismiss a Cabinet officer without the Senate's concurrence.

Be it enacted by the Senate and House of Representatives of the United States of America in Congress assembled, That every person holding any civil office to which he has been appointed by and with the advice and consent of the Senate, and every person who shall hereafter be appointed to any such office, and shall become duly qualified to act therein, is, and shall be entitled to hold such office until a successor shall have been in like manner appointed and duly qualified, except as herein otherwise provided: *Provided,* That the Secretaries of State, of the Treasury, of War, of the Navy, and of the Interior, the Postmaster-General, and the Attorney-General, shall hold their offices respectively for and during the term of the President by whom they may have been appointed and for one month thereafter, subject to removal by and with the advice and consent of the Senate.

SEC. 2. *And be it further enacted,* That when any officer appointed as aforesaid, excepting judges of the United States courts, shall, during a recess of the Senate, be shown, by evidence satisfactory to the President, to be guilty of misconduct in office, or crime, or for any reason shall become incapable or legally disqualified to perform its duties, in such case, and in no other, the President may suspend such officer and designate some suitable person to perform temporarily the duties of such office until the next meeting of the Senate, and until the case shall be acted upon by the Senate, and such person so designated shall take the oaths and give the bonds required by law to be taken and given by the person duly appointed to fill such office; and in such case it shall be the duty of the President, within twenty days after the first day of such next meeting of the Senate, to report to the Senate such suspension, with the evidence and reasons for his action in the case, and the name of the person so designated to perform the duties of such office. And if the Senate shall concur in such suspension and advise and consent to the

removal of such officer, they shall so certify to the President, who may thereupon remove such officer, and, by and with the advice and consent of the Senate, appoint another person to such office. But if the Senate shall refuse to concur in such suspension, such officer so suspended shall forthwith resume the functions of his office, and the powers of the person so performing its duties in his stead shall cease, and the official salary and emoluments of such officer shall, during such suspension, belong to the person so performing the duties thereof, and not to the officer so suspended. . . .

SEC. 6. *And be it further enacted,* That every removal, appointment, or employment, made, had, or exercised, contrary to the provisions of this act, and the making, signing, sealing, countersigning, or issuing of any commission or letter of authority for or in respect to any such appointment or employment, shall be deemed, and are hereby declared to be, high misdemeanors, and, upon trial and conviction thereof, every person guilty thereof shall be punished by a fine not exceeding ten thousand dollars, or by imprisonment not exceeding five years, or both said punishments, in the discretion of the court. . . .

Was the act applicable to Johnson? He would probably only serve until the end of the term to which Lincoln had been elected, but was he not President just as legally as Lincoln had been, and did he not have a right to form his own Cabinet? In any case, he felt the law was unconstitutional, and he meant to test it when he fired Secretary of War Edwin Stanton on February 21, 1868, and appointed Lorenzo Thomas temporary Secretary. The Senate had already disapproved Stanton's dismissal once; the House quickly passed articles of impeachment, and on March 13 the Senate's trial of Andrew Johnson began. The vote would be along party lines, and the Republicans held a two-thirds majority in the Senate, enough for conviction. Journalist Georges Clemenceau, who would one day become the Premier of France, described slightingly the attempt of one of Johnson's attorneys, Benjamin R. Curtis, to cope with the situation in which Congress had placed the President.

. . . Mr. Curtis . . . took up only two essential points. He contends that the law known as the Tenure of Office Bill does not apply in the case of Mr. Stanton, because the latter was appointed Secretary of War by Mr. Lincoln, and not by the present President. Whence he naturally concludes that the removal of Mr. Stanton was a perfectly legal act, and that Mr. Johnson violated none of the provisions of the Tenure of Office Bill. Then, after having established this point to his own satisfaction, he turns right around and seeks to prove that Mr. Johnson, in removing Mr. Stanton, violated the same law deliberately, with the plan of forcing the Supreme Court to give a decision on his action.

I confess I cannot see how Mr. Curtis can reconcile his two lines of defense. I looked in vain all through his speech for anything which might serve as a transition between these two points of view. He merely says, in conclusion, that he realizes some people will think they see a contradiction in his double argument, but that he himself sees none. I doubt whether the Senate will be satisfied with this simple affirmation. . . .

The Critical Vote

By the time the impeachment trial had reached the day of verdict, six Republican senators had announced their intention to vote against conviction. Although the Radicals had only thirty-five sure votes, one less than they needed, Ben Wade, president pro tempore of the Senate and next in line to the powers and duties of the Presidency, had already selected a Cabinet. The only senator whose vote was still in doubt—Edmund G. Ross of Kansas—later described the climactic scene of the trial.

. . . That day, May 15, 1868, was fateful. There had been none such in nearly a hundred years of the history of the Government. It was to determine judicially a question of varying phases which had never before been brought for solution in the courts—what should constitute "high crimes and misdemeanors in office" on the part of the National Executive; what latitude should be allowed him in the expression of personal opinion in his differences with co-ordinate branches of the Government; how far he might lawfully go in the exercise of his personal judgment in the administration of the powers and duties of his great office; whether his oath of office permitted him to interpret the Constitution for himself in the absence and anticipation of judicial determination, or whether he should be governed by Congressional interpretation of that instrument. In a large sense, the independence of the executive office as a co-ordinate branch of the Government was on trial. . . .

The hours seemed to pass with oppressive tedium awaiting the time for the assembling of the Senate and the beginning of the vote. It came at last, and found the galleries thronged to their utmost with a brilliant and eager auditory. Tickets of admission were at an enormous premium. Every chair on the floor was filled with a Senator, a Cabinet officer, a member of the President's counsel, or a representative, for the House had adjourned and its anxious members had at once thronged to the Senate chamber. Every foot of available standing room in the area and about the senatorial seats was occupied. . . .

Pages were flitting from place to place with messages. . . . Little groups were gathered here and there in subdued conversation, discussing the situation and the probable result and its attendant consequences. The intensity of public interest was increased by the general impression that the entire official incumbency and patronage of the Government in all its departments, financial and political, had been pledged in advance and on condition of the removal of the President. . . .

The Chief Justice, with apparent emotion, propounded the query, "How say you, Senator Ross, is the respondent, Andrew Johnson, guilty or not guilty under this article?"

At this point the intensity with which the gaze of the audience was centred upon the figure then on the floor was beyond description or comparison. Hope and fear seemed blended in every face, instantaneously alternating, some with revengeful hate predominating as in the mind's eye they saw their dreams of success, of place, and triumph dashed to earth; others lighted with hope that the President would be relieved of the charges against him, and things remain as they were. Not only were the occupants of the galleries bending forward in intense and breathless silence and anxiety to catch the verdict, but the Senators in their seats leaned over their desks, many with hand to ear, that not a syllable or intonation in the utterance of the verdict should be lost.

Conscious that I was at that moment the focus of all eyes, and conscious also of the far-reaching effect, especially upon myself, of the vote I was about to

In 1866, President Johnson traveled through the East and Midwest, trying to gain support for his policy of gentle reconstruction of the South. Johnson was often booed by the crowds, who wildly applauded his traveling companion, General Grant.

give, it is something more than a simile to say that I almost literally looked down into my open grave. Friends, position, fortune, everything that makes life desirable to an ambitious man, were about to be swept away by the breath of my mouth, perhaps forever. Realizing the tremendous responsibility which an untoward combination of conditions seemed to have put upon me, it is not strange that my answer was carried waveringly over the air and failed to reach the limits of the audience, or that a repetition was called for by distant Senators on the opposite side of the chamber. Then the verdict came —"Not guilty"—in a voice that could not be misunderstood. . . .

Line of Succession

The order of presidential succession after the Vice President had been established in 1792. It consisted of the president pro tempore of the Senate, followed by the Speaker of the House of Representatives, followed by no one—although it was possible that at any given moment there might be neither a president pro tempore nor a Speaker. The impeachment of President Andrew Johnson demonstrated another flaw, which the acquitted Chief Executive futilely called to the attention of Congress in a special message that was read out on July 18, 1868.

. . . Recent events have shown the necessity of an amendment to the Constitution distinctly defining the persons who shall discharge the duties of President of the United States in the event of a vacancy in that office by the death, resignation, or removal of both the President and Vice-President. It is clear that this should be fixed by the Constitution, and not be left to repealable enactments of doubtful constitutionality. It occurs to me that in the event of a vacancy in the office of President by the death, resignation, disability, or removal of both the President and Vice-President the duties of the office should devolve upon an officer of the executive department of the Government, rather than one connected with the legislative or judicial departments. The objections to designating either the President *pro tempore* of the Senate or the Chief Justice of the Supreme Court, especially in the event of a vacancy produced by removal, are so obvious and so unanswerable that they need not be stated in detail. It is enough to state that they are both interested in producing a vacancy, and, according to the provisions of the Constitution, are members of the tribunal by whose decree a vacancy may be produced.

Under such circumstances the impropriety of designating either of these officers to succeed the President so removed is palpable. The framers of the Constitution, when they referred to Congress the settlement of the succession to the office of President in the event of a vacancy in the offices of both President and Vice-President, did not, in my opinion, contemplate the designation of any other than an officer of the executive department, on whom, in such a contingency, the powers and duties of the President should devolve. Until recently the contingency has been remote, and serious attention has not been called to the manifest incongruity between the provisions of the Constitution on this subject and the act of Congress of 1792. Having, however, been brought almost face to face with this important question, it seems an eminently proper time for us to make the legislation conform to the language, intent, and theory of the Constitution, and thus place the executive department beyond the reach of usurpation, and remove from the legislative and judicial departments every temptation to combine for the absorption of all the powers of government. . . .

Fifteenth Amendment

The logical step after freeing the slaves was to give Negroes the right to vote. The Radicals, moreover, saw the establishment of a Republican party in the South, supported by Negro voters, as excellent insurance of their continued dominance in American government. The Fifteenth Amendment, which enfranchised Negroes, was declared ratified by the states on March 30, 1870.

SECTION 1.   The right of citizens of the United States to vote shall not be denied or abridged by the United States or by any State on account of race, color, or previous condition of servitude.

SECTION 2.   The Congress shall have power to enforce this article by appropriate legislation.

Congress Wins

Ulysses S. Grant permitted Congress the role that it had sought—primacy over the President. The Ku-Klux Klan Act passed in 1871 "gave" the Chief Executive a number of powers that earlier Presidents of the United States had regarded as one of their constitutional prerogatives.

. . . SEC. 3.   That in all cases where insurrection, domestic violence, unlawful combinations, or conspiracies in any State shall so obstruct or hinder the execution of the laws thereof, and of the United States, as to deprive any portion or class of the people of such State of any of the rights, privileges, or immunities, or protection, named in the Constitution and secured by this act, and the constituted authorities of such State shall either be unable to protect, or shall, from any cause, fail in or refuse protection of the people in such rights, such facts shall be deemed a denial by such State of the equal protec-

tion of the laws to which they are entitled under the Constitution of the United States; and in all such cases, or whenever any such insurrection, violence, unlawful combination, or conspiracy shall oppose or obstruct the laws of the United States or the due execution thereof, or impede or obstruct the due course of justice under the same, it shall be lawful for the President, and it shall be his duty to take such measures, by the employment of the militia or the land and naval forces of the United States, or of either, or by other means, as he may deem necessary for the suppression of such insurrection, domestic violence, or combinations; and any person who shall be arrested under the provisions of this . . . shall be delivered to the marshal of the proper district, to be dealt with according to law.

SEC. 4.   That whenever in any State or part of a State the unlawful combinations named in the preceding section of this act shall be organized and armed, and so numerous and powerful as to be able, by violence, to either overthrow or set at defiance

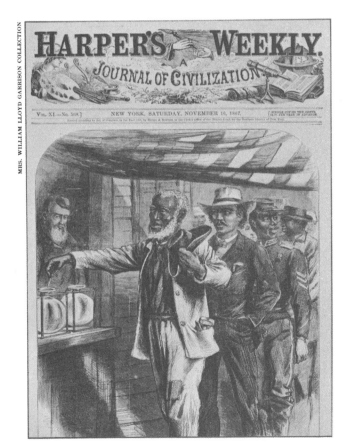

Southern Negroes voted in special elections held in 1867. The magazine cover above celebrates their enfranchisement.

the constituted authorities of such State, and of the United States within such State, or when the constituted authorities are in complicity with, or shall connive at the unlawful purposes of, such powerful and armed combinations; and whenever, by reason of either or all of the causes aforesaid, the conviction of such offenders and the preservation of the public safety shall become in such district impracticable, in every such case such combinations shall be deemed a rebellion against the government of the United States, and during the continuance of such rebellion, and within the limits of the district which shall be so under the sway thereof, such limits to be prescribed by proclamation, it shall be lawful for the President of the United States, when in his judgment the public safety shall require it, to suspend the privileges of the writ of habeas corpus, to the end that such rebellion may be overthrown. . . .

Corruption

Behind the back of the complaisant Grant, his appointees and cronies enriched themselves by hundreds of thousands of dollars. The President had been compelled to fire one of them, Thomas Murphy, as collector for the Port of New York in 1871 because Murphy's demonstrated corruption had proved too great an embarrassment. Yet in 1875 Murphy was still part of Grant's inner circle, and the President was trying to help him with a transaction that was, to say the least, irregular. It stemmed from the American rental of a harbor in the Dominican Republic. Secretary of State Hamilton Fish, one of the few distinguished statesmen who served in Grant's administration, recalled the unsavory episode.

. . . He [Grant] said that Murphy was nearly ruined, and had advanced some $40,000 or $50,000 on account of the rent, and that some others (without naming them) had also made advances; that the money ought to be paid; and that Conkling [Senator Roscoe Conkling of New York] had spoken with him and suggested that I should bring the matter to the notice of the Committee on Foreign Relations. . . .

He asked if it could not be paid out of the contingent fund of foreign intercourse. I explained to him that the appropriation only amounted to about $100,000, and with the strictest economy the ex-

penditures could only be kept $2,000 below it. He suggested that an appropriation for $150,000 might be made without indicating its object.

I thought that it would be impossible, and he asked whether I could not suggest such an appropriation, informing the Administration Senators of its object. I replied that I could not; that the present temper of Congress and the public was such that no appropriation of the kind could be expected, and that it would be very damaging to him and the Republican Party for the Administration to propose an appropriation for the St. Domingo Treaty [already colored with scandal].

The President admitted that he was precluded from asking but thought that I might.

I replied that that would be more injurious to him than a direct proposal from himself, as I should only do it, if at all, under his instructions and it would be regarded as an indirect evasion, on his part, of the responsibility.

I called his attention to the fact that St. Domingo had never made any demands directly or indirectly from the government for the second year's rent. He said that it had been paid, he supposed, by Murphy and others. I had never, however, heard any other than Murphy's allegation of its having been paid by himself.

He finally remarked that he supposed that the only thing would be for the party to make application to Congress, to which I replied that I could suggest nothing, but that the Administration should take no part in it.

Growing Pains

It was clear that any President, whether or not he hoped to administer a graft-free government, would have to contend with many men who were chiefly concerned with personal gain. After Grant, bulwarks against corruption were gradually created. But it still required a great deal of money, "wisely" spent, to win a presidential election. And after the campaign the new Chief Executive had to deal with the party bosses who demanded re-

wards for their support. The Gilded Age Presidents accepted, at least in part, the realities of the situation. A commitment to total reform, they knew, could entangle them in bitter fights over patronage and pork-barrel legislation that would leave them little time to administer what was becoming a huge and complex government.

A Candidate's View

The reform governor of Ohio, Rutherford B. Hayes, was nominated for President by the Republicans in 1876. His diary and letters provide rare insight into the progress of an especially hard-fought campaign, one that ended in the closest finish in United States history.

August 13. Sunday.—Last night, with Attorney-General John Little, I met Senator Morton [Oliver P. Morton of Indiana] at Bradford Junction, on his request, to talk over the political situation. . . . Morton regards the situation as grave; that if Indiana is Democratic in October, our chance is not over one in ten of success in the country in November; that if we carry Indiana in October, our chances of carrying the country in November are forty-nine in fifty; in short, that we lose the Presidency in November if we lose Indiana in October. . . .

I said, "And now the remedy?" He after some further talk said, "*Money and speakers.*" Money to pay men to travel and organize, to print and circulate documents, etc., etc. To my question, "How much is needed to do the work required to carry the State?" he replied one thousand dollars to a county will do it, or . . . one hundred thousand dollars. I asked, "How much is generally used?" He replied, "Four years ago we had from outside the State fifty-five thousand dollars." . . .

On the whole, his talk was not encouraging. The use of money, I have little faith in, and I am confident no such large sum can be raised. I mean to go through cheerfully and firmly and with clean hands. If defeated, there will be no bitterness in the disappointment, and I shall have my self-respect and an approving conscience. . . .

Candidate Hayes was nonetheless inclined to cooperate with Senator Morton, and that same day he wrote a letter to a friend about the crucial Indiana election.

. . . An important matter. Indiana is close. If we carry it the victory is ours in the Nation almost beyond a question. If we lose it, with the South gone, (*as it is, all but one or two States*) our chances are small. The Greenback organizations draw more from us than from the Democrats. It needs organization, speakers, documents, and perhaps at two points the establishment of Republican newspapers. Think of it, the important town of Terre Haute has no Republican paper! For all this, money is required, *and now.* Will you see Mr. Forbes [J. M. Forbes of Boston] and spread this before him? Our National Committee needs funds for the general campaign. Ascertain what is doing. If anything is done or to be done? I do not believe in any miscellaneous use of money in elections. But for the objects named it is necessary.

Few holds were barred. Hayes wrote his long-time friend William H. Smith in Chicago about one opposition ploy.

MY DEAR S—:—I have just seen the [Chicago] *Times* of Saturday. Leroy's attempt to blackmail me can't need much attention. Hastings can give you all that is needed. But I *suspect* the letters purporting to be from me are none of them given correctly. *Certainly the letter of November 16, 1869, is a forgery. No such letter was ever written.* It is made out of whole cloth. If it becomes important I can find the whole of Leroy's letters at my house in Fremont. *It is all a fraud.* Write me if it needs my personal attention. . . .

During the last month of the tense campaign against Samuel Tilden, Hayes revealed in his diary a calm, even ruminative attitude toward most electoral eventualities.

Columbus, October 4, 1876.—Birthday. Fifty-four years of age. The good omen of the day is that Colorado, the first State to elect electors (or rather a Legislature that will elect electors), has been carried by the Republicans. "First gun for Hayes," is the headline of the *Journal.* . . .

Columbus, October 22, 1876. Sunday.—Only two Sundays more before the Presidential election. I am surprised, whenever I think of it, to find myself so cool, so almost indifferent about it. It would be a calamity, I am sure, to give the Democrats the Government. But public opinion, the press, the march of events, will compel them to do better than their character and principles indicate. Here is our safety. Public opinion, the fear of losing the public confidence, apprehension of censure by the press, make all men in power conservative and safe.

On personal grounds, I find many reasons for thinking defeat a blessing. I should stand by my Letter [of Acceptance], I should hew to the line; but what conflicts and annoyances would follow! I do not fear my pluck or constancy a particle. But to be deceived by the rogues, to find many a trusted reformer no better than he should be,—here would be humiliations and troubles without end.

The huge registration in New York City looks sinister. It seems to look to our defeat in that State.

Another danger is imminent: A contested result. And we have no such means for its decision as ought to be provided by law. This must be attended to hereafter. We should not allow another Presidential election to occur before a means for settling a contest is provided. If a contest comes now it may lead to a conflict of arms. I can only try to do my duty to my countrymen in that case. I shall let no personal ambition turn me from the path of duty. Bloodshed and civil war must be averted if possible. If forced to fight, I have no fears of failure from lack of courage or firmness.

Sunday, October 29.—Returned last night from Ohio Day at the Centennial. It was an enthusiastic and prodigious crowd which greeted me. I managed to shake some four thousand people by the hand and to make half a dozen speeches from steps, windows,

Tilden's backers threatened war if he was denied the Presidency, but he urged acceptance of the electoral decision.

and roof of the Ohio Building, without saying anything that I regret—without "slopping over." . . .

I return feeling that with the probabilities of fraud and violence—fraud, North; violence, South—the chances are that we shall lose the election. . . . But I have made a good fight. . . .

Columbus, November 7, 1876.—Dies iræ!—A cold but dry day. Good enough here for election work. I still think Democratic chances the best. But it is not possible to form a confident opinion. If we lose, the South will be the greatest sufferer. Their misfortune will be far greater than ours. I do not think a revival of business will be greatly postponed by Tilden's election. Business prosperity does not, in my judgment, depend on government so much as men commonly think. But we shall have no improvement in civil service—deterioration rather, and the South will drift towards chaos again.

Saturday, November 11.—The election has resulted in the defeat of the Republicans after a very close contest. . . .

I went to bed at 12 to 1 o'clock [election night]. Talked with Lucy, consoling her with such topics as readily occurred of a nature to make us feel satisfied on merely personal grounds with the result. We soon fell into a refreshing sleep and the affair seemed over. Both of us felt more anxiety about the South—about the colored people especially—than about anything else sinister in the result. . . .

But I took my way to my office as usual Wednesday morning, and was master of myself and contented and cheerful. During the day the news indicated that we carried California; soon after, other Pacific States; all New England except Connecticut; all of the free States West except Indiana; and it dawned on us that with a few Republican States in the South to which we were fairly entitled, we would yet be the victors. . . .

Hayes Elected

The Southern states whose results were in doubt were Florida, Louisiana, and South Carolina. As Republican canvassing boards began recounts, men from both parties flocked there to see that "justice was done."

Among them was Senator John Sherman, reformer and astute politician. Hayes wrote to him on November 27.

. . . You feel, I am sure, as I do about this whole business. A fair election would have given us about forty electoral votes at the South—at least that many. But we are not to allow our friends to defeat one outrage and fraud by another. There must be nothing crooked on our part. Let Mr. Tilden have the place by violence, intimidation, and fraud, rather than undertake to prevent it by means that will not bear the severest scrutiny. . . .

The boards, however, produced predictably Republican returns, while both sides shouted fraud—and not without cause. The Democrats made it clear that they would fight the matter further when the electoral votes were counted in Congress. To settle the dispute Congress set up an electoral commission. The key question was: Would it accept the results reported by the Republican authorities in the three Southern states, or would it instead conduct its own investigation of the voting there?

Columbus, February 8, 1877.—Yesterday the Electoral Commission decided not to go behind the papers filed with the Vice-President in the case of Florida. The question was well argued on our side. Judge Matthews was notably able and successful. Mr. Evarts' argument was worthy of his fame. I read the arguments in the *Congressional Record* and can't see how lawyers can differ on the question. But the decision is by a strictly party vote—eight Republicans against seven Democrats! It shows the strength of party ties. The general situation is now regarded as much more favorable to us, and now our friends are very confident of success.

Breaking the Bosses

The tide of reform was running strong in 1880 when James Garfield was elected to succeed Hayes. But the old-line Stalwart Republicans were not taking their medicine with equanimity, and even before he took office Garfield found himself in the midst of a bitter patronage fight with the New York wing of his party, which included Vice President Chester A. Arthur and party boss Senator Roscoe Conkling. Garfield brought the squabble

to a boil soon after he became President by nominating reformer William H. Robertson as collector for the Port of New York. Garfield explained his position in a letter to his long-time friend Burke Hinsdale on April 4, 1881.

. . . This was my philosophy of the case: President Grant surrendered New York patronage to Mr. Conkling—defeat in that State was the result. President Hayes gave the majority of the patronage to his opposers and the result was not so disastrous but it widened the breach between the opposing wings of the Republican party and made a constant petty warfare between himself and Mr. Conkling in which both sides became unduly irritated. After a careful survey of the whole field I thought that both Presidents had made a mistake by enlisting their influence on one side or the other. I determined, therefore, to recognize Mr. Conkling very generously and fully. This I did by appointing from the list of his friends the Postmaster General, the Postmaster at New York, the Minister to France, and filling nine vacancies in the State with persons whom he recommended.

To have stopped there would have been regarded as not only a surrender to him but as putting to the sword all those Independent Republicans who followed me at Chicago in resisting the unit rule and in advocating the right of individual delegates to the free exercise of their judgment in the Convention. Thereupon I determined to recognize the other side in a conspicuous manner. I knew that there lay before me a struggle of a year and a half over Merritt's position. It would have become vacant just when the State of New York would be entering upon the gubernatorial struggle and the appointment of Merritt's successor would have brought the contest in the midst of a great political inflammation of feeling. I thought it better, therefore, to provide for Merritt in such a manner that he could not consider himself slighted and put in his place an abler man and the leader of the N.Y. Independents. This brings on the contest at once and will settle the question whether the President is registering clerk of the Senate or the Executive of the Nation.

It is probable that the contest will be sharp and bitter but I prefer to have the fight ended now and the collectorship of New York settled for the term. Summed up in a single sentence this is the question; shall the principal port of entry in which more than

90% of all our customs duties are collected be under the direct control of the Administration or under the local control of a factional Senator. I think I win in this contest, and having won the ground will be cleared around me and Senators will understand my attitude as well as theirs. . . .

An Acting President?

On July 2, 1881, Garfield was shot by a Stalwart who wanted to make Chester Arthur President. With a bullet in his back, Garfield suffered through the summer, unable to function as Chief Executive. Secretary of State James G. Blaine began to urge that the Vice President step in as Acting President. But the circumstances, combined with Tyler's precedent regarding succession, made such a move impossible for Arthur. The New York Times *argued against replacing the President.*

Washington, Sept. 1.—Under the circumstances, a very significant prominence was given from here in dispatches last night to the statement that it had been in some way arranged that Vice-President Arthur was soon to be invited here to act as President by Gen. Garfield. The matter cannot be properly called sensational, so far as the press is concerned, since it was doubtless founded upon the talk of a Cabinet officer, but the fact is that the question has not been submitted to the President and certainly will not be for the present. In the next place, if a case should arise where the public interests really demanded an extensive signature, the papers might be taken to him now and would be. His absence from the executive office has not yet been as long as when President Hayes visited the Pacific coast, when no public interests suffered. One Cabinet officer, in speaking of this matter to-day, said that if he had a half-hour in which to talk with the President he could transact all needed business with him in one minute. The *Star*, in giving the drift of talk on this subject, has a paragraph . . . . to the effect that grave differences have been found to exist among Cabinet officers in regard to the propriety of urging a consideration of the subject at this time. The truth will probably hereafter be found to be that not over two Cabinet officers have displayed any special anxiety to have Mr. Arthur in some way called to act. It is

only just to Gen. Arthur to say that it is not believed that he or his friends here have been parties to this Washington attempt to give prominence to this matter, and this is beyond question the most significant feature of the whole matter. . . .

Hartford, Conn., Sept. 1.—Commenting on the Washington report, to-day, that the Cabinet was considering plans by which Vice-President Arthur should assume the Presidential functions . . . ex-Senator Eaton said to THE TIMES's correspondent to-night that he was surprised at the propositions made, contemplating, as they do, a notification from the President himself that he is suffering from disability. "Under the Constitution," said the ex-Senator, after quoting the clause referring to the death or disability of the Chief Executive, "there can be no disability that the President can be conscious of. It must be a disability, as, for example, if he were insane, which is patent to everybody except himself. So long as he possesses reasoning powers and can direct what should be done in his place he cannot be held under the Constitution to be disabled. It is, therefore, absurd to talk about plans which require his own intelligence and direction to carry into effect. If he is suffering from disability, such as is clearly evident to those about him and to the country, the Vice-President, under the Constitution, must assume the functions of the office, and no legislation is needed to enforce this duty. . . ."

Elevation

Garfield died on September 19. Many observers were surprised when his successor dissociated himself from some of his Stalwart cronies—notably Conkling—and fought against partisan patronage, graft, and government waste. On August 1, 1882, Arthur vetoed a major piece of pork-barrel legislation, the Rivers and Harbors bill, which was nevertheless passed over his objection.

. . . My principal objection to the bill is that it contains appropriations for purposes not for the common defense or general welfare, and which do not promote commerce among the States. These provisions, on the contrary, are entirely for the benefit of the particular localities in which it is proposed to make the improvements. I regard such appropriation of the public money as beyond the powers given by the Constitution to Congress and the President.

I feel the more bound to withhold my signature from the bill because of the peculiar evils which manifestly result from this infraction of the Constitution. Appropriations of this nature, to be devoted purely to local objects, tend to an increase in number and in amount. As the citizens of one State find that money, to raise which they in common with the whole country are taxed, is to be expended for local improvements in another State, they demand similar benefits for themselves, and it is not unnatural that they should seek to indemnify themselves for such use of the public funds by securing appropriations for similar improvements in their own neighborhood. . . .

The appropriations for river and harbor improvements have, under the influences to which I have alluded, increased year by year out of proportion to the progress of the country. . . .

. . . It being the usage to provide money for these purposes by annual appropriation bills, the President is in effect directed to expend so large an amount of money within so brief a period that the expenditure can not be made economically and advantageously.

The extravagant expenditure of public money is an evil not to be measured by the value of that money to the people who are taxed for it. They sustain a greater injury in the demoralizing effect produced upon those who are intrusted with official duty through all the ramifications of government. . . .

A Succession Act

Through the operation of chance and politics there had been neither a Senate president pro tempore nor a Speaker of the House on the day Garfield died; thus there was no one in the line of succession after Vice President Arthur. Soon after Grover Cleveland became President, his Vice President, Thomas A. Hendricks, died and a similar situation existed. In 1886 Congress at last acted to eliminate the possibilities created by the Succession Act of 1792. The new law stipulated:

. . . That in case of removal, death, resignation, or inability of both the President and Vice-President of the United States, the Secretary of State, or if there be none, or in case of his removal, death, resignation, or inability, then the Secretary of the Treasury, or . . . then the Secretary of War, or . . . then the Attorney-General, or . . . then the Postmaster-General, or . . . then the Secretary of the Navy, or . . . then the Secretary of the Interior, shall act as President until the disability of the President or Vice-President is removed or a President shall be elected: *Provided,* That whenever the powers and duties of the office of President . . . shall devolve upon any of the persons named herein, if Congress be not then in session, or if it would not meet . . . within twenty days thereafter, it shall be the duty of the person upon whom said powers and duties shall devolve to issue a proclamation convening Congress in extraordinary session, giving twenty days' notice of the time of meeting.

SEC. 2. That the preceding section shall only be held to describe and apply to such officers as shall have been appointed by the advice and consent of the Senate . . . [and] are eligible to the office of President under the Constitution, and not under impeachment by the House . . . at the time the powers and duties of the office shall devolve upon them. . . .

Money Troubles

In what was, for the last third of the nineteenth century, a rare show of executive self-assertion, Grover Cleveland called Congress into special session in August, 1893, and demanded repeal of the Sherman Silver-Purchase Act. The law, which had been enacted in 1890, based American currency on a two-metal standard, and Cleveland blamed it for the financial crisis the country faced. In his message to the Congress the President declared:

. . . With plenteous crops, with abundant promise of remunerative production and manufacture, with unusual invitation to safe investment, and with satisfactory assurance to business enterprise, suddenly financial distrust and fear have sprung up on every side. Numerous moneyed institutions have suspended because abundant assets were not immediately available to meet the demands of frightened depositors. Surviving corporations and individuals are content to keep in hand the money they are usually anxious to loan, and those engaged in legitimate business are surprised to find that the securities they offer for loans, though heretofore satisfactory, are no longer accepted. Values supposed to be fixed are fast becoming conjectural, and loss and failure have invaded every branch of business.

I believe these things are principally chargeable to Congressional legislation touching the purchase and coinage of silver by the General Government. . . .

It is of the utmost importance that such relief as Congress can afford in the existing situation be afforded at once. The maxim "He gives twice who gives quickly" is directly applicable. It may be true that the embarrassments from which the business of the country is suffering arise as much from evils apprehended as from those actually existing. We may hope, too, that calm counsels will prevail, and that neither the capitalists nor the wage earners will give way to unreasoning panic and sacrifice their property or their interests under the influence of exaggerated fears. Nevertheless, every day's delay in removing one of the plain and principal causes of the present state of things enlarges the mischief already done and increases the responsibility of the Government for its existence. Whatever else the people have a right to expect from Congress, they may certainly demand that legislation condemned by the ordeal of three years' disastrous experience shall be removed from the statute books. . . .

The repeal of the Sherman Silver-Purchase Act did not prevent the serious depression of 1893 to 1897. And in January, 1895, a drain on American gold reserves brought the country to the verge of disaster. Cleveland again seized the initiative from a slow-moving Congress. He arranged a high-interest loan from J. P. Morgan that brought fifty million dollars in gold into the Treasury—and provoked considerable criticism. Later, the New York Evening Post *came to Cleveland's defense:*

How near the country was, the last week in January, to crashing down to a silver basis, may not be generally known. Bankers knew it, business men knew it, the President knew it. If he had not acted promptly the crash would have been on us before this. Gold was being drawn from the Treasury at the rate of $7,000,000 a week. The next week $10,000,000 would have gone; the week after, the last dollar. There was no time for prolonged negotiations. If bids had been invited for a further issue of 5 per cent bonds, the first danger would have been that the end of the Treasury gold would be in sight before any bids came in, the second danger would [have] been that no bids would come in. This last, in fact, was almost a certainty . . . Congress was standing there like a lot of boys playing with dynamite. No help was to be had from them. The bankers had got tired of flinging their gold into the bottomless pit. If ever there was an emergency in public finance, if ever extreme measures and great sacrifices were justifiable to save the public credit, the last week in January was the time. President Cleveland did just what any banker would have done in analogous circumstances in private business.

A World Power

In 1888 presidential candidate Benjamin Harrison called the United States "an apart nation" and suggested that it would be best to remain uninvolved in world affairs. But in the last decade of the nineteenth century America was beginning to recognize its status as a major industrial nation and to feel colonial and missionary urges. The role of a world power would greatly enhance the powers and duties of the President.

Scruples

In the first annual message to Congress of his second term, President Grover Cleveland outspokenly shunned a policy of annexation by other than democratic means.

. . . It is hardly necessary for me to state that the questions arising from our relations with Hawaii have caused serious embarrassment. Just prior to the installation of the present Administration the existing Government of Hawaii had been suddenly overthrown and a treaty of annexation had been negotiated between the Provisional Government of the islands and the United States and submitted to the Senate for ratification. This treaty I withdrew for examination and dispatched Hon. James H. Blount, of Georgia, to Honolulu as a special commissioner to make an impartial investigation of the circumstances attending the change of government and of all the conditions bearing upon the subject of the treaty. After a thorough and exhaustive examination Mr. Blount submitted to me his report, showing beyond all question that the constitutional Government of Hawaii had been subverted with the active aid of our representative to that Government and through the intimidation caused by the presence of an armed naval force of the United States, which was landed for that purpose at the instance of our minister. Upon the facts developed it seemed to me the only honorable course for our Government to pursue was to undo the wrong that had been done by those representing us and to restore as far as practicable the status existing at the time of our forcible intervention. With a view of accomplishing this result within the constitutional limits of executive power, and recognizing all our obligations and responsibilities growing out of any changed conditions brought about by our unjustifiable interference, our present minister at Honolulu has received appropriate instructions to that end. . . .

AGAIN ON DECK·
Executive-Officer CLEVELAND Reports for Duty on the SHIP OF STATE & Is Warmly Welcomed·
"Thanks, Captain! Glad to get back and never better in my life"

REPEAL & REFORM

Cleveland was welcomed back to the Presidency by this 1893 cartoon. No other man has served nonconsecutive terms.

War with Spain

President William McKinley was also uneasy about his country's desire for expansion. For weeks after the sinking of the American battleship Maine *at Havana in February, 1898, he resisted pressure from the yellow press and refused to advocate war against Spain. But in April, after Spain had agreed to all American demands regarding Cuba, he capitulated to the clamor and sent to Congress a strange and contradictory war message.*

. . . The present revolution is but the successor of other similar insurrections which have occurred in Cuba against the dominion of Spain, extending over a period of nearly half a century, each of which during its progress has subjected the United States to great effort and expense in enforcing its neutrality laws, caused enormous losses to American trade and commerce, caused irritation, annoyance, and disturbance among our citizens, and, by the exercise of cruel, barbarous, and uncivilized practices of warfare, shocked the sensibilities and offended the

humane sympathies of our people. Since the present revolution began, in February, 1895, this country has seen the fertile domain at our threshold ravaged by fire and sword in the course of a struggle unequaled in the history of the island and rarely paralleled as to the numbers of the combatants and the bitterness of the contest. . . .

Our trade has suffered, the capital invested by our citizens in Cuba has been largely lost, and the temper and forbearance of our people have been so sorely tried as to beget a perilous unrest among our own citizens, which has inevitably found its expression from time to time in the National Legislature, so that issues wholly external to our own body politic engross attention and stand in the way of that close devotion to domestic advancement that becomes a self-contained commonwealth whose primal maxim has been the avoidance of all foreign entanglements. All this must needs awaken, and has, indeed, aroused, the utmost concern on the part of this Government. . . .

. . . I ask the Congress to authorize and empower the President to take measures to secure a full and final termination of hostilities between the Government of Spain and the people of Cuba, and to secure in the island the establishment of a stable government, capable of maintaining order and observing its international obligations, insuring peace and tranquillity and the security of its citizens as well as our own, and to use the military and naval forces of the United States as may be necessary for these purposes. . . .

The issue is now with the Congress. It is a solemn responsibility. I have exhausted every effort to relieve the intolerable condition of affairs which is at our doors. Prepared to execute every obligation imposed upon me by the Constitution and the law, I await your action.

Yesterday, and since the preparation of the foregoing message, official information was received by me that the latest decree of the Queen Regent of Spain directs General Blanco, in order to prepare and facilitate peace, to proclaim a suspension of hostilities, the duration and details of which have not yet been communicated to me.

This fact, with every other pertinent consideration, will, I am sure, have your just and careful attention in the solemn deliberations upon which you are about to enter. If this measure attains a successful result, then our aspirations as a Christian, peace-loving people will be realized. If it fails, it will be only another justification for our contemplated action.

"Our Flag Is There"

When the Philippines fell to Commodore George Dewey's forces during the brief Spanish-American War, President McKinley agonized over their future. Some Americans—and many Filipinos—advocated immediate independence for the conquered islands, but there was considerable demand at home that they be annexed to the United States. McKinley finally decided that it was America's duty to "civilize and Christianize" the Philippines. He defended his decision in a speech:

. . . We have gone through a war, the celerity of which and the results of which are scarcely recorded of any other war in history. The American arms triumphed on land and on sea, with unprecedented exemption from disease and death on the part of our soldiers and sailors. We are proud of the army and the navy. They have brought us great responsibili-

ties; they have brought us new acquisitions and new territory; and it is for us to accept those responsibilities, meet them with manly courage, respond in a manly fashion to manly duty, and do what in the sight of God and man is just and right.

One tribe, and a small fraction of that tribe, is questioning the sovereignty of the United States in the island of Luzon. The very people we emancipated from oppression assailed our flag and shot our soldiers. The shedding of blood is anguish to my soul. The giving up of the lives of our bravest and best young men wrings my heart. The shedding of the blood of the misguided Filipinos is a matter of sorrow to all of us. And yet they are resisting the sovereignty of the United States over a territory which we acquired, not by conquest alone, but by the solemn treaty of peace sanctioned by the Congress of the United States. When our authority is undisputed in every part of that archipelago hostilities will stop. May that time soon come!

It is said we could have peace if we would give them independence and a government of their own under their own sovereignty. It is said that if the President would do this we would have peace. The President has no power, even if he was disposed, which he is not, to alienate a single foot of territory which we have honestly acquired, or give up sovereignty over it to any other peoples. That power belongs to the people. It is vested in Congress, which represents the people, and no such power was ever given to the Chief Executive by the people, by Congress, or by the Constitution, and to use it would be a base usurpation of prerogative by the Chief Executive of the government. And then, if we were going to cede the islands away, to whom would we cede them? There is no government there but ours. . . .

My fellow-citizens, the Philippines came to us not of our seeking: none of us ever dreamed, when this war commenced, that we were to have either Porto Rico or the Philippine Islands. We went to war for civilization and for humanity, to relieve our oppressed neighbors in Cuba. I was one of those who held back until the last moment, hoping that war might be averted. I did not want to involve my country in bloodshed. But the war came, and a few of those who wanted it most are now trying to shirk its responsibilities. Man plans, but God Almighty executes. We cannot avoid our responsibility. . . . We have the Philippines, and our flag is there. . . .

"GOODNESS GRACIOUS! I MUST HAVE BEEN DOZING!"

Powers and Perils

Every American boy, the saying goes, may someday be President of the United States. Not every American man, however, wants the job. The necessity of working under ceaseless pressure and constant scrutiny, of dealing with complex issues and unpredictable crises does not appeal to everyone; nor does the prospect of humiliation by Congress, vilification by the opposition, or possible death by assassination. The Theodore Roosevelt or John F. Kennedy who enjoys being at the center of power and bearing the Presidency's enormous burdens is the exception, not the rule. More typical is the man who finds the pressures crushing; like Wilson or Polk he may lose his health as a result. Or, like William H. Taft (shown in the 1910 cartoon above snarled in the intricacies of the office as Roosevelt looks on), he may admit, "I'll be damned if I am not getting tired of this," and wish he were someplace and someone else.

233

The Nation Personified

The President of the United States is the nation's Chief of State as well as its Chief Executive, and as such he must perform a host of ceremonial functions. He must receive visiting royalty and heads of state, award medals to astronauts and other national heroes, and be photographed with delegations of citizens seeking to publicize worthy causes. He is expected to throw out the first baseball each spring, and to turn on the lights of the national Christmas tree each December. He may also—if he wishes—use the enormous prestige of the Presidency to provide moral leadership, as John Fitzgerald Kennedy did in May, 1963, when he appeared on television to remind the American people that the denial of civil rights to Negroes was "a moral issue" that demanded immediate redress. "The Presidency is more than executive responsibility," Herbert Hoover told the voters in 1932. "It is the symbol of America's high purpose. The President must represent the Nation's ideals. . . ."

The appearance of a President makes a ceremony an event. Above, William Howard Taft touches a golden belt to open the Gunnison Tunnel in Montrose, Colorado, in 1909.

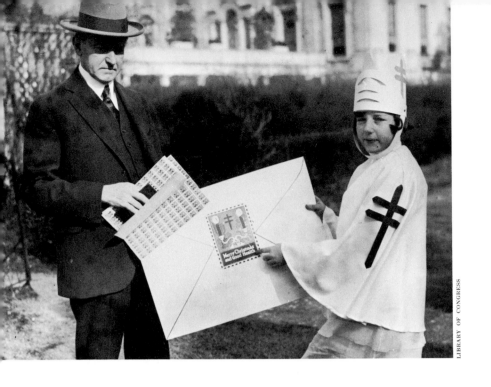

At left, President Calvin Coolidge purchases Christmas Seals from the Christmas Seal Girl of the Year on the White House lawn. Most modern Chief Executives have lent the prestige of the Presidency to charitable causes. Perhaps the most effective support was Franklin Delano Roosevelt's endorsement of the March of Dimes, in which, as a victim of polio, he took a personal interest. Below, President Harry S. Truman, his wife, Bess, and his daughter, Margaret, chat with Princess Elizabeth—the future Queen of England—and Prince Philip, the Duke of Edinburgh, during a concurrent visit to Canada in 1951.

The government is the nation's greatest consumer and bank depositor, and its patronage is prized. The cartoon above deals with Jackson's decision in 1833 to deposit Treasury surpluses in state banks; the beggars are bankers, and the implication is that they will have to bribe Jackson's advisers to get the deposits. Below, politicians and businessmen beg for Grant's patronage. Opposite, Puck *commends President Grover Cleveland, who placed an additional thirteen thousand federal jobs under the merit system.*

A NICE FAMILY PARTY.

Dispenser of Patronage

Federal patronage—the awarding of government jobs to the faithful—is one of the few weapons a President has to keep the various echelons of his party in line. John Quincy Adams believed that merit should determine appointments, and as a result he lost all chance of re-election. Later Presidents adhered to the rotation principle, replacing thousands of federal employees with their own supporters. Dealing with the hordes of office seekers took a major part of the President's time. Lincoln, besieged by applicants, remarked, "It is not the rebellion that is killing me, but the Pepperton post office." In the late nineteenth century, a civil service merit system was introduced, and since then more and more jobs have been exempted from the spoils system. But patronage power remains one of the American Chief Executive's most effective tools and greatest headaches. As William Howard Taft complained, a job appointment often results in "nine enemies and one ingrate."

TO PROSPERITY

Many Presidents, including William McKinley (above), have resented Congress' ponderousness in dealing with their programs. But Congress must take a long time to act because so many factions have a voice in determining what the legislature will finally do.

The President versus Congress

"Sometimes," said Theodore Roosevelt, "I wish I could be President and Congress too." "Well," reflected his cousin Franklin later in the century, ". . . he is not the only President that has had that idea." Friction between the executive and legislative branches has consistently characterized American government. Part of the explanation is that checks and balances imply competition. But an equally important reason is that while members of Congress represent states and parts of states, the President has a national constituency—and national and sectional interests are not always the same. Being President, observed John Kennedy, "is much easier . . . when Congress is not in town. . . ."

The Chicago Tribune, *which published the cartoon above in 1951, took a dim view of President Truman's claim that Congress was restricting his powers. Truman, the cartoon implies, did not have the stature necessary to wield presidential authority properly.*

Foreign Affairs

The President, according to the Constitution, is empowered, "by and with the Advice and Consent of the Senate, to make Treaties, provided two thirds of the Senators present concur. . . ." While the letter of this provision cannot be circumvented, the implication that the President and the Senate should make all foreign policy together has for the most part been ignored. The Senate's insistence on giving more advice than it was asked for annoyed President Washington; and like him, subsequent Chief Executives have depended on the advice of their appointees— and usually of a few key senators—in the conduct of foreign affairs. Treaties must still be approved by the whole Senate, but treaties comprise only one area of international relations. After John Adams resisted partisan and congressional pressures and virtually singlehandedly maintained peace with France, his successor Jefferson accepted the precedent and announced that the responsibility for diplomacy was "executive altogether." One hundred and forty years later, Harry Truman said succinctly: "I make American foreign policy." As chief diplomat, the President can employ executive agreements to avoid Senate interference. He can make trade restrictions or end them, send military equipment and money abroad, and even commit American troops to battle, as in Korea. Growing secrecy in international matters, the ubiquity of multinational alliances, and the importance of the summit conference have made the executive agreement more potent than ever. Indeed, the President and the Premier of the Soviet Union can even decide the future of a third nation without its knowledge. Such was the case with Laos, which was neutralized in 1962 as a result of talks between John F. Kennedy and Nikita Khrushchev.

The cartoon at left, drawn about 1809, attacked Jefferson and his protégé Madison, who tried to avoid war with England or France by imposing a series of embargoes on foreign commerce. At top left, Jefferson and Madison are portrayed as tools of Napoleon (who had less to lose from the embargoes than had the British). At top right, Congress hotly debates the issue. The section at lower left deals with the sea battle in 1807 between the U.S.S. Chesapeake and the British Leopard. The portion at lower right implies that the embargoes hurt no one but the United States.

President McKinley reluctantly called for war with Spain in 1898. It was a brief and one-sided conflict. Secretary of State William R. Day signed the Peace Protocol ending the fighting on August 12 that same year. A week later, the signing was re-enacted for photographers (above). The clean-shaven President stands to the right of Secretary Day.

Judge *magazine honored Theodore Roosevelt for his key role in bringing about the construction of the Panama Canal. Below,* Punch *reflects on President Woodrow Wilson's efforts to lead the reluctant United States into the League of Nations. Wilson's failure to do so was disastrous both for history and for himself.*

Twentieth-century Presidents have expressed their willingness to go anywhere and confer with anyone to restore or maintain world peace. At left, Franklin D. Roosevelt confers with King Ibn Saud of Saudi Arabia aboard a cruiser in 1945. The cooperation of nonbelligerents was essential to the Allied effort during World War II, and F. D. R. was a master of the art of persuasion. Above, John F. Kennedy addresses the General Assembly of the United Nations during the international body's financial crisis of 1961. Like his predecessor and successor, Kennedy was also involved with the diplomacy of the Summit. Below, President Lyndon B. Johnson meets Aleksei N. Kosygin, the Soviet Premier, at a summit meeting held in Glassboro, New Jersey, in June, 1967.

Commander in Chief

There is nothing in the Constitution that requires the President of the United States to know one end of a rifle from another, but there is a provision that makes him Commander in Chief of the armed forces and therefore the nation's principal military strategist. Both the system and the electorate's response to it have worked out well, if somewhat paradoxically. Every declared war that the nation has waged has been won (or at least not lost) under the leadership of a President whose military knowledge was cursory at best: Madison, Polk, Lincoln, McKinley, Wilson, Franklin Roosevelt. Each of those wars (plus the Revolution and excluding World War I) produced a military hero who became a peacetime President: George Washington, Andrew Jackson, Zachary Taylor, Ulysses S. Grant, Theodore Roosevelt, and Dwight D. Eisenhower. Furthermore, the soldier-Presidents have, during their years in the White House, strengthened the concept of civilian control over the military.

Although strategy is formulated in Washington, some Presidents have visited wartime battlefields. The 1865 sketch above records the unexpected arrival of Lincoln. Roosevelt (above, right) went to Sicily in 1943 and Lyndon Johnson (right) to Vietnam in 1966.

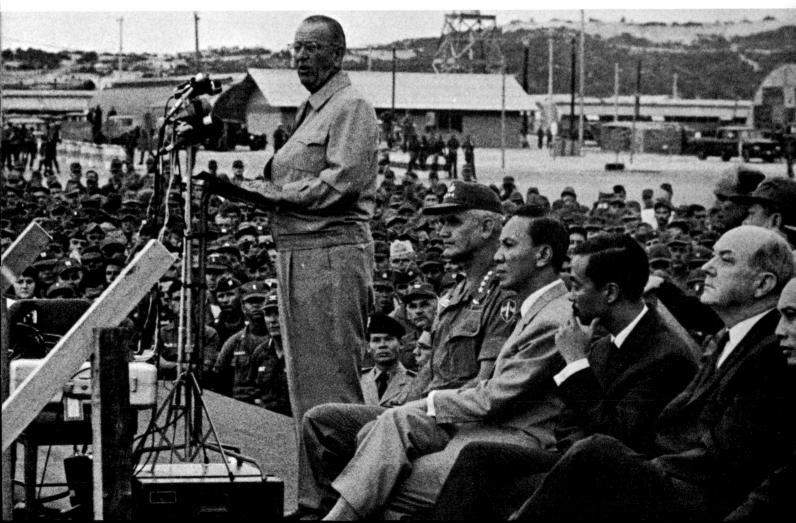

Keeper of the Peace

Insurrections have been rare in American history, but violence has not. Until the Civil War, a threat of force was generally adequate to prevent bloodshed, but later Presidents were frequently compelled to dispatch federal troops to keep the peace. Rutherford B. Hayes used force against railroad strikers in 1877, for instance, and Herbert Hoover ordered the Army to expel the bonus marchers from Washington, D. C., in 1932. Dwight D. Eisenhower sent troops to Little Rock to maintain order in 1957, and during the troubled summer of 1967, federal troops were needed to restore peace in riot-torn Detroit.

In 1794 a group of Pennsylvania farmers refused to pay a tax on whisky and caused some disorder during their brief rebellion. President Washington (opposite) assembled troops, the insurrection was put down with no deaths and little bloodshed, and the two "rebels" who were convicted were pardoned. During the summer riots of 1967 President Johnson sent the Army to Detroit, Michigan (below), at the request of the governor, George Romney. Federal troops proved to be more effective in controlling the riots than local National Guard units.

Protector of Prosperity

Americans regard the President as the guardian of the economy and expect him to preserve or restore prosperity. But he is not equipped to satisfy such demands. Congress may thwart him, as it did Cleveland (below) when he tried to reduce protective tariffs. The Supreme Court may cripple his program, as it did F. D. R.'s. Big business and labor may defy him. The President can, of course, suggest legislation, exert persuasion, and take executive action to deal with strikes, trusts, and emergencies. But by doing so he incurs the wrath of important segments of the electorate, who seek revenge at election time.

SOME POLICIES.

President Taft, left, instituted a record number of suits against trusts and monopolies. The Wilson button above indicates why big business opposed him in 1912. Below is a Chicago Tribune cartoon of 1950 condemning Truman, Congress, and union leader John L. Lewis for not taking any action to end a nine-month-long series of strikes by coal miners.

Party Leader

The candidate is nominated by a party, conducts a partisan campaign, may win the election by the votes of only half the electorate (or even less), and then must become President of all the people and appear to be above partisanship. At the time of elections, however, he is expected to carry his party's standard again for other candidates. He may learn, as Franklin Roosevelt did, that his personal popularity is not always transferable. He may find, as Dwight Eisenhower did, that his programs have much greater success when the opposition has a majority in Congress. But in any case, he is the party chief and must go through the motions, for without the support of his party, the President's power shrinks. The two Adamses were strong men; so were John Tyler, Andrew Johnson, Chester A. Arthur, and William Howard Taft. Theirs was, however, a strength of will, the strength to defy the party rather than keep it in line; and all were weaker as Chief Executives than as men.

As the 1944 cartoon above indicates, Socialist presidential candidate Norman Thomas complained that President Roosevelt was using every occasion to give campaign speeches.

Above, President Eisenhower and Republican National Chairman Leonard Hall study the returns after the congressional elections of 1954. Below are President Kennedy, Vice President Johnson, and their wives at a breakfast in Fort Worth during a political trip contrived to patch up division among Texas Democrats. That same day—November 22, 1963—Kennedy was assassinated.

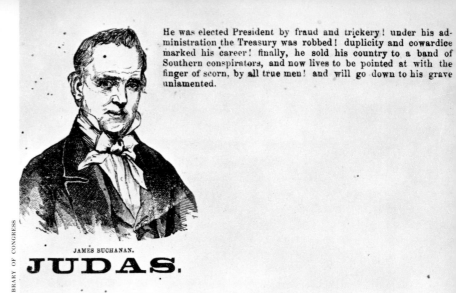

He was elected President by fraud and trickery! under his administration the Treasury was robbed! duplicity and cowardice marked his career! finally, he sold his country to a band of Southern conspirators, and now lives to be pointed at with the finger of scorn, by all true men! and will go down to his grave unlamented.

JAMES BUCHANAN.

JUDAS.

Beset by troubles he could not handle, President James Buchanan was called a Judas on the envelope at top right, when in fact he was only inept. Above is a grotesque caricature of Andrew Jackson. In the vicious cartoon at right, Senate Majority Leader Alben Barkley advises Franklin Delano Roosevelt to disguise his desire to be a dictator. F. D. R., an undogmatic believer in the "try-anything" style of government, was attacked as a fascist by the Left and a Communist by the Right.

"WASHINGTON"

ROOSEVELT COMPARED TO THE FATHER OF OUR COUNTRY —

"LINCOLN."

COMPARED TO THE GREAT EMANCIPATOR —

"NO! NO! NO!" TAKE IT OFF! SOME. BODY MIGHT SEE YOU!"

I LIKE THIS ROLE BEST!

— BUT NOT COMPARED TO THE GREAT DICTATOR

Target of Spleen

While both major parties in America are oriented to the politics of the center, the language of partisanship leans to extremes. The opposition seldom calls a laissez-faire President too weak when it can instead label him a tool of some special interest, and strong Presidents are invariably proclaimed to be tyrants: Washington and Jackson were called monarchists, Lincoln and the two Roosevelts, dictators. "Traitor" is a loosely employed noun, as Thomas Jefferson, Harry S. Truman, and many other Presidents could testify. Truman was remarkably philosophical about such hyperbole. "The President," he once said, ". . . cannot spend his time replying to personal attacks and insinuations. If he did, his time would be fully occupied with nothing else."

BERT ANDREWS

Above, actors portray President and Mrs. Johnson in MacBird, *a bitter satire that paralleled Shakespeare's* Macbeth. *Although the play was not the first use of theater to attack a President,* MacBird *was probably the most vicious and surely the most publicized.*

Abroad as well as at home, Presidents have been abused by those who have disapproved of United States actions and policies. Most Australians welcomed President Lyndon Johnson enthusiastically when he visited Melbourne in 1965, but he was also jeered by dem-

onstrators angry at American involvement in Vietnam. Protestors hurled sacks of red and white paint at the President's limousine (above) as he drove past them. Despite elaborate safety precautions, Presidents can never be totally safe from such attacks.

Martyrdom

Of the eight Presidents who died in office, four—Lincoln, Garfield, McKinley, and Kennedy—were victims of assassination. Jackson and Truman survived assassination attempts while in office, and Franklin Delano Roosevelt while President-elect. Most Presidents, however, while acknowledging the ever-present possibility of their being murdered, have been fatalistic. "If I am killed," said Abraham Lincoln, "I can die but once; but to live in constant dread of it, is to die over and over again." This attitude has been justified by the unpredictableness of the American assassin, who has tended to be propelled by vague, psychopathic, and usually misplaced motives.

The souvenir teardrop above symbolizes the nation's grief after the murder of Abraham Lincoln in 1865. At right is the coffin of John Kennedy in the Capitol rotunda in 1963.

The pressures and pace of the Presidency leave many of its occupants with a distaste for inaction when they are no longer in office. Martin Van Buren, thumbing his nose at a picture of former ally Andrew Jackson in the caricature above, made during his retirement, tried without success to regain the Presidency and once ran on a third-party ticket—a precedent followed by Fillmore and Theodore Roosevelt. The latter, like Grant in the cartoon at left, first tried extensive travel abroad to compensate for the sudden idleness, but neither found travel a substitute for the Presidency. Opposite, Herbert Hoover receives a medal from Congressman Joseph Martin at the 1956 Republican convention.

The Plight of Former Presidents

The transition from President to ex-President is seldom an easy one. One day the Chief Executive is among the world's most powerful men, and the next day he is a private citizen. He may not want to follow the precedent of Washington, Jefferson, and Madison and gracefully retire into elder statesmanship, but there is no ready political niche waiting for him. Several retiring Presidents, however, have refused to be inactive. Andrew Johnson, who might understandably have secluded himself in bitterness, instead returned to the Senate. William Howard Taft, who had admitted he would rather be Chief Justice than President, attained his desire. Herbert Hoover helped settle displaced persons after World War II and served as a consultant on government reorganization. Noblest of all was John Quincy Adams, who returned to Congress and was for seventeen years the tireless "Old Man Eloquent."

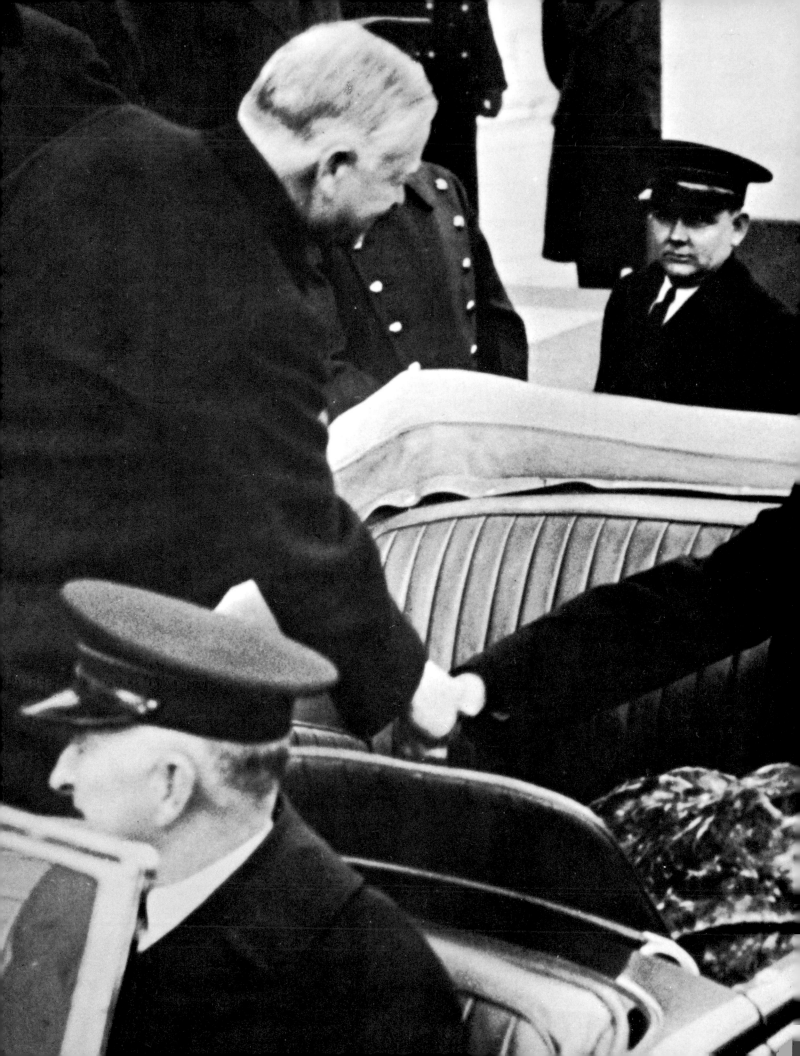

PART

EXPANSION OF AUTHORITY

"I recognize that democratic processes are necessarily and rightly slower than dictatorial processes. But I refuse to believe that democratic processes need be dangerously slow."

FRANKLIN D. ROOSEVELT

On Inauguration Day, 1933, Hoover shakes hands with his successor, F. D. R., who was to bring new strength to the Presidency.

CHAPTER EIGHT

Changing Factors

In the thirty years before 1900 little reliance had been placed on the President as a decisive force, at least not as a benevolent force. Even in 1900 it was possible for a Columbia University professor of government, Frank J. Goodnow, to publish *Politics and Administration*, a study that described the Chief Executive as merely one of several parts of the nation's administrative system. But a prodigious change was in the making.

Woodrow Wilson's *Congressional Government*, written while Chester Arthur was in the White House, spoke of the executive as a semi-impotent branch, "taken into partnership with the legislature upon a salary which may be withheld, and . . . allowed no voice in the management of the business. It is," he said, "simply charged with the superintendence of the employees." Although Wilson was critical of the resultant situation—government with no clear party leadership and no effective executive direction—he did not suggest that any great alteration was likely. Fascinated by the notion that institutions have an organic quality akin to that of living creatures, he portrayed the growth of congressional power as natural and inevitable. Those who believe in such silent, organic developments rarely propose ambitious reforms, for there would be no point in trying to rearrange matters prescribed by nature. Wilson's early views were therefore limited to an analysis of the regrettable consequence of American political evolution, and to a not very sanguine recommendation that something closer to the British method of ministerial responsibility should be aimed at.

In 1900, when *Congressional Government* reached its fifteenth printing, Wilson wrote a new preface in which he began to sing a different tune. His ideas, he explained, had been formulated some years previously; "inasmuch as they describe a living system, like all other living things subject to constant subtle modification . . . of form and of function, their description of the government . . . is not as accurate now as I believe it to have been at the time I wrote it." President McKinley, Wilson believed, was "at the front of affairs, as no president, except Lincoln, has been since the first quarter of the nineteenth century. . . ." Presidential speeches and messages, which had often carried no great weight with Congress or the public, were suddenly relevant and important. "Upon his choice, his character, his experience hang some of the most weighty issues of the future."

Eight years later, when he was president of Princeton University, Wilson expounded his revised conception in a set of published lectures, *Constitutional Government in the United States*. The theme of organic growth was advanced to explain not why Congress was dominant but why the President might be. The American government had evolved through decades of "intimate, almost instinctive, coordination of the organs of life and action." At times the Presidency had been powerful, at others, passive. Yet in general, Wilson asserted, "we have grown more and more inclined from generation to generation to look to the President as the unifying force in our complex system, the leader both of his party and of the nation." Nor would there be a reverse swing of the pendulum: "We can never again see him the mere executive he was in the thirties and forties." The President must "always stand," said Wilson, "at the front of our affairs, and the office will be as big and as influential as the man who occupies it."

Wilson's revised opinions had been foreshadowed in a remarkable book by a Pittsburgh editor, Henry Jones Ford, whom Edward Corwin called "the real herald of the twentieth-century presidency." In *The Rise and Growth of American Politics*, published in 1898, Ford boldly announced that the rise of presidential authority was preordained: "It is the product of political conditions which dominate all the departments of government, so that Congress itself shows an unconscious disposition to aggrandize the presidential office. . . . The truth is that in the presidential office, as it has been constituted since Jackson's time, American democracy has revived the oldest political institution of the race, the elective kingship. It is all there: the precognition of the notables and the tumultuous choice of the freemen, only conformed to modern conditions."

Ford and Wilson sketched the Presidency more or less as it appears today. Yet twenty or even ten years earlier such statements about executive supremacy would have seemed ridiculous. Wilson's analysis in *Congressional Government* was, for all his special pleading on behalf of the British parliamentary system, an accurate version of the federal balance of power in the 1880's. The Presidents of the Gilded Age accepted the situation. Hayes's diary revealed an embryonic sense that there were fresh needs to be satisfied. He favored federal legislation providing for universal free education, more federal subsidies for internal improvements, and national supervision of state elections. But his horizons were limited like those of nearly all his countrymen. This 1879 entry was typical of his memorandums to himself: "While I maintain inflexibly the authority of the Executive department against all attempts to cripple it by other departments, I must not magnify it at the expense of the just prerogatives of either the judicial or legislative departments."

Some observers, including Wilson, subsequently held that the Presidency had begun to reawaken in Grover Cleveland's administrations. In his *Constitutional Government* Wilson praised Cleveland as the only President between 1865 and 1898 who had "played a leading and decisive part in the quiet drama of our national life." He added, however, that Cleveland had "owed his great rôle in affairs rather to his own native force and the confused politics of the time, than to any opportunity of leadership naturally afforded him by a system which had subordinated so many Presidents before him to Congress." By the time he entered the White House, however, Wilson was not willing to give that much credit to Cleveland. Remarking to a group of senators in 1913 that he himself was actually the first Democratic President since Buchanan, Wilson dismissed Cleveland as "a conservative Republican." Historically, Wilson was more correct than Ford in describing the Presidency as an office that during most of its existence had been somewhat negative and subordinate. Certainly in Hayes's and Cleveland's day, the administrations of Jackson and Lincoln seemed departures from the norm.

What happened at the end of the century to redefine the Presidency so that before long the admired styles were Jacksonian and Lincolnian and the long interludes of quiescence were regarded as unhealthy? Several factors contributed to the transformation. Wilson suggested one obvious explanation in his 1900 preface: "Much the most important change . . . is the result of the [1898] war with Spain . . . the greatly increased power and opportunity for constructive statesmanship given the President, by the plunge into international politics. . . . When foreign affairs play a prominent part in the politics and policy of a nation, its Executive must of necessity be its guide: must utter every initial judgment, take every first step of action . . . suggest and in large measure control its conduct."

He re-emphasized the point in his 1908 book (though in another decade the words would return to haunt him): "The initiative in foreign affairs, which the President possesses without any restriction whatever, is virtually the power to control them absolutely. The President cannot conclude a treaty with a foreign power without the consent of the Senate, but he may guide every step of diplomacy, and to guide diplomacy is to determine what treaties must be made. . . . He need disclose no step of negotiation until it is complete, and when in any critical matter it is completed the government is virtually committed. Whatever its disinclination, the Senate may feel itself committed also."

The United States had "risen to the first rank in power and resources." Wilson's words again had a prophetic ring: "The other nations of the world look askance upon her, half in envy, half in fear, and wonder with a deep anxiety what she will do with her vast strength." As for the Chief Executive: "Our President must always henceforth be one of the great powers of the world, whether he act greatly and wisely or not. . . . We have but begun to see the presidential office in this light; but it is the light which will more and more beat upon it. . . ."

Wilson was not entirely right; heralds of change frequently exaggerate the completeness and permanence of a new order. But his basic point was irrefutable, as the early history of the Presidency had demonstrated. A crisis in foreign relations magnified presidential authority. Cleveland, aghast at the prospect of a war with Spain over Cuba, had announced that he would not countenance such a blunder. McKinley was at first almost as reluctant as his predecessor. In such situations, of course, presidential power could only be manifested by acting in a popular direction. John Adams had been denied a second term in 1800 partly because he had resisted the pressure to go to war with France in 1797 and 1798. Madison, reluctant at first to yield to congressional hotheads who demanded war with England, had eventually been swayed. McKinley dared not go against public sentiment.

Yet once war had been declared the President was unquestionably "at the front of affairs." The country always insisted upon rapid victory. The apparent sluggishness of Lincoln's war measures provoked Congress into establishing the aggressive Joint Committee on the Conduct of the War in 1861. Even so, Congress had to entrust Lincoln with the authority to make many decisions on his own initiative. In a foreign war, as opposed to a civil war, the President's freedom of action was correspondingly greater. Only he could drive the war machine; he alone held the tangled threads of strategy, supply, and diplomacy. During a war the lights burn late on Capitol Hill; they burn later still in the President's Mansion.

The Spanish-American War was even less essential to America's vital interests than the War of 1812. Viewed, however, merely as a step toward presidential aggrandizement, it was highly opportune. As Wilfred E. Binkley observed, in *The President and Congress*, the "splendid little war" was over so quickly and so cheaply that it failed to generate any congressional resentment against executive usurpation. The anti-imperialists could not sustain a sizable protest movement when the victory seemed so dazzling—indeed so providential, as if God had willed the events of Manila Bay and San Juan Hill no less firmly than He had willed Andrew Jackson's rout of the British at New Orleans in 1815. National and executive aggrandizement coincided so exactly in 1898 that the one both disguised and validated the other. Before the majority of Americans had any clear idea of what was happening, their nation had acquired an overseas empire. The Caribbean and the Far East were thenceforward American spheres of influence. The United States had become one of the big-navy nations. It had taken up "the white man's burden" of responsibility for subject peoples in Puerto Rico, Hawaii, and the Philippines. And the chief of the new American empire was the President.

In writing about the transformation of the Presidency in 1908, Woodrow Wilson did not say that *every* President would inevitably become the nation's overlord. But he realized that the President was "at liberty . . . to be as big a man as he can. His capacity will set the limit. . . ." Wilson's words were undoubtedly composed with Theodore Roosevelt uppermost in his mind. Roosevelt was the most flamboyant personality who had ever reached the Presidency and during his administration the Presidency was constantly in the public eye. His performance was doubly remarkable because he came to power via the dim shadows of the Vice Presidency.

T. R., himself highly newsworthy, used every means of dramatizing his office. The press was of particular importance. Newspaper circulation had more than doubled in the United States between 1870 and 1890, and doubled again in the next twenty years. Mark Sullivan wrote in *Our Times*: "Roosevelt's fighting was so much a part of the life of the period, was so tied up to the newspapers, so geared into popular literature, and even to the pulpit . . . as to constitute, for the average man, not merely the high spectacle of the Presidency in the ordinary sense, but almost the whole of the passing show, the public's principal interest." He sought to educate and stimulate as well as to entertain. He was the first President to treat the press as a sort of auxiliary federal information service. About twenty years before his administration, reporters had begun to spend a great deal of time at the Executive Mansion. McKinley had given them a table and some chairs in an outer reception room. When Roosevelt commissioned an executive office wing to be added to the White House, he was careful to provide a properly equipped press room. As soon as he was in office Roosevelt began to cultivate a close understanding with certain Washington correspondents. A later President would have been accused of playing favorites; T. R. had the advantage of pioneering, and the chance therefore to make his own rules. By previous standards the rules were refreshingly informal and generous. Sometimes he would invite a large group of journalists to hear his views on some topical issue. Half a dozen trusted correspondents often sat and talked with him in the late afternoon while he was being given his daily shave; lather, towel, and razor had no effect on his flow of conversation.

Roosevelt employed all the attention-getting devices available to him. If radio and television had existed he would undoubtedly have used them to catch the ear and eye of the public. If the telephone had been universal he would surely have played the instrument with a relish equal to Lyndon B. Johnson's. He did extremely well, however, with the existing media. He would produce stories to fill the newspapers' Monday vacuum. He gained the confidence of the press by off-the-record briefings. Sometimes he leaked information, as when he wished to overcome resistance to his plan to create a Department of Commerce and Labor in 1903. Or he would test a tentative idea in the newspapers so that he could gauge the popular reaction before fully committing himself. His secretary, William Loeb, Jr., became also a skillful press secretary, coordinating the flow of news from the executive departments and suggesting approaches and limitations to the correspondents. And so long as the tone of the reporting was sympathetic Roosevelt welcomed personal stories about himself, his family, and their friends.

He was not the first President to travel about the country. But unlike his predecessors, Roosevelt took advantage of his frequent tours to bombard the nation with patriotic and vigorous speeches on matters dear to his heart, including railroad legislation. Those who could not hear him in person could promptly read his views, column after column, in their local newspapers. In the less hectic intervals of his career, T. R. was a ready contributor to magazines, another vital medium. Since their editors were usually sympathetic and reform-minded, he could count on a steady flow of encouraging articles.

Everything that he said or did intrigued the American public. With his Wild West, Rough Rider picturesqueness, his multifarious enthusiasms, his cropped hair, incongruous spectacles, and ferocious smile, and the almost absurd vehemence of his life, he was the answer to a cartoonist's prayer. Harrison, Cleveland, and McKinley had been worthy figures; but how could an artist have portrayed them without being tedious or distorting them beyond recognition? Roosevelt was perhaps the first man in American history to enjoy being President. He communicated his enjoyment, his bubbling energy, his righteous wrath, and his sense of the fitness of all that he did in every possible way. He was accordingly the most visible Chief Executive that America had known. So far as Roosevelt was concerned, his capacity to fill the executive role was limitless.

One wonders what the Presidency would have become if by some improbable but not inconceivable chain of circumstances the Democrats had won the election of 1900; and if their candidate that year had been not William Jennings Bryan but another contender, Admiral George Dewey, the hero of Manila Bay. Dewey, in announcing that he was prepared to serve, remarked that the office of President was "not such a very difficult one to fill." Assuming a Republican victory, what if instead of Roosevelt the party chiefs had nominated one of their alternative choices for McKinley's running mate—Cornelius N. Bliss, former Secretary of the Interior, or Senator William B. Allison of Iowa, both of whom refused to run. Presumably Dewey, Bliss, or Allison would have fallen far short of Roosevelt in executive leadership, and the office would have entered another period of eclipse. They would probably have more closely resembled William Howard Taft than Roosevelt. They would have remained within the conventional ramparts, and might have proved as maladroit as Taft in handling communications with the public. Taft, of course, suffered from having to follow T. R. in the Presidency; reaction against Roosevelt's dominance perhaps forced Taft to formulate a more restricted interpretation of the office than he would otherwise have adopted. Nevertheless, his opinion that "there is no undefined residuum of power" in the Presidency was deeply held and deeply grounded in American constitutional dogma.

Archie Butt, the charming military aide who did his best to work loyally for both T. R. and Taft, said:

The Surgeon, the Patient, and the Nurse

The contrasting styles of the aggressive Roosevelt and the careful Taft inspired the 1909 cartoon above.

"Mr. Roosevelt understood the necessity of guiding the press to suit one's own ends; President Taft has no conception of the press as an adjunct to his office." Butt had the unhappy duty of shepherding the newspaper reporters who accompanied the President —or as Taft saw it, pursued him—on his summer holiday to Beverly, Massachusetts, in 1909. One of the reporters claimed he heard Taft snarl, "Must I see those men again! Didn't I see them just the other day?" Taft shared Roosevelt's delight in travel, but saw in it an escape from official obligations. "If it were not for the speeches," he significantly remarked on one occasion, "I should look forward with the greatest pleasure to this trip." Taft's inadequacy for this aspect of his job was epitomized in Elmer E. Cornwell, Jr.'s, *Presidential Leadership of Public Opinion*, published in 1965: "He could not be persuaded to return the greetings of a crowd, or even to turn his head and notice that people were there hoping for a sign of recognition. . . . That he should be unaware of the need for so elementary a gesture, or unwilling to give it . . . suggests how far he was from being able to exploit the potential of the office under the conditions that had obtained since the advent of the new journalism and the White House incumbency of the redoubtable Rough Rider."

Nor did Taft make use of a third factor that, in addition to the growing importance of foreign affairs and the power of personal magnetism and publicity, led to increased executive vitality. The point, touched upon by Wilson in *Constitutional Government*, was that the President spoke for the whole country. Members of Congress represented merely local and sectional fragments of the nation—and partisan fragments at that. The President was the head of a party, but in becoming President he necessarily took a larger role: he was the voice not of a party but of an entire people. In the unending tussle between the Executive and the legislature, Congress was equipped with formidable constitutional weapons. It could be overborne, said Wilson, "only because the President has the nation behind him, and Congress has not. He has no means of compelling Congress except through public opinion. . . . That part of the government . . . which has the most direct access to opinion has the best chance of leadership . . . and at present that part is the President."

Roosevelt had already based his claims for executive authority on the theory that the President (and only the President) embodied all the people. He and Wilson knew that it was a traditional assertion of presidential prerogative—an assertion heavily relied on by Jackson and Lincoln and particularly effective in periods of national emergency. Garfield had almost touched on it during a clash with Senator Conkling over the right to make federal appointments in Conkling's state. The Executive, said Garfield, was "a whole independent function of the government": in a Senate of seventy-six members Conkling was merely "1/76 of 1/2 of another independent branch of the government with which compound vulgar fractions the President is asked to compromise." But Garfield's quarrel with Conkling was confined to governmental matters; he sought no wider sanction than executive independence in Congress. Garfield's predecessor Hayes had claimed in his diary that while he was "not liked as a President by the politicians in office, in the press, or in Congress, [he was] content to abide the judgement—the sober second thought of the people." In another instance he reminded himself to rebut a congressman by citing "Jackson's claim to *represent* the Nation." Hayes was using an old, somewhat conservative expression when he spoke of "sober second thought."

In their *Dictionary of American Political Terms*, Hans Sperber and Travis Trittschuh traced the phrase back to the Federalists, indeed as far back as "reminiscences from classical authors like Tacitus' remark that the Germans discussed public affairs at their banquets but made decisions only after a night's rest had restored them to sobriety. . . ." That this was the sense Hayes intended seems evident from a subsequent diary notation: "Newspaper and other abuse is not comforting. . . . But the second thought of the best people is I believe with me." The "people" were the "best people": those who had second thoughts.

In 1874, when Garfield was a congressman, he had said that it was "not part of the functions of the national government to find employment for people. . . ." As President he held the same view. So did Cleveland, who declared in his second Inaugural Address: "The lessons of paternalism ought to be unlearned and the better lesson taught that while the people should patriotically and cheerfully support their Government its functions do not include the support of the people." To them, there was no reciprocal bond between the President and the people.

Cleveland's laissez-faire aphorism, applauded in the 1880's, would within twenty years sound mean and stony to men of good will. The statement was a world away from the vocabulary of Theodore Roosevelt. To Garfield and Cleveland "the people" seemed to mean the shiftless poor, those without the moral fiber to fend for themselves. Roosevelt's conception, though not exactly a plea for the underprivileged, was a stewardship exercised by the President for the whole people against whatever evils threatened them. "I was bent," he said in his autobiography, "upon making the Government the most efficient possible instrument in helping *the people* of the United States to better themselves in every way. . . . I believed . . . in real and thoroughgoing democracy, and I wished to make this democracy industrial as well as political. . . . I believed in the people's rights. . . ." Such words as "crisis," "leadership," "the people" were acquiring new shades of meaning. They would be used again and again in the twentieth century to justify bold executive action.

Another factor that influenced the President's role was the gradual transformation of party politics. The dominant feature of American politics from Jackson's day to the end of the century was the search for consensus. Except for brief periods the struggle lay between two parties that maintained an extraordinarily close balance in presidential elections, but that were fluid and miscellaneous in internal composition. Since the control of the Presidency was the apex of the party system, the tendency was to avoid divisive questions and to nominate "available" men. The Democratic party's rule, introduced in 1836, that a successful nominee must receive two thirds of the delegates' votes in the national convention, was an additional guarantee that noncontroversial candidates would be selected. As a result, the President was apt to be a symbol rather than a leader. To the extent that politics reduced itself to patronage and pork-barrel operations, and to elections won with soap (bribery), the Presidency could preserve its prestige only by seeming removed from the fray— and thus from national life. The dignity of the office was becoming spinsterish.

It cannot be claimed that a total change was wrought at the beginning of the twentieth century. But in the 1890's new economic issues aroused new passions. The Populist party secured over one million votes in the 1892 presidential election, and within a few years some of its reform proposals made their way into the mainstream of national politics. Some scholars suggest that the national party system entered its fourth stage in 1896; the second had begun with Jackson, and the third with the emergence of the Republican party in the 1850's. Paradoxically, the elections of 1896 and 1900 seemed such resounding victories for solid Republican principles that an opportunity for vigorous leadership was created within the more conservative of the two major parties. In other words, the defeat of Bryanism gave the Republicans control of both houses of Congress; and McKinley, unlike his recent predecessors, was able to establish both a fruitful relationship with Congress and enough of a hold over his party to ensure that he would be renominated. (Correspondingly, the Democrats offered a more coherent opposition.) The majorities won by Roosevelt in 1904 and Taft in 1908 were substantial; and the Republicans again retained control of both houses of Congress. When friction developed within the Republican party between the conservative and reform wings, it was, though disruptive, at least more meaningful than the Stalwart–Half-Breed split of the 1880's. And when the Democrats recovered and fought back in the 1912 presidential election with Wilson, a candidate as incisive as Roosevelt and a good deal more so than Taft, the party spirit seemed to have borrowed a fresh lease on life from the alliance of the people and the Chief Executive. There was no prodigious difference between the progressivism of Roosevelt and that of the Wilsonian Democrats. But there was a considerable difference between progressivism and the Standpatter Republicanism represented by Taft in the three-cornered contest of 1912. (It was actually four-cornered: the Socialist party candidate, Eugene V. Debs, won 900,000 votes.) After sluggish decades the parties were trying to outbid one another on the grand scale. Their platforms were at last composed of real programs instead of being confined to tariff scales, veterans' benefits, and the like. The rise of Debs was alarming enough to persuade alert politicians that the reforms they offered must be genuine. Wilson was lucky to win in 1912 and was again lucky in 1916. No less fortunately for him and for the emergence of a strong Executive, in both elections he carried a Democratic Congress into office. The guerrilla warfare of previous party politics seemed to have broadened into something more stable and more significant. Since 1916 every presidential election except those of 1948 and 1960 has been of landslide proportions. Winners have had a clear mandate —if they cared to assert themselves.

Another related factor was also discussed in Wilson's early *Congressional Government*. Wilson believed that American federal government was congressional in the main. The biennial election of the Speaker of the House of Representatives attracted nationwide interest. Newspapers printed almost as much about the rival candidates for the speakership as about presidential candidates, "having come to look upon the selection made as a sure index of the policy to be expected in legislation." Even later, in his 1908 book, *Constitutional Government*, Wilson devoted several pages to the almost autocratic authority of the Speaker and to the "condescension with which the older members of the Senate" regarded the President: "Dominate the affairs of the country though he may, he seems to them at most an ephemeral phenomenon. . . . A member of long standing in the Senate feels that he is the professional, the President an amateur." Though by 1908 he classed the President as one of the "active elements" in the federal government, Wilson agreed that there were two other active elements: "the Speaker of the House

with all that he represents as spokesman of the party majority in the popular chamber . . . and the talkative, debating Senate. . . ."

The question is why Congress, so dominant for a generation, did not continue to hold the reins alone. The answer is that it brought about its own downfall. The Senate grew more pontifical, rather than wiser, and more obstructionist. "Of all things that can be imagined as absurd and inconsistent with . . . the proper operation of our Government," Cleveland once exploded, "the Senate . . . reaches the extreme." Although there were good men in the Upper House there were too many Conklings and Platts. The public grew weary and then angry at a legislative body whose complacency and venality mocked the high hopes of the Founding Fathers. The 1892 Populist demand for the direct election of senators (instead of election by state legislatures) was eventually recognized as a reasonable reform and was put into effect by the Seventeenth Amendment in 1913. As for the House of Representatives, the more apparent authority it accumulated the more unwieldly, discordant, and ludicrous it became. Its calendar was jammed with business that never reached the floor, having been buried in committee or blocked by minority opposition. Matters were made even worse by slender party majorities and by abrupt shifts in the balance of power. The object of the House rules, said Speaker Thomas B. Reed, "appears to be to prevent the transaction of business." In 1890 the tough-minded Reed, exasperated by Democrats who refused to answer voice calls and thus denied the House a quorum, proposed that attendance, not votes, should determine a quorum. McKinley, then in Congress, supported him by remarking that "sullen silence" was not the way to conduct public business: "We have done it—all of us. I am not saying that you gentlemen on the other side are doing differently from what we have done. . . . I have sat here and filibustered day after day in silence, refusing to vote, but I cannot now recall that I ever did it for a high, or a noble or a worthy purpose." An opposing Texas Democrat dragged in the old phrase "sober second thought." House rules, he said with more partisan fervor than accuracy, were intended to "cause the House to halt, to pause, to reflect, and in some instances . . . to go back and inquire of the sober second thought of the people again. It is on the sober thought of the people our Government rests."

"Czar" Reed won his battle against the House obstructionists. But the Speaker was only a majority appointee; and the more he sought to assume control of the crazy quilt of committees and coteries the more resentment he aroused. Although Representative George Norris showed courage and tactical skill in depriving the dictatorial Speaker Joe Cannon of his power to appoint the crucial Rules Committee in 1910, the reform in some ways did more harm than good. The House needed a comprehensive reorganization. To weaken its only unequivocal source of leadership was merely to encourage fresh abuses.

Congress had, then, proved its inability to provide constructive government. Congressmen in general were, rightly or wrongly, despised and distrusted by the public. Many were in fact ignorant, pompous, corruptible. Those of superior quality were too often preoccupied with factional bickering. The two houses could not function creatively even as single units, let alone work in tandem. An adroit President, with the public behind him could, for a while anyway, force the legislative branch to follow his initiatives or risk defeat in the next election. By 1900 the moment was nearly ripe for an alliance between the President and the People—the People with a capital P.

The impulse did not come from the President or from any branch of the federal government. Roosevelt's enthusiasm for the Progressive cause developed mainly after he had left the White House. Professor Wilson's pronouncements during the Roosevelt years were hardly radical. He disapproved of what he thought Bryan typified within the Democratic party. In 1907, sounding much like Cleveland, he said in a speech that "free men" were better able to take care of themselves "than any government had ever shown or was ever likely to show in taking care of them." The development of the reform spirit was gradual and various. It burgeoned among despairing farmers; among city dwellers appalled by the misery and graft that seemed inseparable from urban living; among intellectuals such as Henry George, Edward Bellamy, and Henry Demarest Lloyd, who were groping for an explanation of America's economic and social ills, and for a cure. There was a revived demand for efficient, honest government: a demand first voiced and first satisfied at the local and state level. Here and there, with amazement and then with jubilation and renewed zeal, reformers discovered that boss government could be overthrown. The collective power of the electorate was still irresistible if only it could be harnessed. If legislatures could not be trusted, voters might initiate their own legislation or show their reaction by means of a referendum or recall.

The public had been at the mercy of privileged groups, robber barons who had established themselves across the pathways of American life and levied a toll on all who came by. The railroads battened upon the farmers, as did the mortgage holders and all the other middlemen. Giant industry, with its web of combinations and trusts, grew fat at the expense of the consumer. The ordinary citizen paid more than necessary for everyday articles because of the indirect subsidy of high tariffs. He paid too much for sidewalks and water supply and streetcar systems because of crooked bids and franchises. Vested interests were protected by the courts in the sacred name of private property; or so it seemed to a growing number of puzzled and outraged citizens. If the beneficiaries of unbridled laissez faire had not somehow been held in check the United States would soon have gone the way of every other society in the world's long, melancholy history. It would have become not a democracy but a plutocracy; and by a tragic irony the plutocracy would have been created by invoking such catchwords of democracy as liberty and individualism.

There was much disagreement on how to achieve fundamental improvements. The situation in the House of Representatives posed the problem in miniature. So-called democracy produced corrupt chaos. But strong leadership might produce dictatorship. Some reformers in the 1890's tended to lump the Presidency with other dangerous centralizing forces. The remedy appeared to be that proposed by Henry Demarest Lloyd in a Populist speech in 1894: "The people [must] get the control of their industries as of the government." Then, he continued in more extreme terms than most would find acceptable, "we will have the judges and the injunctions, the president and the house of representatives. There will be no senate; we will have the referendum, and the senate will go out when the people come in."

The control of industry was more complicated than Lloyd's fiery oratory indicated. The control of government was easier to envisage because of the popular sovereignty of the ballot box. Although Lloyd, not conceiving of the possibility of direct election, would have got rid of the Senate, he was prepared to define the Presidency and the Lower House as potentially democratic parts of the government. The next, more positive stage was to recognize that the Chief Executive might be a champion around whom to rally. The idea of the People's President was reborn; and it was no accident that the reputation of Andrew Jackson, which had been occluded for some decades, was made to shine again in the writings of historians. Frederick Jackson Turner identified Jackson with the quintessential feature of American democracy: its frontier atmosphere. By degrees the President came to be again considered the people's advocate within the federal government—the means by which the delays and evasions of Congress could be short-circuited. Participation in the democratic process was necessary but it was not sufficient. There must be leadership and there must be a leader in the Capital; for in some way or other the federal government must redress the balance between the underprivileged and the overprivileged.

The agreement that the Executive must accomplish the task was greatly hastened by the drama of the Spanish-American War, which was on the whole a popular war. With Roosevelt in the White House the drama was heightened; the executive office became a continuous theatrical show. A few spectacular performances—notably his ending of the anthracite coal strike in 1902 by threatening to seize the mines if the owners refused to agree to arbitration, and his protracted assault on the Northern Securities Company (he insisted that corporations must "subserve the public good")—convinced Americans of liberal temperament that whatever Roosevelt's deficiencies, he was determined to use the Presidency for the general good. His actual achievements were open to dispute. Some reformers felt that he was more bark than bite, and that he was still very much a politician. One of the muckraking journalists, Ray Stannard Baker, was enchanted by Roosevelt's "energy and gusto" and was flattered to receive from him letters praising his articles. "But as the years passed," Baker wrote, "Roosevelt's typical reaction, that of balancing the blame, without going to the root of the matter, and of seeking the 'devil in the mess,' satisfied me less and less. His actions often seemed to me to be based not upon principles well thought out, but upon moral judgments which were, or seemed to me to be, too hasty. His notion of a

square deal was to cuff the radical on one ear and the conservative on the other, without enlightening either."

Such criticisms should be seen in a larger perspective. One important point about T. R. was that he was a patrician. Of unassailably good family and cushioned by a moderate private income, he had an aristocrat's disdain for parvenu wealth. In his early days he had also an unconscious paternalism toward the lower classes. Although his invariable "balancing the blame" formula was partly a matter of political calculation, it came naturally to one of his background. He was genuinely unimpressed by millionaires. The rags-to-riches saga dazzled most Americans, including such self-made men as General Grant and Mark Twain, and disposed them to consider the bonanza as a symbol of Americanism. Roosevelt's symbols of Americanism were of another type, not always more subtle but sometimes more altruistic. Previously the nation had tended to believe that presidential candidates ought to be men of humble background who had risen by their own exertions. Roosevelt had certainly exerted himself, from the cowpunching days in the badlands of Dakota to his passage through the political badlands of New York State. But he was not a Jackson, a Lincoln, or a Garfield. In the twentieth century, Americans would turn increasingly to presidential aspirants—Franklin D. Roosevelt, Adlai E. Stevenson, John F. Kennedy, Nelson A. Rockefeller—who could be called patrician in that they were at least one generation removed from the effort of toiling for a living and of establishing a dynasty. Since the cost of campaigning rose astronomically, wealthy candidates were selected partly because they stood more chance of surviving the expensive ordeal of primary contests. The trend embodied also, however, a tacit agreement that other things being equal, a candidate with an assured social position was more likely to have a lofty vision of the United States than one still en route to the Social Register. Although Wilson was not an aristocrat, his professional milieu and his demeanor were those of a gentleman; he too stood above the daily round.

"Crisis," "leadership," and "the people" were key words in the changing conception of the Presidency. So were "nation" and "nationalism." Roosevelt's authentic concern for all the people was not only that of a patrician and a politician but also that of an avowed and clamant patriot. "The people" and "the nation" were interchangeable terms for him; but he did not fully explore the implications of his belief until he was no longer President. While he was in the White House its purest form was perhaps exemplified in his passion to conserve the national land and resources as steward of the people. Otherwise it tended to encourage the jingo side of T. R. He himself, however, saw no contradiction: a true People's President had to be the guardian of every facet of nationhood. He made a revealing statement of this dual conception in an article, "How I Became a Progressive," which was published shortly before the 1912 election:

"I too often found that men who were ardent for social and industrial reform would be ignorant of the needs of this nation as a nation, would be ignorant of what the navy meant to the nation, of what it meant to the nation to have and to fortify and protect the Panama Canal, of what it meant to the nation to get from the other nations of mankind the respect which comes only to the just. . . . I feel that the Progressive party owes no small part of its strength to the fact that it not only stands for the most far-reaching measures of social and industrial reform, but . . . also for the right and duty of this nation to take a position of self-respecting strength among the nations of the world. . . ."

As Roosevelt implied, not all Progressives shared his concern for the place of America in the world at large. Some disapproved, with reason, of his pugnacity over Panama. But none could object to his role as mediator in international disputes. There was something grand in the notion of the United States as a virtuous great power, implanting a new standard of morality in international affairs. In this instance, as in other ways, the idea of nationality struck a responsive chord in the emotions of millions of different sorts of Americans. There was a readiness to agree that at home as abroad there was a need for discipline, for concerted activity, for Presidents who would govern as well as rule. In the revised vocabulary of the era the concepts of "crisis," "leadership," "the people," and "the nation" were joined in a sudden fondness for the word "mastery"—meaning benevolent yet energetic leadership of the people. Wilson employed it in 1908 ("That part of the government . . . which has the most direct access to opinion has the best chance of leadership and mastery"); Walter Lippmann analyzed the contrast between bad and good in national life in his 1914 book

Drift and Mastery. Lippmann, a brilliant young man recently out of Harvard, was one of a group who should perhaps be called liberals rather than progressives. Lippmann, the journalist Herbert Croly, and a few others were distinctly urban and urbane in outlook. They applauded Roosevelt for his executive assurance, his internationalism, and for his reluctance to lay the blame for the nation's maladies upon any single sector. In *A Preface to Politics*, written in 1913, Lippmann described Roosevelt as a "colossal phenomenon" in American politics, "the working model for a possible American statesman at the beginning of the Twentieth Century."

These were compliments that might have been proffered by any one of dozens of admirers. The novel feature of Lippmann's analysis was its cool sophistication. He seemed to blend the amusement of a satirist with the involvement of a prophet. He said, for example: "Critics have often suggested that Roosevelt stole Bryan's clothes. That is perhaps true. . . . It would not be unfair to say that it is always the function of the Roosevelts to take from the Bryans." The thesis of Lippmann and Croly, who teamed up as editors of the *New Republic*, was that the American republic had to be made new. Croly's 1909 book, *The Promise of American Life*, accorded exactly with the emerging Roosevelt variant of progressivism and was read by him with delight. The book explained America's fundamental problem. For over a century Americans of the Jeffersonian persuasion had insisted that democracy was a concomitant of agrarianism and states' rights. Americans interested, on the other hand, in a strong federal government had tended to typify selfish business interests. There had to be a realignment; it had to be understood that democratic society was best sustained by a powerful regulatory government. What Roosevelt ridiculed as "sincere rural toryism" was an anachronism. Jeffersonian ends had to be attained by Hamiltonian means. The ideals upheld by John Quincy Adams were at last to be vindicated.

Roosevelt was not alone during the Progressive Era in urging the United States forward toward something that sounded disturbingly like a garrison state, animated by the warrior virtues of manliness, discipline, and patriotic ardor. After all, Henry George's *Progress and Poverty* and Edward Bellamy's *Looking Backward* had presupposed a central authority firm enough to introduce and maintain the panaceas they proposed. Liberals such as Croly could talk as unselfconsciously as the martial Roosevelt of America's "historic mission," secure in the conviction that their prognosis was economically, intellectually, and emotionally viable. By their methods the United States would substitute "mastery" for the apathy and inefficiency of the old days of drift. When they and Roosevelt talked of nationalism they meant a combination of many things, each of them good. They were not, of course, advocating a warrior nation; they were merely reacting emphatically against the errors of the past.

It followed that Roosevelt's "New Nationalism" made a greater appeal to certain progressives than the seemingly old-fashioned "New Freedom" of Woodrow Wilson. The Democratic leader appeared to be attempting to turn the clock back: to be pretending that the complex structure of finance and industry could be dismantled and that a few ethical pronouncements would restore the country to a Jeffersonian idyl. Wilson was in fact seeking to base his 1912 campaign on grounds different from Roosevelt's for partly tactical reasons. He was in good Democratic company. The arguments he developed were both venerable and weighty. Indeed the polarity between regulation and the combination of laissez faire and moralism has persisted to the present day.

Nevertheless, T. R. and Wilson stood on basically similar ground. For somewhat different reasons both could take pride in executive descent from Andrew Jackson. Notwithstanding the states' rights side to Jackson that particularly pleased the Southern Democrat in Woodrow Wilson, it was the quality of leadership in Jackson's Presidency that inspired Wilson no less than Roosevelt. And Wilson too was a stealer of clothes; Arthur S. Link has said that his ambition was stronger than his commitment to any given issues. He too meant to be masterful, and had proved to himself and the nation while governor of New Jersey that at his best he was an adroit executive. He too was genuinely moved by the sufferings of America's submerged millions—although in common with the majority of his fellow countrymen he saw no special urgency in the woes of the most submerged group of all, the Negro Americans. He too could at moments convey with an eloquence and fire as stirring as T. R.'s his determination to fight for a better America. Many who heard his Inaugural Ad-

dress in March, 1913, were deeply moved. "This is not a day of triumph," he said, "it is a day of dedication. . . . Men's hearts wait upon us; men's lives hang in the balance; men's hopes call upon us to say what we will do. Who shall live up to the great trust? Who dares fail to try? I summon all honest men, all patriotic, all forward-looking men, to my side. God helping me, I will not fail them, if they will but counsel and sustain me!"

Once in office Wilson plunged into its duties with an unmistakable zest. If Roosevelt was the first President to have truly enjoyed executive responsibility, Wilson was the second. He seized the initiative at once by calling Congress into special session, addressing it in person (which had not been done since John Adams' day), and compelling the legislators to enact the only palpable reduction of the tariff since the Jacksonian Era. He proceeded to reform the nation's banking system by securing the passage of the Federal Reserve Act in 1913.

President Wilson in due course revealed certain deficiencies that diminished his effectiveness. He was still half convinced by his own New Freedom slogans. He therefore alarmed progressive Democrats by seeming to be ready to abandon further programs of reform. He was addicted to the self-hypnosis of the orator who feels that by delivering a fine, impeccably high-minded speech he has fulfilled his duty to mankind. Croly attacked him in a *New Republic* article entitled "Presidential Complacency" as the possessor of "a mind which is fully convinced of the everlasting righteousness of its own performances and which surrounds this conviction with a halo of shimmering rhetoric." The accusation had an uncomfortable core of truth when it was written in 1914, and would seem disquietingly apropos five years later when Wilson was endeavoring to make the Senate "swallow its medicine" by ratifying the Treaty of Versailles. Another of Wilson's weaknesses was that in adversity he was stubborn to the point of folly. So long as matters were going his way he was a superb Executive—clear-witted, shrewd, persuasive, even charming. When resistance stiffened, Wilson's gaiety and guile disappeared. He was to pay the price in 1919.

It would be a mistake, though, to attribute entirely to Wilson's personality tendencies that lie deep in the American psyche, and that more particularly are characteristic of the Presidency. The presidential term is short and its scope limited even in the hands of Executives as forceful as Roosevelt and Wilson. Those who reach the Presidency have for the most part necessarily achieved a certain oratorical skill. They are apt, therefore, to exaggerate the accomplishments of their administration, knowing that they are expected to bring the millennium overnight and to proclaim the millennium by fiat.

By the same token, even the most popular and favorably situated Chief Executives are restricted in their capacity to move forward and to maneuver. The Presidency resembles an unwieldy vessel which can navigate only when it has built up a head of steam and is proceeding at a brisk speed. When the pressure is dissipated and the speed drops, the craft is at the mercy of the elements—or in this case, of Congress. The captain is then apt to complain of sabotage. Wilson blundered in his handling of the Senate over the Treaty of Versailles. But by the nature of things he was bound to have difficulty. The domestic crisis of the Progressive years was over, or thought to be over. So was the crisis of the Great War. Leadership no longer seemed so vital. The formulas of laissez faire no longer looked so tarnished. The alliance between the President and the people had lost its clarity. A revived legislative branch was ready to interpose itself between the two, in order to cure the short circuit. The loss of presidential magic was nicely illustrated in an exchange between Wilson and a hostile member of the Senate Committee on Foreign Relations. The senator asked the President whether the United States could not arrange with Germany a bilateral peace that would take no account of the multilateral Treaty of Versailles. "We could, sir," Wilson answered, "but I hope the people . . . will never consent to it." But, the senator coldly reminded him, "there is no way by which the people can vote on it." Since Congress refused to accept that the President spoke for the people, Wilson had no recourse but a speaking tour; he discovered to his dismay, however, that his enemies, too, could go on speaking tours.

The nation, a little jaded by crusades, was ready to be told by Warren G. Harding (in his 1921 State of the Union address) that "during the anxieties of war, when necessity seemed compelling, there were excessive grants of authority and an extraordinary concentration of powers in the Chief Executive." The intellectuals, disillusioned by the war and by the way in which both the New Nationalism and the

Wilson was optimistic and self-confident when he became President in 1913; he left office a sick and broken man.

New Freedom appeared to have degenerated into the New Chauvinism and the New Conventionalism of 1917 to 1919, transferred their talents to more private spheres. They could hardly be blamed when the rest of America was doing the same.

Yet the United States had changed, or would from that time on be more responsive to change when "necessity seemed compelling" once again. The demonstration of executive energy of the Progressive Era had left a legacy. There were the examples of Roosevelt and Wilson, examples that posterity would not quite forget, although the America of Harding and Coolidge appeared to put them in moth balls. And there were two culminating developments that would have enormous repercussions. One was Wilson's almost unchallenged assumption of war powers on a scale that dwarfed anything Lincoln had done. The other Wilsonian transformation took place in 1916, when the Republicans repudiated progressive principles and left the field open to the Democrats. Thenceforward the Democrats could always claim to be the party with a heart; the Republicans could too easily be portrayed as the party of the purse. The division was somewhat unfair; yet it preserved for future occasions something of the spirit of the turn of the century. There was still potentially a People's party; and its candidate, if victorious, could again present himself as the People's President.

CHAPTER NINE

The President and World Power

In foreign affairs the executive branch has always had considerable scope for action. But traditions of national isolationism and congressional intransigence have limited the executive freedom of maneuver, sometimes drastically. The interaction of these elements—executive initiative and popular or congressional resistance—defined the great part of the story of the Presidency and foreign policy until 1945. Traditional attitudes have not entirely disappeared since then, but the whole nature of the story has altered. Power has become the dominant factor. Executive power has enlarged to an extent that would have amazed and possibly dismayed Theodore Roosevelt and Woodrow Wilson. But the power of the United States has also enlarged on an unbelievable scale and with unbelievable rapidity. New problems, different in kind as well as in degree from those of previous decades, burst upon the postwar scene. "We inhabit a world of original horrors," wrote Edmund Stillman and William Pfaff in 1961 in their book *The New Politics: America and the End of the Postwar World*. Their title reflected a widespread conviction that an unprecedented situation called for fresh terminology. Some writers began to distinguish between the "modern" and the "postmodern" world. Some wrote almost with nostalgia of the preatomic days when even a thousand bombers were insufficient to wipe out a city, and when the United States was not blamed for every mischance from China to the Congo.

The year 1945 may therefore be regarded as the great divide in discussing the Presidency and foreign affairs. The Founding Fathers had recognized a fact

that is still operative. It was undeniable, though somewhat disquieting, that the President had to be given a great deal of discretionary authority. All writers concerned with executive aspects of government agreed that secrecy and dispatch were essential in certain fields, especially in foreign policy. John Jay used these words in the sixty-fourth essay of *The Federalist*, in which he argued that the President must inevitably have a free hand—even if the other hand was in the grip of the Senate. "Thus," Jay reassured his readers, "we see that the Constitution provides that our negotiations for treaties shall have every advantage which can be derived from talents, information, integrity, and deliberate investigations, on the one hand, and from secrecy and despatch on the other." In 1816, though not always on other occasions, the Senate was in complete accord with Jay's view. Its Foreign Relations Committee declared in a report: "The President is the constitutional representative of the United States with regard to foreign nations. He manages our concerns with foreign nations and must necessarily be most competent to determine when, how, and upon what subjects negotiations may be urged with the greatest prospect of success. . . . The committee . . . think the interference of the Senate in the direction of foreign negotiations calculated to diminish that responsibility and thereby to impair the best security for the national safety. The nature of transactions with foreign nations . . . requires caution and unity of design, and their success frequently depends upon secrecy and dispatch. . . ." The committee clearly had in mind Washington's explanation of his refusal to allow the

House of Representatives to examine papers relating to Jay's Treaty. Such precedents were also remembered in the twentieth century. They were cited by Justice George Sutherland in the 1936 Supreme Court opinion *United States v. Curtiss-Wright Export Corporation*, a remarkably positive opinion from a body that had not hesitated to strike down the administration's program of domestic legislation. As a result of the American Revolution, Sutherland contended, the powers of "external sovereignty" had passed directly to the federal government of the United States and therefore were not dependent upon the delegation of powers from the states affirmed in the Constitution. "In this vast external realm," said Sutherland, "with its important, complicated, delicate and manifold problems, the President alone has the power to speak or listen as a representative of the nation." In international affairs the President must often be allowed a "freedom from statutory restriction which would not be admissible were domestic affairs alone involved."

Grants of power within the Constitution, or interpreted as derivable from the Constitution, greatly extended the President's control. The clause "he shall receive Ambassadors and other public Ministers" enabled him to confer recognition upon (or to withhold recognition from) other countries. It was Theodore Roosevelt who extended recognition to Panama in 1903, two days after the province had rebelled against its parent state, Colombia. Wilson recognized the independence of Czechoslovakia in 1918, even though that state had never existed before and was still nominally part of the Austro-Hungarian Empire. It was F. D. R. who recognized the Soviet Union in 1933, sixteen years after diplomatic relations had been terminated following the Russian Revolution. President Truman made a powerful gesture of friendship when he recognized the state of Israel in May, 1948.

The President could escape some of the complications of making treaties by entering into executive agreements with other nations. Such agreements were as legally valid as treaties, although they either involved no congressional participation or required at most a simple majority vote in both houses. They could even replace a treaty defeated by the Senate. This device was used in 1845, after the Senate had declined to ratify the treaty—between the United States and the Republic of Texas—which annexed Texas to the Union. President Tyler recommended that the treaty be accepted by joint resolution, and after some legislative skirmishing his proposal was adopted. Executive agreements became more and more an accepted practice. From 1789 to 1889 the federal government negotiated 275 treaties and accepted almost the same number (265) of executive agreements. In the next fifty years, the balance changed decisively: there were 524 treaties ratified in that period, and 917 executive agreements. The trend would become even more apparent. From 1940 to 1954 the respective figures were 139 as against 1,948. President Theodore Roosevelt brought the Dominican Republic under American protection in 1905 after the Senate had failed to approve a treaty to that effect. And in 1940—in perhaps the most famous of all executive agreements—Franklin Roosevelt concluded the arrangement by which Great Britain, a belligerent, acquired fifty ostensibly overage destroyers from the neutral United States, in return for the right to establish American bases on British territory in the Western hemisphere.

A comparable presidential prerogative was the capacity to deliver statements of policy that were not binding in theory, but that could in practice commit the United States as firmly as a treaty. An early instance was the Monroe Doctrine of 1823, which was announced in President Monroe's annual message to Congress. A later addition, subsequently known as the Roosevelt Corollary, was first expounded at a dinner in New York, when former Secretary of War Elihu Root read a letter from T. R. about United States relations with Latin-American republics. "Brutal wrongdoing," the guests heard over coffee and cigars, "or an impotence which results in a general loosening of the ties of civilized society, may finally require intervention by some civilized nation, and in the Western Hemisphere the United States cannot ignore this duty." The dinner took place in May, 1904; not until his annual message in December did Roosevelt officially inform Congress—in virtually the same words as those of his letter—that the nation was thenceforward to be a hemispheric policeman. His cousin Franklin went further still at the beginning of 1942, when he joined the representatives of twenty-five other nations in signing the Declaration of the United Nations. The United States was thus committed to a promise that it would wage war against Germany with the rest of the signatories, make no peace until Hitler's Third Reich was destroyed, and then decide upon peace terms jointly, not separately. The President had in effect contracted an alliance without the consent of Congress.

Sundry other devices gave the Chief Executive exceptional freedom of action. Diplomatic appointments were subject to Senate confirmation, and occasionally the Senate had signified its disapproval. This had been done, mainly out of spite, when Andrew Jackson named Martin Van Buren as minister to London. To avoid humiliation or delay and to gain the benefit of personal advice, Presidents have therefore employed private emissaries. President Washington assigned Gouverneur Morris to confer with the British government. Polk chose Nicholas Trist for a "confidential" mission to negotiate peace terms with Mexico in 1847. Woodrow Wilson sent his confidant Colonel Edward House (whose title was bestowed by the governor of Texas as a mark of friendship, not of military prowess) on several journeys to Europe before and during World War I, and then included him in the American delegation to the Versailles Peace Conference. Franklin Roosevelt, who had grown to lean on Harry Hopkins during the New Deal years, retained him as an unofficial roving ambassador to London and Moscow.

The Commander-in-Chief clause (Article II, Section 2) of the Constitution provided Presidents with still more powers. Control of the Army and Navy permitted Jefferson to wage small undeclared wars against the Barbary States of North Africa, and enabled Polk to precipitate the Mexican War by ordering American troops to occupy disputed terrain. It permitted T. R., Taft, Wilson, and their successors to land expeditionary forces in various Caribbean countries and to maintain Marines in Cuba, Haiti, the Dominican Republic, and Nicaragua for years at a stretch. Theodore Roosevelt decided to sail the American fleet around the world; when a congressman threatened to withhold a naval appropriation, the President blithely answered that he had sufficient funds on hand to send the fleet halfway, and would let Congress determine whether to leave the ships stranded on the other side of the globe. President Truman responded to the invasion of South Korea by committing United States forces to an undeclared war on a far bigger scale than the sanctioned wars of 1846 and 1898.

War powers could in moments of emergency be stretched to astounding limits. In 1917 and 1918 President Wilson asked for and obtained almost totalitarian control of the American economy. He successfully asserted his right to dictate the organization of agriculture, industry, labor, and railroads. When a group of senators, alarmed by evidences of inadequate planning, suggested the establishment of a special war council, Wilson met the challenge to his authority by drafting an alternative bill. The Wilson measure, duly enacted in May, 1918, as the Overman Act (the name was appropriate since the President thereby made himself the nation's *Übermensch*), empowered him to manage the plethora of new executive agencies exactly as he saw fit. As World War II loomed, F. D. R. did what he wished and sought sanction afterward. The destroyers-for-bases agreement of 1940 violated at least two American statutes and, according to critics, usurped power specifically reserved to Congress by the Constitution. Roosevelt's Attorney General, Robert Jackson, pointed to the all-purpose Commander-in-Chief clause by way of answer: the President was entitled to "dispose" the armed forces to the best of his judgment, and disposing them might include disposing *of* them by executive agreement. Jackson cited other statutes as well, and argued that the bases were far more essential to national defense than the destroyers. Congress acquiesced to the extent of overtly relinquishing its constitutional rights to the President in the Lend-Lease Act of April, 1941, which empowered him to "sell, transfer title to, exchange, lease, lend, or otherwise dispose of . . . any defense article" to any country whose survival he deemed vital to the defense of the United States.

By 1945 F. D. R. wielded greater authority than any other elected official on earth. His enemies in the United States asserted that he had trampled on every law and precedent in the nation's history—not least on the unwritten law that limited Presidents to two terms in office. Certainly he had gone further than any of his predecessors, but not very much further, under the circumstances, than Lincoln or Wilson had during earlier wars. In essence, Roosevelt had merely confirmed dramatically Jefferson's pronouncement: "The transaction of business with foreign nations is executive altogether." And since the distinction between foreign and domestic affairs almost disappeared in situations of total war, Roose-

CABOT LODGE

PEACE TREATY

This cartoon from the New York Sun *credited Henry Cabot Lodge with defeating the peace treaty and the League.*

velt's jurisdiction reached into every corner of national life. Jefferson would no doubt have been aghast, but he would have understood.

Jefferson's dictum was, of course, not entirely correct. The Executive might be the moving force in foreign policy, he might enlarge his domain, he might demonstrate endless ingenuity in getting his own way. But constitutionally he was limited by the Senate's voice in the ratification (if not the negotiation) of treaties and in the appointment of officials, and by the control of appropriations exercised by the House of Representatives. Beyond Congress lay the impalpable but overwhelmingly significant factor of public opinion. The President's apparent autonomy was circumscribed. In none of the instances mentioned above was a seemingly autocratic Chief Executive able to depart in any significant way from the route prescribed by congressional sanction, by historic conceptions of policy, and by the popular mood of his own day. John Tyler, a lame-duck President in early 1845, could not have imposed upon the Senate the joint resolution annexing Texas if it had not been for the popular mandate for annexation that had given Polk victory in the recent election. Polk himself would not have risked war with Mexico if he had not been fairly confident that the expansionists were ascendant in the United States. Although Lincoln was bitterly condemned for acting

unconstitutionally, he knew that he would earn far more opprobrium if through punctilio he allowed the South to secede from the Union. For all his swagger Theodore Roosevelt had a canny regard for popular support. His Caribbean activities, like some of his other ventures in foreign policy, satisfied the popular appetite for excitement without real involvement. As for Wilson, his fate at the hands of the anti-League members of the Senate was an object lesson to Presidents tempted to overreach themselves; he had failed to make the necessary gestures of compromise and he had been punished. The next wartime President, F. D. R., would not have made the destroyer deal with Britain had he not been sure that the majority of Americans sympathized with the British cause.

In short, the President was like a man fettered to a heavy vehicle. Once the vehicle was moving he could add his own motive force to increase the speed. He could ease its progress by kicking small obstacles out of the way. He could change its direction a little. But he could not start it moving by himself, nor could he stop it.

For most of America's history the vehicle was almost stationary; and its movement was obstructed by Congress and by the public. The metaphor is unfortunate if it suggests that congressional dissent was invariably obstructionist. The Constitution obliged Congress to act in resistance to the Executive. While Congress could be wrong, so could the President. The Whigs were justified in querying the necessity of the war with Mexico. Grant's administration was so inept that the Senate was probably wise to refuse to sanction the purchase of the Dominican Republic, which Grant recommended. Although Senator Henry Cabot Lodge opposed Wilson's League of Nations out of personal and partisan spite, Wilson had behaved with arrogant rashness; and some features of the Versailles Treaty ran counter to cherished notions of America's role in world affairs. After John Quincy Adams, few Presidents until Theodore Roosevelt's day showed much knowledge of foreign affairs or had occasion to travel abroad for private purposes, let alone on official business. The comment made about Calvin Coolidge, that he had "not an international hair in his head," could have been applied to several nineteenth-century Presidents. Their inexperience was, moreover, not always remedied by their Secretaries of State. As the senior post in the Cabinet, the Secretaryship was often regarded as a

"UNDER WHICH FLAG?"

James Cox, the Democratic nominee in 1920, supported the League, but voters preferred Harding's isolationism.

sop to a disappointed rival whom it was important to placate. Lincoln chose William H. Seward for this reason (though the appointment proved a good one). Political necessity induced Wilson to make William Jennings Bryan his first Secretary of State, although he had considered Bryan a reckless and unreliable politician and he might well—if he had been a Republican opposition figure instead of a Democratic President—have echoed the view of a New York newspaper that Bryan was "about as well fitted to be Secretary of State as a cherub is to skate or a merman to play football." In fact Bryan performed quite creditably. But the appointment could have turned out lamentably, as did McKinley's selection of John Sherman. McKinley picked Sherman, a man on the verge of senility, because he wanted to reward Mark Hanna, his Ohio guide, philosopher, and friend. When Hanna declined the Secretaryship, indicating that he preferred to enter the Senate, McKinley's solution was to move Sherman (also of Ohio) into the Cabinet and to arrange that Hanna be given Sherman's Senate seat. In the mercifully brief period of his Secretaryship, Sherman was a liability whose work had to be done by an assistant.

Nevertheless, the broad statement is true: executive liberty of action was frequently nullified by legislative and national tendencies toward inaction—or reaction. John Hay, Secretary of State from 1898 to 1905, found that educating congressmen in the new realities of American commitments was extremely painful. At one point he wondered whether the Senate would ever consent to ratify another treaty. A man with little stomach for the fray, Hay complained that a treaty entering the Senate resembled a bull entering the arena in a bullfight. The animal's death was certain; the only question was the precise manner and timing of the slaughter. Hay's friend Henry Adams said disdainfully: "The Secretary of State exists only to recognize the existence of a world which Congress would rather ignore; of obligations which Congress repudiates whenever it can; of bargains which Congress distrusts and tries to turn to its advantage or to reject. Since the first day the Senate existed it has always intrigued against the Secretary of State whenever the Secretary has been obliged to extend his functions beyond the appointments of Consuls in Senators' service."

The United States as a whole was profoundly isolationist until World War II. The only alliance of its early history—with France—was formally terminated in 1800, and for some years previous had been regarded as a dangerous liability. Not until 1942 did Americans enter into another full alliance; during World War I the nation fought with the "Allies," but technically as only an "associated power." The average nineteenth-century American believed that foreign nations were corrupt, unstable, class-ridden, selfish, and trapped in a cycle of dynastic wars. His own country must beware of becoming caught in the same snares; it belonged spiritually as well as geographically to another hemisphere. The Monroe Doctrine epitomized the sense of separation and the determination to remain separate from Europe's entanglements. Xenophobia was endemic in America. To call something un-American was not merely to note its strangeness but to pass judgment on its depravity. Radical ideas were commonly believed to be foreign in origin. Suspicion of Britain, the nation with whom the United States had the most dealings, was heightened by the American Civil War, during which both North and South believed that the British behaved with a hostile bias. Later, Irish-American enmity toward England supplied another stimulus to Anglophobia. Not until the twentieth century, when Britain's authority was waning rapidly, was it widely understood that the security of the United States had in fact been strengthened by British sea power.

Anxious to avoid the errors of Europe, and believing itself liberated from Old World necessities, the United States maintained a relatively small Army and Navy. Some citizens argued that by the same token the nation ought to dispense with its foreign service. Consular appointments might be retained, since the United States was engaged in world trade; but conventional diplomacy with its apparatus of functionaries seemed an unnecessary extravagance. Such was the view expressed in 1884 by Henry George in his *Social Problems*. America did not abolish the foreign service, but the level of diplomatic and consular appointments remained extremely low, as it had been since the War of 1812. A career service never properly developed in the nineteenth century. Salaries were too low—and would remain so until well after World War I—to attract men who had no private income. Appointments were generally regarded as party awards, made either to politicians such as James Buchanan or, increasingly, to wealthy citizens who had contributed to party funds. Every major nation was represented by an ambassador at the capital city of other major powers, and by a minister or chargé d'affaires in countries of lesser importance. But until 1893 no American diplomat ranked higher than a minister. In London, Paris, Berlin, or Rome the American minister would find himself outranked by numerous ambassadors from other countries. Belatedly the United States began

to acknowledge that if it viewed itself as an important nation it must ensure that others saw it in the same light. The American missions in Britain, France, Germany, and Italy were raised to embassies in 1893. In the next twelve years the United States upgraded its diplomats in Russia, Mexico, Austria-Hungary, Brazil, Japan, and Turkey.

The slow growth of professionalism in diplomacy was not accompanied by any apparent growth of internationalism in the American people. The Allies owed much to the United States for aid in World War I. Indeed their subsequent grievance was that they felt they owed too much, in the concrete form of war and postwar debts. Even the much-traveled and philanthropic Herbert Hoover, who had toiled to organize relief programs in Europe, became convinced that the Old World was a source of little but trouble. American doughboys reached the same conclusion. So in the 1920's did the average civilian. Europeans were dirty, ungrateful, dishonest. Uncle Sam had been taken for a ride. Let there be no more "foreign wars" for the United States, no more Presidents like Wilson, re-elected because "He kept us out of war" only to drag his country into the war within a few months. At the next presidential election the voters chose by an overwhelming majority Warren G. Harding, who campaigned on the slogan "America first," and was sustained by Republican publicity that declared: "This country will remain American. Its next President will remain in our own country. . . . We decided long ago that we objected to foreign government of our people."

The flow of immigrants to the United States was drastically—and selectively—reduced by the immigration acts of 1921 and 1924. It could be contended that America was more isolationist in those three years than ever before. Nor was there any basic difference of outlook between the Republicans and the Democrats. A small minority of liberals, including ex-Secretary of State Elihu Root and the journalist Walter Lippmann, strove to remind their countrymen of the blunder made in repudiating the Treaty of Versailles. The majority remained indifferent. In 1932 presidential candidate Franklin D. Roosevelt expressed the common attitude when he announced on behalf of the Democrats: "We are opposed to any official participation in purely European affairs or to committing ourselves to act in unknown contingencies."

Although Roosevelt's words were probably not weighed with any particular care, it is worth noting that he referred to aloofness from *European* affairs. American isolationism was, in fact, qualified. The Monroe Doctrine warned Europe against interference in the Western hemisphere; it also proclaimed American noninterference in Europe. It is unlikely that Monroe or his Secretary of State, John Quincy Adams, meant at that time to define the entire hemisphere as a United States sphere of influence. Certainly their country ignored for half a century and more the possibility, elusive though it may have been, of leading in the establishment of Pan-Americanism. The actions of Polk and others, however, revealed that the United States did assert a special claim to territory in *North* America. By degrees the claim spread further south, into the Caribbean. It hung equivocally over Cuba. It encouraged Cleveland and his Secretary of State Richard Olney to take a highly pugnacious tone with Britain during the Venezuela dispute of 1895. Theodore Roosevelt felt that it justified his role in creating an independent Panama and in building the Panama Canal. It led to the Roosevelt Corollary, and to a series of interventions in Caribbean affairs that persisted well into the limp administrations of Harding and Coolidge. Not until 1928 did the United States begin a serious attempt to institute friendly instead of hectoring relations with Latin America; and by then, unfortunately, the damage had been done. Pan-Americanism was a chimera; talk of good neighbor policy provoked cynical disbelief even when it was sincere. Perhaps the narrow, high-minded isolationism of Senator William Borah or of Senator George Norris was preferable to Theodore Roosevelt's brand of American involvement. To resentful Latin Americans and to some European critics, the United States seemed unable to discern a middle ground between self-righteous neutrality and the blatant dollar diplomacy that had been practiced in the Caribbean.

The other exception to isolationism concerned the Pacific. It was an American, not a British or French, naval expedition that opened Japan to the outside world in the 1850's. The first American doctrinal contribution to international affairs (excluding the Monroe Doctrine, which was merely a unilateral declaration) was McKinley's Open Door policy regarding China. Thereafter the United States, which had taken possession of the Philippines, American Samoa, and Hawaii, liked to think of itself as a Pacific power, and believed with some reason that it had treated China more benevolently than the European nations, which jostled for special rights within the Chinese domain. Except for the relatively brief presence of the American Expeditionary Forces in France, service overseas for the armed forces came to mean service in the Pacific or the Caribbean. (During the years of mounting tension in Europe, from 1935 to 1939, Major Dwight D. Eisenhower was stationed in the Philippines as assistant to General Douglas MacArthur.) It cannot be said, however, that more than a small section of the American public had more than a vague awareness of conditions in the contemptuously named "banana republics" of Central America, or of events in the Far East. The editor of the Brooklyn *Daily Eagle* in the 1930's kept on his desk a memorandum that read: "Always remember that a dogfight in Brooklyn is more important than a revolution in China." A California editor, changing "Brooklyn" to "Oakland," might have substituted "Europe" for "China." An editor in Kansas or Illinois might have been happy with either "Europe" or "China."

There is no need to dwell upon the change that took place. After World War I the United States retreated psychologically within its frontiers, with the exceptions noted above. As World War II approached, President Roosevelt, who was engrossed in a domestic depression, had to educate himself in foreign problems before he could begin to educate the public. Prewar American initiatives such as the "cooling-off" treaties devised by Bryan, and the Kellogg-Briand Pact of 1928 (formulated by Coolidge's Secretary of State, Frank B. Kellogg) followed John Hay's Open Door letter in being virtuous mutual declarations that negotiation and arbitration were preferable to warfare. Such treaties suffered from the same weakness that had afflicted Wilson's League of Nations (which had been further debilitated by American abstention) and would later afflict the United Nations organization: they entailed no real surrender of national sovereignty. The most admirable of the American initiatives—the summoning of an international conference in Washington at the end of 1921 —led to some actual disarmament and to a number of treaties, including a four-power agreement to consult in the event of "aggressive action" in the Pacific. The Senate ratified all the treaties. But it attached to the four-power agreement with Britain, France, and Japan a reservation that "there is no commitment to armed force, no alliance, no obligation to join in any defense." The subsequent aggression by Japan in the Far East, Italy in Africa, and Germany in Europe made the pious hopes of the Bryans and Kelloggs appear pathetically optimistic. Moreover, such agreements were not even presidential inspirations. Harding did not grasp the fine points of international diplomacy. When as President-elect he was queried on his future foreign policy, he replied, "You must ask Mr. Hughes about that." His Secretary of State, Charles Evans Hughes, was the formulator of whatever action was taken.

On the eve of World War II the United States was easily the greatest industrial power in the world and had one of the largest navies. But the nation counted for disproportionately little in the places where momentous decisions were being made. No American representative was invited to attend the fateful meeting between Hitler, Chamberlain, Mussolini, and Daladier at Munich in 1938. Beginning in 1934 Congress had passed various neutrality acts designed to keep the United States out of war. Even when war broke out in Europe and Hitler won victory after victory, many reputable Americans strove to maintain neutrality. They were equally anxious to avoid embroilment with Japan and so resented Roosevelt's undisguised aversion to the Axis powers that they later accused him of having dragged America into war by obliging the Japanese to attack Pearl Harbor. Isolationist motives had always been mixed. It is only fair to observe that not all so-called isolationists were purblind. Some feared that war would breed war—that conflict would acquire a ghastly momentum and become an addictive habit. Some pointed to World War I as proof that wars solved nothing. Some mourned the loss of the peaceable, virtuous tradition of America at its best. If they were softheaded, they feared the results of a national indulgence in hardheadedness; and they had some cause.

But the war came. By the spring of 1945 it was almost over in Europe and the end was in sight in the Far East. The death of Roosevelt in April shocked the world. But the extent of the shock was a measure of the Allies' dependence upon the United States. Harry Truman's manful assumption of presidential responsibility left no serious hiatus in leadership. Moreover, he had inherited a secret weapon, the atomic bomb, which ended Japanese resistance almost overnight. The bomb appeared to endow America with prodigious power for good. In 1889 an American writer, Frank R. Stockton, had produced a fantasy entitled *The Great War Syndicate*. Stockton had envisaged a future war in which American scientists invent an invincible weapon called the Instantaneous Motor. This early version of the atomic bomb, in his tale, is used to win a war against Britain, decisively but without loss of life, and then to form the basis of an Anglo-American alliance that guarantees global peace.

In 1945 a comparable dream was possible. That year the United Nations organization was formed at a meeting held in San Francisco. The headquarters of the old League of Nations, which it superseded, had been at Geneva; the headquarters of the United Nations would be in New York. Optimists believed that a better world was genuinely in the making. The defect of previous American proposals for disarmament and arbitration was that while apparently internationalist, they were at heart isolationist. They sought paper solutions that would have permitted the United States to remain detached from world concerns. They decreed peace but had no provision for deterring aggression. In 1945, however, the traditional benevolence of American policy was backed by overwhelming power. With America in the lead, working through the United Nations and other international agencies, the world might at last be made truly safe for democracy.

The dream quickly faded. The triumphant months of 1945 gave birth to a host of intractable problems, any one of which was enough to occupy the full energies of the President. Instead of peace America faced an apparently interminable cold war, which was at times terrifyingly close to full-scale war and was always perplexing and frustrating. International communism confronted the American vision of international democracy. Before long Russia too had an atomic bomb. From the horrible missiles of Hiroshima and Nagasaki the two superpowers developed thermonuclear weapons of still more nightmarish destructive capacity. Other powers began to acquire nuclear capability of their own. Ultimate weapon succeeded ultimate weapon. The American defense budget, amounting to some eleven billion dollars in 1948, had more than quadrupled by 1953. It crept upward to over forty billion dollars before Eisenhower left the White House. During his Presidency military spending accounted for more than half of the federal budget.

Such astronomical outlays proved unavailing, or so it seemed. In some instances it was possible to say, especially in the immediate postwar years, that American action had achieved decisive results. European recovery was certainly hastened by the Marshall Plan. Greece would almost certainly have become Communist if the United States had not taken over Britain's defense role in the eastern Mediterranean. The vigorous policy of containment, formulated under President Truman, was at least negatively effective. But in general the situation was comfortless. The Communist bloc interpreted American activity as aggressive imperialism. Non-Communist countries, especially those such as Britain and France that had until recently been major powers, were resentful of American hegemony. Before the war it had been difficult to persuade the United States to enter into international agreements for collective security. After the war the United States, immensely richer and stronger than other free nations, had the task of persuading them to join and support defense pacts. Everything had happened too quickly. During World War II Roosevelt had criticized British and French "imperialism." Within a few years the United States was compelled to try to bolster former European possessions whose societies and economies were alarmingly precarious. The so-called uncommitted nations, well aware of the competing claims of America and Russia, naturally endeavored to play one against the other. Everything was expected of the United States, yet every sign of "interference" provoked hostility.

The situation was deeply disappointing to Americans. Accustomed to thinking of themselves as the anti-imperialist, democratic wave of the future, they began to be treated in some quarters as bloated reactionaries. There, said Reinhold Niebuhr, lay "the irony of American history." Their ideology was apparently outmatched by that of communism; and the very proofs of free society urged by the Americans— wealth and stability—were both envied and despised by much of the rest of the world. Angered and impatient, some Americans, led by Senator Joseph McCarthy of Wisconsin, hunted for scapegoats within the federal government. Others became "hawks" urging what they called preventive war.

The United States, they said, held a temporary superiority in nuclear weapons; why not use them before it was too late?

Only twelve years after the Korean War ended, the United States was more heavily committed than ever in the Far East, this time in Vietnam. The easing of tension with Russia was inhibited by the Vietnam conflict and was more than offset by the increasing hostility of Communist China. The rehabilitation of Europe's economic strength prompted America's allies to question the necessity of the North Atlantic Treaty Organization. Charles de Gaulle evicted NATO forces from France. There was increasing talk of Europe as a "third force" poised between America and the Communists and affiliated to neither. Yesterday's innovation in foreign policy became today's orthodoxy and tomorrow's straitjacket. The containment theory sketched by Truman's advisers hardened into the brinkmanship of the Eisenhower era. Fidel Castro's Cuba accused the United States of every crime in the calendar. In 1967 the Arab countries briefly claimed that their defeat in the six-day war with Israel had been effected by American (and British) intrigue.

Such were the predicaments of the United States, and therefore of the Presidency, in the nuclear age. Such changes profoundly affected the executive branch of government and its responses to global crisis (the adjective "global" has become part of everyday American discourse). The most obvious effect was the vesting of still more power in the President. As the advance warning of enemy attack dwindled in defense calculations from days to hours, and from hours to minutes, the need for secrecy and dispatch was the more readily acknowledged. The intricacy of foreign affairs baffled the ordinary citizen. The electorate, and even Congress, seemed obliged to entrust decisions to the President, for only he with his access to fresh, detailed, and confidential information could be presumed to know what was happening in Cuba, Iran, Guatemala, and all the other places that suddenly claimed the headlines.

For long stretches of the nineteenth century one-term Presidencies were the norm. But in the twentieth century, the desire for continuity of leadership in external policy and the prestige accruing to the Executive made it almost impossible to defeat a President seeking re-election—and it was assumed that each President would expect to be renominated.

General Eisenhower's prominence as the former head of multinational armies gave him an immense advantage over Governor Adlai Stevenson of Illinois in the 1952 election, although Stevenson had served in the State Department and had been actively involved in the United Nations. As a candidate again in 1956, and as a possible candidate in 1960, Stevenson necessarily made himself a foreign policy expert. (After the Democratic victory in 1960 he hoped to become Secretary of State but was instead appointed ambassador to the United Nations.) Any presidential aspirant strove to demonstrate his firsthand knowledge of international issues. In the 1960 campaign the Republican candidate Richard Nixon frequently mentioned his Moscow visit, during which he had publicly argued with Premier Nikita Khrushchev. Although F. D. R.'s onetime Vice President John Nance Garner had remarked that the office was "not worth a pitcher of warm spit," his successors after 1953—Nixon, Lyndon B. Johnson, Hubert Humphrey—began to travel abroad on official business so often that they ceased to be negligible functionaries in that sphere. As Vice President, Truman had known nothing of the atomic bomb project. Subsequent Vice Presidents could no longer be left ignorant of vital matters affecting national security. The office therefore promised to become again a route to the Presidency, as it had been in the earliest days of the republic. There were signs too, judging from the careers of Nixon, John F. Kennedy, Lyndon Johnson, and Barry Goldwater, that membership in the Senate—and especially of its Foreign Relations Committee—formed a more attractive qualification for presidential nomination than the governorship of a state.

As in earlier decades, the President's relations with Congress were sometimes strained. He tended to bypass the legislative branch through executive agreements. Presidents and their emissaries traveled abroad with increasing readiness. Eisenhower inaugurated a new postwar era of summit diplomacy, particularly in his second administration. He attended a summit conference at Geneva in 1955. In 1959, having flown to the capitals of Western Europe to explain his purpose, he invited Premier Khrushchev to the United States and in September held private talks with the Russian leader at his summer retreat, Camp David. At the end of the year President Eisenhower visited eleven nations—Italy,

Turkey, Pakistan, Afghanistan, India, Iran, Greece, Tunisia, France, Spain, and Morocco—in less than three weeks. The display was both personal and symbolic of America's purpose. Eisenhower distributed scores of gold medallions inscribed on one side, "In Appreciation, D. D. E.," and on the other, "Peace and Friendship in Freedom." In February, 1960, he flew fifteen thousand miles on a similar good-will tour of Latin America. He had already prevailed upon Khrushchev to attend a summit meeting in Paris and he was preparing to visit the Soviet Union when Russian-American relations were abruptly jarred by the news that Soviet antiaircraft had shot down an American U-2 reconnaissance plane that had been engaged on a secret and illicit mission over Russian territory.

President Kennedy was somewhat skeptical as to the value of summit meetings. But he too appeared in European capitals, where he received wild acclaim, and peered across the Berlin Wall. He too was forced to reckon with the harsh truth announced by Khrushchev: "There are only two nations which are powerful—the Soviet Union and the United States." In the Cuban Missile Crisis of October, 1962, the American President and the Russian Premier were linked in a strange, ambivalent intimacy. They were as close as two chess players, each contributing to the pattern of play and each endeavoring to read the other's mind. The hot line from Washington to

THE RIVAL SALESMEN AND THE WATCHING WORLD

A 1959 cartoon in the Chicago Tribune *depicted President Eisenhower and Nikita Khrushchev as competing salesmen.*

Moscow—which includes a telephone on the President's desk—was a constant reminder that in moments of emergency, decision rested with the White House, not with Congress. Whether or not Presidents wished to treat directly with other heads of state, circumstances dictated conduct. The need for tact, if nothing else, in dealing with friendly or uncommitted nations obliged Presidents to include them in travel itineraries. Conversely, the White House was subject to an unending stream of visits from foreign heads of state, each anxious to convince his own people of his privileged standing with the United States.

It was inevitable that Congress should at times react sharply to executive dominance in foreign affairs. President Truman and Secretary of State Dean Acheson were assailed by neoisolationists who disapproved of foreign aid, or of involvement in Korea, or of the government's apparent failure to gain an immediate victory in the cold war. This national mood found expression in a constitutional amendment proposed in 1953 by Senator John Bricker of Ohio. Designed to prevent the President from making executive agreements without previous congressional authorization, the Bricker Amendment also voiced a more judicial uneasiness that treaties might be enforced as domestic law without the sanction of Congress. But in essence it was an attempt to reduce presidential authority and to reclaim the rights of Congress; and it was enthusiastically supported by the Chicago *Tribune*, the Daughters of the American Revolution, and other self-styled guardians of patriotism. According to Emmet John Hughes, a White House adviser under Eisenhower, the President became seriously worried. "The whole damn thing," he exclaimed at one point, "is senseless and plain damaging to the prestige of the United States. We talk about the French not being able to govern themselves—and *we* sit here wrestling with a *Bricker* Amendment." Not least among Eisenhower's irritations was the inability of otherwise cooperative senators to see the problem through the President's eyes. The Republican Majority Leader, Senator William Knowland of California, voted for a substitute version of the amendment even after receiving a note from the President saying that he was "unalterably opposed" to it, and that it would constitute a declaration that "our country intends to withdraw from its leadership in world affairs." Eisenhower's alarm

was understandable; the diluted version of the Bricker Amendment was approved by sixty senators in February, 1954—only 1 vote short of the necessary two-thirds majority. Vice President Nixon reported that among those in favor was Senator Lyndon B. Johnson. "He says he doesn't think it's wise at all, but he's going to vote for it. And you ask him why, and he says simply: 'Because all my people in Texas want it.'"

The controversy gradually abated, but the basic issue was periodically revived. In his own Presidency Lyndon B. Johnson found himself on the receiving end. During the summer of 1967 Senator J. William Fulbright, chairman of the Foreign Relations Committee, submitted a resolution that would have required any American overseas commitment to be approved beforehand by Congress. Introducing his resolution, he said that the executive branch had "acquired virtually unrestricted power to commit the U.S. abroad politically and militarily." Senator Fulbright maintained that if Congress had been consulted, American intervention in Vietnam and in the Dominican Republic might have been avoided, and so might the 1961 Bay of Pigs fiasco, in which the United States connived at an invasion of Cuba by anti-Castro exiles.

One reason for the Senate's annoyance was that recent Presidents had, far from ignoring Congress, made increasing use of congressionally approved executive agreements in international affairs. The process eliminated the traditional treaty-making procedure; and it gave a stronger voice to the House of Representatives, which formerly could participate only obliquely by giving or withholding appropriations. For the same reason a concerted assault on executive prerogative was unlikely to come from Congress as a whole. Moreover, beginning with President Truman's administrations, there was a marked tendency to formulate policy on bipartisan lines. The Republican Senator Arthur H. Vandenberg of Michigan led the way by giving staunch support to Truman's overseas programs. Eisenhower and his successors were careful to consult prominent congressmen, including the minority as well as the majority members of the Senate's Foreign Relations and the House's Foreign Affairs committees. Such treatment raised a problem for congressmen; although it gave them a better grasp of certain matters, it drew Congress into a greater rapport with the

White House than some might have wished. If the price of confidential briefing was legislative silence, some of them would rather not pay it. A paradox developed. Eisenhower had a genuine wish to curb what he regarded as the executive usurpations of F. D. R. But when he from the best of motives sought to involve Congress in decision making, the legislators from a mixture of motives revealed that they would rather not be implicated.

Some congressional resolutions, such as one in 1955 that gave the President discretionary authority to respond to Communist China's threatened assault on Formosa, muffled debate instead of promoting it. One disquieting feature of the cold war was that perpetual crisis inhibited discussion. Criticism of the administration was apt to be interpreted as evidence of disloyalty; it was condemned as bringing aid and comfort to the enemy. The psychology of actual war—that of being either for or against one side—was applied to a situation that continued year after year. President Johnson's response to the attacks by Senator Fulbright and others was to argue that he had not exceeded his powers in sending half a million Americans to fight in Vietnam. He had merely followed the implications of the 1964 Gulf of Tonkin Resolution, which had received almost unanimous approval—and which Fulbright himself had piloted through Congress. The President, knowing that he held the whip hand, challenged Congress to rescind the resolution. Unless public opinion swung toward his Senate critics, their gesture against him was doomed to failure. Testifying before the Foreign Relations Committee, the Under Secretary of State, Nicholas Katzenbach, made two points. One was that throughout American history "the voice of the United States in foreign affairs was that of the President." The second was that "whatever the powers of the President to act alone on his own authority . . . there can be no question that he acts most effectively when he acts with the support and authority of the Congress." While these assertions were true, they did not really answer the congressional complaint that more and more the President determined policy and Congress made it effective by voting favorably—a vote it dared not refuse.

In this climate of protracted crisis, attitudes inevitably hardened and became ridden with clichés. Both the executive and the legislative branches developed the habit of overdramatizing problems.

Their intention was partly, no doubt, to convey complex ideas in the simplest possible way, so as to render them intelligible to the electorate. They also felt that public approval and congressional appropriations would be more easily secured if needs were presented as crash programs designed to combat some immediate Communist menace to the free world. Sometimes legislation not directly related to international problems was given a crisis coloration. A 1958 bill, for example, although stimulated by the shock of Russia's successful launching of Sputnik I, was largely a step toward federal support for education. But it was christened the National Defense Education Act. Foreign observers, misinterpreting such domestic nuances, were given additional reason to believe that the United States, from the President downward, was in the grip of an anti-Communist hysteria. It is likely that the men in Washington underestimated the sophistication of the public. They might gain short-run advantages from exploiting the hopes and fears of the electorate. In the long run, however, they risked creating what became known in the mid-1960's as a credibility gap between official language and actuality.

If the President's tasks were complicated by his relations with Congress, they were further complicated by his relations with the executive branch. In theory he was the Executive, but he was only the chief figure in a welter of agencies and bureaus concerned in some way with foreign affairs. There was the State Department's vastly expanded realm. There was the secret domain of the Central Intelligence Agency. There was the United States Information Agency. There was the Defense Department, which had been established in 1947 as a consolidation of the War and Navy departments. There were the Army, Navy, Air Force, and Marine chiefs of staff, each representing his military constituency with competitive zeal. There was, in President Eisenhower's words, a "permanent armaments industry of vast proportions," employing three and a half million people by 1961. In 1956 the sociologist C. Wright Mills published a study called *The Power Elite*, in which he argued that Congress and the public had ceased to have any effective voice in American affairs: the nation was run by an interlocking directorate of "warlords" and executive officials, most of whom—like Eisenhower's Secretary of Defense Charles E. Wilson—were corporation heads. Just before leaving the Presidency in 1961, Eisenhower was sufficiently concerned to warn America of the dangerous potential of "the military-industrial complex"—a typically "civilian" response from a former "warlord."

The Secretary of Defense had become a major executive figure. Robert S. McNamara, who held the post under Presidents Kennedy and Johnson, wielded a formidable authority in his dealings with both the Pentagon and Congress. But the chief Cabinet office, in protocol and in practice, was still that of the Secretary of State. Since Herbert Hoover's day the State Department had been headed by men of some stature: Henry L. Stimson, Cordell Hull, Edward R. Stettinius, James F. Byrnes, George C. Marshall, Dean Acheson, John Foster Dulles, Christian Herter, and Dean Rusk. But the relationship between the President and the Secretary was not simple. President Truman was irked by Byrnes's view of himself as "an Assistant President in full charge of foreign policy." "Apparently he failed to realize," said Truman, "that the President is required to assume all responsibility for foreign affairs. The President cannot abdicate that responsibility, and he cannot turn it over to anyone else." Truman was particularly annoyed when Secretary Byrnes, on his return

from a foreign ministers' conference in Moscow in December, 1945, prepared to discuss his mission over national radio before reporting on it to the White House.

At the other extreme was Eisenhower's cordial relationship with Dulles, which rested on the Secretary's virtual autonomy in determining policy. True, the two operated in close harmony, conferring almost daily when Dulles was in Washington. Dulles was tremendously industrious and was a tireless advocate of the idea of personal contact: he traveled over half a million miles in his six years at the head of the State Department. He was courteous in his dealings with the President. When Eisenhower's heart attack in 1955 made the President more or less a passenger in the executive branch for six months, Dulles was able to continue without difficulty. The reason for this smooth transition seems, however, to have been that Dulles' policies were the President's, rather than vice versa. At any rate, Dulles was the conspicuous architect of massive retaliation and brinkmanship—policies that seemed too doctrinaire to have been conceived by a man of Eisenhower's temperament. Although he was somewhat conservative on domestic issues, Eisenhower was, generally speaking, liberal, if naïvely so, in foreign policy. It seems

In June, 1954, President Eisenhower (center) and Secretary of State John Foster Dulles (left) conferred with Prime Minister Winston Churchill and Foreign Secretary Anthony Eden of Great Britain. They posed for photographers on the White House lawn.

more than coincidence that he embarked on his world travels and summit meetings almost immediately after the death of Secretary of State Dulles in 1959.

Between the extremes of attempted dominance and accepted dominance lay the ideal conduct of General George C. Marshall and Dean Acheson, men of strong will and bold ideas who enjoyed considerable freedom of action but who managed to efface themselves in the interests of presidential prerogative. They were fortunate in working with President Truman, who repaid their loyalty with generous appreciation: it was he who insisted that the European recovery program be called the Marshall Plan because he wanted the Secretary to be given "full credit for his brilliant contributions. . . ." Acheson and Marshall were in this respect luckier than F. D. R.'s Secretary, Cordell Hull, who for nearly twelve years endured the humiliation of being left out in the cold. On the pretense that the wartime summit meetings at Casablanca, Cairo, and Teheran were military, not diplomatic, in emphasis, Roosevelt did not take Hull with him. Worse still, Hull was not even informed of the result of the conferences. He was not told of the atomic bomb project. He had little idea of the vital matters discussed between the President and his lend-lease "expediter," Averell Harriman. Nor were Cabinet meetings valuable to him (or to most other executive heads in the previous twenty-five years: the real business was nearly always transacted elsewhere). Roosevelt Cabinets, another official said, were "a solo performance by the President, interspersed with some questions and very few debates."

Hull was treated thus because the President regarded him as unduly conservative. What he gained from relative obscurity was immunity from the kind of malevolent hostility that enveloped Marshall and Acheson. Hull's recourse was a familiar one in the executive milieu. Debarred from the chance to shape policy, he became a champion of the career diplomats congregated in the State Department—a bureaucrat instead of a decision maker. Although they were loyal to their subordinates as well as to the President, Marshall and Acheson had to witness a drastic slump in the prestige and morale of the State Department, for they bore the brunt of the McCarthy attack on "striped-pants diplomats" with "phony British accents." Dulles' intransigent position on communism may have been unconsciously conditioned by a desire to protect the department against a recurrence of the onslaught. At any rate, it was several years before professional diplomacy was again securely established in the United States.

Even then there was a fundamental difficulty in the position of the Secretary of State vis-à-vis the President. The preponderance of foreign affairs meant that it was essential to appoint a distinguished public servant to the post and to keep him in it in order to develop his grasp of the great range of tangled responsibilities. But as Harry Truman said, the President could not abdicate responsibility. The Secretary of State was therefore apt to be a frustrated figure, treated with more respect than Cordell Hull and yet still left to work out the almost impossible compromise between overassertion and a meek retreat into the fastnesses of executive bureaucracy. Under John F. Kennedy, Secretary of State Rusk had a somewhat thankless tenure. For he was not merely obliged to shape a proper relationship with the President; he had to compete with other advisers on the White House staff such as the brilliantly clear-witted McGeorge Bundy, the President's special assistant for National Security Affairs. Holding the same office under President Johnson, Rusk again endured the inevitable lot of Secretaries of State appointed by strong-minded Presidents in periods of international tension. He resembled Tantalus in the old fable: each time he was about to drink, the water was apt to recede.

In the last resort, perhaps, an exact balance between the President and his advisers depended upon the chemistry of temperament rather than upon organization charts. The President sought out those whose ideas and style most pleased him. Although there was nothing intentionally devious in the process, the President's entourage was reminiscent of the court of Versailles in the days of Louis XIV. Those who had his ear acquired renown; those who were not in the running occupied themselves with obsessive speculation on the personal history of the foremost courtiers.

Certainly the organization charts lacked permanence. President Eisenhower, who had been accustomed to a military command structure, liked to have issues presented via a neat committee hierarchy and a chief of staff (Sherman Adams from 1953 until 1958). He held weekly meetings of the National

Security Council, a body established in Truman's time. He was probably more systematic than his successor John F. Kennedy, although the incoming Democratic administration announced its intention to make the mechanism function more efficiently. Kennedy arranged fewer meetings of the National Security Council than President Eisenhower—sixteen in the first six months of his administration—and sometimes encouraged the Council to deliberate in his absence in order to promote uninhibited argument. McGeorge Bundy explained in September, 1961: "Much that used to flow routinely to the weekly meetings of the Council is now settled in other ways—by separate meetings with the President, by letters, by written memorandums, and at levels below that of the President. President Kennedy has preferred to call meetings of the NSC only after determining that a particular issue is ready for discussion in this particular forum."

Another of Kennedy's advisers, Theodore Sorensen, shed light on the matter in his witty book *Decision-Making in the White House*, published in 1963. "For years agencies and individuals all over town have felt affronted if not invited to a National Security Council session. The press leaps to conclusions as to who is in favor and who is not by scanning the attendance lists of meetings, speculating in much the same fashion . . . as the Kremlinologists who study the reviewing stand at the Russian May Day Parade. . . . Yet in truth attendance at a White House meeting is not necessarily a matter of logic. Protocol, personal relations, and the nature of the forum may all affect the list. Some basic foreign policy issue, for example, may be largely decided before it comes to the National Security Council—by the appointment of a key official, or by the President's response at a press conference, or by the funds allocated in the budget."

Presidents who might once have had difficulty in procuring expert advice on esoteric international questions were instead swamped with guidance from a plethora of executive offices. Such advice was often bewildering or highly technical in form. As Kennedy remarked in the course of a television address, "No matter how many advisers you have, the President must finally choose." The burden is his. "The advisers may," he said with dry wit, "move on to new advice." By the mid-1960's the burden was nearly intolerable. However devoted and wise his assistants,

at the moment of decision the President was alone. Most of his decisions were, fortunately, less than cataclysmic. But always in a corner of his mind was the knowledge that he might someday have to press the button that would spell the destruction of civilization. The aim of his foreign policy was to see that he never had to press it. Beneath this supreme negation came all the other restrictions of a power seemingly illimitable and yet circumscribed by the actions of his predecessors, by public opinion and national habit, by Congress, by the sensibilities of allied nations, and by sudden developments outside his ken. The President's principal nightmare in 1967 was the American commitment in Vietnam. Neither withdrawal nor further involvement appeared to be acceptable.

On the whole the Presidents of the post-modern era achieved the abrupt transition from isolation to total responsibility with dignity and moderation. In an imperfect world it was unlikely that the leader of any other nation placed in the President's position would have performed as creditably. They had made mistakes. The nation had not always appreciated what was at stake. Flexibility had sometimes been lacking. The experts on holocaustic war revealed an almost excessive readiness to think the unthinkable —talking airily of casualties measured in tens of millions. But in retrospect the Truman policies seemed firm without being unduly truculent, the Eisenhower ones ponderous without being disastrous, the Kennedy initiatives intelligent and mature. Kennedy's handling of the Cuban Missile Crisis was a high point in crisis diplomacy; imaginative experiments such as his Peace Corps showed the world that there was much more to the United States than dollars and ballistic missiles. Until the escalation—one of the most ominous of words in the new vocabulary of the post-modern era—of the war in Vietnam, there had been light ahead. The cold war was dissolving into new alignments, some of them distinctly hopeful. Lyndon Johnson may well have remembered the words of Abraham Lincoln on the eve of his great crisis: "This too shall pass." In the meantime, however, the President had power without glory. He was a man tethered to a heavy vehicle that seemed to be building up a terrible momentum. There was no apparent way to stop it. The President's task was to find a way. The task of the United States, and of mankind elsewhere, was to help him.

The Presidency and the Union

During the twentieth century the foreign and domestic responsibilities of the Presidency have become so inextricably related that it is almost impossible to separate them. Eisenhower's warning against the "military-industrial complex" is a conspicuous instance; some commentators believe that the great Depression of the 1930's was solved only by the compulsions of a world crisis that forced the United States into a wartime economy, and that the cold war has been the main economic safeguard against another sizable depression. Within the executive branch, the Departments of the Treasury, of Agriculture, of Commerce, and even of the Interior (through its control of petroleum uses) may all have an important say in foreign policy. Conversely, of course, foreign affairs may determine the shape of America's domestic development. Premier Khrushchev certainly thought that his activities could sway the American electorate. It is conceivable that if the U-2 piloted by Francis Gary Powers had eluded the Soviet antiaircraft gunners in May, 1960, the Republican candidate, Vice President Richard Nixon, might have won the presidential election the following November; the incident was a serious embarrassment to the Eisenhower administration. It can also be argued that John F. Kennedy, the Democratic candidate in 1960, would not have been elected, or even nominated, if Americans had not been prepared to discard one of their old isolationist fears: fear of the alleged determination of the Roman Catholic papacy to influence adherents in the United States. Foreign and domestic crises have usually kept step with one another, especially since 1945. The exten-

sion of presidential authority has constituted a response to both, equally and inseparably. It has been one of the indicators of an astonishing transformation in the whole tone of the American Union.

However, there is a range of internal issues that are mainly conditioned by domestic considerations. The stock market crash of 1929 and the decade of economic adversity that ensued were part of a worldwide malaise; but the Depression naturally turned the gaze of Americans inward. A bread line in Brooklyn had an understandable and necessary priority in the newspapers over a revolution in China. It was near at hand, it was urgent, and it was doubly grim after the complacent assurances of the 1920's that an era of permanent American prosperity was in sight. President Hoover was booed for telling audiences that the national economy was basically sound, that federal regimentation would destroy liberty, and that (as he later phrased the matter in his memoirs) the Depression had been caused by "miasmic infections" from "the boiling social and economic caldron of Europe. . . ."

The presidential memory was longer than that of the average citizen. Hoover could have found sanction for his outlook in the words of several previous Chief Executives, including Garfield and Cleveland. Franklin D. Roosevelt, elected in 1932, deliberately reached back to a conception of his office defined between Cleveland's terms and, in F. D. R.'s words, the "hear-nothing, see-nothing, do-nothing" administrations of the 1920's. Pledging himself and the nation to a new deal in his acceptance speech at the Democratic convention, he adapted the Square Deal formula of his distant cousin Theodore. During a 1932 campaign address he reiterated T. R.'s view that the Presidency was a pulpit—"a bully pulpit" in T. R.'s breezy phrase—from which to reach and educate the nation. Many of F. D. R.'s speeches were couched in the idiom of "Roosevelt the First" and of Woodrow Wilson, and they evoked the precedents of Jackson and Lincoln. F. D. R.'s first Inaugural Address called for "a leadership of frankness and vigor." He was to be a people's President, representing all the country but especially the poor.

Nor was his sense of the past confined to rhetoric. F. D. R. had served in Wilson's administration. Many of the men who came to work for him in Washington were veterans of the Progressive crusades. Some of the sweeping measures that passed through Congress with dazing rapidity in 1933, and at subsequent stages of Roosevelt's Presidency, derived their sanction from the control of the American economy entrusted to Wilson by such measures as the Overman Act of 1918. Roosevelt's methods of communicating with the public were chiefly those already exploited by predecessors. Even Calvin Coolidge, who is said to have succeeded in his ambition to be "the least President" the United States had ever had, was shrewdly aware of the value of good publicity. He held press conferences with even greater frequency than F. D. R. did, was always willing to have his photograph taken, and exploited the novel possibilities of radio broadcasting. "I am very fortunate," he told a senator, "that I came in with the radio. I can't make an engaging, rousing, or oratorical speech to a crowd as you can. . . but I have a good radio voice, and now I can get my messages across to them without acquainting them with my lack of oratorical ability. . . ." Coolidge's annual message to Congress in December, 1923, was the first to be broadcast, and he delivered other well-received talks from time to time. President Hoover gave twenty-one radio addresses in his four-year term.

Nevertheless, F. D. R. went beyond anything that his predecessors had done to energize and dramatize the Presidency. The contrast with Hoover's dour manner was amazingly marked. One of Roosevelt's Brain Trust advisers, Rexford G. Tugwell, described him as "not a made President, but a born one. . . . No monarch. . . unless it may have been Elizabeth or her magnificent Tudor father, or maybe Alexander or Augustus Caesar, can have given quite that sense of

serene presiding, of gathering up into himself, of really representing, a whole people. He had a right to his leeways, he had a right to use everyone in his own way, he had every right to manage and manipulate the palpables and impalpables. . . . He had touch with something deeper than reason. . . ."

The Roosevelt touch was brilliantly demonstrated in his relations with the press. Coolidge had been considerate with newspapermen; Hoover had attempted to convey information efficiently. Roosevelt treated them with affection, informality, and humor, and with basic respect. His mastery of the press conference, at which he abolished the previous practice of demanding written questions, was so complete that his critics alleged he had bemused the fourth estate and had turned hardened journalists into gushing sycophants. Whatever the truth of this complaint, he certainly succeeded in keeping them informed of what his administration was doing. The result was apparent in the fullness of reporting; Roosevelt's name was rarely absent from the front pages. Nor did he generally use his press contacts to nag Congress, although he employed every means at his disposal to attract public interest in and support for his programs. His references to the legislative branch were usually in the best traditions of executive courtesy. Indeed, oddly enough, F. D. R. prodded Congress in public somewhat less than the "do-nothing" Coolidge, despite the latter's claim that "I have never felt it was my duty to attempt to coerce Senators or Representatives. . . ."

Roosevelt's rapport with the nation was even more triumphantly demonstrated in his radio broadcasts. As governor of New York he had already begun to anticipate the famous "fireside chats" of the New Deal era. He was keenly aware that most newspaper publishers were Republicans, whatever the sympathies of their reporters. Unlike newspapers, Roosevelt told the president of the National Broadcasting Company in 1933, radio "can not misrepresent or misquote. It is far reaching and simultaneous in releasing messages given it for transmission. . . ." Many members of his administration, including the forceful Harold Ickes, were also frequent and skillful broadcasters. Roosevelt devised his annual messages with quite as much attention to their radio audience as to his live audience in Congress, and he delivered the addresses in the evening, when most Americans were at leisure. The fireside talks were, however, the

The National Recovery Administration, which supervised a system of fair competition codes, inspired a song in 1933.

high point of his contacts with the American public. Coolidge and Hoover had sounded stiff, and their remarks platitudinous. F. D. R. perfected a style that was direct, lucid, friendly, and informative. Anxious not to blunt their effect by overdoing them, he gave only twenty-seven fireside chats in his twelve White House years, six of them in the first eighteen months of the New Deal. So great was the impression they created that many people believed in retrospect that they had been almost weekly occurrences. His voice could be heard in every street in the land and his words lingered in the nation's imagination. His concern was that the federal government, under a Democratic administration, should not only be active but should be *considered* active.

The activity was undeniable, especially in the first Hundred Days, March through June, 1933, which witnessed an unparalleled quantity of legislation. It was the beginning of the "alphabet soup" of New Deal agencies—CCC (the Civilian Conservation Corps), FERA (the Federal Emergency Relief Administration), AAA (the Agricultural Adjustment Administration), TVA (the Tennessee Valley Authority), N.R.A. (the National Recovery Administration). Some, such as the N.R.A., fell by the wayside; others, such as WPA (the Works Progress Administration), were created later.

The result was an immense extension of federal power and of executive functions. Roosevelt outlined the change in his April, 1939, message to Congress: "Forty years ago in 1899 President McKinley could deal with the whole machinery of the Executive Branch through his eight cabinet secretaries and the heads of two commissions; and there was but one commission of the so-called quasi-judicial type in existence. He could keep in touch with all the work through eight or ten persons. Now, forty years later, not only do some thirty major agencies (to say nothing of the minor ones) report directly to the President, but there are several quasi-judicial bodies which have enough administrative work to require them also to see him on important executive matters." The first of these bodies were the Civil Service Commission, established in 1883, and the Interstate Commerce Commission, instituted in 1887. In Wilson's time came the Tariff Commission, the Federal Reserve apparatus, the Federal Trade and Power Commissions, and various war agencies, including the War Industries Board. Under Hoover were formed the Reconstruction Finance Corporation and the Federal Farm Board. The New Deal added a swarm of other corporations, agencies, commissions, and banking organizations.

Some of F. D. R.'s predecessors had tried to reform the increasingly cumbersome structure of the executive branch, but with little success. F. D. R. had a great deal of trouble before Congress finally passed the Reorganization Act of 1939, which enabled him to divide the executive office of the President into six main groups. One of these, the Bureau of the Budget, had been created in 1921 within the Treasury Department; under F. D. R. it was moved into the immediate orbit of the President. Another division, the White House Office, was to include a number of secretaries and personal assistants. A third was designated the National Resources Planning Board. At the end of the list, provision was made "in the event of a national emergency, or threat of a national emergency," for "such office for emergency management as the President shall determine." This sixth division, the OEM (Office for Emergency Management), was created in 1940. Like his strong predecessors, Roosevelt stressed the existence of a crisis to justify bold executive measures. He used the word "emergency" to define a supercrisis. Under the OEM were eventually massed the panoply of bodies that

During John F. Kennedy's administration, federal marshals were ordered to accompany James Meredith when he registered as a student at the University of Mississippi. Previously, the state-supported school had not permitted Negro students to enroll.

helped to make wartime Washington so hectic—and so bewildering to the casual visitor. There were under the umbrella of the OEM, for instance, the Office of Production Management, the Office of Civilian Defense, the Office of Defense Transportation, the Board of Economic Warfare, the Office of Price Administration, and the National War Labor Board. This entire mushrooming administrative empire lay within the executive office of the President. No wonder that as Roosevelt was renominated for a third and then a fourth term, he was increasingly called a dictator by his opponents.

During and since his administrations there have been spectacular demonstrations of presidential authority. In September, 1942, F. D. R. made one of the most extreme claims of presidential prerogative ever propounded. Congress had passed the Emergency Price Control Act and had incorporated a farm parity provision to which the President objected. In fact, he threatened to repeal the act on his own if Congress failed to accept his wishes within the near future. The legislators bowed to his will—a will Roosevelt expressed in these words: "The President has the powers, under the Constitution and under Congressional acts, to take measures necessary to avert a disaster which would interfere with the winning of the war. . . . When the war is won, the powers under which I act automatically revert to the people —to whom they belong." As John P. Roche has remarked, such a claim was essentially the same as that advanced by Locke in the seventeenth century

on behalf of royal prerogative ("the power to act according to discretion for the public good, without the prescription of the law and sometimes even against it"). In less sensational episodes F. D. R., followed in the same spirit by Truman, was prompt to veto bills he did not like. There is a story that Roosevelt used to ask his aides to look out for a piece of legislation he could veto, in order to remind Congress that it was being watched.

In every subsequent administration a President has aroused a clamor of excitement over some sudden demonstration of his supremacy. Truman electrified the nation, and infuriated a fair portion of it, when he dismissed General MacArthur in April, 1951. MacArthur was the most eminent American soldier of his day. He had been allowed considerable latitude in expounding his views on the need for the United States to give priority to Asian affairs and to substitute all-out war for the limited strategy being pursued in Korea. He returned home to receive a hero's welcome and the rare compliment of an invitation, which he accepted, to address Congress. But the dismissal stood; there was no way of evading Truman's decision. MacArthur was General of the Army, but the President was still the Commander in Chief. "It is fundamental," said Truman, "that military commanders must be governed by the policies and directives issued to them in the manner provided by our laws and Constitution. In time of crisis, this consideration is particularly compelling." If anyone was to justify actions unsanctioned by the law on the grounds that a crisis existed, it was the President: only one could play at that game.

In September, 1957, Eisenhower appeared on television to announce another critical decision: "Whenever normal agencies prove inadequate to the task and it becomes necessary for the Executive Branch of the Federal Government to use its powers and authority to uphold Federal Courts, the President's responsibility is inescapable. In accordance with that responsibility, I have today issued an Executive Order directing the use of troops under Federal authority to aid in the execution of Federal law at Little Rock, Arkansas. . . ."

Governor Orval Faubus of Arkansas, supported by the state legislature, had refused to abide by the ruling of a federal court that under a Supreme Court ruling of 1954, racial segregation had to end in the public schools of Little Rock. The federal government, upheld by the Court, had for a decade honorably attempted to combat racial discrimination. The Little Rock school board was among those in the South that had begun to move toward integration, only to be thwarted by what Eisenhower described as "certain misguided persons." American rights, he said, depended upon "the certainty that the President and the Executive branch of Government will . . . insure the carrying out of the decisions of the Federal Courts, even, when necessary with all the means at the President's command." Federal authority was paramount, at least in the circumstances he outlined. States' righters might fulminate; but on the day Eisenhower explained his action, paratroopers were patrolling the streets of Little Rock. President Kennedy employed federal marshals to enforce the law at the University of Mississippi in 1962.

One of Kennedy's boldest exercises of authority was his handling of the steel industry in April, 1962. Delicate negotiations had persuaded the steelworkers to accept a wage increase modest enough to avoid inflationary consequences for the national economy. Kennedy had been actively involved in these consultations. At the moment when matters seemed to be under control the steel companies suddenly announced a substantial increase in the price of steel.

On this occasion Kennedy made his intention to tame the steel companies unmistakable. He deployed the whole arsenal of executive weapons. The Attorney General (the President's brother Robert F. Kennedy) threatened antitrust proceedings. The Defense Department declared that federal contracts would be given only to companies which had not raised their prices. Democratic spokesmen from both houses of Congress announced that judiciary committees were to investigate the steel companies' machinations. The President discussed the situation at length and with scathing eloquence at a press conference—knowing that it was an excellent method of mobilizing public opinion. His introductory statement invoked the national emergency as his reason for insisting that the new prices "constitute a wholly unjustifiable and irresponsible defiance of the public interest." The emergency was manifold: Kennedy referred to "grave crises in Berlin and Southeast Asia," to the sacrifices expected of American servicemen, and to the struggle for "economic recovery and stability." He implied that the "tiny handful of steel executives," in their "pursuit of private power and profit," were a group of Benedict Arnolds. The price increases were swiftly cancelled; Kennedy had used executive pressure in lieu of the statutory authority that he did not possess.

The episode illustrates the expansion of executive responsibility as well as of the executive capacity to maneuver. The President, Herbert Hoover had gloomily observed in 1933, "has become increasingly the depository of all national ills, especially if things go wrong." What was true then was even truer thirty years later. Everyone looked to the President to rectify wrongs, indeed to prevent the existence of wrongs. The health of the economy had become his responsibility. Prices and wages and taxes and tariffs and stockpiles were his daily diet. It is not surprising that Presidents should sometimes appear to devote a disproportionate amount of energy and enthusiasm to small, noncontroversial questions. The sheer relief is like that of a circus lion tamer playing with a puppy after his act is over.

All Presidents since F. D. R., with the exception of General Eisenhower, have been experienced politicians with a keen appreciation of the congressional viewpoint. Although Eisenhower was criticized for political naïveté, he too was by temperament and training an advocate of executive-legislative consensus. Consensus, one of Lyndon B. Johnson's favorite words, was equally applicable to the Eisenhower techniques, at least in his conception of them. A President, he explained to his associates, does not lead "by hitting people over the head. Any damn fool can do that, but it's usually called 'assault'—not 'leadership'. . . . I'll tell you what leadership is. It's *persuasion*—and *conciliation*—and *education*—and *patience*. It's long, slow, tough work. That's the only kind of leadership I know—or believe in—or will practice." In his 1960 book *Presidential Power*, which is said to have been carefully read by President-elect John F. Kennedy, Richard E. Neustadt emphasized that the Founding Fathers did not create a government of "separated powers," but a government of "separated institutions *sharing* powers."

By the middle of the twentieth century the executive and legislative branches were well aware of the complexity of their interrelationship. Congressional sophistication was increased by such devices as the establishment in 1946 of the Legislative Reference Service and by making heavy demands on executive officers, some of whom spent much of their time testifying before congressional committees. Congress was reconciled to the fact that some four fifths of the thousands of bills and resolutions that came before it in each session emanated from the executive branch. The majority and minority leaders in both houses were closely involved in shepherding legislation. Mike Mansfield, the Democratic Majority Leader in the Senate, said in 1962 that his chief function was "to interpret the President's program to Members of the Senate . . . to interpret the attitudes of the Senate with respect to his program to the President and to try to obtain a definite decision on the legislation the President desires." The Minority Leader, Everett Dirksen, sounded equally compliant. "The majority leader and I," he recalled of the operations of the Eighty-seventh Congress, "used to go to the telephone, or to the White House. When the President of the United States said, 'There is no further business,' Congress went home. But if the President said, 'You did not finish your business,' we remained. The Congress would not dare to go home if the President said that the job had not been finished."

For their part, Presidents took great trouble to maintain amicable relations with Congress. Lyndon Johnson frequently stressed his determination to avoid the mistakes made by Woodrow Wilson in 1918 and 1919, in failing to name Senate spokesmen to his team of peace negotiators, and by F. D. R. in 1937, when he alienated Congress in attempting to create a more liberal Supreme Court. Other Presidents were no less familiar with such cautionary

tales. Eisenhower held a series of breakfast meetings for congressmen. Anxious to consolidate his slender victory in the 1960 election (the Democrats lost twenty seats in the House of Representatives), Kennedy held individual discussions at the White House with every committee chairman, briefing sessions on important bills for Democratic supporters, and foreign policy briefings for bipartisan groups. He entertained groups of congressmen for morning coffee.

Johnson surpassed his predecessors in demonstrations of esteem. He attended the funerals of Senator Harry Byrd's wife in Virginia and of Representative Emanuel Celler's wife in New York, and he even managed to fly to Georgia for the funeral of a nephew of his old associate Senator Richard Russell. At the close of the Eighty-eighth Congress he invited the entire membership to a gala White House occasion that included a specially produced Broadway show. Kennedy and Johnson prided themselves on their intimate links with Capitol Hill—links maintained through the activities of a squad of liaison assistants. The columnist Joseph Alsop, explaining Johnson's success in securing the passage of the 1964 Civil Rights bill, said that in addition to indefatigable executive lobbying by staff aides, "the President . . . left no Congressman unturned . . . presidential telephone calls to individual members . . . of both houses . . . have been almost incessant."

The highly professional Chief Executives of the mid-twentieth century likewise recognized the importance of capitalizing on party loyalty, no matter how imperfect it might be. President Kennedy rewarded a Tennessee New Frontier congressman, who was running for re-election in 1962, by appointing him special ambassador to represent the United States at the independence ceremonies in Trinidad: an exotic gesture, but one that brought valuable publicity to the Tennessean. The entire Kennedy family lavished praise upon Representative Charles A. Buckley of New York. Buckley was temperamentally poles apart from the New Frontier, but as chairman of the House Public Works Committee he was too important to be flouted. And it is significant that President Kennedy's final, fatal visit to Texas in November, 1963, was on party business: his aim was to patch up the bitter factional quarrel that existed between the supporters of Vice President Lyndon Johnson and those of Senator Ralph Yarborough.

Yet often every technique, every pressure exerted

by the President was inadequate. The central thesis of Richard Neustadt's book *Presidential Power* is suggested by its subtitle: *The Politics of Leadership*. Professor Neustadt quoted two revealing observations by President Truman. The first was an epitome of his White House experiences: "I sit here all day trying to persuade people to do the things they ought to have sense enough to do without my persuading them. . . . That's all the powers of the President amount to." The second was a comment made in 1952 on the fate awaiting General Eisenhower if he won the forthcoming election: "He'll sit here, and he'll say, 'Do this! Do that!' *And nothing will happen.* Poor Ike—it won't be a bit like the Army. He'll find it very frustrating."

Neustadt analyzed some of the apparent demonstrations of presidential authority, such as the dismissal of MacArthur and the dispatch of federal troops to Little Rock. His point was that although such actions were in a sense decisive, they were actually confessions of failure, steps taken reluctantly when more satisfactory expedients had failed. Presidential power is severely limited; in domestic as in foreign affairs, frustration has been more usual than triumph. (Although Kennedy seemed to have abased the steel industry, steel price increases were introduced a year later.) Neustadt concluded that consummate political skill is required of the Chief Executive; General Eisenhower could therefore be considered an unsuccessful President because he failed to grasp the essential balance between persuasion and leadership. But mere political skills are not enough; some extra quality of charm, magnetism, or imagination must disclose itself.

Looking back over the Presidency in the middle third of the twentieth century, it becomes clear that despite the vast growth in the activities of the federal government and of the executive branch, the Presidency has not escaped its traditional shackles. In fact, the President has in some respects been still further restricted by the spread of executive offices. As Neustadt insisted, the Congress and the President still have different "constituencies" and different ideas as to why certain things should be done (or not done). The President has in general come to represent liberal and international ideas, while Congress— and particularly the House of Representatives—has in general continued to be conservative and national (or local) in outlook. A recent example is the block-

ing by the House in 1967 of a reciprocal arms arrangement between the American and British defense departments. This compact would have enabled Britain to offset some of the costs of purchasing United States military aircraft by selling British military and naval equipment to the United States. The agreement was largely nullified by an amendment to the Defense Appropriations bill that required all naval vessels to be built in American yards. The amendment was introduced by Representative John W. Byrnes of Wisconsin, who was determined that an order for seven minesweepers should go not to a foreign country but to yards in his own state.

Many other examples may be cited. One of the most resounding setbacks to presidential authority was suffered by Franklin Roosevelt in 1938. Previously, backed by a handsome Democratic majority in Congress, he had seemed invulnerable. Suddenly he was in trouble over an executive reorganization bill submitted to Congress in 1937. Most of its proposals were sensible, and a new bill was approved in 1939. But the first bill seemed to disgruntled legislators and citizens to confer altogether too many powers on Roosevelt. For example, he proposed that the executive branch absorb some of the independent regulatory commissions. Although the Senate reluctantly passed the bill, President Roosevelt enraged the Upper House by suggesting at a press conference that the votes of some senators were open to purchase. In the House of Representatives one hundred Democrats, including the powerful chairman of the Rules Committee, deserted the administration. A Missouri Democrat, who had been begged to trust the President, shouted: "Assurances are not worth a continental when they come from men who care no more for their word than a tomcat cares for a marriage license in a back alley on a dark night." A Kentucky representative cried, "Let us tell the world that the Congress is not impotent." If Congress did not stop relinquishing authority to Roosevelt, declared another speaker, members "might just as well stay at home and endorse Executive desires by mail." In April, 1938, after the House defeated the bill, F. D. R.'s whole New Deal government seemed to be in disarray. Everyone except jubilant Republicans was angry with everyone else. Underlying resentments burst to the surface. The fragility of presidential rule was all at once painfully apparent. As often happens in such crises, the President struck his associates as a gambler who had lost his touch: he ignored warnings and advice, he confused his followers, his words were maladroit. One recurrent problem that led to such blunders was explained in the memoirs of F. D. R.'s successor Harry Truman. The President, said Truman, "will hear a hundred voices telling him that he is the greatest man in the world for every one that tells him he is not. A President, if he is to have clear perspective and never get out of touch, must cut through the voices around him, know his history, and make certain of the reliability of the information he gets."

Truman himself had a hard time with Congress. He lacked the Rooseveltian aura, his ambitious legislative programs were challenged, and for the first time since 1932 the Republicans controlled both houses of Congress after the 1946 election. He fought back boldly. A clever stratagem, announced in his acceptance speech at the Democratic nominating convention in 1948, was to summon the "last, worst 80th Congress" back into special session: "On the 26th day of July, which out in Missouri we call 'Turnip Day,' I am going to call Congress back and ask them to pass laws to halt rising prices, to meet the housing crisis—which they are saying they are for in their [Republican] platform. At the same time, I shall ask them to act upon other vitally needed measures, such as aid to education, which they say they are for; a national health program; civil rights legislation, which they say they are for; an increase in the minimum wage, which I doubt very much they are for; extension of the Social Security coverage . . . which they say they are for. . . ."

The tactic worked. Truman was elected President in his own right, and the Democrats regained control of Congress. But the Eighty-first Congress proved as intransigent on some points as the Eightieth, especially on the question of policy toward communism. The President maintained a robustly liberal and international position; Congress by contrast seemed ready to believe wild theories of conspiracy and subversion. Thus Congress passed the Internal Security Act of 1950, which attempted to curb Communist (or other radical or totalitarian) activities in the United States and to debar suspect aliens. Truman vetoed the bill in an eloquent message: "Our position in the vanguard of freedom rests largely on our demonstration that the free expression of opinion, coupled with government by popular consent, leads

to national strength and human advancement. Let us not, in cowering and foolish fear, throw away the ideals which are the fundamental basis of our free society."

His appeal was brushed aside; the next day his veto was overridden. The bill, slightly amended, emerged in 1951 as the McCarran Act. Senator Pat McCarran (a Democrat from Nevada) also sponsored the McCarran-Walter Act of 1952, which virtually retained the discriminatory provisions of immigration legislation of the 1920's, proposed complex screening methods to keep out "subversives," and empowered the Attorney General to deport unwelcome immigrants. Again President Truman sent the bill back with a rousing veto. "In no other realm of our national life," he declared, "are we so . . . stultified by the dead hand of the past as we are in this field of immigration. We do not limit our cities to their 1920 boundaries; we do not hold corporations to their 1920 capitalizations; we welcome progress and change . . . except in the field of immigration. . . ." Again, however, Congress overrode his veto.

Nor were more placatory methods invariably successful. President Eisenhower gained such favor with the public during his first administration that he was re-elected in 1956 by a margin of over nine and a half million votes. But the Democrats kept control of Congress and increased their hold in the mid-term elections of 1958. Throughout his Presidency Eisenhower sought to cooperate with the legislative branch. Yet legislators, journalists, and all the other President watchers in Washington soon perceived that he was more likable than formidable. He made no move to dissociate himself from the excesses of Senator Joseph McCarthy. Exasperated by the unresponsiveness of congressional Republicans, he pondered in 1953 whether it might not be better to form a new party. But he took no steps toward doing so—and in any case the dream was unrealistic. One of his associates noted that congressmen "were scared of Roosevelt, and even Truman. They're not scared of Ike." More assertive in his last two years, he was nevertheless too negatively inclined to clash head on with Congress. What he gained in popularity among congressmen he lost in authority.

John F. Kennedy obliquely attacked Eisenhower's conception of the Presidency in a speech at the National Press Club in January, 1960. The nation, he said, could not "afford a Chief Executive who is praised primarily for what he did not do, the disasters he prevented, the bills he vetoed." The President "must know when to lead Congress, when to consult it and when he should act alone." They were bold words. But Kennedy himself, once in the White House, was criticized for failing to dominate Congress. Carroll Kilpatrick, a sympathetic Washington correspondent, maintained that while the record of Kennedy's first two years with Congress "was not without notable successes . . . there were notable failures as well, and the amount of energy he expended in gaining as much as he did was enormous. The President's power struggle with Congress was almost equal to that of his struggle with the Communist leaders abroad." Despite a substantial Democratic majority, the administration's omnibus farm bill was killed in the House by 10 votes and the Medicare bill was defeated in the Senate by 5 votes. Among other unsuccessful pieces of presidential legislation were bills to create a Department of Urban Affairs and to provide federal aid for public schools and for higher education. Contemplating these and other disappointments, Kennedy's able assistant Theodore Sorensen wryly remarked that a President "is free to choose only within the limits of permissibility, within the limits of available resources, within the limits of available time, within the limits of previous commitments, and within the limits of available information." Congress might contribute to each of these limits. In 1962 Sidney Hyman, an expert on the Presidency, predicted that in domestic affairs the legislative branch would continue to claim dominance "in defiance of the President, in defiance of the public opinion he mobilizes, and in defiance of the fact that the sum of all local and regional interests do not necessarily add up these days to the national interest." His prediction was borne out by the legislative history of Lyndon Johnson's administration. In his first presidential address to Congress, Johnson promised the legislators "the full cooperation and support of the Executive branch. . . . As one who has long served in both Houses of the Congress, I firmly believe in the independence and integrity of the legislative branch. . . . I shall always respect this. It is deep in the marrow of my bones. With equal firmness, I believe in the capacity and I believe in the ability of the Congress, despite the divisions of opinions which characterize our nation, to act—to act wisely, to act vigorously, to act speedily when the

need arises. The need is here. The need is now. I ask your help." Johnson established an astonishing record in his first year; he persuaded Congress to enact most of the principal measures desired by Kennedy.

The appeal succeeded. And having gained a crushing victory over Senator Goldwater in the 1964 election, President Johnson moved on to his own Great Society with its far-reaching schedule of plans for social justice, economic improvement, and beautification of the landscape. Portions of his program, including an increased and extended national minimum wage and the establishment of a new Department of Transportation, were quite briskly enacted. Professor Robert Lekachman wrote in June, 1965: "Lyndon B. Johnson is without question more lovingly immersed in domestic issues, and more effective in getting his programs through Congress, than any American President since Franklin Roosevelt in his first term of office." The statement was, however, qualified. Lekachman went on to say that President Johnson's prescription for the Great Society "is the drive not toward the transformation of society but toward the expansion of the economic machine. This is not an ignoble vision. But it is a highly conservative one." The reforms Johnson proposed were, in other words, relatively modest, relatively inexpensive, and relatively superficial. There was little to raise the hackles of Congress. Lekachman concluded his survey: "Although there is no special reason to condemn a conservative politician for choosing the path of conciliation, there is every reason to avoid confusing rhetoric with the program of social action that is desperately needed."

By 1967 Lyndon Johnson's domestic legislation was widely criticized for being more shadow than substance. The Great Society was derided as a catch phrase. Preoccupied by the agonizing dilemma of Vietnam, the President had ceased his previous barrage of flattery and cajolery on Capitol Hill. Executive-legislative relationships require constant attention; like plants in a hot, arid zone they wilt unless watered daily. Congress complained of neglect and hostility, and responded with comparable hostility. Its rough handling of the Defense Appropriations bill was in part a way of showing its displeasure.

The problems engendered by the expansion of the executive side of the federal government have already been mentioned in the previous chapter. Nineteenth-century Presidents had sometimes been irritated by the devious resistances encountered among federal bureaucrats. The situation was far worse by the 1930's. "Half of a President's suggestions," according to Jonathan Daniels, a former aide of Franklin D. Roosevelt's, "which theoretically carry the weight of orders, can be safely forgotten by a Cabinet member. And if the President asks about a suggestion a second time, he can be told that it is being investigated. If he asks a third time, a wise Cabinet officer will give him at least part of what he suggests. But only occasionally, except about the most important matters, do Presidents ever get around to asking three times." Permanent officials were often able to impose their own ideas on executive heads, or at least prevent them from making changes. F. D. R. had to recognize this situation as a fact of life:

"The Treasury is so large and . . . ingrained in its practices that I find it is almost impossible to get the action and results I want. . . . But the Treasury is not to be compared with the State Department. You should go through the experience of trying to get any changes in the thinking . . . of the career diplomats and then you'd know what a real problem was. But the Treasury and the State Department put together are nothing compared with the Na-a-vy. . . . To change anything in the Na-a-vy is like punching a feather bed. You punch it . . . until you are finally exhausted, and then you find the damn bed just as it was before you started punching."

President Truman encountered the same difficulty. Career officials, he said in his memoirs, "regard themselves as the men who really make policy and run the Government. They look upon the elected officials as just temporary occupants. . . . It has often happened in the War and Navy Departments that the generals and the admirals, instead of working for and under the Secretaries, succeeded in having the Secretaries act for and under them. And it has happened in the Department of State."

Different Presidents have tried different expedients to solve the problem. Starting with Roosevelt's Executive Reorganization bill, a steady stream of proposals were considered. In 1947 Congress established the Commission on Organization of the Executive Branch with the approval of President Truman, who named ex-President Hoover to head it. The Hoover Commission reported in 1949 that the executive branch was "cut up into a large number of

agencies, which divided responsibility and which are too great in number for effective direction from the top." The line of command downward from the President, and of responsibility up to the President, had "been weakened, or actually broken, in many places and in many ways." The federal government, which had almost overnight become "the most gigantic business on earth," was creaking under the strain.

Remedial legislation was enacted. The President's annual salary was increased in 1949 to $100,000 (plus a tax-free allowance of $50,000), and that of the Vice President to $30,000 plus a $10,000 allowance. (In 1955, the Vice President's salary was raised to $35,000. Possibly this was a gauge of his increased importance. From 1789 to 1909 the Vice President's salary had been only one fifth of the President's, and from 1909 to 1949 less than one sixth.) The administrative Reorganization Act of 1949 conceded that the President must have authority over his own branch and empowered him to make significant alterations.

But there was a major snag. Congress, understandably anxious to retain a degree of control, restricted the act to a four-year span, and renewed it for periods of two years in 1953, 1955, and 1957. It stipulated that plans for executive reorganization must be submitted for congressional approval. The renewal proposal of 1959 was defeated in the Senate, and the President's grant of authority therefore lapsed. The renewal was defeated because Congress had grown more and more uneasy at the implications of permitting the President to run his own household when that household was "the most gigantic business on earth." It rejected twelve of the fifty-one reorganization plans submitted by Truman, and three of the seventeen devised by Eisenhower. At President Kennedy's request, Congress consented in 1961 to a further vesting of authority for a two-year period. Four of Kennedy's nine plans were rejected. One of these would have established the new Cabinet-rank Department of Urban Affairs. Many congressmen were suspicious of such a creation; some were hostile because the President had intimated that he intended to appoint a Negro, Robert Weaver, Secretary of the Department.

When the Reorganization Act was given a further two-year lease in 1963, Congress denied to the President authority to institute new departments of Cabinet rank. President Johnson managed to implement the Kennedy scheme by establishing the Department of Housing and Urban Development in 1965, and he was successful in placing Robert Weaver at its head. But he had to promote a separate bill to get his way; and—perhaps prudently—he did not name Mr. Weaver until the bill became law.

The executive branch, or at least the executive office centered in the White House, was more adequately staffed than in the past. But the burgeoning of functions and personnel tended to cancel out the streamlining that had been theoretically achieved. More than ever the President's problem was to select key issues from the immense quantity of documents moving about the so-called corridors of power in Washington. Eisenhower's solution was to rely on his executive heads, and especially upon his assistant Sherman Adams, to preselect and digest such issues for him. He kept a clean desk and a tidy organization chart. The disadvantage was that he risked isolating himself unduly. How could he be sure that the proper issues were reaching him? Cabinet and committee meetings were supposed to bring him in contact with all his chief officials and with their areas of responsibility. But were committees a satisfactory way of handling executive business? President Kennedy thought not. Reverting to styles reminiscent of F. D. R., though with considerably greater concern for administrative clarity, he sought to break through the elaborate hierarchy of the federal government. Kennedy sought advice from a wide variety of sources, often drawing upon the views of men outside the government. He would telephone an official directly, bypassing the head of the department or agency; he encouraged energetic subordinates to communicate directly with him. Up to the time of his death the technique was working reasonably well because so many of his officials respected and admired him. If he had continued this procedure, however, he might have exposed his administration to some of the defects that disturbed F. D. R.'s underlings—confusion, duplication of effort, factionalism, undermining of authority. There was indeed no perfect way for a President to pick his way through the mazes of Washington. If he could work a twenty-four-hour day seven days a week he would still not have time for more than a fraction of the matters demanding his attention.

Even in less burdensome periods most Presidents professed to have been overworked. In a private memorandum which Truman wrote in April, 1950, he

Robert Weaver became the first Negro Cabinet member when President Johnson selected him to head the newly formed Department of Housing and Urban Development in 1965.

observed that "eight years as President is enough and sometimes too much for any man to serve in that capacity." It was not merely that executive heads became fatigued. There was, he felt, a subtler difficulty. Presidents were too subject to the lure of power, by which he presumably meant the glamour of the office: "It can get into a man's blood just as gambling and lust for money have been known to do." Truman seems to have thought F. D. R. wrong to have broken precedent by running for a third term; unless Presidents honored the code of restraint followed by Washington, Jefferson, and Jackson, he said, "we will start down the road to dictatorship and ruin." Although he probably could have secured renomination in 1952, he decided not to; he had already been in office for nearly eight years.

The same thoughts had, however, occurred to Congress, which had proposed what in 1951 became the Twenty-second Amendment to the Constitution: "No person shall be elected to the office of the President more than twice, and no person who has held the office of President, or acted as President, for more than two years of a term to which some other person was elected President shall be elected to the office of the President more than once." The amendment had not been adopted when Truman recorded his views, and he was specifically exempted from its ruling. But he knew it was likely to be ratified and was opposed to it: the two-term tradition, he said, "should continue not to be a Constitutional amendment, but by custom based on the honor of the man in the office." The logic of this statement is not altogether clear. President Truman may have felt that decisions on re-election were best left to the Executive and the electorate. No doubt he considered the amendment a posthumous revenge exacted by a Republican Congress upon the dead Democratic leader F. D. R. A further tactical aspect undoubtedly struck him. He said in his memoirs that while he had decided as early as 1949 not to run again in 1952, he "could not share this decision with anyone. By the very nature of his office, this is one secret a President must keep to himself to the last possible moment." If he disclosed it prematurely he was apt to set off a furious contest among aspirants for the succession; and his own influence would dwindle. Most commentators have agreed with Truman that the Twenty-second Amendment was a mistake. Whether or not they are correct, the amendment should be added to the list of factors that have circumscribed presidential potency.

The President must reckon with every branch of government. Apart from legislative and executive complications, he might also encounter difficulties with the third branch—the judiciary. Much of F. D. R.'s New Deal legislation was invalidated by a Supreme Court of which the majority did not share his social and political attitudes. His scheme of 1937 and 1938 to end the deadlock by threatening to alter the composition of the Court aroused violent opposition and alienated even some of his liberal admirers. He discovered to his cost that the Court enjoyed as much prestige as the Presidency—in fact perhaps more, because it was further removed from the world of politics. Roosevelt's exasperation with the Supreme Court was well-founded. But in questioning the impartiality of the judiciary he unwittingly laid open to question the rectitude of the President. Here was another of the paradoxes of executive prerogative. Leadership depended upon vigorous presidential activity. Activity was, however, not always compatible with the appearance of rectitude. The standing of the office rested partly on the notion that the President must be in some sense an "appellate" President, a Chief Magistrate with a magistrate's

dispassionate aloofness. To attack the excessive power vested in the "nine old men" was to invite the response that they were guardians, not aggressors, and so were less dangerous than one man, the President, whose power might take aggressive forms.

By the end of F. D. R.'s administration, and with remarkable strength and near-unanimity after the appointment of Chief Justice Earl Warren in 1953, the Supreme Court moved into an era of positive liberalism. It thus became an ally of the almost innately liberal executive branch, especially in the realm of civil rights. Before this change occurred, however, President Truman suffered a sharp reminder that the Court as well as Congress might on occasion resist executive decrees. During World War II Roosevelt had now and then taken over factories in order to avert strikes and maintain essential production. In 1952 President Truman was faced with a strike in the steel industry. The Korean War was in progress, and Truman's advisers agreed with him that the threatened strike—precipitated in his view by the obstinacy of the steel companies—constituted a national emergency. He therefore issued an Executive Order for the seizure of the steel mills by the government and on the same day delivered an explanatory radio address to the nation. "I believe," he said afterward, "that the power of the President should be used in the interest of the people, and in order to do that the President must use whatever power the Constitution does not expressly deny him." Congress, he insisted, had obliged him to intervene by refusing to act constructively.

The steel owners and most of the newspapers disagreed. The volume of protest was so great that the Supreme Court decided to hear testimony in a suit challenging the President's authority. Chief Justice Fred Vinson declared that Truman had simply performed his constitutional duty to "take Care that the Laws be faithfully executed" and had sustained the honorable tradition of Washington, Jefferson, Jackson, Lincoln, Wilson, and the two Roosevelts. Only two justices sided with him. The other six, including Hugo Black and Felix Frankfurter, ruled that the President had exceeded his powers. Frankfurter approvingly cited the opinion of Justice Brandeis in *Myers v. United States* (1926): "The doctrine of the separation of powers was adopted by the Convention of 1787, not to promote efficiency but to preclude the exercise of arbitrary power. The purpose was, not to avoid friction, but, by means of the inevitable friction incident to the distribution of the governmental powers among three departments, to save the people from autocracy." The irony of this statement was that the majority opinion in *Myers v. United States* upheld presidential authority against that of Congress. The majority opinion in the 1952 steel case obliged the President to return the companies to their operators; he was rapped on the knuckles for dictatorial conduct.

Neither the man nor the institution was crushed. President Truman continued to believe that he had been right. Within a few years the Warren Court was beginning to rule consistently that America's interests were best served by a strong, benevolent federal Executive, rather than by private enterprise or state and local autonomy. The action of the 1952 Court revealed, however, that the third branch was still capable of contesting the prerogatives of the executive branch and that constitutional precedents were still susceptible of more than one interpretation. Moreover the activism of the Warren Court, though far preferable to the stubbornness of the New Deal Court, was not an unmixed blessing for the Presidency. Some perceptive commentators thought it tended to weaken its own prestige by venturing into areas best left to Congress and the White House. And a President such as Eisenhower, with passive or "appellate" inclinations, showed a disturbing readiness to shelter behind the armor of the Court instead of leading public opinion himself. His argument in justifying his intervention at Little Rock was that the President was merely enforcing a Supreme Court decision. "Our personal opinions about the decision," he said, apparently including the Executive in the word "our" and not affirming any executive attitude, "have no bearing on the matter of enforcement. . . ." The danger was that the White House might abdicate responsibility and shift to the Court a burden that it should not be expected to carry.

In the mid-twentieth century the news media were often called the fourth branch of government. Newspapers, periodicals, radio, and television performed important if miscellaneous functions. Not least of these was the presentation to the public of the President's views. As has already been noted, Presidents became increasingly alert to the opportunities afforded by the news media. A President was guaranteed immediate and comprehensive coverage of

everything he did and said. The partisan political advantages were great. In the mid-term elections of 1962, as Louis Koenig pointed out, President Kennedy could embark on a campaigning tour with three airliners, four helicopters, a fleet of automobiles, five press assistants, and a squad of forty-four reporters, photographers, and television technicians.

Yet no twentieth-century President, not even F. D. R., was altogether happy with the outcome. For one thing, the influence of the media was not as significant as some journalists liked to think. President Truman won the 1948 election despite a mainly hostile (and predominantly Republican) press. The public, used to a diet of entertainment, tended to be bored by presidential exhortations on television. Relations between the White House and the press corps were apt to wear thin. If the President was uncommunicative, the newspapermen complained of being shut out; if he took trouble to keep them informed, they complained of being taken in—in other words, spoon-fed. The televised press conference exemplified the frustrating situation of the fourth branch in Washington. Such conferences were far too large, too staged, too public to offer genuine contact with the President. The interview conventions of the mass media required journalists to ask about matters on which they could not hope to be given a candid answer. Public figures, above all the President, often struck ordinary citizens as men with nothing to say because the rules of the game compelled them to respond evasively. Journalists in search of good copy usually exaggerated the fascination of new Presidents, and before long began to exaggerate the failings of the incumbent. For their part, Presidents often proved oversensitive to press reports. Harry Truman occasionally lost his temper with journalists and told them so. Kennedy, while less peppery, was sufficiently annoyed by the New York *Herald Tribune* to cancel the White House subscription to the paper. Lyndon Johnson was markedly resentful of unfavorable publicity. The news media, in common with the general public, began to complain that instead of receiving guidance by and information about the President, they were being fobbed off with bland substitutes fashioned by public relations officers. They sensed that in an era of ghostwriting and press releases Presidents were too much concerned with their images and too little concerned with reality. Some commentators believed that the "cult of consensus" had led the whole nation, including the Presidency, into an obsession with polls and ratings, with the photogenic, and that this development must have damaging consequences for the nation.

There was, of course, nothing new in the tendency of journalists to become disenchanted with each President once his novelty wore off. They typified a national habit, which was almost as old as the Presidency, to expect too much and react too harshly. Mid-term elections usually showed a swing away from the President's party after the brief honeymoon period. The disenchantment was usually even greater during a President's second term. Calvin Coolidge said in his autobiography: "An examination of the records of those Presidents who have served eight years will disclose in most every instance the latter part of their term has shown very little in the way of constructive accomplishment." This observation is not invariably true—it did not happen in the closing stages of Eisenhower's Presidency—but it has by and large been the case. F. D. R.'s administration reached a low point during his second term. Truman's government, despite his personal resilience, had lost most of its impetus by 1950 or 1951. Although Kennedy might have been an exception, most Washington observers of his administration noted a disparity between what one of them, the journalist Douglass Cater, has called "courageous expectations and cautious operations." Comments by congressmen in the wake of the 1966 mid-term elections indicated a drastic swing away from Lyndon Johnson. "We've had our bellyful of new legislation . . ." said a Democratic leader. "The pendulum has swung too far in the direction of the White House, and now it's time for it to swing back. This will be a people's Congress." The House Republican leader, Gerald R. Ford, Jr., announced that his party's gains were "a repudiation of the President's domestic policies. . . . It's going to be rough going for him around here. Congress will write the laws, not the executive branch."

The post-1945 President, everyone concurred, was the most powerful person in the most powerful nation on earth. Historically speaking, there was no doubt that an aggrandizing office had acquired almost total responsibility, not only for the well-being of the American nation but for that of half the globe. This much was cumulative and probably irreversible. On another scale, however, the office seemed to face a principle of diminution. Enlarged executive powers evoked increased congressional uneasiness. The response to Truman's seizure of the steel mills implied that Presidents could no longer count on being able to impose their will upon the nation by claiming "emergency" powers. In spite of the links between the White House and Capitol Hill, they remained separate political realms.

What, then, was presidential power, or authority? It was a contradictory intangible, compounded of celebrity, frustration, and crushing responsibility. The President was the person of whom too much was expected and on whom everything could be blamed. John F. Kennedy dealt with the predicament at a meeting of newspaper editors in April, 1963, when he was asked for his policy on a possible wage increase for steelworkers. "I know," he said, "that there are important editorial interests . . . who really don't feel that this is the President's business. They have never really defined what his business is, but it is not this. I take a somewhat different view . . . in that if there is a wage demand, it has a number of effects upon the public interest. . . . I find that when things go badly, it becomes our business. When the stock market goes down, letters are addressed to the White House. When it goes up, we get comparatively few letters of appreciation. But when you have high unemployment, it is because the President hasn't gotten the country moving again." He was the symbol of national pride, but he was also the nation's scapegoat. He might be widely popular, like Harding, yet weak and mediocre as Harding was. He might be widely unpopular, like Truman, yet tough and able as Truman was. He might be both popular and competent, as Kennedy might have been had he lived. He might be both unpopular and mediocre. In the eyes of posterity he would be apt to be blamed for errors beyond his ken, although he might also be given credit for achievements that were rather those of his executive associates, or of good men in Congress, or of the nation as a whole. Perhaps it was more accurate to talk of presidential responsibility than of presidential power. At least it seemed so to the White House occupants of the 1950's and 1960's. "All Presidents," the British journalist Alistair Cooke remarked in 1963, "start out pretending to run a crusade, but after a couple of years they find they are running something much less heroic, much more intractable: namely, the Presidency."

Program for the Peace of the World

By *PRESIDENT WILSON* January 8, 1918

I. Open covenants of peace, openly arrived at, after which there shall be no private international understandings of any kind, but diplomacy shall proceed always frankly and in the public view.

II. Absolute freedom of navigation upon the seas, outside territorial waters, alike in peace and in war, except as the seas may be closed in whole or in part by international action for the enforcement of international covenants.

III. The removal, so far as possible, of all economic barriers and the establishment of an equality of trade conditions among all the nations consenting to the peace and associating themselves for its maintenance.

IV. Adequate guarantees given and taken that national armaments will reduce to the lowest point consistent with domestic safety.

V. Free, open-minded, and absolutely impartial adjustment of all colonial claims, based upon a strict observance of the principle that in determining all such questions of sovereignty the interests of the population concerned must have equal weight with the equitable claims of the government whose title is to be determined.

VI. The evacuation of all Russian territory and such a settlement of all questions affecting Russia as will secure the best and freest coöperation of the other nations of the world in obtaining for her an unhampered and unembarrassed opportunity for the independent determination of her own political development and national policy, and assure her of a sincere welcome into the society of free nations under institutions of her own choosing; and, more than a welcome, assistance also of every kind that she may need and may herself desire. The treatment accorded Russia by her sister nations in the months to come will be the acid test of their goodwill, of their comprehension of her needs as distinguished from their own interests, and of their intelligent and unselfish sympathy.

VII. Belgium, the whole world will agree, must be evacuated and restored, without any attempt to limit the sovereignty which she enjoys in common with all other free nations. No other single act will serve as this will serve to restore confidence among the nations in the law which they have themselves set and determined for the government of their relations with one another. Without this healing act the whole structure and validity of international law is forever impaired.

VIII. All French territory should be freed and the invaded portions restored, and the wrong done to France by Prussia in 1871 in the matter of Alsace-Lorraine, which has unsettled the peace of the world for nearly fifty years, should be righted, in order that peace may once more be made secure in the interest of all.

IX. A readjustment of the frontiers of Italy should be effected along clearly recognizable lines of nationality.

X. The people of Austria-Hungary, whose place among the nations we wish to see safeguarded and assured, should be accorded the freest opportunity of autonomous development.

XI. Rumania, Serbia and Montenegro should be evacuated; occupied territories restored; Serbia accorded free and secure access to the sea; and the relations of the several Balkan States to one another determined by friendly counsel along historically established lines of allegiance and nationality; and international guarantees of the political and economic independence and territorial integrity of the several Balkan States should be entered into.

XII. The Turkish portions of the present Ottoman Empire should be assured a secure sovereignty, but the other nationalities which are now under Turkish rule should be assured an undoubted security of life and an absolutely unmolested opportunity of autonomous development, and the Dardanelles should be permanently opened as a free passage to the ships and commerce of all nations under international guarantees.

XIII. An independent Polish State should be erected which should include the territories inhabited by indisputably Polish populations, which should be assured a free and secure access to the sea, and whose political and economic independence and territorial integrity should be guaranteed by international covenant.

XIV. A general association of nations must be formed under specific covenants for the purpose of affording mutual guarantees of political independence and territorial integrity to great and small States alike.

1901 - 1968
The Presidency in Documents

At the end of 1918, the year in which his Fourteen Points (above) were published, Wilson sailed for Europe to attend the talks he hoped would result in lasting peace. His brother-in-law wrote him a letter that spoke for millions: "Your vision of the new world that should spring from the ashes of the old is all that has made the war tolerable. . . . [It has] filled our imaginations, and has made the war not a tragedy but a sacrament."

The Modern Presidency

With Theodore Roosevelt's accession to the Presidency in 1901 the office entered its modern era. Although Roosevelt himself was a major factor, the time was ripe for enlarging the functions of the Chief Executive. Technological revolutions, rapid population growth, and urbanization were creating problems in America that local governments could not solve, while rapidly improving communications were shrinking distances and making centralized control increasingly possible. The size and power of the United States of America also brought it to a position of responsibility in world affairs, for the great oceans no longer served as isolating moats.

A Big Stick

Roosevelt viewed the Presidency as a "big stick" and as a podium. He tackled difficulties with a freewheeling, happy ferocity exemplified by his handling of the coal strike of 1902, which could have resulted in a serious coal famine. Below is part of a letter from T. R. to Governor W. Murray Crane of Massachusetts, outlining the President's plan of action; communicated to the mine owners, it had forced arbitration and settlement.

. . . The position of the operators, that the public had no rights in the case, was not tenable for a moment, and what most astounded me therein was their ignorance of the fact that their violence and unreason and their inability or refusal to consider the terrible nature of the catastrophe impending over the poor were all combining to produce a most dangerous feeling in the country at large—a feeling which might have effect in great social disturbance. Among the trades unions generally, the wageworkers generally, there was beginning to be ugly talk of a general sympathetic strike, which, happening at the beginning of winter, would have meant a crisis only less serious than the civil war. Even without such a crisis the first long-continued spell of bitter weather meant misery and violence in acute form in our big cities. I

did not intend to sit supinely when such a state of things was impending, and I notified Knox and Root that if the contingency arose where I had to take charge of the matter, as President, on behalf of the Federal Government, I should not ask even their advice, but would proceed to take certain definite action which I outlined to them. I explained that I knew that this action would form an evil precedent, and that it was one which I should take most reluctantly, but that it was the only one which I could see which would be effective in such an emergency; and that I should feel obliged to take it rather than expose our people to the suffering and chaos which would otherwise come. I told them that they should both write letters of protest against it if they wished, so as to free themselves from responsibility—for that I should act just as if we were in a state of war. Knox, however, having made up his mind to embark with me on a policy of intervention, was thoroughgoing and instantly acquiesced in my plan. This plan was to summon Governor Stone [William A. Stone of Pennsylvania] to take action, on the one hand by the use of his troops to put down all violence and disorder, and on the other hand by calling together the Pennsylvania legislature and getting them to act in any way that was necessary to bring about a reopening of the mines; on the theory that wherever the fault might lie the present system of management had failed and the needs of the country would brook no delay in curing the failure. Then I would also inform him that if he could not deal with the situation, I could, and would. Root told me that there were 10,000 regulars which I could put in at once, and I had seen old General Schofield and told him that if I put in the regulars I intended at the same time to seize the mines and to have him take charge and run them as receiver for the government. I do not know whether I would have had any precedents . . . but in my judgment it would have been imperative to act, precedent or no precedent—and I was in readiness. . . .

The Canal

The bumptious United States, personified by Roosevelt, wanted to dig a canal across Central America. The methods the President employed to gain title to the necessary land—encouraging and then recognizing Panama's secession from Colombia—may have been extralegal, but Roosevelt believed that Might, to a great degree, meant Right. Otto Gresham, a Chicago attorney, raised questions about those methods in a letter, to which President Roosevelt replied on November 30, 1903.

. . . Now, how anyone can conceive that Colombia has the slightest right in the matter I do not understand. We have been more than just, have been generous to a fault, in our dealings with Colombia. It seems incredible to me that anyone could take the position which you speak of as being taken by some men, provided those men have either red blood or common sense in them. Are these men ignorant of the fact that General Reyes (a clipping concerning whom you enclose) and President Marroquin [of Colombia] are now endeavoring to get us to break faith with Panama, just exactly as they themselves broke faith with us, on the specific ground that they will do for us the precise thing which they contemptuously and unanimously refused to do last summer?

The case in a nutshell is this: The government of Colombia was solemnly pledged to give us the right to dig that canal. The government of Colombia now, through Reyes and through their minister, asserts that it will instantly carry out that pledge and ratify the treaty we proposed—or if necessary a treaty even more favorable to us; yet last summer the government refused to ratify this treaty, and said that in view of the unanimous adverse action of the Colombian Congress it had no power to do what we desired. Of course this means that it was guilty of deliberate bad faith. The Colombians have not been badly treated; they have been well treated, and have themselves behaved badly; and if Congress should appropriate money to indemnify them my present feeling is that I should veto the appropriation. If Colombia and Panama should come to an agreement, that is another matter; but the United States owes Colombia nothing in law or in morals. The Colombians need not come here to ask justice from me. They have received exact justice, after I had in vain endeavored to persuade them to accept generosity. In their silly efforts to damage us they cut their own throats. They tried to hold us up; and too late they have discovered their criminal error.

By the way, on the score of morality it seems to me that nothing could be more wicked than to ask us to surrender the Panama people, who are our friends, to the Colombian people, who have shown themselves our foes; and this for no earthly reason save because we have, especially in New York City and parts of the Northeast, a small body of shrill eunuchs who consistently oppose the action of this government whenever that action is to its own interests, even though at the same time it may be immensely to the interest of the world, and in accord with the fundamental laws of righteousness—which is now a synonym for anemic weakness.

Responsibility and Power

Roosevelt had announced, after the 1904 election, that he would not be a candidate again. But as his second term waned, there were many who urged him to stand for re-election in 1908. In a letter to historian George Trevelyan, President Roosevelt discussed his views on the office of the Presidency and the third-term question.

. . . Now, my ambition is that, in however small a way, the work I do shall be along the Washington and Lincoln Lines. While President I have *been* President, emphatically; I have used every ounce of power there was in the office and I have not cared a rap for the criticisms of those who spoke of my "usurpation of power"; for I knew that the talk was all nonsense and that there was no usurpation. I believe that the efficiency of this Government depends upon its possessing a strong central executive, and wherever I could establish a precedent for strength in the executive, as I did for instance as regards external affairs in the case of sending the fleet around the world, taking Panama, settling affairs of Santo Domingo and Cuba; or as I did in internal affairs in settling the anthracite coal strike, in keeping order in Nevada this year when the Federation of Miners threatened anarchy, or as I have done in bringing the big corporations to book—why, in all these cases I have felt not merely that my action was right in itself, but that in showing the strength of, or in giving strength to, the executive, I was establishing a precedent of value. I believe in a strong executive; I believe in power; but I believe that responsibility should go with power, and that it is not well that the strong executive should be a perpetual executive.

Above all and beyond all I believe as I have said before that the salvation of this country depends upon Washington and Lincoln representing the type of leader to which we are true. I hope that in my acts I have been a good President, a President who has deserved well of the Republic; but most of all, I believe that whatever value my service may have comes even more from what I *am* than from what I *do*. I may be mistaken, but it is my belief that the bulk of my countrymen, the men whom Abraham Lincoln called "the plain people"—the farmers, mechanics, small tradesmen, hard-working professional men—feel that I am in a peculiar sense their President, that I represent the democracy in somewhat the fashion that Lincoln did, that is, not in any demagogic way but with the sincere effort to stand for a government by the people and for the people. Now the chief service I can render these plain people who believe in me is, not to destroy their ideal of me. . . . However certain I might be that in seeking or accepting a third term I was actuated by a sincere desire to serve my fellow countrymen, I am very much afraid that multitudes of thoroly honest men

THE HEIR PRESUMPTIVE.

Theodore Roosevelt (*to* William H. Taft, *his candidate for the Presidency*). "THERE, SONNY, I'VE FIXED YOU UP SO THEY WON'T KNOW THE DIFFERENCE BETWEEN US."

President Theodore Roosevelt's enormous popularity enabled him to designate his own successor, William Howard Taft.

who have believed deeply in me, (and some of whom, by the way, until I consented to run might think that they wisht me to run) would nevertheless have a feeling of disappointment if I did try to occupy the Presidency for three consecutive terms, to hold it longer than it was deemed wise that Washington should hold it. . . .

Retrenching

Roosevelt might have felt differently had he not believed that his hand-picked successor, William Howard Taft, was a very stout version of himself. This assumption, however, proved to be poor judgment, for although Taft believed in Roosevelt's reforms, he did not have Roosevelt's flair nor did he approve of all Roosevelt's methods. Somewhat uncertainly, and with a sense of foreboding—as the letter to T. R., below, indicates—Taft set about building a legal structure to support the Roosevelt ideas.

My dear Theodore:

If I followed my impulse, I should still say "My dear Mr. President." I cannot overcome the habit. When I am addressed as "Mr. President," I turn to see whether you are not at my elbow. When I read in the newspaper of a conference between the speaker and the President, or between Senator Aldrich and the President, I wonder what the subject of the conference was, and can hardly identify the report with the fact that I had had a talk with the two gentlemen. . . .

Many questions have arisen since the inauguration with respect to which I should like to have consulted you, but I have forborne to interrupt your well-earned quiet and to take up your time when it must have been so much occupied with preparation for your long trip. . . .

. . . Of course I have not the prestige which you had or the popular support in any such measure as you had to enable you to put through the legislation which was so remarkable in your first Congress; but I am not attempting quite as much as you did then, and I am hopeful that what I do offer will be accepted and put through. . . .

I want you to know that I do nothing in the Executive Office without considering what you would do under the same circumstances and without having in a sense a mental talk with you over the pros and cons of the situation. I have not the facility for educating the public as you had through talks with correspondents, and so I fear that a large part of the public will feel as if I had fallen away from your ideals; but you know me better and will understand that I am still working away on the same old plan and hope to realize in some measure the results that we both hold valuable and worth striving for. I can never forget that the power that I now exercise was a voluntary transfer from you to me, and that I am under obligation to you to see to it that your judgment in selecting me as your successor and in bringing about the succession shall be vindicated. . . .

Because effective laws did not exist, Roosevelt had operated by executive fiat in the area of conservation of land and natural resources. Taft discussed the matter in a special message to Congress on January 14, 1910.

. . . The present statutes, except so far as they dispose of the precious metals and the purely agricultural lands, are not adapted to carry out the modern view of the best disposition of public lands to private ownership, under conditions offering on the one hand sufficient inducement to private capital to take them over for proper development, with restrictive conditions on the other which shall secure to the public that character of control which will prevent a monopoly or misuse of the lands or their products. The power of the Secretary of the Interior to withdraw from the operation of existing statutes tracts of land the disposition of which under such statutes would be detrimental to the public interest, is not clear or satisfactory. This power has been exercised in the interest of the public, with the hope that Congress might affirm the action of the Executive by laws adapted to the new conditions. Unfortunately, Congress has not thus far fully acted on the recommendations of the Executive, and the question as to what the Executive is to do is, under the circumstances, full of difficulty. It seems to me that it is the duty of Congress now, by a statute, to validate the withdrawals which have been made by the Secretary of the Interior and the President, and to authorize the Secretary of the Interior temporarily to withdraw lands pending submission to Congress of recommendations as to legislation to meet conditions or emergencies as they arise. . . .

The Tariff

Taft's approach did not please his mentor, who ran against him in 1912. Both lost to Woodrow Wilson, however. Roosevelt had avoided tariff reform as President. Taft had not, but he had run head on into a conservative Congress and had achieved relatively little. The protective tariff was a campaign issue in 1912, and when Wilson and the Democrats won, they moved to abolish protection. To dramatize his concern, Wilson broke a long-standing precedent on April 8, 1913, when he delivered his tariff message to Congress in person.

I am very glad indeed to have this opportunity to address the two Houses directly and to verify for myself the impression that the President of the United States is a person, not a mere department of the Government hailing Congress from some isolated island of jealous power, sending messages, not speaking naturally and with his own voice—that he is a human being trying to cooperate with other human beings in a common service. After this pleasant experience I shall feel quite normal in all our dealings with one another.

I have called the Congress together in extraordinary session because a duty was laid upon the party now in power at the recent elections which it ought to perform promptly, in order that the burden carried by the people under existing law may be lightened as soon as possible and in order, also, that the business interests of the country may not be kept too long in suspense as to what the fiscal changes are to be to which they will be required to adjust themselves. It is clear to the whole country that the tariff duties must be altered. They must be changed to meet the radical alteration in the conditions of our economic life which the country has witnessed within the last generation. . . .

. . . We long ago passed beyond the modest notion of "protecting" the industries of the country and moved boldly forward to the idea that they were entitled to the direct patronage of the Government. For a long time—a time so long that the men now active in public policy hardly remember the conditions that preceded it—we have sought in our tariff schedules to give each group of manufacturers or producers what they themselves thought that they needed in order to maintain a practically exclusive market as against the rest of the world. Consciously or unconsciously, we have built up a set of privileges and exemptions from competition behind which it was easy by any, even the crudest, forms of combination to organize monopoly; until at last nothing is normal, nothing is obliged to stand the tests of efficiency and economy, in our world of big business, but everything thrives by concerted arrangement. Only new principles of action will save us from a final hard crystallization of monopoly and a complete loss of the influences that quicken enterprise and keep independent energy alive.

It is plain what those principles must be. We must abolish everything that bears even the semblance of privilege or of any kind of artificial advantage, and put our business men and producers under the stimulation of a constant necessity to be efficient, economical, and enterprising, masters of competitive supremacy, better workers and merchants than any in the world. Aside from the duties laid upon articles which we do not, and probably can not, produce, therefore, and the duties laid upon luxuries and merely for the sake of the revenues they yield, the object of the tariff duties henceforth laid must be effective competition, the whetting of American wits by contest with the wits of the rest of the world. . . .

Safe For Democracy

The Underwood Tariff, passed that October, markedly lowered duties and provided for a graduated income tax to supply the revenue that would be lost thereby. In December a banking and currency reform act was signed into law. But Wilson gradually found his attention being drawn away from domestic problems and toward the war in Europe. The United States, treated increasingly by Germany as a belligerent, showed considerable forbearance; but at last, just after his inauguration for a second term, President Wilson responded to the German submarine war on neutral shipping by asking Congress, on April 2, 1917, to declare war.

. . . American ships have been sunk, American lives taken, in ways which it has stirred us very deeply to learn of, but the ships and people of other neutral and friendly nations have been sunk and overwhelmed in the waters in the same way. There has been no discrimination. The challenge is to all

mankind. Each nation must decide for itself how it will meet it. The choice we make for ourselves must be made with a moderation of counsel and a temperateness of judgment befitting our character and our motives as a nation. We must put excited feeling away. Our motive will not be revenge or the victorious assertion of the physical might of the nation, but only the vindication of right, of human right, of which we are only a single champion.

When I addressed the Congress on the twenty-sixth of February last I thought that it would suffice to assert our neutral rights with arms, our right to use the seas against unlawful interference, our right to keep our people safe against unlawful violence. But armed neutrality, it now appears, is impracticable. Because submarines are in effect outlaws when used as the German submarines have been used against merchant shipping, it is impossible to defend ships against their attacks as the law of nations has assumed that merchantmen would defend themselves against privateers or cruisers, visible craft giving chase upon the open sea. . . . Armed neutrality is ineffectual enough at best; in such circumstances and in the face of such pretensions it is worse than ineffectual; it is likely only to produce what it was meant to prevent; it is practically certain to draw us into the war without either the rights or the effectiveness of belligerents. There is one choice we cannot make, we are incapable of making: we will not choose the path of submission and suffer the most sacred rights of our nation and our people to be ignored or violated. The wrongs against which we now array ourselves are no common wrongs: they cut to the very roots of human life.

With a profound sense of the solemn and even tragical character of the step I am taking and of the grave responsibilities which it involves, but in unhesitating obedience to what I deem my constitutional duty, I advise that the Congress declare the recent course of the Imperial German Government to be in fact nothing less than war against the government and people of the United States; that it formally accept the status of belligerent which has thus been thrust upon it; and that it take immediate steps not only to put the country in a more thorough state of defense but also to exert all its power and employ all its resources to bring the Government of the German Empire to terms and end the war. . . .

We are accepting this challenge of hostile purpose

because we know that in such a government, following such methods, we can never have a friend; and that in the presence of its organized power, always lying in wait to accomplish we know not what purpose, there can be no assured security for the democratic governments of the world. . . . The world must be made safe for democracy. Its peace must be planted upon the tested foundations of political liberty. We have no selfish ends to serve. We desire no conquest, no dominion. We seek no indemnities for ourselves, no material compensation for the sacrifices we shall freely make. We are but one of the champions of the rights of mankind. We shall be satisfied when those rights have been made as secure as the faith and the freedom of nations can make them. . . .

The Pendulum Swings Back

The war over, Wilson assumed the role of world leader with courage and enthusiasm. But he tried to cram the Treaty of Versailles and the League of Nations down the throat of a Senate that would have preferred to take it in small bites, if at all. One ultimate result was a diminution of the Executive that lasted fourteen years. More immediate consequences were an impassioned wrangle between Wilson and the Senate, in which both sides appealed to the electorate in speaking tours, and the nearly fatal illness of the exhausted President.

A Disabled President

Aboard the presidential train on September 26, 1919, Wilson fell ill, possibly suffering a slight stroke. Rushed back to the Capital, he was felled by another stroke on October 2, and for weeks those who were permitted to know the seriousness of the situation despaired for his life. The nation faced critical postwar problems, but the President was in no condition to deal with them. Secretary of State Robert Lansing, already out of favor for daring to consider compromise on the treaty issue, decided that despite the difficulties presented by the Tyler succession precedent, Vice President Thomas R. Marshall should stand in for the Chief Executive. Wilson's secretary, Joseph Tumulty, later told part of the story.

. . . A few days after the President returned from the West and lay seriously ill at the White House, with physicians and nurses gathered about his bed, Mr. Lansing sought a private audience with me in the Cabinet Room. He informed me that he had called diplomatically to suggest that in view of the incapacity of the President we should arrange to call in the Vice-President to act in his stead as soon as possible, reading to me from a book which he had brought from the State Department . . . the following clause of the United States Constitution:

In case of the removal of the President from office, or his death, resignation, or inability to discharge the powers and duties of the said office, the same shall devolve upon the Vice-President.

Upon reading this, I coldly turned to Mr. Lansing and said: "Mr. Lansing, the Constitution is not a dead letter with the White House. I have read the Constitution and do not find myself in need of any tutoring at your hands of the provision you have just read." When I asked Mr. Lansing the question as to who should certify to the disability of the President, he intimated that that would be a job for either Doctor Grayson or myself. I immediately grasped the full significance of what he intimated and said: "You may rest assured that while Woodrow Wilson is lying in the White House on the broad of his back I will not be a party to ousting him. He has been too kind, too loyal, and too wonderful to me to receive such treatment at my hands." Just as I uttered this statement Doctor Grayson appeared in the Cabinet Room and I turned to him and said: "And I am sure that Doctor Grayson will never certify to his disability. Will you, Grayson?" Doctor Grayson left no doubt in Mr. Lansing's mind that he would not do as Mr. Lansing suggested. I then notified Mr. Lansing that if anybody outside of the White House circle attempted to certify to the President's disability, that Grayson and I would stand together and repudiate it. I added that if the President were in a condition to know of this episode he would, in my opinion, take decisive measures. That ended the interview. . . .

Wilson did not step aside, nor did he become well enough to function in any meaningful way as President for several months. He never made a complete recovery.

Enlarging the Suffrage

The Nineteenth Amendment, giving American women the right to vote, was declared ratified on August 26, 1920.

The right of citizens of the United States to vote shall not be denied or abridged by the United States or by any State on account of sex.

Congress shall have power to enforce this article by appropriate legislation.

Scandal

Warren G. Harding, whose handsomeness was noted by the new women voters, was elected President in 1920. The personal tragedy of his administration ended with his death in the summer of 1923. Secretary of Commerce Herbert Hoover later recalled his last days:

. . . In June of 1923 I was in the West on an inspection trip. One day I received a telegram from the President saying that he had decided to change the personnel which had been announced as accompanying him on his forthcoming trip to Alaska, and asking if Mrs. Hoover and I would join the party. He added that the other guests would be Speaker Gillett [Frederick H. Gillett] of the House, Secretary of Agriculture Wallace [Henry Cantwell Wallace, father of Franklin Roosevelt's future Vice President], Secretary of the Interior [Hubert] Work, Admiral [Hugh] Rodman, and a respectable gentleman from Ohio named Malcolm Jennings, with their wives. I was naturally surprised, as it had been announced that Daugherty [Harry Daugherty, the Attorney General], Jesse Smith, and others of his cronies were to be the guests. Mrs. Hoover and I joined the party at Tacoma on July 3. . . .

One day after lunch when we were a few days out,

Harding asked me to come to his cabin. He plumped at me the question: "If you knew of a great scandal in our administration, would you for the good of the country and the party expose it publicly or would you bury it?" My natural reply was, "Publish it, and at least get credit for integrity on your side." He remarked that this method might be politically dangerous. I asked for more particulars. He said that he had received some rumors of irregularities, centering around Smith, in connection with cases in the Department of Justice. He had followed the matter up and finally sent for Smith. After a painful session he told Smith that he would be arrested in the morning. Smith went home, burned all his papers, and committed suicide. Harding gave me no information about what Smith had been up to. I asked what Daugherty's relations to the affair were. He abruptly dried up and never raised the question again.

The President grew more nervous as the trip continued. Despite his natural genius for geniality, he was now obviously forcing gaiety. He sought for excitement from the receptions, parades, and speeches at every port, and all along the railway to Fairbanks. To the rest of us, these events were at least some relief from the everlasting bridge game. . . .

On July 27, Hoover related, President Harding stopped in Seattle, Washington, for receptions and speeches.

. . . Again the crowds were enthusiastic. But Daugherty turned up and had an hour with him. In the afternoon we went to the Stadium, where the President was to deliver the speech on Alaska. There were sixty thousand cheering people. I sat directly behind him. When he was about half through his address he began to falter, dropped the manuscript, and grasped the desk. I picked up the scattered pages from the floor, gave him the next few quickly, and, knowing the text, sorted out the rest while he was speaking. He managed to get through the speech. As soon as he finished, Speaker Gillett, Secretary Work, the White House physician, Dr. Sawyer [Charles E. Sawyer], and I hustled him to the special train, put him to bed, and canceled the engagements for the evening. . . .

After a report from Dr. Sawyer that the President was suffering from some bad sea food and that he would require two days to recover, we announced it to the press and canceled the engagements in Port-

Caricaturists usually depicted former professor Woodrow Wilson (left) as a schoolmaster and Warren G. Harding (center) as either an average fellow or a Roman senator in a toga; President Herbert Hoover (right) was portrayed as stout and upright.

land and directed the train to run through to San Francisco.

The next morning we were somewhere in southern Oregon when Dr. Joel Boone, a very competent young naval surgeon who had accompanied the party to look after the guests and crew, came to me and stated that he believed that the President was suffering from something worse than digestive upset, but that Dr. Sawyer would not have it otherwise. Boone was much alarmed, so I took him to Secretary Work, who had been a physician in his younger days. Work insisted on going into the President's room and soon sent for Boone. They came out and asked me to arrange that some heart specialists should meet the train in San Francisco. . . .

. . . The doctors, despite Sawyer, at once diagnosed the case as a heart attack. In their view, it was most serious; and I therefore called Secretary Hughes [Secretary of State Charles E. Hughes] and told him it might be desirable for him to keep in touch with Vice President Coolidge. . . .

Then Harding seemed to rally, and on August 1 Hoover phoned Hughes to tell him the crisis had been passed.

That evening, however, while Mrs. Harding was reading him a magazine article, the nurse saw he had broken out with perspiration. Throwing back the

blankets, she began to bathe his chest, when she perceived that he was dying. . . . The doctors could do nothing—in a few minutes he was dead. The cause was undoubtedly a heart attack. . . . People do not die from a broken heart, but people with bad hearts may reach the end much sooner from great worries. . . .

Impending Disaster

Harding's successor Calvin Coolidge had a conservative attitude toward his office. Watching a stock market that seemed desperately in need of regulation, he waited for the proper authorities to act, and spoke in contradiction of his own views. Following is the recollection of H. Parker Willis, Coolidge's cousin, about a visit he had with the Chief Executive at a time when the large amount of brokers' loans to stock speculators was causing considerable alarm in the nation's financial community.

After the business which we had had in hand had been disposed of, Mr. Coolidge invited me to come back to luncheon. I did so, and after luncheon sat down with him in his study for a while, and he asked me a number of questions about pending financial affairs. It so happened that two or three days before that he had given out at the White House a statement that brokers' loans were not at all too large. On the occasion of this visit to Washington I had been testifying before the Senate committee that I thought they were very much too large. President Coolidge . . . remarked that my opinion had seemed to show a great difference from his, but he added:

"If I were to give my own personal opinion about it, I should say that any loan made for gambling in stocks was an 'excessive loan.' "

I replied: "I wish very much, Mr. President, that you had been willing to say that instead of making the public statement you did."

"Why did you say that?" Mr. Coolidge queried.

"Simply because I think it would have had a tremendous effect in repressing an unwholesome speculation, with which, I now see, you have no sympathy."

Mr. Coolidge thought this over for a moment or so and then he said: "Well, I regard myself as the representative of the government and not as an individual. When technical matters come up I feel called on to refer them to the proper department of the government which has some information about them and then, unless there is some good reason, I use this information as a basis for whatever I have to say; but that does not prevent me from thinking what I please as an individual."

Depression

The Great Depression was as serious a crisis as America had ever faced. A revolutionary change in approach was called for, but President Hoover chose to place responsibility for most of that change on the individual citizen working through local institutions. His annual messages brimmed with assurances that this course was right and effective. The following selection is from his State of the Union address of December, 1932.

. . . It seems to me appropriate upon this occasion to make certain general observations upon the principles which must dominate the solution of problems now pressing upon the Nation. Legislation in response to national needs will be effective only if every such act conforms to a complete philosophy of the people's purposes and destiny. Ours is a distinctive government with a unique history and background, consciously dedicated to specific ideals of liberty and

to a faith in the inviolable sanctity of the individual human spirit. Furthermore, the continued existence and adequate functioning of our government in preservation of ordered liberty and stimulation of progress depends upon the maintenance of State, local, institutional, and individual sense of responsibility. We have builded a system of individualism peculiarly our own which must not be forgotten in any governmental acts, for from it have grown greater accomplishments than those of any other nation.

On the social and economic sides, the background of our American system and the motivation of progress is essentially that we should allow free play of social and economic forces as far as will not limit equality of opportunity and as will at the same time stimulate the initiative and enterprise of our people. In the maintenance of this balance the Federal Government can permit of no privilege to any person or group. It should act as a regulatory agent and not as a participant in economic and social life. The moment the Government participates, it becomes a competitor with the people. As a competitor it becomes at once a tyranny in whatever direction it may touch. We have around us numerous such experiences, no one of which can be found to have justified itself except in cases where the people as a whole have met forces beyond their control, such as those of the Great War and this great depression, where the full powers of the Federal Government must be exerted to protect the people. But even these must be limited to an emergency sense and must be promptly ended when these dangers are overcome. . . .

. . . I would emphasize again that social and economic solutions, as such, will not avail to satisfy the aspirations of the people unless they conform with the traditions of our race, deeply grooved in their sentiments through a century and a half of struggle for ideals of life that are rooted in religion and fed from purely spiritual springs.

Inauguration Day

The Twentieth Amendment was sent to the states on March 2, 1932, and was ratified on February 6, 1933.

Section 1. The terms of the President and Vice-President shall end at noon on the 20th day of

January, and the terms of Senators and Representatives at noon on the 3d day of January, of the years in which such terms would have ended if this article had not been ratified; and the terms of their successors shall then begin.

Section 2. The Congress shall assemble at least once in every year, and such meeting shall begin at noon on the 3d day of January, unless they shall by law appoint a different day.

Section 3. If, at the time fixed for the beginning of the term of the President, the President elect shall have died, the Vice-President elect shall become President. If a President shall not have been chosen before the time fixed for the beginning of his term, or if the President elect shall have failed to qualify, then the Vice-President elect shall act as President until a President shall have qualified; and the Congress may by law provide for the case wherein neither a President elect nor a Vice-President elect shall have qualified, declaring who shall then act as President, or the manner in which one who is to act shall be selected, and such person shall act accordingly until a President or Vice-President shall have qualified.

Section 4. The Congress may by law provide for the case of the death of any of the persons from whom the House of Representatives may choose a President whenever the right of choice shall have devolved upon them, and for the case of the death of any of the persons from whom the Senate may choose a Vice-President whenever the right of choice shall have devolved upon them. . . .

Recovery and War

Hoover had been confident of national recovery—but in a platitudinous, laissez-faire fashion. Franklin Delano Roosevelt reinforced his sense of assurance with highly visible experiment and action. By the time the United States was called upon to enter World War II, it had found its footing again; President Roosevelt, who was deeply identified with American resilience, seemed the ideal man to lead the country through its newest crisis, and he remained the Chief Executive until he died.

The Whole Truth

Roosevelt quickly created an atmosphere of personal communication, of partnership with his countrymen, which was to be the hallmark of his Presidency. Not only did he act; he also explained himself and voiced his confidence often. Below are selections from his first Inaugural Address, delivered on March 4, 1933.

I am certain that my fellow Americans expect that on my induction into the Presidency I will address them with a candor and a decision which the present situation of our Nation impels. This is preeminently the time to speak the truth, the whole truth, frankly and boldly. Nor need we shrink from honestly facing conditions in our country to-day. This great Nation will endure as it has endured, will revive and will prosper. So, first of all, let me assert my firm belief that the only thing we have to fear is fear itself—nameless, unreasoning, unjustified terror which paralyzes needed efforts to convert retreat into advance. In every dark hour of our national life a leadership of frankness and vigor has met with that understanding and support of the people themselves which is essential to victory. I am convinced that you will again give that support to leadership in these critical days.

In such a spirit on my part and on yours we face our common difficulties. They concern, thank God, only material things. Values have shrunken to fantastic levels; taxes have risen; our ability to pay has fallen; government of all kinds is faced by serious curtailment of income; the means of exchange are frozen in the currents of trade; the withered leaves of industrial enterprise lie on every side; farmers find no markets for their produce; the savings of many years in thousands of families are gone.

More important, a host of unemployed citizens face the grim problem of existence, and an equally great number toil with little return. Only a foolish optimist can deny the dark realities of the moment.

Yet our distress comes from no failure of substance. We are stricken by no plague of locusts. . . . Plenty is at our doorstep, but a generous use of it languishes in the very sight of the supply. Primarily this is because the rulers of the exchange of mankind's goods have failed, through their own stubbornness and their own incompetence, have admitted their failure, and abdicated. Practices of the unscrupulous money changers stand indicted in the court of public opinion, rejected by the hearts and minds of men.

True they have tried, but their efforts have been cast in the pattern of an outworn tradition. Faced by failure of credit they have proposed only the lending of more money. Stripped of the lure of profit by which to induce our people to follow their false leadership, they have resorted to exhortations, pleading tearfully for restored confidence. They know only the rules of a generation of self-seekers. They have no vision, and when there is no vision the people perish. . . .

Restoration calls . . . not for changes in ethics alone. This Nation asks for action, and action now. . . .

Our greatest primary task is to put people to work. This is no unsolvable problem if we face it wisely and courageously. It can be accomplished in part by direct recruiting by the Government itself, treating the task as we would treat the emergency of a war, but at the same time, through this employment, accomplishing greatly needed projects to stimulate and reorganize the use of our natural resources.

Hand in hand with this we must frankly recognize the overbalance of population in our industrial centers and, by engaging on a national scale in a redistribution, endeavor to provide a better use of the land for those best fitted for the land. The task can be helped by definite efforts to raise the values of agricultural products and with this the power to purchase the output of our cities. It can be helped by preventing realistically the tragedy of the growing loss through foreclosure of our small homes and our farms. It can be helped by insistence that the Federal, State, and local governments act forthwith on the demand that their cost be drastically reduced. It can be helped by the unifying of relief activities which to-day are often scattered, uneconomical, and unequal. It can be helped by national planning for and supervision of all forms of transportation and of communications and other utilities which have a definitely public character. There are many ways in which it can be helped, but it can never be helped merely by talking about it. We must act and act quickly.

Finally, in our progress toward a resumption of work we require two safeguards against a return of the evils of the old order; there must be a strict

A 1935 Supreme Court decision put an end to the National Recovery Administration and its familiar blue eagle (above).

supervision of all banking and credits and investments; there must be an end to speculation with other people's money, and there must be provision for an adequate but sound currency.

There are the lines of attack. I shall presently urge upon a new Congress in special session detailed measures for their fulfillment, and I shall seek the immediate assistance of the several States. . . .

But in the event that the Congress shall fail to [act], and in the event that the national emergency is still critical, I shall not evade the clear course of duty that will then confront me. I shall ask the Congress for the one remaining instrument to meet the crisis—broad Executive power to wage a war against the emergency, as great as the power that would be given to me if we were in fact invaded by a foreign foe. . . .

Reforming the Court

Program after program was turned out by the New Deal production line as Roosevelt sought to spur economic recovery. Congress cooperated throughout his first term, and did not begin to put on the brakes until the President overreached himself politically. The New Deal's main stumbling block had been the Supreme Court, which in 1935 began voiding important progressive legislation. President Roosevelt decided to try to reform the Court, but he sent the proposed legislation to Congress without even discussing it with Democratic leaders there—and then compounded the error by intervening in a fight over the selection of a Senate Majority Leader. On March 9, 1937, the President took his case to the American people by means of another radio broadcast.

. . . I am reminded of that evening in March, four years ago, when I made my first radio report to you. We were then in the midst of the great banking crisis.

Soon after, with the authority of the Congress, we asked the Nation to turn over all of its privately held gold, dollar for dollar, to the Government of the United States.

Today's recovery proves how right that policy was.

But when, almost two years later, it came before the Supreme Court its constitutionality was upheld only by a five-to-four vote. The change of one vote would have thrown all the affairs of this great Nation back into hopeless chaos. In effect, four Justices ruled that the right under a private contract to exact a pound of flesh was more sacred than the main objectives of the Constitution to establish an enduring Nation. . . .

. . . [Long ago] the Court itself admitted that [denying a law's constitutionality] was an extraordinary power to exercise and through Mr. Justice Washington laid down this limitation upon it: "It is but a decent respect due to the wisdom, the integrity and the patriotism of the legislative body, by which any law is passed, to presume in favor of its validity until its violation of the Constitution is proved beyond all reasonable doubt."

But since the rise of the modern movement for social and economic progress through legislation, the Court has more and more often and more and more boldly asserted a power to veto laws passed by the Congress and State Legislatures in complete disregard of this original limitation.

In the last four years the sound rule of giving statutes the benefit of all reasonable doubt has been cast aside. The Court has been acting not as a judicial body, but as a policy-making body. . . .

What is my proposal? It is simply this: whenever a Judge or Justice of any Federal Court has reached the age of seventy and does not avail himself of the opportunity to retire on a pension, a new member shall be appointed by the President then in office, with the approval, as required by the Constitution, of the Senate of the United States.

That plan has two chief purposes. By bringing into the judicial system a steady and continuing stream of new and younger blood, I hope, first, to make the administration of all Federal justice speedier and, therefore, less costly; secondly, to bring to the decision of social and economic problems younger men who have had personal experience and contact with modern facts and circumstances under which average men have to live and work. This plan will save our national Constitution from hardening of the judicial arteries. . . .

The Third Term

With the flames of war burning in Europe and Asia, F. D. R. believed that the nation needed a liberal, experienced President. He therefore agreed to run for a third term, thereby breaking the precedent set by Washington. In its issue of July 29, 1940, Newsweek *noted some of the reactions to President Roosevelt's decision.*

Renomination of President Roosevelt for a third term was greeted with mixed reaction by the nation's press, cheers from Latin America, China, and Great Britain, and sneers from the Axis Powers.

In the United States, The St. Louis Globe-Democrat saw a "revolutionary tendency to do away with the barriers to the encroachment of despotic powers." The Indianapolis Star regretted that "from being President of all the people, he defies tradition to become the champion of those to whom partisan success weighs more than national safeguard." The New York Times added: "There are large numbers of independent voters to whom the doctrine of any man's indispensability is distasteful, and for whom the third-term issue will be important and decisive."

In the solidly Democratic South, The Raleigh (N.C.) News and Observer declared "the people want him," and The Birmingham (Ala.) Age-Herald insisted "we have the right to decide that departure from that [third-term] tradition will better serve our basic American ideals and objectives." The New

Orleans Times-Picayune charged that "the break-down of the time-tried and tested barrier against third terms imperils the nation's free institutions and menaces democracy itself."

Across the Atlantic, the German and Italian press dismissed Mr. Roosevelt's renomination in a few words. The Nazi Foreign Office organ Diplomatische Politische Korrispondenz termed it "no surprise in the case of a man who loves power as he does." . . .

Pearl Harbor

Christmas, 1941, was less than three weeks away when the tidal wave of war struck America. Roosevelt addressed Congress and a stunned nation on December 8:

Yesterday, December 7, 1941—a date which will live in infamy—the United States of America was suddenly and deliberately attacked by naval and air forces of the Empire of Japan.

The United States was at peace with that nation and, at the solicitation of Japan, was still in conversation with its government and its Emperor looking toward the maintenance of peace in the Pacific. Indeed, one hour after Japanese air squadrons had commenced bombing in Oahu, the Japanese ambassador to the United States and his colleague delivered to the Secretary of State a formal reply to a recent American message. While this reply stated that it seemed useless to continue the existing diplomatic negotiations, it contained no threat or hint of war or armed attack.

It will be recorded that the distance of Hawaii from Japan makes it obvious that the attack was deliberately planned many days or even weeks ago. During the intervening time the Japanese Government has deliberately sought to deceive the United States by false statements and expressions of hope for continued peace.

The attack yesterday on the Hawaiian Islands has caused severe damage to American naval and military forces. Very many American lives have been lost. In addition American ships have been reported torpedoed on the high seas between San Francisco and Honolulu.

Yesterday the Japanese government also launched an attack against Malaya.

Last night Japanese forces attacked Hong Kong.

Last night Japanese forces attacked Guam.

Last night Japanese forces attacked the Philippine Islands.

Last night the Japanese attacked Wake Island.

This morning the Japanese attacked Midway Island.

Japan has, therefore, undertaken a surprise offensive extending throughout the Pacific area. The facts of yesterday speak for themselves. The people of the United States have already formed their opinions and well understand the implications to the very life and safety of our nation.

As Commander-in-Chief of the Army and Navy, I have directed that all measures be taken for our defense.

Always will we remember the character of the onslaught against us.

No matter how long it may take us to overcome this premeditated invasion, the American people in their righteous might will win through to absolute victory.

I believe I interpret the will of the Congress and of the people when I assert that we will not only defend ourselves to the uttermost but will make very certain that this form of treachery shall never endanger us again.

Hostilities exist. There is no blinking at the fact that our people, our territory and our interests are in grave danger.

With confidence in our armed forces—with the unbounding determination of our people—we will gain the inevitable triumph—so help us God.

I ask that the Congress declare that since the unprovoked and dastardly attack by Japan on Sunday, December 7th, a state of war has existed between the United States and the Japanese Empire.

United Nations

America and her allies were winning the war and also thinking about ways to prevent future conflicts. On October 21, 1944, Roosevelt expressed his views on maintaining peace to the Foreign Policy Association:

. . . The power which this Nation has attained—the political, the economic, the military, and above all the moral power—has brought to us the responsibility, and with it the opportunity, for leadership in the community of Nations. It is our own best interest, and in the name of peace and humanity, this Nation cannot, must not, and will not shirk that responsibility.

Now, there are some who hope to see a structure of peace completely set up immediately, with all the apartments assigned to everybody's satisfaction, with the telephones in, and the plumbing complete—the heating system, and the electric ice boxes all functioning perfectly, all furnished with linen and silver—and with the rent prepaid.

The United Nations have not yet produced such a comfortable dwelling place. But we have achieved a very practical expression of a common purpose on the part of four great Nations, who are now united to wage this war, that they will embark together after the war on a greater and more difficult enterprise, an enterprise of waging peace. We will embark on it with all the peace-loving Nations of the world—large and small.

And our objective, as I stated ten days ago, is to complete the organization of the United Nations without delay, before hostilities actually cease.

Peace, like war, can succeed only where there is a will to enforce it, and where there is available power to enforce it.

The Council of the United Nations must have the power to act quickly and decisively to keep the peace by force, if necessary. A policeman would not be a very effective policeman if, when he saw a felon break into a house, he had to go to the Town Hall and call a town meeting to issue a warrant before the felon could be arrested.

So to my simple mind it is clear that, if the world organization is to have any reality at all, our American representative must be endowed in advance by the people themselves, by constitutional means through their representatives in the Congress, with authority to act.

If we do not catch the international felon when we have our hands on him, if we let him get away with his loot because the Town Council has not passed an ordinance authorizing his arrest, then we are *not* doing our share to prevent another world war. I think, and I have had some experience, that the people of this Nation want their Government to work, they want their Government to act, and not

merely to talk, whenever and wherever there is a threat to world peace. . . .

The Bomb

On April 12, 1945, Roosevelt died. His successor Harry S. Truman was astonished to learn for the first time of the existence of an atomic bomb, then almost ready for use. The decision to employ the new weapon against Japan was his. On July 24, 1945, the following order was sent to the Pacific Theater by the War Department:

1. The 509 Composite Group, 20th Air Force will deliver its first special bomb as soon as weather will permit visual bombing after about 3 August 1945 on one of the targets: Hiroshima, Kokura, Niigata and Nagasaki. To carry military and civilian scientific personnel from the War Department to observe and record the effects of the explosion of the bomb, additional aircraft will accompany the airplane carrying

An Arizona newspaper cartoon in 1943 took a dim view of the wartime alliance of Roosevelt, Stalin, and Churchill.

the bomb. The observing planes will stay several miles distant from the point of impact of the bomb.

2. Additional bombs will be delivered on the above targets as soon as made ready by the project staff. Further instructions will be issued concerning targets other than those listed above. . . .

.

Succession

When Truman took office, the Secretary of State, Edward R. Stettinius, Jr., became next in line to the powers of the Presidency. He had never been elected to a public office, although he had been part of the Roosevelt administration since 1939; nor was he a seasoned diplomat, since Roosevelt had been more or less his own Secretary of State, especially after the resignation of Cordell Hull in 1944. This situation worried Truman. No man who had never had a constituency, he felt, should serve as Chief Executive. He assigned Stettinius to the United Nations and named a former congressman and senator, James F. Byrnes, to replace him. But Truman was still not satisfied. He believed that no President should be able to appoint his own potential successor. So he began a campaign to change the line of succession so that the Speaker of the House and the president pro tempore of the Senate preceded the Cabinet. The new succession bill became law on July 18, 1947.

Be it enacted by the Senate and House of Representatives of the United States of America in Congress assembled, That . . . if, by reason of death, resignation, removal from office, inability, or failure to qualify, there is neither a President nor Vice President to discharge the powers and duties of the office of President, then the Speaker of the House of Representatives shall, upon his resignation as Speaker and as Representative in Congress, act as President.

. . . The same rule shall apply in the case of the death, resignation, removal from office, or inability of an individual acting as President. . . .

. . . If, at the time when . . . a Speaker is to begin the discharge of the powers and duties of the office of President, there is no Speaker, or the Speaker fails to qualify as Acting President, then the President pro tempore of the Senate shall, upon his resignation as President pro tempore and as Senator, act as President.

. . . An individual [thus] acting as President . . . shall continue to act until the expiration of the then current Presidential term, except that—

(1) if his discharge of the powers and duties of the office is founded in whole or in part on the failure of both the President-elect and the Vice-President-elect to qualify, then he shall act only until a President or Vice President qualifies; and

(2) if his discharge of the powers and duties of the office is founded in whole or in part on the inability of the President or Vice President, then he shall act only until the removal of the disability of one of such individuals.

. . . If, by reason of death, resignation, removal from office, inability, or failure to qualify, there is no President pro tempore to act as President . . . then the officer of the United States who is highest on the following list, and who is not under disability to discharge the powers and duties of the office of President shall act as President: Secretary of State, Secretary of the Treasury, Secretary of War, Attorney General, Postmaster General, Secretary of the Navy, Secretary of the Interior, Secretary of Agriculture, Secretary of Commerce, Secretary of Labor.

. . . An individual acting as President under this subsection shall continue so to do until the expiration of the then current Presidential term, but not after a qualified and prior-entitled individual is able to act, except that the removal of the disability of an individual higher on the list contained in [the last] paragraph . . . or the ability to qualify on the part of an individual higher on such list shall not terminate his service. . . .

The Cold War

Twice the United States had been drawn by war into an active role in world affairs. But in the mid-1940's there could be none of the reversion to isolationism that had followed the first great war. Considering the crucial part that America had already played in defeating aggression, it was not surprising that the nation viewed itself, grimly, as an unofficial police force to the world. The wartime affection for Russia was quickly supplanted by bitter distrust, as its determination to extend communism became apparent. The President of the United States became the chief policeman, protecting countries undermined by the war or as yet undeveloped against the power and sometimes understandable appeal of communism. At the same time, the United States became self-conscious about its own image. Domestically, the contrast between American ideals and practice caused concern, and concern brought change, especially for American Negroes, who were demanding full equality.

The Truman Doctrine

At the end of World War II, the Soviet Union installed puppet governments in each of the Eastern European nations it had liberated. In Greece and Turkey, Russian-supported Communists threatened to subvert the established governments. The economic condition of both nations made a long-range solution necessary. Great Britain had once been able to give aid to Greece and Turkey, but could no longer do so. President Truman believed that the responsibility for providing financial and military aid had thus fallen to the United States, as he told Congress in a message in March, 1947:

. . . I am fully aware of the broad implications involved if the United States extends assistance to Greece and Turkey, and I shall discuss these implications with you at this time.

One of the primary objectives of the foreign policy of the United States is the creation of conditions in which we and other nations will be able to work out a way of life free from coercion. This was a fundamental issue in the war with Germany and Japan. Our victory was won over countries which sought to impose their will, and their way of life, upon other nations.

To ensure the peaceful development of nations, free from coercion, the United States has taken a leading part in establishing the United Nations. The United Nations is designed to make possible lasting freedom and independence for all its members. We shall not realize our objectives, however, unless we are willing to help free peoples to maintain their free institutions and their national integrity against aggressive movements that seek to impose upon them

totalitarian regimes. This is no more than a frank recognition that totalitarian regimes imposed upon free peoples, by direct or indirect aggression, undermine the foundations of international peace and hence the security of the United States. . . .

I believe that our help should be primarily through economic and financial aid which is essential to economic stability and orderly political processes. . . .

It is necessary only to glance at a map to realize that the survival and integrity of the Greek nation are of grave importance in a much wider situation. If Greece should fall under the control of an armed minority, the effect upon its neighbor, Turkey, would be immediate and serious. Confusion and disorder might well spread throughout the entire Middle East.

Moreover, the disappearance of Greece as an independent state would have a profound effect upon those countries in Europe whose peoples are struggling against great difficulties to maintain their freedoms and their independence while they repair the damages of war.

It would be an unspeakable tragedy if these countries, which have struggled so long against overwhelming odds, should lose that victory for which they sacrificed so much. Collapse of free institutions and loss of independence would be disastrous not only for them but for the world. Discouragement and possibly failure would quickly be the lot of neighboring peoples striving to maintain their freedom and independence.

Should we fail to aid Greece and Turkey in this fateful hour, the effect will be far reaching to the West as well as to the East. . . .

War in Korea

On June 25, 1950, Communist forces made another probe into free-world territory—South Korea. Two days later President Truman outlined the American response.

In Korea the Government forces, which were armed to prevent border raids and to preserve internal security, were attacked by invading forces from North Korea. The Security Council of the United Nations called upon the invading troops to cease hostilities and to withdraw to the 38th parallel. This they have not done, but on the contrary have pressed the attack. The Security Council called upon all members of the United Nations to render every assistance to the United Nations in the execution of this resolution. In these circumstances I have ordered United States air and sea forces to give the Korean Government troops cover and support. . . .

. . . I have ordered the 7th Fleet to prevent any attack on Formosa. As a corollary of this action I am calling upon the Chinese Government on Formosa to cease all air and sea operations against the mainland. The 7th Fleet will see that this is done. The determination of the future status of Formosa must await the restoration of security in the Pacific, a peace settlement with Japan, or consideration by the United Nations.

I have also directed that United States Forces in the Philippines be strengthened and that military assistance to the Philippine Government be accelerated.

I have similarly directed acceleration in the furnishing of military assistance to the forces of France and the Associated States of Indochina and the dispatch of a military mission to provide close working relations with those forces. . . .

The U.N. troops drove the North Koreans back almost to the Chinese border. Douglas MacArthur, the commanding general, did not expect the Chinese to enter the conflict, but enter it they did, and swept down the peninsula. Unlike President Truman, MacArthur did not agree with the United Nations' policy of not attacking Chinese territory, and involved himself increasingly in a public dispute on the issue—eventually in direct disobedience of orders. On April 11, 1951, Truman acted:

With deep regret I have concluded that General of the Army Douglas MacArthur is unable to give his wholehearted support to the policies of the United States Government and of the United Nations in matters pertaining to his official duties. In view of the specific responsibilities imposed upon me by the Constitution of the United States and the added responsibility which has been entrusted to me by the United Nations, I have decided that I must make a change of command in the Far East. I have, therefore, relieved General MacArthur of his commands and have designated Lt. Gen. Matthew B. Ridgway as his successor.

322

This Truman cartoon by Herblock was titled "The Tumult And The Shouting Dies; The Captains And The Kings Depart."

Full and vigorous debate on matters of national policy is a vital element in the constitutional system of our free democracy. It is fundamental, however, that military commanders must be governed by the policies and directives issued to them in the manner provided by our laws and Constitution. In time of crisis, this consideration is particularly compelling. . . .

No Third Term

In reaction against the four consecutive terms of F. D. R., the Republican Congress passed the Twenty-second Amendment, which was ratified on February 26, 1951.

No person shall be elected to the office of the President more than twice, and no person who has held the office of President, or acted as President, for more than two years of a term to which some other person was elected President shall be elected to the office of the President more than once.

But this Article shall not apply to any person holding the office of President when this Article was proposed by the Congress, and shall not prevent any person who may be holding the office of President, or acting as President, during the term within which this Article becomes operative from holding the office of President or acting as President during the remainder of such term.

Nuclear Responsibility

Knowledge of how to build nuclear weapons was bound to spread. Russia soon ended America's monopoly, and the world was haunted by the specter of a war to end not only war, but life as well. Arms were being stockpiled and other nations were joining the race; there was universal concern about radioactive fallout from nuclear tests in the atmosphere. The United Nations asked that the atomic powers try to scale down the competition. President Eisenhower responded for the United States in December, 1953, in a speech to the world organization.

. . . The United States, heeding the suggestion of the General Assembly of the United Nations, is instantly prepared to meet privately with such other countries as may be "principally involved," to seek "an acceptable solution" to the atomic armaments race which overshadows not only the peace, but the very life, of the world.

We shall carry into these private or diplomatic talks a new conception.

The United States would seek more than the mere reduction or elimination of atomic materials for military purposes.

It is not enough to take this weapon out of the hands of the soldiers. It must be put into the hands of those who will know how to strip its military casing and adapt it to the arts of peace. . . .

I therefore make the following proposals:

The Governments principally involved, to the extent permitted by elementary prudence, to begin now and continue to make joint contributions from their stockpiles of normal uranium and fissionable materials to an International Atomic Energy Agency. We would expect that such an agency would be set up under the aegis of the United Nations.

The ratios of contributions, the procedures and other details would properly be within the scope of the "private conversations" I have referred to earlier. . . .

The Atomic Energy Agency could be made responsible for the impounding, storage, and protection of the contributed fissionable and other materials. The ingenuity of our scientists will provide special safe conditions under which such a bank of fissionable material can be made essentially immune to surprise seizure.

The more important responsibility of this Atomic Energy Agency would be to devise methods whereby this fissionable material would be allocated to serve the peaceful pursuits of mankind. Experts would be mobilized to apply atomic energy to the needs of agriculture, medicine, and other peaceful activities. A special purpose would be to provide abundant electrical energy in the power-starved areas of the world. Thus the contributing powers would be dedicating some of their strength to serve the needs rather than the fears of mankind.

The United States would be more than willing—it would be proud to take up with others "principally involved" the development of plans whereby such peaceful use of atomic energy would be expedited. . . .

Little Rock

Eisenhower's greatest disappointment as President, he said later, was his failure to ease the nuclear crisis. But he had made a start upon which his successors could build. Domestically, his administration also saw another beginning: increased federal activity in securing civil rights for American Negroes. In 1954 the Supreme Court reversed an earlier ruling and declared that segregated public schools were unconstitutional. The President was apprehensive about imposing an emotional upheaval on the South, and did not throw the moral weight of his office behind desegregation until the fall of 1957, when Orval Faubus, the governor of Arkansas—in defiance of a federal court order—used the National Guard to preserve segregation in Little Rock high schools. On this bold challenge, Eisenhower acted.

. . . SECTION 1. I hereby authorize and direct the Secretary of Defense to order into the active military service of the United States as he may deem appropriate to carry out the purposes of this Order, any or all of the units of the National Guard of the United States and of the Air National Guard of the United States within the State of Arkansas to serve in the active military service of the United States for an indefinite period and until relieved by appropriate orders.

SEC. 2. The Secretary of Defense is authorized and directed to take all appropriate steps to enforce any orders of the United States District Court for the Eastern District of Arkansas for the removal of obstruction of justice in the State of Arkansas with respect to matters relating to enrollment and attendance at public schools in the Little Rock School District, Little Rock, Arkansas. In carrying out the provisions of this section, the Secretary of Defense is authorized to use the units, and members thereof, ordered into the active military service of the United States pursuant to Section 1 of this Order.

Sec. 3. In furtherance of the enforcement of the aforementioned orders of the United States District Court for the Eastern District of Arkansas, the Secretary of Defense is authorized to use such of the armed forces of the United States as he may deem necessary. . . .

Cuban Crisis

A détente between the United States and the Soviet Union seemed possible when John F. Kennedy became President. But shortly after his inauguration in 1961, Kennedy approved a plan conceived by the Eisenhower administration for the invasion of Communist Cuba by Cuban exiles. The operation failed completely, and the Russian government subsequently began supplying Cuba with technicians and intermediate-range missiles. When the United States discovered that the Caribbean island had become a Russian missile base, some Americans urged an immediate invasion of Cuba. Kennedy decided on a moderate first step to give the Russians an opportunity to back off gracefully; he announced an arms "quarantine" of Cuba, and ordered the Navy to intercept Soviet merchantmen and turn back any that carried weapons. The gamble worked; Chairman Khrushchev announced that the missiles would be removed. Kennedy quickly replied with a hopeful message about the future.

I am replying at once to your broadcast message of October twenty-eight, even though the official text has not yet reached me, because of the great importance I attach to moving forward promptly to the settlement of the Cuban crisis. I think that you and I, with our heavy responsibilities for the maintenance of peace, were aware that developments were approaching a point where events could have become unmanageable. So I welcome this message and consider it an important contribution to peace.

The distinguished efforts of Acting Secretary General U Thant have greatly facilitated both our tasks. I consider my letter to you of October twenty-seventh and your reply of today as firm undertakings on the part of both our governments which should be promptly carried out. I hope that the necessary measures can at once be taken through the United Nations, as your message says, so that the United States in turn will be able to remove the quarantine measures now in effect. I have already made arrangements to report all these matters to the Organization of American States, whose members share a deep interest in a genuine peace in the Caribbean area. . . .

Mr. Chairman, both of our countries have great unfinished tasks and I know that your people as well as those of the United States can ask for nothing better than to pursue them free from the fear of war. Modern science and technology have given us the possibility of making labor fruitful beyond anything that could have been dreamed of a few decades ago.

I agree with you that we must devote urgent attention to the problem of disarmament, as it relates to the whole world and also to critical areas. Perhaps now, as we step back from danger, we can together make real progress in this vital field. I think we should give priority to questions relating to the proliferation of nuclear weapons, on earth and in outer space, and to the great effort for a nuclear test ban. But we should also work hard to see if wider measures of disarmament can be agreed and put into operation at an early date. The United States Government will be prepared to discuss these questions urgently, and in a constructive spirit, at Geneva or elsewhere.

Test Ban Treaty

Eight months later the hope for a sustained peace was reinforced by a treaty. President Kennedy announced it in a broadcast to the nation on the night of July 26, 1963.

. . . In these years, the United States and the Soviet Union have frequently communicated suspicions and warnings to each other, but very rarely hope. Our representatives have met at the summit and at the brink; they have met in Washington and in Moscow, at the United Nations and in Geneva. But too often these meetings have produced only darkness, discord or disillusion.

Yesterday, a shaft of light cut into the darkness. Negotiations were concluded in Moscow on a treaty to ban all nuclear tests in the atmosphere, in outer space and under water. For the first time, an agreement has been reached on bringing the forces of nuclear destruction under international control—a goal first sought in 1946 when Bernard Baruch submitted our comprehensive plan to the members of the United Nations.

That plan, and many subsequent disarmament plans, large and small, have all been blocked by those opposed to international inspection. A ban on nuclear tests, however, requires on-the-spot inspection only for underground tests. This nation now possesses a variety of techniques to detect the nuclear tests of other nations which are conducted in the air or under water. For such tests produce unmistakable signs. . . .

The treaty initialed yesterday, therefore, is a limited treaty which permits continued underground testing and prohibits only those tests that we ourselves can police. It requires no control posts, no on-site inspection and no international body.

We should also understand that it has other limits as well. Any nation which signs the treaty will have an opportunity to withdraw if it finds that extraordinary events related to the subject matter of the treaty have jeopardized its supreme interests; and no nation's right to self-defense will in any way be impaired. Nor does this treaty mean an end to the threat of nuclear war. It will not reduce nuclear stockpiles; it will not halt the production of nuclear weapons; it will not restrict their use in time of war.

Nevertheless, this limited treaty will radically reduce the nuclear testing which would otherwise be conducted on both sides; it will prohibit the United States, the United Kingdom, the Soviet Union and all others who sign it from engaging in the atmospheric tests which have so alarmed mankind; and it offers to all the world a welcome sign of hope. . . .

An End to Poll Taxes

The Twenty-fourth Amendment, sent to the states in August, 1962, eliminated one bar to Negro voters. It was ratified after Kennedy's death, on January 23, 1964.

Section 1. The right of citizens of the United States to vote in any primary or other election for President or Vice President, for electors for President or Vice President, or for Senator or Representative in Congress, shall not be denied or abridged by the United States or any State by reason of failure to pay any poll tax or other tax.

Section 2. The Congress shall have the power to enforce this article by appropriate legislation.

The Tonkin Resolution

By August, 1964, several thousand American troops had been sent to South Vietnam to serve as military advisers. They were helping the South Vietnamese in their fight against Communist guerrillas, who were being aided by North Vietnam. That summer, United States ships cruising in the Gulf of Tonkin became targets for North Vietnamese torpedo boats. Kennedy's successor, Lyndon B. Johnson, ordered retaliatory air attacks on the North Vietnamese torpedo bases, and then asked Congress to authorize him to give whatever military aid he believed necessary to South Vietnam. On August 10, 1964, Congress passed the following resolution, later the subject of a heated debate.

. . . *Resolved by the Senate and House of Representatives of the United States of America in Congress assembled*, That the Congress approves and supports the determination of the President, as Commander in Chief, to take all necessary measures to repel any armed attack against the forces of the United States and to prevent further aggression.

SEC. 2. The United States regards as vital to its national interest and to world peace the maintenance of international peace and security in southeast Asia. Consonant with the Constitution of the United States and the Charter of the United Nations and in accordance with its obligations under the Southeast Asia Collective Defense Treaty, the United States is, therefore, prepared, as the President determines, to take all necessary steps, including the use of armed force, to assist any member or protocol state of the Southeast Asia Collective Defense Treaty requesting assistance in defense of its freedom.

SEC. 3. This resolution shall expire when the President shall determine that the peace and security of

'All I'm trying to do is to limit our conflict to this small area.'

Critical of United States Far Eastern policy in general and the war in Vietnam in particular, The Observer *of London viewed President Lyndon Baines Johnson as an unreasonable St. George who was toying dangerously with the restive dragon of Asia.*

the area is reasonably assured by international conditions created by action of the United Nations or otherwise, except that it may be terminated earlier by concurrent resolution of the Congress.

Death and Disability

When John F. Kennedy died, the two men in the line of succession immediately after Lyndon Johnson were both older than seventy, and were widely regarded as inappropriate presidential possibilities. Because Johnson had once had a heart attack, and because the nation had become tragically aware of the Chief Executive's vulnerability, the situation caused considerable worry. The need for a constitutional amendment dealing with presidential disability was also obvious; Eisenhower and Kennedy had worked out informal arrangements in letters to their Vice Presidents, but this was at best a makeshift solution. Congress therefore passed the Twenty-fifth Amendment, which was submitted to the states on July 6, 1965, and was ratified early in 1967.

Section 1. In case of the removal of the President from office or his death or resignation, the Vice President shall become President.

Section 2. Whenever there is a vacancy in the office of the Vice President, the President shall nominate a Vice President who shall take the office upon con-

firmation by a majority vote of both houses of Congress.

Section 3. Whenever the President transmits to the President pro tempore of the Senate and the Speaker of the House of Representatives his written declaration that he is unable to discharge the powers and duties of his office, and until he transmits to them a written declaration to the contrary, such powers and duties shall be discharged by the Vice President as Acting President.

Section 4. Whenever the Vice President and a majority of either the principal officers of the executive departments or of such other body as Congress may by law provide, transmit to the President pro tempore of the Senate and the Speaker of the House of Representatives their written declaration that the President is unable to discharge the powers and duties of his office, the Vice President shall immediately assume the powers and duties of the office as Acting President.

Thereafter, when the President transmits to the President pro tempore of the Senate and the Speaker of the House of Representatives his written declaration that no inability exists, he shall resume the powers and duties of his office unless the Vice President and a majority of either the principal officers of the executive department or of such other body as Congress may by law provide, transmit within four days to the President pro tempore of the Senate and the Speaker of the House of Representatives their written declaration that the President is unable to discharge the powers and duties of his office. Thereupon Congress shall decide the issue, assembling within 48 hours for that purpose if not in session. If the Congress, within 21 days after receipt of the latter written declaration, or, if Congress is not in session, within 21 days after Congress is required to assemble, determines by two-thirds vote of both houses that the President is unable to discharge the powers and duties of his office, the Vice President shall continue to discharge the same as Acting President; otherwise, the President shall resume the powers and duties of his office.

"We Shall Overcome"

As he said often, Lyndon Johnson wanted to be the President who brought a hope for a better life to all Americans who lacked decent housing, food, medical care, jobs, education, and—perhaps above all—the civil rights attendant to full citizenship. During a voter-registration drive in Selma, Alabama, early in 1965, local whites and government officials had tried to make the registration of Negroes as unpleasant and as difficult as possible. A white clergyman from Boston, who had gone to Selma to help the drive, was beaten on March ninth, and died two days later. On the fifteenth, President Johnson addressed Congress and his countrymen and, by using a line from a hymn identified with the civil rights movement—"We Shall Overcome"—dramatically made himself a champion of that cause.

Mr. Speaker, Mr. President, members of the Congress, I speak tonight for the dignity of man and the destiny of democracy.

I urge every member of both parties, Americans of all religions and of all colors, from every section of this country, to join me in that cause.

At times, history and fate meet at a single time in a single place to shape a turning point in man's unending search for freedom.

So it was at Lexington and Concord. So it was a century ago at Appomattox. So it was last week in Selma, Alabama.

There, long suffering men and women peacefully protested the denial of their rights as Americans. Many were brutally assaulted. One good man—a man of God—was killed.

There is no cause for pride in what has happened in Selma. There is no cause for self-satisfaction in the long denial of equal rights of millions of Americans. But there is cause for hope and for faith in our democracy in what is happening here tonight.

For the cries of pain and the hymns and protests of oppressed people have summoned into convocation all the majesty of this great Government—the Government of the greatest nation on earth.

Our mission is at once the oldest and the most basic of this country—to right wrong, to do justice, to serve man. . . .

The Constitution says that no person shall be kept from voting because of his race or his color. We have all sworn an oath before God to support and to defend that Constitution. We must now act in obedience to that oath.

Wednesday, I will send to Congress a law designed to eliminate illegal barriers to the right to vote. . . .

But even if we pass this bill the battle will not be over.

What happened in Selma is part of a far larger movement which reaches into every section and state of America. It is the effort of American Negroes to secure for themselves the full blessings of American life.

Their cause must be our cause too. Because it's not just Negroes, but really it's all of us who must overcome the crippling legacy of bigotry and injustice. And we shall overcome.

As a man whose roots go deeply into Southern soil, I know how agonizing racial feelings are. I know how difficult it is to reshape the attitudes and the structure of our society. But a century has passed—more than 100 years—since the Negro was freed.

And he is not fully free tonight. . . .

A century has passed since the day of promise, and the promise is unkept. The time of justice has now come, and I tell you that I believe sincerely that no force can hold it back. It is right in the eyes of man and God that it should come, and when it does, I think that day will brighten the lives of every American.

For Negroes are not the only victims. How many white children have gone uneducated? How many white families have lived in stark poverty? How many white lives have been scarred by fear, because we wasted energy and our substance to maintain the barriers of hatred and terror? . . .

These are the enemies: poverty, ignorance, disease. They are our enemies, not our fellow man, not our neighbor. And these enemies too—poverty, disease and ignorance—we shall overcome. . . .

My first job after college was as a teacher in Cotulla, Texas, in a small Mexican-American school. Few of them could speak English. . . .

My students were poor and they often came to class without breakfast and hungry. And they knew even in their youth the pain of prejudice. They never seemed to know why people disliked them. . . .

And somehow you never forget what poverty and hatred can do when you see its scars on the hopeful face of a young child.

I never thought then, in 1928, that I would be standing here in 1965. It never even occurred to me in my fondest dreams that I might have the chance to help the sons and daughters of those students, and to help people like them all over this country.

But now I do have that chance. And I'll let you in on a secret—I mean to use it. . . .

Why Vietnam?

Johnson's Voting Rights bill was passed. So was other progressive domestic legislation of the Great Society. But during his first full term, Johnson's Vietnam policy became the subject of an angry national debate. United States troops in greater and greater numbers were being committed to the war—not as advisers but as fighting men—and American aircraft were bombing more and more targets in North Vietnam. To many Americans it seemed that this war was both unconstitutional and pointless. Others believed that the war effort should be increased. The President answered some of his critics in a speech at Johns Hopkins University in April, 1965.

. . . We fight because we must fight if we are to live in a world where every country can shape its own destiny. And only in such a world will our own freedom be finally secure.

This kind of a world will never be built by bombs or bullets. Yet the infirmities of man are such that force must often precede reason—and the waste of war the works of peace.

We wish that this were not so. But we must deal with the world as it is, if it is ever to be as we wish.

The world as it is in Asia is not a serene or peaceful place. The first reality is that North Vietnam has attacked the independent nation of South Vietnam: its object is total conquest.

Of course, some of the people of South Vietnam are participating in attack on their own government, but trained men and supplies, orders and arms flow in a constant stream from north to south. This support is the heartbeat of the war and it is a war of unparalleled brutality. . . .

The confused nature of this conflict cannot mask the fact that is: it is the new face of an old enemy.

Over this war and all Asia is another reality: the deepening shadow of Communist China. The rulers in Hanoi are urged on by Peking. This is a regime which has destroyed freedom in Tibet, which has attacked India and has been condemned by the United Nations for aggression in Korea.

It is a nation which is helping the forces of violence in almost every continent. The contest in Vietnam is part of a wider pattern of aggressive purposes. . . .

Why are we in South Vietnam?

We are there because we have a promise to keep.

Since 1954 every American President has offered support to the people of South Vietnam. We have helped to build, and we have helped to defend. Thus, over many years we have made a national pledge to help South Vietnam defend its independence. And I intend to keep that promise. . . .

We are also there to strengthen world order. Around the globe, from Berlin to Thailand, are people whose well-being rests in part on the belief that they can count on us if they are attacked. To leave Vietnam to its fate would shake the confidence of all these people in the value of an American commitment; and in the value of America's word.

The result would be increased unrest and instability—and even wider war.

We are also there because there are great stakes in the balance. Let no one think for a moment that retreat from Vietnam would bring an end to conflict. The battle would be renewed in one country and then another. The central lesson of our time is that the appetite of aggression is never satisfied.

To withdraw from one battlefield means only to prepare for the next. We must say in Southeast Asia, as we did in Europe, in the words of the Bible, "Hitherto shalt thou come; but no further." . . .

The Presidential Image

"When a man assumes a public trust he should consider himself as public property." Not all Presidents have been enthusiastic advocates of Jefferson's dictum; but it has been a difficult one to ignore, since neither the press nor the voters recognize a line between the public and private President. He is, to the people, their nationhood personified. His tastes, avocations, manner of entertaining—his style—are or ought to be, they believe, representative of the behavior of the people at their best. Calvin Coolidge viewed his expected role cynically. "I think," he is reported to have remarked on one occasion, "the American public wants a solemn ass as a President and I think I'll go along with them."

Host for the Nation

Andrew Jackson was the People's President, and it seemed fitting that on the day of his inauguration in 1829 the doors of the White House should be opened to the common man. At the reception, food and drink vanished as soon as they were served; glassware, china, and furniture were shattered by the boisterous mob. The new President, astonished and trapped, was finally rescued by friends who locked arms, formed a flying wedge, and led Jackson out. Since then, Presidents have understandably preferred to entertain only invited guests. Their problem has been to do so in a way that is dignified and elegant yet does not appear excessively lavish. Jefferson, who believed in democratic informality, was criticized for wearing "yarn stockings and slippers down at the heels" while receiving the British ambassador; Martin Van Buren, on the other hand, was denied re-election in 1840 partly because the sumptuous banquets he gave offended many voters. For modern Presidents the solution has been to provide the proper formality and pomp at state dinners at the White House, and to demonstrate their informality by inviting dignitaries to their own homes. Thus F. D. R. served hot dogs to the king of England at Hyde Park, and Lyndon Johnson entertained the chancellor of Germany at a barbecue on his ranch.

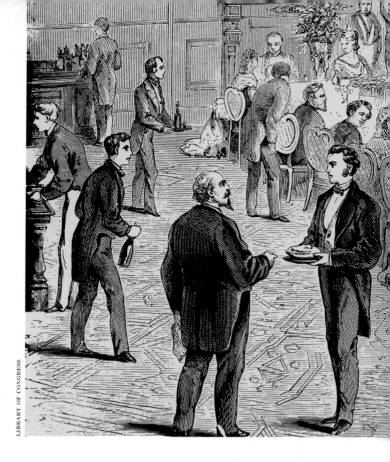

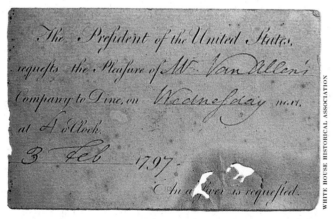

Above is an invitation to dine with President and Mrs. Washington at the Executive Mansion in Philadelphia in 1797. Their formal levees were criticized as being too reminiscent of royal receptions. At top right is a depiction of a banquet given by Ulysses S. Grant in the ornately decorated state dining room of the White House. At right, Theodore Roosevelt toasts Prince Henry of Germany (who is standing at President Roosevelt's right) at an all-male state dinner in 1902.

President and Mrs. Kennedy brought a new youthful elegance to White House social

affairs. Here they chat before a dinner for French Minister of Culture André Malraux.

The Common Touch

The ideal President, Americans seem to believe, is an ordinary man who does an extraordinary job: he is calm, firm, and decisive in the face of world crises and the pressures of office, but he never forgets that he is just an average citizen raised temporarily to high office. A President seeking re-election is always careful, therefore, to demonstrate that he is at heart just one of the boys. As Clinton Rossiter has pointed out, the President of the United States is not really required to be a college graduate, but he ought to like "baseball, detective stories, fishing, pop concerts, picnics, and seascapes."

At left, Rutherford B. Hayes sits in a chair made from horns and hide, a gift from frontiersman Seth Kinsman. Above, Theodore Roosevelt stops for breakfast with cowboys on a Colorado trail. While both men displayed the dignity expected of a Chief Executive, Teddy Roosevelt could do so and still seem to be a regular fellow—a valuable political knack.

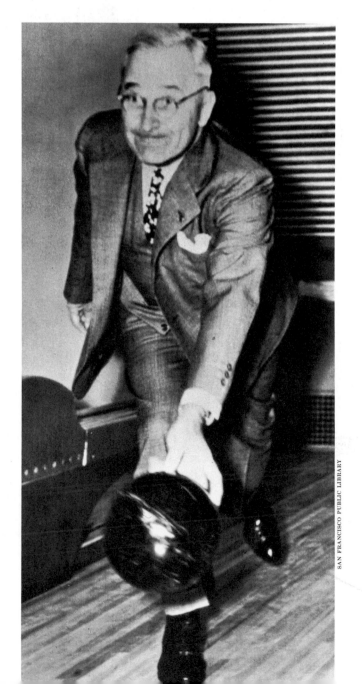

The fez of the Shriners, the fun-loving Masons, fit Warren Harding (top) perfectly. Despite a corrupt administration, Harding, who loved poker and race horses, was a popular President in the roaring twenties. In more serious times Franklin Roosevelt (above in 1935) took pride in more public-spirited activities: here he models the cap and medal that signify long-term membership in the Hyde Park, N.Y., Fire Department. In 1946 President Harry Truman (right) inaugurated the new White House bowling alleys; seven pins fell.

Because of television and jet airplanes, the modern President enjoys—or suffers through —an unprecedented intimacy with the American people. Young, handsome, and eloquent, John F. Kennedy was able to bear up well under this personal scrutiny. Appearing on a California beach (below) shortly after his election in 1960, Kennedy inspired a response that in earlier years might have been reserved for Rudolph Valentino.

Refreshing the Soul

The President needs to escape the pressures of office occasionally, to be alone, to have an opportunity, as Herbert Hoover put it, "for refreshment of one's soul and clarification of one's thoughts. . . ." John Quincy Adams liked to begin his eighteen-to-twenty-hour-long working day with a solitary, predawn swim in the Potomac; allegedly a lady reporter found him out one morning and refused to let the nude President emerge from the water until he had granted her an interview. During his prepresidential years, Harry Truman took a long walk each day "to take stock." But after he became the Chief Executive, reporters usually followed him on his strolls, which became mobile press conferences, not relaxation. Most Presidents, therefore, have left Washington when they wanted privacy and exercise. There have been presidential golfers, hunters, sailors, and swimmers, but the favorite recreation has been fishing, perhaps because—as Hoover said—it is "the silent sport."

The 1882 cartoon above pokes fun at the frequent fishing trips of President Arthur. The lithograph at right portrays Theodore Roosevelt during a hunt in Arizona in 1905.

Several Presidents have considered it their duty to remind Americans that regular physical exercise is important. "A strong body makes the mind strong," said Thomas Jefferson, who was slender and seldom ill; his sentiments were echoed by John F. Kennedy, who remarked, "Physical fitness goes with mental fitness. It goes with energy." Theodore Roosevelt also preached the virtues of the strenuous life and practiced what he preached. Not all American Presidents have been models of physical fitness, however. Like Dwight Eisenhower, William Howard Taft (left) was a frequent golfer, but his three-hundred-pound figure set the wrong kind of example. Calvin Coolidge, below, worked out in the Capitol gym; his waistline, however, seems to have been less responsive to exercise than that of his colleague. The day after his victory in the election of 1964, President Lyndon Johnson (right, astride his horse, Lady B.) let off steam by lassoing a Hereford yearling at his ranch on the Pedernales River in Texas.

Reaching the People

When Franklin Delano Roosevelt wanted to explain directly to the American people the whys and hows of his program to resolve the banking crisis of 1933, microphones were promptly installed in his White House office; the President's calm, confident voice was heard in millions of homes. Similarly, when John F. Kennedy felt it necessary to speak out against the violent reactions of some white communities to peaceful demonstrations by Negroes in 1963, television cameras were moved into his office and millions of Americans saw and heard the President appeal directly to them in a moving plea for justice.

Until the third decade of the twentieth century, American Presidents knew no such luxury; their activities, programs, pleas, and explanations reached the people only through a middleman, the press. Every Chief Executive has been a great believer in the freedom of the press. Jefferson called it "one of the great bulwarks of liberty"; Jackson saw it as "the Palladium of our liberties"; Eisenhower said that he would die for it. Nevertheless, a sensitivity to criticism and a hostility toward the press seem endemic to the office. "The man who never looks into a newspaper is better informed than he who reads them, inasmuch as he who knows nothing is nearer the truth than he whose mind is filled with falsehoods and errors," Jefferson remarked. And the freedom of the press that Eisenhower would have given his life to preserve included "the freedom of newspapers that call me everything that is a good deal less than . . . a gentleman." "Misrepresentation" and "exaggeration" are words commonly used by Presidents in describing press coverage and editorial criticism of government affairs. "We may be sure that in tomorrow's prints . . ." Lincoln said, "all the little Colt's revolvers will have grown into horse-pistols."

On election night, 1920, radio station KDKA in Pittsburgh announced that Warren G. Harding (at right, making a phonograph recording) was the next President, and asked those who heard the broadcast to write and say so. Harding's two successors, Calvin Coolidge and Herbert Hoover, made radio speeches, but neither fully appreciated its real potential.

The intimacy with the people that Franklin Roosevelt achieved through his fireside chats and masterful use of radio was indispensable to his popularity. Even when he officially addressed an assembly—such as the joint session of Congress in 1945, above—he seemed to be speaking first and most directly to the people at home. Kennedy used television in much the same way, and like F. D. R., he helped temper the hostility of many newspaper publishers by maintaining an easygoing and co-operative relationship with the working press. At top right, he holds a session for photographers. Uncomfortable in his early confrontations with the press, Lyndon B. Johnson avoided televised conferences for some time; but in 1967 the Chief Executive tried to project a new, more sympathetic image, as The New York Times *reported (right).*

President Johnson at his news conference yesterday. H manner led many people to phone White House in prais

A New Presidential Sty

With a microphone concealed in his coat, the President could leave lectern. Sometimes he gestured and frowned.

He waved his arms. His voice ranged from angry volume to modest gentleness. This, some said, was "the real Johnson."

That Was 'the Real Johnson,' His Old Friends Say

On the Road

To see and be seen by the people and to put to practical advantage whatever personal charisma they might possess, many Chief Executives have undertaken grand tours of the nation. Washington made such a trip to demonstrate that the United States was a truly unified nation with one President and one set of common goals. In 1817 James Monroe embarked on an even more triumphant series of journeys through a much larger America and created, according to his contemporaries, a national "Era of Good Feelings."

The appearance of the President makes a day a holiday; and some Chief Executives have scheduled tours in order to bolster their personal popularity, rally public sentiment behind their legislative programs, or appeal directly to the people for their support of some special issue. Facing Senate hostility to the League of Nations, Woodrow Wilson planned a cross-country trip to "appeal to Caesar" (the people). Despite bad health he arranged a crowded itinerary, spoke several times a day, and suffered a paralytic stroke. Harry Truman, however, helped secure his renomination and then won a surprising victory in the election of 1948 because of his whistle-stop meetings with the people.

Special events such as world's fairs, the dedication of national monuments, labor conventions, and days of national celebration and consecration also provide an opportunity for Presidents and people to look each other over. "I have come to the conclusion," said Taft, "that the major part of the work of a President is to increase the gate receipts of expositions and fairs and bring tourists into the town."

Andrew Jackson's trip to New England in 1853 and the common man's affection for him inspired the satirical cartoon at the top of the page. At right, President and Mrs. McKinley attend a festival in Los Angeles after a cross-country tour in 1901. When McKinley was assassinated that year, his successor Theodore Roosevelt found himself with limited congressional and party support. But a 1903 tour demonstrated his enormous popularity (at far right he speaks in Wyoming) and he won renomination and an easy re-election.

347

Bundled up against the cold, the monumental William H. Taft (who disliked making per-

sonal appearances) arrives to inspect the United States Military Academy at West Point.

Woodrow Wilson (above) visited California during his nationwide tour to gain support for the League. Below, the popular Eisenhowers acknowledge cheers along a parade route. At right is John F. Kennedy in Ireland, the home of his ancestors.

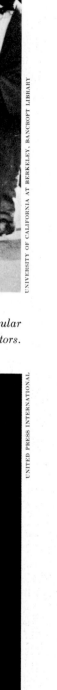

The President's Lady

As soon as Washington was inaugurated, the Presidency existed in spirit as well as in law. The role of the First Lady was less easily defined. Martha Washington was a correct hostess but was politically inactive; Abigail Adams, on the other hand, was so interested in the affairs of state that some officials wondered seriously if she should be called Mrs. President. It was Dolley Madison who set a standard by which future First Ladies would be judged. Her vivaciousness and the casual informality of her entertaining were so popular that her successor Elizabeth Monroe was deeply resented for her return to aristocratic formality. Since then, First Ladies have varied greatly. There have been eccentrics, such as Mary Lincoln, who have hampered their husbands; homebodies, such as Bess Truman; and others, especially Eleanor Roosevelt, who have played an important role in the nation's affairs. In the era of television, Presidents' wives have been highly visible, helping to set the image of the administration and win friends and votes for their husbands. But clearly the First Lady can make her own rules for behavior; Americans insist only that her first interest always be her husband and her family.

Dolley Madison served as hostess for Jefferson, a widower, and then moved into the White House as First Lady in 1809. Above left is a detail from her portrait by Stuart. "Lemonade Lucy" Hayes (above right, in a painting by Daniel Huntington) was a charming woman who regarded the White House as primarily her family's home; she therefore banned all alcoholic beverages. The lovely Frances Folsom Cleveland, posing for Augustus St. Gaudens in the photograph at right, married Cleveland when she was twenty-one and he was Chief Executive. Their wedding greatly increased her husband's popularity.

Edith Bolling Galt Wilson (below with the President) married Woodrow Wilson in 1915, the year after his first wife's death, and became the closest thing to a woman Chief Executive that the United States has had; when President Wilson lay half-paralyzed and semiconscious from the effects of a stroke, it was the First Lady who decided which officials and which documents he could see and when he was well enough to conduct national business. Making no excuses, Mrs. Wilson admitted frankly that her husband's health was the only matter that concerned her. Grace Coolidge, shown posing with a pigeon outside the White House at right, presented a sharp contrast to her husband: she was as gay as Coolidge was earnest, as warm as he was dour.

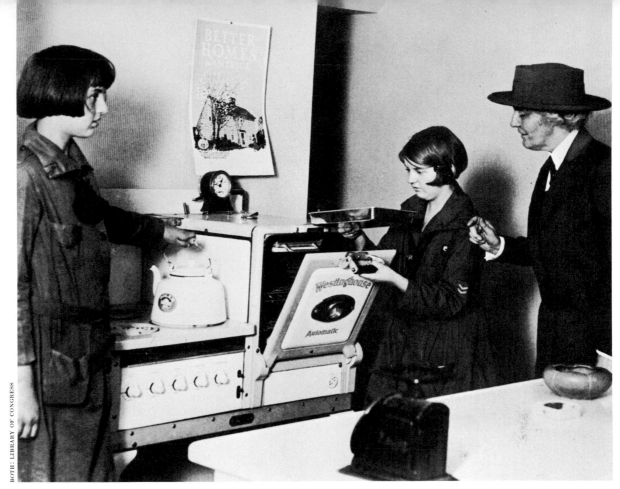

Above, Lou Hoover, First Lady and President of the Girl Scouts of America, bakes cookies with a pair of young ladies. At right is a 1940 cartoon that pokes gentle and affectionate fun at Eleanor Roosevelt, who was without doubt the busiest First Lady in history. Her husband, confined to his wheel chair, employed Mrs. Roosevelt as his legs, dispatching her frequently to scenes of strikes and national disasters. A spokesman for the country's underprivileged and oppressed, the First Lady offended countless special-interest groups, including the Daughters of the American Revolution (from which she resigned), as she fought bigotry and privilege, and sought social justice for all Americans. Her observations and opinions were revealed to the nation in Mrs. Roosevelt's popular column, "My Day."

The First Lady can be as busy as she wants to be. Invitations to address meetings and appear at dedications pour into the White House, and she may choose from them arbitrarily or pursue a specific cause. Above are Bess Truman and her daughter, Margaret, at an airplane christening. At the top of the opposite page, Jacqueline Kennedy attends a National Gallery of Art exhibit; at right, Interior Secretary Stewart Udall watches Lady Bird Johnson plant a tree to stimulate publicity for her national beautification project.

NATIONAL PARK SERVICE/ABBIE ROWE

WIDE WORLD

Family Assets

Americans like their Presidents to be family men, and a close-knit family is a political asset. The mischief of their youngsters, White House weddings, the advent of grandchildren—all make good copy for the newspapers and lend popularity to the Chief Executive. Sometimes, however, being a father can result in problems for the President. James Monroe's snobbish daughter Eliza created a minor diplomatic crisis by disregarding protocol, and Harry S. Truman, who usually took criticism well, threatened to punch one newspaper critic who had reviewed his daughter Margaret's singing unfavorably.

PERSONALLY SELECTED
AMERICAN-DESIGNED FASHIONS
BY THE MISSES WILSON

MISS MARGARET WILSON
The Eldest Daughter

MISS JESSIE WILSON
The Next Youngest Daughter

MISS ELEANOR WILSON
The Youngest Daughter

7667
Selected by Miss Margaret Wilson

7666
Selected by Miss Jessie Wilson

7665
Selected by Miss Eleanor Wilson

(Page 29)

In the Ladies' Home Journal *feature at left, Woodrow Wilson's three daughters describe their preferences for certain American fashions. At the top of the opposite page, Caroline and John F. Kennedy, Jr., watch a concert from a White House balcony with their parents. The performers were the pipers of the Black Watch Royal Highland Regiment of Scotland; seventeen hundred youngsters from child-care agencies also attended. At right, President Lyndon Baines Johnson watches his elder daughter, Lynda Bird, cut the cake after her marriage to Captain Charles Robb, a Marine, in December, 1967. Johnson's daughter Luci was also married during his administration.*

THE FUTURE OF THE PRESIDENCY

*"When I ran for the Presidency
of the United States,
I knew that this country faced
serious challenges, but
I could not realize — nor could
any man realize who does not
bear the burdens of this office —
how heavy and constant
would be those burdens."*

JOHN F. KENNEDY

The immense burdens of the Presidency are symbolized by this photograph of John F. Kennedy.

CHAPTER ELEVEN

Conscience of the Nation

Ever since the Presidency was instituted its working has been under discussion. Critics at one extreme have echoed the belief of certain delegates to the 1787 Constitutional Convention that a single Executive placed too much power in the hands of one man. Such was the view, for example, of Augustus B. Woodward, who proposed in 1809, in his *Considerations on the Executive Government of the United States of America*, a plural, elected Executive of five men, each to preside annually, in rotation. The plan was similar to that adopted in the Swiss constitution of 1848. Henry C. Lockwood's *The Abolition of the Presidency* expressed a similar alarm in 1884 and likewise recommended government by an executive council. At the other extreme, especially in the middle third of the twentieth century, it has been argued that the problem is not to curb the President but to remove some of the factors that make his leadership ineffective. In the previous two chapters it has been shown that even in the field of foreign affairs the President is not a free agent, while in domestic matters he is even more restricted.

Are reforms desirable? Are they feasible? Are they likely? The common response is unenthusiastic. As Theodore C. Sorensen observed in his 1963 study *Decision-Making in the White House*: "There are already enough proposals to reorganize the Presidency to stretch from here to Utopia. . . ."

One obvious consideration is that the problems of post-1945 Presidents are essentially the problems of a nation with an advanced economy and a polyglot society—a nation compelled to play a principal role in a world that is undergoing rapid and prodigious transformation. No amount of administrative regrouping would return the United States to the days of laissez faire and isolationism. Truman grasped this harsh fact when he placed on his desk the reminder that "the buck stops here." Whether there was a single desk or five or fifty desks, the Executive would still have to exert himself to the utmost.

A second consideration is that whatever the theoretical shortcomings of the American system of government, those of other countries are no better. Woodrow Wilson dreamed of reorganizing the government on the British model. But the British scholar Harold Laski, lecturing on the Presidency at the University of Indiana in 1938 and 1939, maintained that "anyone who knows the life of a political party from within Great Britain will not feel inclined to cast a stone at the American system." Judged by results, American methods were just as likely to produce outstanding leaders when the hour demanded them. As for the interference of Congress in foreign policy, Laski said: "A president eager for imperialist adventure . . . might easily, in the absence of Senate control, be a source of grave danger to the American people. And this view is, I suggest, reinforced by experience of systems like that of Great Britain where the control of foreign affairs is, in fact, 'executive altogether.' For the only real control of the House of Commons is of a *post-mortem* nature. It is presented by the cabinet with a *fait accompli*, rejection of which involves the defeat of the government and a subsequent general election. There is no instance in modern times where the government has had an assured majority, upon which its supporters have been willing to take that risk." More recent observations would seem to confirm Professor Laski's skepticism. In his *The Chief Executive*, published in 1964, Louis W. Koenig devoted a chapter to comparing American Presidents with chief executives in other countries. He pointed out defects in British practice that worry the British themselves. Prime ministers may be mediocre figures. The method of selecting a prime minister, as revealed in 1963 when Harold Macmillan made way for Sir Alec Douglas-Home, is clumsy, slow, and somewhat secretive. "The House of Commons," Professor Koenig asserted, "has been reduced to a passivity which even the most resolute critic of Congress would not wish upon it. In its tightly restricted capacity, the House resembles the American electoral college, registering the popular will in choosing a government and then automatically ratifying its program and voting the funds it asks for." Koenig saw the British civil service, once the envy of American political scientists, as "ingrown, uninspired, uncreative, and out of step with the fast pace of Britain's problems." Developments in former colonies such as Nigeria suggest that even if the British model were ideal for the mother country it is not necessarily suitable for export. As for non-English-speaking nations, none seems to offer executive styles alluring enough for the United States to try to copy them.

In a more positive view of the matter, a third common line of reasoning is that the American Presidency in fact works well. The process of selection is thorough and democratic. Aspirants have little chance to hide their weaknesses in the preconvention months, and none once the major parties have chosen their candidates. Only men of rare stamina and political maturity, it is argued, can survive the grueling test of presidential campaigns. In office the President has as much power as is good for any man. It is necessary in a federal government—so the argument goes—that Congress should represent local attitudes. If it did not the administration in Washington might become dangerously remote and monolithic. Moreover, the United States has fifty mini-Presidents—the governors of its fifty states—and, on a lower level, numerous mayors of cities. That each of these tends to act as a small-scale President is cited to prove that the real Presidency is an office well adapted to American needs. The states and cities also serve as laboratories for political experiment.

Some suggested reforms, including the adoption of a plural Executive, have already been tried and found wanting at the local level.

A fourth contention is that even if the Presidency did not work reasonably well it would be naïve to suppose that any fundamental revision of the executive office could be introduced at this late stage in the nation's development. The federal government has been in existence for nearly two hundred years. Far from crumbling through the decades, it has been strengthened by the cement of tradition. The nation is deeply averse to revolutionary political change. Both national and world history appear to confirm the practical wisdom of the almost unanimous popular feeling that any change should be gradual and organic, and that it should be introduced not by theoreticians but by the men who must live with it at either end of Pennsylvania Avenue. Indeed, most of the academics who specialize in American government would agree with the conclusion of Professor Arthur N. Holcombe, who wrote in 1950 in *Our More Perfect Union* that "there is no rational basis for loss of confidence in the soundness and practical utility of the . . . great principles upon which the government . . . was established. . . . They have given character to a system of government under which the men in power have been able to control one another without losing their ability to control the governed." Professor Clinton Rossiter, who like Holcombe would like to see improvements here and there, thinks that Leave your Presidency alone! is a sensible slogan. Efforts to change the system strike him as a futile occupation in the American context. "The Presidency is in a state of sturdy health, and that is why we should not give way easily to despair over the defects men of too much zeal or too little courage claim to discover in it." Sir Denis Brogan, a distinguished British student of American politics, felt in 1933 that the President should be given a more compelling mandate for action and that a national referendum on each major issue would be the way to accomplish it. But Brogan wrote at a time of exceptional crisis and would presumably not wish to be held to an idea of half a lifetime ago.

By the same token, yesterday's actual reforms are often today's nuisances. In the Progressive Era, the presidential primary seemed a valuable means of enabling ordinary citizens to voice their sentiments on possible candidates. In the 1950's Clinton Rossiter wrote: "I am inclined to agree with Adlai Stevenson, who speaks to the point with matchless authority, that the presidential primaries are a 'very, very questionable method of selecting presidential candidates.' Rather than have a handful of primaries spread carelessly over the months between February and July, it might be the wiser and even more democratic thing to have none at all. . . . It is, by almost any standard, one of the failures of our political system." Reforms are apt to misfire. The primary contest may, for instance, give an unfair advantage to a candidate with abundant personal resources. Certainly this was true of John F. Kennedy in 1960. Although he might have defeated Senator Hubert Humphrey in the primaries in any case, Kennedy and his family left nothing to chance.

Wisdom aside, self-interest is too much involved to encourage reform. Any executive-legislative regrouping would entail a loss of prerogative for someone or for some institution. Why should the President, or the independent regulatory commissions, or the Senate, or the House of Representatives acquiesce in a diminution of their authority? The 1946 mid-term elections confronted President Truman with a Republican majority in both houses of Congress. Senator Fulbright, predicting with some justification that the result would be legislative stalemate, offered a solution. He suggested that Truman appoint a Republican as his Secretary of State and then immediately resign from the Presidency. There was at the time no Vice President; the Secretary of State was next in line for the Chief Magistracy. If Truman had been ready to oblige, the country would have had a unified Republican government—in theory at least. Not surprisingly, Truman ignored Fulbright's plan; nor did Congress or the public show any sympathy for the senator's eccentric panacea.

A fifth answer to implied criticisms of the *status quo* is that modest revisions are actually being made or are likely to be made in the near future. Thus no significant group defends the operations of the Electoral College or insists that it operates faultlessly. In 1950 there was considerable support in the Senate for a proposed constitutional amendment that would have abolished the Electoral College altogether. The electoral vote would have remained, but it would have been divided within each state according to the proportion of the popular votes cast in the state for presidential candidates. As Rossiter explained, "If the electors are puppets, they are useless; if they are free agents, as several Southern states have tried to make them, they are 175 years out of date." It is doubtful whether the nation will go the whole way in this direction, if only because the present method of giving a state's entire electoral vote to the leading candidate pleases the Northern urban interest, which would be reluctant to yield. President Johnson is among those who, while not doing away entirely with the Electoral College, would wish to make sure through a constitutional amendment that its members vote en bloc, as puppets rather than as so-called free agents.

One of the acknowledged weaknesses of the mechanism for electing a President prescribed in the Twelfth Amendment is the hiatus between the casting of popular votes early in November and the formal meeting of the Electoral College six weeks later. Chaos could result if the winning candidate were to die in the interval. There is a further lame-duck gap between the meeting of the college and the inauguration of the President. This transitional period, has, however, been shortened by about six weeks by the Twentieth Amendment, which became law in 1933. A good deal of thought has been given to the problem of achieving a smooth transition from one administration to the next. Lincoln, contemplating the likelihood of defeat in 1864, decided that if it was necessary in order to avert a breakdown of the war effort, he would resign immediately after the election and yield the office to his rival, General McClellan. In 1916 Woodrow Wilson, faced with a comparable defeat by the Republican candidate, Charles Evans Hughes, might have resigned (and persuaded his Vice President to do the same) after nominating Hughes as Secretary of State. After the Democrats lost the 1920 presidential election, his former Secretary of State William Jennings Bryan urged Wilson—an exhausted invalid—to follow the same procedure in handing over the White House to the victorious Warren G. Harding. No doubt Senator Fulbright was familiar with these precedents, if precedents they were, when he requested President Truman to abdicate.

Future Presidents will probably be no more compliant than Truman was. But the expedient is there in case of emergency. (Certainly Truman is likely to be the last Vice President to be hurled into the Presidency without previous introduction. Since the

1950's, Vice Presidents have been kept informed of all important presidential business.) In Truman's own words: "It is a terrible handicap for a new President to step into office and be confronted with a whole series of critical decisions without adequate briefing. I thought it was an omission in our political tradition that a retiring President did not make it his business to facilitate the transfer of the government to his successor." President Hoover did attempt to consult with President-elect Roosevelt at the end of 1932, though he met with a rather evasive response. Truman was determined to avoid the errors of the past. In 1952 he arranged for the Democratic candidate, Adlai Stevenson, to attend Cabinet meetings and to be regularly briefed on foreign affairs by the Central Intelligence Agency. He offered the same facilities to the Republican contender, Dwight D. Eisenhower. Although Eisenhower declined the invitation (like F. D. R., he wished to preserve his freedom of maneuver), he readily accepted a post-election invitation to name deputies who would liaise with the outgoing administration on budgetary and other matters. President Eisenhower in turn provided facilities for President-elect Kennedy at the end of 1960 and met him twice at the White House.

BALTIMORE *Sun*

"Lyndon Johnson says you're out of date!"

This cartoon appeared in the Baltimore Sun *in 1965, after Johnson had said that the Electoral College was outmoded.*

The value of such transitional discussions is limited, especially when the change of President is also a change of party. The incoming Chief Executive is understandably anxious not to appear to be in accord with an administration whose programs he has just finished denouncing. Nevertheless, on major foreign issues and on certain domestic matters a degree of bipartisan continuity has now been established. The expenses of the transition have been provided for by Congress, in answer to a request by President Kennedy. It seems certain that such behind-the-scenes collaboration will increase within modest limits.

The sudden death of F. D. R. in 1945 and of John F. Kennedy in 1963 and the illnesses suffered by Eisenhower and Lyndon Johnson have directed attention to the related problems of presidential succession and disability. Succession at the time of Roosevelt's death was governed by an act of 1886 that designated the Secretary of State next in succession after the President and Vice President, followed in order of seniority by the remaining Cabinet Secretaries. It was pointed out in 1945 that Truman, a former Vice President, would be able to name his own immediate successor through his right of Cabinet appointment. This circumstance seemed undemocratic, to Congress and to Truman himself. After some complex skirmishing between the parties and the two houses of Congress, the 1947 Succession Act interposed the Speaker of the House and then the president pro tempore of the Senate between the Vice President and the Secretary of State. The Speaker was given preference because he had already won the suffrage of his own congressional district and that of a majority of the four hundred and thirty-five members of the House of Representatives. But the change illustrates the dangers of well-meant reforms. Doubt has been expressed as to whether either figure can be deemed an "Officer of the United States." Constitutionally, if the verdict were negative, he might not be entitled to assume the full powers of the Presidency for the whole of the term remaining to him. If President Johnson had died in the year between the assassination of Kennedy and his own election, he would have been followed in the White House by Speaker John W. McCormack, a man of seventy-two who, whatever his other qualifications, was hardly presidential timber. Both the Speaker and the Senate president pro tempore are likely to be elderly figures chosen through seniority and for party loyalty rather than because they are outstanding. Statisticians offer the consolation that the death of both President and Vice President in the same administration should not occur more than once in every eight hundred and forty years.

Until recently, presidential disability has been treated with remarkable nonchalance. It has been more than merely an academic question: four Presidents have been assassinated, four others (William Henry Harrison, Taylor, Harding, Franklin D. Roosevelt) have died in office, and several have been seriously incapacitated through illness. Garfield, after having been shot by Guiteau, lingered for two and a half months before he finally died—two and a half months during which there was virtually no President. Woodrow Wilson, having suffered a paralytic stroke in October, 1919, was bedridden for most of his remaining eighteen months in the White House. Senator Albert Fall of New Mexico was not far wrong when he told colleagues in the Foreign Relations Committee, "We have petticoat Government! Mrs. Wilson is President!" The President was paralyzed; so was the United States government. President Eisenhower's three illnesses, although he made excellent recoveries, were further indications that it was time to clarify the problem. In his second annual message, in January, 1965, Lyndon Johnson referred to the need for "laws to insure the necessary continuity of leadership should the President become disabled or die." In the summer of that year Congress approved a new constitutional provision (which became law as the Twenty-fifth Amendment in February, 1967). The amendment entitles the President to nominate a Vice President, subject to confirmation by Congress, whenever the office is vacant. The Vice President is empowered to assume the duties of President whenever the President declares himself disabled or is ruled by the Vice President and a respectable contingent of department heads or other prominent persons to be disabled. The amendment likewise describes the procedure by which a President may resume his office.

Harry Truman, who urged action on the problems of presidential succession and disability, also had views on the employability of ex-Presidents. He was impressed by Herbert Hoover's wide knowledge of men and affairs, which was revealed in the work of the Hoover Commission. Former Presidents were the people, he said, "to whom we must look for help and counsel. That is why we must not shelve or thrust into obscurity men with such unique experience." (Former Vice Presidents and Speakers might also, he thought, play a useful part.) Truman suggested that "Congress should pass enabling legislation designating former Presidents of the United States *as Free Members of the Congress*," with the right to attend sessions or committees of either house, though with no voting right. Part of his proposal has found sanction. In 1963 three Democratic senators and one Republican sponsored a proposal that ex-Presidents

<table>
<tr><td>"All the News That's Fit to Print."</td><td>The New York</td></tr>
</table>

VOL. LXVIII...NO. 22,526.   •••   NEW YORK, SATURDAY, SEPTEMBER , 27, 1919. TWENTY-F

PRESIDENT SUFFERS NERVOUS BREAK
SPEEDING BACK TO WASHINGTON
STEEL STRIKE WEAKENS; BRITISH RAIL

Bold headlines in The New York Times *on September 27, 1919, announced Woodrow Wilson's collapse during a speaking tour designed to gain support for the League of Nations. His "nervous breakdown" was probably a stroke; he never regained his health.*

should be regarded as senators at large and be given seats in the Senate. Their scheme was reduced to an agreement—reached a few weeks before the death of President Kennedy—to change the rules of the Senate in order to permit former Presidents to address the Senate after notifying the presiding officer.

Other connections, previously mentioned, have developed between Congress and Presidents in office. A Chief Executive who takes sufficient trouble can maintain close contact with the legislative branch. If the tendency to nominate for the Presidency men who are serving or have served in Congress—Truman, Nixon, Kennedy, Goldwater, Johnson—continues, it is possible that prior service in Congress, especially in the Upper House, might become an unwritten law of the American federal system.

It is arguable, too, that Congress may undergo changes which will improve the quality of membership or will at least make members more representative of public opinion. If the Electoral College method of choosing a President gives an advantage to large, urban states, each with its big bloc of electoral votes, election to Congress has been overweighted in the interests of small states and of rural areas. Although empowered to compel reapportionment so as to take account of shifts of population, the House was too much influenced by parochialism to take action. There was no redistricting in Illinois between 1901 and 1948. When changes were finally made, the Chicago area contained over half the population of the

state but had only ten representatives as against fifteen for the rest of Illinois. A special message to Congress from President Truman in January, 1951, requesting legislation to provide for more equal districts, failed to accomplish reorganization. Similar proposals again failed to pass Congress in 1959. The 1960 census disclosed glaring discrepancies. One Michigan congressional district that included part of Detroit had 803,000 inhabitants, while another in the rural north of the state had a population of only 177,000.

The Supreme Court stepped into the breach with a series of decisions involving federal as well as state legislative districting. In 1964 in *Wesberry v. Sanders* the Court ruled that although "it may not be possible to draw congressional districts with mathematical precision," this difficulty was "no excuse for ignoring our Constitution's plain objective of making equal representation for equal numbers of people the fundamental goal for the House of Representatives." If the winds of change keep blowing, the Congress of A.D. 2000 could be a considerably more alert body with a less standpat and more contemporary outlook on the nation's needs.

Signs of change are apparent also in the conception of the kind of person who may be eligible for the Presidency. Until the 1960's a set of implicit assumptions narrowed the field of candidates. Professor Sidney Hyman, writing in 1959, listed "Nine Tests for the Presidential Hopeful." They were: "1. The rule

COURTESY OF *The New York Times*

UNITED PRESS INTERNATIONAL.

𝕿𝖎𝖒𝖊𝖘.

THE WEATHER

Fair Saturday and Sunday; warmer Sunday; moderate northeast to southeast winds.

For weather report see next to last page.

…GES.   TWO CENTS   …   THREE CENTS   FOUR CENTS

DOWN, TOUR CANCELED;
FOR A NEEDED REST;
WAY MEN WALK OUT

In September, 1955, President Dwight Eisenhower (right) suffered a coronary occlusion. A month later, he was well enough to pose for photographers. He wore pajamas on which was embroidered the answer to an anxious nation's question: much better thanks.

of political talent and experience. 2. The rule of governors. 3. The rule of big swing states. 4. The rule of northern monopoly. 5. The rule of multiple economic interests. 6. The rule of happy family life. 7. The rule of the small town. 8. The rule of English stock. 9. The rule of Protestantism." He did not suggest that all nine conditions would have to be or could be fulfilled by major party nominees. General Eisenhower, for example, was not politically experienced in federal or in state government, and like Herbert Hoover was not of English but of Swiss-German ancestry. Adlai Stevenson might seem to have broken rule six by having been divorced. Nevertheless, political astrologers did once pay keen attention to such considerations. As Clinton Rossiter noted, they were also hesitant to back aspirants who were conspicuously wealthy.

It is too early to suggest that the rules will alter fundamentally. Yet the events of the 1960's have made some of them appear relatively unimportant. John F. Kennedy was neither the first Roman Catholic candidate nor the first candidate to exemplify a big-city background. Al Smith, who was nominated by the Democrats in 1928, was a Catholic and a New Yorker. But unlike Smith, Kennedy won; and he was wealthy, as were the two contenders in 1964, Lyndon Johnson and Barry Goldwater. Johnson, a Texan, was acutely aware that Southerners were virtually ineligible for nomination; the desire to escape the "Texas trap" might have influenced him to accept the vice presidential nomination in 1960. Only accident made him the Democratic nominee for President in 1964. Again, however, he won. And in the same year the Republicans chose Barry Goldwater, some of whose ancestors had been Jewish.

None of the things feared of Presidents who were members of minority or special-interest groups happened. General Eisenhower displayed no bias toward the armed services; indeed he was probably more impartial than F. D. R., who had revealed a boyish attachment to the United States Navy that sometimes irked Army spokesmen. John F. Kennedy revealed so little indication of his personal religious affiliation that some Catholic leaders accused him of prejudice against the Roman faith. Lyndon B. Johnson suppressed all trace of Southernness in securing the passage of the Civil Rights Act of 1964. In fact, it would seem that a minority-group President, out of caution, is even more likely than a centrally placed

incumbent to behave with judicial impartiality.

The rules will not disappear altogether. Candidates will still have to be widely acceptable and have a power base from which to operate. Wealth has become an asset rather than a liability, because of the grace, the cosmopolitan style, and the aura of success it confers upon a candidate, as well as its obvious other advantages. If present tendencies persist, divorce may be no great handicap, but a candidate will still benefit from having an attractive and intelligent wife and preferably some young children. Franklin Roosevelt gained greatly from the activities of his wife, Eleanor. The personalities of Mrs. Kennedy and Mrs. Johnson have reinforced the expectation that the First Lady will contribute appreciably to life in the White House and in the nation.

In a speech to Chicago Populists, Henry Demarest Lloyd prophesied in 1894: "Women will vote, and some day we will have a woman president when the people come in." Women do have the vote, but the odds are that they will prefer to give it to a male candidate. Once second-class citizens, they are today powerful and respected. They have achieved recognition somewhat as Catholicism and Judaism have achieved a near-parity of *official* esteem in American public discourse. It is quite likely that the major parties will in the near future deliberately pick someone Catholic or Jewish as a vice presidential candidate, and it is conceivable that they will one day choose a woman for the second office. The chances would be increased if women had as prominent a place in public life as they have in some other countries. The same may be said of Negro Americans. They are not likely to be nominated for the Presidency before A.D. 2000. But a Negro Vice President could conceivably be put forward, and the chances will be much increased if and when there are several Negro senators and governors to choose from. Nor would the relegation of such minority figures to the vice presidential office be evidence of discrimination. In the next generation the majority of Americans will, after all, continue to be white Protestants. There is nothing sinister in expecting the man in the White House to be drawn from the majority, so long as there is what might be called a sporting chance of his being replaced by a minority deputy.

The fluidity of the situation has stimulated some speculation in fiction. Eugene Burdick's novel *The 480*, published in 1964, has as its hero a tough, capa-

In 1964, Senator Margaret Chase Smith entered several presidential primaries and received a few votes at the Republican convention. She knew that she had no chance of winning, but wished to point out that a lady candidate was a possibility.

ble American engineer, vaguely reminiscent of the young Hoover, who becomes a presidential candidate. His beautiful Eurasian wife, who was interned by the Japanese during the war, survived imprisonment only by prostituting herself to the camp guards. When his enemies discover this information they attempt to use it as blackmail to compel him to abandon his campaign. At the end of the novel Thatch, the hero, has made the surrender announcement in order to spare his wife's feelings; but she tells him that he must stick to his guns. Equally equivocal is the theme of Irving Wallace's 1965 novel *The Man*. Wallace imagines a future United States not very different from that of the 1960's. The Vice President dies of a heart attack. Named president pro tempore of the Senate is Douglass Dilman, a Negro, selected for the empty honor in an effort to appease the Negro protest movement. The President of the United States and the Speaker of the House of Representatives travel overseas to attend a Russo-American summit conference. They are both accidentally killed. According to the succession law of 1947, Dilman becomes President. The Secretary of State, an intimate friend of the dead President's, is next in line; but for the 1947 Succession Act he would be President. He wants the office. Dilman's enemies scheme against him and finally impeach him. Having demonstrated his integrity of character and his capacity to handle a series of domestic and foreign crises, Dilman is acquitted. When popular novelists begin to exploit a theme, it is fairly certain that the general public is almost ready to accept the theme as actuality.

As has been noted, criticisms of the Presidency are usually met with the answers that the office is adversely affected by difficulties, national and international, which would exist in any case; that although executive government has had unsatisfactory features in other countries, in America it works well; that even if it did not, sweeping reforms are neither feasible nor desirable; and that modest improvements are being gradually introduced.

This note would be a cheerful one to end on. But if one really wishes to look into the future he must envisage pessimistic as well as optimistic developments. The American political system is certainly resistant to change. An admirer would say that it is organic or stable. A critic would say that because it is so highly conservative, it is anachronistic—dangerously so in a world of constant, rapid change. The problem of the Presidency is thus dual. The federal government should strike a balance between executive efficiency and legislative democracy. It should also be stable—that is, effective, systematic, dignified, respected—and yet swiftly and sensitively responsive to an unstable national and international situation. Most reform proposals focus upon the first of these aspects—the balance between Executive and legislature, efficiency and democracy, authority and consent. In doing so they naturally tend to the verdict that matters are as satisfactory as could be expected.

If, however, the second aspect is emphasized, matters look less rosy. The governmental conservatism of Americans is then seen not as a cause for congratulation but for alarm. The parade, year after year and decade after decade, of reform recommendations appears as a proof not of the simple-mindedness of professors of political science but of the real need for reform. After all, it is not only academics who want improvement; Presidents and congressmen often share their views. President Johnson has been called a political animal—a man steeped in practical politics, which is defined as "the art of the possible." It can be assumed that he was not shadowboxing in his annual message of January, 1966, when he asked that the term of representatives be extended to four years. The change had already been advocated by many political scientists. Books such as Senator Joseph S. Clark's *The Senate Establishment*, which appeared in 1963, and Representative Richard Bolling's *House Out of Order*, published two years later, provide firsthand evidence of the grave defects of Congress. The Presidency too has received some fairly basic criticism from liberals for almost the first time in this century. One does not have to be a Jeremiah to maintain that the United States in the 1960's, while economically vigorous, is socially and politically in the doldrums. The mood of national alarm and despondency may be temporary. If not, and if the uneasiness increases, the nation might seek far-reaching remedies that would almost certainly embrace the federal government.

It is therefore worthwhile to examine some of the analyses of the Presidency made in the past quarter of a century, and to reflect on which might actually be applied before A.D. 2000.

The majority of them are concerned with strengthening the Presidency by bringing it into harmony with Congress. Most of these proposals suggest a parliamentary system roughly akin to that of Britain. Thomas K. Finletter, for example, in *Can Representative Government Do The Job?* (1945) recommends lengthening the term of the President and congressmen and providing for a dissolution of the federal government, to be followed by a national election, if the President and Congress fail to reach agreement on crucial elements of the legislative program. Professor C. Perry Patterson, in *Presidential Government in the United States: The Unwritten Constitution* (1947), advocates the creation of a Cabinet executive council chosen by Congress from among its membership and headed by a prime minister. Although the President would continue to supervise administration and to initiate policy, his views would be mediated by the Cabinet, which would be directly responsible to Con-

gress. In *Bureaucracy in a Democracy* (1950), Professor Charles S. Hyneman suggests the establishment of a central advisory council that would be selected by the Chief Executive from among congressional leaders of his own party, certain executive officials, and a few prominent citizens from outside the government.

Herman Finer's *The Presidency: Crisis and Regeneration* (1960) would initiate sweeping changes. Finer feels that "the gravest problem of America's government is the inadequacy of the President, any President." He advocates that all executive heads and members of Congress be elected simultaneously for a four-year period. The executive branch would consist of a President and eleven Vice Presidents (all eligible for re-election), who must all be past or present members of Congress. The President and his eleven associates would function as the Cabinet. The Cabinet would have collective responsibility for executive decisions, whereas the existing principle, says Finer, is that "the President alone is responsible and that his convictions are to dominate the administration; but if he lacks the personal qualities, and has not the kind of assistance such a man would need, he will surely fail." Congress under his scheme would cease to be "a congeries of local interests" and become a truly national legislative body, with the majority party genuinely in accord with the party executive as represented by the presidential dozen.

Professor James MacGregor Burns, in *The Deadlock of Democracy: Four-Party Politics in America*, focuses upon the weaknesses of the party structure. He believes that "to see the pattern of power at the national level only in terms of two parties is grossly misleading. The balance between one or two parties . . . and (at the national level) over a thousand personal parties (one for the President, one for each member of Congress, and at least one for each rival for the office, in both parties) . . . has been struck not in a two-party power system, nor in a multi-party system, but in what is essentially a four-party system. The four national parties are the presidential Democrats, the presidential Republicans, the congressional Democrats, and the congressional Republicans." The presidential party of the defeated candidate is woefully weak. The party aligned with the victorious candidate is powerful within limits and is especially dominant for the brief period of the national party convention. The outlooks of the congressional parties are very different from those of the presidential parties: "An executive impetus and a legislative tendency confront each other at every junction. The executive impetus is to combine legislative and administrative power, to coordinate functions, to exert control from the top. . . . The legislative instinct is pluralistic. Congress and the state legislatures, under the control of the legislative parties, seek to fragmentize the executive by means of individual or committee influence over administrative units, or control of specific budgetary items, or through hobbling the executive's power to reorganize. . . . This bewildering array of countervailing and overlapping powers compels American political leaders to piece together a new patchwork of party fragments, factional chieftains, congressional votes, constitutional usage, and bureaucratic officials in order to put through each major new program."

Burns hopes for an integration of the four-party system into a two-party system. He would end the seniority principle in Congress and seek to place effective control in the hands of leaders and whips elected for their ability instead of availability. He proposes constitutional amendments that include a four-year term for representatives and a repeal of the Twenty-second Amendment (the anti-third-term rule). Although no President would be indiscreet enough to ask for the repeal of the Twenty-second Amendment, the four-year term for the House has obvious attractions for the House and for the executive branch. Hence, in his annual message to Congress in January, 1966, Lyndon Johnson said: "To strengthen the work of Congress I strongly urge an amendment to provide a 4-year term for Members of the House of Representatives which should not begin before 1972. The present 2-year term requires most Members of Congress to divert enormous energies to an almost constant process of campaigning. . . . Today, too, the work of government is far more complex than in our early years, requiring more time to learn and more time to master the technical tasks of legislating. And a longer term will serve to attract more men of the highest quality to political life. The Nation, the principle of democracy, and I think each congressional district, will all be better served by a 4-year term for Members of the House, and I urge your swift action."

The aim of such proposals is to overcome the excessive separation and the mutual institutional antipathy of President and Congress. Some would argue that only Constitution worship blinds us from perceiving that the Founding Fathers erred from the start. Less radical critics maintain that while the delegates at Philadelphia built extremely well, they could not be expected to devise a government suitable to the needs of a totally different society. And some of the ancillary devices they did not contemplate—the party system, the Cabinet—have likewise grown hoary and require revision.

Another contention is that the framers of the Constitution failed to conceive clearly what the role of the Executive should be and that this basic ambiguity has persisted ever since. Some of the implications have been discussed in previous chapters. Contemporary thinking on the matter has been shaped by twentieth-century experience, which has then been read back into American history by scholars. The lessons presented to us in the dominant liberal style may be summed up as follows:

—Strong Presidents (such as Washington, Jefferson, Jackson, Lincoln, Wilson, the two Roosevelts) have promoted national unity, prosperity, democracy, and responsibility.

—Weak Presidents (such as Pierce, Buchanan, Grant, Harding, and Coolidge) have, no doubt unwittingly, countenanced national disunity, economic selfishness, social conservatism, and irresponsibility in both domestic and international affairs.

—The Whig conception of the Presidency is therefore unsound.

—A strong Executive must be a single Executive; schemes for a plural Executive threaten a reversion to America's parlous days under the Articles of Confederation.

—Historically, the legislative branch has sought to weaken executive authority through jealous obstructionism.

—The executive branch is the hero of the story of American federal government; Congress is the villain.

An example of this attitude is found in Emmet John Hughes's account of the Eisenhower administration, *The Ordeal of Power.* Asked on one occasion to characterize his great predecessor Abraham Lincoln, Eisenhower praised his "modesty and his humility" and cited with approval Lincoln's meek remark after he had been slighted by his Army commander: "I would hold General McClellan's horse if

NUCLEAR HAZARDS

MOSCOW TEST-BAN TALKS

Herblock drew the cartoon above in 1963, after the Kennedy administration had begun talks aimed at a nuclear test ban.

he would just win the Union a victory." For John F. Kennedy, Hughes points out, "the Civil War President excited a wholly different image." Kennedy cited Lincoln's instruction to his Cabinet when he had decided to issue the Emancipation Proclamation: "I have gathered you together to hear what I have written down. I do not wish your advice about the main matter—that I have determined for myself." For Eisenhower, says Hughes, the supreme symbol of the Presidency "would be not the sword of authority but the shield of rectitude."

Which of the two attitudes toward the Presidency is preferable? A knowledge of American history and present expectations make one opt for authority. Strong Presidents have often been less popular during their own time than weak Presidents. Lincoln was execrated, Harding was applauded. The judgment that counts is that of posterity; and posterity is probably right. If decisive leadership had been lacking in the White House, the United States might have become another sort of country, and an inferior one, pervaded by the spirit of what Emerson termed "village littleness." This is the spirit that infuses many of the activities (or inactivities) of Congress at its narrowest. It is expressed in such legislative slogans as To get along, go along (go along, that is, with the rest) and Vote your district first.

But there are drawbacks to the display of presidential authority. Strong Presidents run a far greater

risk of assassination, or at least of provoking unhealthily fierce opposition on Capitol Hill and among the population. Most of this opposition is irrational and deplorable, but not all of it. One modern French writer, Amaury de Riencourt, claims in *The Coming Caesars* (1957) that "it is in Washington and not in London, Paris, or Berlin that the Caesars of the future will arise. It will not be the result of conspiracy, revolution, or personal ambition. It will be the end result of an instinctive evolution in which we are all taking part like somnambulists." His thesis is that "as society becomes more equalitarian, it tends increasingly to concentrate absolute power in the hands of one single man." He believes that Americans are particularly disposed to accept the rule of a Caesar: "They always tend to personalize issues, and in every walk of life they look up to the 'boss.' . . . wars are the main harbingers of Caesarism. . . . In grave emergencies, leadership can never be collective, and we are now living in an age of permanent emergency. Presidential power in America has grown as American power and expansion have grown, one developing within the other." Today, says Riencourt, "one man is directly in command . . . of more than half the globe's economic and technical power"; he wields an imperial prerogative as vast as that of the Roman emperors in the ancient world. The chief factor, this writer emphasizes, is psychological, not political or strategic. "It is the growing 'father complex' . . . the willingness to follow . . . the leadership of one man. It is the growing distrust of parliaments, congresses, and all other representative assemblies, the growing impatience of Western public opinion at their irresponsibility, lack of foresight, sluggishness, indecisiveness."

Riencourt's thesis consists of half-truths and it need not be accepted as a convincing prophecy. Even in the executive branch, government proceeds largely by committee bureaucracy. In Congress the committee structure is almost the whole story; and some, though mercifully not all, of the committee chairmen wield power not by taking action but by impeding it. The federal government combines dashes of Caesarism with quantities of inertia. The worst threats to American democracy have come not from Presidents but from demagogues of the McCarthyite variety. Yet there is some truth in Riencourt's account. The situation is perilous not so much because absolute executive prerogative exists but rather because it seems erratic, discontinuous, and capricious—even in the hands of a first-rate President, and especially in the hands of a mediocrity. One source of danger is the American *fear* of Caesarism—a fear that might induce self-appointed patriots to re-enact the tale of Brutus and Cassius (or, in the American context, of John Wilkes Booth or Lee Harvey Oswald). Another undeniable danger is that a President might, with the best of intentions, commit the world to catastrophe. This act, the work of a moment, could be called Caesarism, but the word is not really applicable: such a possibility is the supreme nightmare of our time, for which the past provides no parallel. The danger that is closest to Caesarism in Riencourt's use of the term is that of involvements on the Vietnam scale. Their most terrifying feature, however, is not that they may be thrust upon the American people by a despotic President, but that public and congressional sentiment may accord so readily with that of the Chief Executive, and even impel him toward belligerence.

There are other elements of presidential power to which less apocalyptic commentators have addressed themselves. Finer, Edward S. Corwin, and a few other mid-twentieth-century scholars have tried to go beyond the simple reassurances of the liberal idea that the stronger the President, the better. They maintain, as did Henry C. Lockwood in *The Abolition of the Presidency* in the late nineteenth century, that the American public is too ready to entrust the Presidency to men whom they have endowed with superhuman attributes. Along with Woodrow Wilson in his first book, *Congressional Government*, they hold that no one man is capable of reaching wise decisions on all the issues that confront him. Finer's plan to institute more effective party government is also a plan to diminish the power of the single Executive. He would ask why we applaud an anecdote that shows that Lincoln did not consult the Cabinet on a matter of such prime importance as the Emancipation Proclamation. He would no doubt agree with General Eisenhower's view that the prestige of the Presidency is based upon rectitude as well as authority. It is often said that the Presidency is an ennobling office, whose occupants behave with a dignity one might not have expected in light of the previous conduct of some. Chester Arthur's sudden probity may have owed more to his sense of the elevation of the office than to his awareness of its powerfulness.

The Whig conception cannot be entirely dismissed. Presidents who descend from their eminence to give legislative or partisan battle may bring the Chief Magistracy into disrepute; or so such Presidents as Taft and Eisenhower have honestly believed.

The modern President, says Finer, is given more advice than he can assimilate, and responsibility for more decisions than any single person ought to possess. His veto power is excessive. Worse still, he is "chosen by the most ramshackle, the flimsiest method ever used to select the supreme leader of a nation." The electorate seeks impossible qualities in its candidates and admires them for the wrong reasons: "Because the President is expected to play a dual role, demigod and astute politician, the voters disregard the immensity of the responsibilities with which he is vested as they seek to assess his charm. . . . The combination of the two roles, national symbol and political leader, is too emollient, too disarming, to be healthy for the mightiest democracy in the world." Corwin too feels that "presidential power has been at times dangerously *personalized*," in making leadership subject to the particular personality of whatever President happened to be selected by "our haphazard method."

In a broad sense, the Presidency has suffered from the cult of personality, a cult intensified by the inordinate publicity given to the Chief Executive

ENLARGING THE PRESIDENTIAL CHAIR

The Presidency was considered a big job in 1928, when this cartoon appeared. It has grown far more complex since then.

and his entourage. This fact in itself is no proof of Caesarism. American popular interest in the occupants of the White House is on approximately the same level as British interest in the occupants of Buckingham Palace, which is, of course, not the center of power in British government. But the American appetite for gossipy information about the President, harmless in itself, is related to a disquieting exaggeration. There is a tinge of hysteria in the quadrennial excitements that attend each new administration. It is expected that with each new President the office will somehow undergo a transformation. The limitations of his role are temporarily forgotten. The immensely complex federal structure is dramatized and personalized as if it consisted of only one man, remotely attended by shadowy subordinates and challenged only by a rabble of scheming congressmen.

The inevitable disenchantment is the more painful in consequence. Having failed to be all things to all men, the President is condemned both for weakness and for arrogance. Paradoxically, the more contemporary Presidents respond to the public demand for a dazzlingly attractive executive image, the less likely they are to attempt genuinely forceful leadership. The trenchancy of Harry Truman's utterances comes as a shock when one reads them again, since Americans have grown accustomed to the discreet, affable words of his successors. The American people, vaguely worried by the vast potential of executive power, are also vaguely disappointed that power is so blandly wielded. If the worst has not befallen the nation, neither has the best. Yet such apparent mildness ought to be comforting. Professor Corwin, in the 1957 revision of his influential book *The President: Office and Powers*, was induced to modify previous strictures. He had proposed an executive council; by 1957 an "institutionalized Presidency" seemed to be actually coming into existence, with the President "merged with—albeit not submerged in—a cluster of institutions designed to base government . . . on conference and consensus." Perhaps Dwight D. Eisenhower was more sensible than some of his critics realized; perhaps a dose of modesty and humility was not such a bad prescription for the White House of the future.

Corwin ended his 1957 edition by refusing to predict whether the "institutionalized Presidency" would become permanent. In a changing world, he said, "the incalculables are too many and too formidable." Since 1957 the liberal view of the Presidency has wavered somewhat. It is still maintained that the country needs first-rate men on the Lincolnian and Rooseveltian models. On the other hand, worries of the kind that dominated liberal discussion in the last third of the nineteenth century have been expressed —misgivings that in our century have until now mainly been confined to conservatives. They are more or less epitomized in Herman Finer's analysis. Underlying them is the reflection that no one man should be either expected or empowered to bear so much responsibility. It has been assumed as a liberal axiom that presidential authority would always be benevolent. Now, pondering the awful dilemmas of the contemporary scene, Americans of good will wonder if a President might not also use his authority in harmful ways, and if so how he could be stopped. They again discuss the brake instead of the accelerator—not surprisingly, considering the velocity of modern events. Disability amendments are all very well. But a close reading of Gene Smith's excellent account of Woodrow Wilson's illness, *When the Cheering Stopped*, suggests that the national government could still be paralyzed or warped if something happened to the Chief Executive. Suppose that the President was not physically incapacitated nor certifiably insane, but became by degrees increasingly jaded, increasingly exasperated by Congress, and increasingly apathetic? He could be removed from office at the next election, but possibly not until serious harm had been done. "It hasn't happened yet" is only a partial consolation; "it can't happen here" is a foolish form of optimism.

Which, then, is the better guide to future developments, optimism or pessimism? If the latter, there is still a dilemma. Reformers offer two propositions: that the federal government, Congress in particular, is slow, overcautious, and negative, and that the President is given too much isolated authority. How is it possible to remedy the one without intensifying the other? The optimistic recommendation for the future of the Presidency is that things should be left alone because things are fine. The pessimistic view may be that things should be left alone because changes might aggravate an already unsatisfactory situation. The wisdom of optimism might arrive via a different route at the same conclusion as the wisdom of pessimism.

All books about the Presidency, including this one, conclude inconclusively. It can never be an ideal institution. So far, in comparison with chief magistracies in other countries, it has been a great success. Its future success, like its past development, involves many factors—among them the fundamental decency of American life, the devotion of many thousands of executive officials, and the labors of Congress when the legislators are in a constructive, responsible mood. This is not to say that Capitol Hill is constructive only when agreeing with the White House; the important consideration is that Congress should agree or disagree with the President for the right reasons, not because of narrow partisanship or excessive touchiness.

Reform *is* needed. Whatever its precise shape, thoughtful citizens seem to concur that one need is for a closer link between the executive and legislative branches. Congress has perhaps unfairly been dubbed the "sapless branch." The metaphor may be extended. Can there be a tree that has branches but no trunk? Which division is the trunk of the federal government? Should there not be less reference to *separation* of powers and more to *association* of powers?

Another need is for improved counseling within the executive branch, and if possible a more visible sharing of executive responsibility. If this change were to lead to a slight diminution of the Presidency it would be beneficial for everyone. The presidential limelight is too glaring and it makes other governmental figures too penumbral. There is much to be said for a House of Representatives elected quadrennially; a good deal of the present Capitol–White House animosity is futile. Cabinet-type reforms are a more dubious proposition, although they are worth aiming at. Professor Finer, for instance, would empower the President to dismiss any of his eleven vice presidential Cabinet members, having also provided that they should be popularly elected to their office. One can imagine the constitutional wrangling that would arise from this single feature in Finer's scheme.

Among the shrewdest comments on attitudes toward government is Alexis de Tocqueville's: "I have come across men of letters who have written history without taking part in public affairs, and politicians who have concerned themselves with producing events without thinking about them. I have observed that the first are always inclined to find general causes, whereas the second, living in the midst of disconnected daily facts, are prone to imagine that everything is attributable to particular incidents, and that the wires they pull are the same as those that move the world. It is to be presumed that both are equally deceived." Neither the reformers nor the pragmatists are entirely correct in their estimates of the Presidency; neither liberals nor conservatives, neither optimists nor pessimists. Changes are worth introducing; the climate of reform is valuable. But the most ingenious paper reforms amount to nothing, as do the most sophisticated attempts at consensus, voter satisfaction, and the like, unless certain broad considerations are given weight. Although the Presidency has been profoundly altered since George Washington's day, these considerations are still true; they are truisms, but they can bear reiterating.

The nation is apt to get the President it deserves. An America obsessed with popularity ratings is likely to pick a Chief Executive because he looks the part—and will get a man who in turn is obsessed with popularity ratings. A brutal nation merits a brutal Executive. A complacent country ought not to complain if the White House is occupied by a garrulous bore. Only if Americans pursue excellence in their own lives have they the right to hope for an excellent President.

Whatever his capacity, the President will be a human being committed to almost superhuman effort. The wise course is for the man himself and the United States to recognize that he cannot be superhuman. There are only twenty-four hours in his day. Apart from the hours he needs for sleep and work, he must find time to sit and think. The greatest task of the Presidency is not that of Commander in Chief or party leader or legislative leader or director of foreign policy or chief of the executive branch or head of state (to list the "six hats" that President Truman said he had to wear). Each of these is important. But the President must, if he is to be the fitting head of a morally great nation, do something more that transcends these roles. He must speak to the United States as well as for it. He must find words to lift men out of their everyday selves. He must be the nation's conscience, its chief teacher, a seer rather than a Caesar. Such figures are rare. The task of America is to nurture some, and to discover at least one every four years.

ACKNOWLEDGMENTS

Professor Marcus Cunliffe wishes to thank Beth Biddle for preliminary research; Anita Sinkins for secretarial help; his wife, Mitzi, for shrewd comment, ebullient companionship, and for typing almost the whole manuscript despite the distractions of a summer in Provence; and Toni, Shay, and J. J. for reinforcement. He also wishes to thank the many admirable scholars whose works he consulted.

If the book had a formal dedication, it would be to his esteemed parents.

The Editors are grateful to the following individuals and organizations for their invaluable assistance in the picture research for this project:

Chicago Historical Society: Mary Frances Rhymer
Chicago *Tribune*
Cincinnati Historical Society: Eleanor Wirmel
Denver Public Library: Alys Freeze
J. Doyle DeWitt
Free Library of Philadelphia: Robert Looney
Harding Memorial Association: Warren C. Sawyer
Harvard College Library: Gregory Wilson
Henry E. Huntington Library and Art Gallery: Edward Carpenter Stanley King
Library of Congress: Virginia Daiker; Renata Shaw
Metropolitan Museum of Art: Margaret Nolan
National Park Service: Nash Castro
National Portrait Gallery: Robert G. Stewart
New-York Historical Society: Carolyn Scoon; Wilson G. Duprey; Martin Leifer; Thomas Dunnings; Wilmer Leech
New York Public Library: Romana Javitz
Franklin D. Roosevelt Library: Elizabeth B. Drewry; Joseph Marshall
San Francisco Public Library: William Ramirez
Shelburne Museum: Bradley Smith
Smithsonian Institution: Meredith Johnson
Society of California Pioneers: William Long
State Historical Society of Colorado: Kathleen Pierson
Tennessee State Library & Archives: Harriet C. Owsley
United States Capitol, Architect's Office: Mrs. Florian Thayn
United States Defense Department: Colonel Robert A. Webb
University of California at Berkeley, Bancroft Library: John Barr Tompkins
University of California at Los Angeles, Special Collections: Wilbur Smith
Robert Weinstein
Wells Fargo Bank: Irene Simpson
The White House: James R. Ketchum
White House Historical Association: Hillory A. Tolson

The Editors also make grateful acknowledgment for permission to use material from the following books:

The Adams-Jefferson Letters, Vol. I, edited by Lester J. Cappon. Copyright 1959 by The University of North Carolina Press. The excerpt on page 121 reprinted by permission of The University of North Carolina Press.
American Reconstruction 1865–1870 and the Impeachment of President Johnson by Georges Clemenceau and edited by Fernand Baldensperger. Copyright 1928 by The Dial Press, Inc. The excerpt on pages 220–21 reprinted by permission of The Dial Press, Inc.
Beckoning Frontiers by Marriner S. Eccles. Copyright 1951 by Alfred A. Knopf, Inc. The excerpt on page 300 reprinted by permission of Alfred A. Knopf, Inc.
The Collected Works of Abraham Lincoln, Vols. I, IV, and V. Copyright 1953 by The Abraham Lincoln Association. The excerpts on pages 136, 216–17, 218–19 reprinted by permission of Roy P. Basler.

The Coming Caesars by Amaury de Riencourt. © Copyright 1957 by Amaury de Riencourt. The excerpt on page 372 reprinted by permission of Coward-McCann, Inc.
Concerning Civil Government, Second Essay by John Locke (Vol. 35 of *Great Books of the Western World* of Encyclopædia Britannica, Inc.). The excerpt on pages 27–29 reprinted by permission of Encyclopædia Britannica, Inc.
The Deadlock of Democracy by James MacGregor Burns. © Copyright 1963 by James MacGregor Burns. Published by Prentice-Hall, Inc., in hardcover and in a specially revised Spectrum Paperback. The excerpts on pages 370, 371 reprinted by permission of Prentice-Hall, Inc., Englewood Cliffs, New Jersey.
Decision-Making in the White House by Theodore Sorensen. © Copyright 1963 by Columbia University Press. The excerpt on page 290 reprinted by permission of Columbia University Press.
Dialogues of Plato translated by Benjamin Jowett, fourth edition, Volume IV. The excerpt from "Laws" on page 26 reprinted by permission of The Clarendon Press, Oxford.
Diary and Letters of Rutherford Birchard Hayes, Vol. III, edited by Charles R. Williams. Copyright 1924 by Ohio State Archeological and Historical Society. The excerpts on pages 225–27 reprinted by permission of The Ohio Historical Society.
The Diary of Gideon Welles, Vol. I, edited by Howard K. Beale. Copyright 1960 by W. W. Norton & Company, Inc. The excerpt on page 219 reprinted by permission of W. W. Norton & Co., Inc.
The Diary of John Quincy Adams, edited by Allan Nevins. Copyright 1951 by Allan Nevins. The excerpt on page 132 reprinted by permission of Allan Nevins.
Garfield-Hinsdale Letters, edited by Mary L. Hinsdale. Copyright 1949 by The University of Michigan Press. The excerpt on pages 227–28 reprinted by permission of The University of Michigan Press.
Hamilton Fish: The Inner History of the Grant Administration by Allan Nevins. Copyright 1936 by Dodd, Mead & Company, Inc. The excerpt on page 224 reprinted by permission of Dodd, Mead & Company, Inc.
The Letters of Theodore Roosevelt, edited by Elting E. Morison. Vol. III, Copyright 1951 and Vol. VI, Copyright 1952 by the President and Fellows of Harvard College. The excerpts on pages 306, 307, 308 reprinted by permission of Harvard University Press.
The Life and Times of William Howard Taft, Vol. I, by Henry Pringle. Copyright 1939 by Farrar & Rinehart, Inc. The excerpt on pages 308–9 reprinted by permission of Charles P. Taft.
The Memoirs of Herbert Hoover, Vol. II. Copyright 1952 by The Macmillan Company. The excerpt on pages 312–13 reprinted by permission of The Macmillan Company.
"My Case for the Republican Party, 1964" by Barry Goldwater from the October 17, 1964 issue of *Saturday Review*. The excerpt on page 170 reprinted by permission of *Saturday Review*.
The Oxford Translation of Aristotle translated by Benjamin Jowett. The excerpt on pages 26–27 reprinted by permission of The Clarendon Press, Oxford.
A Puritan In Babylon by William Allen White. Copyright 1938 by The Macmillan Company. The excerpt on pages 313–14 reprinted by permission of The Macmillan Company.
The Records of the Federal Convention of 1787 edited by Max Farrand. © Copyright 1966 by Yale University Press. The excerpts on pages 32–43 reprinted by permission of Yale University Press.
The Spirit of Laws, Book XI, by Charles de Secondat, Baron de Montesquieu, translated by Thomas Nugent, revised by J. V. Prichard. The excerpt on page 29 reprinted by permission of G. Bell & Sons, Ltd., London.
"Third-Term Echoes" from the July 29, 1940 issue of *Newsweek*. The excerpt on pages 317–18 reprinted by permission of Newsweek, Inc.

Front endsheet: A section of President Abraham Lincoln's manuscript of the Gettysburg Address; Library of Congress

Back endsheet: Franklin Delano Roosevelt's manuscript of his first Inaugural Address; Franklin D. Roosevelt Library.

BIBLIOGRAPHY

Agar, Herbert, *The Price of Union.* Boston, Houghton Mifflin, 1950.

Binkley, Wilfred E., *The Man in the White House.* Baltimore, Johns Hopkins Press, 1959.

————*The President and Congress.* New York, Alfred A. Knopf, 1947.

Borden, Morton, ed., *America's Ten Greatest Presidents.* Skokie, Ill., Rand McNally, 1961.

Brown, W. Burlie, *The People's Choice: The Presidential Image in the Campaign Biography.* Baton Rouge, La., Louisiana State University Press, 1960.

Brownlow, Louis, *The President and the Presidency.* Chicago, Public Service Administration, 1949.

Bryce, James, *The American Commonwealth,* 2 vols., 3rd rev. ed. Macmillan, 1893–1895.

Burns, James MacGregor, *The Deadlock of Democracy: Four-Party Politics in America.* Englewood Cliffs, N.J., Prentice-Hall, 1963.

————*Presidential Government: The Crucible of Leadership.* Boston, Houghton Mifflin, 1965.

Cavaioli, Frank J., *West Point and the Presidency.* New York, St. John's University Press, 1962.

Chambers, W. N., *Political Parties in a New Nation: The American Experience, 1776–1809.* New York, Oxford University Press, 1963.

Cornwell, Elmer E., Jr., *Presidential Leadership of Public Opinion.* Bloomington, Ind., Indiana University Press, 1965.

Corwin, Edward S., *The President: Office and Powers, 1787–1957,* 4th rev. ed. New York, New York University Press, 1957.

Coyle, David C., *Ordeal of the Presidency.* Washington, Public Affairs Press, 1960.

Donald, Aida DiPace, ed., *John F. Kennedy and the New Frontier.* New York, Hill & Wang, 1966.

Donald, David, *Lincoln Reconsidered.* New York, Alfred A. Knopf, 1956.

Donovan, Robert J., *The Assassins.* New York, Harper & Brothers, 1955.

Feerick, John D., *From Failing Hands: The Story of Presidential Succession.* New York, Fordham University Press, 1965.

Fenno, Richard F., Jr., *The President's Cabinet.* Cambridge, Mass., Harvard University Press, 1959.

Finer, Herman, *The Presidency: Crisis and Regeneration.* Chicago, Chicago University Press, 1960.

Ford, Henry Jones, *The Rise and Growth of American Politics: A Sketch of Constitutional Developments.* New York, Plenum Publishing Corp., 1898.

Fuess, Claude M., *Calvin Coolidge: The Man from Vermont.* Hamden, Conn., The Shoe String Press, 1940.

Geyelin, Philip, *Lyndon B. Johnson and the World.* New York, Frederick A. Praeger, 1966.

Harnsberger, Caroline T., ed., *Treasury of Presidential Quotations.* Chicago, Follett Publishing Co., 1964.

Hayes, Rutherford B., *Hayes: The Diary of a President,* T. Harry Williams, ed. New York, D. McKay, 1964.

Holcombe, Arthur N., *Our More Perfect Union: From Eighteenth-Century Principles to Twentieth-Century Practice.* Cambridge, Mass., Harvard University Press, 1950.

Hughes, Emmet John, *The Ordeal of Power.* New York, Atheneum, 1963.

Hyman, Sidney, "Nine Tests for a Presidential Hopeful." *The New York Times Magazine,* (January 4, 1959).

Johnson, Donald B. and Walker, J. L., eds., *Dynamics of the American Presidency.* New York, John Wiley & Sons, 1964.

Johnson, Walter, *1600 Pennsylvania Avenue.* Boston, Little, Brown and Co., 1960.

Kallenbach, Joseph E., *The American Chief Executive: The Presidency and the Governorship.* New York, Harper & Row, 1966.

Kane, Joseph N., *Facts About the Presidents: A Compilation of Biographical and Historical Data.* New York, H. W. Wilson, 1959.

Koenig, Louis, *The Chief Executive.* New York, Harcourt, Brace & World, 1964.

Kurtz, Stephen G., *The Presidency of John Adams.* Philadelphia, University of Pennsylvania Press, 1957.

Laski, Harold J., *The American Presidency: An Interpretation.* New York, Harper & Brothers, 1940.

Leuchtenburg, William E., ed., *Franklin D. Roosevelt: A Profile.* New York, Hill & Wang, 1967.

Link, Arthur S., *Wilson,* 5 vols. Princeton, N.J., Princeton University Press, 1947–1965.

Lipset, Seymour Martin, *The First New Nation.* New York, Basic Books, 1963.

Lockwood, Henry C., *The Abolition of the Presidency.* New York, R. Worthington, 1884.

McCormick, Richard P., *The Second American Party System: Party Formation in the Jacksonian Era.* Chapel Hill, N.C., University of North Carolina Press, 1966.

Manchester, William, *Death of a President: November, 1963.* New York, Harper & Row, 1967.

May, Ernest R., ed., *The Ultimate Decision: The President as Commander in Chief.* New York, G. Braziller, 1960.

Neustadt, Richard E., *Presidential Power: The Politics of Leadership.* New York, Signet Books, The New American Library, 1964.

Peck, Harry Thurston, *Twenty Years of the Republic 1885–1905.* New York, Dodd, Mead & Co., 1906.

Peterson, Merrill D., *The Jefferson Image in the American Mind.* New York, Oxford University Press, 1960.

Polk, James K., *Polk: The Diary of a President 1845–1849.* Allan Nevins, ed. London, Longmans, Green & Co., 1929.

Riencourt, Amaury de, *The Coming Caesars.* New York, Coward-McCann, 1957.

Roche, John P. and Levy, Leonard, eds., *The Presidency.* New York, Harcourt, Brace & World, 1964.

Roseboom, Eugene H., *A History of Presidential Elections,* 2nd ed. New York, Macmillan, 1964.

Rossiter, Clinton, *The American Presidency,* rev. ed. New York, The New American Library, 1960.

Schlesinger, Arthur M., Jr., *The Age of Jackson.* Boston, Little, Brown and Co., 1950.

————*The Age of Roosevelt,* 3 vols. Boston, Houghton Mifflin, 1957–1960.

Sherrill, Robert, *The Accidental President.* New York, Grossman Publishers, 1967.

Silva, Ruth C., *Presidential Succession.* Ann Arbor, Mich., University of Michigan Press, 1951.

Sinclair, Andrew, *The Available Man: The Life Behind the Masks of Warren Gamaliel Harding.* New York, Macmillan, 1965.

Smith, Gene, *When the Cheering Stopped: The Last Years of Woodrow Wilson.* New York, William Morrow, 1964.

Sorenson, Theodore C., *Decision-Making in the White House: The Olive Branch or the Arrows.* New York, Columbia University Press, 1963.

Stillman, Edmund and Pfaff, William, *The New Politics: America and the End of the Postwar World.* New York, Coward-McCann, 1961.

Thach, Charles, Jr., *The Creation of the Presidency 1775–1789: A Study in Constitutional History.* Baltimore, Johns Hopkins Press, 1922.

Tourtellot, Arthur, ed., *The Presidents on the Presidency.* Garden City, N.Y., Doubleday, 1964.

Truman, Harry S., *Memoirs,* 2 vols. Garden City, N.Y., Doubleday, 1955, 1956.

Tugwell, Rexford G., *The Enlargement of the Presidency.* Garden City, N.Y., Doubleday, 1960.

White, Leonard D. *The Federalists: A Study in Administrative History.* New York, Macmillan, 1948.

————*The Jacksonians: A Study in Administrative History 1829–1861.* New York, Macmillan, 1954.

————*The Jeffersonians: A Study in Administrative History 1801–1829.* New York, Macmillan, 1951.

————*The Republican Era: A Study in Administrative History.* New York, Macmillan, 1958.

Wilmerding, Lucius, Jr. *The Electoral College.* New Brunswick, N.J., Rutgers University Press, 1959.

Wilson, Woodrow, *Congressional Government.* Cleveland, Ohio, Meridian Books, The World Publishing Co., 1956.

————*Constitutional Government in the United States.* New York, Columbia University Press, 1961.

Wright, Benjamin F., ed., *The Federalist.* Cambridge, Mass., The Belknap Press, Harvard University Press, 1961.

INDEX

ratification of, 12, 13, 15, 18, 19, 20, 22, 24, 25, 45, 47, 48, 63, 69, 72, 111
and removal power, 78
separation of powers, 76, 109, 279
signing of, 21, 43, 67
and treaty-making power, 114, 241, 276
and war-making power, 136
See also Constitutional Convention and individual framers
U.S. House of Representatives, 43, 74, 75, 79, 88, 90, 94, 101, 106, 121, 124, 126, 130–31, 142, 187, 188, 193, 270–72, 277, 296, 297, 299, 364, 367
and appropriations control, 279, 286
and 1800 election, 83, 94, 138
and 1824 election, 94, 105, 141
and election of President, 13, 41, 42, 44, 82, 108, 117–20 *passim*
and four-year term, 370–71, 375
Foreign Affairs Committee, 286
and impeachment, 41, 43
of Andrew Johnson, 191, 220–22
and removal power, 78
Rules Committee, 271, 297
Speaker of the House, 43, 102, 195, 198, 222, 229, 270, 271, 320, 326, 365–66
and treaty-making power, 81, 286
and war-making power, 39
U.S. Senate, 13, 36, 38, 40, 43, 74, 76, 78, 83, 94, 101, 115, 121, 174, 175, 176, 180, 184–88 *passim*, 193, 198, 199, 230, 270–72 *passim*, 274, 279, 286, 287, 296, 297, 299, 300, 314, 364, 367
and "advice and consent," 12, 42, 44, 65, 76, 114–15, 241
and Bank of the U.S., 94, 174
and censure of Jackson, 129–30, 174, 175
and diplomatic appointments, 278, 279
and election of President and Vice President, 41–42, 44, 82, 118, 120
and foreign policy, 22, 276, 279, 280, 286, 363
Foreign Relations Committee, 275, 276–77, 285, 286, 287
and impeachment, 41, 43
of Andrew Johnson, 220–22
and League of Nations, 279, 285, 311
and Majority Leader, 296

and president pro tempore, 43, 198, 222, 229, 320, 326, 365–66
President of the Senate, 40, 41, 42, 44, 117–18, 120
and presidential succession, 132–33
and removal power, 78, 186, 220
and treaty-making power, 15, 42, 44, 65, 114–15, 241, 265, 277–80 *passim*, 282–83
and Treaty of Versailles, 274, 275, 311
and war-making power, 39
U.S. Supreme Court, 87, 127, 173, 174, 180, 221, 250, 277, 295, 296, 302, 306, 316, 367
Chief Justice, 40, 41, 43, 222
and civil rights, 302, 323
establishment of, 75
and New Deal legislation, 277, 302, 316–17
and separation of powers, 76

V

Van Buren, Martin, 83, 91, 93, 96, 104–11 *passim*, 127, 129, 130–32 *passim*, 136, 142, 144, 147, 174–77 *passim*, 198, 201, 260, 278, 330
Vandenberg, Arthur H., 286
Versailles Peace Conference, 278, 289
Veto power, 35, 80, 174, 196
See also the President
Vice President, the, 13, 42, 82, 83, 119, 171–72, 198–99, 285, 364–68 *passim*
election of, 40–41, 44, 82–83, 118–20
as President of the Senate, 13, 41, 42, 43, 83, 114
salary of, 74–75, 300
and succession, 41, 42, 44, 82–83, 85, 132–33, 222–23
Vietnamese War, 246, 256–57, 284, 286, 287, 290, 299, 325–26 *passim*, 328, 373
Virginia Plan, 32–33, 35, 65

W

Wade, Benjamin F., 98, 186, 221
Wallace, Henry A., 164, 165
War of 1812, 89, 92, 102–3, 123, 140, 266, 281
War powers, 97, 98, 278
See also the President
Ward, John Williams, 88
Warren, Earl, 302, 303
Washington, George, 16, 17, 20, 24, 46, 71, 72–82 *passim*, 83, 85, 86, 87, 90, 92,

93, 98, 102, 103, 111, 113, 139, 172, 181, 197, 199, 203, 246, 261, 278, 301, 302, 307, 308, 330
and American monarchy, 19, 171
and annual messages, 80
appraisal of, 75–76
and Cabinet, 74–80 *passim*
and Cherokee Indians, 114–15
as choice for first President, 20, 48, 49, 69, 72, 137, 138
as Commander in Chief of Continental Army, 20, 24, 199
during Presidency, 16
confidence of contemporaries in, 15, 20, 24, 48, 115
and Congress, 76, 80, 81, 114–15
and Constitutional Convention, 12, 14, 20, 23, 32, 40, 49, 72, 76
criticism of, 171–72, 255
Farewell Address, 22–23, 76, 86, 100
and federal appointments, 77, 78, 193
first inauguration, 3, 69, 73, 74, 75, 352
first term, 72–76 *passim*
and foreign affairs, 80–81, 241, 276–77
and Hamilton, 79–82 *passim*
influence on future of Presidency, 76, 80, 86, 87, 114–16
and neutrality proclamation, 115
and political parties, 100, 101, 103
and precedents, 71, 73–78 *passim*, 80–82 *passim*, 85
third-term precedent, 85, 181, 317
and protocol, 73–74
and Revolutionary War, 62, 69, 137
and second term, 80, 81, 85, 86, 100
as strong President, 170, 183, 185, 371
and tours, 75, 346
unanimous re-election of, 113
and veto, 80
and Whisky Rebellion, 82, 115–16, 249
Washington, Martha, 71, 73, 330, 352
Weaver, Robert, 300–301
Webster, Daniel, 85, 87, 91, 92, 94, 107, 142, 173, 176, 177, 197, 198, 199, 211
Weed, Thurlow, 104, 111
Welles, Gideon, 200, 216, 219
Wheeler, William A., 199
Whig party, 84, 85, 94, 95, 97, 105, 106, 107, 108–9, 110, 112, 131, 134, 136, 142, 144, 146, 147, 172, 175, 176, 177, 185, 197, 199, 203, 206, 279

Whig conception of Presidency, 185, 371, 373
Whisky Rebellion, 16, 82, 115, 116, 249
White, Leonard D., 75, 95, 96
Williamson, Hugh, 37, 38, 40, 41, 42
Willkie, Wendell L., 163
Wilmerding, Lucius, Jr., 82
Wilson, Edith, 354, 366
Wilson, Edmund, 177
Wilson, James, 12, 21, 33, 34, 35, 41, 42, 51, 58, 62, 65
Wilson, Woodrow, 133, 181, 206, 208, 233, 265, 271, 272, 273, 274–75 *passim*, 277, 278, 281, 292, 293, 302, 313, 354, 358, 362
and annual messages, 80
appraisal of, 274
and Cabinet, 280
and Congress, 274
and executive authority, 276
first Inaugural Address, 274
and foreign affairs, 278
and Fourteen Points, 305
illness of, 311–12, 346, 354, 366, 374
and succession problem, 133, 311–12
and League of Nations, 243, 279, 311, 346, 350
and the New Freedom, 159, 274, 275
and 1912 election, 158, 251, 269–70, 274
and 1916 election, 158, 270, 281, 364
and Overman Act, 278
prepresidential writings of, 193, 195–99 *passim*, 264–66 *passim*, 268, 270, 373
second inauguration, 310
and Senate and the Treaty of Versailles, 274, 275, 296, 311
as strong President, 159, 182, 192–93, 274–75 *passim*, 371
and tariff and banking reform, 158, 309–10
and Versailles peace talks, 305
and wartime powers, 275, 278, 292
and World War I, 158, 246, 310–11
Wiltse, Charles M., 173
Wirt, William, 89–90, 95, 103, 106
Woodward, Augustus B., 362
World War I, 160, 179, 246, 275, 278, 280, 281, 282, 283, 310–11, 314, 320
World War II, 245, 277–78, 280, 282, 283, 284, 302, 315, 317, 318, 321

Z

Zangara, Giuseppe, 178, 180

Nor need we shrink from ~~being~~

~~w~~of our country today.   This

as it has endured, will reviv

first of all let me assert my

thing we have to fear is fear

unjustified terror which para

convert retreat into a

~~to bring about prosperity one~~